CW01270361

COPTIC DOCUMENTARY TEXTS
FROM KELLIS

Volume 2

Dakhleh Oasis Project: Monograph 16

COPTIC DOCUMENTARY TEXTS FROM KELLIS

Volume 2

P. Kellis VII
(P. Kellis Copt. 57–131)

Edited by

Iain Gardner, Anthony Alcock and Wolf-Peter Funk

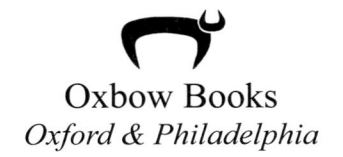

Oxbow Books
Oxford & Philadelphia

Published in the United Kingdom in 2014 by
OXBOW BOOKS
10 Hythe Bridge Street, Oxford OX1 2EW

and in the United States by
OXBOW BOOKS
908 Darby Road, Havertown, PA 19083

© Oxbow Books and the individual authors 2014

Hardcover Edition: ISBN 978-1-78297-651-6; Digital Edition: ISBN 978-1-78297-652-3

A CIP record for this book is available from the British Library

Library of Congress Cataloging-in-Publication Data

Coptic documentary texts from Kellis / edited by Iain Gardner, Anthony Alcock and Wolf-Peter Funk.
    volumes cm. -- (Dakhleh Oasis Project monograph ; 16)
 In English and Coptic; some material translated from Coptic. Coptic romanized.
 Includes index.
 Digital photographs of the texts are provided on the accompanying disc.
 Contents: House 3 -- Letter on a wooden board (with traces of an earlier text in Syriac), P. Kellis Copt. 57 -- Texts perhaps additional to groups published in volume 1, P. Kellis Copt. 58-60 -- Manichaean letters, P. Kellis Copt. 61-63 -- Letters by Pamour (and Maria), P. Kellis Copt. 64-72 -- Letters by Pegosh (brother of Pamour), P. Kellis Copt. 73-79 -- Letters from Philammon to Theognostos (Louishai) and Hor, P. Kellis Copt. 80-82 -- Letters from Theognostos, P. Kellis Copt. 83-84 -- Letters from and to Ploutogenes, P. Kellis Copt. 85-91 -- Kyra/Loihat/Timotheos group, P. Kellis Copt. 92-93 -- Individual and unplaced documents and letters, P. Kellis Copt. 94-121 -- List of other (not edited) Coptic fragments from House 3 -- House 4 -- Letters, P. Kellis Copt. 122-124 -- Inventory, P. Kellis Copt. 125 -- Invocation, P. Kellis Copt. 126 -- List of other (not edited) Coptic fragments from House 4 -- Temple enclosure -- Letters, P. Kellis Copt. 127-128 -- Varia, P. Kellis Copt. 129-131 -- List of other (not edited) Coptic fragments from the temple enclosure.
 ISBN 978-1-78297-651-6
 1. Coptic manuscripts--Egypt--Kellis (Extinct city) 2. Coptic manuscripts (Papyri)--Egypt--Kellis (Extinct city) 3. Coptic language--Texts. 4. Kellis (Extinct city) 5. Manichaeism--History--Sources. I. Gardner, Iain. II. Alcock, Anthony. III. Funk, Wolf-Peter.
 PJ2195.C667 2014
 893'.2--dc23
                       2014019806

All rights reserved. No part of this book may be reproduced or transmitted in any form or by any means, electronic or mechanical including photocopying, recording or by any information storage and retrieval system, without permission from the publisher in writing.

Printed in the United Kingdom by Berforts Information Press

For a complete list of Oxbow titles, please contact:

UNITED KINGDOM
Oxbow Books
Telephone (01865) 241249, Fax (01865) 794449
Email: oxbow@oxbowbooks.com
www.oxbowbooks.com

UNITED STATES OF AMERICA
Oxbow Books
Telephone (800) 791-9354, Fax (610) 853-9146
Email: queries@casemateacademic.com
www.casemateacademic.com/oxbow

Oxbow Books is part of the Casemate Group

Front cover: P. Kellis Copt. 78
Back cover: P. Kellis Copt. 122

CONTENTS

Preface...1
Introduction...4
Abbreviations..16

HOUSE 3

Letter on a wooden board (with traces of an earlier text in Syriac)
P. Kellis Copt. 57 17

Texts perhaps additional to groups published in Volume 1
P. Kellis Copt. 58 - 60 20

Manichaean letters
P. Kellis Copt. 61 - 63 29

Letters by Pamour (and Maria)
P. Kellis Copt. 64 - 72 39

Letters by Pegosh (brother of Pamour)
P. Kellis Copt. 73 - 79 83

Letters from Philammon to Theognostos (Louishai) and Hor
P. Kellis Copt. 80 - 82 118

Letters from Theognostos
P. Kellis Copt. 83 - 84 135

Letters from and to Ploutogenes
P. Kellis Copt. 85 - 91 143

Kyra / Loihat / Timotheos group
P. Kellis Copt. 92 - 93 164

Individual and unplaced documents and letters
P. Kellis Copt. 94 - 121 172

List of other (not edited) Coptic fragments from House 3..259

HOUSE 4

Letters
P. Kellis Copt. 122 - 124 263

Inventory
P. Kellis Copt. 125 280

Invocation
P. Kellis Copt. 126 284

List of other (not edited) Coptic fragments from House 4..289

TEMPLE ENCLOSURE

Letters

P. Kellis Copt. 127 - 128 290

Varia

P. Kellis Copt. 129 - 131 299

List of other (not edited) Coptic fragments from the Temple Enclosure 306

Indices:
- Native words 307
- Loan words 339
- Greek words in Greek context 344
- Personal names 346
- Geographical names (and provenances) 350
- Conjugations 351
- Triadic pronominals (PTN) 357
- Subject index (English language) 360

Inventory numbers 361

Note concerning the photographs 365

P. Kellis addenda and corrigenda 365

Plates 367

PREFACE

This volume is the culmination of over twenty years of work. The three authors have spent many seasons in the Dakhleh Oasis working on the texts, individually, in pairs, or on occasion all together. Out of season we have continued to work at home (in Australia, Germany and Canada), exchanging drafts and ideas and sudden realisations. It has been enormously interesting and intellectually rewarding, and our first thanks are given to C.A. Hope of Monash University whose archaeological fieldwork recovered the texts and who entrusted their publication to ourselves. Colin has been generous and supportive, and is of course the authority on the site of Ismant el-Kharab.

Further, we are indebted in many ways both personal and professional to all our colleagues on the Dakhleh Oasis Project. It has been one of the most stimulating and friendly environments one could hope to have, and we are fortunate to have received this opportunity. We cannot mention everyone by name, but in particular we are most grateful to A.J. Mills, who inaugurated and led the Dakhleh Oasis Project from the start (of which the excavations at Ismant el-Kharab developed as a constituent part). Also Lesley Mills, who has ensured such a warm and welcoming atmosphere at the various dig houses over the years; Gillian Bowen, for her infectious energy and interest in our work; and all the other leading colleagues on the project for their incredible expertise on everything under the Saharan sun, especially Olaf Kaper, Fred Leemhuis, Mary McDonald, Rufus Churcher, and many others with much affection. We are also grateful for the support given by all the members of the Supreme Council of Antiquities who have facilitated our work in Egypt over many years.

A special thanks is due to our papyrological colleagues working on the Greek texts recovered from both this site and elsewhere in the Oasis. We have worked closely for many years with both Klaas Worp and Roger Bagnall, and profited constantly from their incomparable knowledge of fourth-century Egypt. Both have read drafts of this volume, as also have C.A. Hope and G.E. Bowen, and we are most grateful for the help and suggestions from all. The Coptic texts in this volume must be read together with the Greek documents published by our colleagues, which enrich and clarify content and context in a great many ways.

Over the years we have used photographs taken variously by Bruce Parr, Robert Colvin and Colin Hope. A selection of these are reproduced as plates in the volume. However, a major step forward occurred in early 2009 when Jay Johnston of the University of Sydney visited Dakhleh and took the digital photographs supplied with this volume on disc. This has made a crucial difference to our being able to complete the volume, and we are indeed grateful to her and also to Michael Myers for post-production of the images in Sydney.

We have at various times received financial grants (for travel, accommodation, consumables and so on) from a number of learned and charitable institutions, and we are enormously grateful for this necessary aid to our work to: The Australian Research Council; The Australian Academy of Humanities; Fonds de recherche du Québec - Société et Culture; The Egyptology Society of Victoria; The Seven Pillars of Wisdom Trust; The Faculty of Arts at Monash University; The School of Letters, Art and Media at the University of Sydney. We also wish to thank the various institutions at which we have worked for both the time and facilities to complete this publication, especially The University of Sydney.

A few final comments may be made about the process of producing this volume. The research has been collaborative and no individual author is responsible for any single text or group of such. Anthony Alcock was the first to view and study many of the fragments that had been recovered, and his early draft translations helped each of us to see how we might read and understand them. The overall project to produce both volumes in the series has been led by Iain Gardner, and during 2010 and 2011 he worked to collate the material we had generated over the years into a coherent and ordered compilation, including the writing of all the introductory material found here, so as to actually achieve a final publication of these important documents. He is largely responsible for the collation of fragments, the reconstruction and description of actual documents, and arranging them into groups according to familial relations or other criteria. Wolf-Peter Funk generated an invaluable concordance for all the Coptic texts, and his work especially on dialect and his linguistic expertise placed the project on secure foundations. He has also produced the indices. Final responsibility for the volume is taken by Iain Gardner, with the warmest of thanks to his colleagues and friends of many years.

Iain Gardner, Sydney
Anthony Alcock, Kassel
Wolf-Peter Funk, Québec
February 2013

INTRODUCTION

The purpose of this volume is to complete the publication of Coptic documents recovered at the site of Ismant el-Kharab (ancient Kellis) by the excavations directed by C.A. Hope. This archaeological project began in 1986 and almost from the start (1987) Coptic material was recovered. The first finds from House 1, House 2 and the North Building were relatively minor, with much the greatest mass from House 3 in the 1990-91 and 1991-92 seasons. There were then some important pieces from House 4 in the 1992-93 season; after which only occasional and mostly rather poor fragments during the following years, all from the Temple area and mainly from strata relating to domestic purposes after the Tutu Temple itself had fallen into disuse about the 330s C.E. The final pieces published here were recovered in 1997, and although archaeological work has continued at various places across the site there have been no publishable finds of Coptic since that year. What is noticeable is that texts written in Coptic have been found only in structures of particular purpose (domestic) and from a clearly defined time-span (second half of the IVth century with ancient Kellis deserted by 400 C.E.). Of course, texts in other languages and scripts are similarly associated with particular find sites and time-spans, with Greek material the most ubiquitous at the site overall. Interestingly, neither the churches nor the Christian cemeteries have yielded Coptic material (but one may note that such were mostly found to be devoid of any texts whatsoever).

This is the second volume of *Coptic Documentary Texts from Kellis*, and really they form two halves of a single work. In particular, the first volume ended part-way through the publication of texts that had been recovered from House 3, and this sequence continues directly through the greater part of the second. The two volumes together present much the largest quantity of Coptic documents dated prior to 400 C.E. to have ever been made available to modern scholarship. In the following fairly brief introduction we shall not repeat the extensive detailed sections found in the introduction to the first volume. That would tend to being repetitive; and, besides, the volume is already too large and too long-delayed for such an undertaking. Details about prosopography, or weights and measurements, or commodities, can be tracked through the indices; and we have also included sub-introductions to each section that will provide direction to the reader. Instead, in the following pages we will attempt some summary remarks about the finds of Coptic documentary material from Ismant el-Kharab as a whole. Whether there were particular circumstances at play in ancient Kellis, and whether these findings can be regarded as statistically significant or applicable to the situation elsewhere, are relevant questions; but in the absence of anything really comparable they are difficult to answer. We will make such suggestions as seem to be warranted by the available evidence, even though they may be somewhat hypothetical. We hope to show that the finds have wider utility for an understanding of the development of Coptic in its crucial early phase.

Although the quantity of material recovered is remarkable, especially in comparison with the relative paucity of Coptic documents from this period elsewhere available, it presents various problems for the historian (and indeed for the papyrologist). There are the obvious difficulties of poorly preserved fragments, incomplete documents, missing text, uncertain readings and so on. Further, the great majority of the documents are letters or memoranda belonging to late fourth-century villagers writing to family, friends and associates. Little is given in the way of explanatory context, much is presumed knowledge between persons who knew each other well. In comparison to Greek documents of the same period, there are not really any dates given, witnesses cited, authorities invoked or legal processes involved. There are a certain number of epistolary conventions, which do make easier the reading of difficult passages and reconstruction of fragmentary lines, but they are mostly to do with rather mundane and formulaic matters of greeting and farewell. All of this makes for difficult reading, a considerable amount of repetition and obscurity, and major problems in terms of reconstructing the relationships between the persons concerned (especially as the authors rarely provide patronymics and are rather fond of abbreviated names). Nevertheless, concentrated study of the material provides a remarkable opportunity to understand the lives of ordinary persons, and the peculiar features of the collection (especially in terms of language, gender, religion and occupation) make a real contribution to our understanding of a pivotal moment in late antique society.

In the first volume[1] we made as detailed a study of the dating as seemed possible. Although we now have more extensive data, our conclusions remain the same in all essential details. That is: the archaeological context (stratigraphy, ceramics, coins etc.) corresponds to general historical processes (including the spread of Christianity), as well as dating mechanisms such as palaeography, to make a fourth century date for almost all the Coptic documents certain. Efforts to be more exact than that largely depend on analysis of the economic data in the documents (specifically the commodity prices in a period of high inflation) and cross-referencing through prosopography to dated Greek contracts from the same find sites. These factors enabled us to make more precise conclusions, and we argued that the evidence places the great majority of the Coptic documents, indeed all about which we can ascertain substantial data, in an approximate quarter century from ca. 355-380+ C.E. This gives a satisfying and rather tight chronological context, and one that corresponds to broader historical changes during the decades leading up to the accession of Theodosius.

We can detail the gross number of texts corresponding to find site:[2]

---

[1] See especially the summary in CDT I, pp. 8-11.

[2] For the archaeological context of documents from Houses 1-3: C.A. Hope, 'The Archaeological Context', in CDT I, pp. 96ff. For House 4: G.E. Bowen, C.A. Hope and O.E. Kaper, 'A Brief Report on the Excavations at Ismant el-Kharab in 1992-93, *Bulletin of the Australian Centre for Egyptology*, 4, 1993: 25-6. On the dating of the structure: C.A. Hope, 'Observations on the Dating of the Occupation at Ismant el-Kharab', in C.A. Marlow, A.J. Mills, eds., *The Oasis Papers I*, Oxbow Books, Oxford 2001: 54-5. For the Temple area: All but one of the documents derive from Area D/8 which is not technically a part of the actual Temple complex in that its function does not relate it to the religious activity carried out there, and also it cannot be accessed from the Temple. It appears to post-date the use of the Temple for religious purposes. Cf. C.A. Hope, 'Excavations in the Settlement of Ismant el-Kharab in 1995-1999', in C.A.Hope, G.E. Bowen, eds., *Dakhleh Oasis Project: Preliminary Reports on the 1994-1995 to 1998-1999 Field Seasons*, Oxford 2002: 199-204. For D/2 (the *mammisi*): There is an overview of the

Group 1 = Houses 1, 2 and 3 (including the North Building). The house 'numbers' represent nothing more that the sequence in which the structures were excavated. These structures are contiguous, and although in strict archaeological terms they represent different building histories, as regards the textual finds there are such common features across them (including fragments of single documents found in separate structures and the strong probability of family relationships across the buildings) that we see little point for our purposes here in distinguishing them. Of course, much the greatest quantity of textual material (Greek as well as Coptic) came from House 3.

Group 2 = House 4. This structure is also in the domestic Area A at Ismant el-Kharab, and of the same approximate date as the previous, though of more elaborate construction. However, it is several hundred metres away, and must be supposed to have had distinct series of inhabitants.

Group 3 = Area D. This corresponds to some scattered finds of Coptic documents from sites evidencing domestic re-use within the old Temple area. Dating can not be so exact for these pieces, but they would still come from the same half century 340-390 C.E. as the groups 1 and 2. This is probable because the evidence we have is that the Temple dedicated to Tutu fell into disuse in the 330s. The Coptic documents will postdate this event. However, apart from this, there is little unity to this group (although they do make an interesting contrast in terms of dialect and to some extent orthography as compared to group 1).

Total numbers of Coptic texts (including literary pieces)

<u>Group 1</u> (Houses 1-3 and North Building):

Letters:	177
(of which are published:	110)
Accounts, lists, etc.:	6
Writing exercise:	1

---

decoration and function of the room is O.E. Kaper, 'Pharaonic-style Decoration in the Mammisi at Ismant el-Kharab: New Insights after the 1996-1997 Season', in Hope and Bowen, eds., op. cit. 2002: 217-23.

Jar stopper:	1
New Testament:	2
Works of Mani:	2
Other Manichaean literature:	10
Magic (?):	2
Coptic / Syriac glossaries:	2
(other Syriac:	6)

Group 2 (House 4):

Letters:	3
(of which are published:	3)
Accounts, lists:	1
Other Manichaean literature:	1
Magic:	1

Group 3 (Temple area):

Letters:	19
(of which are published:	3)
Accounts, lists:	1
Magic:	1
('Old Coptic' letter	1)
(other Syriac:	1)

There are a number of issues with this list, including matters of genre (e.g. 'magic' is itself problematic), but also with the totals given. In particular, it is probably impossible to give an absolute total number of documents (n.b. this is a calculation of the number of discrete <u>productions</u>, not of the number of actual texts). For instance, we list here 177 letters from Group 1, of which 110 are now published. These figures must necessarily remain open to debate. Firstly, there is the question of genre: For instance, **69** is really a kind of affidavit rather than a letter; **123** is essentially a receipt, though in epistolary form; and then there are other pieces that are just notes of various kinds or primarily concerned with recording business dealings (e.g. **114**). Further, as one moves down from the well-preserved pieces of clear purpose the remains become increasingly fragmentary, until at the extreme end one is left with small scraps which could conceivably be joined to other pieces, or even in the worst cases where one is unsure if it is Coptic or Greek (when only a couple of letters are hardly visible). Nevertheless, we think it important to try to calculate the gross number of original documents, as it gives an idea of the magnitude of the find and also enables some statistics to be calculated.

In what follows we are concerned exclusively with the documentary texts proper, that is the letters and the associated accounts and lists. As already noted, the boundaries between these categories are somewhat blurred, in that some of the 'letters' are hardly more than memoranda themselves, and may provide very similar information to the 'accounts' but contained within epistolary conventions. Certainly, the household accounts were produced by some of the same persons as the letters. On this matter of blurred boundaries, one must of course emphasise that some of the Greek documents (and literature) from the same sites, especially group 1, were undoubtedly produced by the same people as some of the Coptic. We will return to the question of bilingualism below.

To turn now to the question of what writing surface was used. Of the 183 letters and accounts found from group 1 sites, 163 were written on papyrus, 8 on wooden boards, 1 on parchment and 1 is an ostracon. However, this total is derived from 177 letters and 6 accounts, but of the 8 for which wooden boards were used 4 of those were in fact accounts (i.e. 4 out of 6) and 4 were letters (i.e. 4 out of 177). It is apparent that wood was preferred for the accounts. This point is confirmed (though statistically useless) from group 2 where the 3 letters are on papyrus and the 1 account is on wood. Issues of genre are more complicated in group 3 and we refrain from including that data here. In fact, evidence elsewhere confirms that the use of wooden boards for writing letters was unusual.[3]

---

[3] See the recent listing by K.A. Worp, *A New Survey of Greek, Coptic, Demotic and Latin Tabulae Preserved from Classical Antiquity*, version 1.0 (February 2012) = Trismegistos

Incidentally, as an aside regarding the literary material: The 2 New Testament texts and the 2 by Mani are all on papyrus, i.e. from codices; however, the 2 Coptic-Syriac glossaries are on wooden boards, and of the 11 listed as 'other Manichaean literature' (which are mostly psalms and prayers) 7 are on wooden boards. This use of wood may partly be accounted for in terms of communal usage and catechetical purpose.

For both papyrus and wood there is evidence of a great deal of re-use, and writing material was obviously a valuable and sometimes scarce commodity. In the archive there are some extreme examples where almost every available square centimetre has been used (e.g. **19**, **58**, **94**), and certainly one can find correlations between patterns of papyrus usage and sub-sets of authors / scribes, which may be related to socio-economic factors. For instance, **29** is marked by its expansive margins, and we note that the author Piene is in the entourage of the Teacher (the Manichaean leader in Egypt) with whom he will travel to Alexandria. Writing to his mother in distant and provincial Kellis, the format is a kind of statement about how well her son is doing. In contrast, the group entitled 'Petros' letters repeatedly evidence the author using scrap pieces of second-hand papyrus, to which practice he himself refers in **39**, 20.

There is need for a systematic typology of the papyrus sheets used for the letters found at Ismant el-Kharab. We do not have all the data available that would be needed to achieve this (especially across time-spans and languages / scripts). However, it is apparent that a great many of the Coptic letters used sheets of approximately the same height, between 260-280 mm. The width then varies, with some very thin (about 50-60 mm.) e.g. **36**; others about twice as wide (110-120 mm.) e.g. **20**; and others thrice (about 170-180 mm.) e.g. **19**. Height is almost always greater than width, with the papyrus generally folded in half and then rolled into the characteristic tube shape that would be tied with the address

---

Online Publications #6 (http://www.trismegistos.org/top.php). It is noticeable that letters are almost non-existent amongst the types of texts represented in Greek and Coptic from Egypt, with the rather interesting exception of those from Douch in the Khargeh Oasis.

visible on the outer surface. Sometimes the same author (or perhaps better the scribe) used papyrus of almost exactly the same dimensions, and wrote in the same format, and often indeed phrasing, for the letter. This is valuable evidence that should be collated as regards scribal practice and 'workshops'. Equally, it would be interesting to look across the multiple letters sent by a single more prolific author from the archive (e.g. Makarios or Pamour or Pegosh) to determine patters of format and style. It is apparent that authors utilised particular scribes or workshops on multiple occasions, and at other times (for whatever reasons?) went elsewhere.

When we first envisaged this introduction one of the issues that we most wanted to investigate and discuss was the social usage of language in Egypt's bilingual culture of late antiquity. However, it has been found difficult to detail this statistically. In part, this is because there is no account of the actual numbers of Greek documents found at Ismant el-Kharab either according to category or according to find site. The reason is presumably that Greek documentary papyri are much more common, not just from Ismant el-Kharab but generally from Egypt; and thus there is less interest in accounting for the many hundreds of small fragments without information value. On this matter one can consult Klaas Worp's introductory comments to his *Greek Papyri from Kellis I* (= P. Kellis I).

Another problem is the difficulty of calculating numbers according to categories of letters, by which we mean that it had originally been hoped to give figures and percentages separated into family letters, business letters and religious. These would then be compared across the language divide. However, such calculations prove extremely difficult partly because such purposes are greatly mixed in the letters, and partly because so many of them are only partially preserved. For such reasons the following comments are not as statistically grounded as one would wish, and rely to some extent on impressions of the material based on our two decades of work.

P. Kellis I published 90 documents in Greek from the 'group 1' sites, which volume represents the majority (though certainly not all) of the better-preserved papyri and texts on wooden boards that were found there. Compared with the Coptic texts from group 1 it must first be emphasised that the Greek documents evidence a much greater time-span of approximately one hundred years from about 290-390 C.E. Whilst it is possible that a few of the Coptic texts might come from the first part of the fourth century, all the available evidence focuses their production in a narrower time-span of approximately 355-380+ C.E, that is (roughly) only the final third of the period represented by the Greek documents. There are two reasons for this difference that immediately occur. The first and demonstrable reason is that no legal or higher administrative documents of formal character survive in the Coptic archive (**69** is the closest to such and thus of especial interest), whereas in the Greek there are many petitions and leases and contracts. This is precisely as one would expect: The use of Coptic for legal purposes is not generally to be found before the mid-sixth century.[4] The occupants of the house have preserved documents of lasting value, and these are written in Greek. The second and unprovable reason is that widespread use of Coptic even for more informal purposes such as letters and household accounts, at least for the social groups represented here, may not have begun until about the mid-fourth century. This is an important issue to pursue, but problematic because of the lack of precise dates for such material.

To turn now purely to the letters preserved in Greek, we count 25 published in P. Kellis I. Unfortunately we do not know the total number of such that were found. However, there are published 110 Coptic letters from the same group 1 sites, and even given that what is 'publishable' in fourth century Coptic (due to relative scarcity) is different to what is regarded as 'publishable' in Greek, it would appear that this particular social group favoured letter-writing in Coptic in the latter half of the fourth century. Indeed, if we can be indulged recording our impressions here (which are difficult to quantify), most of the Greek letters are of prosaic purpose and a number are indeed listed as 'business letters'. Of course, these exist in the Coptic archive as well, but it is a clear impression that Coptic was favoured for the personal and the familial.

---

[4] See the discussion in R.S. Bagnall, *Everyday Writing in the Graeco-Roman East*, Berkeley 2011: 86.

Let us be as exact as we can. For religion, which amongst this group is essentially Manichaeism (and one wonders to what extent this makes a special case), there is only one Greek letter published that contains explicit evidence of such faith: P. Kellis I Gr. 63. Interestingly, this piece is not related in terms of prosopography to the Manichaean believers familiar from the Coptic archive, and also the editor dates it on both prosopographic and palaeographic grounds to the first part of the fourth century. This raises the hypothesis that by the latter half of the century Coptic had become the preferred vehicle for such expressions of faith.[5] Indeed, we count at least 23 of the 110 Coptic letters from group 1 to be published that have reasonably explicit expressions of Manichaean faith, by which we mean reference to the 'Paraclete' or the 'Light Mind' or suchlike; (of course prosopographical grouping shows that a much higher percentage of the total were written by people who can reasonably be supposed to have been Manichaeans).

As regards gender: this is one matter that can to some extent be statistically demonstrated. One can calculate the number of the Coptic letters from group 1 that were either written by or to a woman, or which directly address (not just name or greet) a female recipient. Of the 177 total many are too fragmentary to be of any use, but our admittedly rather rough count (i.e. including a number of assumptions that can not always be clearly demonstrated) of the others came to 43 out of 98. We might give some latitude for error and say in excess of 40%. Using the same criteria, we count 2 out of the 25

---

[5] There is at least one other Greek letter from House 3 with strong religious terminology, but it was deemed too poorly preserved to be publishable. The terminology is broadly Christian (i.e. rather than 'pagan'), but that characterisation could easily include Manichaeism in this context. There is also the unanswerable question as to why certain authors occasionally used Greek rather than Coptic. P. Kellis I Gr. 67, 71 and 72 can all be included in sub-sets of the Coptic letters. For instance, 71 clearly belongs with at least 9 other letters in Coptic written by Pamour and his wife Maria from the Nile valley to family in Kellis. Why this letter was in Greek we can not say.

Greek letters in this category, i.e. less than 10%. We think that these figures are significant; and that for this social group in the latter 4th century there is a correlation between Coptic, family, gender and religious expression. It is well known that women are relatively invisible (with important exceptions) in the Greek documentary record from late antique Egypt.[6] However, this is certainly not the case in the Coptic archive discussed here.

Of course, there are unique features to this material. As regards the social group represented by our group 1 texts there are a preponderance of letters written by men (husband, fathers, brothers and sons) working in the Nile valley and writing to their womenfolk in Kellis. At the same time, the women in Kellis seem to have been involved in textile production, and at least one of the household accounts is explicitly written by a woman (**44**). This combination of circumstances and female economic activity may not be standard, as equally it has been asserted that gender relations in the Manichaean community (analogous perhaps to the medieval Cathars and other sectarians) were atypical.

In sum, the documents published in these two volumes break new ground in certain important respects. In the first place, they provide what is really a unique insight into the social and economic relations of a sectarian group within a late antique village, and furthermore the opportunity to study that group's interaction with other communities with whom they lived side-by-side. Equally, as regards religious culture, one is presented with a snap-shot of faith and practice at a crucial moment of major transformation (i.e. to a Christian, and indeed 'Coptic', culture). Whilst this picture is not necessarily entirely representative of the situation elsewhere, it is nevertheless illuminating as regards its complexity and the variety of competing forces that are evident.

---

[6] However, see J. Rowlandson, *Women and Society in Greek and Roman Egypt. A Sourcebook*, Cambridge 1998; also R.S. Bagnall, R. Cribiore, *Women's Letters from Ancient Egypt. 200 B.C - A.D. 800*, with Contributions by E. Ahtaridis, Ann Arbor 2006.

Further, these documents are a major step forward in redressing the imbalance caused by reading the history of fourth century Egypt from Greek, male, urban or monastic sources (to list a number of the more obvious problems). Here there is a voice for the indigenous population, women are very visible, and the experience of life on the (supposed) periphery, i.e. the Oasis and village, weighs against the preponderance of sources from metropolitan centres and seats of authority whether ecclesiastical or secular.

Finally, the texts in these two volumes provide data by which to test many of the standard assumptions about life in late antiquity, about literacy and the role of women, about communications and travel, about a multilingual society and normative forms of belief and practice, even about emotion and expression in ancient letter-writing. We hope in these publications to have given a voice to these documents, to have achieved the understanding that they surely deserve.

ABBREVIATIONS

CD	W.E. Crum, *A Coptic Dictionary*, Oxford 1939.
CDT	*Coptic Documentary Texts from Kellis* (i.e. the series of which this is the second volume and P. Kellis V is the first).
DOP	The Dakhleh Oasis Project.
frg/s.	Fragment/s of papyrus.
Inv #	Object inventory and papyrus deposit numbers used by the DOP. These correspond to the glass frames in which papyri are conserved.
KAB	R. Bagnall, (ed.), *The Kellis Agricultural Account Book*, (= P. Kellis IV Gr. 96), DOP monograph 7, Oxford 1997.
1Keph	H.-J. Polotsky, A. Böhlig, W.-P. Funk, eds., *Kephalaia*, Stuttgart 1940, 1966, 1999, 2000.
KLT	*Kellis Literary Texts* (i.e. the series in which P. Kellis II and VI have been published).
lh / rh	left hand / right hand (here generally used of margins).
LSJ	H.G. Liddell, R. Scott, *A Greek-English Lexicon*, new ed. H.S. Jones, Oxford 1940 (9th ed. plus 1996 revised supplement).
Namen	M. Hasitzka, *Namen in koptischen dokumentarischen Texten* (resource at http://www.onb.ac.at/files/kopt_namen.pdf).
PsBk2	C.R.C. Allberry, ed., *A Manichaean Psalm-Book II*, Stuttgart 1938.
r	Recto (generally the start and principal part of a document).
tr	Transverse (here generally text written in the margin of a letter)
v	Verso (generally the address of a letter and sometimes additional text)
SCA #	Supreme Council for Antiquities (previously Egyptian Antiquities Organisation, EAO) registration number. The SCA numbers have been recorded for some wooden boards and ostraca as an aid to finding these pieces in the official inventory books and storage facilities. In contrast, substantial finds of papyrus were generally grouped together in the inventory books under a single SCA #; and this is why such are not recorded here.

HOUSE 3

The great majority of texts edited and published in this volume are from House 3. The situation was the same in CDT I (= P. Kellis V). This is because the excavations at this domestic structure in Area A, which took place over two field-seasons (1990-91 and 1991-92), recovered such an enormous quantity of inscribed material. In contrast, there have been relatively few texts written in Coptic found elsewhere in Ismant el-Kharab; and the causes and implications of this are discussed in the introduction. What it does mean is that the documents in the two volumes need to be studied together to achieve an holistic understanding of the material, and readers will find here constant cross-references to texts from the first volume.

It is also important to reference the many documents written in Greek, and also recovered from House 3, published by Klaas Worp in P. Kellis I. Some of these were written by or for or sent to the very same persons as in the Coptic letters and business accounts. Translations of the most important of these are provided in this volume for ease of reference; but this does not substitute for studying that earlier volume. However, it may be noted that the Greek documents from House 3 cover a full century from the end of the third to the end of the fourth. As far as can be determined, the Coptic documents are all to be dated to the final forty years of habitation, from approximately 355 C.E. Whether this fact tells us anything about the spread of Coptic as a medium for writing, or is simply the result of the kinds of texts kept by the inhabitants, is a difficult but interesting question.

Mention must also be made of the KAB (= P. Kellis IV), written in Greek and edited by Roger Bagnall. Although this was found in House 2, it is to be dated either to the early 360s or later 370s, and thus belongs to exactly the same period as the many Coptic letters published in these two volumes. The account refers to a great many persons from Kellis and its vicinity, as well as detailing prices and commodities, and some of these are most probably the same individuals as in the Coptic documents. Finally, one should consult KLT I and II (= P. Kellis II and VI). These literary texts in Coptic, Greek and Syriac, of which again the majority were recovered from House 3, provide evidence of the reading of the inhabitants, which was primarily religious and most specifically Manichaean (on the whole). Some of the texts may actually have been written by persons we encounter in the Coptic letters, a number of which refer to the copying of such material.

LETTER ON A WOODEN BOARD
(WITH TRACES OF AN EARLIER TEXT IN SYRIAC)

P. Kellis Copt. 57

Inv #: A/5/280 + A/5/260

SCA #: 2113

Location: House 3, room 11, deposit 3

Preservation: An almost square wooden board in two parts. Coated, and written on both sides (A and B). 68 x 70mm; lh and upper margins of 6mm.

Content: A short letter written in Coptic; but poorly preserved. Above the first line (and perhaps also at its start?) there are traces of Syriac from a previous text of unknown type. The positioning of the Syriac may indicate that this board has been cut anew from a larger tablet on which the earlier text was inscribed, and thus suggests that the former was no longer regarded as of value.

Address: No address.

Names: P- (?); Pshai;

Text:

	traces of Syriac text
A1	ⲡⲁⲓⲱⲧ ⲙ̄ⲙⲉ[ⲣ]ⲓ̣ⲧ ⲉⲧ`ⲧⲁⲓ̈ⲁⲓ̈ⲧ ⲛ̄
2	ⲧⲟⲧ ⲧⲟ̣[ⲛ]ⲟ̣ⲩ ⲡ . . . ⲁⲛⲁⲕ
3	ⲡϣⲁⲓ̈ ϩⲙ̄ ⲡⲭ̣[ⲁⲓ̈ⲥ ⲭⲁⲓ]ⲣⲉⲓ̣ⲛ̣
4	[†]ϣⲓ̣ⲛⲉ ⲁⲣⲁⲕ ⲧⲟ̣ⲛⲟ̣[ⲩ . .] . . . .
5	[. .] . ⲁⲓ̈ⲱⲡ ⲁ̣ . . . [. . .] . . .
6	[. . .] . . . . [. . . . .] .
7	†ϣⲓⲛⲉ ⲁ̣ . [. .] . . . . ⲕⲏ
8	. . ⲓ̈ . . [. . . . .] . . . . .
9	. . ⲛ̣ⲧⲁⲣ[. . . . .] . . .
10	. . . . . [. . . . .] . ⲡ[. . .]ⲟϣ
B11	ϫⲉ ⲙ̄ⲡⲟⲩⲧⲉⲥ ⲛⲏⲓ̈ ⲡⲁϫⲉⲩ ϫⲉ
12	ϣⲁⲧ[ⲉ]ⲕϫⲟⲥ †ⲥⲁⲩⲛⲉ ⲅⲁⲣ
13	ⲛ̄ⲧⲕ̄ⲙⲛ̄ⲧⲙⲁⲓ̈ⲣⲱⲙⲉ ϫⲉ
14	ⲕⲁⲛ[.]ⲉ̣ . . . . ⲧ̄ⲕ̄ ⲁⲩⲛⲁϭ
15	ⲛ̄ϩⲱ̄ⲃ ⲛ̣ . [.] . . . . ⲙ ⲛⲏⲓ̈
16	ⲙⲛ̄ⲕ . . [. .] . . . .
17	ⲣ̄ⲡϩⲱⲃ ⲕ̄[. . .] . . . . . .
18	ⲙ̄ⲡⲱⲣ̄ⲣⲁ[ⲙⲉⲗⲉⲓ] . . . .
19	ϫⲉ †ⲭⲣⲓⲁ [. . . .] . . . . . .

———

12 ϣⲁⲧ[ⲉ]ⲕϫⲟⲥ: ϣ- ex ϩ- corr.

———

(A) My loved father, who is greatly honoured by me, P- (?). (It is) I, Pshai; in the Lord, - greetings.

I greet you warmly ... (5) ... I counted (?) ... I greet ... (10) ... (B) for they did not give it to me. They say: "(Not) until you say so". For I know your love of people, that ... a great (15) thing ... for me ... do the thing you ... Do not [neglect to] ... for I am in need [of] ...

Commentary:

13   ⲙⲛ̄ⲧⲙⲁⲓ̈ⲣⲱⲙⲉ: i.e. equivalent to the Greek φιλανθρωπία.

TEXTS PERHAPS ADDITIONAL TO GROUPS PUBLISHED IN VOLUME 1

There follow three pieces that may belong to groups of texts published in CDT I. It is most probable that **58** is another letter by Orion[7] (**15-18**); but the connections suggested for the others are rather speculative. The pieces have no particular association with each other beyond this organisational matter. If they do not belong to previous groups they can be counted as unplaced within the general corpus.

P. Kellis Copt. 58

Inv #: P 17EE

Location: House 3, room 10, deposit 3

Preservation: A mostly complete business letter written on two sides (both ^, thus with side B perpendicular to side A), now breaking along the folds. The remains are 113 x 95 mm.; but the original dimensions were probably about 10 mm. greater at the top of side A (and thus ca. 123 x 95 mm.). We think that only one or two lines are missing at the start of A; and perhaps five or so letters at the end of each line on side B. Line 37 must be the final one.

Content: Substantially of business content and concerning textiles. In this it is similar to P. Kellis Copt. **18** (written by Orion to Tehat). The hand is also very much the same, and the find spot is identical (see the summary on p. 336 of P. Kellis V). Consequently, although neither sender nor recipient are named in **58**, we are fairly certain that the author is again Orion and the recipient may well be Tehat. It is also reasonable to identify the person of Lauti in this piece with the Lautine of the other (**18**, 3; see also **17**, 4); and we think that there is a certain brother Saren common to both pieces. On the other hand,

---

[7] In CDT I the name was always spelt Horion for Ὡρίων, following K.A. Worp's usage in P. Kellis I. However, on reconsideration, we regard this spelling to be a better choice.

Talaphanti connects it to the Makarios family, so that the text can be associated with two of the main groups represented in CDT I.

Address: No visible address, and it is difficult to see how there could have been space for one.

Names: Erakl<ei> (Herakles); Lauti (= Lautine?); Saren; Talaphanti; Tharre (?);

Text:

A(x + 1) [. . . .] . . . ⲛⲕⲗⲉϥⲧ ⲉⲛⲁⲛⲟⲩ ⲛ̄ⲑⲉ ⲛ̄ⲧⲉⲧ
2 ⲁ̣ⲧⲉⲧⲛ̄ⲧⲛ̄ⲛⲁⲩⲥ ⲛⲏⲓ̈ ⲁⲃⲁⲗ ϩⲁⲧⲛ̄ⲥϩⲉⲓ̈ ϫⲉ ⲁ
3 ϣⲱⲡⲉ ⲉⲕⲟⲩⲁϣⲥ̄ ⲕⲁⲥ ⲛⲉⲕ ⲏ ⲙ̄ⲙⲁⲛ ⲙ̄ⲛ̄ⲧ
4 ϣⲁⲙⲧⲉ ⲛ̄ϣⲉ ⲛ̄ϭⲛϭⲱⲣ ϩⲁⲓ̈ⲥϩⲉⲓ̈ ϭⲉ ⲛⲏⲧⲛ̄ ⲙ̣̄
5 ⲡϩⲟⲟⲩ ⲉⲧⲙ̄ⲙⲟ ϫⲉ ϩⲁⲓ̈ⲧⲉⲉⲥ ⲙ̄ⲛⲥ̣ⲛⲏⲩ ⲙ̄ⲧⲉⲧⲛ̄
6 ⲟⲩⲱ †ⲛ̣ⲁ†ⲥⲟⲩⲛⲧⲥ ⲛⲏⲧⲛ̄ ϩⲁ ⲗⲁⲩ† ϫⲟⲥ ⲛⲏⲓ̣̈
7 ϫⲉ ⲡⲉⲧⲉ̣ⲕⲟⲩⲁϣϥ †ⲛⲁⲛ̄ⲧϥ̣ ⲛⲉⲕ ⲙ̄ⲙ̣ⲛ̣[ⲧ]
8 [ⲥ]ⲛⲁⲩⲥ̣ ⲛ̄ϣⲉ̣ ⲙ̄ⲡⲓϫⲓ ⲥⲉϫⲉ ⲛ̄ⲧⲟⲧϥ̄ ⲡⲁϫⲉⲓ̈ ϫⲉ ⲙⲛ̄
9 ⲭⲣⲓⲁ †ⲛ̣ⲟⲩ ϭⲉ ⲧⲉⲧⲛⲁⲧⲁⲣⲱϣⲉ ⲛ̄ϩⲉ ⲛⲓ̣ⲙ̣
10 [. . ⲡⲙⲁ ⲉ]ⲧⲉⲧⲛⲁϭⲛⲧⲟⲩ ⲙ̄ⲙⲁϥ ⲙ̄ⲛ̄ϣⲧⲁⲉⲟⲩ
11 [ϩⲁⲧⲉⲧⲛ̄]† ⲛⲏⲓ̈ ⲛ̄ⲟⲩⲱ ⲛⲓⲙ ⲉϣⲱⲡⲉ ⲉⲥⲉ ⲛⲁϣⲏ̣
12 [ⲣⲉ . . . . ⲛⲉ]ϥϩⲁⲙⲧ ⲛ̄ⲧⲉⲧⲛ̄ⲧⲉⲟⲩ ϩⲁ ⲛ̄ⲕⲉⲭⲣⲓ
13 [ⲁ . . . .]ⲧⲛ̄ⲛⲁⲩ ⲛⲏⲧⲛ̄ ⲉⲧⲃⲉ ⲡⲓϩⲱⲃ †ⲛⲁϫⲓ
14 ⲧⲟⲩ ⲁⲛ̣ⲁ . . . . . . †ⲣⲁⲝⲓⲟⲩ ⲁⲛ ⲙ̄ⲙⲱⲧⲛ̄
15 ⲙ̄ⲡⲓⲕⲉⲟⲩⲉ ⲁⲛⲟ ϫⲉ ⲛ̄ⲧⲉⲧⲛⲁϭⲛ̄ ϩⲏⲛⲉ ⲥⲛ̄ⲧⲉ ⲉⲛⲁ
16 ⲛⲟⲩⲟⲩ ⲉⲩϣⲙⲁⲧ ⲉⲓⲥ ⲡ†ⲕⲙⲁ ⲁⲓ̈ⲧⲛ̄ⲛⲁⲩϥ ⲛⲏⲧⲛ̄
17 ⲏ ⲛ̄ⲧⲁϥ ϫ̣ⲉ ⲛ̄ⲧⲉⲧⲛⲁϭⲛ̄ ⲥⲁⲣⲧ ⲙ̄ⲡⲟⲩⲁⲟⲩⲉⲛ ⲛ̄ⲧⲉⲧⲛ̄
18 ⲧⲣⲟⲩϩⲉⲥⲧⲟⲩ ⲉⲩϣⲙⲁⲧ ⲧⲟⲛⲟⲩ ⲛ̄ⲑⲉ ⲛ̄ⲛⲉⲧⲉϣⲁ ⲑⲁⲣⲣⲏ̣
19 ⲛ̄ⲧⲁⲗⲁⲫⲁⲛⲧⲓ ⲧⲁⲛⲁⲩ ⲛ̄ⲛⲥϩⲟⲛⲉ ⲧⲉⲧⲛⲟⲩⲱϣ ⲕⲱⲧⲉ
20 ⲁⲛ ⲛ̄ⲥⲉϭ̣ⲁⲣⲧ ⲙ̄ⲡⲓⲙⲁ ⲥϩⲉⲓ̈ ⲛⲉⲛ   ἔρρ(ωσο)

B21 ⲛⲓϩⲏⲛⲉ ⲙⲛ̄ ⲛⲓ[ⲕⲗⲉ]ϥ̣ⲧ ⲛⲉⲡⲛ̄ϭⲁⲛ ⲛⲉ ⲥ̣ⲁⲣⲏⲛ ⲉϥⲛⲁⲓ̈ ϭⲉ ⲉ[. . . . . .]
22 ϩⲉⲗϭⲏⲧ ⲧⲟⲛⲟⲩ ⲧⲟ[ⲛⲟⲩ] . ϭ̣ϣⲱⲛ ⲏⲣⲁ̣ⲕⲗ<ⲉⲓ̣> ⲁⲥϩⲉⲓ̣ ⲁⲧⲣⲟⲩⲓ̈ ⲁⲟⲩⲁϩⲉ ⲧⲁ̣[ⲃⲱⲕ ⲁ]

23 ⲙⲉⲩ ⲛ̄ⲧⲁⲛⲟ ⲁⲣⲱ[ⲧ]ⲛ̄ ϥⲟⲩⲱϣ ⲛ̄ϩⲛⲉ ⲁⲥⲙ̄ⲛ̄ⲧⲟⲩ ⲛ̄ϩⲛ̄ⲑⲱⲣⲁϫ [. . . . .]

24 ⲧⲏ ⲛ̄ⲧⲱⲧⲛ̄ ⲁⲛ ⲉⲧ[ⲛ̄]ⲁⲟⲩⲁϫⲟⲩ ⲙⲛ̄ ⲡⲟⲩⲣⲱϣⲛ̄ ⲙⲛ̄ⲁ̣ ⲥ̣ⲛⲟ ⲛ̣̄[. . . . ⲣ]

25 ϣⲱⲛ ⲟⲩⲙⲛⲁ ⲙⲛ̄[.] . . ⲉ ⲛ̄ⲥⲁⲧⲉⲣⲉ̣ ⲛ̄ϣ†† ⲛⲁϭ ⲙⲛ̄ ⲡⲓⲣⲱϣⲛ̣ [. . . . .]

26 ⲙ̄ⲡⲓⲙⲁ ⲉϥⲛⲁⲧⲏ[ⲛⲁ]ⲩⲥ ⲁⲛ ⲛⲏⲧⲛ̄ ⲁⲟⲩⲁϫⲉ ⲟⲩⲉ ⲃⲁⲗ ⲙ̄ⲙ . . . [. . . . .]

27 ⲡⲃⲉⲕⲉ ⲥⲱϩ\ⲉ/ ϫⲉ . [. .]ϩⲓⲥⲉ ⲁⲣⲁ̣ⲓ ⲙⲛ̄ ⲟⲩϩⲁⲗⲁⲕ[ⲁ]ⲧⲓ ϫⲉ ϫⲁⲩϥ . [. . . . .]

28 ⲙ̄ⲡⲓϫⲓⲧϥ̄ ϣⲁⲧⲉⲧ[ⲉ]ϥ ⲛⲏⲧⲛ ⲁϣⲱⲡⲉ ⲧⲉⲧⲛ̄ⲣ̄ ⲡϩⲱⲃ ϣ[. . . . ⲙ]

29 ⲙⲁⲛ ⲇⲉ ⲧⲉⲧⲛⲁⲕⲁ̣[.] . ⲛ̄ⲗⲁⲩⲉ \ⲉⲛ/ . . . . ⲟⲩⲧⲉ̣ ϩⲓⲧⲛ ⲛ̄ⲣⲱⲙⲉ ⲡ[. . . . . .]

30 ⲁⲡϥ̄ⲧⲱϭⲥ ⲧⲉⲧⲛ̄ϫ̣[. .] ⲛ̄ⲟⲩⲣⲙ̄ⲙ̄ⲙ̣̄[ⲛ]ⲉ ⲡⲉ<ⲧ>ⲛ̄ⲣⲁⲙⲉⲗⲓ ⲙ̄ⲙⲁϥ ⲧϩⲏⲙ[ⲉ . . . . .]

31 ⲁⲣⲁϥ ϫⲉ ⲉⲟⲩⲁⲥⲡ[. . . . . . ⲙ̄]ⲡⲉϥⲧⲉⲥ ⲡⲁϫⲉϥ ϫⲉ ⲙⲛ̄ ⲫ[. . . . . .]

32 ϫⲁⲩⲥ ⲛⲏⲓ̈ ⲁⲟⲩⲁϩⲉ̣ . . . ⲁⲕⲣⲓ]ⲃⲱⲥ ⲙⲛ̄ ⲧⲥⲡⲟⲩⲇⲏ ⲉⲧⲉⲧⲛ̄ⲓⲣⲉ̣ [ⲙ̄ⲙⲁⲥ †]

33 †ⲉⲁⲩ ⲛⲏⲧⲛ̄ ⲧⲟϩ\ . . /ⲗ[. . . . . ⲁ]ⲙⲉⲗⲓ ⲁⲗⲁⲩⲉ ⲛ̄ϩⲱⲃ ⲛ̄ⲣ[. . . . . .]

34 ⲁⲙⲉⲗⲓ ⲁⲛⲏϩⲉ ⲁϩ[. . . . . . ⲙ̄]ⲙⲱⲧⲛ̄ ⲁⲣⲁϥ ⲙⲁⲥⲧⲁⲡⲁ[ϭ ϩⲱⲃ]

35 ⲛⲓⲙ ⲛ̄ϣⲁⲣⲡ ⲙ̄ . [. . . . .]ⲧⲛ̄ⲛⲁⲩ ⲧϩⲁⲓ̈ⲧⲉ ⲛ̄ . [. . . . . .]

36 ϣⲓⲛⲉ ⲁⲛⲉⲓ ϩⲁⲧⲏⲧ[ⲛ̄ ⲧⲏⲣⲟⲩ ϣⲓ]ⲛⲉ ⲁ[.]ⲁ . [. . .]ⲉ ⲙⲛ . [. . . . . . .]

37 ϣⲓⲛⲉ ⲁⲡ . . [. . . . .]

———

8 ⲙ̄ⲡⲓϫⲓ ⲥⲉϫⲉ: the text has been emended before ϫⲓ, and we suppose that the first person sing. is intended although it is by no means clear   21 ⲉϥⲛⲁⲓ̈: apparently ⲉϥⲛⲁⲓ̈, but probably no superlinear stroke was intended   27 ⲥⲱϩ\ⲉ/: ⲥ- ex ϩ- corr.   29 ⲙⲁⲛ: -ⲛ ex corr.

———

(A) ... good cowl, like the one which you (pl.) sent off for me. You wrote: "If you like it keep it, or else 1300 talents". So, I wrote to you (5) that day that I had given it to the brothers. Do you have no news? I will give you its price. Lauti told me: "The one that you (sing.) want I will bring it to you for 1200 (talents)". (But) I did not take word from (i.e. 'make an agreement with') him. I said that there is no need. Now, then, will you (pl.) satisfy me in every way? (10) [Wherever] you might find them, it is not possible for me to do them.

[Have you] given me all the news? If so, my children (?) ... his money and you can spend (it) on the other needs ... send you (a message) about this matter. I will receive them for ...

I also ask of you (15) this other (thing), to see whether you can find two good and fine fabrics - see the sample I sent you - or else, can you find wool of their colour and have it spun very fine, like the ones that

Tharre (daughter?) of Talaphanti makes for the women. Also, would you search (20) for wool at the place? Write to us. Farewell.

(B) These fabrics and these cowls belong to our brother Saren. Now, as he will come (would you be?) so very kind ... bid (?) Erakl(ei) to write to get them to come to the Oasis; and I shall [(also?) go] there and see you. He wants the fabrics to be made (into) jerkins ... Also, you are to cut them with their cloak(s): two *mna* for [each?] (25) cloak, one *mna* ... *staters* for large warp and this cloak. (Wool?) from the place he will also send to you, - to cut one from the ... the weaving wage so that [they can] spin for me with a distaff ... send it ... I did not receive it so that I could [give] it to you. If you will do the work ... But, if not, you can not keep (?) anything ... not even (?) from the men. ... (30) for its dye (?).

Can you send an honest man, - <you> did not neglect it? The freight ... to him, so that if they ... He has not given it. He said that there is no ... Send it to me to the Oasis ... precisely, with the speed with which (habitually) you do [it. I] salute you ... [Do not] neglect any work ... never neglect ... you to him. She can not make me settle any [matter] (35) before ... send the garment ...

Greet [all] these with you. Greet ... and ... Greet ...

Commentary:

One must read carefully the other pieces written by this author, (who we think is Orion, see **15-18**), to have a feeling for his context.

1-10   The sense of this somewhat complicated section seems to be something like this: The author has given a cowl as a free gift to some 'brothers'; which probably should be understood as alms given to the local Manichaean elect. Now, the weaving workshop that originally sent it to him and to whom he is writing (using the plural 'you', but perhaps specifically meaning Tehat) want its price from him. Orion (as we presume) is aggrieved, because he thought that the option of a gift had been clearly stated in their previous correspondence. He also points out that he could have had the same for less from Lauti. Nevertheless, it does not appear to be an enduring problem, because he turns to other news (l. 11); and then in l. 14 begins to discuss further business he would like to conduct with the workshop.

10   A generic place expression (thus ⲡⲙⲁ) would seem to be the most likely antecedent of the resumptive pronoun in ⲛ̄ⲙⲁϥ; but how this relates to the preceding context, and what 'they' are, remains obscure to us.

11   ⲉϣⲱⲡⲉ ⲉⲥⲉ: 'If so, ..'; lit. 'If yes, ..'. In our understanding, Orion has now finished with the previous matter of the disputed cowl, and in l. 11 signals a change of topic. Nevertheless, the purpose of the following incomplete passage (before a new matter is introduced with ϯⲣⲁϩⲓⲟⲩ ⲁⲛ 'I also ask ..' in l. 14) is difficult to follow.

18   ⲑⲁⲣⲣⲏ: This should be a personal name according to syntax, i.e. 'Tharre (daughter) of Talaphanti'. Cf. perhaps the name Θαραθης (discussed in H.J. Thissen, 'Zwischen Theben und Assuan. Onomastische Anmerkungen', *ZPE*, 90, 1992: 292-296 [294]). However, such a name is not found elsewhere in the House 3 documents, and one might prefer another reading (e.g. instead of ⲑⲁ- one could try ⲉⲧⲃ-, but we can make no sense of this). Could it somehow have a meaning such as 'the workshop' or 'quarter' of Talaphanti? On the latter name see P. Kellis V (p. 45).

19   ⲥϩⲟⲛⲉ: For this previously unattested word used for 'women' in the House 3 Coptic archive see the note and further references ad loc. **20**, 50. Whether it has any specific meaning within a Manichaean context, or is some kind of variant for ⲥⲱⲛⲉ or ⲥϩⲓⲙⲉ, is unknown.

20   ⲙ̄ⲡⲓⲙⲁ, lit. 'at this place': Perhaps one could translate as 'local', i.e. is the author simply asking his recipients to look out for some 'local wool'? The meaning may be the same at ll. 25-26, reading [ⲧⲥⲁⲣⲧ] | ⲙ̄ⲡⲓⲙⲁ. In general, it is difficult to determine whether the wool referred to in the many documents about weaving found in House 3 was local or imported from the Nile valley. It may be worth noting that wool is not mentioned in the KAB, but that could simply be because it was a record of crops and harvests rather than goods produced by animals (poultry being the most notable exception). It does occur in a number of Greek documents, including P. Kellis I 71, where Pamour in the valley writes to Pshai in the Oasis and promises to send each year a present of wool for a cloak as payment for the hire of a girl servant. The Greek word ἐρέα indicates that the wool was from sheep rather than goats, whereas the Coptic ⲥⲁⲣⲧ could be from either animal (CD 356b). In the indices to P. Kellis I see also ἐρίδιον and perhaps πορφύρα (purple-dyed wool?).

ἔρρ(ωσο): We presume that side A is the recto (with the opening greetings lost), if only in the sense that it was written first; and side B the verso (with the farewell greetings partially preserved), in that it will have been written after. In that case this formulaic farewell here was either written in before the actual letter was started, or side B has been added as an afterthought. Compare **17** (also written by Orion); although there are a number of similar examples of this in the archive.

21 Saren (ⲥⲁⲣⲏⲛ): We think that this must be the same person named as a presbyter in **18**, 22-23. In this case, the text there must be emended to remove the lacuna in the midst of his name, and (see the plate) the relevant small fragment pushed further left to cover the apparent gap. This will make some slight changes to the printed Coptic text of ll. 21-23, but we have not been able to autopsy the papyrus anew.

22 Erakl (ⲏⲣⲁⲕⲗ⟨ⲉⲓ⟩?): Presumably for Herakles, if we have read this correctly; but whether the same person as in **38** or **48** is unknown. In P. Kellis I Gr. 14 (dated 356 C.E.) an Aurelius Herakles witnesses a contract for an Aurelius Orion. This corresponds rather exactly to the dating that we assigned to the Orion letters in P. Kellis V.

23 ⲑⲱⲣⲁⲝ: The term is only found this once in the Coptic texts from Ismant el-Kharab, and we have translated it as 'jerkin(s)' following LSJ 814a. However, R. Livingstone, who is undertaking a study of the textiles from ancient Kellis, suggests that it might have been a scarf. She quotes U. Rothe: 'A heavy scarf was sometimes worn by Romans in cold weather. Most commonly it is seen worn by soldiers tucked into the collar of their paenula, but it was sometimes worn with the tunica alone' (*Dress and Cultural Identity in the Rhine-Moselle Region of the Roman Empire*, Archaeopress, Oxford, 2009: 41). Whilst this reference is obviously from the other end of the Roman world, Livingstone has no evidence of anything like a jerkin from her research.

27 ϩⲁⲗⲁⲕ[ⲁ]ⲧⲓ: i.e. ἠλακάτη, LSJ 767b, 'distaff' (a cleft stick used for spinning); noting the spelling and contemporary date of ἀλακάτιον (a diminutive form) in P. Oxy. 1740.8, LSJ 60a. Alternatively, one might consider ⲗⲁⲕⲟⲧⲉ, CD 140a, a 'liquid measure, mostly of wine'; but the context favours the former identification.

27-30 Under magnification it is apparent that there must be a slight crease or overlay of the papyrus, as recorded by the digital photograph; so that parts of the letters are obscured. This extends through the following words: l. 27 ϩ|ⲁⲗⲁⲕ[ⲁ]ⲧⲓ; l. 28 |ⲧⲉⲧⲛⲁⲣ̄; l. 29 ⲟⲩⲧ|ⲉ; l. 30 ⲁ|ⲙⲉⲗⲓ.

30 ⲟⲩⲣⲙⲛ̄ⲙ̄[ⲓ]ⲉ: The reading is difficult.

P. Kellis Copt. 59

Inv #: P 40

Location: House 3, room 8, deposit 1

Preservation: A small rectangular fragment from the upper lh corner of a Coptic letter on papyrus. The restoration suggested for ll. 1-2 (and the position of the address on the v) would indicate that the papyrus letter has split along a midway vertical fold. What remains is similar to the upper rh corner fragment of **36** (see the plate); and one suspects that the original dimensions and shape of this piece would have been similar to that one.

Content: This may be another letter by Ouales to Psais and Andreas (**35-37**), thus the speculative restoration of ll. 1-2 corresponding to **36**. The principal connection is prosopographical; but note something of a similar style with the opening in Greek.

Address:
verso

  τοῖς κυρίοις μου ἀδελφ[οῖς
   To my master brothers ...

Names: An[dreas] (?); [Ouales?]; Pshai;

Text:

1   τοῖς κυρίοις [μου ἀδελφοῖς]
2   Ψάϊτι Ἀγ[δρέᾳ Οὐάλης]
3   χαίρειν αι[. . . . .]
4   ⲣⲉ ⲟⲩⲉ ⲙ̄ⲙⲱ[ⲧⲛ . . . .]
5   . . . . . . ⲁⲛ̄[. . . . .]
6   ⲙ̄ⲙⲱⲧⲛ̄ ⲉⲓ . [. . . . .]
7   . ⲙⲁⲛ . vac ⲁⲛ[. . . . .]
8   ⲁⲧⲣⲛ̄ⲉⲓ ⲁ . . . [. . . . .]

House 3   27

9   [. . . .] . . [.] . [. . . . .]

To [my] master [brothers], Psais (and) Andreas (?). [From Ouales]; - greetings.

I ... [Let] one of you (pl.) ... (5) ... you ... I / We (?) ... to cause us to come to ...

Commentary:

7   ⲁⲛ[: This is probably the beginning of a new sentence, to be resolved either as 'I' (ⲁⲛ[ⲁⲕ); or, in view of the first plural in l. 8, as 'we' (conjugation base uncertain).

P. Kellis Copt. 60

Inv #: P 56C(a)ii

Location: House 3, room 9, deposit 3 west doorway

Preservation: 9 small rectangular strips of papyrus from a single letter written in a rather tiny script, which has broken along the folds. 4 of the strips join across the top, from which the opening lines of the text can be read (and reconstructed) with reasonable accuracy. The remaining scraps can not be placed and provide no coherent sense. They are not transcribed. There are also traces of another text on the verso.

Content: This may be another 'Petros' letter, (**38-41**). Notably, the find site is identical (see the summary on p. 336 of P. Kellis V); and the address corresponds to that of **38**. The style of the introduction is also similar; in that it is written to a mother by her son, but without the names of either sender or recipient. Also, all the pieces share the characteristics of being tightly-written on small 'scrap' pieces of papyrus.

Address:
verso

[τῇ τιμιω]τάτῃ μου μητρὶ   [X]   ὁ υἱός σου
To my most honoured mother. [X] Your son.

Names: None.

Text:

1 [ⲧⲁⲙⲟ ⲙ̄]ⲙⲉⲣⲓ[ⲧ]˙ ⲁⲛⲁⲕ ⲡⲉ{ⲕ}ϣⲏⲣ[ⲉ]
2 [ⲡⲉⲧⲥϩ]ⲉ̣ⲓ̈ ⲛⲉ ϩⲙ̄ ⲡⲭⲁⲓ̈ⲥ ⲭⲁⲓⲣⲉⲓⲛ
3 [ϩⲁⲑⲏ] ⲛ̄ϩⲱⲃ ⲛⲓⲙ˙ ϯϣ[ⲓ]ⲛⲉ ⲁⲡ[ⲁ]
4 [ⲓ̈ⲱⲧ] ⲙⲛ̄ ⲛⲉⲧϩⲙ̄ ⲡⲏⲓ̈ ⲧⲏⲣⲟⲩ ⲕ[ⲁⲧⲁ]
5 [ⲛⲟⲩⲣ]ⲉ̣ⲛ̣ [[.]]ⲙⲛ̄ⲛⲥⲱ̣ⲥ̣ ϯⲡ̄ . . [. . . .]
6 [. . . .] . ⲥ ⲙ̄[ⲡ]ⲉ̣ⲧ̣ⲛ̄ϯ [ⲡϩ]ⲱⲃ ⲛⲏ[ⲓ̈ . . . .]
7 [. . .] ⲛ̄ⲉϣ [. . . .] . ⲉⲓⲥ . [. . . . . . .]
8 [. . . . .]ⲩⲁⲛ ⲛ̣ . [. . . . . . .]
9 [. . . . .] . ⲱⲡ[. . . . .]
10 [. . . . .] . . [. . . . .]

[My] loved [mother]: (It is) I, your son, [who] writes to you; in the Lord, - greetings.

[Before] everything: I greet [my father] and all who are in the house [by (5) their] names. Next: I am ... you did not give [the] thing to me ... why ... (10) ...
(*remainder of the text not ordered and too fragmentary for useful translation*)

Commentary:

1   ⲡⲉ{ⲕ}ϣⲏⲣ[ⲉ]: The masc. form of the second person sing. must be in error and we have deleted it. Not only do we know from the address that the son is writing to his mother, but in l. 2 he correctly uses the fem. form (ⲛⲉ).

3   [ϩⲁⲑⲏ]: Although this is the most common form used in the formula throughout the archive as a whole, one might note that **39**, 3 uses ϩⲓⲑⲏ and **40**, 2 ϣⲁⲣⲡ in its place.

5-6   Perhaps ϯⲡ̄ ϣ[ⲡⲏⲣⲉ | ϫⲉ ⲡ]ϣⲥ: 'I am surprised at how (you did not ...)'.

7   Probably ⲛ̄ⲉϣ [ⲛ̄ϩⲉ.

MANICHAEAN LETTERS

In CDT I there were a number of authors who expressed their Manichaean faith explicitly, such as Orion, Makarios and Matthaios, Ouales; but their letters were (in good part) about other things, such as family and business matters. There were also letters where the faith or Manichaean 'connection' seemed to be paramount, and in these there was maintained a level of deliberate anonymity (notably **31** and see the introductory comments to that section). It is similar in this second volume (CDT II): There are again instances where the author's faith is explicit, or can be supposed with reasonable surety, although it is not their primary concern (such as **71**, Pamour writing to Partheni); and there are letters that we can specifically term Manichaean (this present section, **61-63**). Still, the examples of both types in CDT II are fewer. One could speculate about the reasons: accidents of preservation; a need for greater circumspection; a prevalence of business purposes; possibly a diminution of faith in a younger generation (but this is very uncertain). For instance, we know that Philammon was closely linked to persons of clear Manichaean belief and practice (such as Apa Lysimachos and Ision), but in his three well-preserved letters published here (**80-82**) he says nothing that is really explicit. Nevertheless, commonalities of style and association make his faith virtually certain.

In this present section the prize letter is one written by The Teacher, by whom we understand the leader of the Manichaean community in Egypt. Whereas various unnamed references to 'The Teacher' amongst the Makarios family letters of volume I might be thought to indicate reverence, now it becomes apparent that anonymity is a deliberate feature. It is unknown whether this new letter is written by the same person referred to there, as it might well be from a different time-frame. However, the issue of deliberate anonymity in Manichaean literature would be worthy of a further study. For instance, it is notable that in the codex *The Kephalaia of the Teacher* (n.b.) Mani is rarely named, usually being referred to by the circumlocutions 'apostle', 'enlightener', 'master', 'father'. 'Manichaios' may not have been his personal birth-name, but rather a religious one that was given to him ('hidden vessel' is a recent suggestion for its etymology from the Aramaic).[8] In the personal letters from Kellis we have examples of the author introducing himself simply as 'your father' (thus **31**, **32**), a highly unusual practice and in each instance with a clear Manichaean context.[9]

The other two pieces in this section are very fragmentary, and 'anonymity' may simply be a result of preservation. They exhibit characteristic phrases of Manichaean sentiment, which should be compared with other examples of the genre. Some provisional discussion of Manichaean epistolary conventions can be found in I. Gardner, 'A Letter from the Teacher: Some Comments on Letter-Writing and the Manichaean Community of IVth Century Egypt', in L. Painchaud, P.-H. Poirier, *Coptica – Gnostica – Manichaica. Mélanges offerts à Wolf-Peter Funk*, Québec 2006: 317-323.

P. Kellis Copt. 61

Inv #: P 27B + P 8

Location: House 3, room 6, deposit 2

Preservation: 10 fragments of a Coptic letter on papyrus, (2 ex P8). N.B. The placing of the fragments as recorded by the digital photograph is somewhat misleading. The sequence of lines in the transcript must be noted carefully.

Content: A Manichaean letter by 'The Teacher'. Detailed discussion by I. Gardner, op. cit., 2006.

---

[8] On this question see J. Tubach, M. Zakeri, 'Mani's name', in J. van Oort et al., *Augustine and Manichaeism in the Latin West*, Leiden 2001: 272-286. There is no general consensus about the matter.

[9] Probably also P. Kellis Gr. I 67; see the comments by I. Gardner in *ZPE* 159, 2007: 225.

Address:

verso

Πλουτ]ογενίωι καὶ Πεβο

To ... (?) Ploutogenios and Pebo

Names: Drousios; Pebo; Ploutogenios; 'The Teacher';

Text:

1 ⲡⲥⲁϩ ⲙⲛ̄ ⲛ[ⲥⲛ]ⲏⲩ ⲉⲧʼⲛⲙ̄ⲙⲏ[ⲓ̈]
2 ϣⲁ ⲙ̣ⲡⲣⲉⲥⲃ[ⲩⲧ]ⲉⲣⲟⲥ ⲧⲏⲣⲟⲩ ⲛ[ⲁ]
3 ϣⲏ[ⲣ]ⲉ ⲛⲁⲙⲉ[ⲣⲉⲧ]ⲉ ⲡⲗⲟⲩⲧⲟⲅⲉⲛ̣[ⲓⲟⲥ]
4 ⲙⲛ̄ [ⲡ]ⲉⲃⲟ ⲙ[ⲛ̄ ⲛ̄]ⲕⲁⲕⲉⲩⲉ ⲧⲏⲣⲟⲩ
5 \ . . . ⲁⲛ̄/ ⲕⲁⲧ̣[ⲁ ⲛⲟⲩⲣⲉⲛ ϩⲙ̄] ⲡⲭⲁⲓ̈ⲥ ⲭⲁⲓⲣⲉⲓⲛ
6 ⲛ̄ⲟⲩ[ⲁⲓ̈ϣ ⲙⲉⲛ ⲛⲓⲙ] ⲁⲉⲓⲟⲩⲏ̣ⲩ ⲉⲉⲓ
7 ϩⲏ[ⲛ ⲁⲉⲓⲉⲓⲣⲉ ⲙ̄ⲡ̄ⲣ̄ⲡⲙⲉ]ⲩⲉ ⲛ̄ⲧⲙⲛ̣̄ⲧϩⲉⲗϭⲏⲧ
8 ⲛ̄[ⲧⲉⲧⲛ̄ⲙⲛ̄]ⲧ̣ϣⲏⲣⲉ ⲙⲛ̄ ⲡⲧ̣ⲁϫⲣⲟ ⲙ̄
9 ⲡ[ⲉⲧⲛ̄ⲛⲁϩ]ⲧ̣ⲉ ⲁⲉⲓϣⲗⲏⲗ ⲛ̄ⲥ̣ⲏⲩ ⲛⲓⲙ
10 ϣ[ⲁ ⲓⲏⲥⲟⲩ]ⲥ̣ ⲡⲉⲭ̄ⲣ̄ⲥ̄ ϫⲉ ⲉϥ[ⲛ̄]ⲁϩⲁ[ⲣⲏϩ]
11 ⲁⲣ[ⲱⲧⲛ̄] ⲛⲏⲓ̈ ϩⲛ̄ ⲡⲓⲥϯⲛⲟⲩϥⲉ ⲁⲣⲉ[ⲧⲛ̄]
12 [ⲧⲁⲓ̈ⲁⲓ̈ⲧ ⲛ̄]ⲧⲛ̄ⲟⲩⲁⲛ̣ [ⲛⲓ]ⲙ̣ [ⲛ̄ⲧⲱⲧ]ⲛ̄ ⲕⲁ̣[ⲧⲁ]
13 [ⲧⲉⲧⲛ̄]ⲡⲟⲗⲓⲧⲓⲁ ⲛ̄[. . . . .]
14 [. . . .] ⲙ̣ⲁϣⲉ ⲛ̄[ⲧⲉⲧⲛ̄ . . . .]
15 [. . . ϫⲉ] ⲛⲉⲧⲛ̄ⲉⲓ ⲁϩ[ⲟⲩⲛ . . . .]
16 [. . ⲁⲛ]ⲏϩⲉ ϯⲣ̄[. . . . .]
17 [. . .]ⲉ̣ⲱⲥ ⲡⲟⲩⲉ ⲡ̣[ⲟⲩⲉ . . . .]
18 [. . .]ⲉ̣ ⲉ . [. . . . .]

(likely to follow immediately)

19 ⲧⲛ̄ϯⲛ[. . . .]
20 ⲣⲟⲩϣⲁ̣[. . . . .]
21 ϫⲉⲛⲁϣ[. . . . . ⲙⲏ]
22 ⲡⲱⲥ ⲛ̄ⲧ̣[ⲉⲧⲛ̄ . . . .]

23   ϣⲉⲛϩ[. . . . .]
24   . . . . . [. . . . .]

unplaced frg

(x +)25   . . . .]ϣⲛ̄[. . . . .
26   . . . .]ⲉⲓⲣ[. . . . .

tr27   ⲛ̄ⲙ̄ⲧⲁⲛ[. . . . .] ⲛ̄ⲧⲱⲧⲛ̄ ϩⲱ[ⲧⲧⲏⲛⲉ . . . .]
28   ⲙⲛ̄ ⲛ̄ⲕ[ⲁⲕⲉⲩⲉ ⲧⲏⲣⲟⲩ ϩ]ⲓ ⲟⲩⲥⲁⲡ ⲥⲟⲩϣ[. . . . . .]
29   ⲉⲧϩⲁⲧⲛ̄[. . . . .] ⳨ⲣⲟⲩⲥⲓⲟⲥ ϯϣⲓⲛ[ⲉ . . . . . .]

The Teacher, and the brothers who are with me: To all the presbyters, my children, my loved ones; Ploutogenios and Pebo and all the others (5) … according to their names; in the Lord, - greetings.

[Now, every] time I am afar (it is) as if I am near. [I remember] the gentleness of your (pl.) sonship and the strength of your faith. I pray always (10) to Jesus Christ: That he will guard you for me with this fragrance; as you are [honoured] by everyone corresponding to [your] conduct … go and … (15) … lest you ever come in … I am … each one … (20) …

(25) … (tr) … You yourselves … and [all] the others together. … Drousios. I greet …

Commentary:

1   The incipit ('The Teacher, and the brothers with me, to …') contrasts markedly with the normal epistolary style of the period. It is clearly modeled on that of Mani in his *Epistles*; (which were canonical scriptures for this community).

3   The -ios ending to the name 'Ploutogenios' is here restored following the address, but one should note that standard lists do not record any other attestation of this (cf. http://www.trismegistos.org/nam). Still, the phonetic value at this period would have been identical to that of the expected spelling 'Ploutogenes'.

5   \ . . . ⲁⲛ̄/: It does not seem possible to read ϩⲱⲟⲩ ⲁⲛ. Also, it is difficult to understand the significance of what appears to be a superlinear stroke stretching across from the final letter inserted in the margin to the initial ⲕ- in the regular line. Perhaps it is some kind of correction mark.

11   ⲥⲧⲛⲟⲩϥⲉ 'fragrance': Presumably metaphorical or figurative for 'excellent conduct', see also CD 363a. One may consider a possible play on words with the phonetically similar ⲥⲓⲧⲛⲟⲩϥⲉ 'good reputation', which occurs in comparable contexts elsewhere (i.e. with Manichaean authors). Thus **19**, 2,7; **31**, 20-21, where the full ⲥⲁⲓⲧ ⲉⲧⲛⲁⲛⲟⲩϥ is found; P. Kellis I Gr. 63, 6-7, where εὐφημία can be paralleled; also e.g. *1Keph*. 259, 11 and 380, 13.

15-16   The most likely sense of this fragmentary clause seems to be: '... so that you never get into (some sort of trouble or bad habits)'. This may well have been preceded by an admonition in l. 14: '.. walk (i.e. 'behave') and ...'.

Verso   The position where the names of the recipients are written on the address suggests that the title (or otherwise) of the sender of the letter may not have been recorded. Alternatively, the normal sequence may have been reversed; as indeed is true in the highly stylised opening to the letter.

P. Kellis Copt. 62

Inv #:   P 4 + P7 + P7A

Location: House 3, room 6, deposit 2

Preservation: 6 fragments of a Coptic letter on papyrus, plus a scrap. 4 of the main pieces can be joined so as to reconstruct a long thin strip down the upper rh edge of the page. Some complete lines can be restored corresponding to the well-known style of such pieces, and indicate the original width to have been not much greater than twice what is preserved.

Content: Strong religious sentiment, reminiscent in tone and terminology of other Manichaean letters from the archive.

Address:

verso

．．．．．．．．．．］   Χ   Προ[．．．．．．．

To ... X Pro- ...

Names: Pro-; Pshai;

Text:

1   [ⲡⲁ . . . ⲉⲧⲧⲁⲓ]ⲁⲓⲧ
2   [. . . . . ⲛ̄ϩⲣ̄ⲕⲏⲧ
3   [. . . . .]ⲉ̣ ⲡⲁ
4   [. . . . .] . ⲧ
5   [. . . . . ⲭⲁⲓ]ⲣⲉⲓⲛ
6   [ϩⲁⲑⲏ ⲙⲉⲛ ⲛ̄ϩ]ⲱⲃ ⲛⲓⲙ ϯϣⲓ
7   [ⲛⲉ ⲁⲡⲁ . . . ⲁⲩ]ⲱ ϯϣⲗⲏⲗ ⲁ
8   [ⲡⲛⲟⲩⲧⲉ ⲛ̄ⲧⲙⲏ]ⲉ ϩⲁ ⲡⲕ[ⲟⲩ]
9   [ϫⲉⲓⲧⲉ ⲛ̄ⲥⲏⲩ ⲛⲓ]ⲙ̣ ϫⲉⲕⲁ̣[ⲥ]
10   [ⲉϥϩⲁⲣⲏϩ ⲛ̄ϥ̄]ⲣⲁⲓⲥ ⲁⲣⲁ[ⲕ]
11   [. . . . . ⲁⲧⲛ̄ⲟⲩ]ⲁ̣ϣⲧⲛⲉ [ⲙⲛ̄]
12   [ⲛⲉⲛⲉⲣⲏⲩ ϩⲛ̄] ⲟⲩⲉⲓⲣⲏ[ⲛⲏ]
13   [. . . . . ⲛ]ⲉ̣ⲛⲉⲣⲏⲩ ϩⲛ̄ ⲡⲁ
14   [. . . . .] ϩⲛ̄ ⲧϥ̄ⲉⲕⲕⲗ
15   [ⲥⲓⲁ . . . . . . ϫ]ⲱⲕ ⲁⲃⲁⲗ ⲙ̄ⲡⲉ
16   [ⲧⲛ̄ . . . .] ϣⲁ ⲑⲁⲏ ⲁⲡⲥ̄
17   [. . . . . . ⲛⲉⲛⲉ]ⲣⲏⲩ· ϩⲛ̄ ⲧϥ̄[. .]
18   [. . . . .]ⲧⲉ̣ . [. . .]
19   [. . . . .]ϥ̄ ⲛ[. . . . .]
20   [. . . . .]ⲉⲓ[. . . . . .]
21   [. . . . .]ⲟ̣ⲩ[. . . . . .]

tr22   . . . .] . ⲙ[.] . . . ⲡϣⲁⲓ ⲡ[. . . . .

1 unplaced frg. (with a section of the address on the verso)

```
x+1       . . . . . . . . . . . ] . [ . . .
2         . . . . . . . . ]ⲱⲛ . [ . . .
3         . . . . . . . ⲉ]ⲡⲏⲩ [ . . .
4         . . . . . . . . ] . . . [ . . .
5         . . . . . . . . ] . . [ . . . .
```

[My] honoured … peaceful … (5) – greetings.

[Now, before] everything: I greet [my] … and I pray to [the God of truth] for your [health always]; so that (10) [he may guard (?) and] watch you [(until) we] greet [one another in] peace; … one another in … in his church, (15) … perfect your … until the end. … one another, in his … (20) …

(tr) … Pshai …

Commentary:

Address: After the central cross one usually finds the name of the sender or recipient (thus here 'Pro-'). However, one should note that there is no name of this sort in the extant Coptic archive from House 3.

2   ϩⲣ̄ⲕⲏⲧ: This will be a quality ('peaceful' or 'calm') ascribed to the recipient by the author. Interestingly, this particular term is not found elsewhere in the archive from House 3, but it makes good sense as a Manichaean virtue (and can be added to the list made in CDT I pp. 80f.). Compare e.g. *1Keph.* 183, 29.

P. Kellis Copt. 63

Inv #: P 14 + P 22 + P 51C + P 62

Location: House 3, room 7, deposit 1 (P14 + P 22); room 9, deposit 3, east wall (P51C); room 6, deposit 3 (P 62).

Preservation: Thirteen fragments of a coated papyrus text (perhaps more than one text, but all of the same distinctive appearance). Some fragments can be joined, for which see the transcriptions (as the digital photograph does not indicate the correct placings). The suggested width of the text follows a minimal restoration in the first three lines. It is entirely possible (even probable) that additional terms were used in the opening greetings, and consequently that the lines were somewhat longer throughout.

The scrap recorded as containing ll. 33-35 seems to have been lost from the glass frame before the photograph was taken in January 2009.

Content: Manichaean letter (or letters?), with characteristic terminology.

Address: None preserved.

Names: None preserved.

Text:

(top centre frg)

1   [ⲧⲁϣⲉⲣⲉ] ⲙ̄ⲙ[ⲉⲣⲓⲧ ⲉⲧ]
2   [ⲁⲓ̈ ⲛⲧⲟ]ⲧ̣` ⲧⲟⲛ[ⲟⲩ ⲛⲣⲉⲛ]
3   [ⲉⲧϩⲁⲗϫ̄ ϩⲛ̄ ⲣⲱ[ⲓ̈ ⲛ̄ⲛⲉⲩ ⲛⲓⲙ]
4   [ⲧⲁϣⲉⲣ]ⲉ̣ ⲙ̣̄ⲙⲉ[ⲣⲓⲧ . . .]
5   [. . . . .] ⲧⲉϯⲟ̣[ⲩⲁϣⲥ ϩⲛ̄]
6   [ⲡⲁϩⲏ]ⲧ̣ ⲙⲛ̄ ⲡ[. . . . . .]
7   [. . . . .] . ⲛ̄ . . [. . . . . .]
8   [. . . . .] . . [. . . . . . .]

(5 frgs. reconstructed down rh edge)

(x+)9   [. . . . .] . [. .]
10   [. . . . . ⲛ̄]ⲛ̣ⲉⲩ ⲛⲓⲙ̣
11   [. . . . . . . ⲛ]ⲁϣ[ⲗ]ⲏ̣ⲗ ⲉⲓ̈
12   [. . . . . . .]ⲣⲉ ⲁⲅⲁⲑⲟⲛ
13   [ⲛⲓⲙ . . . .] . ⲓ̈ ϫⲉ ⲛⲛⲉⲣ̄
14   [. . . . . . .]ⲉ̣ⲧⲉ· ϫⲉ . .

15 [. . . . . ϩ]ⲙ̄ ⲡⲥⲱⲙⲁ

16 [. . . . . .]ϥ· ⲧⲛ̄ϩⲏⲛ ⲁ

17 [. . . . . .] . ⲛ ϫⲉ ⲡⲉ̣ⲧⲟⲩ

18 [. . . . . .]ⲧϥ̄· [[ⲥ]]ⲉϣⲁⲩ

19 [. . . . .] . ⲉ ⲙ̄ⲡⲣ̄ⲧⲉ ⲉⲁ

20 [. . . . .] ⲁⲃⲁⲗ ϩⲛ̄ ⲡⲉⲛⲁϩ

21 [ⲧⲉ . . . .]ⲧⲉ· ϫⲉ ⲛ̄ⲧⲁⲩ

22 [. . . . . .] ⲙⲛ̄ⲧⲣⲉ ⲡⲣⲱⲙⲉ

23 [. . . . .]ⲧϥ̄ ⲛ̄ⲗⲁⲩⲉ [. . .]

24 [. . . . . . .] . [. . . . . . .]

(2 frgs. joined down rh edge)

(x+)25 [. . . . .]ⲉ̣[ⲧⲃ]ⲏⲧⲥ· ϫⲉ

26 [. . . . .]ⲟⲩⲁⲉⲓϣ

27 [. . . . . ϭⲁ]ⲁ̣ⲛ̄ⲃⲁⲗ ⲛⲓⲙ

28 [. . . . .] ⲙ̄ⲙⲉ

(frg. from rh edge)

(x+)29 [. . . . . . .] . ⲁⲧⲗⲩⲡⲏ·

30 [. . . . ⲡ]ⲛ̣ⲁϩⲧⲉ· ⲙⲛ̄ ⲡⲥⲁ

31 [ⲩⲛⲉ . . .]ⲧϥ̄· ϫⲉ ⲛ̄ⲧⲁϥ ⲡⲉ

32 [. . . . .]ϯ̄. [. . . . . .]

(frg. from rh edge)

(x+)33 [. . . . . ⲧ]ⲟⲛⲟⲩ

34 [. . . . .]ⲟⲩⲛⲁϭ

35 [. . . . .] ⲉⲓⲧⲉ

(unplaced frg.)

(x+)36   ] . ⲩⲉ ⲛ̄[

37   ⲉⲧ]ⲁⲓ̈ⲧ· [

38   ] ϯⲛⲁ[

39   ] . ⲁⲗ[ⲗⲁ

40	]ⲛ ϩⲓⲛ[
41	]ⲉ ⲛ̄ⲛ̣[
42	]·[

(unplaced frg., perhaps a different text)

(x+)43	ϩ]ⲟⲟⲩ ⲛ̄ⲧ·[
44	]ⲧⲉⲯⲩⲭⲏ [
45	]ⲛⲉ ⲛ̄ϩⲁ[
46	]· ϫⲉ ⲛ̄ⲛ[
47	]·ⲉ· ⲛ̄ⲥⲉ·[
48	]·[

(unplaced frg., perhaps a different text)

(x+)49	]·····[
50	ⲧ]ⲁϣⲉⲣⲉ ⲙ̄[ⲙⲉⲣⲓⲧ
51	] ⲡⲁϣⲏⲣⲉ [

[My loved daughter who is] very [precious to me. The sweet name] in [my] mouth [at all times. My] loved [daughter] … (5) …, the one who I [love in my heart] and my … (10) ... at all times ... my prayers, while I ... [all] good things ... lest you ...

(*remainder of the text is too fragmentary for useful translation*)

Commentary:

1-3   Although mostly destroyed, the introductory greetings can be restored with fair certainty according to familiar patterns, e.g. compare **16**, 4; **17**, 1-3.

15-16 Probably a reference to the theme of being 'far' apart in the body, yet 'near' in spirit (ⲟⲩⲏⲩ / ϩⲏⲛ); variations of this are characteristic of the Manichaean letters, e.g. **19**, 69-70; **31**, 24-25; **61**, 6-7; **85**, 3-4.

20   ⲡⲉⲛⲁϩ[ⲧⲉ: 'your (fem.) faith', note the female recipient as with other Manichaean letters of similar type (cf. **31**, 27 ['faith' paired with 'knowledge' as here also at ll. 30f.]; **32**, 3).

27   ϭⲁ]ⲁ̄ⲛ̄ⲃⲁⲗ: see **65**, 14 and the note to **71**, 4-9. The sense here is presumably to protect or guard from 'all mishap'.

LETTERS BY PAMOUR (AND MARIA)

Pamour is the author of a series of letters, to which a certain Maria (who was surely his wife) often adds a postscript. One must read together with these P. Kellis I Gr. 71, (copied below for ease of reference), which clearly belongs to this same group. Further, Pamour (Pamouris) generally addresses his letters to various brothers, particularly Pshai (Psais) and Pegosh (Pekysis); but including also others such as Theognostos and Andreas, who may or may not be direct siblings. Persons named Partheni, Kapiton, Philammon and Hor also feature prominently. Thus, this present group of letters is followed by a number written by Pegosh, the brother of Pamour, (with which P. Kellis I Gr. 72 must be included). One can then expand out to other groups, such as the three letters written by Philammon to Theognostos and Hor, which will lead to two letters written by Lysimachos (one to Theognostos and one to Hor), to another two written by Theognostos himself; and so on.

This far, the connections between the persons are certain. As one expands further it becomes more problematic. The latter part of CDT II contains many 'unplaced' documents by persons such as Psais to Partheni or Psais to Andreas. Many of these will belong to the core Pamour group with which we have started; but, given that there are certainly multiple persons with names like Psais (especially common), it becomes increasingly difficult to be sure that one is always dealing with the same characters. There is also the further problems of multiple or abbreviated names. Whilst it is clear that Theognostos is also called Louishai (as will be seen); is Heni (or Eni) the same as Partheni, or Iena (or Gena) the same as Ploutogenes?[10]

---

[10] The phenomenon of 'truncated' names is a feature also evident in the Greek ostraca from Ain es-Sabil; see the discussion in O. Trim. I (*Ostraka from Trimithis*, ed. R.S. Bagnall, G.R. Ruffini, New York 2012), p. 60.

However, despite these issues, we may say that the Pamour and related groups take us to the heart of events recorded by the House 3 Coptic archive, which must be dated in the main (perhaps even in its entirety) to the decades from the 350s to the 380s C.E. Many of the Greek documents from this period also belong to these same persons and their histories. In terms of the family stemma reconstructed by K.A. Worp in P. Kellis I (p. 51) we are dealing with Pamour 'III', son of Psais 'II' (who will be the 'father Pshai' of many of these Coptic letters) and of Tapollos (who almost certainly appears in the Coptic documents as 'mother Lo'[11]).

One major question, that naturally will arise for the reader, is how does this family and their correspondents relate to the Makarios family and their circle that dominated much of CDT I? In the first volume the most fully-drawn characters were the couple Makarios and Maria, and their sons Matthaios and Piene; whilst in the second it is Pamour and Maria, with their various brothers and sisters.

If we attempt to relate the two core couples, we must first consider whether Makarios could be the same as Pamour? But there is no evidence to support this. Makarios writes from the Nile valley to his wife Maria in Kellis, and that group of letters (including those of their sons Matthaios and Piene) would appear to have been saved by and thus to have 'belonged to' Maria. In contrast, Pamour's wife Maria is with him in the valley, from where they both write letters to Pshai and Pegosh and so on in Kellis. They never mention any persons called Matthaios and Piene. In fact, there is clear evidence of there being two Marias. In P. Kellis I Gr. 71 Pamour addresses directly a 'mother Maria', and then his wife Maria adds her own greetings to the letter.

In sum, our interpretation is that the Makarios family correspondence dates from the later 350s C.E. (the evidence for this is discussed in some detail in CDT I). Probably it was preserved for some years by his wife Maria who lived as an elderly relative in House 3. In contrast, the core Pamour documents belong to a younger generation. Perhaps they

---

[11] See also P. Kellis I Gr. 87 for an instance of this in the Greek papyri.

were mainly written ten or fifteen years later, and thus never mention Makarios or Matthaios; but the old woman was still alive in the house. Finally, as regards the religious affiliation of these persons: Manichaean faith is vitally alive and a central concern for Makarios and his sons; in contrast, whilst there is still evidence for it in the Pamour documents, it is rarely so overt. Whether this is a result of increased circumspection, or a diminishing of faith, we simply can not say.

Translation of P. Kellis I Gr. 71 (by K.A. Worp):

To his most honoured and truly most longed-for lord brother Psais, Pamouris sends greetings in God. First of all I and my wife and sons each individually send many greetings to your reverence, being well up until now through the providence of God. Greet for us our lord brother Theognostos and his son Andreas. About your coming to (?) us, most honoured one, every day we ... from long ago since you wrote. And, I swear by God, it was on your account that I remained here, not departing for Antinoopolis to transact pressing business with my brother Pekysis. But look, he summoned me there many times and since I was expecting you, I did not leave. Indeed I wrote this very thing to him too that "I am expecting my brother and his children here". So don't neglect to come. Please bring with you a small hatchet and a bronze oven dish. Please greet each by name for me. I am amazed that, while so many have come to us, you have not deemed us worthy of even a letter for such a long time; but I myself, too, had decided not to write, and yet I was unable to endure, particularly since Philammon is here. Or don't you know that we are thirsting for your letters? Greet Kapiton for me and Psais, the son of Tryphanes, with their wives and children. Give many greetings for me to mother Maria and the little Tsempnouthes. Please send the girl to me. I am giving you her travel money and each year I will give you a present of wool for a cloak as her hire. Farewell, my lord.

Please get ten loom weights from Kame and give them to Psais, the son of Tryphanes. I wonder, mother Maria, why you have not written to me: "I received the hanging (?) from Psais". Accept this other one from Philammon and a little pot of fish.

Mother Maria, please send me the dish and the iron ring because I want to put it on the loom. I Maria greet my lady mother and sister along with her children. My children also greet you. Farewell.

P. Kellis Copt. 64

Inv #: P 9

Location: House 3, room 1, deposit 1

Preservation: Reused papyrus, with traces of earlier text clearly visible on both sides (e.g. read ⲡⲱⲁⲓ at v5). There now remains the lower two-thirds of a letter, broken along both the vertical and horizontal folds (thus six-ninths remain with the upper three folds missing). The dimensions of the remains are 168 x 125 mm.; but the original can be calculated at ca. 240 mm. vertical.

Content: Pamour writes to his brother Pshai (Psais), according to the address. Probably he also addressed other persons in the introductory greetings, (such as Theognostos?). Unfortunately, these are lost; but compare e.g. **72** and P. Kellis I Gr. 71. His wife Maria adds a fairly extensive postscript, which should be closely compared to others that she appends to Pamour's letters (**65**, **66**, **71** and P. Kellis I Gr. 71); as well as Pamour and Maria's greetings added to Pekysis' letter to Kapiton sent from Aphrodite (**77**). We think that in this present letter also (and generally so in this group of documents) Pamour and Maria are in the Nile valley.

The principal purpose of these closely related series of letters is to maintain contact between various members of the extended family. One supposes that Pamour is writing to the Oasis, and indeed there are occasional references to it (e.g. **65**, 37) and comments that one can interpret as being about travel from the one place to the other. Extensive greetings are sent or relayed, and insofar as there is real 'content' it is mainly concerned with various possessions and goods that are needed or missing. Often there are complaints that such and such has not been sent, and these (which appear rather terse to the modern reader) are interspersed with family news and other remarks about health or other difficulties.

Address:

verso

        ἀδελ]φῶι   X   Ψαῖϣι Παμοῦρ

                    ὁ ἀδελφός σου

      To [my master] brother X Psais. Your brother Pamour.

Names: Chares; Jnapllo (Senapollo); Lo; Marie; Pamour; Parthene; Philammon; Pshai; Tagoshe;

Text:

approximately twelve lines missing

x+1	ⲕⲁⲧⲁ . [. . . . . . .]ⲉ̣ⲧϥ . [. .] . ⲉ ⲉⲧⲁ̣ⲓ̣
2	ϩⲱⲃ ⲡ[ⲓ]ⲱⲧ` ⲡϣⲁⲓ ⲉⲧⲃⲏ[ⲧ]ϥ̄ ⲧⲛ̄ⲛⲁⲩϥ
3	ⲟⲩⲛ ⲛⲏⲓ̈ ⲙ̄ⲡⲱⲣⲧⲉ ϩⲗⲁⲙ[ⲗ]ⲉⲙ ϣⲱⲡⲉ
4	ⲙⲛ̄ ⲡⲉⲣⲏⲩ· ⲙ̄ⲙⲁⲛ ⲁⲓ̈ϣⲓⲛⲉ ⲛ̄ⲥⲁ ⲛ̄ϩⲛⲁⲩ
5	ⲉ ⲡⲁϫⲉⲩ ϫⲉ ⲁⲧⲉⲧⲛ̄ⲧⲉⲓ̈ⲧⲟⲩ ⲁⲃⲁⲗ· ⲉϩⲉ ϭⲉ
6	ⲙ̄ⲙⲁⲛ ϯⲛ̄ϣⲓⲛⲉ ⲛ̄ⲥⲁ ⲛⲉⲓ̈ ⲉ̣ⲛ· ϣⲡⲉ ⲙ̄
7	ⲙⲁⲛ ⲛ̄ⲧⲁϥ ⲛ̄ⲧⲁ ⲡⲁⲓⲱⲧ ϣⲁⲛⲉⲧ ϫⲉ ⲛⲓϫⲓ
8	ⲗⲁⲩⲉ ϩⲁⲣⲁϥ· ϩⲓⲉ ⲧⲛ̄ⲟⲩⲏⲧⲉ̣ [ⲁ]ⲣⲁⲩ· ⲉⲛϣ̣ⲓ
9	ⲛⲉ ⲙ̄ⲙⲉ̣ⲧⲉ ⲛ̄ⲥⲁ ⲡⲉⲧⲉⲡϣⲛ̣̄ ⲧⲕⲉⲗⲉ
10	ⲕⲙⲉ ⲁⲛ ⲛ̣̄ϩⲛⲟ ⲛ̄ϩⲁⲙⲧ` ⲉ̣ⲧⲁⲧⲉⲧⲛ̄ⲧⲛ̄
11	ⲛⲁⲩⲥ ⲛⲏⲓ̈ ⲉⲓⲥϩⲏⲧⲉ· ⲙ̄ⲛ[ⲓ]ⲙⲁ· ⲡⲉⲧⲉ
12	ⲧⲛ̄ⲟⲩⲱϣⲧⲉⲥ ⲛⲉϥ ⲧⲛ̄[ⲛ]ⲁⲩ ⲛⲏⲓ̈ ⲧⲁ
13	ⲧⲉⲥ ⲛⲉⲩ· ϣⲡⲉ ⲁϥϣⲁⲛⲉⲧ` ⲛⲁⲙⲏⲉ
14	ⲛⲉⲧⲉⲧⲛ̄ⲏⲡ ϩⲱⲧ` ⲁⲛ ⲛ̄ⲧⲁⲙⲁⲓ ⲉⲧⲉⲧⲛ̄ϯ ⲙ̄
15	ⲙⲁⲩ· ϯⲛ̣ⲟⲩ ⲛ̄ⲧⲱⲧⲛ̄ ⲡⲉⲧⲥⲁⲩⲛⲉ ⲉⲧⲃⲉ
16	ⲧⲕⲁ̣ . [.] . . . . . . ⲡⲉⲧⲉⲧⲛ̄ . . . ⲉ ⲥ̣ ⳨ⲟⲩ
17	ⲁⲛ ⲛⲓⲙ̣ ϩⲓϣⲱⲥ ⲧⲛ̄ⲛⲁⲩⲥ̣ ⲛⲏⲓ̈ ⲧⲁⲧⲛ̄
18	ⲛⲁⲩ ⲥⲟⲩⲛ̄ⲧⲥ̄ ⲛⲏⲧⲛ̄ ⲁⲛ· ϯϣⲓⲛⲉ ⲁⲡⲁⲣ
19	ⲑⲉⲛⲉ ⲙⲛ̄ ⲛⲉⲥϣⲏⲣⲉ· ⲁⲛ[ⲁ]ⲕ ⲙⲁⲣⲓⲉ
20	ⲡⲉⲧⲥϩⲉⲓ̈ ⲉⲧϣⲓⲛⲉ ⲁⲧⲉⲥⲙⲟ ⲙ̄ⲙⲉⲣⲓⲧ`
21	ⲙⲛ̄ ⲧⲥ̣ϣⲉⲣⲉ· ⲙⲛ̄ ⲧⲁϭⲱⲛⲉ ⲙⲛ̄ ⲛⲉⲥ

22 ϣⲏⲣⲉ ⲙⲛ̄ ⲧⲁϭⲟϣⲉ ⲙ[ⲛ̄] ⲧⲥ̄ϣⲉⲣⲉ
23 ⲙⲛ̄ ⲗⲟ ⲙⲛ̄ ⲧⲥ̄ϣⲉⲣⲉ· ⲙⲛ̄ ⲧⲁⲙⲟ ⲭⲁⲣⲏⲥ
24 ⲙⲛ̄ ⲛⲉⲥϣⲏⲣⲉ ⲕⲁⲧⲁ ⲡⲟⲩⲣⲉⲛ·
25 ⲙⲁⲗⲓⲥⲧⲁ ⲡⲁⲥⲁⲛ ⲡⲁⲭⲁⲓⲥ [ⲡ]ϣⲁⲓ̈ ⲛ̄ⲧⲁⲕ
26 ϭⲉ ⲡⲁⲥⲁⲛ· ⲡϣⲁⲓ̈ ⲙⲛ̄ ⲧⲁⲙⲟ ⲉⲓⲥ ⲟⲩⲭⲁ`
27 ϭⲉ ⲁⲟⲩⲉ ⲁⲓ̈ⲙⲁϩⲥ̄ ⲭⲉⲓ̈ⲛⲁⲧⲉⲥ ⲙ̄ⲡⲁⲓⲱⲧ`
28 ⲫⲓⲗⲁⲙⲙⲱⲛ ⲁⲛ̄ⲧⲥ̄ ⲛⲏⲧⲛ̄ ⲛ̄ⲧⲟ ϩⲱⲉ
29 ⲧⲁⲙⲟ ⲧⲛ̄ⲛⲁⲩ ⲟⲩϣⲁϣ ⲛ[ⲏ]ⲓ̈ ⲙ̄ⲙⲁⲛ ⲁⲡⲱⲓ̈ ⲥⲱⲣ/ⲙⲉ\
tr30 [. . . . . ⲭ]ⲗϭⲉ ⲡⲁⲥⲁⲛ ⲡϣⲁⲓ̈ ⲙ̄ⲡⲱⲣϭⲱ ⲉⲙⲡⲉⲕⲉⲓ ⲁⲃⲁⲗ ⲧⲛ̄ⲛⲟ ⲁⲣⲁⲕ·
31 [. . . . .] . ⲛ ϯⲧⲱⲛⲉ ⲁⲛ· ⲉϣⲱⲡⲉ ⲟⲩⲛ ϭⲁⲙ ⲉⲧⲉⲧⲛ̄ⲧⲛ̄ⲛⲁⲩ ϯⲕⲟⲩ⟨ⲓ̈⟩ ⲛⲏⲓ̈
32 [. . . . .]ⲁ ⲧⲛ̄ⲛⲁⲩⲥ ⲙⲛ̄ ⲡⲁⲓⲱⲧ ⲫⲓⲗⲁⲙⲙⲱⲛ ⲭⲉ ⲁⲛϯ ⲭⲛ̄ⲁⲡⲗⲗⲟ ⲛ̄ⲟⲩϩⲉⲓ·

---

10 ⲉⲧⲁⲧⲉⲧⲛ̄ⲧⲛ: final -ⲧ- ex -ⲛ- corr.   23 ⲧⲥ̄ϣⲉⲣⲉ: -ⲥ- ex corr.   27 ⲁⲟⲩⲉ: ⲁ- smudged or erased?   ⲙⲁϩⲥ̄: -ϩ- ex corr.   29 ⲟⲩϣⲁϣ: -ⲁ- smudged

---

...] about which I have sent father Pshai. Send it to me, therefore; do not let any complication occur among us. For sure, I sought after the items (5) they say that you (pl.) have sold. Very well then, we are not seeking these ones. If, indeed, my father did exclude me so that I would receive nothing from him, then we renounce them; we are only seeking for what is ours.

Also, the other (10) piece of copper vessel that you sent me is here. Whoever you want to give it to: Send me (instructions) and I will give it to them.

If he really has excluded me, - you were supposed to inform me too if you are selling them.

(15) Now, you are the one who knows about the ... the one that you ... each one on it. Send it to me and I also will send its price to you. I greet Parthene and her children.

I, Marie, (20) am the one who writes, who greets her beloved mother and her daughter; and my sister and her children, and Tagoshe and her daughter, and Lo and her daughter, and my mother Chares and her children according to name. (25) Especially my brother, my master Pshai. So, you, my brother Pshai, and my mother: See (i.e. 'Here is') a cloth bag for one (of you). I filled it so that I could give it to my father Philammon to bring to you. You, too, my mother: Send a (measuring) jar to me, for mine is lost. (tr30) ...

cloth bag. My brother Pshai, do not delay your coming (so that) we may see you. … I am also sick. If it is possible, can you send this little (girl) to me? … send her with father Philammon, for we have given Jnapollo to a husband.

Commentary:

Address: There probably was room for the usual [(τῶι) κυρίωι μου ἀδελ]φῶι vel sim. The form of the name Ψαϊωι is an uncertain reading; obviously one expects Ψαϊτι, but it cannot be that. However, see the address to **72** and the note ad loc. with further references.

2   This 'father' Pshai will be a different person to the one named on the address of the letter (i.e. the author's brother). Here, as elsewhere in these pieces, he may well be the Psais 'II' of K.A. Worp's reconstructed stemma in P. Kellis I (p. 51). Note also that Pamour uses two different verbs in sequence (ϩⲱⲃ and ⲧⲛⲛⲁⲩ), though both are translated here as 'send'. Probably the first means 'send a message', whilst the second indicates to send (i.e. 'transport') the thing itself.

5-6   ⲉϩⲉ ϭⲉ ⲙ̄ⲙⲁⲛ: 'So, yes indeed' or 'very well then'. This phrasing, apparently hitherto unattested and a striking feature of some letter-writers' diction, is found four times in this corpus: **105**, 46 and **108**, 26 (with ⲁϩⲉ); **64**, 5-6 and **92**, 15-16 (with ⲉϩⲉ). The closest literary parallel to this phraseology may be found in Nag Hammadi Codex I,2 *(Epistle of James)*, where the expression ⲥⲉ ⲙ̄ⲙⲁⲛ is regularly used to translate an introductory: 'Amen/Verily (I say unto you ...)' (NHC I 10:1,15; 13:8; 14:14). Combining another word for 'yes' with the truth reinforcer, this parallel confirms that the element ⲙ̄ⲙⲁⲛ in our phraseology is the assertive particle 'verily, indeed' (and not the negative particle or an alternative 'else'). With the additional ϭⲉ in it, the phrase seems to be a textual marker that brings a foregoing discussion of an open issue to a conclusion and at the same time emphasises the veracity of what follows. In this instance it marks the transition from stating the reported sale of the items to an emphatic renouncement of any further pursuit of the matter. One may also compare the similar cluster ⲙ̄ⲙⲁⲛ ⲁⲛ ⲙ̄ⲙⲁⲛ at **48**, 30 (which probably does not mean 'or else').

9-10   We do not know what this 'piece' (CD 139a ⲗⲉⲕⲙⲉ) of copper vessel might be. One should note Crum's following entry of ⲗⲟⲕⲙ, given as 'meaning unknown' from a list with other utensils; perhaps we are rather dealing with some specific item here.

13-15   ϣⲡⲉ ⲁϥϣⲁⲛⲉⲧ` ... ⲉⲧⲉⲧⲛ̄† ⲛ̄ⲙⲁⲩ`: Pamour's thoughts have now returned to his earlier frustration with his father. The exclusion may well have been to do with the distribution of property, such as happens with a will. The obvious sense to expect would be that Pamour had counted on them to tell him at the time when they sold (or perhaps 'distributed' or 'administered') the items; see l. 5.

15-17   Unfortunately, the text is much destroyed along the central fold at l. 16. But it is probable that Pamour's meaning is something like: 'You are the one who knows the price of everything. Whatever you think, add each one to the bill. Send it to me, and I will return you the total cost'.

23   The name Lo is quite frequently found in these letters. It seems probable that it is another example of an abbreviated name, which appears to have been a rather common practice especially in the Coptic letters of this archive. We think that her full name may be Tapollos (this follows a suggestion of Worp in P. Kellis I p. 54). The latter name is never found in the Coptic archive, but was that of Pamour (III)'s mother according to the Greek information (see the reconstructed stemma in P. Kellis I p. 51). It is notable that in her greetings Maria begins with a number of the senior women, i.e. her own mother (Maria), Tagoshe (= Takysis), Lo (= Tapollos) and Chares (ⲭⲁⲣⲏⲥ, fem., for 'Charis'). We think that this gives some sense of the true generational context. See also P. Kellis I Gr. 87, 3 and notes ad loc.

30-31   Maria asks her brother Pshai not to delay his coming, and to send the little girl (presumably as a housemaid and general assistant). Both these elements feature in Pamour and Maria's letter in Greek (P. Kellis I Gr. 71), and we strongly suspect that they are the same events and that the two letters were written at about the same time. In this case the girl is Tsempnouthes (Coptic Jemnoute), see further **65**, 39-41 note ad loc.

P. Kellis Copt. 65

Inv #: P 45 + P 21 + P 36 + P 43 + P47 + P 56C

Location: House 3, room 5, deposits 1 + 3 + 4 and room 9, deposit 3 west doorway.

Preservation: Ten papyrus fragments, which can be joined or placed so as to recover extensive remains of a letter written in Coptic. The lower half is mostly complete, but a large central section of the upper half is missing. Perhaps about five lines are entirely lost between the remains of the upper and lower parts.

Content: The concerns, style and persons mentioned in the letter are consistent with the other pieces written by Pamour to his brothers. The introductory prayer (ll. 7-15) has formulaic elements that should be counted as Manichaean (on which see I. Gardner, A. Nobbs, M. Choat, 'P. Harr. 107: Is this Another Greek Manichaean Letter?', *Zeitschrift für Papyrologie und Epigraphik*, 131, 2000: 118-124). This example may, in particular, be compared to that written by Pamour to Partheni in **71**. The actual 'content' of the letter again concerns details of various items and small-scale transactions that can be difficult to follow. The reference to the Oasis in l. 37 indicates that these letters passed between scattered and traveling family members, some of whom were there (presumably based in Kellis) and others in the Nile valley. Pamour's wife Maria adds her usual postscript, greeting her mother and other women in the family as well as the men.

Address:
verso

    ἀπ(όδος) τῳ[
    Deliver to [...

Names: Andreas; Ham; Jemnoute; Kapitou; Lamon; Lioushai (?) Theognos(tos); Lo; Maria; Pamour; Pegosh; Philammon; Pshai; Tapshai;

Text:

1 ⲡⲁϫⲁⲓⲥ ⲡⲁⲥⲁⲛ ⲙⲉⲣⲓⲧ ⲉⲧⲁⲓ̈ ⲛ̄ⲧⲟ
2 ⲟⲧ ⲧⲟⲛⲉ ⲡⲉϭⲱϣ ⲙⲛ̄ ⲡϣⲁⲓ̈ ⲙⲛ̄
3 ⲡⲁⲥⲁⲛ ⲁⲓⲟⲩϣⲁⲓ ⲑⲉⲟⲅⲛⲱⲥ
4 ⲙⲛ̄ ⲡⲁⲕ[ⲉⲥⲁ]ⲛ̣ ⲁⲛⲇⲣⲉ[ⲁ]ⲥ ⲁⲛⲁⲕ
5 ⲡⲁⲙⲟⲩ[ⲣ ⲡⲉⲧⲥϩⲉⲓ̈ ϯϣⲓⲛⲉ] ⲁⲣⲱ
6 ⲧⲛ̄ ϩⲙ̄ ⲡ[ϫⲁⲓⲥ ⲭⲁⲓⲣⲉⲓⲛ] vac
7 ϩⲁⲑⲏ ⲛ̣[ϩⲱⲃ ⲛⲓⲙ . . . . . ϯϣ]ⲗⲏⲗ
8 ⲁⲡⲓⲱⲧ [ⲡⲛⲟⲩⲧⲉ ⲛ̄ⲧⲙⲏ]ⲉ ϫⲉⲧⲉ
9 ⲧⲛⲁⲱⲛ[ϩ ⲛ̄ⲟⲩⲛⲁϭ] ⲛ̄ⲟⲩⲁⲓ̈ϣ
10 ⲉⲧⲉⲧⲛ̄[ⲟⲩⲁϫ ϩⲙ̄ ⲡⲥⲱⲙ]ⲁ ⲉⲧⲉⲧⲛ̄
11 ⲧⲁⲗⲏⲁ [ϩⲙ̄ ⲡⲡⲛⲉⲩⲙⲁ] ⲉⲧⲉⲧⲛ̄ⲟⲩ
12 ⲁϫ̄ ϩⲛ̄ ⲧ̣[ⲯⲩⲭⲏ . . . . . .]ⲃⲁⲗ ⲛ̄ⲛⲉ
13 ⲡⲓⲃⲟⲗⲗⲁ[ⲩⲉ ⲙ̄ⲡⲇⲓⲁⲃⲟ]ⲗⲟⲥ ⲙⲛ̄
14 ⲛ{ⲛ̄}ϭⲗⲁⲛ[ⲃⲁⲗ . . . . . ⲙ̄]ⲡⲥⲁⲧⲁ
15 ⲛⲁⲥ· ⲛ . . [. . . . . ⲟⲩ]ⲱϣⲉ [ⲁ]ⲧⲛ̄
16 ⲛⲁⲩ ⲛⲏⲓ̈ ϫ̣[. . . . .] . . ⲙ̄ⲙⲁⲩ
17 [. .] . . . [. . . . .

(about 5 lines missing)

23 . . . . [. . .] . . . . [ϩⲁ]
24 ⲗⲉⲕ ⲙ̄ⲃⲁⲛⲓⲡⲉ ⲉϯ[. .]ⲧ . . . . ϩ[ⲁⲧⲉ]
25 ⲧⲛ̄ⲥϩⲉⲓ̈ ⲛⲉⲛ ⲉⲧⲃⲉ ⲛ̄[ϩ]ⲛⲉⲩ . [. .] .
26 . ⲩ ⲁⲙⲏⲧ ⲛ̄ϣⲉ . . . . ⲧⲛ̄ . . . . [ϣ]
27 ⲡⲉ ⲟⲩⲛ ⲁⲕⲁ ⲛ̄ϩⲁⲙ ⲛ̄ϣⲁ . ⲧⲛ̄ⲛ̣[ⲁⲩϥ]
28 ϯϣⲓⲛⲉ ⲁⲡ[ⲁ]ⲓ̈ⲱⲧ ⲡϣⲁⲓ̈ ⲧⲟⲛⲉ ⲙⲛ̄
29 ⲛⲉϥϣⲏⲣⲉ ϯϣⲓⲛ[ⲉ] ⲁⲛⲉⲑⲁⲧⲏⲕ
30 ⲧⲏⲣⲟⲩ ⲡ[ⲟ]ⲩⲉ ⲡⲟⲩⲉ ⲕⲁⲧⲁ ⲡ[ⲟ]ⲩⲣⲉⲛ
31 ⲉⲧⲃⲉ ⲉⲩ [ⲁ]ϥⲧⲛ̄ⲛⲁⲩ ⲕ̣ⲁⲡⲓⲧⲟⲩ ⲛⲉⲕ
32 ⲉⲧⲃⲉ ⲧⲓⲙⲏ ⲛ̄ⲛ̄ⲥⲓⲥⲟⲩⲡⲉ ⲙ̄ⲡⲉ
33 ⲕⲥϩⲉⲓ̈ ⲛⲉⲛ ϫⲉ ⲧⲉⲓ̈ⲧⲟⲩ ⲛ̄ⲟⲩⲏⲣ ϯⲛⲟⲩ
34 ⲁⲩⲟⲩⲉ ⲉⲓ ⲛⲏⲓ̈ ⲛⲓϩⲟⲟⲩⲉ ϫⲉ ⲙⲁⲛⲧⲉⲓⲧⲟⲩ
35 ⲁⲉⲓⲟⲩⲉⲛ ⲁⲣⲁⲩ ⲁϭⲛ̄ⲧⲥ̄ ⲉⲁⲩⲧⲉⲕⲟ
36 ϯⲛⲟⲩ ⲥ̣ϩⲉⲓ̈ ⲛⲉⲓ̈ ϫⲉ ⲧⲉⲓ̈ⲧⲟⲩ ⲁⲃⲁⲗ ϩⲛ̄

37 [ⲟ]ⲩⲁϩⲉ ϣⲓⲛⲉ ⲁⲡⲁⲥⲁⲛ ⲕⲁⲡⲓⲧⲟⲩ ⲧⲟ
38 ⲛⲉ ⲙⲛ̄ ⲛⲉϥϣⲏⲣⲉ ⲙⲛ̄ ⲧⲉϥϩⲓⲙⲉ
39 [ⲁ]ⲛⲁⲕ ⲙⲁⲣⲓⲁ ϯϣⲓⲛⲉ ⲁⲧⲁⲙⲉⲩ ⲧⲁ
40 ϫⲁⲓⲥ ⲧⲟⲛⲉ ⲙⲛ̄ ⲧⲁϣⲉⲣⲉ ϫⲉⲙ̄ⲛⲟⲩ
41 [ⲧ]ⲉ ϯϣⲓⲛⲉ ⲁⲡⲁⲥⲁⲛ ⲡⲉϭⲱϣ
42 [ⲧⲟⲛⲉ] ⲧⲁⲥⲱⲛⲉ ⲙⲛ̄ [ⲛⲉⲥ]ϣⲏⲣⲉ
43 ϣⲓⲛⲉ ⲁⲗⲟ ⲙⲛ̄ ⲧⲉⲥϣⲉⲣⲉ ϣ[ⲓ]ⲛⲉ
44 ⲁⲧⲁⲡϣⲁϊ ⲙⲛ̄ ⲛⲉⲥϣⲏⲣⲉ vac
45 ϣⲓⲛⲉ ⲁ‹ⲡⲁ›ⲓⲱⲧ ⲫⲓⲗⲁⲙⲙⲱⲛ ⲙⲛ̄ [ⲧⲉ]ϥ
46 [ϩⲓⲙⲉ] ⲙⲛ̄ ⲛⲉϥϣⲏⲣⲉ ⲡⲟⲩⲉ ⲡⲟⲩⲉ
47 ⲕⲁⲧⲁ ⲡⲉϥⲣⲉⲛ· ϯϣⲓⲛⲉ ⲁⲗⲁⲙⲱⲛ
48 ⲙⲛ̄ ⲧⲁⲙⲟ ⲧⲁⲡϣⲁϊ: ἐρρῶσθαί
49 σαι εὔχομαι πολλοῖς
50 χρόνοις   vac
tr51 ⲛ̄ⲧⲁⲕ ϩⲱⲕ ⲡⲉϭ[ⲱ]ϣ ⲉϣⲱⲡⲉ ⲉⲕⲙ[. . . . .] . . . [.] ⲉⲕⲛⲏⲩ ⲁⲃⲁⲗ [. . . . .
52   vac   . . . . [. . . . .] . . . ⲛ̄ⲕⲟⲩⲓ̈ vac
53   vac   . . . .] . [.] ⲥⲛⲧⲉ ⲛ̄[.] . . . [. . . . . .

———

1 ⲙⲉⲣⲓⲧ for ⲙ̄ⲙⲉⲣⲓⲧ   6 ϩⲙ̄: looks more like ϩⲛ̄   32 ϯⲙⲏ: for ⲧⲧⲓⲙⲏ   34 ϩⲟⲟⲩⲉ: second -ⲟ- ex -ⲩ- corr.   40 ⲧⲟⲛⲉ: -ⲉ ex -ⲟ corr.   42 [ⲧⲟⲛⲉ]: perhaps [ⲧⲟⲛⲉ ‹ⲙⲛ̄›] or [. . ⲙⲛ̄] etc.   48 ⲧⲁⲙⲟ: looks more like ⲧⲙⲱ

———

My master, my loved brother, very precious to me; Pegosh and Pshai, and my brother Lioushai (?) Theognos, and my other brother Andreas. I, (5) Pamour, [am the one who writes. I greet] you (pl.) in the [Lord; - greetings].

Before [everything: ... I] pray to the Father, [the God of truth], that you will live [for a long] time; (10) being [healthy in the body], rejoicing [in the spirit], healthy in the [soul, safe] from the snares of the devil and the adversities of Satan.

(15) ... please send to me ... them ... (20) ... iron ring ... (25) You have written to us about the things ... ten hundred ... If there is any sesame from Ham ..., send [it].

I greet [my] father Pshai warmly and his children. I greet all those who are with you (sing.), (30) each one by name. Why did he send Kapitou to you about the price of the jujubes? You did not write to us saying how much to sell them for! Now, someone has come to me lately (lit. these days) saying: "We shall not sell them". (35) I opened them to find out whether they had perished. Now, write (about) these, saying (whether to) sell them in the Oasis. Greet my brother Kapitou warmly, with his children and his wife.

I, Maria, I greet my mother, my (40) lady, warmly; with my daughter Jemnoute. I greet my brother Pegosh [warmly, (and?)] my sister and [her] children. Greet Lo and her daughter. Greet Tapshai and her children. (45) Greet <my> father Philammon and his [wife] and his children, each one by his name. I greet Lamon and my mother Tapshai. I pray for your health for many (50) years.

(tr) You, too, Pegosh: If you … you are coming …

Commentary:

Address: This clearly starts with the letters ⲁⲡ, the latter perhaps with a line struck through it. We have resolved this as an abbreviation ἀπ(όδος); see the index s.v. ἀποδίδωμι for other examples of similar forms in this archive. One might expect (e.g.) a supralinear delta next to the pi, but amongst the addresses to these Coptic letters there is simply found ⲁⲡ/ (or similar).

3   The exact spelling of the name Lioushai (ⲗⲓⲟⲩϣⲁⲓ) is very difficult to read, but we are convinced that it was this or some form close to it. It is followed immediately by Theognos, which is probably complete in itself (i.e. with no letters missing). One needs to compare **81**, where Theognostos is given on the address but Louishai (ⲗⲟⲩїϣⲁї) is clearly written at l. 2; and **82**, where Loishai (ⲗⲱїϣⲁї) is read on the address, but Shai is found in l. 3. From these three letters we conclude that the one person, who is often named Theognostos by Pamour and his circle, could also be called Louishai (we may have variant spellings) or simply Shai. See also perhaps **95**, 18.

7-15   Pamour's prayer can be reconstructed in most of its details by comparison with the parallels: **25**, 12-26; **29**, 7-13; **32**, 19-24; **71**, 4-9; **72**, 4-5; P. Harr. 107, 4-12; (also noting **31**, 12-16 and elements in **62** and **63**). The core elements are: prayer to the God of truth; the trichotomy of body, soul and spirit associated with qualities of health, joy and gladness; to be kept safe from Satan and all the evils of the world; and hope for life eternal. Although there are some variations in detail, and the prayer can be abbreviated or amplified, there are enough formulaic qualities to use it as a marker of Manichaean faith. Indeed, we suppose that such was intended by the authors. Certainly, the trichotomy can be traced back to IThess. 5:23, and variations occur in other papyrus letters of the period; but the combination of elements so characteristic of these Kellis pieces (and notable in P. Harr. 107) is likely to have been in imitation of Mani himself. Evidence for this assertion can be drawn now from the remains of one of his *Epistles* preserved in Middle Persian: cf. 'Second fragment (M501p + M 882c + M1402 + M9152)' l. 4, as reconstructed by W. Sundermann, 'A Manichaean Collection of Letters and a List of Mani's Letters in Middle Persian', in *New Light on Manichaeism*, ed. J.D. BeDuhn, Leiden 2009: 259-277 (pp. 271-273). Sundermann's translation of the opening of the letter reads (slightly adapted): '... to the most beloved ... at ease and healthy you remain ... so that with the aid of the angels you, most beloved, [in spirit (?)] are well, and as for the body content and happy'. Thus, e.g., Matthais to Maria at **25**, 12-22: 'This is my prayer to the Father, the God of Truth, and his beloved Son the Christ, and his Holy Spirit and his light angels: That he will watch over you together, you being healthy in your body, joyful in heart and rejoicing in soul and spirit, all the time we will pass in the body'.

23-24 In P. Kellis I Gr. 71, 50-51 there is also a request for an iron ring (κρίκιον), which is something to do with a loom.

27 ϩⲁⲙ ⲛ̄ϣⲁ . : More probably a personal name (Ham) than some quality of the sesame; e.g. derived from the word for a craftsman (CD 673b-674a) or an abbreviated form of Sheham (cf **73**, 20 note ad loc.). It may be followed either by a patronym or toponym.

31, 37 Kapitou: It seems probable that this is the same person as Kapiton, a commonly occurring character in these letters. See further the note at **66**, 42.

34-37 There may be an implied reproach here (l. 34), i.e. this person exclaims that they can not sell the jujubes in that condition. Consequently, Pamour opened up a sample to see if they were spoilt. Following this, it may be questioned whether he then does indeed intend to sell products that are rotten. An alternative translation and interpretation may be considered: 'I opened them to find that they were rotten. Now, write to these (people), saying: "Sell them (in the future) in the Oasis"'.

39-41 Maria begins her postscript by greeting 'my mother ... and my daughter Jemnoute', as she also does in **71**, 26-27. In **64**, 19-21 it was her mother and her daughter (unnamed); and see also **77**, 35-36 for the same. In **66**, 21-23 she begins with her sister and daughter (unnamed), and one wonders if the mother has now died. It is worth paying close attention to these parallels. Although, in general, the usage of terms such as 'mother' or 'sister' in these letters is so broad as to be of little use for establishing exact family relations, in these instances Maria is so consistent that we think that the data will be reliable. But if the daughter is Jemnoute, what is Maria's mother called? She never actually names her. Here P. Kellis I Gr. 71 is vital evidence. Again Maria adds her customary postscript (ll. 52-53) greeting her mother, and in this instance her sister (both unnamed). However, earlier in the letter (ll. 41-43) Pamour has sent his greetings to 'mother Maria and the little Tsempnouthes', the latter being the Greek form of the name Jemnoute (variously Jnpnoute et al). We are therefore fairly certain that Pamour's wife Maria, when she greets her mother in her postscripts, is greeting the elder Maria. One should note also occurrences of the same name in the Makarios family letters.

P. Kellis Copt. 66

Inv #: P 59A + P59B/C

Location: House 3, room 3, deposit 3.

Preservation: A mostly complete letter, if somewhat poorly preserved in places and now disintegrating into a number of fragments. There are clear traces of previous text. The placing of some fragments as recorded by the photograph is misleading, and the order in the transcription should be followed instead. The text is coarsely written, and the scribe has made a number of errors. The original dimensions were 280 x 60 mm.

Content: Pamour writes to his brother Pegosh, with a lengthy postscript (more than half the letter) by Maria. A possible context for this piece (see the notes further for details of this reconstruction) is that Pegosh is in Aphrodite, and Pamour and Maria have written to him there from elsewhere in the Nile valley where they are doubtless engaged in trade. In this case, the letter has been transferred to Kellis at a later date, together with other documents belonging to members of this Oasis family who apparently resided in Aphrodite in the 360s - 380s C.E.

Address:

verso

τῷ κυρίῳ μου   X   ἐγὼ Παμοῦρ
ἀδελφῷ Πεκύσι   [ὁ ἀδελφ]ός σου
To my master brother Pekysis.   X   I, Pamour, your brother.

Names: Chares; Io; Maria; Pamour; Pebo; Pegosh; Philamou; Pshai; Pshmnoute;

Text:

1 [ⲡⲁⲥ]ⲁⲛ ⲙ̄ⲙⲉⲣ[ⲓ]ⲧ` ⲉⲧ[ⲁⲓ̈]
2 [ⲁⲓ̈ⲧ] ⲛ̄ⲧⲟⲧ` ⲧⲟⲛⲟⲩ ⲡⲁⲥⲁⲛ
3 [ⲡⲉϭ]ⲱϣ ⲁⲛⲁⲕ ⲡⲉⲕⲥⲁⲛ
4 [ⲡⲁ]ⲙⲟⲩⲣ ⲉⲓ̈ϣⲓⲛⲉ [ⲁ]ⲣⲁⲕ
5 [ϩⲙ̄ ⲡ]ϫⲁⲓ̈ⲥ ⲡⲛⲟⲩⲧⲉ
6 vac   ⲭⲁⲓⲣⲉⲓⲛ
7 [ⲛ̄ⲧ]ⲁⲣⲓϭⲓⲛⲉ ⲛ̄ⲧⲉⲩⲭⲏ ⲁ
8 [ⲃⲁⲗ] ϩⲓⲧⲛ̄ ⲡⲁⲥⲁⲛ [ⲡ]ⲉⲃⲟ
9 ⲁ[ⲓ̈]ϣⲁⲧⲡ̄ⲧ ⲉⲓ̈ⲥϩⲉⲓ̈ ⲛⲉ[ⲕ]
10 ⲛ . . ⲁⲥ ⲡ[ⲉ]ⲃⲟ ⲥϩ . [.]ⲩⲉⲓ
11 ϣⲓⲛⲉ ⲛ[ⲏⲓ̈] ⲧⲟⲛⲟ[ⲩ] ⲁⲧⲉⲕ
12 ϩⲓⲙⲉ ⲙⲛ̄ [ⲛ]ⲉⲕϣⲏⲣⲉ ⲕⲁ
13 ⲧⲁ ⲡⲟⲩⲣ[ⲉⲛ] ⲁⲕϩⲁⲃ ⲟⲩ
14 . [.]ⲙⲉ ⲙ[ⲛ̄ ⲟ]ⲩⲗⲉϯⲉ ⲛ̄
15 ϫⲏϭⲉ ⲙ̄[ⲡ]ⲣⲱⲙⲉ ϩⲏ
16 ⲧⲉ ϯⲉⲓⲣ[ⲉ] ⲙ̄ⲡⲉ[ϥ]ⲕⲱ
17 ⲧⲉ ϣⲓⲛⲉ [ⲛⲏⲓ̈ ⲁⲡ]ⲁⲓ̈ⲱ⟨ⲧ⟩
18 ⲡϣⲁⲓ̈ ⲙ[ⲛ̄ . . . .] .

19 ⲙ̄ⲙⲉ[ⲣⲓⲧ . . . .] . .
20 ϯⲛ̄ⲛⲁⲩ ⲧ[.] . . [ⲛⲉ]ⲕ
21 ⲁⲛⲁⲕ ⲙ[ⲁ]ⲣⲓⲁ ϯϣⲓ
22 ⲛⲉ ⲁⲧⲉⲥ[ⲱ]ⲛⲉ ⲙ̄ⲙⲉⲣⲓⲧ
23 ⲙⲛ ⲧⲁϣ[ⲉ]ⲣⲉ ϫⲓ ⲡⲓ
24 ⲥⲁⲩ ⲛⲉ [ⲛ̄]ϭⲁⲗⲙ ⲛ̄ϫⲏ
25 ϭⲉ ⲛ̄ⲧⲟⲧ[ϥ ⲙ̄ⲡ]ⲉⲃⲟ ⲛⲉⲧⲁ
26 ⲧⲉⲟⲩ ⲁⲩ[. . .]ⲩ ⲛⲉⲓ̈ ⲛⲉⲧ
27 ⲉⲛⲏⲩ ⲁⲃⲁⲗ ⲙ̄ⲡⲉ
28 ϯⲛ̄ⲛⲁⲩ ⲟⲩⲉⲡⲓⲥⲧⲟⲗⲏ
29 ⲉⲧⲛ̄ϣⲓⲛⲉ ⲁⲣⲁⲓ̈ ⲛⲁϣⲏ
30 ⲣⲉ ϣⲓⲛⲉ ⲁⲣⲟ ⲧⲟⲛⲟⲩ ϣⲓ
31 ⲛⲉ ⲛⲏⲓ̈ ⲁⲧⲁⲥⲱⲛⲉ
32 ⲙⲛ̄ ⲡⲓⲱⲧ ⲛ̄ⲛⲉⲥϣⲏ
33 ⲣⲉ ⲛⲁⲡⲛ̄ⲏⲓ̈ ⲧⲏⲣⲟⲩ
34 ϣⲓⲛⲉ ⟨ⲁ⟩ⲣⲱⲧⲛⲉ ϣⲓⲛⲉ
35 ⲁⲡⲁⲓ̈ⲱⲧ ⲡϣⲁⲓ̈ ⲙⲛ̄
36 ⲛⲉϥϣⲏⲣⲉ ⟨ⲁⲛⲁⲕ⟩ ⲓ̈ⲟ ϯϣⲓ
37 ⲛⲉ ⲁⲣⲱⲧⲛⲉ ⲙⲛ̄ ⲧⲥ
38 ϣⲉⲣⲉ ⟨ⲉ⟩ϣⲁⲧⲉⲛ̄ⲛⲉⲩ
39 ⲁⲡⲁⲥⲁⲛ ϣⲓⲛⲉ ⲁⲣⲁϥ
40 ϣⲛ̄ϩ ⲛ̄ⲧⲉⲙⲟⲩⲛ
41 ⲁⲃⲁⲗ ⲛ̄ⲛⲟⲩⲛⲁ[ϭ
tr42   vac   [ⲁ]ⲛⲁⲕ ⲙⲁⲣⲓⲁ ⲉⲓ̈ϣⲓⲛⲉ ⲁⲡⲁⲓ̈ⲱⲧ ⲫⲓⲗⲁⲙⲟⲩ ⲙⲛ̄ ⲧϥϩⲓⲙⲉ ⲙⲛ̄ ⲛⲉϥϣⲏⲣⲉ
v43 ϣⲓⲛⲉ ⲛⲏ⟨ⲓ̈⟩ ⲁⲡⲁⲓ̈ⲱⲧ ⲡϣⲙⲛⲟⲩⲧⲉ ⲙⲛ ⲧϥϩⲓ[ⲙⲉ]
44 ⲙⲛ ⲛⲉϥϣⲏ⟨ⲣⲉ⟩ ϫⲓ ⲛⲉⲕ ⲛ̄ϯⲥⲁϣⲃⲉ ⲛ̄ϣⲁⲧⲥ̄ ⲛ̄ⲧⲃ̄ⲧ
45 ⲛ̄ⲧⲟⲧϥ ⲙ̄ⲡⲉⲃⲟ ϫⲓ ϯⲥ̄ⲛⲧⲉ ⲛ̄ϣⲁⲧⲥ̄ ⲉⲩⲡⲁⲣⲭ
46 ⲛ̄ⲧⲟⲧϥ ⲛ̄ⲃⲟ ⲛ̄ⲧⲉⲛ̄ⲧⲉⲩ ⲛ̄ⲭⲁ[ⲣⲏⲥ]

---

39 ⲧⲥ|ϣⲉⲣⲉ: understand ⲧⲉⲧⲛ-   46 perhaps ⲛ̄⟨ⲡⲉ⟩ⲃⲟ, or else 'Bo' is just a shortened form

(To) [my] loved brother, very [honoured] by me; my brother Pegosh. I am your brother Pamour (and) I greet you (5) [in the] Lord God; - greetings.

When I found the prayer from my brother Pebo, I hastened to write to [you] (10) ... Pebo (?) ... Greet for me warmly your wife and your children by their names. You have sent a ... and a small amount of (15) dye for the man. Look, I am working around it. Greet [for me] my father Pshai and [my] loved ... (20) send the ... to you.

I, Maria, I greet my loved sister (?) and my daughter. Take for yourself these six sticks of dye (?) (25) from Pebo. The ones that you gave have ...; these are the ones coming out (now). You did not send a letter greeting me! My children (30) greet you warmly. Greet for me my sister and the father and her children. Everyone in our house greets you. Greet (35) my father Pshai and his children. <I (?)>, Io, I greet you and <your> daughter. If you should see my brother, greet him. (40) Live and stay (well) for a long (time).

(tr) I, Maria, I am greeting my father Philamou and his wife and his children. (v) Greet for me my father Pshmnoute and his wife and his children. Take for yourself these seven portions of fish (45) from Pebo. Take these two separate portions from Bo and give them to Chares.

Commentary:

7-10   Perhaps what is meant is that Pamour has received a heartfelt 'prayer' for news sent from Pegosh via Pebo. Now he hurries to reply, and this letter will be conveyed back again by Pebo (see the poorly preserved l. 10). Alternatively, it may be that Pamour has an actual copy of a prayer that he wants to send. Compare the example of the ritual text copied and sent in **35** (especially noting there Ouales' comments in ll. 28ff.).

This Pebo may be the same person as the Aurelius Pebos son of Tithoes, who is from Kellis but residing in Aphrodite, where he signs contracts on behalf of Pamour and Pekysis (P. Kellis I Gr. 42-44). See further the comm. ad ll. 21-23.

14   . [.]ⲙⲉ: There is hardly enough room to read ⲗⲉⲕⲙⲉ 'fragment'.

16-17 'I am working around it', i.e. 'I am taking care of it'.

21-23 If our reading of l. 22 is correct, this is the only occasion where Maria does not start by greeting her mother. It seems probable that either the mother Maria has died by this stage, or else that this particular letter is not sent to Kellis. We know from other letters that Pegosh is at least some of the time in the Nile valley. P. Kellis I Gr. 71, 16-18, explicitly places him in Antinoopolis. And then, in **77**, Pamour and Maria add their greetings to a letter by Pegosh sent to Kapiton from Aphrodite. N.B. A number of the documents found in Kellis refer to the village of Aphrodite (in the Antaiopolite nome), and especially important are the dated Greek contracts published by K.A. Worp in P. Kellis I (30, 32, 42, 43, 44, from the 360s - 380s C.E.). These should certainly be read in conjunction with the letters by Pamour, Pegosh and their circle.

23-24   It is tempting to read: 'Receive this knowledge .. (ϫⲓ ⲡⲓⲥⲁⲩⲛⲉ)'; but compare the syntax at ll. 44 and 45.

24-25   Alternatively, ϫⲗϭⲉ 'cloth bag' could be a better reading than ϫⲏϭⲉ 'dye', (compare e.g. Maria at **64**, 26-27); but, in that case, one may want to read ⲙⲛ̄ ‹ⲧ›ϫⲗϭⲉ ('Receive these six ... and the cloth bag'). It does not seem possible to read '6 *mna* of dye'; but one might consider ϭⲁⲗⲙⲁ 'jar' instead of ϭⲁⲗⲙ 'stick' (with the final -ⲁ squeezed in very small).

26   ⲧⲉⲟⲩ ⲁⲩ[. . .]ⲩ: or ⲧⲉⲟⲩⲁⲩ [. . .]ⲩ ('The ones that you) uttered ...').

41   There appears to be no space for the expected ⲛ̄ⲟⲩⲁⲓⲱ following ⲛ̄ⲛⲟⲩⲛⲁ[ϭ].

42   The form Philamou is surely for Philammon. One can compare Kapitou in **65**, who we believe to be the same Kapiton as commonly occurs in this group of letters. See also Lamou in **19** (Lammon?), and Amou in **19** and **45** (Ammon?).

43   Perhaps this is the same Pshemnoute (and his wife Kyria) who are prominent in the Makarios family letters, see CDT I pp. 29, 42; but in that case the letter must be sent to Kellis.

44   A number of these letters refer to the sending of portions of fish, which must certainly have been salted or pickled or dried in some manner for preservation. Cf. the short note by A. Alcock, 'Pickling', *Discussions in Egyptology*, 57, 2003.

46   Chares (i.e. Charis) may be the wife of Philammon (Philamou?); see CDT I pp. 23, 38-39.

P. Kellis Copt. 67

Inv #: P 60D

Location: House 3, room 9, deposit 4.

Preservation: A substantial Coptic letter; but, although the dimensions of the papyrus are mostly preserved, the text itself is badly abraded. The hand and general design is very similar to **68** (also from Pamour), and perhaps **76** (from Pagosh, but the brothers could have used the same scribe). The original dimensions were 280 x 106mm. It is now broken across the central fold, and disintegrating along the verticals.

Content: Pamour writes to Pagosh, greeting also Theognostos and Pshai. Probably Maria has added her customary long postscript, though we can not read her name in the extant text.

Address:

verso

  ἀπ(όδος) Πακύσι   X   Παμοῦρ
  Deliver to Pakysis.   X (From) Pamour.

Names: Chares; Pagosh / Pakysis; Pamour; Philas; Plousiane (?); Pshai; Shai (?); Tagoshe; Tapshai; Theognos; -ou (Philamou?);

Text:

1 ⲁⲛⲁⲕ ⲡⲁⲙⲟⲩⲣ ⲡⲉ[ⲧⲥϩⲉ]ⲓ̈ [ⲉⲓ̈]
2 ϣⲓⲛⲉ ⲁⲡⲁⲥⲁⲛ ⲡ[ⲁ]ϭⲱϣ ⲧⲟⲛⲟⲩ
3 vac   ⲭⲁⲓⲣⲉⲓⲛ   vac
4 ϩⲁⲑⲏ ⲛ̄ϩⲱⲃ ⲛⲓⲙ †[ⲧⲱ]ⲃϩ ⲁⲡⲛⲟⲩ
5 ⲧⲉ ϫⲉϥⲛⲁⲣⲁⲓ̈ⲥ ⲁ[ⲣ]ϣ[ⲧ]ⲛ̄ ⲛ̄ⲟ[ⲩ]
6 ⲛⲁϭ ⲛ̄ⲟⲩⲁⲓ̈ϣ †ϣ[ⲓⲛ]ⲉ ⲁⲡ[ⲁⲥ]ⲁⲛ
7 ⲑⲉⲟⲅⲛⲟⲥ ⲙⲛ̄ ⲡⲁ[ⲥⲁ]ⲛ ⲡϣⲁⲓ †ⲣ̄

8   ⲁϩⲓⲟⲩ ⲙⲙⲱⲧⲛ̅ ⲧ[ⲟⲛ]ⲟⲩ ⲁⲣⲓ ⲟⲩ[. .]
9   ϣ . ⲩ . . . . ⲙ̅ⲙ̅ . ⲁ . ⲁ . [. .]ⲣⲓ . ⲕ [. . . .]
10 . . ⲛ̅ . . . . . ⲁϣⲏⲣⲉ . [. . . .] . . . [. . . .]
11 . . ⲃⲏϣ . ⲗ . . . ⲁⲛ[. . . .] . . . . . . [. . .]
12 ⲛ̅ⲥⲟⲩⲝ̣ . . [. .] . . ⲛⲁ[.] . . . . ϣ .
13 [. . ⲉ]ⲡ[ⲓⲥ]ⲧⲟⲗⲁⲩⲉ . . [. .] . . . . . .
14 . . . . . ⲉ ⲧⲛ̅ⲥⲁ̣[. .] . . . . . .
15 . . . . . ⲛⲉ ⲉⲓ̈ⲣⲓⲙ[ⲉ .] . . . .
16 ϣ ⲁⲩ . . ⲁϩⲱⲃ ⲧ̣ϣ[.] . ⲉ . . . ϭ̣ ⲁ
17 ⲡⲁⲥⲁⲛ ⲡⲁϭⲱϣ [ⲙ]ⲛ̅ ⲧϩⲓⲙⲉ
18 ⲙ[ⲛ̅] ⲛⲉϥϣⲏⲣⲉ ⲧⲣⲙⲁⲓ̈ϩⲉ ⲭ[ⲉ]
19 [ⲙ̅ⲡ]ⲉⲧⲛ̅ⲉⲓⲃⲁⲗ . ⲁⲛ[.]ϩⲁⲧ· ⲧ̣[.]
20 . . . [. . . .] ⲁⲕⲭⲟⲥ ⲛⲏⲓ̈ ⲭ̣[ⲉ . . . .]
21 . . . .
22 [. . . . . .] . . ⲭⲁⲣ[ⲏⲥ] . . . . ⲛ̣ . ⲡ̣ .
23 [. . . . . ⲕ]ⲁ̣ⲧⲁ ⲧⲑⲉ ⲉ̣[.] . . . .
24 [. .]ⲥⲛ[. .] . . [.]ⲧⲕⲟⲩ . . . . . ϩⲟ . . .
25 . . ⲁⲓ̈ . [.]ⲟⲩ ⲧϣⲓⲛⲉ ⲁ . . . .
26 [.]ⲁⲓ̈ⲝ̣ . [.] . . ⲩ ⲧⲣⲙⲁⲓ̈ϩⲉ ⲭⲉ . . .
27 [.]ⲃⲁⲗ . [.] . . ϥⲉ ⲛⲉⲓ̈ ⲛⲉⲕ ⲉⲓ̈ . . ⲩ
28 ⲫⲓⲗⲁⲥ ⲛ̅ⲧⲟⲧⲕ ⲛ̅ⲧⲁⲕ ⲙⲛ̅ ⲡⲕ[ⲉ] ⲡⲁ
29 ϭⲱϣ . . . ⲛ ⲛ̅ⲧⲁⲕ ⲡⲗⲟⲩ[ⲥⲓⲁ]ⲛⲉ
30 ⲟⲩⲡⲉⲧ[.] . . ⲡⲉ ⲉⲕⲛ̅ . . . .
31 ⲁⲛⲓϥ † . . . ⲗ ϭⲛ̅ⲡ̣ . ⲛ̅ . . . .
32 ⲃ̣ⲁⲩ . . [.]ⲟⲩϣϣ ⲟⲩ . . . . ⲕⲏ . . . . .
33 . ⲛⲏ . . ϣⲓⲛⲉ ⲁⲧⲁϭⲟϣⲉ . . . . . .
34 . . . ⲱⲧ ϣⲓⲛⲉ ⲁⲡⲁ[ⲥⲁⲛ] ϣⲁ̣ⲓ̈ ⲙⲛ̅] ⲧ̣ⲁ̣
35 [ⲡ]ϣⲁⲓ̈ ⲙⲛ̅ ⲛⲟⲩϣⲏⲣⲉ . . . . . ⲧⲛ
36 [. . . . . . .]ⲧⲛⲉ ⲭⲉ . . . . ⲉ
37 . . . . . [. .] . . ⲧⲛⲟⲩ ϭ[ⲉ] . . . .
38 . . . [. .] . . ⲟⲩ ⲙⲛ̅ ⲧϥ̣[ϩⲓⲙ]ⲉ . . . .
39 . . ⲛ . . [ϣ]ⲏⲣⲉ ⲙⲛ̅ . . [.] . [. . .] . . ⲧ[.]

House 3   59

```
40       ϣ[ερε †]ϣινε ⲁⲡⲁϭⲁⲛ . . . . . . .
41       [ . . . . ] . ⲁ̣ι . . . . ⲛ̣ . [ . ] . . . . [ . . ] ⲙ̣ⲛ̄
42       [ . . . ⲛ]ⲁ̣ⲡ̣ⲛ̣ⲏⲓ̈ ⲧⲏⲣⲟⲩ [ . . . . . . . . . ]
43       [ vac?   ⲱⲛ]ϩ ⲟⲩⲭⲉⲓ̈
tr44     ⲡϣ . . . ⲁ̣[ . . ] . ⲁ̣ⲁⲓⲡ . . . . . [ . . . . . . . . . . ] . . . . . ⲡϭϩⲱⲃ ⲉⲧ . . . . [ . . ] . [ . ] . . . [
45       . [ . . ] . [ . . ] . . . . . . . . . . . . [ . . . . . . . . . . . . ]ⲥⲉⲣϣⲉⲩ ⲥⲟⲩ . . .
v46      . [ . . . . ⲡⲁ]ⲥⲁⲛ ⲡⲁϭϣϣ ⲓ̄ⲥ ⲡ†ⲱⲡ ⲙ̄ⲡ . . . .
47       [ . ] . ⲧⲛ̣ⲛⲁⲩⲥⲉ ⲙⲛ̄[ⲡ]ⲣⲱⲙⲉ ⲛ̄ⲧⲟⲧ̣ . . . .
48       . [ . . . . . . . ] . . . . . [ . ]ϣⲉ ⲁϣⲉ . . . .
49       [ . . . . . . . ] . . . . . . [ . . ]ⲕⲉⲧⲛⲉϥ . . . .
50       ⲁ̣ⲛⲁ̣[ⲕ . . . ] . . . . . †ϣ[ⲓ]ⲛⲉ ⲁⲣⲱⲧⲛ̄ ⲧⲏⲣⲧⲛⲉ
51                . . . . . . . . . . . . . . . . . . . .
52       . . . [ . . . . . . . . . . . . . . . . . . . . ]
53       . . . . . . [ϣ]ⲁⲏⲗ ϩⲁ . . . ⲧⲕ . . . . . . .
54                . . . . . . . . . . . . . . . . . . . .
55                . . . . . . . . . . . . . . . . . . . .
56       . . . . . . . . . . . . . . ⲉ . . . †ϣⲓⲛⲉ
57       . . . . . . . . . . . . . . . ⲛⲟⲩⲥⲛⲏⲩ
58       . . . . . . . . . . . . . ⲁⲛⲓⲧ . ⲛ̣ⲉ†ⲣⲭⲣⲓⲁ
59       ⲛⲉⲧ . . [ . . . . . . . . . . . . . . . . ⲡⲁ]
60       ϩⲱⲃ ϩⲱⲧ ⲁⲛ vac ⲉⲧⲉⲧⲛ̄ⲟⲩⲁϣ ⲥϩⲉⲓ̈ ⲛⲏⲓ̈
```

———

23 ⲧⲑⲉ sic, for ⲧϩⲉ

———

I, Pamour, am the [one who writes], greeting my brother Pagosh warmly; - greetings.

Before everything: I pray to God (5) that he will guard you (pl.) for a long time. I greet my brother Theognos and my brother Pshai. I beg you greatly: Do ... (10) ... my son ... letters ... (15) I am weeping ... send. I ... to my brother Pagosh and his wife and his children. I am astonished that you have not come out ... (20) ... You (sg.) told me that ... Chares ... just as ... (25) ... I greet ... I am astonished that ... Philas from you. You and also (?) Pagosh ... You, Plousiane (?), (30) ... you ... Bring it, ... wish ... greet Tagoshe ... greets my father Shai (?) and (35) Tapshai and their children. ...

So, now, ... [I greet] -ou and his wife ... children and ... and her (40) daughter (?). I greet my brother ... and ... All in our house [greet you]. Live and be well.

(tr) ... (45) ... they are well ... (v) ... [my] brother Pagosh: Here is the account for the ... send them with a man from ... (50) ... I, ..., I greet you all ... [I am (?)] praying for your ... (55) ... I greet ... their brothers ... I am in need ... (60) also my own thing. Please will you (pl.) write to me.

Commentary:

Address: Although one cannot be sure (due to the poor preservation), the wording may well have been as simple as this (i.e. with nothing missing). The style of the address on **76** is very much the same.

1 To start the letter simply with ⲁⲛⲁⲕ is not so remarkable, but it is certainly less common in this archive than starting with the name and relationship of the recipient (ⲡⲁⲥⲁⲛ, ⲧⲁⲙⲟ, etc.). Again, one may compare **76**, 1.

3 Note how ⲭⲁⲓⲣⲉⲓⲛ is positioned by itself in the centre of the line. It is characteristic of a number of these letters, compare e.g. **76**, 5.

7 For the abbreviated form of the name Theognos (i.e. without an ending -tos) see also **65**, 3; **73**, 20.

17 ⲧϩⲓⲙⲉ: The reading is very uncertain. One would expect ⲧϥϩⲓⲙⲉ; but since the form ϩⲓⲙⲉ (without initial sigma) is a relational term anyway, it might also have been used without the possessive.

28 Perhaps Philas could be a hypocoristic form for Philammon? In the archive we have ample evidence for shortening the name to the final element (e.g. Partheni > Heni; Tapollos > Lo). For the name 'Philammon' one is tempted to look to Lammon / Lamou, but apparently this practice might also work from the start of the name (cf. Theognostos > Theognos at l. 7 in this very letter).

29 ⲡⲗⲟⲩⲥ[ⲓⲁ]ⲛⲉ: This reading is very uncertain.

30 The ink traces are very ambiguous. Perhaps ⲟⲩⲡⲉⲧ[ϣ]ϣⲉ ⲡⲉ ('What is fitting is for you to ...') or ⲟⲩⲡⲉⲧ[ⲁ]ⲛⲓⲧ ⲡⲉ ('It is a good thing that you ...').

33ff. One might suppose that about here Maria (ⲁⲛⲁⲕ ⲙⲁⲣⲓⲁ) adds her own greetings, as in many of the letters by Pamour.

38   -ⲟⲩ (and his wife): Perhaps Philamou, compare **66**, 42.

P. Kellis Copt. 68

Inv #: P 61CC

Location: House 3, room 8, deposit 4.

Preservation: Coptic letter on papyrus. The basic dimensions of the piece are apparent (280 x 82mm.), but the text itself is badly abraded. The hand and general design is very similar to **67** (by Pamour) and perhaps also **76** (by Pagosh).

Content: There is little coherent sense to be made from the poorly preserved text. Since neither the address nor the initial greetings can be read, the author and recipient are uncertain. But the similarity of design to **67**, and especially of the uncial script, suggests that the letter was probably sent by Pamour. Perhaps Maria also added her customary postscript to her husband's letter, (note the greetings to various women in the lower part of the main text).

Address:
verso

       traces α   X   ἀπ(όδος) Π . . . . .
           ... X Deliver to P-

Names: Gouria (or Goure?); Martha; Pagosh; Tapshai;

Text:

1   [. . . . . .] . . [. . .] . [. .]
2   [. . . . . .]ⲛ̣[. . . .]ⲛ[. .]
3   [. . . . . . .] . [. . .] . [. .]
4   [. .] . [. . .]ⲧⲛ̣ⲉ[. . . . .]

5   vac   ⲭⲁⲓ[ⲣ]ⲉⲓ̣ⲛ̣ vac

6   ϩⲁⲑ[ⲏ] ⲛ̄ϩⲱⲃ ⲛ̣[ⲓⲙ †]

7   ϣⲓⲛ[ⲉ] ⲁⲣⲁ[ⲕ] ⲡ[ⲁⲥ]ⲁ̣ⲛ̣ [. . . .]

8   †ϣ[ⲓ]ⲛⲉ ⲁ[ⲡ]ⲁ[ⲥ]ⲁⲛ [ⲡ]ⲁⲭⲁ̈ⲓ̈[ⲥ]

9   ⲧⲟⲛ[ⲟⲩ] †ⲣⲙ[ⲁ]ⲓ̈ϩⲉ ⲭⲉ [. .]

10   ϩⲁ . ⲛ . ⲁⲩ . ⲉ ⲁⲕⲏⲙⲉ̣ [.]

11   ϩⲁ . . [.]ⲧ̣ ϩⲛ̄ ⲟⲩⲁϩⲉ ⲙ̄[. .]

12   ⲡⲉ̣[. . .]ⲡ̣ vac †[ϣⲓⲛⲉ]

13   ⲁⲧⲁⲙ̣ . [. . .] . . . [. . . . .] . ⲉ

14   [.]ⲕⲉ ϩⲁ . . [. . .] . [. . . . . .]

15   [ⲧ]ⲛ̄ⲛⲁⲩⲥ . . [. . .] . [. . . . . .]

16   [. .]ϣⲓⲛⲉ . [. . . .] . . [. . . . .]

17   [. .] . ϣ . . [. . . .] . . [. . . . .]

18   [. . .]ⲥ̣ⲁ . ⲁ[. . .]ⲁ̣ⲓ̈[. .] . [. . .]

19   [. . . .]ⲙⲟ . [. . .] . ⲣ̣[.] . [.] . [. .]

20   [. .]ⲏ̣ⲣⲉ . . [. . . . .]

21   [. .] . ⲙⲛ̄ⲛ[. . .] . . . . [. .]

22   [. .]ⲥ̣ⲱⲛⲉ ⲙ̣ⲁⲣⲑⲁ ⲙ̄ⲛ̄

23   [. .]ⲙⲟ ⲛⲉ̣ . . . . ⲙⲟ̣ [. .]

24   ⲡⲁϭⲱϣ . [.] . . ⲥϣ[. .]

25   [.] . . ⲙ . . . . . . ⲉ . [. .]

26   ⲧ[.] . . . . . ⲛ[. .] . . . [.]

27   ⲛⲉ . ϣⲏⲣⲉ̣ . . . ⲧⲛ . . [.]

28   ⲧⲁ[ⲡ]ϣⲁ̈ⲓ̈ ⲙ̣ⲛ̣ⲛ . [. . . . . .]

29   ϣⲉ ⲁⲧⲛ̄ⲙ[ⲟ] ⲧ̣ⲁⲡϣⲁ̣[ⲓ̈] ⲧ[ⲟ]

30   ⲛⲟⲩ ⲙ̄ⲛ̄ [ⲧⲛⲙⲟ] ϭⲟⲩ[ⲣⲓⲁ ⲙ̄ⲛ̄]

31   ⲛⲉⲥϣⲏⲣⲉ ⲁⲛⲛⲁ[. .]

32   ⲧⲛ̄ⲣ . . . [.] ⲧⲏⲣⲛⲉ̣ ⲁⲛ ⲛ̄

33   ⲧⲛ̄ⲙⲁϩ[.] . [.]ⲣ̣[.]ⲧⲛ̄ ⲁⲃⲁⲗ

34   ϩⲓⲧⲁϩ . [. .]ⲙ̣ . . . . ϣⲁ

35   . ⲛⲧⲁ . . . ⲓ̈ⲡⲉ . [.]ⲉ̣[. .]ⲛ

36   . ⲉⲧⲛ̄ⲣⲗⲩⲡⲏ ⲉⲧⲃⲉ̣ . . [.]

37	... ϣine ⲁⲧⲛ̄ⲥⲱⲛⲉ [ⲙⲛ̄]
38	ⲡⲛ̄ⲥⲁⲛ ϫⲉ ⲙ̄ⲡⲉ[..]
39	vac ⲛⲉⲛ ϫⲉ ⲛ̄ⲧⲉϥ..[...]
40	vac ⲙ̄ⲙⲁ.[...]
41	...[.].[.......]
v42	traces
43	traces
44	traces
45	traces
46	.[..]ⲧⲙⲏⲧⲉ ⲛϣⲁⲧⲥ..[...] vac ⲉ...
47	.[..].ⲡ ⲁⲧⲛ......ⲉ ⲁⲡⲥϩⲗ̄ⲗ[ⲟ]

---

11 the letter before ϩⲛ̄ looks like a large Γ; but we suppose that one should read -ⲧ   38-40 lh margin bends inwards (and thus nothing precedes ⲡⲛ̄ⲥⲁⲛ?)   40 perhaps there is nothing after the lacuna?

(I, Pamour, am the one who writes?) ... ; (5) - greetings.

Before everything: [I] greet you, my brother ... I greet my brother, my master, warmly. I am astonished that (10) ... to Egypt ... in the Oasis ... I [greet] my mother ... (15) send ... greet ... (20) ... sister Martha and ... Pagosh ... (25) ... children ... Tapshai ... our mother Tapshai (30) very much, and [our mother] Gouria [and] her children. ... and we are all ... and ... (35) ... we are grieving about ... greet our sister and our brother, for ... (40) ... (v) ... (45) ... ten portions ... to her old man.

Commentary:

Address: All that can really be read is what appears to be a final -α (before what we think must be the central cross). Otherwise, only traces survive, and any readings are very uncertain.

30   Gouria: ϭⲟⲩ[ⲣⲓⲁ or ϭⲟⲩ[ⲣⲉ? Cf. 'Kyria' at P. Kellis V p. 29; also **82**, 27, and the comment in the introduction to that piece.

P. Kellis Copt. 69

Inv #: P 78Hi (ex P78H)

Location: House 3, room 6, deposit 3.

Preservation: The document is complete in one rectangular piece of papyrus: 143 x 99 mm.

Content: The text is best described as something like an affidavit. It is not a letter, being without the typical epistolary formulae, greetings, address etc. At the same time, it lacks features that one would expect in a legal document, such as witnesses, signatures or date. Perhaps it is a private agreement or a draft?

The subject of the document would seem to be the ownership of property, either inherited by two brothers from their father or otherwise provided by him. Pamour would seem to be in actual possession of the property, perhaps to be used as start-up capital for trade in the Nile valley; but the purpose of the document is to confirm that it actually belongs to his brother Pagosh. The exact details of the agreement are somewhat difficult to follow; but it certainly reminds one of Pamour's comments in **64**, where he states that he renounces any claim to items from which he has been excluded by his father.

Address: No address, verso blank.

Names: Pagosh; Pamour;

Text:

1 ⲁⲛⲁⲕ ⲇⲉ ⲡⲁⲙⲟⲩⲣ ⲡⲉⲧⲥϩⲉⲓ ⲙ̄ⲡⲁ
2 ϭⲱϣ ⲡⲁⲥⲁⲛ· ⲉⲡⲓⲇⲏ ϩⲁϩ ⲛ̄ϩⲛⲁ
3 ⲟⲩ ‹ⲟⲩ›ⲉϩ ⲁⲣⲁⲓ ⲁⲓⲃⲱⲕ· ⲁⲕⲏⲙⲉ· ⲁϥⲉⲓ
4 ⲁϩⲟⲩⲛ ⲟⲩⲧⲱⲓ̈ ϯⲛⲟⲩ ϭⲉ ϯⲥϩⲉⲓ ⲛⲉⲕ

```
5      ϫⲉ ϩⲛⲟ ⲛⲓⲙ ⲉϥϣⲟⲡ· ⲛⲉⲛ· ⲉϥⲟⲩ
6      ⲧⲱⲛ ⲙⲛ ⲛ[ⲉ]ⲛⲉⲣⲏⲩ ϩⲁ ⲡⲛⲓⲱⲧ·
7      ⲉⲓⲧⲉ ⲛϩⲛⲟ ⲛϩⲁⲙⲧ· ⲉⲓⲧⲉ ⲡⲉⲧⲛ
8      ⲧⲉⲛ ⲧⲏⲣϥ· ⲕⲟ ⲙⲡϥϫⲁⲓⲥ· ⲉⲓⲧⲙ
9      ⲧⲛⲛⲁⲩ ⲛⲓϩⲛⲁⲩⲉ ⲛⲉⲕ· ⲟⲩⲃⲉ ⲧϩⲉⲗ
10     ⲉⲧⲁⲓⲧⲉⲥ ⲁ . . . ⲕ ⲧⲉⲩ ⲙⲡⲟⲩϫⲁⲓⲥ
11     ⲉⲧⲁⲕⲉⲓ ϩⲟⲩⲛ ⲟⲩⲧⲱⲓ ⲉⲧⲃⲏⲧⲟⲩ
```

And I, Pamour, am writing to Pagosh, my brother. Since many items are attributed (?) to me, I have gone to Egypt. He (i.e. Pshai?) entered into an agreement with me. Now, therefore, I am writing to you (5) that every item we have, between us mutually on account of our father, whether of bronze or all that is ours, you are its owner. If I do not send these items to you, (held) against the servant girl (10) whom I gave to you, (then you are still entitled to?) pay them to (as?) their owner, concerning which you have entered in to an agreement with me.

Commentary:

1   The use of the enclitic particle ⲇⲉ at the very start of this document strikes us as odd. Perhaps it implies that what we have is a response to some other (lost) text.

2   'Since': The conjunction ⲉⲡⲓⲇⲏ may simply be functioning to introduce the content part of the letter, but its being initial here is probably a coincidence. The clause is better understood as to provide the reason for the author's travel to the Nile valley.

2-3   ϩⲛⲁⲟⲩ: These 'items' seem to be what the document is really about, see also ll. 5, 7 and 9 (pl.). The term is frustratingly vague; but note that it is also used in **64**, 4-5, a text that may well provide some background to this present document. They appear to be material possessions, perhaps 'vessels' of some kind. We presume the sense here is that it is because Pamour has a substantial number of such items that he has gone to Egypt, no doubt to engage in trade. However, if one was to take the term in an abstract sense as 'debts' (on which see **72**, 20 and the note ad loc.), the entire meaning of this piece would change: 'Because I have many debts, I went to Egypt ...' etc.

3-4   ⲁϥⲉⲓ ⲁϩⲟⲩⲛ ⲟⲩⲧⲱⲓ: The subject of this clause appears to be unstated. We think that it must be a reference to a third peson whose identity would be obvious to the persons concerned. The most obvious candidate would be Pamour and Pagosh's brother

Pshai, who would presumably have had a share in any matter to do with the distribution of the family's material possessions. Further, there must be some technical usage here of the verb ⲉⲓ ('come') plus ⲁϩⲟⲩⲛ ('in') with ⲟⲩⲧⲱ// ('between'). The literal translation of 'he came in between me' makes no sense. In fact, the Ancient Egyptian *r-jwd* (from which ⲟⲩⲧⲉ- / ⲟⲩⲧⲱ// is derived) can have the sense of obligation. Thus, *ntj r-jwd.j* 'which is incumbent upon / with me'. We propose a meaning such as 'he entered into (an agreement) with me', i.e. a business arrangement or finance deal. This would be similar to the colloquial English of 'he came in with me'. Note also the same in l. 11; indeed, ⲟⲩⲧⲱ// is used three times in this short document.

5-6 ⲉϥⲟⲩⲧⲱⲛ ⲙⲛ̄ ⲛ[ⲉ]ⲛⲉⲣⲏⲩ: 'between us mutually' (i.e. the three of us); or, less likely, 'between us and our comrades'.

9 ⲛⲉⲁ: This must be for the Greek νεᾶνις, presumably here meaning a 'servant girl'.

10 It is difficult to read ⲁⲧⲟⲧⲕ. Indeed, the letters look as if they may have been deliberately erased. Still, syntax and sense require something of this sort.

P. Kellis Copt. 70

Inv #: P 78J + P 59E/F + P 67

Location: House 3, room 6, deposit 3; room 3, deposit 3.

Preservation: Twelve fragments survive of a large, finely written, letter on papyrus. It has broken along the horizontal and vertical folds, and some significant pieces have not been found (see the photograph). Nevertheless, what remains can either be joined or securely arranged to recover substantial sections of the text; (only 1 small fragment has not been placed). The dimensions and line count are not absolutely certain; but it was approximately 280 x 110 mm., with probably no complete lines missing between ll. 12 / 13 or 28 / 29.

Content: The letter is written to Pshai, but the identity of the author can not be known for certain. We think it is Pamour, primarily due to various of the persons mentioned in the letter, noting such as Theognostos, Kapiton, Partheni and especially 'mother Maria' in l. 14 (see our comments at the start of this group of letters). But the author might also be his brother Pagosh. From l. 3 and the address it seems certain that the name begins with a ⲡ-. Another point to consider is that Lo is named as sister in ll. 43-44, whereas elsewhere (see **64**, 23 note ad loc.) we have suggested that this is an abbreviated form of the name of the brothers' mother Tapollos. Still, it is not certain who actually is making the greeting at ll. 43ff. Despite these issues, we think that this letter must belong to this general group of documents. The very fine script is of particular interest, when compared to the rather coarse production of many of the other pieces. This confident and rather beautiful writing has similarities to that in **29** (sent by Piene).

Address:

verso

        ] . . . . . Ψαϊωι

        Παμ[οῦρ]

(To) ... Psais. (From) Pamour (?).

Names: Chares; Kapiton; Lo; Maria; Pamour (or Pagosh?); Partheni; Patuse; Pshai; Theognostos; Titoue; -alous;

Text:

1   ⲡⲁⲥⲁⲛ ⲙ̄[ⲙⲉⲣⲓⲧ ⲉⲧⲁⲓ̈ ⲛ̄ⲧⲟⲧ ⲧ]ⲟⲛⲟⲩ ⲡⲣⲉⲛ

2   ⲉⲧϩⲁⲗϭ [ϩⲛ̄ ⲣⲱⲓ̈ ⲛ̄ⲛⲟ ⲛⲓⲙ ⲡⲁ]ϫⲁⲓ̈ⲥ ⲡϣⲁⲓ̈

3   ⲁⲛⲁⲕ ⲡ[ⲁⲙⲟⲩⲣ ⲡⲉⲧⲥϩⲉⲓ̈] ⲭⲁⲓⲣⲉⲓⲛ

4   ϩⲁⲑ[ⲏ ⲛ̄ϩⲱⲃ ⲛⲓⲙ †ϣⲓⲛⲉ] ⲁⲣⲁⲕ ⲧⲟⲛⲟⲩ

5   ⲙⲛ̄ [. . . . . ⲡⲁ]ⲥⲁⲛ ⲑⲉⲟⲅⲛⲱⲥⲧⲟⲥ

6   ⲙⲛ̄ ⲡ[. . . . . . . ⲛⲉⲧⲙ̄ⲡ]ⲓⲙⲁ ϣⲓⲛⲉ

7   ⲁⲣⲱ[ⲧⲛ̄ . . . .] ⲙⲛ̄ ⲛⲉⲥⲕⲉⲕⲟⲩⲓ̈

8   ⲛ̄ϣⲏⲣⲉ . . . .]ⲥⲛⲏⲩ ⲉⲓⲧⲉ

9   ϩⲁⲩⲧ [ⲉⲓⲧⲉ ⲥϩⲓⲙⲉ ⲙⲛ̄ ⲧⲁⲥⲱⲛ]ⲉ ⲡⲁⲣⲑⲉⲛⲓ

10 ⲙⲛ̄ ⲛⲉ[ⲥϣⲏⲣⲉ ⲕⲁⲧⲁ ⲡⲟⲩ]ⲣⲉⲛ ϯϣⲓⲛⲉ
11 ⲁⲡⲁⲥⲁ[ⲛ . . . . ⲙⲛ̄ ⲧϥϩⲓ]ⲙⲉ ⲙⲛ̄ ⲛⲉϥ
12 ϣⲏⲣⲓϣ[ⲧ . . . . ϣⲓ]ⲛⲉ ⲁⲡⲁ
13 [. . . . . .]ϩⲓⲛⲉ [. . . . .] . . .
14 [. . . . .]ⲁⲧⲁⲙⲁ ⲙⲁⲣ[ⲓⲁ] ⲙⲛ̄ [ⲡ]ⲓⲱⲧ ⲛ̄ⲡⲁ
15 [. . . . . ⲥ]ⲁⲛ ⲡⲁⲧⲩⲥⲉ ⲙⲛ̄ ⲡⲁⲥⲁⲛ ⲕⲁⲡⲓⲧⲱⲛ
16 [ϯⲣ̄ϣⲡⲏ]ⲣⲉ ϫⲉ ⲡⲱⲥ ⲁⲓ̈ϩⲱⲛ ⲁⲧⲟⲧⲧⲏⲛ[ⲉ]
17 [ⲁⲧⲛ̄]ⲁⲩ ⲟⲩⲕ[ⲟⲩⲥ] ⲛ̄ⲛⲏϩ ⲛⲏⲓ̈ ϫⲉ ⲡⲛⲏ[ϩ]
18 [. . . .]ϯⲣⲁⲙⲡⲉ ⲧⲟⲛⲟⲩ ⲛ̄ⲛⲓⲙⲁ ⲙ̄ⲡⲉ
19 [ⲧⲛ̄ϩⲓⲥⲉ ⲙ̄]ⲙⲱⲧⲛ̄ [ⲁ]ⲧⲛ̄ⲛⲁⲩ ⲛⲏⲓ̈
20 [. . . . .] . [.] ⲉⲓⲛⲏϫ` ⲁⲃⲁⲗ ⲉⲧⲃⲉ ⲡ[ⲉⲓ̈]
21 [. . . . .] ⲛ̄ⲛⲏϩ· ⲡⲗⲏⲛ ⲉϣⲱⲡⲉ ⲧⲉⲧⲛ̄
22 [. . . .]ⲧⲛ̄ⲛⲁⲩϥ ⲙⲁⲣⲉ ⲡⲟⲩⲉ ⲡⲟⲩⲉ . . .
23 [. . . .] Γ̄ ⲡ̄ⲙⲉⲩⲉ ⲛ̄ⲧⲙⲛ̄ⲧⲥⲁⲛ ⲧⲉⲡ . .
24 [. . . .] . ϯⲛⲁ[ⲧⲛ̄]ⲛⲁⲩϥ ⲛⲏⲧⲛ̄ ⲙ̄ⲡⲉ\ⲉ/ⲗⲗⲟⲥ
25 [. . . .] . ⲁϣϥ̄ [ⲁⲩ]ⲱ ϯⲣ̄ϣⲡⲏⲣⲉ ϫⲉ ⲡⲱⲥ
26 [ⲙ̄ⲡⲉ . .] . . . [. .] ⲟⲗⲱⲥ ⲛ̄ⲧⲛ̄ ⲭⲁⲣⲏⲥ
27 [. . . . .] . . ϭⲱ . [.] . ϩⲁ ⲟⲩⲏⲣ
28 . [. . . . .] . ⲉ[. . .]
29 ⲁⲡⲛⲟⲩⲃ ⲟⲩⲧⲉ . [. . . . .]
30 ϫⲓ ϯϫⲗϭⲉ ⲛⲏⲧⲛ [. . .] . . [. .] . . . . . ⲁⲗⲟⲩ[ⲥ]
31 ⲉϣⲱ[ⲡ]ⲉ ⲇⲉ ⲁϩⲁ[. .]ⲉⲣⲟⲩ ϯ ⲡⲗⲉϯⲉ ⲛ̄ϩⲛⲛⲉ
32 ⲛⲏⲧⲛ̄ [ⲛ̄ⲓ̈]ⲉ ⲙⲁϫⲉ [. .] . ⲁⲗⲟⲩⲥ ϫⲉϥⲁⲧⲉϥ`
33 ⲥϩⲉⲓ ⲛⲏ[ⲓ̈ ϯ]ϣⲓⲛ[ⲉ ⲁⲡ]ⲁⲭⲁⲓ̈ⲥ ⲡⲁⲓ̈ⲱⲧ ⲡϣⲁⲓ̈
34 ⲙⲛ̄ ⲛⲉϥ[ϣⲏⲣⲉ ⲧⲏⲣⲟⲩ ⲕ]ⲁⲧⲁ ⲡⲟⲩⲣⲉⲛ ϯⲣ̄ⲗⲩⲡⲏ
35 . . . [. . . . .]ⲛ̄ϫ ⲉϩⲟⲩϣⲉⲧⲕ ⲙ̄ⲡⲓϩⲟⲩⲟ
36 [. .] . . [. . . . .]ϩⲓⲥⲉ ⲁⲣⲁⲕ ϫⲉ ⲙ̄ⲡⲣ̄ⲃⲱⲕ
37 ⲁ̣[. .] . [. . . . .]ⲁ̣ⲓ̈ ⲁⲗⲗⲁ ⲕⲁⲛ ⲁⲕⲥⲱϭ
38 ϫ̣[. . . . . ⲉⲧⲃⲉ] ⲡϣⲉϫⲉ ⲇⲉ ⲙ̄ⲡⲗⲉϯⲉ
39 ⲛ[. . . . . ⲁ]ⲗⲗⲁ ⲛ̄ⲧⲁⲩⲧⲉϥ ⲛⲏⲓ̈
40 ϫ[. . . . .]ⲕϭⲛ ⲁⲣⲓⲕⲉ ⲁⲣⲁⲓ̈ ϩⲓϩⲓⲥⲉ
41 ⲁⲛ̣[. . . . .] . ` ⲙ̄ⲡⲟⲩⲁⲡⲧ̄ ⲁϥⲓⲧⲥ

42   ⲭ[. . . . .]ⲙ̄ⲡⲛⲁ ⲛ̄ⲧⲉ ⲗⲟ·

tr43   ⲉⲣϣⲁ ϯⲧⲟⲩⲉ ⲁⲡⲧ ⲁϥⲓⲧⲥ̄ ⲡⲁⲩ . [. . . . .] . ϯϣⲓⲛⲉ ⲁⲧⲁⲥⲱⲛⲉ ⲙ̄ⲙⲉⲣⲓⲧ

44   ⲗⲟ· ϯⲣ̄ϣⲡⲏⲣⲉ ϫⲉ ⲙ̄ⲡⲉⲧⲛ̄ⲥϩⲉⲓ̣ [. . . . .] ⲧⲟ̣ⲛⲟⲩ ϩⲁⲣⲁⲥ ⲏ ⲣⲱ ⲟⲗⲱⲥ ϫⲉ ⲛⲥ̄ϣⲟⲡ

45   ϯϣⲓⲛⲉ ⲁⲡⲁⲥⲁⲛ [. . . . .] ⲧⲏⲣⲟⲩ ⲕⲁⲧⲁ ⲡⲟⲩⲣⲉⲛ

plus one small frg. unplaced.

(To) my [loved] brother, [who is] very [precious to me]; the name that is sweet [in my mouth all the time; my] master Pshai. (It is) I, [Pamour (or Pagosh?) who writes]; - greetings.

Before [everything: I greet] you warmly (5) and ... my brother Theognostos and ... (All) [those] here greet you (pl.) ... and also her small children ... siblings, whether male [or female; and my sister] Partheni (10) and [her children (all) by] name. I greet my brother ... [and his] wife and his half-brothers ... greet my ... wife ... my mother Maria and the father of (15) ... brother Patuse and my brother Kapiton.

[I am] astonished how, (when) I ordered you [to send] me a *chous* of oil, because oil is very (scarce) here this year, you did not [trouble] yourselves to send me (20) ... I am cast down because of this (shortage) of oil, except if you ... send it. Let each one (of us) remember (our) brotherhood ... (the cost?) I will send to you. (As for) the item (25) ..., and I am astonished how [you did not] ... at all from Chares ... for how much ... the gold nor ... (30) Take this cloth bag for you ... -alous. But if ... has given the small portion of fabric to you, then -alous says that he can pay. Write to me.

[I] greet my master, my father Pshai and [all] his [children] by their names. I am aggrieved (35) ... that they have demanded more from you ... trouble to you (sing.), saying: 'Do not go to ...'. ... but even if you were rigid ... However, [concerning] the matter of the small portion of ... but they gave it to me (40) ... you (should not?) find fault with me. I toiled to ... they did not allow me to take it ... of Lo. (tr) If Titoue allows me to take it ... I greet my loved sister Lo. I am astonished that you did not write ... very much about her, or indeed at all whether she exists! (45) I greet my brother ... all by their names.

Commentary:

Address: The reading of Pamour's name on the address is most uncertain, though possible. Pakysis is another possibility (Pekysis with an -e- is less likely), and perhaps preferable given what seems to be a long vertical stroke remaining from the third letter of the sender's name (i.e. a -ⲕ- rather than -ⲙ-). But it is really very difficult to reach any conclusion from these scant remains.

14 .]ⲁⲧⲁⲙⲁ: We have translated as '.. my mother Maria'. Of course, it looks very much like ⲕ]ⲁⲧⲁ ⲙⲁ 'in each place'; but this kind of distributive ⲕⲁⲧⲁ (very common in Sahidic and elsewhere) seems to be absent in these letters.

15 The reading of the name Patuse is not entirely certain, but it is probably correct. Whilst this form is not found elsewhere in the archive, the closely related 'Pauese' is found in a letter by Pegosh (**78**, 29); and compare also Πετῆσις (P. Kellis I Gr. 8 and 9). These are all slight variations of the same common name, which etymologically indicates dedication to Isis (similarly the fem. Taese and contrast Petosiris).

18 Perhaps ϣⲁⲧ 'is lacking' in the lacuna (and see comm. ad l. 21).

21 Similarly to l. 18, perhaps ϣⲱⲱⲧ 'shortage' in the lacuna.

30, 32 It seems that a personal name ending -alous (or possibly -aleus) must be read in these two instances. For understanding ⲙⲁϫⲉ in l. 32 as ⲡⲁϫⲉ-, see the references collected at **114**, 2.

37 ⲁⲕⲥⲱϭ: We have translated this as 'you were rigid'. The verb ⲥⲱϭ is commonly used for being physically paralysed; but, with no real context, we can not know whether this is meant or something more abstract.

P. Kellis Copt. 71

Inv #: P 81C + P 93D

Location: House 3, room 6, deposit 4.

Preservation: A substantial letter written on reused papyrus. The Coptic script is quite plain, though competent enough and easy to read. It is rather similar to that of **72** (also sent by Pamour), and may have been written by the same scribe. Whilst the script and construction of the latter piece appear a little more refined, this may simply be a matter of somewhat different circumstances at the time of writing. The text of **71** has been abraded in many places, but often there is enough preserved for us to reconstruct the sense. The document has been reconstructed to be mostly complete. Smaller fragments have been added to restore the upper third, whilst the major piece of papyrus preserves the lower two-thirds. The dimensions are 272 x 175mm.

Content: The letter is sent by Pamour to his 'sister' Partheni, and also to 'my son Andreas'. The name Partheni occurs frequently in the archive, especially in the letters of Pamour and his circle; and it may also be that the name Heni (which again is common) is simply a contraction of the same. It is unclear to us how many persons there were with this name (or names). Certainly we should not assume that all occurrences in the archive refer to the same woman; but the evidence of **75** would suggest strongly that the wife of Pamour's brother Pegosh (Pekysis) was called Partheni. In this present letter then it is a reasonable supposition that Pamour (and Maria in her postscript) are addressing their sister-in-law, to use present-day terminology. Also, where in the content of the letter Pamour repeatedly refers to 'him' and 'my brother', he is in fact writing to Partheni about her husband Pegosh. 'Father Pshai' is also presumably their (common) father, i.e. Psais II in K.A. Worp's stemma (P. Kellis I p. 51). However, the figure of Andreas is more problematic. The name occurs frequently in the archive, with many instances in the Pamour and Pegosh letters; but, whilst he is obviously an important figure, we have found it difficult to ascertain his exact relationship to the core characters.

The letter is a good example of the 'Manichaean style'. There is the formulaic prayer to the 'God of Truth' (see the comments on **65**); and there is also an instance of the exclamation ⲧⲟⲩⲉⲱⲧⲉ ⲙ̄ⲡⲛⲟⲩⲧⲉ ('Praise God!' or similar) which is only found in texts of known Manichaean authorship (see further the comments at p. 80 of CDT I). However, as regards the actual content of this letter, it is difficult to reconstruct the events that lie behind it. Something would seem to have happened to Pegosh, and now Pamour and Maria are writing to Partheni and perhaps encouraging her to come. Presumably she is in Kellis, whilst the others are in the Nile valley; but the details of what this is all about are very unclear to us. Our attempted translation is, accordingly, very uncertain at times. It may be that the contents of **72**, especially Pamour's remarks to

Pshai about 'your sister' (is this in fact their common sister-in-law Partheni?), can cast some light on the events.

Address:

verso

   ἀπ(όδος) τῇ κυρίᾳ μου   X   Παρθενει
       ἀδελφῇ

   Deliver to my sister X Partheni.

Names: Andreas; Bes; Jnpnoute; Maria; Noe; Pamour; Partheni; Pshai (x2)?;

Text:

1 [ΤΑΣ]ѠΝΕ ΜΜΕΡΙΤ ΕΤΤΑΪΑΪΤ ΝΤΟΤ ΤΟΝΟΥ ΑΝΑΚ ΠΑΜΟ[ΥΡ]
2 ϮϢΙΝΕ ΑΤΑΣѠΝΕ ΠΑΡΘΕΝΙ ΜΝ ΝΕΣϢΗΡΕ ΚΑΤΑ ΠΟΥΡΕΝ
3 ΜΑΛΙΣΤΑ ΠΑϢΗΡΕ ΑΝΔΡΕΑΣ ϮϢΙΝΕ ΑΡѠΤΝ 2Ν ΠΧΑΪΣ
4 ΠΝΟΥΤΕ ΧΑΙΡΕΙΝ   vac   2ΑΘΗ Ν2ѠΒ ΝΙΜ ϮϢΛΗ[Λ]
5 ΑΠΙѠΤ ΠΝΟΥΤΕ Ν[Τ]Ε ΤΜΗΕ ΧΕΤΕΤΝΑѠΝ2 ΝΗΪ ΝΟΥ
6 ΝΑ6 ΝΟΥΑΪѠ Μ[Ν Ο]ΥΚΑΙΡΟΣ ΕΝΑϢѠϤ ΕΡΕΤΝΟΥΑΧ
7 2Ν ΠΣѠΜΑ ΑΡΕΤΝΡΑΥΤ 2Ν ΤΨΥΧΗ ΕΡΕΤΝΤΑΛΗΛ
8 2Ν ΠΝΕΥΜΑ ΑΡΕΤΝΟΥΑΧ ΑΒΑΛ ΜΠΙΡΕΣΜΟΣ ΤΗ
9 ΡΟΥ ΜΠΣΑΡΤΑΝΑΣ ΜΝ Π6ΑΜΒΑΛ ΝΤΕ ΠΜΑΝΒѠΝΕ
10 ϮΝΟΥ 6Ε 2ΑΠΡΑ Ν[Ν]6ΕΧΕ ΤΗΡΟΥ ΕΤΑΡΕΣΑ2ΟΥ ΝΗΪ Ε[ΤΒΗ]
11 ΤϤ ΣѠΤΜΕ ΝΣΕ ΝΕΤΑΪΤΕΟΥΑΥ ΑΡΑϤ ΝΝΙΜΑ ΕΙϢΑ[Ϯ]
12 [ΟΥ]ѠΝ2 ΝΕΥ ΝΑΜΗΕ ΑΠΑΣΑΝ Ε2Ε Ϯ[[6Ο]]ΧѠ ΜΜ[ΑΣ]
13 ΧΕ ΕΡΟΥΚΑΕ ΕΙΣ . [. .] ΕΙΕ ΜΑΡΟΥΧΙΤΕ ѠΠ ΤѠΡΕ ΧΕ ΝΤΑΪ
14 ΑΠΙΜΑ ΕϢΑΝΤΑΕΙ ϮΝΟΥ 2ѠΒ ΝΙΜ ΑΡΑϤ ΕϢΑΤΕ
15 ΠΒΑΡѠ2Ε ΝΤΕ ΑΒΑΛ ΤΝΑϮ 2ѠΒ ΝΙΜ ΑΤΠϤ ϮΧΙΤϤ Α
16 ΑΤΠϤ ΝΕϤ [[ΝΤΟΤϤ ΜΠΒΑΡѠ2Ε]] 2ΑΠ . . . . ΟΥ . . . .
17 [. . . .] \2Α ΠΑΣΑΝ/ ΕΑϤΤΕΟΥΑϤ vac ΝΕ ΠΙѠΤ ΠϢΑΪ 2Μ . . . . . Ṣ
18 . . . ΟΥΒΕ ΝΚΟΥΝΑϤΪ ΑϤΧΟΣ ΝΗΪ ΧΕ ΑΝΟ ΑΡΑΥ . .
19 . . . . . Α ΠϢΑΪ ΧΟΣ ΧΕ ϮΝΑΚΑΥ ΑΒΑΛ Ν[. . . .]
20 . ΑΪΧΟΣ ΧΕ ΜΠѠΡ Π2ѠΒ ΝΕΣΑΒΤΕ \ΕΝ/ ΑΚΑΥ

21 ϨⲀⲦⲎⲔ ⲘⲠⲤⲚⲞ ⲔⲀ ⲠⲞⲨⲈ ⲚⲈⲔ ⲚⲔϯ ⲠⲞⲨⲈ ⲘⲠⲀⲤⲀⲚ
22 ⲈϢⲀⲚⲦⲈ ⲚⲞϬ ⲈⲒ ⲀⲂⲀⲖ ⲀⲚⲒ ⲠⲞⲨⲈ ⲚⲘⲘⲈ ⲈⲢⲈ
23 ⲦⲚⲚⲈⲨ ⲄⲀⲢ ⲘⲘⲈⲨ ϪⲈ ⲦⲈⲦⲚⲀⲂⲰⲔ ⲚⲦⲈⲦⲚⲘⲒϢⲈ
24 ϪⲈ ⲦⲀⲨⲂⲰⲖⲔ ⲢⲰ ⲀⲢⲰⲦⲚ ⲈⲨ ⲚⲈ ⲚⲒⲚⲀϬ ⲚϨⲂⲎⲨ
25 ⲞⲨⲈ ⲈⲦⲈⲦⲚⲈⲨ ⲀⲒϪⲞⲤ ⲄⲀⲢ ⲀⲢⲰⲦⲚ ϪⲈ Ⲡϥ̄ⲦⲀ ⲚⲀϮ
26 ⲖⲀⲔⲈ ⲀⲢⲰ̄ⲦⲚ vac ⲀⲚⲀⲔ ⲘⲀⲢⲒⲀ ⲦⲈⲦⲤϨⲈⲒ ⲈⲤϢⲒⲚⲈ
27 ⲀⲦⲈⲤⲘⲈⲨ ⲘⲚ̄ ⲦⲀϢⲈⲢⲈ ϪⲚⲠⲚⲞⲨⲦⲈ ⲀⲚⲀⲔ ϬⲈ ⲘⲀⲢⲒⲀ
28 ⲦⲈⲦⲤϨⲈⲒ ⲈⲤϢⲒⲚⲈ ⲀⲦⲀⲤⲰⲚⲈ ⲦⲀⲬⲀⲒⲤ ⲠⲀⲢⲐⲈⲚⲒ
29 ⲀⲤϨⲈⲒ ϬⲈ ⲚⲎⲒ ϪⲈ ϮⲚⲎⲨ ⲀⲂⲀⲖ ⲀⲘⲎ Ⲛ̄ⲦⲞ ⲦⲚⲀⲔⲀⲈ
30 ⲀⲦⲀϢ . . Ⲛ̣Ⲁ . . ⲈⲚ ⲠⲘⲀ Ⲣ̄ϢⲈⲨ ϤϢⲚ̄Ⲧ ⲀⲂⲀⲖ vac
31 ϢⲒⲚⲈ ⲀⲠⲀⲒⲰⲦ ⲠϢⲀⲒ ϢⲒⲚⲈ ⲀⲢⲘ̄ⲢⲈⲞⲨ[[ⲎⲨ]]ⲚⲦⲞⲨ ⲔⲀⲦⲀ
32 ⲚⲞⲨⲢⲈⲚ ϪⲞⲤ ⲘⲠⲀⲢⲐⲈⲚⲒ ϪⲈ ⲀⲒϪⲒ ⲚⲈϨⲀⲒⲦⲈ Ⲛ̄Ⲧⲟ̣Ⲧϥ̣ [Ⲛ̄]
33 ⲂⲎⲤ ⲚⲈⲐⲀⲦⲚⲀⲨⲤⲞⲨ ⲚⲎⲒ ⲀⲒϪⲒⲦⲞⲨ ⲚⲦⲞⲦϥ̄ ⲠⲚⲈⲨ
34 Ⲛ̄ⲦⲢⲒϪⲀⲨ ⲀⲂⲀⲖ ϮⲚⲀⲦⲢⲞⲨ⟨Ⲛ̄⟩ ⲦⲖⲈⲠⲤⲈ ⲚⲈ Ⲛ̄ⲤⲀⲢⲦ vac
35 ⲰⲚϨ Ⲛ̄ⲦⲈⲦⲚ̄ⲞⲨϪⲈⲒⲦⲈ ⲚⲎⲒ ⲚⲞⲨⲚⲀϬ ⲚⲞⲨⲀⲒϢ

tr36   vac   Ⲧ̣ⲞⲨⲈϢⲦⲈ Ⲙ̄ⲠⲚⲞⲨⲦⲈ ⲀⲒ
37 ⲈⲒϢⲀⲚⲦⲈ . [.] . . ⲉ̣ . . . . [. . .] . . ⲀⲚⲈⲦⲚⲀ . . . . ϨⲀ ⲠⲒⲰⲦ̣ . . . [. . . .] . . . . . .
[. . . . . .]
38 [. . .]ⲖⲞⲨ[.]ⲘⲰ . . . . Ⲛ̄ ⲘⲠⲚ̄ . . . . [.] . ⲀⲚⲚⲀⲦⲒϬ . [. . . . .]
39 [Ⲟ]ⲨⲚ ⲞⲨⲖⲀⲨⲈ Ⲛ . . [. . . . . .] ϪⲈ ϮϢⲰⲚⲈ . . . . . ⲁ̣ . . . Ⲛ̣ . ⲀϢ[Ⲓ]ⲚⲈ [. . . . .
. . .]

---

8 ⲠⲚⲈⲨⲘⲀ for ⲠⲠⲚⲈⲨⲘⲀ; Ⲙ̄ⲠⲢⲈⲤⲘⲞⲤ for Ⲛ̄Ⲛ- 12 ⲀⲠⲀⲤⲀⲚ: -ⲤⲀ- ex -Ⲛ- corr. 15 ⲀⲦⲠϤ as it seems, read ⲖⲀⲦⲠϤ 25 ⲈⲦⲈⲦⲚⲈⲨ: Ⲉ⟨ⲦⲀ⟩ⲦⲈⲦⲚⲈⲨ 31 ⲀⲢⲘ̄ⲢⲈⲞⲨ[[ⲎⲨ]]ⲚⲦⲞⲨ: there seems to have been a scribal correction (apparently with the intention to change the singular to an otherwise unattested plural form, or perhaps one should suppose somehow Ⲧ⟨ⲎⲢ⟩ⲞⲨ?); also one should read Ⲁ⟨Ⲛ⟩ⲢⲘ̄ⲢⲈⲞⲨⲎ-

---

(To) [my] beloved sister, who is greatly honoured by me. (It is) I, Pamour. I greet my sister Partheni and her children by name, especially my son Andreas. I greet you (pl.) in the Lord God; - greetings.

Before everything: I pray (5) to the Father, the God of Truth, that you will live for me a long time and a great period, being healthy in the body, flourishing in the soul and rejoicing in spirit, safe from all the temptations of Satan and the adversities of the evil place.

(10) Now, therefore, with respect to all the matters which you (fem. sg.) have written to me concerning him, listen to what I told him here. If I should truly make known to them about my brother - indeed I am saying, if they allow you ... - then let them take you as surety, since you (will by then) have come here. If now you do come, everything (will be) on him. When (15) the pack-animal has brought you out, I will deliver everything to be loaded; and I will take it to load it for him [[from the pack-animal]], on account of the ... for my brother, as he has told it. Father Pshai was ... the little ones. He said to me: "See them ...". Pshai said: "I will leave them ... ". (20) I said: "Do not (do that). The matter would not be right to leave them (both) to you. Of the two, keep one for yourself and give one to my brother". If Noe shall come out, bring (that) one with you (fem. sg.). For you (pl.) see (?) there that you can go and fight; in that they were indeed angry with you. What are these big things (25) that you have done? For I said to you: "The endless (?) ... to you".

(It is) I, Maria, who is writing; greeting her mother and my daughter Jnpnoute. Indeed, I, Maria, am the one who is writing, greeting my sister, my lady Partheni. So, you wrote to me: "I am coming out". Come then! I will (not?) let you (30) ... The place is worthwhile. It is cut off (?). Greet my father Pshai. Greet all the neighbours by name. Tell Partheni that I have received the garments from Bes. The things that you sent me I have received from him. When I have cause to send out I shall make them <bring> to you the portion of wool. (35) Live and be healthy for a long time.

(tr) Praise God, truly! If I ... for father ... There is some ... for I am sick ...

Commentary:

Address: If we presume that Παρθενει is a dative, then one should of course read the name as 'Parthenis'. However, in this Coptic archive the name is always given as Partheni or Heni.

4-9   On the formulaic and Manichaean character of this opening prayer see our comments at the introduction to **65**, and the note and references to **65**, 7-15. For 'the temptations of Satan' see **25**, 20-21. The term ϭⲁⲛⲃⲁⲗ (ϭⲁⲁⲛⲃⲁⲗ) 'adversity' is unusual and a distinctive terminological feature of these prayers; see also **65**, 14, perhaps **63**, 27, and noting **80**, 22. One should compare the occurrence at *PsBk2* 208, 9, where it is used of a disaster at sea; and *1Keph.* 244, 9 where it seems to refer to some kind of rebellion by the archons. Thus, whilst the basic meaning will be something like a typhoon (CD 810a 'wave'?), its semantic range certainly tends towards a spiritual catastrophe. In this present passage it is used for the characteristic dangers of 'the evil place'. Probably, this latter term here does not mean hell, but rather the evil world in which we must live and where Satan rules (see e.g. 1Jo 5:19).

9   ⲥⲁⲣⲧⲁⲛⲁⲥ: Forms of Satan's name with (ⲡ)ⲥⲁⲣ- as a first syllable have so far only been known from manuscripts of Middle Egyptian provenance; notably, the Schøyen codex of Matthew (dialect *M*): ⲡⲥⲁⲣⲇⲁⲛⲁⲥ at Mt. 12: 26 and 16: 23 (see H.-M. Schenke, *Das Matthäus-Evangelium im mittelägyptischen Dialekt des Koptischen (Codex Schøyen)*, Oslo, 2001) and the Cologne codex of Testament literature (non-standard Sahidic): ⲡⲥⲁⲣⲧⲁⲛⲁⲥ at Job 5: 22; 6: 17 and *passim* (see Gesa Schenke, *Der koptische Kölner Papyruskodex 3221, Teil I: Das Testament des Iob,* Papyrologia Coloniensia 33, Paderborn 2009).

15-16 ⲃⲁⲣⲱϩⲉ: On the identity of the pack-animals (camels?) see comm. ad **20**, 54; but here one might better undertand reference to the driver himself.

19   This Pshai may well not be the same as 'father Pshai' mentioned just before (l. 17). Instead, one is inclined to identify him the recipient of **72**, and to suppose that the events discussed here relate to those in the following letter.

20   ⲙ̄ⲡⲱⲣ ⲡϩⲱⲃ ⲛⲉⲥⲁⲃⲧⲉ \ⲉⲛ/: In order to understand this somewhat problematic line in its proper context, we assume the verb ⲥⲁⲃⲧⲉ to be used in its larger, metaphorical, meaning as 'set in order' (see CD 323ab, including 'make εὔθετος', thus 'well-disposed, smooth, right'), here used intransitively and thus turned into passive.

25-26 ⲡϥ̄ⲧⲁ ⲛ̄ⲁⲧⲗⲁⲕⲉ: Perhaps ϥ̄ⲧⲁ is an unattested noun form related to ϥⲱⲧⲉ 'sweat'? In this case, the meaning could be something like: "The endless sweat (i.e. 'labour') is upon you". Still, the entire section from ⲭⲉ to ⲁⲣⲱⲧⲛ̄ looks like it may have been erased.

26-27 On this greeting by Maria to her mother (Maria) and daughter Jnpnoute (= Tsempnouthes) see further **65**, 39-41 note ad loc.

30   One can only speculate about the significance of these comments. The text certainly appears to say that the place (where Pamour and Maria are) is 'of value' and

'cut off'. Perhaps ⲣϣⲉⲩ here means 'prosperous'; but the connotation of ϣⲏⲧ ⲁⲃⲁⲗ is hard to fathom. Possibly it implies 'shortage' or 'need'; i.e. if the family are traders, then the twin circumstances of a village where there is money but a lack of goods would be an attractive proposition.

32   The phrasing ('Tell Partheni') appears odd in a letter addressed to the same, but presumably the scribe is simply and rather literally copying down what Maria is saying.

33   Bes: This could be the same person as that Besas who has traveled between Pamour and Pegosh in P. Kellis I Gr. 72, 46.

33-34 The final letter of ⲡⲛⲉⲩ has a strange anchor-like shape, but this must be the correct interpretation. The phrase about the hour to 'send out' (ϫⲁⲩ ⲁⲃⲁⲗ) may well refer to the time of shipment of goods.

36   This line is written transverse on the lower part of the sheet. There appears to be nothing prior to it. It consists of what seems to be a typically Manichaean expression ⲧⲟⲩⲉϣⲧⲉ ⲙ̄ⲡⲛⲟⲩⲧⲉ ('Praise God!', see further the references and comments in P. Kellis V at p. 80). It is then followed by ⲁⲓ̈, which must be for ϩⲁⲓ̈ⲟ 'verily' (CD 636b-637a); see this form at Mt. 21: 30 in dialect *M* (Codex Scheide).

verso The faint remains of a line of Greek text can clearly be seen running transverse to the address across the lower part of the document. It has been read by K.A. Worp as: 'Contract for the teaching of letters' (ὁμολογία μαθήσεως γραμμάτων). Obviously, the papyrus has been reused for the writing of this letter in Coptic.

P. Kellis Copt. 72

Inv #: P 91A/B

Location: House 3, room 6, deposit 5.

Preservation: This complete and extensive letter, written in Coptic on papyrus, is one of the better pieces in the archive. It has now broken into eleven fragments along the vertical and horizontal folds, but the original dimensions were 265 x 142 mm. There are clear underlying traces of an earlier letter, including ⲧⲁⲙⲟ ⲙⲁⲣⲓⲁ in the final greetings (now on the verso of the current letter). Thus that previous text most probably had also belonged to the same family group. The script of **72** is similar to the previous piece (**71**: sent from Pamour to Partheni). It may well have been written by the same scribe and one might suppose that it comes from a similar context in place and time.

Content: The letter contains many of the elements familiar from other examples in the archive, especially the comments about being far away and the heartfelt wishes to see one another again. The reference to the God of Truth indicates Manichaean belief. Almost certainly Pamour is in the Nile valley, whilst Pshai and Theognostos are in Kellis. The 'father Pshai' must again be 'Psais II' according to Worp's stemma (P. Kellis I p. 51), and there are greetings and references to other familiar figures such as Kapiton (brother-in-law to the brothers Pamour and Pegosh?).

Insofar as the letter has a real point or content, it is an appeal to Pamour's 'brother' Pshai to help his 'sister'. Given the similarities of this piece to **71**, we are inclined to identify this woman with Partheni, the recipient of that earlier letter and probably the wife of Pegosh. Interestingly, there is no mention of Pegosh in this present letter; nor does Maria add her customary postscript. The Pshai to whom Pamour is writing is presumably the same as in **64** and P. Kellis I Gr. 71. Whether he is literally Pamour and Pegosh's brother, perhaps the eldest son of their common father ('Psais II'), is not entirely clear to us.

Address:
verso

τῷ δεσπότῃ μου   X   Ψαΐωι Παμοῦρ

To my master X Psais. (From) Pamour.

Names: Apa L(ysimachos?); Hor; Jnpnoute; Kapiton; Lammon; Pamour; Pshai (x 2); Theognostos; Titoue;

Text:

1 τῶι δεσπ[ότ]ῃ μου ἀδελφῶι Ψάϊωϊ καὶ
2 Θεογνώστωι Παμοῦρ ἐν θ(ε)ῷ χαίρειν
3 ϨΑΘΗ ΜΕΝ Ⲛ̄ϨⲰⲂ ⲚⲒⲘ ϮϢⲒⲚ[Ⲉ] ⲀⲢⲰⲦⲚ̄ ⲦⲞⲚⲞⲨ·
4 ϮϢⲖⲎⲖ ⲀⲠⲒⲰⲦ ⲠⲚⲞⲨⲦⲈ Ⲛ̄[Ⲧ]Ⲉ ⲦⲘⲎⲈ ϨⲀ ⲠⲈⲦⲚ̄
5 ⲞⲨϪⲈⲒⲦⲈ ⲦⲈⲦⲚ̄Ⲙ̄Ⲛ̄ⲦⲤⲀⲚ Ⲉ[Ⲧ]Ⲉ ⲘⲚ̄ ⲔⲢⲀϤ \Ⲛ̄ϨⲎⲦⲤ/ ⲘⲚ̄
6 ⲖⲀⲨⲈ ⲄⲀⲢ ⲤⲀⲨⲚⲈ· ⲀⲦ‹ⲀⲄ›ⲀⲠⲎ ⲈⲦⲢⲦⲀⲢⲦ ϨⲚ̄ ⲠⲀ
7 ϨⲎⲦ ϢⲀⲢⲰⲦⲚ̄ ⲈⲒⲘⲎⲦⲒ ⲀⲠⲚⲞⲨⲦⲈ Ⲛ̄ⲞⲨⲀⲈⲦϤ
8 Ⲛ̄ⲦⲀϤ ⲈⲦⲤⲀⲨⲚⲈ ⲈⲠⲘⲈⲒⲈ ⲈⲒⲔⲀϢⲦ ⲀⲂⲀⲖ ϨⲎⲦ
9 ⲦⲎⲚⲈ ⲈⲒⲞⲨⲰϢ ⲚⲈⲨ ⲀⲢⲰⲦⲚ̄ ⲀⲖⲖⲀ ⲈⲠⲒⲆⲎ ⲦⲈ
10 ⲦⲚ̄ⲞⲨⲎⲨ Ⲙ̄ⲘⲀⲒ ϮⲚⲀϢⲚⲈⲨ ⲀⲢⲰⲦⲚ ⲈⲚ ⲈⲒⲤϨⲈ
11 ⲚⲒ ⲚⲈⲔ/ ϨⲚ̄ ⲚⲈⲒⲤϨⲈⲒ Ⲛ̄ⲔⲘⲈⲒⲘ ⲚⲈⲦϪⲒ ϢⲒⲚⲈ ⲈⲦⲚ̄ϢⲒ
12 ⲚⲈ ϢⲀⲦⲈ ϨⲞ ⲞⲨⲰϢⲦ ϨⲞ· ϮⲚⲞⲨ ϬⲈ ⲠⲀⲤⲀⲚ ⲠϢⲀⲒ
13 ⲈⲒⲈ Ⲛ̄ϨⲂⲎⲨⲈ ⲚⲈ ⲚⲈⲒ ⲈⲦⲀⲒⲦⲈⲨ ⲀⲦⲞⲦⲔ̄ ⲈⲔⲚⲎⲨ
14 ⲀⲂⲀⲖ ϨⲒⲦⲞⲦ ϪⲈ Ⲙ̄ⲠⲢ̄ⲘⲀϨⲔ̄ ⲠϨⲎⲦ Ⲛ̄ⲦⲔ
15 ⲤⲰⲚⲈ ϨⲚ̄ⲖⲀⲨⲈ ⲀⲒϪⲞⲤ ⲀⲢⲰⲦⲚ̄ ϪⲈ Ⲙ̄ⲠⲢ̄
16 ⲂⲰⲔ ⲦⲈⲦⲚ̄ⲦⲀ ⲘⲀ ⲘⲀ ⲀⲢⲰⲦⲚ̄ ϨⲀⲦⲚ̄ⲂⲰⲔ
17 ϨⲀⲦⲚ̄ⲠⲢⲤ ⲠϨⲈⲤ ⲀⲢⲰⲦⲚ· ϮⲚⲞⲨ ⲦⲈⲦⲚ̄
18 ⲎⲠ ⲈⲚ ⲀⲢ̄ϨⲰⲂ Ⲛ̄ϮϨⲈ ⲈϢⲰ‹ⲠⲈ› Ⲛ̄ⲔⲘⲘⲈ
19 ⲚⲀⲘⲎⲈ ⲈⲤⲞⲨⲰϢⲈ ‹Ⲁ›ⲈⲒ ⲀⲔⲎⲘⲈ ⲈϢⲰⲠⲈ
20 ⲀⲚ ⲈⲔⲤⲀⲨⲚⲈ ϪⲈ ⲞⲨⲚ ϨⲚⲈⲨ ⲀⲢⲀⲤ ⲈⲘⲠⲞⲨ
21 ⲔⲀⲤ ⲀⲒ ⲈⲦⲂⲎⲦϤ̄ ⲈⲒⲈ ⲦⲈ[Ⲉ]ϤⲚ̄ⲦⲀⲔ
22 ϨⲀⲢⲀϤ Ⲛ̄Ⲕ̄ⲤϨⲈⲒ ⲚⲎⲒ ϪⲈ ⲀⲒϮ ⲞϮⲚⲀⲦⲚ̄
23 {Ⲧ}ⲚⲀⲨϤ ⲚⲈⲔ Ⲛ̄ϬⲖⲀⲘ ϢⲒⲚⲈ ⲚⲎⲒ ⲀⲠⲀⲒⲰⲦ
24 ⲠϢⲀⲒ ⲀⲦϤ̄ϨⲒⲘⲈ Ⲙ̄ⲠⲈϤϢⲎⲢⲈ ϢⲒⲚⲈ ⲀⲠⲀ
25 ⲤⲀⲚ ⲔⲀⲠⲒⲦⲰⲚ ⲀⲦϤ̄ⲤϨⲈⲒⲘⲈ vac ⲘⲚ̄ ⲚⲈϤ
26 ϢⲎⲢⲈ ⲀⲔⲤϨⲈⲒ ⲚⲎⲒ ϪⲈ ⲀϢⲰⲠⲈ ⲠⲘⲀ ⲘⲀ
27 ⲦⲚ̄ ⲈⲒⲈ ⲤϨⲈⲒ ⲚⲎⲒ ϮⲚⲞⲨ ⲈⲒⲤϨⲎⲠⲈ
28 ϮⲤϨⲈⲒ ⲚⲈⲔ ⲈϢⲰⲠⲈ ⲈⲔⲞⲨⲰϢ ⲈⲒ ⲀⲂⲀⲖ Ⲁ
29 ⲘⲞⲨ ⲠⲀⲤⲀ ϢⲎ ϪⲚ̄ ⲀⲂⲀⲖ ϢⲒⲚⲈ
30 ⲀⲠⲀϢⲎⲢⲈ ⲖⲀⲘⲘⲰⲚ ⲘⲚ̄ ⲦϤ̄ⲤϨⲈⲒⲘⲈ
31 ⲠⲀϢⲎⲢⲈ ϮⲦⲞⲨⲈ ϢⲒⲚⲈ ⲀⲢⲰⲦⲚ̄ ϤⲚⲒⲘⲀ ϨⲀⲦⲎⲒ

```
32      ϢΙΝΕ ΝΗΪ ΤΟΝΟΥ ΑΝΑCΝΗΥ ΚΑΤΑ ΝΟΥ{ΝΟΥ}ΡΕΝ
33      ΕΙC ϮΟΥ ΝΝΕΒΑΤ ϮϢѠΝΕ ΠϨΜΑΤ ΠΝΟΥΤΕ ϢΗΠ
34      ΑΪΛΟ ѠΝϨ ΝΚΟΥΧΕΙΤΕ ΝΗΪ ΝϨΟΥΝΑϬ ΝΟΥΑΙϢ
tr35    ΧΝ ΝΑΑΠΑ Λ . ΜΝ ϨѠΡ ϢΙΝΕ ΑΠΑCΑΝ ΠϢΑΪ ΤΟΝΟΥ ΧΝΠΝΟΥΤΕ ΤΡΝΤΑΝΑΪΕΤΟΥ
36               vac        [Π]CCΑΝ CΝΕΥ ΠΔΙΑΚѠΝ ϢΙΝΕ ΑΡΑΚ
```

———

11-12 ϢΙ|ΝΕ: -Ν- ex corr.   14 ΜΑϨΚ̄: Ν- ex Α- corr.   24 ΜΝ̄ΕϤ-, i.e. ΜΝ̄ ΝΕϤ-   25 ΑΤϤϹϨΕΙΜΕ: Α- ex corr. or erased?   29 ΠΑϹΑ: first -Α- ex corr?   36 ΠΔΙΑΚѠΝ: -Ν ex -Κ corr.

———

To my lord brother Psais, and Theognostos. (From) Pamour, in God; - greetings.

Before everything: I greet you (pl.) warmly. I am praying to the Father, the God of Truth, for your (5) health; your brotherhood in which there is no guile. For no one knows the love for you that pierces my heart, save God alone. He is the one who knows the love (with which) I am looking out for you and wanting to see you; but, since (10) you are far from me, I will not be able to see you. (Instead), I am writing to you (sg.) with these obscure (?) letters, which carry greeting after greeting until (the time when) face greets face.

So, now, my brother Pshai, are matters as I handed them over to you (sg.) when you left me, (saying): "Do not cause pain to the heart of your (15) sister in any way"? I told you (pl.): "Do not go and make every place pay you". (But) you went and you extended the muck to you. Now, you are not supposed to act like this. Do you truly know if she wants to come to Egypt? Also, if (20) you know that she has a debt because of which she is not allowed to come, then pay it, you on her behalf; and write to me, "I have paid whatever". I will send it to you (i.e. I wll repay you) quickly.

Greet for me my father Pshai, his wife and his children. Greet my (25) brother Kapiton, his wife and his children.

You wrote to me: "When the place is quiet, then write to me". Now (that it is), see, I am writing to you. If you want to come out, come ...

Greet (30) my son Lammon and his wife. My son Titoue greets you. He is here with me. Greet warmly for me my brothers, each one by name. I have been ill for five months; by the grace of God I have recovered. Live, and be of good health for me for a long time.

(tr. 35) From those of Apa L(ysimachos?) and Hor: Greet my brother Pshai warmly. Jnpnoute, the woman from Tanaietou; her two brothers; the deacon; (they all) greet you.

Commentary:

Address: One should perhaps note the somewhat strange Greek name form in the dative Ψαῖωι, here and in l. 1 (i.e. as if from Ψάϊος rather than Ψάϊς). Similarly, the address of **115**; and probably **64** and **70**.

11 ⲛ̄ⲕⲙⲉⲓⲙ: We think that this must be a variant form of ⲕⲙⲏⲙⲉ 'dark(ness)' or 'black(ness)'; and not the conjunctive ⲛ̄ⲕ- plus some verb such as ⲙⲉⲓⲉ 'love', or ⲙ̄ⲙⲉ 'understand' (cf. l. 18). However, it is not clear whether the meaning is literal (perhaps referring to letters in black ink) or more abstract (we have translated it as 'obscure'). It is probably too ambitious to understand 'Egyptian', i.e. as Coptic or even as written from Egypt (CD 110a). A second issue is whether it is attributive, which is how we have translated it; or otherwise whether it is the start of a cleft sentence with a nominal plural as vedette: 'It is the black things (ink strokes?) that carry ...' etc. A very different approach would be to understand ⲕⲙⲉⲓⲙ as a place name (Akhmim?).

11-12 ⲉⲧⲛ̄ϣⲓⲛⲉ: This is a second occurrence in the Pamour letters of an unclear ⲉⲧⲛ̄ϣⲓⲛⲉ (see also **66**, 29). Unfortunately, we have not been able to find a common interpretation, fitting them both.

12 ϣⲁⲧⲉ ϩⲟ ⲟⲩⲱϣⲧ ϩⲟ: 'until face greets face'. For similar phraseology see the examples at CD 647a, as well as *1Keph*. 206: 17; 220: 10; 235: 16. In none of these instances, however, is the connective term verbal. For ⲟⲩⲱϣⲧ with a simple ϩⲟ cf. **90**, 7. It probably stands for a respectful, possibly affectionate, encounter.

17 ϩⲁⲧⲛ̄ⲡⲣ̄ⲥ ⲡϩⲉⲥ ⲁⲣⲱⲧⲛ: 'you extended the muck to you'. The exact connotation of this is presumably colloquial (perhaps 'you have covered yourself with dung'?). Our understanding of Pamour's complaint is that he thinks Pshai has been harsh in his (financial?) demands where he should have been generous, and that this reflects badly on him.

20 ⲟⲩⲛ ϩⲛⲉⲩ ⲁⲡⲁⲥ: 'that she has debts' or 'that she owes something'. The following context makes it sufficiently clear that ⲁⲡⲁ// is here predicated in the common

sense of 'debt'. This implies that the zero-determmined ϩⲛⲉⲩ functions as an indefinite pronoun (for which normally ⲟⲩⲁⲛ is used in the debt formula).

26-27 ⲁϣⲱⲡⲉ ⲡⲙⲁ ⲙⲁⲧⲛ̄: 'When the place is quiet ..'. It is possible that we are over-interpreting the meaning of 'the place' (i.e. as the village or town from which Pamour is writing). Possibly, the meaning could be as prosaic as: 'When you have a moment ..'. But from what follows it does seem that they are discussing travel to an actual destination. Compare also **71**, 30.

29 ⲡⲁϛⲁ ϣⲏ ⲝⲛ̄ ⲁⲃⲁⲗ: The reading of ⲡⲁϛⲁ is uncertain, but the word does appear separated from the following ϣⲏ. Perhaps one could read ⲡⲁⲥⲁ<ⲛ> (thus '.. come my brother'); and then understand ϣⲏ for ϣⲉ 'go', which is well-enough attested even in the south. Although this would still not make sense of what is actually written, it might suggest some overall meaning such as 'come my brother - go out from there'. An alternative approach would be to read ⲡⲙⲁ ϣⲏⲝⲛ̄ ⲁⲃⲁⲗ. Although what follows ⲡⲙⲁ ('the place') remains incomprehensible to us, one might compare the phrasing at **71**, 30 of ⲡⲙⲁ ⲣ̄ϣⲉⲩ ϭⲱϣⲧ ⲁⲃⲁⲗ (more comprehensible but still difficult, see the note ad loc.).

35 ⲝⲛ̄ ⲛⲁⲁⲡⲁ ⲗ . : Although the final letter here is difficult to determine, we do not think that one should read a form of the name Jnapollo (even though such does appear at **64**, 32, also written from Pamour to Pshai). Instead, our understanding of the meaning is that greetings are sent from (ⲝⲛ̄) 'those of' (poss. pronoun ⲛⲁ-) Apa L(ysimachos) and Hor, in which case one should suppose an abbreviation mark and thus ⲛⲁⲁⲡⲁ ⲗ/. For a reference to Lysimachos in this volume (and indeed many of the other characters in this present piece) see **82**, 38-39; and further on this person the discussion by I. Gardner, 'P. Kellis I 67 Revisited', *ZPE*, 159, 2007: 223-228 (especially p. 224). It will be seen that there are a number of documents in the archive that place Apa Lysimachos in the Nile valley, and that he is closely associated with Hor and Theognostos. One should read as background his two surviving letters: P. Kellis V Copt. **30** (written to Hor) and P. Kellis I Gr. 67 (to Theognostos). Pshai appears in both of these. Apa Lysimachos is also an important figure in the Makarios family letters, and he links those to the major groups in the present volume (particularly the core sets of letters by Pamour, Pagosh and Philammon).

Having said all that, it is not obvious who exactly are 'those of Apa Lysimachos and Hor'. Some speculation might be in order. The senior member of the Manichaean community in Egypt, 'The Teacher' (see **61**), certainly travelled up and down the Nile valley with a retinue of assistants. This is indicated, *inter alia*, by the boy Piene when he talks about 'following' after him (thus **29**, 13-17); but the same practice was a feature of lower levels of the hierarchy also, amongst whom we should count Apa Lysimachos as a Manichaean elect. This characteristic, the senior figure accompanied by young acolytes, provided ample fuel for anti-Manichaean polemic of course (for example, read al-Biruni, *The Chronology of Ancient Nations*, ed. C. E. Sachau, London 1879: 209). We think it plausible that the 'those of' in this letter refer to members of the retinue who were known to the Kellis recipients of this letter. Some support for this theory can be derived from **82**, 37-40 where Philammon writes to his recipient '.. I asked Apa Lysimachos, (and) he said that we might not stay here'. If this is correct, then it is of particular interest for our understanding of Philammon, and indeed the religious and socio-economic relations between the Kellis believers and the church. On this network of persons and their correspondence (especially Lysimachos, Theognostos, Hor, Ision) see also the introduction in this volume to the letters by Philammon (**80-82**). Further, one might compare P. Oxy. 31 2603 (especially its reference to 'the company of Ision and Nikolaos'); the context for that letter is explored by I. Gardner, 'Once More on Mani's *Epistles* and Manichaean Letter-Writing', *Zeitschrift für Antikes Christentum* (forthcoming).

ⲧⲁⲛⲁⲓⲉⲧⲟⲩ: This seems to be a place name, unless somehow one were to understand ⲛⲉⲓⲉⲧ// ('blessed'). As a toponym, the word bears some resemblance to modern-day Teneida at the eastern end of the Oasis, although that name is commonly derived from ⲧ-ϩⲉⲛⲉⲧⲉ ('the monastery'); on which see further the note at **123**, 17.

LETTERS BY PEGOSH (BROTHER OF PAMOUR)

This group of letters should be read together with the previous. As we have already seen, the two brothers Pegosh and Pamour are in the Nile valley from where they write these many letters to family members and associates in Kellis. The style of letters, the persons named and the topics discussed are very similar throughout. The time-frame must be within an approximate twenty-year span from the 360s into the 380s. Pegosh's wife was probably named Parthene (see **75**). Further information can be derived from the documents published in P. Kellis I, since this Pegosh is clearly the same person as Pekysis the brother of Pamour 'III', son of Psais 'II' and grandson of Pamour 'I', according to the stemma reconstructed in that volume by K. A. Worp (p. 51). Text 44 there (pp. 130-132) details a loan of money to this Pekysis, which is dated 26/04 in 382 C.E. One should also read text 76. We include here Worp's translation of P. Kellis I Gr. 72, since it certainly belongs with the following letters in Coptic:

To my lord brother Pamouris, Pekysis your brother. Before all I greet you very much, praying for your health. Your wife greets you and your son Horos and his little sister. Your brother Horos greets you and Theognostos and Psais and all our family and we are in good health thanks to God's grace. Perhaps you heard about our son Horos that he is a liturgist just now and for that very reason you did not want to come to us, in view of the performance of the liturgy. So come, and he does not need you for that. I wonder why you have not sent me even one fleece, though you know that we had no other one in hand; you did not send it, neither to me nor to your own son. For not only he himself has no spare time for the service of the liturgy, but I myself have no spare time for even an hour because of such things. I am baffled by your carelessness towards us. For if you had bought the small amount of purple dye and only by sack, you did not send this. Remarkable: for you could buy a linen cloth and put it (the purple) in there and send that off to us. Please buy for me the little amount of nicely coloured wool. Greet for me my brother Philammon, if he is with you. Do what you are doing. I pray for your health and well-being in many years to come. (tr) And I'll come to you quickly for this, because you appeared heavy-headed. (v) And we were very sorry not receiving ... through the persons who now have come down to us, I mean Nestorios and Besas, the son of Syros. For the whole day on which they arrived he (?) still showed ...

N.B. It is to be emphasised that there are a number of letters edited later in this present volume (in the 'individual and unplaced' group) that are written <u>to</u> a Pegosh (such as **108**), and also some <u>to</u> a Pamour. Almost certainly some of these belong to these earlier groupings of letters sent by Pamour and Pegosh. Further, **120** is sent by a Pekos to a Pamour, and these could again be our very same brothers. In this latter case the letter has not been included in the present section as it remains uncertain whether it is simply a variant spelling of the name Pegosh / Pekysis, or actually the name of a different person (the form Πεκως is recorded elsewhere).

P. Kellis Copt. 73

Inv #: P 52J

Location: House 3, room 9, deposit 3.

Preservation: There remains approximately the upper two-thirds of a papyrus letter, in one piece. The ink is quite faded, and the document is now breaking along the vertical folds. The dimensions are 188 x 142 mm.; but the original height can be calculated from the centre fold as approximately 256 mm.

Content: Pegosh writes to Pshai, greeting Andreas and Theognostos. The latter two persons are paired together in a number of documents, and generally appear in close proximity to Pshai as well; compare e.g. the starts of **65**, **79** and P. Kellis I Gr. 71. They are all in Kellis. The content of this letter is about the care of two orphaned girls. The use of pronouns, and the modern reader's lack of background knowledge, can make the details difficult to follow. In our endeavour to make sense of events and instructions we have presumed a mixture of direct and indirect speech (i.e. in the English translation); but sometimes Pegosh's meaning remains frustratingly obscure. Still, we suppose that the orphaned girls must be in the Oasis. Their uncle (who apparently was not there when the mother died) heard of his sister's death and suggested Pegosh as guardian for one of the girls, though he will need to persuade the head of his household (since he himself is still quite young as indicated by his being called a 'boy' or at least a 'young man' κογϊ in l. 7). Pegosh is pleased to take on the responsibility, and is now writing to Pshai to find out if it is going ahead. Still, it remains not entirely clear to us whether Pshai is himself the same person as the 'father', i.e. head of the household. Probably he is not, since Pegosh has written to the boy that he needs to persuade 'my father'; whereas he addresses Pshai as brother. In that case the 'father' is probably that elder Pshai whom we have noted in other letters of the Pamour and Pegosh archive (i.e. Psais 'II' in Worp's stemma). In all this, we are somewhat reminded of the girl who is to be sent out to Pamour and Maria (see **64**, 30-31 note ad loc.).

Address:

verso

       τῷ τιμιωτάτῳ   X   ἀδελφῷ . . . . . [.] . . .
          vac?   εἰς Κέλλιν . . . . . .

To my honoured X brother ...
                        To Kellis ...

Names: Andreas; Pegosh; Philammon; Pine; Pshai; Pfiham (?); Theognos; Theognostos;

Text:

1   ⲡⲁⲥⲁⲛ ⲙⲙⲉ[ⲣⲓⲧ] ⲉⲧⲁⲓ̈ [ⲛⲧⲟⲧ ⲧⲟⲛⲟⲩ]

2   ⲡϣⲁⲓ̈ ⲁⲛⲁⲕ ⲡⲉϭⲱϣ ϯϣ[ⲓⲛⲉ ⲁⲣⲁ]ⲕ

3   ⲧⲟⲛⲟⲩ ϩⲛ̄ ⲡϫⲁⲓ̈ⲥ ⲭⲁ[ⲓⲣⲉⲓ]ⲛ

4   ϩⲁⲑⲏ ⲛ̄ϩⲱⲃ ⲛⲓⲙ ϯϣⲓⲛⲉ ⲁⲡⲁ]ϣⲏ[ⲣⲉ] ⲁⲛⲇⲣ[ⲉⲁⲥ]

5   ϯϣⲓⲛⲉ ⲁⲡⲁⲥⲁⲛ ⲑⲉⲟⲅⲛⲱⲥ[ⲧⲟⲥ] ⲧⲟⲛⲟ[ⲩ . . .]

6   ϯⲛⲟⲩ ϭⲉ ϯϣⲓⲛⲉ ⲙⲙⲁⲕ ⲡⲁ[ⲥⲁⲛ] ⲙⲙⲉⲣⲓⲧ

7   [ϫⲉ] ⲉϣ ⲧⲉ ⲑⲉⲡⲓ[ⲇ]ⲏ ⲁ ⲡⲕⲟ[ⲩⲓ̈] ⲥⲱⲧⲙ[ⲉ]

8   ϫⲉ ⲁϥⲥⲱⲛⲉ ⲙⲟⲩ [ⲁ]ⲥⲕⲁ ⲥⲛⲧⲉ ⲛϣⲉⲣⲉ

9   ⲁϥⲥⲱⲧⲙⲉ ⲙⲁⲭⲉϥ ϫⲉ ⲥϩⲉⲓ̈ ⲛⲉϥ ⲛϥ̄ⲧⲛⲛⲁⲩ

10   ⲟⲩⲓ̈ⲉ ⲛⲏⲓ̈ ⲛ̄ϩⲏⲧⲟⲩ ⲛⲧⲁⲕⲁⲥ ⲛⲏⲧⲛⲉ

11   ⲡ̄ⲛⲓϣⲉⲣⲉ ⲙⲁⲭⲉϥ ϯⲛⲁϥⲓ ⲡⲥⲣⲁⲩϣ ⲛⲑⲉ

12   ⲛⲟⲩϣⲉⲣⲉ ⲁϥϫⲟⲥ ⲛⲟⲩⲥⲁⲡ ⲛⲥⲛⲉⲩ ⲛⲉ

13   ⲁⲓ̈ⲁϩⲉ ⲁⲓ̈ⲥϩⲉⲓ ⲛⲉϥ ϫⲉ ⲕⲛⲁⲡⲓⲑⲉ ⲙⲡⲁ

14   ⲓ̈ⲱⲧ ⲓ̈ϣϫⲉ ⲕⲏⲕ ⲛϩⲏⲧ ⲧⲁⲡϩⲱⲃ ⲁⲩⲱ

15   ϯⲙⲁⲓ̈ⲉ ϩⲱⲧ ϫ[ⲉ] ⲕⲡⲓⲑⲉ ⲉⲡⲓⲇⲏ ⲉϥ

16 ⲟⲩⲁϣⲥ ⲁⲉⲥ ⲛⲥⲁϫⲟ ϫⲉⲧⲛⲁⲣ ⲡϣⲙϣⲉ
17 ⲛⲧⲉⲕⲕⲗⲏⲥⲓⲁ ⲁⲩⲱ ⲡⲉⲓⲱⲧⲡ ϫⲁⲃⲁⲧ ⲁ
18 ⲡϩⲉⲡ ⲓϣϫⲉ ⲕⲡⲓⲑⲉ ⲛⲓⲉ ⲧⲉⲧⲛⲁⲛ ⲡⲓⲛⲉ
19 ⲛϥⲛⲧⲥ ⲛⲏⲓ ⲁⲃⲁⲗ· ϣⲓⲛⲉ ⲛⲏⲓ ⲧⲟⲛⲟⲩ
20 ⲁⲡⲛⲥⲁⲛ ⲡϥⲓϩⲁⲙ ⲡⲛⲥⲁⲛ ⲑⲉⲟⲅⲛⲱⲥ
21 [ϥ]ⲛⲁⲧⲉⲩⲟ ϩⲱⲃ ⲛⲓⲙ ⲁⲣⲁⲕ ϥⲛⲁⲥⲉϫⲉ
22 [ⲛ]ⲙⲙⲉⲕ ⲉⲧⲃⲉ ⲧⲕⲟⲩⲓ̈ ⲁⲩⲱ . . . ⲧⲣⲁ . ⲧⲓ .
23 [. . .] ⲁⲡϩⲱⲃ ⲉ[ⲧⲁⲓ̈ ϫ]ⲉ ⲉⲛⲁⲡϩ ⲡⲱⲛϩ ⲛϣⲁⲁ
24 [ⲛⲏϩⲉ . . . .]

(tr)25 ϯϣⲓⲛⲉ ⲁⲡⲁⲓ[ⲱⲧ] ⲫⲓ[ⲗ]ⲁⲙⲙⲱⲛ [ϯ]ϣⲓⲛⲉ ⲁⲡⲁ[. . . . .]
26 ⲁⲓⲥⲱⲧⲙⲉ ϫⲉ ϥⲛⲁ . . . ⲧⲁϣⲉⲣⲉ ⲁⲕⲡ[. . . .]
27 ⲓⲱⲧ ⲙ̄ⲡ . . . ⲛⲁ . [

---

7 ⲑⲉⲡⲓ[ⲇ]ⲏ: i.e. ⲑⲉ ⲉⲡⲓ[ⲇ]ⲏ   14 read ⲧⲁ⟨ⲣ̄⟩ⲡϩⲱⲃ   15 read ϯ⟨ⲣ̄⟩ⲙⲁⲓ̈ϩⲉ

(To) my beloved brother, revered [greatly by me], Pshai. I, Pegosh, greet you warmly in the Lord; - greetings.

Before everything: I greet my son Andreas. (5) I greet my brother Theognostos warmly. So, now, I greet you my loved [brother, for] how is it since the boy heard that his sister had died and left two daughters? (When) he heard, he said: "Write to him that he may send (10) one of them to me", so that I can keep her for you. He said I will take care of her like a daughter. He said it a second time. I have waited. I wrote to him: "Will you persuade my father if you are content for me <to do> the thing?". And (15) I myself am wondering whether you are persuaded? Because he wants to do it head-over-heels so that you will perform the service for the church, and this is a hard burden at the judgement. If you are persuaded, then will you bring Pine and he can bring her out to me.

Greet for me warmly (20) our brother Pfiham. Our brother Theognos will tell you everything. He will speak to you about the girl and ... the [great (?)] matter, so that we may attain life eternal ...

(tr 25) I greet my father Philammon. I greet my ... I heard that he will ... my daughter. You have ... father ...

Commentary:

5   ⲑⲉⲟⲅⲛⲱⲥ[ⲧⲟⲥ]: The lacuna may be too short for all three letters, and perhaps instead one might read ⲑⲉⲟⲅⲛⲱⲥ[ⲧⲉ].

9, 11   ⲛⲁϫⲉϥ: i.e. ⲡⲁϫⲉϥ. See CD 285a and the references collected at **114**, 2. This is only the end product of a 'nasilisation' process for ⲡⲁϫⲉ//, which makes it sometimes into ⲙ̄ⲡⲁϫⲉ// (as attested, *inter alia*, four times in the Heidelberg codex of *Acta Pauli*, in the neighbouring dialect *L6*), perhaps before it becomes fully assimilated into ⲛⲁϫⲉ// (as here and in the closely related dialect *A*, see Sophonias 1, 2f.).

12   The construction is not quite clear. Perhaps a literal translation would be: 'He said it once, (and then a) second (time)'. But the final ⲛⲉ remains without explanation.

16-17   The somewhat unusual construction of ⲛⲥⲁϫⲟ must indicate an impetuous 'headlong' desire, (we have translated 'head-over-heels'), to do this deed as a service for the church; but that involves postulating an artificial 'absolute' form of the suffixal adverb ⲛ̄ⲥⲁϫⲱ// (*B, S*), ⲥⲁϫⲱ// (*B, L4*), cf. CD 756b. Alternatively, one might consider ⲛⲥⲁϫⲟ (CD 384a), perhaps to mean 'officially'. Either way, we are strongly reminded of kephalaion 80 ('The Chapter of the Commandments of Righteousness') where it is instructed that as the second work of the catechumenate: 'A person will give a child to the church for the (sake of) righteousness, or his relative [or member] of the household; or if he can rescue someone beset by trouble; or buy a slave, and give him for righteousness (*1Keph*. 193: 5-8)'.

17-18   ⲡⲉⲓⲱⲧⲡ ϫⲁⲃⲁⲧ ⲁⲡϩⲉⲡ: This is an unusual phrase, but we think the meaning is to do with a heavy religious duty to fulfil, and one of considerable weight at the time of judgement. The matter is of some particular interest when considering the nature of Manichaeism, its appeal and demands on the believers.

20   From the context should we suppose that this Theognos is a different person to the Theognostos greeted in l. 5?

ⲡϥⲓϩⲁⲙ: Whilst the text clearly reads like -ϥ-, it may be noted that in **46** there is found the name Shiham. No other occurences of either name are recorded Hasitzka's *Namen*. It is plausible that this is an Aramaic name (cf. Shechem, Gen. 34:13).

P. Kellis Copt. 74

Inv #: P 56C(a)i

Location: House 3, room 9, deposit 3 west doorway.

Preservation: This is a single strip of papyrus with the scant remains of a letter written in Coptic. However, it also preserves the address on the verso.

Content: Nothing can be said about the content.

Address:

verso

                ] Πεκῦσις Ψάϊς ὁ ἀδελ-
                      φός σου

   (To) ...   ] (From) Pekysis (son of) Psais, your brother.

Names: Pekysis, son of Psais;

Text:

1	]ϣιne ⲁⲣⲁⲕ [
2	ϩ]ine vac . [
3	] . . ne ⲁ . . [
4	]ϣe . . . ⲁ . [
5	] . . . . . [
6	] . n̄ⲗ . . [
7	]ⲉⲁ . . . [
8	] . ⲗ . . . [
9	] . . . . . [
10	] . ⲙⲟ . . [
11	]ϭⲏⲗⲉ ⲁ[

12   ] . . ⲛⲉ . [
13   ]ϭⲛϭ[

Commentary:

Address   We think that the preserved portion of the address gives only the name of the sender, i.e. Pekysis son of Psais; even though this means that the writer has been sloppy in failing to decline the name of the father (i.e. it appears to be nominative where it should be genitive). Of course, the alternative is to suppose that Psais has written to Pekysis, in which case the scribe has simply been sloppy as regards giving the appropriate form Πεκύσι for the recipient. It is difficult to decide either way; but, although the addition of the patronymic is rather uncommon in the Coptic Kellis letters, we have compared the next piece (**75**) where there is a definite example of the same. Here the address is complete:

κυρία μου ἀδελφῇ   X   Παρθενε Πεκῦσις Ψάϊς
                              Παμοῦρ

To my lady sister X Parthene. (From) Pekysis, (son of) Psais, (grandson of) Pamour.

From the opening of that letter we can be certain that the author was indeed Pegosh (Pekysis); and that, although first he formally greets his father and brothers, he is really writing to his wife Parthene. Thus, from these two examples we confirm that Pekysis is the son of Psais and grandson of Pamour, which corresponds precisely to the Greek evidence in P. Kellis I (see p. 51).

3   Probably one can read again †]ϣⲓⲛⲉ ⲁ.

11   ϭⲏⲗⲉ: Perhaps this is an instance of the name 'Kellis' (apparently spelt ϭⲏⲗⲁ at **50**, 40 and maybe ϭⲏⲗⲏ at **108**, 27).

P. Kellis Copt. 75

Inv #: P 56D

Location: House 3, room 9, deposit 3.

Preservation: A letter written in Coptic on papyrus. It is complete in one piece, though now almost broken at the centre fold. Whilst the surface is slightly abraded in places, virtually the entire text can be read. The dimensions are 270 x 55 mm., with an upper margin of 6 mm. Traces of a previous text are clearly visible on the verso.

Content: The excellent preservation makes this an exemplary piece in the House 3 archive. Pegosh writes to his wife Parthene. First he greets his father and brothers, (presumably) according to the conventions of a somewhat patriarchal society. But the major content of the letter concerns his directions to Parthene about the textile trade. Notably, Kapitou (i.e. Kapiton) adds a note to Tagoshe (his wife?) about a similar matter. This all corresponds closely to the context apparent in other letters and documents from House 3. The women are in Kellis, where they are engaged in weaving and the making of garments. Many of the men are away in the Nile valley. The remarkable number of letters found at House 3 can in good part be understood against this background of absence, trade and transport requests.

Address:

verso

  κυρίᾳ μου ἀδελφῇ   X   Παρθενε Πεκῦσις Ψάϊς

           Παμοῦρ

To my lady sister X Parthene. (From) Pekysis, (son of) Psais, (grandson of) Pamour.

Names: Kapitou; Pane; Parthene; Pegosh (= Pekysis, son of Psais, grandson of Pamour); Tagoshe; the man of Mono (?);

Text:

1 ⲁⲛⲁⲕ ⲡⲉϭⲱϣ
2 ϯϣⲓⲛⲉ ⲁⲡⲓⲱⲧ
3 ⲙⲛ̄ ⲛⲁⲥⲛⲏⲩ
4 ϯϣⲓⲛⲉ ⲁⲧⲁ
5 ⲥϩ/ⲓⲙⲉ ⲙⲛ̄ ⲛⲉⲥ
6 ϣⲏⲣⲉ ⲕⲁⲧⲁ

7   ⲡⲟⲩⲣⲉⲛ ϫⲓ
8   ⲡⲓⲥⲁⲩ ⲛ̄ⲙ̄
9   ⲙⲛⲁ ⲛ̄ⲥⲁⲣⲧ
10 ⲙⲛ̄ ⲙⲏⲧⲉ
11 ⲥⲉ ⲛ̄ⲡⲗⲉⲧⲓ
12 ϫⲓⲧⲟⲩ ⲧⲟⲧϥ
13 ⲙ̄ⲡⲁⲛⲉ
14 ⲟⲩⲁϫϥ ⲛ̄ⲥⲧⲓ
15 ϫⲁ ⲉⲛⲁⲛⲟⲩϥ
16 ⲧⲉⲧⲛ̄ⲛⲁⲩϥ
17 ⲛⲏⲓ̈ ⲁⲓ̈ⲙⲁϩϥ
18 ⲛ̄ⲧⲉϥϩⲙⲉ
19 ϯⲣ̄ⲑⲁⲩⲙⲁⲍⲉ ⲛ̣
20 ⲛⲓ̣ⲣⲱⲙⲉ ‹ⲉ›ⲧⲉ̣ ⲛ̄
21 ⲡⲉ̣ⲧ̣ⲛ̣̄ⲛⲁⲩ ⲟⲩⲉⲡⲓⲥⲧⲟ
22 ⲁⲛ ⲛⲏⲓ̈ ⲛ̄ⲧⲟⲧⲟⲩ
23 ⲡⲥⲁⲡ̇ ⲅⲁⲣ ⲉⲧ˙ϣⲁⲓ̈
24 ϫⲓ ⲧⲉⲧⲛ̄ⲉⲡⲓⲥⲧⲟⲗⲏ
25 ⲁⲡ̄ⲥ̄ ⲛ̄ⲧⲱⲧⲛ̄ ⲛⲉ̣
26 ϣⲁⲣⲓⲛⲟ ⲁⲣⲁⲩ ⲡϩⲟⲟ[ⲩ]
27 ⲧϩⲓⲉⲓⲃⲁⲗ ϩⲓⲧⲟⲧⲧⲏⲛ̣[ⲉ]
28 ⲉⲧⲃⲏⲧ ⲉϣⲱⲡⲉ [ⲉ]
29 ⲧⲉⲧⲛⲁϭⲛ̄ ⲡⲉⲧⲛⲁ
30 ⲧⲉϥ ⲛⲏⲧⲛ̄ ϩⲁ ϩⲃⲁⲥ
31 ⲉⲓ{ⲧ}ⲉ ⲕⲁⲗⲱⲥ ⲉϣϣ
32 ⲡⲉ ⲁⲛ ⲙ̄ⲙⲁⲛ ⲛ̄ⲓ̈ⲉ̣ ⲙ̣
33 ⲙⲁⲛ ϩⲓⲛⲟ ⲁⲡⲉⲧⲣϣⲉ̣ⲩ̣
34 ⲡⲣⲙ ⲙ̄ⲙϣⲛϣ ⲇ[ⲉ]
35 ⲙ̄ⲛⲓⲙⲁ ϩⲓϣⲛⲧϥ
36 ⲁⲣⲱⲧⲛ̄ ⲡⲁϫⲉϥ
37 ϫⲉ ⲧⲉⲧⲛ̄ⲣ̄ϣⲉⲩ ⲕⲁ
38 ⲡⲓⲧⲟⲩ ⲡⲉⲧⲥϩⲉⲓ̈ ⲛ̄ⲧⲁ

39	ϭⲟϣⲉ ⲉϥϣⲓⲛⲉ ⲁⲣⲟ
40	{ἐρ-}
tr41	ⲡⲓϣⲏⲙ ⲛ̄ⲥⲁⲣⲧ ⲧϩⲓⲧⲛⲛⲁⲩϥ ⲛⲉ ⲟⲩⲁϫⲉϥ ⲛ̄ⲥⲧⲓⲭⲁ ⲧⲉⲧⲛ̄ⲛⲁⲩϥ ⲙⲛ̄ ⲛⲁⲡⲉϭⲱϣ †ϣⲓⲛⲉ ⲁⲡⲁⲓⲱⲧ ⲙⲛ̄ ⲛⲉϥⲥⲛⲏⲩ
v42	ⲉϣⲱⲡⲉ ϩⲁϫⲓ ⲡϩⲛⲟ ⲛ̄ⲧⲟⲧϥ̄ ⲙ̄ⲡⲣⲱⲙⲉ ⲥϩⲉⲓ ⲛⲏⲓ ⲉϣⲱⲡⲉ
43	ⲁⲛ ⲙ̄ⲡⲉⲥϩⲉⲓ̈ ⲛⲏⲓ̈ ⲙⲛ̄ ⲥⲉϫⲉ ⲥⲙⲛ̄ⲧ ⲉⲧⲃⲉ ⲡⲛⲟⲩⲃ· ἐρρῶ-
44	σθαί σε εὔχομαι πολλοῖς χρόνοις κυρία μου Παρ[θενε]

(It is) I, Pegosh. I greet father and my brothers. I greet my (5) wife and her children by their names. Take these six *mna* of wool (10) and sixteen coils. Take them from Pane, cut it (i.e. the wool) for a (15) good *sticharion*; and send it to me. I have paid him for its freight.

I am amazed by (20) these people, with whom you did not send any letter to me. For any time I shall receive a letter of yours (pl.), (25) count on it, yours are the ones I shall look for (?). The day I came away from you (pl.) (it was?) on my own account.

If you (pl.) can find anyone who will (30) pay you for cloth, then good. If not, then not. I have seen something useful (i.e. 'of good quality'?). And, the man of Mono (35) is here: I asked him about you (pl.). He said that you are well.

It is Kapitou who (now) writes to Tagoshe, greeting her. (40) {Farewell.} (tr) The small quantity of wool that I sent you (fem. sg.): Cut it for a *sticharion*, and send it with (the belongings of) Pegosh. I greet my father and his brothers. (v) If you have received the item from the man, write to me. And if you did not write to me there is no word confirmed about the gold.

I pray that you will be well for many years, my lady Parthene.

Commentary:

Address: See the note to the address of **74**.

1-7   The opening formalities are brief and 'business-like'. In l. 7 Pegosh comes rapidly to the point with an imperative: ϫⲓ 'Take'. One wonders whether the peremptory style is itself an indication of the intimacy of the relationship, formalities being reserved for relatively distant relationships?

2   One suspects that 'my father' (ⲡⲁⲓ̈ⲱⲧ) was intended.

5-6   'Her children' may imply a previous marriage, but probably this is reading too much into it. On such usage see the discussion by E. Dickey, 'Literal and Extended Use of Kinship Terms in Documentary Papyri', *Mnemosyne* 57, 2004: 131-176 [167-168].

11   ⲡⲗⲉⲧⲓ: This may be for πλεκτή, LSJ 1415b. Admittedly, the noun is not recorded in the Greek papyri from Egypt, but there is found the adjectival κ[ίστη]ν πλεκτήν in P. Mert. II 72, 21 (a list of marriage goods). We have translated 'coils', as the range of meaning includes twisted rope, nets and mats. It could indicate wool that has been spun, in contrast to ⲥⲁⲣⲧ. Perhaps one might translate as 'hank', which is also coiled and used to indicate a measure.

13   The reading of the name 'Pane' is uncertain, and no other instance of this is found in the archive. Perhaps it is another name; or one might consider whether ⲡⲁ- is rather the possessive article, followed by a short noun (brother, son or whatever).

19   The handwriting changes notably at this point. Perhaps it is to do with a change of writing implement, and a sudden realization that space is short. But we think that there must be a new scribe, with the hand now being more fluent and cursive, and a marked slant to the letters that were previously rather square and upright.

19ff.   It is probable that Pegosh's meaning has been condensed here. Presumably, he was shocked not at the travelers from the Oasis, but at the fact that they had not brought any letter; or perhaps he means that he expressed his surprise to them.

25ff.   Again, Pegosh's meaning is very condensed. But the basic sense must be that he is really looking forward to a letter from his wife, and he wants her to be in no doubt about it. He seems to say that the reason he is away is all for her sake.

28ff.   Pegosh's instructions to Parthene are to sell the cloth if she can; but, if not, at least it will be useful in other ways.

34   ⲙⲱⲛⲱ: Perhaps one might read ⲙⲉⲙⲛⲱ. An alternative approach would be to read ⲱϩ[ⲉ] | ⲛ̄ⲛⲓⲙⲁ, i.e. 'the man from *mon* is staying here'. In this case it could be that the intended meaning was something like 'the employee of Ammon' (or Lammon, or even Philammon).

40   {ἐρ-}: As in other instances in the archive, this abbreviated Greek farewell must have been written on the papyrus sheet before the Coptic text. It makes no sense here,

interrupting the obvious flow of the letter which continues down the side and then overleaf.

42-43 The details of this transaction are not very clear to us, though see further on this **69**, 2-3 note ad loc. Kapitou is seeking some confirmation about it (l. 43 might be more loosely translated as '.. and if you do not write, then there is no agreement about the money [i.e. gold coins = *solidi*?)'; though it is not obvious whether this refers to what has been handed over by Tagoshe, or the amount that he himself must pay.

P. Kellis Copt. 76

Inv #: P 56E

Location: House 3, room 9, deposit 3 west doorway.

Preservation: A large letter on papyrus, written in Coptic. It is mostly complete, with dimensions of 280 x 82 mm. However, the document is breaking into strips along the folds, (it is completely separated at the centre); and the text itself is badly abraded, especially in the upper half. The hand and general design is very similar to **67** and **68**, which are both by Pamour; and one supposes that all three pieces are products of the same workshop in the Nile valley.

Content: Pagosh writes to Partheni, but (as in **75**) begins with greetings to males in the household, before continuing with instructions to his wife about the textile business. There seems to be a postscript by Chares; but, unfortunately, these final lines (especially the verso) are poorly preserved, and of little help for reconstructing the family relations. See further the note at l. 44.

Address:

verso

    ἀπ(όδος) Παρθ[ενι] Χ . . . ⲡⲁϭⲱϣ

    Deliver to Partheni. X From Pagosh.

Names: Chares; Heni; Hor; (mother) Maria; Pagosh; Pamour; Pollon; Shai; Tiberi;

Text:

1   ⲁⲛⲁⲕ ⲡⲁϭⲱϣ ⲡⲉⲧⲥϩⲉⲓ̈ [ⲉ]ⲧϣⲓⲛⲉ
2   ⲁⲡⲁⲥⲁⲛ ⲙ̅ⲙⲉⲣⲓⲧ ⲉⲧⲧⲁⲓ̈ⲁⲓ̈ⲧ
3   ⲛ̅ⲧ[ⲟ]ⲧ ⲧⲟⲛⲟⲩ ϩⲱⲣ ⲙⲛ̅ ⲛⲉⲕϣⲏⲣⲉ
4   ⲉⲩⲥⲁⲡ ⲕⲁⲧⲁ [ⲡⲟ]ⲩⲣⲉⲛ
5   ⲭⲁ[ⲓ]ⲣⲉⲓⲛ
6   ϩⲁⲑⲏ ⲛ̅ϩⲱⲃ [ⲛ]ⲓ̅ⲙ ϯϣ[ⲓ]ⲛⲉ ⲁⲣⲱⲧⲛ̅ ⲧ[ⲟ]
7   ⲛⲟⲩ [ⲁ]ⲩⲱ ϯ[ϣⲗ]ⲏⲗ [ⲁ]ⲡ̣ⲛ[ⲟⲩ]ⲧⲉ ϫⲉϥ
8   ⲣⲁⲓ̈ⲥ ⲁⲣⲱⲧ[ⲛ . . .] . [.] . [.]ⲉⲛⲁⲣⲓ̣ . ⲛ̅
9   ⲕⲉ[ⲥ]ⲁⲡ ⲉ[.] . . . . . . [.]ϭⲉ ⲁ[ⲛⲁⲕ]
10   ⲡⲉⲧⲥϩⲉⲓ̈ ⲛⲏ[ⲧⲛ̅ . .]ⲉⲧ . ⲟⲩ . . . ⲁ
11   ϩⲟ . ⲛ̣ⲓ̣ⲥ . . [. . .] ⲛ̣̅ϩⲏⲧϥ ⲁⲩⲱ [ⲟ]ⲩ̣[ⲁ]ⲓ̈ϣ
12   ⲛⲓ[ⲙ] ϩⲓⲧⲉ[ⲟ]ⲩ . [. . .]ⲧ ⲉϥⲙⲏϩ ⲛ̅[.] . . [ϩ]ⲓ̣
13   ⲧⲉⲟⲩ ⲙ̅ⲡ[. . . .] . . ⲧ[.]ⲥⲱ . . . .
14   ⲧⲉ[ⲧ]ⲁⲩⲧⲁⲧ . . ⲛ̣ . . . . ϩⲭ . . ϩ . ⲛ[ⲏ]ⲓ̈
15   ϫⲉ ⲙ̅ⲡⲉϥⲛ̅ⲧϥ . . . . . . ϫⲟ· ⲉϥ[.]ϫⲉ[.]ⲉ̣
16   ⲙⲉⲛ ⲙ̅ⲡⲉⲕ . . . . ⲙⲡ . . ⲱⲛⲉ ϫⲉ
17   ⲛ̣[.]ⲧ ⲉⲧⲁⲓ̈ⲉⲟⲩ . . . ϫ . [.] . ⲉϥⲉⲛ[. .] .
18   ϣⲁⲣⲉⲛ̅ⲧⲁ . . . . . [. .] . . ⲁ . . [. . .]
19   ⲙ̣ⲉ ⲉϥⲁⲡ . . ⲛⲏⲓ̈ ⲙⲡ . . . . . † . . .
20   [. . .]ϯⲙⲏ[. .] ⲙ̅ⲙⲁⲩ ϯⲛⲁⲧⲣⲉϥϩⲱϥ
21   ⲟ[ⲩ]ⲁⲛ ⲉϣⲱⲡⲉ ϩⲁⲧⲛ̅ϥⲓ ⲥⲁⲣⲧ ⲛ̅ⲧⲟⲧϥ
22   . . ⲁⲩⲧⲉ ⲛ̅ϩⲙⲉⲥⲁϣϥⲉ ⲛ̅ϣⲉ ⲁⲩⲱ ϩⲁ
23   ⲕⲥ̣ϩⲉⲓ̈ ⲛⲏⲓ̈ ϫⲉ ⲙ̅ⲡⲟⲩϫⲓ ⲛ̅ⲥⲁⲣⲧ ⲉⲧϩⲓ
24   ⲧ[ⲛ̅]ⲛⲁⲩⲥⲉ ϫⲉ ⲥⲉϩⲁⲩ ⲉϭⲉ ⲧⲁⲩⲧⲉ ⲉϩⲓ
25   ⲥⲁ̣ⲧⲡⲟⲩ ϩ[ⲛ̅]ⲟⲩϭⲁⲛ ϯⲛⲁⲣ̅ ⲛ̅ⲧⲁⲕ ⲡⲁⲥⲁ̅
26   ϣⲁⲓ̈ ⲛ̅ⲟⲩⲥⲁⲣⲧ ϩⲓⲧⲛⲛⲁⲩⲥ ⲟⲩⲛ† ϩⲙⲉ
27   ⲙ[ⲛ̅] ⲙⲛ̅ⲧⲏ ϩⲓⲱⲥ ⲉϣⲱⲡⲉ ⲉⲕⲟⲩⲁϣⲥ
28   ⲛ̅[ⲓ̈]ⲉ̣ ϥⲓⲧⲥ ⲛⲉⲕ ⲉϣⲱⲡⲉ ⲁⲛ ⲉⲕⲟⲩⲱϣ

29 ⲧⲉⲥ ⲛ̄ϩⲉⲏ[ⲓ] ⲟⲩⲁϫⲉⲥ ⲁⲛ ⲥⲧⲛ̄ⲛⲁⲩⲥ
30 ⲉ[.] . ⲧⲉⲥ· ϯⲧⲣⲟⲩⲛ̄ⲕⲉⲟⲩⲓ̈ ⲁⲛ ⲛⲉⲕ ⲟⲩ̄
31 [ϣ]ⲁⲙⲧ ⲗ[ⲁ]ⲃ[ⲏ]ⲥ ⲛ̄ⲧⲃ̄ⲧ ⲙⲛ̄ ϩⲙⲉ ⲛ̄ⲉⲓ ⲛ̄
32 ⲕ . ⲥⲉ ⲛ̄[. .]ⲛ ⲛ̄ϩⲏⲧⲥ ϩⲓⲧⲉⲥ ⲛ̄ⲭⲁⲣⲏⲥ
33 . [.]ⲡ̄ⲛⲁ[. .]ⲣⲛ̄ⲉ ⲥⲉⲣ ⲡⲓ ⲡⲉⲧⲛⲁⲓ̈ϣⲙ
34 [ⲙⲛ̄]ⲛ̄ⲥⲱ[ⲥ] ϯϣⲓⲛⲉ ⲁⲣⲟ ⲙⲛ̄ ⲛⲁϣⲏⲣⲉ
35 [. .] ⲙ̄ⲡⲉⲛϫⲓ ⲛⲉⲓ̈ ⲛⲁⲙⲏⲉ ⲛ̄ⲧⲟⲧⲧⲏⲛⲉ
36 [.]ⲉⲓ̈ⲛ . . ⲉⲓϣⲡⲉ ϩⲉ ⲛ̄ⲧⲉⲧⲉⲥ ⲛⲉⲥ ⲙ̄
37 [ⲡ]ⲕⲁⲥ ⲉⲧϩⲙⲁⲥⲧ ⲙⲁⲣⲥⲟⲩⲁϫⲉⲥ ⲁⲛ
38 ⲥⲧⲛ̄ⲛⲁⲩⲥ ϯⲛⲁⲧ[ⲣ]ⲟⲩⲛ̄[ⲧⲥ . .] . . .
39 [.] . ⲛⲟⲩ . . ϣⲓⲛⲉ ⲁⲡⲁϣⲏ[ⲣⲉ . .] . . .
40 [. .] ⲥϩⲉⲓ̈ ⲛⲏⲓ̈ ⲉⲧⲃⲉ ϯ . . . . [. . . . . .]
41 ϩⲁ ⲧⲓⲃⲉⲣⲓ ⲁϣⲧϥ ⲛⲓϣⲏⲣ[ⲉ . . . . . .]
42 . . ⲙⲛ̄ⲧⲟⲩ ⲁⲡⲟ[ⲫⲁ]ⲥⲓⲥ [vac?]
43 ⲱⲛϩ ⲟⲩⲭ[ⲉ]ⲓ̈[ⲧⲉ . . . .]
tr44 ⲁⲛⲁⲕ ⲭⲁⲣⲏⲥ ϯϣⲓⲛⲉ ⲁⲣⲁⲕ ⲡⲁⲓ̈ⲱⲧ ⲡⲁ . [. . . . ⲙⲛ̄] ⲛⲉⲕϣ[ⲏ]ⲣ[ⲉ ⲕⲁ]ⲧⲁ ⲡⲟⲩⲣⲉ‹ⲛ› ⲁⲓ̈ϫⲓ ⲧϫⲗϭⲉ ⲛ̄
45 ⲧⲟⲧϥ ⲙ̄ⲡⲁϭⲱϣ . . [.] . . . . ⲉ[.]ⲧⲉ ⲙ̄ⲡⲁ[. . . .]ⲣⲱⲙⲉ ⲁⲧ . . . . . ⲥⲕ ϯϣⲱⲡ ⲙ̄ⲡⲉⲕϩⲙⲁⲧ
46 vac   vac   ϩⲱ[ⲃ ⲉⲕ]ⲟⲩⲁϣϥ . . . . ϯⲛⲁⲉϥ ⲉⲓ̈ⲣⲉϣⲉ
v47 ϯϣⲓⲛⲉ ⲁⲧⲁⲙⲟ ⲙⲁⲣⲓⲁ ⲧⲟⲛⲟⲩ ⲡⲁⲙⲟⲩⲣ . . .
48 [. . . . .] . . . [. . . . . .] . . . . .
49 . . . . ⲛ̣ . . . . . . ⲁϫⲟⲥ ⲛⲉⲩ̣
50 ϫⲉ ⲙⲁⲣⲟⲩⲧⲛ̄ⲕ ⲟⲩⲁⲩⲉ ⲛ̄ⲕⲧⲛ̄ⲛⲁⲩϥ ⲛⲏⲓ̈ . . .
51 . . . .
52 ⲙ̄ⲡⲣ̄ⲣⲁⲙⲉⲗⲓ ⲁⲧⲛ̄ⲛⲁⲩ ⲡⲣⲏϣ ⲛⲏⲓ̈ ⲁⲧⲛ̄ϫ[.]
53 ϭⲥ . ⲛⲛⲁ . ⲛ . ⲁⲩ ⲡϩⲛⲟ ⲙ̄ⲡⲉⲧⲛ̄ⲛⲁⲩϥ
54 . . . .
55 . . . .
56 . . . .
57 . . . .

58	. . . .
59	. . . . ⲙ̄ⲡⲟⲗⲗⲱⲛ
60	. . . .
61	. . . .
62	. . . . ⲉ[ⲓ]ⲣⲉ ⲙ̄ⲙⲁⲩ ⲛ̄ⲭⲟⲩ
63	ⲱⲧ ⲛ̄ϣⲉ ⲙ̄ⲡⲁⲧⲟⲩϥⲓⲧⲟⲩ ⲣⲱ ϯϣⲓⲛⲉ
64	vac ⲁⲣ . . . .

---

22 ⲛ̄ϩⲙⲉⲥⲁϣϥⲉ: ⲛ̄- ex corr.   33 ϛⲉⲣ: -ϛ- ex corr. (or read -ⲙ-?); -ϣⲙ: -ϣ- ex corr. (with correction mark above?)   52 ⲙ̄ⲡⲣ̄ⲣⲁⲙⲉⲗⲓ: -ⲡ- looks like -ⲛ-

---

(It is) I, Pagosh, who writes (and) greets my loved brother who is greatly honoured by me: Hor, and your children together by their names, (5) - greetings.

Before everything: I greet you (pl.) warmly, and I pray to God that he may watch over you ... again ... I (10) am the one who writes to you ... in it, and always I have given them full ... I have given them to ..., the one that he has ... for me; (15) in that he did not bring it ... which I did ... should ... as he ... to me for the ... (20) ... them, I will make him send someone. If you (pl.) took wool from him ... 4700 (talents); and you (sg.) wrote to me that they did not accept wool that I had sent them, saying "they are bad"; even though I had (25) selected them in a low place (?). I will do <...> you, my brother Shai, for wool I have sent. I have 40 and 15 on it. If you want it then take it for yourself. Or, if you want, give it to Heni to cut and send it (30) ... pay her. Also, I am having another one brought for you. There are three traps (?) of fish and forty pairs of ... in it. I have given it to (or 'paid'?) Chares ...

After (all that), I greet you (fem.) and my children. (35) Truly, we did not receive these (things) from you (pl.). ... if yes, and you (fem.) give to her the half that remains, let her cut it also (and) send it. I will have it brought ... (I?) greet my son ... (40) Write to me about the ... Tiberi has hung it. These children ... They have no verdict. Live and be well (for a long time).

(tr) (It is) I, Chares. I greet you, my father ... and your children by their names. I received the cloth bag (45) from Pagosh, ... I am grateful to you. Anything you want (here, ask and) I will do it joyously. (v) I greet my mother Maria warmly. Pamour greets ... Speak to them, (50) so that they may give you (sg.)

some; and you send it to me. ... Do not neglect to send a blanket to me ... the item you (pl.) did not send ... (55) ... Pollon (60) ... make them for 2000. Indeed, they still have not taken them. I greet ...

Commentary:

Address: Interestingly, it seems that Pagosh's name is given in the Coptic form. There are a number of bilingual addresses in the archive; see particularly **103** (again Coptic ⲡⲉϭⲱϣ in an otherwise Greek formula), **82** (likewise with ⲗⲱⲓϣⲁⲓ), and perhaps P. Kellis I Gr. 67 (Lysimachos in Syriac script, but probably the lost remainder of the address was in Greek).

22   4700: I.e. the payment (in talents); similarly the 2000 in ll. 62-63.

25   The real cause of the dispute is not very clear. It seems that wool Pagosh has supplied has been rejected as of poor quality, which of course he denies. The word ϭⲁⲛ (CD 819b) would imply a valley rather than on the heights, and perhaps Pagosh's meaning is that it has come from well-fed sheep. But this seems rather far-fetched, and a derivation somehow from ϭⲛⲟⲛ 'be soft' or 'smooth' (CD 821ab) could make better sense.

There seems to be an omission of the object after ⲡ̄-; or else {ⲡⲛ̄} needs to be deleted, to read ϯⲛⲁ{}ⲧⲁⲕ 'I will make you pay'.

26   Shai: Possibly this is Theognostos / Louishai, who often appears with Heni (see the following lines). However, the name is common.

30   Perhaps 'another one' means another shipment of goods.

31   ⲗⲁⲃⲏⲥ: The word is used here and in two other of Pegosh's letters (**78**, 43 and **79**, 41), in every instance for a certain quantity of fish. See also **109**, 34. The term contrasts with the more generic ϣⲁⲧϭ̄ 'portion' (e.g. **66**, 44, 45 and **110**, 49). We suggest that it may be for λαβίς (LSJ 1021a), and give this translation of 'trap' following the usage in CD 277a (ⲡⲁϣ and λαβή). An alternative would be to understand λέβης, a 'kettle' or 'pot'; another is ἀλάβης (LSJ 59b and CD 148b s.v. ⲗⲉⲓϭⲓ), which is a kind of Nile fish. One should also note that in P. Kellis I Gr. 71, 49 is found the term κυθρίδιον; i.e. 'a small pot of fish'. Presumably the fish were packed in salt or pickled in brine.

33   ⲥⲉⲣ ⲡⲓ ⲡⲉⲧⲛⲁⲓϣⲙ: This line of text is mostly incomprehensible to us. The scribe may be thought to suggest a word break around the letters ⲥⲉⲣ, so one might read this

section as for ⲥⲉⲣ̄ ⲛⲉⲓ̈ 'and they will do this'. Note the strange stroke at the top of the -ⲉ immediately prior to this. Then, before the final -ⲛ of the line it looks like a -ⲗ- has been corrected to -ⲱ- (though this could be interpreted in other ways), and there is a slightly odd superlinear stroke that may be intended to indicate the correct reading; but the various possible combinations of letters suggest nothing sensible. If one ignored these final two letters as a garbled attempt to start the [ⲙⲛ̄]ⲛ̄ⲥⲱ[ⲥ] that follows in l. 34, then ⲡⲉⲧⲛⲁⲓ̈ could be read as 'the one who will come'.

36-38 It seems that Pagosh has returned to his earlier thoughts about the wool, especially the option of giving it to Heni to cut (l. 29). This afterthought breaks up the greetings he has started in l. 34, and which now continue in l. 39.

40-42 Pagosh's final comments here look intriguing, but there is not enough of the text remaining to understand the content. The name 'Tiberi' will be for Tiberios.

44   Although the reading is not entirely clear, we think that this postscript is by Chares (i.e. Charis, fem.). This might imply that she is Pagosh's wife (and that our suppositions about him being married to Partheni are wrong). But the whole section is poorly preserved and it would be hasty to build too much on this. In (the following) **77** Pamour and Maria add their greetings to the letter. Perhaps the same is true here; the greeting to 'mother Maria' in l. 47 is reminiscent of letters by them, and that line may well continue 'Pamour greets N.N.'. Other evidence we have suggests that Chares is the wife of Philammon; see the note at **66**, 46, and further **80-82**.

46   'Anything you want (here), ask and I will do it joyously'. This formulaic phrase can be supposed from the parallels. See **35**, 48 and **36**, 37-39 (both by Ouales): ϩⲱⲃ ⲉⲕⲟⲩⲁϣϥ ⲛ̄ⲛⲓⲙⲁ ⲕⲉⲗⲉⲩⲉ ⲛⲏⲓ̈ ϯⲛⲁⲉϥ ⲉⲓ̈ⲣⲉϣⲉ. For the Greek counterpart see e.g. P. Kellis I Gr. 7, 18-19; 66, 11-12; 69, 9-10.

47   See the note to **65**, 39-41 on greetings to 'mother Maria'. Here, in this present text, we think that the line must continue with 'Pamour greets N.N.'. In that case, one might wonder whether the writer greeting 'mother Maria' is Pamour's wife (the younger) Maria; but, as noted in the previous discussion referred to above, she never names her own mother. Thus, it is more probable that the speaker here is still Chares. Furthermore, if Pamour does send his greetings, then it means he is with Pagosh (as e.g. he is in **77**). It is for this reason that we have not suggested that his name be read in l. 44 where Chares

greets 'my father Pam–'. (Of course, it is conceivable that what follows 'father' may not be a name at all; but rather ⲡⲁⲙⲉⲣⲓⲧ or suchlike).

P. Kellis Copt. 77

Inv #: P 81F/1 + P 68D

Location: House 3, room 6, deposits 3 + 4.

Preservation: A substantial letter written in Coptic on papyrus. Whilst it has been reconstructed to be mostly complete, (only the lower right hand corner is entirely missing), it has broken along the horizontal folds so that the upper and lower quarters are now detached. Indeed, the upper portion evidences a different preservation context to the remainder, being distinctly darker and more abraded. Otherwise, the script (although somewhat untidy in appearance) is quite well preserved and able to be read with confidence.

Content: Pekysis (i.e. Pegosh) writes from Aphrodite to Kapiton, who is probably his brother-in-law. On this see especially P. Kellis I Gr. 76, at the time of which document it appears that Kapiton and his wife have separated. There Pekysis expresses some antipathy to the man. He also states that Kapiton has been living in Egypt, i.e. the Nile valley; and claims that he does not know if he is still alive. That document is not dated, but in P. Kellis I Gr. 45 we have a loan of money from 386 C.E. made to an Aurelius Kapiton son of Kapiton. The name (sometimes as Kapitou) occurs quite frequently in the letters of the Pamour family, and in general we suppose that they refer to this brother-in-law. Our hypothesis is that the Aurelius Kapiton of 386 C.E., who is said to be from the village of Kellis and residing in the Mothite nome, is the son of Pegosh's brother-in-law. We suppose this because the date is near the end of the period of documentation from Kellis, and the Kapiton of P. Kellis I Gr. 76 is said to have been living for some time in the valley.

In the present Coptic piece, (as in a number of other documents in this volume), Kapiton is clearly still living with his wife (the sister of Pegosh and Pamour). He and his family are warmly greeted. We think that they are in Kellis, especially as - at the end of the letter - Pamour and Maria add their own greetings; the latter to her mother (i.e. the elder Maria) and daughter (i.e. Jemnoute). In sum, we can date this piece to a somewhat earlier year (probably in the 360s - 370s). It provides important evidence that Pegosh and Pamour are in Aphrodite, and support for our reconstruction of the family and their lives.

Address:

verso

   κυρίῳ ἀδελφῷ   X   Καπίτωνι Πεκῦσις

           ἀπὸ Ἀφροδείτης

To master brother X Kapiton. Pekysis, from Aphrodite.

Names: Asklepi; Hapia; Kapiton; Lammon; Maria; Pakous; Pamour; Pekysis; Philammon; Pshai; Shai; Titoue; -isima (?);

Text:

1	τῷ κ[υρίῳ] μο\υ/ τῆς ψυχῆς Καπ[ίτωνι]
2	Πεκῦσ[ις] ὁ ἀδελφό‹ς› σο\υ/ ἐν κ(υρί)ῳ χαίρ[ειν]
3	ϩⲁⲑⲏ ⲛ̄ϩ[ⲱⲃ] ⲛⲓⲙ ϯϣⲓⲛⲉ ⲁⲣⲁⲕ ⲧⲟⲛⲟⲩ ⲙⲛ̄ ⲛ[ⲉⲕ]
4	ϣⲏⲣⲉ ⲁⲩⲥⲁⲡ ⲙⲛ̄ ⲧⲣⲉⲟⲩⲏ ⲧⲏⲣⲥ ϣⲓⲛⲉ ⲛⲏⲓ̈ ⲧ[ⲟ]
5	ⲛⲟⲩ ⲁⲡⲁⲥⲁⲛ ⲕⲁⲡⲓⲧⲱⲛ ⲙⲛ̄ ⲧϥ̄ⲥϩⲓⲙⲉ ⲙⲛ̄ [ⲛⲉϥ]
6	ϣⲏⲣⲉ ϣⲓⲛⲉ ⲛⲏⲓ̈ ⲁⲡⲁϣⲏⲣⲉ ⲗⲁⲙⲙⲱⲛ ⲙⲛ̄ . . . [. . .]
7	. . ⲓⲥⲓⲙⲁ ⲙⲛ̄ ⲡϣⲁⲓ̈ ⲡⲙⲁϩϭ̄[.]ϭ ⲙ̄ . . . . [. . .]
8	. . . . ⲙ̄ . . . [. . .]
9	ⲁⲓ̈ϫⲓ ⲧⲉ[ⲕⲉⲡ]ⲓⲥⲧⲟⲗⲏ ϭⲉ ⲁⲓ̈ⲣⲉϣⲉ ⲧⲟⲛⲟⲩ ϫⲉ ⲁⲓ̈ⲛ̄
10	ⲙⲉ ⲛ̄ϩⲏⲧⲥ̄ ⲁⲡⲕⲟⲩϫⲉⲓ̈ⲧⲉ ⲙⲛ̄ ⲡⲟⲩϫⲉⲓ̈ⲧⲉ ⲙ̄
11	ⲡⲏⲓ̈ ⲧⲏⲣϥ̄ ϫⲛ̄ⲧⲁⲓ̈ⲕⲛ̄ⲧⲏⲛⲉ ⲁⲃⲁⲗ ⲙ̄ⲡⲓ\ϫⲓ/ ⲉⲡⲓ
12	ⲥⲧⲟⲗⲏ ⲛ̄ⲥⲁ ⲧⲉⲓ̈ ⲛ̄ⲧⲟⲧϥ̄ ⲙ̄ⲡⲁⲕⲟⲩⲥ ⲉⲓⲉⲧⲃⲉ ⲉⲩ
13	ⲙ̄ⲡⲉⲧⲛ̄ⲥϩⲉⲓ̈ ⲛⲏⲓ̈ ⲉⲧⲃⲉ ϩⲱⲃ ⲛⲓⲙ ⲁ ⲡⲁⲙⲟⲩⲣ ⲅⲁⲣ
14	ϫⲟⲥ ⲛⲏⲓ̈ ϫⲉ ⲙⲁϫⲓ ϯⲧⲟⲩⲉ ⲙⲡⲉⲓ̈ⲁⲩⲛⲉ ϫⲉ ⲁⲩⲧⲱϣ

15 ⲁϯ ⲧⲕⲟⲩⲓ ϫⲉ ⲁⲅⲉ[ⲓ] ϩⲓⲣⲉⲧⲥ̄ ⲉϣⲱⲡⲉ ϭⲉ ⲁ ϩⲛ̄ⲕⲉ
16 ⲛⲟⲙⲟⲥ ϣⲱⲡ[ⲉ ⲙ̄ⲛ]ⲓϩⲟⲟⲩ ⲉⲓⲉ ⲧⲉⲥ ⲉⲓⲉⲧⲃⲉ ⲉⲩ
17 ⲙ̄ⲡⲕ̄ⲥϩⲉⲓ ⲛⲏⲓ̈ ⲉⲧⲃⲉ ⲡⲥ . ⲟⲕ ⲛ̄ϯⲧⲟⲩⲉ ⲙ̄ⲡⲉⲓⲁⲩ
18 ⲛⲉ ϫⲉ ⲁⲕⲧⲉϥ ⲛⲉϥ ϩⲛ̄ ⲙ̄ⲡⲉ ⲉϥⲙⲏϩ ⲛ̄ϫⲏϭⲉ
19 ϫⲉ ⲟ ⲣ̄ ⲛ̄ⲥⲱⲓ̈ ϫⲉ ⲙ̄ⲡⲓϫⲓ ⲙⲛ̄ ⲧϫⲗ̄ϭⲉ ⲛ̄ⲁ
20 ⲥⲕⲗⲏⲡⲓ ⲉⲧⲃⲉ ⲫⲱⲃ ⲛ̄ϩⲁⲡⲓⲁ ϫⲉ ⲟ ⲙ̄ⲡⲉ
21 ⲧⲛ̄ⲥϩⲉⲓ̈ ⲛⲏⲓ̈ ϫⲉ ⲁⲧⲛ̄ϫⲓ ⲗⲁⲩⲉ ⲛ̄ⲧⲟⲧⲥ̄ ϩⲛ̄
22 ⲙ̄ⲡⲉ ϫⲉ ⲡⲁϫⲉ ⲡⲓⲱⲧ ϣⲁⲓ̈ ϫⲉ ⲟⲩⲣⲁⲙⲡⲉ
23 ⲟⲩϭⲁⲥ ⲡⲁϫⲉⲧⲏⲛⲉ ϫⲉ ⲟⲩⲣⲁⲙⲡⲉ ϫⲟⲥ ⲛⲉϥ
24 ϫⲉ ⲉϣⲱⲡⲉ ⲛⲉⲓ̈ ⲣ̄ ⲉⲛⲉ ⲉⲓⲉ ⲙⲁⲣⲟⲩϣⲱⲡⲉ
25 [. .] . . . . vac ⲉⲓⲥⲏⲧⲉ ⲧⲛ̄ⲙⲓ
26 ϣⲉ ⲙⲛ̄ ⲛ̄ⲛⲉⲣⲏⲟⲩ ⲛⲁ[. . . . .]
27 ⲁⲧⲛ̄ⲛⲁⲩ ⲟⲩⲗⲉⲡⲥⲉ ⲛ̄[. . . . .]
28 ⲙ̄ⲡⲓⲱⲧ ⲫⲓⲗⲁⲙⲙⲱ[ⲛ . . . .]
29 ⲡϣⲁⲓ̈ ϫⲟⲥ ⲛ̄ⲕⲁ[ⲡⲓⲧⲱⲛ . . . .]
30 ⲙ̄ⲛⲓϩⲟⲟⲩ ⲁⲛⲉⲩ [. . . . .]
31 ⲛ̄ⲁⲙⲕⲉⲛⲉⲕ ⲛ̄[. . . . .]
32 ⲡⲕ̄ⲃⲉⲕⲉ ⲛⲁ . [. . . . .]
33 ϭⲉ ⲁⲓ̈ⲧⲉⲥ ⲛ̄[. . . . .]
34 . ⲉϥⲥⲁⲓ̈ϣ . [. . . . .]
        vac
tr35 ⲡⲁⲙⲟⲩⲣ ϣⲓⲛⲉ ⲁⲣⲱⲧⲛⲉ ⲙⲛ̄ ⲧϥ̄ϩⲓⲙⲉ ⲙⲛ̄ ⲛⲉϥϣⲏⲣⲉ ⲙⲁⲣⲓⲁ ϣⲓⲛⲉ ⲁⲧⲥ̄ⲙⲟ ⲙⲛ̄
36 ⲧⲥ̄ϣⲉⲣⲉ ⲁⲛⲉ ⲡⲁⲣ̄ⲧⲁⲃ ⲥⲛⲟ ⲛ̄ⲛⲟⲩⲃⲥ ϩⲱⲥ ⲉⲩⲛⲁⲧⲛⲉ ⲛ̄ⲧⲉⲧⲛ̄ⲧⲛ̄ⲛⲁⲩⲥⲟⲩ ⲛⲏⲓ̈

---

10 ⲡⲟⲩϫⲉⲓⲧⲉ: -ϫ- ex -ⲓ̈- corr.   33 ⲁⲓ̈ⲧⲉⲥ: -ⲥ ex corr.   35 ⲁⲣⲱⲧⲛⲉ: -ⲱ- ex corr.   36 ⲧⲥ̄ϣⲉⲣⲉ: ⲧⲥ̄- ex ⲛⲥ̄- corr.

To the master of my soul, Kapiton; (from) Pekysis your brother, in the Lord; - greetings.

Before everything: I greet you (sg.) warmly and your children together with the whole neighbouhood. Greet for me warmly (5) my brother Kapiton and his wife and his children. Greet for me my son Lammon and ... -isima (?) and Pshai the ...-filler (?) ...

So, I have received your letter. I rejoiced greatly, for I (10) learned from it about your health, and the health of the entire household. Since I left you (pl.), I did not receive any letter, - except this one from Pakous. Then why did you not write to me about everything? For Pamour told me that Titoue from Peiaune says they have determined (15) to sell the girl, because they have come for her (?). Now, if some other laws come about these days, then sell her. Then why did you not write to me about ... of Titoue from Peiaune, whether you sold it to him or not, full of dye? For what? Be after me, for I did not receive (it?) with the cloth bag from (20) Asklepi.

Concerning the matter of Hapia: Why did you not write to me whether you received anything from her or not? For father Shai says: "A year and a half". You say: "One year". Tell her, that if these (terms) please you (fem.), then let them be (25) ... Look, are we fighting with one another ... to send a small amount of ... father Philammon ... Pshai. Tell (?) Kapiton ... (30) these days. Look (?) ... consideration (?) ... your wage ... I gave her to ...

(tr 35) Pamour greets you, and his wife and his children. Maria greets her mother and her daughter. Bring my two *artabs* of jujubes as long as they are settled (?), and send them to me.

Commentary:

1   This is the only instance in the archive of what may seem to the modern reader a rather extravagant phrase: 'To the master of my soul ...'. However, there are examples from elsewhere (e.g. SPP 20 111 τῷ δεσπότῃ μου τῆς ψυχῆς).

4-5   It may be thought strange that Pekysis has first written to Kapiton with greetings in Greek (ll. 1-2), then in Coptic greeted 'you and your children' (ll. 3-4), and now again greets Kapiton and his wife and children. Whilst a bilingual duplication is understandable, the third occasion with its 'greet for me' phrasing may indicate one of the following: (a) there are two Kapitons (see P. Kellis I Gr. 45); (b) in the second instance, i.e. the first Coptic greeting, Pekysis is in fact formally addressing the patriarch of the family (perhaps father Pshai) before turning to his true recipient (compare the start to **75**); (c) the third instance reflects Pekysis' oral instruction to his scribe: 'Greet for me my brother Kapiton ...'. For the latter option compare e.g. **71**, 32 ('Tell Partheni') and possibly l. 29 in the present letter ('Tell Kapiton' [?]).

7   . . ⲓⲥⲓⲙⲁ: Perhaps this is not the ending of a name (-isima), but rather a poorly formed or garbled rendering of ⲧϥ̄ⲥϩⲓⲙⲉ 'his wife'.

ⲡⲙⲁϩⲉ[.]ϭ: or ⲡⲙⲁϩⲉ[. .]ϭ. If this is a description of Pshai's occupation as a 'filler (ⲙⲁϩ- cf. CD 210a)' of something, then the following noun can only be ϭ[ⲱ]ϭ 'cake' or ϭ[ⲣⲁ]ϭ 'seed'. The latter might be possible, but it still seems unlikely. Alternatively, one could read it as the start of a new sentence: 'The place (ⲡⲙⲁ) is ...' (e.g. **71**, 30 note ad loc.). But this is also improbable, not only from context but also for the difficulty of starting a verb with ϩϭ-.

11   We suggest to take the verbal ⲕⲛ̄ⲧ// ⲁⲃⲁⲗ as belonging to a hitherto unattested verb *ⲕⲓⲛⲉ (less likely *ⲕⲱⲛ) related to Bohairic ⲕⲏⲛ; and meaning 'cease for', 'fail' or 'leave'. See also **116**, 3 and **122**, 21.

12, 16 ⲉⲓⲉⲧⲃⲉ: Perhaps this is the writer's form of ⲉⲧⲃⲉ when it is used for questioning. Possibly (but not clear) coalesced from ⲉⲓⲉ (interrogative) + (ⲉ)ⲧⲃⲉ.

14   Peiaune seems most likely to be a toponym, although one could understand it as patronymic. See again at ll. 17f.; also **110**, 50 (Peouaune). It may be worth noting P. Lond. 4 1420, 172, where there is a τόπ(ος) named Παιανε. There is also a Paione[in no. 1419). Both documents are from Aphroditopolites, although much later (VIIIth century).

15   From what follows it appears that some regulations are preventing them doing what they would wish, which apparently is to 'sell the girl' (understanding this as the meaning of † ⲧⲕⲟⲩⲓ); but the force of ⲁⲩⲉ[ⲓ] ϩⲓⲣⲉⲧⲥ̄, lit. 'they have come towards her', esapes us.

17   ⲡⲥ . ⲟⲕ: We can make no sense of this. The final letter may have been corrected. The general context of the sentence suggests that it must be a container of some sort (used for dye).

18   ϩⲛ- in this function (question with alternative) is no doubt related to the regular form ϩⲛ- in dialect *A* (as in ϩⲛ̄ ⲛ̄ⲙⲁⲛ 'or not' Lk. 12:41 *A* ed. Lefort; cf. also *Epist. Apost.* 19, 15), which the etymological dictionaries list along with ϣⲁⲛ- *B* (as in ϣⲁⲛ ⲙⲙⲟⲛ), whereas the normal ⲭⲛ- of the other dialects remains without etymology. But there may also be a phonetic background since the spelling ϩⲛ- is also twice found in *A* as a variant of ⲭⲛ(ⲛ)- 'since' (cf. G. Steindorff, *Die Apokalypse des Elias*, 64). Also at l. 21f. and in **78**, 50.

19   ⲡ̄ ⲛ̄ⲥⲱⲓ̈: We have translated this as: 'Be after me, ...'. Perhaps the meaning is that 'your claim is secondary to mine'.

20   For Hapia (probably the same as Apia) see also **108**, 20. Note that the latter letter is sent from Pshai to Pegosh. It also refers to a Kapiton (spelt Kapidon) and a Philammon. These are, almost certainly, the same group of characters.

29   The imperative is not certain, but 'Pshai told Kapiton' seems even stranger in a letter addressed to Kapiton. See also the note to ll. 4-5. Of course, our restoration of Kapiton's name here is also by no means assured.

31   The reading seems clear enough, but the meaning is entirely obscure.

35   Whilst the letters are not entirely clear, if our transcription is correct then we must suppose either a scribal error to read: 'Pamour greets you and your wife and your children'; or otherwise understand: 'Pamour greets you (as do) his wife and his children'.

36   ⲧⲥ̄ϣⲉⲣⲉ: ⲧⲥ̄- ex ⲛⲥ̄- corr. One might more naturally suppose (see the photograph) that the plural was intended, but we think that it must be the singular (i.e. ⲧⲥ̄-) following Maria's common practice. See further **65**, 39-41 note ad loc.

ⲉⲩⲛⲁⲧⲛⲉ: The use of this verb (CD 195b-196a) in this context seems rather odd, though perhaps it is something to do with the process of treating the jujubes. Alternatively, the verb might be taken as refering to persons, i.e. 'as agreed'; or even in the sense of relieving a debt, i.e. 'as settlement'.

P. Kellis Copt. 78

Inv #: P 92.19 + P 92.22

Location: House 3, room 11, deposits 3 + 4.

Preservation: This is a virtually complete and well-preserved papyrus letter of 268 x 64 mm. It is beginning to break along the folds; and it has been possible to add one small fragment (from P 92.22), in order to help restore the upper right hand strip that is now in the process of disintegrating. N.B. In 2007 the glass frame was found to be broken and the letter was placed with P 91B (= **117**).

The letter is written in a fine and practised hand that shows little variation between the opening in Greek and the majority of the letter in Coptic. Probably the whole was written by the one, bilingual scribe. Note that the name of Pshai is given in its Greek form in l. 14.

Content: The letter is addressed from Pekysis to a father Horos. It is closely related to the following piece (**79**), where are again to be found many of these persons, including both sender and recipient. Since we believe the author to be that same Pegosh, brother of Pamour, as in the other letters of this group, Hor can not be his biological father (who is called Pshai). This Hor is probably also the recipient (together with Theognostos) of the three letters by Philammon (**80-82**), and also no. **30** written by Lysimachos. However, we do not know if he is the same as that Hor to whom Orion writes (**15-17**). There were certainly multiple people with this common name (as is clear from P. Kellis I, and see e.g. no. 72 in that volume). In short, it is difficult to place the recipient of this letter; except that he was obviously a senior member of the extended family for Pegosh, and a close associate of Theognostos, Lysimachos and Philammon.

The above reconstruction, despite its lack of a clear conclusion, certainly situates Hor firmly in Manichaean circles. It is noticeable in this present letter (and in the following) that Pekysis begins with a short form of what we have argued is a characteristic Manichaean prayer (see **65**, 7-15 and note ad loc.). We also note that in both **78** (ll. 16ff.) and **79** (ll. 12 ff.) Pekysis begins with discussion of rolls of papyrus and their expense. The latter parts of both letters are then concerned with other commodities, especially the textile trade that is so central to this archive. These pieces should certainly be read together with those in the following group by Philammon. They are all written in the Nile valley, but presumably sent to Kellis.

Address:

verso

τῶι κυρίωι μου καὶ τιμιωτάτωι   X   πατρὶ Ὥρωι Πεκῦσις

To my master and most honoured X father Horos. (From) Pekysis.

Names: Andreas, (son) of Tone; Antinou; Horos; Lammon; Papnoute; Pauese; Pekysis; Philammon; Psais / Pshai; Shai, (son) of Trouphane; Tagoshe; Theognostos;

Text:

1	τῶι κυρίῳ μου
2	πατρὶ Ὥρωι
3	Πεκῦσις ἐν κ(υρί)ωι χαίρειν
4	ϩⲁⲑⲏ ⲙⲉⲛ ⲛ̄ϩⲱⲃ ⲛⲓⲙ
5	ϯⲥϩⲉï ϯϣⲓⲛⲉ ⲁⲣⲁⲕ ⲧⲟ
6	ⲛⲟⲩ ϯϣⲗⲏⲗ ⲁⲡⲛⲟⲩⲧⲉ
7	ϫⲉϥⲛⲁⲣⲁïⲥ ⲁⲣⲁⲕ ⲉⲕⲟⲩ
8	ⲁϫ ⲛ̄ⲥⲏⲩ ⲛⲓⲙ ϩⲙ̄ ⲡⲉⲕ
9	ⲥⲱⲙⲁ ⲧⲉⲕϯⲩⲭⲏ ⲙⲛ̄
10	ⲡⲉⲕⲡⲛⲉⲩⲙⲁ ϣⲁϯⲛⲟ
11	ⲁⲣⲁⲕ ⲛ̄ⲕⲉⲥⲁⲡ` ⲧⲁ ⲡⲁⲣⲉϣⲉ
12	ϫⲱⲕ` ⲁⲃⲁⲗ` ϣⲓⲛⲉ ⲛ̣[ⲏ]ï ⲁ
13	ⲡⲁⲥⲁⲛ ⲑⲉⲟⲅⲛⲱⲥⲧⲟ[ⲥ] ⲙ̄ⲛ
14	ⲡⲁⲥⲁⲛ ϯⲁïⲥ ⲙⲛ̄ ⲡⲕⲟⲩ[ï] ⲙ̄ⲛ
15	ⲧⲉϥⲙⲟ ⲙⲛ̄ ⲛⲉϥⲥⲛⲏⲩ ⲉⲩ
16	ⲥⲁⲡ ⲕⲁⲧⲁ ⲡⲟⲩⲣⲉⲛ ϩⲁⲕⲥϩⲉï
17	ϭⲉ ⲛⲏï ⲉⲧⲃⲉ ⲛ̄ⲭⲁⲣⲧⲏⲥ ⲙⲛ̄
18	ⲧⲣⲉⲕϫⲟⲥ ϫⲉ ϩⲓⲡ̄ⲣⲁⲙⲉⲗⲓ ⲛ̄
19	ⲙⲁⲛ ⲁⲗⲗⲁ ⲁⲣⲟⲩϫⲏϥ ⲉⲩϫⲱ
20	ⲅⲁⲣ ⲙ̄ⲙⲁⲥ ϩⲓⲑⲏ ⲙ̄ⲡⲟⲟⲩ ϫⲉ
21	ⲙⲛ̄ⲧ‹ⲥ›ⲛⲁⲩⲥ ⲛ̄ϣⲉ ⲛ̄ϭⲛ̄ϭⲱⲣ
22	ⲛ̄ⲧⲁⲣⲓⲛⲟ ϫⲉ ⲙ̄ⲡⲉⲕⲕⲓⲙ`
23	ⲉⲕⲥϩⲉï ⲁïϥⲓ ⲫⲓⲗⲁⲙⲙⲱⲛ

24 ⲁⲓⲃⲱⲕ ⲙ̄ⲡⲕ̄ⲕⲁ ϭⲉⲡⲓϭⲉ
25 ϣⲁⲧⲟⲩϯ ⲡⲓⲥⲁⲓ̈ϣ ⲛⲏⲓ̈
26 ϩⲁ ⲙⲏⲧ` ⲛ̄ϣⲉ ⲙⲛ̄ ⲧⲉⲥⲉ
27 ⲛ̄ⲛⲟⲩⲙⲓⲥ ϩⲁⲕⲥϩⲉⲓ̈ ⲛⲏⲓ̈ ϫⲉ
28 ϫⲓ ⲡⲓⲙⲛ̄ⲧⲏ ⲛ̄ϣⲉ ⲛ̄ϭⲛ̄ϭⲱⲣ
29 ⲛ̄ⲧⲛ̄ ⲡⲁⲩ̄ⲛⲥⲉ ⲕⲧⲉⲓ̈ⲧⲟⲩ ⲛⲏⲓ̈
30 ϩⲁ ⲟⲩⲁⲛ ⲙ̄ⲡⲉϥϯ ⲡⲁϫⲉϥ
31 ϫⲉ ϯⲛⲁϯ ⲉⲛ ⲉⲓ̈ϣⲁⲛⲙ̄
32 ⲙⲉ ⲛⲁⲙⲏⲉ ⲉⲧⲃⲉ ⲡⲛⲟⲩⲃ`
33 ϫⲉ ⲛ̄ⲛⲟⲩⲙⲏⲉ ⲡⲉ ⲡⲥⲁⲓ̈ϯ
34 ⲉⲧⲟⲩⲥⲱⲣ ⲙ̄ⲙⲁϥ ϯⲛⲁⲥϩⲉⲓ̈
35 ⲛⲏⲧⲛ̄ ⲏ ⲙ̄ⲙⲁⲛ ⲁ ⲡⲓⲱⲧ ϣⲁⲓ̈
36 ⲛ̄ⲧⲣⲟⲩⲫⲁⲛⲏ ⲛ̄ⲏⲩ ⲃⲁⲗ ⲛ̄
37 ⲛⲓϩⲟⲟⲩ ⲉϣⲱⲡⲉ ⲧⲉⲧⲛ̄
38 ⲟⲩⲱϣ ⲟⲩⲱⲣⲡ ⲧⲥϩⲓⲙⲉ
39 ϣⲁⲣⲁⲓ̈ ⲛ̄ⲓ̈ⲁ ⲧⲛ̄ⲛⲁⲩⲥ

tr40 ⲙ̄ⲡⲉⲧⲛ̄ϩⲱⲃ` . . . . . . . ⲕ ⲙ̄ⲡⲣ̄ϣⲧⲁⲣⲧⲣ` ϫⲓ ⲡⲓⲥⲁⲓ̈ϣ ⲛ̄ⲭⲁⲣⲧⲏⲥ ⲛ̄ⲧⲛ̄ ⲡⲥⲁⲛ ⲁⲛⲧⲓⲛⲟⲩ

v41 ϫⲓ ϯⲗⲉϯⲉ ⲛ̄ⲥⲁⲣⲧ` ⲛ̄ⲧⲟⲧϥ ⲛ̄ⲁⲛⲇⲣⲉⲁⲥ ⲛ̄ⲧϣⲛⲉ ⲟⲩⲛ ⲙⲁⲃ ⲛ̄ⲛ̄
42 ⲛ̄/ⲙ/ⲙⲛⲁ/ ϣⲁⲧⲛ̄ ⲟⲩⲉ ⲥⲁⲉⲓⲣⲉ ⲛ̄ⲥⲁϣⲃⲉ ⲛ̄ⲥⲁⲣⲧ [[.]]ⲙⲛ̄ ⲙⲉⲗⲁⲛⲓⲟⲛ
43 ⲥⲛⲉⲩ ⲛ̄ϩⲏⲧⲥ ⲙⲛ̄ ϯⲟⲩ ⲗⲁⲃⲏⲥ ⲛ̄ⲧⲏⲃⲧ` ⲙⲛ̄ ⲕⲁⲗⲁⲧⲟⲩⲥ ⲥⲛⲉⲩ
44 [[.]]ⲉ ⲧⲁϭⲟϣⲉ ⲛⲉⲡⲗ̄ⲇ̄ ⲗⲁⲙⲙⲱⲛ ⲁⲃⲁⲗ ⲙ̄ⲡϭⲙ̄ⲛⲧ ⲛ̄ⲙⲙⲛⲁ
45 ⲡⲙⲁⲗⲓⲙⲙⲉ ⲧⲉⲧⲛ̄ⲟⲩⲁϫⲟⲩ ⲛⲏⲓ̈ ⟨ⲛ̄⟩ⲥⲧⲓⲭⲁ ⲉϥⲣ̄ϣⲉⲩ ⲧⲉⲧⲛ̄
46 ⲧⲛ̄ⲛⲁⲩⲥⲉ ⲛⲏⲓ̈ ⲧⲁⲭⲩ ⲙ̄ⲡⲣ̄ϣⲧⲣ̄ⲧⲣ̄ⲧⲏⲛⲉ ⲁⲧⲛ̄ⲛⲁⲩ ϣⲃⲱⲛ
47 ⲛⲏⲓ̈ ⲛ̄ⲧⲁⲕ ϭⲉ ⲡⲁⲥⲁⲛ ⲡϣⲁⲓ̈ ϩⲓϩⲁⲃ ⲡⲓⲱⲧ ⲛⲉⲕ ⲁⲛⲣⲟⲩ ⲉⲧⲃⲉ ⲥⲁⲓ̈ϣ
48 ⲥⲛⲉⲩ ⲛ̄ϩⲙⲁⲥ ⲉϣⲱⲡⲉ ⲟⲩⲁⲛ ϣⲟⲡ ⲧⲛ̄ⲛⲁⲩⲥⲉ` ⲁⲛⲁⲕ
49 ⲡⲁⲡⲛⲟⲩⲧⲉ ϯϣⲓⲛⲉ ⲁⲣⲱⲧⲛ̄ ⲧⲟⲛⲟⲩ ⲙⲁⲣⲉ ⲧⲁϭⲟϣⲉ ⲥϩⲉⲓ̈
50 ϫⲉ ⲛ̄ⲥϫⲓ ⲡⲛⲟⲙⲓⲥⲙⲁⲧⲓⲟⲛ ϩⲛ̄ ⲙ̄ⲡⲉ

---

36 ⲧⲣⲟⲩⲫⲁⲛⲏ: -ⲁⲛⲏ smudged   41-42 ⲙ̄/ⲙ/ⲙⲛⲁ/ sic (one ⲙ too many)   44 ⲛⲉⲡⲗ̄ⲇ̄: -ⲡ- smudged   48 ⲥⲛⲉⲩ: ⲥ- smudged   ⲉϣⲱⲡⲉ ⲟⲩⲁⲛ sic, haplology for ⲉϣⲱⲡⲉ ⲟⲩⲛ̄ ⲟⲩⲁⲛ (common in dialects *B* and *M*, cf. Polotsky, *Grundlagen* I, 69 n. 17)

To my master (and) father Horos; (from) Pekysis, in the Lord; - greetings.

Before everything (5) I write and greet you warmly. I pray to God that he will keep you healthy at all times in your body, your soul and (10) your spirit; until I see you again and my joy is complete. Greet for me my brother Theognostos and my brother Psais, and the little one and (15) his mother and his brothers all together by name.

Now, you (sg.) have written to me about the papyrus rolls. Do not say that I have been negligent, by no means; but they are expensive! For they have been quoting (20) it - till today - at 1200 talents. When I saw that you did not stop writing (about the papyrus), I took Philammon and went. We did not allow any other inducement (25) until they gave me this pair for 1000 (talents) and 16 *nummi*.

You (also) wrote to me: "Take these 1500 talents from Pauese and give them to me (30) for someone". (But) he did not pay. He said: "I will not pay (un)less I receive true information about the gold (i.e. *solidi*), that is to say, whether the reputed quality which they circulate is true. I will write (35) to you (if this is the case) or not".

Father Shai (son) of Trouphane is coming out these days. If you (pl.) want to send the woman to me, then send (a message?). (tr 40) You did not send ... Do not worry. Take the pair of papyrus rolls from brother Antinou. (v) Take this small amount of wool from Andreas, (son) of Tone. There are 30 *mna* less one. It can make seven (lots) of wool; and two small inks there, and five traps of fish and two baskets. (Let) Tagoshe settle (with) Lammon for his 10 *mna* (45) ... and you cut them for me (into) a good *sticharion*, and send them quickly. Do not bother yourselves to send me cereal. Now, you, my brother Pshai: I sent the barley for you. What are we doing about (the) two pairs of clothes? If any are available, send them.

(It is) I, Papnoute. I greet you (pl.) warmly. Let Tagoshe write whether she receives the *nomismation* or not.

Commentary:

11-12 '.. and my joy is (or: 'will be') complete' (ⲧⲁ / ⲛ̄ⲧⲉ ⲡⲁⲣⲉⲱϣⲉ ϫⲱⲕ ⲁⲃⲁⲗ): Cf. IJn. 1: 4, 2Jn 12. The use of the phrase (also **15**, 37-38; **36**, 26; **42**, 13; **82**, 8; **115**, 5) could be supposed a commonplace, but we think that its repeated occurrence may be a specific stylistic element most likely derived from Mani's *Epistles* (which themselves re-used sentiments found in the New Testament). It is one of a number of phrases that recur in particular sets of letters (e.g. those of Orion and Ouales); another example might be the use of † ⲛ̄ⲧⲁⲛ, cf. **115**, 40-41 note ad loc.

19   ⲁⲣⲟⲩϫⲏϥ: We understand an unusual form of the second present. Probably ⲁⲣⲟⲩϣⲓⲧⲉ at **11**, 22 is the same. The text, translation and accompanying note there should consequently be revised, and read: '... your share, for they demand ...'.

20   ϩⲓⲑⲏ ⲙ̄ⲡⲟⲟⲩ: The use of this preposition (here as 'before'?) appears somewhat odd in the context. Does he mean that until today this was the price, but it has now gone up; or simply that this was the price when he last asked?

22-23   For the phraseology of neg. ⲕⲓⲙ + circumstantial to mean 'not cease to ..', see CD 108b (Sah. N.T. only Acts 5: 42, but cf. *1Keph*. 347, 13, 14; 372, 9).

24   ϭⲉⲡⲓⲑⲉ: As written here, this can only be the object noun phrase depending on ⲙ̄ⲡ̄ⲛ̄ⲕⲁ- '(no) other persuading / persuasion'. Note that ⲡⲓⲑⲉ is the only infinitive of Greek origin to be found nominalised (as 'persuasion') in several corpuses of Coptic. Alternatively, but much less likely in the context, ϭⲉ could be taken as absolute '(not) anything else', in which case ⲡⲓⲑⲉ would have to be an imperative: 'Believe (it) / Be persuaded until they give me ...'.

25   ⲡⲓⲥⲁⲓ̈ϣ: This term is used here for purchasing a quantity of papyrus (see also l. 40); presumably it is for two papyrus rolls. See further R.S. Bagnall, *Currency and Inflation in Fourth Century Egypt*, Atlanta, 1985: 68; judging by the texts cited there prices seem to have been calculated on the basis of rolls.

26-27   (Lit.) '.. for ten hundred and sixteen *nummi*': The meaning can scarcely be '1016 *nummi*'. Rather, Pekysis first refers to units of account (i.e. 1000 talents, a substantial discount on the quoted price of 1200), and then to the physical coins. Compare the similar issue at **44**, 31; and see further e.g. O. Douch 1 54.

27-35   It is difficult to understand the matter of the payment via Pauese, as a number of things seem to be taken as understood and some terms have a rather broad lexical range. Our interpretation is that it is about Pauese wanting to wait until he really knows the value of the coins. At the end, Pekysis seems to imply that he will write again if it continues to be an issue; but if it is resolved he will not. However, we may be misunderstanding it.

35-36 ⲡⲓⲱⲧ ϣⲁⲓ ⲛ̄ⲧⲣⲟⲩⲫⲁⲛⲏ: There are a number of variations on this name in the archive, both in Greek and Coptic. It remains rather unclear as to whether one should understand a patronymic ('son of Trouphane') or some kind of alias. See the discussions by Worp in P. Kellis I p. 188 and by ourselves in P. Kellis V pp. 48f. (this includes what is now seen to be an incorrect interpretation of the present text, i.e. that his 'coming forth' would refer to his death). It is apparent that 'Shai' is equivalent here to 'Psais', and virtually certain that we are dealing with the same person as in P. Kellis I Gr. 71 and 73. Furthermore, his appearance as a subscriber to the official document no. 24 in that volume gives us a firm date of 352 C.E. for his lifetime. He also occurs there in the Greek text no. 50; on the other side of which is found a Coptic letter published here as **112**.

37 ⲛⲓϩⲟⲟⲩ: Does this mean that Shai will come soon ('(one of) these days'), or that he is coming out regularly? Presumably the journey is that between the Oasis and the valley.

38-40 Pekysis employs three separate verbs (ⲟⲩⲱⲣⲡ, ⲧⲛ̄ⲛⲁⲩ and ϩⲱⲃ), all of which we translate as 'send'. Elsewhere, there is also found ⲭⲁⲩ. The first term is rather rare in southern dialects, certainly in *L*. A systematic study is probably warranted in order to discern the range of usages; but the distinctions are by no means obvious.

41 This 'Tone' may well be the same as the 'Toni' of **112**, 21; the two letters being connected through the figure of Shai son of Trouphane (as explained *supra* in the note to ll. 35-36).

42-43 ... ⲛⲉⲗⲁⲛⲓⲟⲛ ⲥⲛⲉⲩ ⲛ̄ϩⲏⲧⲥ ⲙⲛ̄ ϯⲟⲩ ⲗⲁⲃⲏⲥ ⲛ̄ⲧϩⲃⲧ: Pekysis says almost exactly the same in **79**, 41, except that there it reads simply ⲛⲉⲗⲁ ⲥⲛⲟ. We suppose that in both instances he is referring to ink, or conceivably a more generic black dye for wool; cf. LSJ 1095a. Nevertheless, the combination of commodities is rather bizarre.

43 ⲗⲁⲃⲏⲥ: see **76**, 31 note ad loc.

ⲕⲁⲗⲁⲧⲟⲩⲥ: We think that this must be κάλαθος, a basket 'narrow at the base' and especially used for wool (LSJ 865a).

45 ⲡⲙⲁⲗⲓⲙⲛⲉ: The reading is clear enough, but we can suggest no interpretation other than that ⲙⲙⲉ could be the verb 'to understand'. Possibly it is some kind of aside

about Tagoshe's debt. The meaning of the final sentence about Tagoshe is equally obscure (ll. 49-50).

45-46   Compare Pegosh's very similar wording at **75**, 14-17.

47   ⲥⲁⲓϣ: Again there is the issue as to what sort of quantity this means (see *supra* l. 25 and note).

48   ϩⲙⲁⲥ: This is probably a variant form of ϩⲃⲁⲥ, 'linen' (CD 659b-660a).

P. Kellis Copt. 79

Inv #: P 92.35G(i) + P 92.22

Location: House 3, room 11, deposit 4.

Preservation: This is a large and mostly complete letter (as reconstructed), written in Coptic on papyrus. It has broken along the main vertical fold; and a few small sections have been lost. One fragment was able to be added from P 92.22. The address seems to have been written by a different scribe, which hand (especially with the extravagant upward diagonal on the epsilon) should be compared to that of **85** and **86**. The principal scribe (i.e. who wrote the letter itself) evidences a competent and practised, but somewhat plainer, style.

There appear to be further ink traces on the verso below l. 45 and to the left; but, as they are not aligned with what has come before, we are in some doubt as to whether they really represent additional text to this letter. In any case, no words can be read.

Content: This letter is closely related to the previous one in terms of the persons involved, the context and content of the letter; and even the find site. In fact, it must have been written at about the same time; so much so, that one wonders if the two documents duplicate identical content. For instance, Pegosh is still explaining that he has not bought the papyrus, because it is so expensive. On the verso of **78** he talks about '30 less 1' *mna* of wool from Andreas, and something about another 10 for Lammon. Here in **79** (l. 38) there is again the '30 less 1' *mna* of wool (but from Papnoute) and 10 for Lampou. Although Andreas is named in the first instance, one notes that Papnoute adds his greetings to that letter. And it does seem probable that Lammon and Lampou are the same person. Clearly, the two letters must be read together, and one may well help to explain the other. But the scribe here is different, for both the main text and the address; and it contrasts to the other letter in some aspects such as format (e.g. there is no introduction in Greek).

Address:

verso

    τῶι δεσπότῃ μου X πατρὶ Ὥρωι

                           Πεκύσιος

To my master X father Horos. (From) Pekusios.

Names: Andreas; Antinou; Hor(os); Lampou (Lamou / Lammon?); Papnoute; Pegosh (Pekusios); Philammon (?); Pshai; Theognostos;

Text:

1 ⲡⲁⲓⲱⲧ ⲡⲁϫⲁⲓⲥ ⲉⲧⲁⲓⲁⲓⲧ ⲛ̄ⲧⲟⲧ
2 ⲧⲟⲛⲟⲩ ⲡⲉⲧⲉⲣⲉ ⲡⲉϥⲣⲉⲛ ϩⲁⲗϭ
3 ϩⲛ̄ ⲧⲁⲧⲁⲡⲣⲟ ⲛϩⲁⲧⲉ ⲛⲓⲙ ⲡⲁⲓⲱⲧ
4 ⲙ̄ⲙⲉⲣⲓⲧ ϩⲱⲣ ⲙⲛ̄ ⲡⲁⲥⲁⲛ ⲑⲉⲟⲅⲛⲱ
5 ⲥⲧⲟⲥ ⲙⲛ̄ ⲡⲁⲥⲁⲛ ⲡϣⲁⲓ ⲙⲛ̄ ⲡⲁⲥⲁⲛ
6 ⲁⲛⲇⲣⲉⲁⲥ ⲁⲛⲁⲕ ⲡⲉⲧⲛ̄ⲥⲁⲛ ⲡⲉϭⲱϣ
7 ⲡⲉⲧⲥϩⲉⲓ ⲉⲧϣⲓⲛⲉ ⲁⲣⲁⲧⲱⲛ ϩⲛ̄ ⲡⲭⲁ̣[ⲥ]
8 ⲡⲛⲟⲩⲧⲉ ⲭⲁⲓⲣⲉⲓⲛ vac ϩⲁⲑⲏ ⲛ̄
9 ϩⲱⲃ ⲛⲓⲙ †ϣⲗⲏⲗ ⲁⲡⲛⲟⲩⲧⲉ ⲁⲧⲣⲉϥ
10 ⲣⲁⲓⲥ ⲁⲣⲁⲕ ⲛ̄ⲟⲩⲛⲁϭ {ⲛ̄ⲟⲩⲛⲁϭ} ⲛ̄ⲟⲩⲁⲓϣ
11 ⲉⲕⲧⲁⲗⲏⲗ ϩⲛ̄ ⲧⲉⲕⲯⲩⲭⲏ ⲙⲛ̄ ⲡⲉⲕ
12 ⲡⲛ̄ⲁ ⲙⲛ̄ⲛⲥⲁ ⲛⲉⲓ ⲁⲛ †ⲥϩⲉⲓ ⲛⲉⲕ ⲉⲉⲓ
13 ⲧⲁⲙⲟ ⲙ̄ⲙⲁⲕ ⲉⲧⲃⲉ ⲡⲥⲉϫⲉ ⲛ̄ⲛ̄ⲭⲁⲣ
14 ⲧⲏⲥ ϫⲉ †ⲛⲁⲣⲁⲙⲉⲗⲓ ⲉⲛ ⲉⲙⲡⲓⲧⲛ̄ⲛⲁⲩ

15 ⲥⲉ ⲛⲉⲕ ⲉⲧⲉ ⲙ̄ⲡⲓⲧⲛ̄ⲁⲩⲥⲉ ⲇⲉ ⲛⲉⲕ
16 ϯⲛⲟⲩ ϫⲉ ⲥⲉⲭⲏϥ ⲉⲉⲓⲁⲙⲁϩⲧⲉ ⲛ̄ⲧⲟⲧ
17 ⲧⲛ̄ϯ ⲕⲉϩⲟⲟⲩⲉ . [. . . . . . .] ⲙ̄ⲙⲁⲥ
18 ϫⲉ ϣⲁⲧⲟⲩⲙ̄ⲧⲁ[ⲛ . . . . .]ⲉ ⲥⲉϯ ⲙ̄
19 ⲙⲁⲩ ⲁⲃⲁⲗ ⲉⲩⲭⲏϥ ⲧⲭⲁϭⲉ ϯⲁⲩⲥ ⲛ̄
20 ϣⲉ ϩⲁ ⲡⲥⲁⲓ̈ϣ ⲉⲟⲩⲕⲁⲗⲁⲙⲟⲛ ϯⲛⲁ
21 ⲧⲛ̄ⲛⲁⲩⲥⲉ ⲛⲉⲕ ⲛ̄[. . . . . .]ⲡⲓⲱⲧ
22 ⲁⲛⲧⲓⲛⲟⲩ ⲁⲉⲓ [. . . . . . .]ⲉ ⲙⲛ̄ ⲡⲉ
23 ⲧⲛ̄ϩⲏⲧⲥ̄ ϩⲓϭⲛ̄ ⲟ[ⲩ . . . . .]ⲉⲣⲉ ⲛ̄ϩⲏ
24 ⲧⲥ̄ ⲙⲛ̄ ϫⲟⲩⲧⲉⲥ[ⲉ] ⲛ̄ⲛⲟⲩⲙⲟⲥ ⲙⲛ̄
25 ⲛⲕⲉϩⲛⲁⲩⲉ ⲉⲧⲛ̄ϩⲏⲧⲥ̄ ⲡⲉⲧⲁⲕϫⲟⲥ
26 ϫⲉ ⲧⲉⲟⲩ ⲁⲃⲁⲗ . . . ⲉⲉⲓⲛⲁϫⲁⲩ
27 ⲥⲟⲩ ⲁⲡⲙⲁⲣⲏⲥ {ⲙ̄ⲙⲁⲩ} ⲥⲉⲛⲁϫⲓⲧⲟⲩ
28 ⲉⲛ ⲙ̄ⲡⲓⲙⲁ ⲁⲉⲓϫⲓ ⲡⲣⲏϣ ⲙⲛ̄ ⲛ̄
29 ϩⲁⲓ̈ⲧⲉ ⲙⲛ̄ ⲧϭⲓϫ ⲛ̄ϣⲃⲱⲛ ⲉⲧⲛ̄ϩⲏⲧϥ̄
30 ⲛ̄ⲧⲁⲕ ϭⲉ ⲡⲁⲥⲁⲛ ⲡϣⲁⲓ̈ ⲁⲕⲥϩⲉⲓ
31 ⲛⲏⲓ̈ ϫⲉ ⲁⲉⲓϫⲓ ⲧϭⲁⲣⲧ̄ ⲁⲕϫⲟⲥ ϫⲉ ⲧⲛ̄
32 ⲛⲁⲩ ⲕⲉⲙ̄ⲙ̄ⲛ̄ⲁ ϭⲛⲟ ⲛⲏⲓ̈ ⲛ̄ϣⲧⲓⲧ
33 ⲉⲓⲉ ⲛ̄ⲕⲥⲁⲩⲛⲉ ⲉⲛ ϫⲉ ϯⲛⲁϭⲛ̄ ⲥⲁⲣⲧ
34 ⲉⲛ ⲙ̄ⲡⲓⲙⲁ ⲉⲓⲙⲏϯ ⲛ̄ⲧⲁϫⲁⲩ . . . \ . ⲉ . . / ⲙⲁ
35 ⲣⲏⲥ ⲡⲛⲟ ⲛ̄ⲧⲣⲓϭⲛ̄ⲧⲥ̄ ⲉⲛⲁⲧⲛ̄ⲛⲁⲩⲥ
36 ⲛⲉⲕ ⲱⲛϩ ⲛ̄ⲧⲉⲧⲛ̄ⲟⲩϫⲉⲓⲧⲉ ⲛ̄ⲟⲩⲛⲁϭ
37 ⲛ̄ⲟⲩⲁⲓϣ ⲕⲁⲧ[ⲁ] ⲛⲉⲛϣⲗⲏⲗ

tr38 ϫⲓ ⲡⲙⲁⲃ̄ ⲛ̄ⲙ̄ⲛⲁ ⲛ̄ⲥⲁⲣⲧ ϣⲁⲧⲛ̄ⲟⲩⲉ ⲛ̄ⲧⲟⲧϥ̄ ⲙ̄ⲡⲁⲡⲛⲟⲩⲧⲉ † ⲙⲏⲧ ⲛⲏⲓ̈ ⲛ̄ⲗⲁⲙⲡⲟⲩ
ϯⲛⲁⲙⲁϩϥ ⲛ̄ⲧⲩϩⲙⲉ ⲙ̄ⲡⲓⲙⲁ

39 ⲕⲁϥ ⲥⲁⲧⲡⲟⲩ ⲛⲉϥ ⲧϩⲉ ⲉⲧⲉϩⲛⲉϥ ⲙ̄ⲡⲣ̄ⲣ̄ⲗⲩⲡⲏ ⲙ̄ⲙⲁϥ ϫⲉ ϯⲟⲩⲁϣ ⲣ̄ ⲉⲛⲉϥ ⲧⲟⲛⲟⲩ
ⲙ̄ⲡⲱⲣϫⲛⲟⲩϥ ⲁϩⲙⲉ ϣⲓⲛⲉ ⲁⲣⲁϥ

40 vac ⲧⲟⲛⲟⲩ ⲙⲛ̄ ⲛⲉϥ . . . .

v41 ϫⲓ ⲡⲓⲙⲉⲗⲁ ⲥⲛⲟ ⲙⲛ̄ ⲡⲓϯⲟⲩ ⲛ̄ⲗⲁⲃⲏⲥ ⲛ̄ⲧⲃ̄ⲧ ⲟⲩⲉ
42 ϩⲛ̄ ⲡϣⲁⲧ ⲛ̄ⲧⲁⲕ ⲇⲉ ⲡⲁⲥⲁⲛ ⲡϣⲁⲓ ⲉϣⲱⲡⲉ ⲁⲕ
43 ϫⲓ ⲧⲗⲉⲡⲥⲉ ⲛ̄ϫⲏϭⲉ ⲉⲓⲉ ⲧⲛ̄ⲛⲁⲩ . . . .
44 ⲧⲕⲉⲗⲉⲡⲥⲉ ⲡⲉϣ ⲛ̄ϩⲉ ⲧⲁⲧⲛ̄ⲛⲁⲩ[ⲥ ⲛⲉⲕ] . . . [ⲫⲓⲗⲁⲙ]

45 ⲙⲱⲛ ϣⲓⲛⲉ ⲁⲡⲉϥⲥⲁⲛ ⲧⲟⲛⲟⲩ ⲛ̄ⲧⲁϥ ⲙⲛ̄ ⲡⲉϥⲓ̈ⲱⲧ ϩⲱⲣ

Address ⲟ̅ⲡⲱⲓ Pap.   7 ⲁⲣⲁⲧⲱⲛ: -ⲱ- perhaps corrected; read ⲁⲣⲱⲧⲛ   20 ϣⲉ: ϣ- ex corr.; ⲉⲟⲩⲕⲁⲗⲁⲙⲟⲛ: -ⲕ- ex -ⲩ- or -ⲁ- corr?   23 ϩⲓϭⲛ̄: ϩ- ex ⲓ- corr.; final -ⲛ- ex corr.   34 ⲉⲓⲙⲏⲧⲓ̣: ⲉ- ex corr.   36 ⲛⲉⲕ̣: -ⲕ ex corr.   39 read (?) ⲕⲁϥ ⟨ⲁ⟩ⲥⲁⲧⲡⲟⲩ (thus elsewhere); or is ⲕⲁϥ- as a construct here grammaticalised (= ⲧⲣⲉϥ-, = ⲙⲁⲣⲉϥ-)?   41 ⲡⲓϯⲟⲩ: ⲡ- ex ϯ- corr.

(To) my father, my master who is honoured by me greatly, the one whose name is sweet in my mouth at every moment: My loved father Hor. Also my brother Theognostos, (5) and my brother Pshai and my brother Andreas. (It is) I, your (pl.) brother Pegosh, who writes greeting you in the Lord God; - greetings!

Before everything: I am praying to God that he can (10) watch over you for a long time, you rejoicing in your soul and your spirit. After these (things): Again I am writing to you, telling you about the matter of the papyrus rolls, that I will not neglect (to purchase them); though I have not sent (15) them to you. But, that is I did not send them to you now, for they are expensive. If I hold my hand (for a few more days?); so that, until they ease off ... they are selling them expensive.

The cloth bag: Buy it at (20) 100 for the pair (?). If there are any reeds (?), I will send them to you ... father Antinou to come ... and what is in it. I have found a ... in it, with 26 *nummi* and (25) the other items that are in it, which you said to sell ... I will send them south ... they will not take them here. I have received the blanket and the garments, and the handful (?) of cereal with it.

(30) So, you, my brother Pshai: You have written to me "I received the wool". You said: "Send another two *mna* of warp". Do you not know that I will not find wool here unless I send ... south. (35) When I can find it we will send it to you (sg.). Live and you (pl.) be well for a long time according to our prayers.

(tr) Take the 30 *mna* of wool, less one, from Papnoute. Give 10 for me to Lampou; I will clear his freight charge here. Let him select as he likes. Do not upset him, for I want to please him very much. Do not question him about (the) freight charge. Greet him (40) warmly and his ...

(v) Take these two inks and five traps of fish; one (is) with the cushion. And you, my brother Pshai: If you have received the small amount of dye, then send ... The other portion: How am I to send it [to you] ...? Philammon (?) greets his brother warmly; he and his father Hor.

Commentary:

16-17   Whilst it is not entirely clear what follows Pegosh's comment that the papyrus is expensive, one may compare the similar section in **78** where is also found a somewhat unusual construction with ϩⲓⲑⲏ ⲙ̄ⲡⲟⲟⲩ (l. 20). If one tries to think about what Pegosh's sense might be, probably he is saying that he wants to hold off buying for a few more days in the hope that the price will go down. Thus a literal meaning would be 'and we give another day', (ⲧⲛ̄-ⲧⲓ- Conjunctive).

20   ⲡⲥⲁⲓϣ: Whether this word simply means a 'pair' in this context, or is used for some other kind of quantity (e.g. 'buy the cloth bags at 100 per bundle'), is uncertain. There is the same problem through **78**, in **81** and elsewhere. CD 374b does list the term separate to 'pair' as a measure.

21   We understand ⲉⲟⲩⲕⲁⲗⲁⲙⲟⲛ as ⲉ- circ. + ⲟⲩ- for ⲟⲩⲛ- + bare noun (instead of a preposition ⲉ- + indef. art.). There are three arguments: (a) it can hardly be linked to the preceding clause but is needed as a protasis to the following; (b) the preposition ⲉ- would normally be ⲁ-; and (c) it seems to be resumed by the plural suffix -ⲥⲉ in ϯⲛⲁⲧⲛ̄ⲛⲁⲩⲥⲉ and thus cannot be an explicit singular. For the omission of ⲛ in ⲟⲩ(ⲛ)-, cf. **33**, 15. In both cases, the omission occurs before velar / palatal /k/ or /c/, where the nasal probably became velarised and less apt for letter spelling (as the orthographical efforts around -ⲅⲕ- and ⲛⲅ- / ⲛⲕ- tend to show).

There are all sorts of possible meanings for κάλαμος ('reed'), cf. LSJ 865b-866a. However, presuming that Pegosh is here talking about the purchase of commodities for trade, there are basically two options: (a) 'reed(s)', whether as general material for thatching or whatever; or in the form of 'reed-pipes' (flutes); or even, most intriguingly, 'reed-pen'; (b) 'rod(s)', especially in the form of 'fishing-rod' or 'measuring-rod'.

21-22   Compare **78**, 40, 'brother Antinou'. One has a slight suspicion that the name could be geographical rather than personal (perhaps talking of some business partner in the city), as Antinoopolis features in a number of the letters (cf. e.g. P. Kellis I Gr. 71, 15-18 '.. not departing for Antinoopolis to transact pressing business with my brother Pekysis'; **116**, 11 ⲛ̄ⲧⲁϥⲃⲱⲕ ⲁⲁⲛⲧⲓⲛⲟⲟⲩ); although obviously that should read ⲡⲱⲧ or ⲡⲥⲁⲛ ⲛ̄ⲁⲛⲧⲓⲛⲟⲟⲩ with a doubled omicron.

29 ⲧϭⲓϫ: We have translated as 'handful'; but probably the term is used here for a specific measure (cf. CD 840ab), like ⲡⲥⲁⲓϣ. The same phrase is found at **24**, 7. In Greek papyri one finds the term δέσμη 'bundle'. The precise meaning of ϣⲕⲱⲛ (some kind of cereal or herb?) is unclear; see also **19**, 41; **78**, 46; CD 553a.

38 ϫⲓ ⲡⲙⲁⲃ̄ ⲛ̄ⲙ̄ⲛⲁ ⲛ̄ⲥⲁⲣⲧ ϣⲁⲧⲛ̄ⲟⲩⲉ ⲛ̄ⲧⲟⲧϥ̄ ⲛ̄ⲡⲁⲡⲛⲟⲩⲧⲉ: Cf. **78**, 41-42 and **96**, 33.

Lampou: If we are correct in supposing that this is the same person as the Lammon of **78**, 44 (i.e. that in both instances Pegosh is referring to the same 10 *mna*), then there is a choice between treating it as some kind of nickname or supposing that Pegosh actually said 'Lamou' (whatever the scribe seems to have written). The latter option is probably more efficient; cf. the note to **66**, 42.

41 See **78**, 42-43 and note ad loc.

44-45 We have supposed that the final greeting may be by Philammon rather than Lammon; because we think that the Lampou of l. 38 is probably the same as the latter (see the note ad loc.), who therefore should not be in the valley with Pegosh. Also, it seems reasonable to suppose that it is Philammon who here sends his greetings to Theognostos and Hor, the same persons to whom he writes in the letters **80-82**. Thus this provides a very nice link to the pieces in the next section.

LETTERS FROM PHILAMMON TO THEOGNOSTOS (LOUISHAI) AND HOR

These three well-preserved letters form a coherent group. They are essentially a sub-set of the main Pamour and Pegosh archive, and many of the same characters reappear (such as Kapiton). Like the two brothers, Philammon is clearly in the Nile valley, writing back to Kellis in the Oasis. In each instance he addresses first Theognostos (who is alternatively called Louishai), and then afterwards Hor(os); later in the letters there may be added other greetings. The letters should be read together with two by Lysimachos, since this important person is an associate of Philammon's in the valley. We have one of his letters to Theognostos in Greek (P. Kellis I Gr. 67) and another to Hor in Coptic (**30**). Since Apa Lysimachos also occurs in the Makarios family letters of the first volume, we are here at the heart of matters regarding the House 3 'clan' and their associates.

From the Makarios group (see the summary in P. Kellis V pp. 38-39) we could deduce that Philammon was married to Charis, and that the couple were of Makarios' generation (and thus older than Pamour and Pegosh). In the following three letters there are no references to Charis; but she does appear in those of the two brothers (notably **64**, **66**, **70** and **76**). There are also no explicit references to Makarios and his family.[12] Our cautious explanation for the latter is that here Philammon is writing at a somewhat later period, current with the Pamour and Pegosh archive, when Makarios and his sons Matthaios and Piene have either died or for whatever reasons are absent from the correspondence. The time-frame is probably the 360s or shortly after that.

Philammon is closely connected to Manichaeans such as Lysimachos and Ision, and more generally the whole extended family. Although he often uses pious expressions, none of

---

[12] However, in **82**, 26-28 Philammon does greet 'my mother Gouria and my sister and her husband and her daughter'. Probably this is the same Kyria, wife of Pshem(p)noute (see the notes at P. Kellis V p. 29), who is close to Makarios' wife Maria (a sister by blood or marriage). One wishes Philammon had named the other persons there.

these are explicit about his faith (beyond Christian commonalities).¹³ In the letters he discusses both family and business matters. As elsewhere in the archive, the actions of the family relative / associate Kapiton cause problems (e.g. P. Kellis I Gr. 76 and Worp's comments there). Travel between the Oasis and valley seems to be quite frequent; and the letters are often concerned with who is going where, and requests for items to be sent.

All the Philammon letters are of a very similar format, in a fluid and professional style. There are occasional Greek inflections (ⲑⲉⲟⲅⲛⲱⲥⲧⲉ, ⲭⲁⲓⲣⲉ); but only a minimum of Greek epistolary formulae such as addresses (even here the Coptic ϫⲱⲓϣⲁⲓ̈ notably intrudes in **82**); ⲭⲁⲓⲣⲉⲓⲛ; once ἐρρ-. Document **82** evidences a hand of considerable proficiency and is similar to (though not the same as) that of **80**. The hand of **81** is somewhat plainer in appearance; but still very competent. The comparative dimensions of the three letters are: 274 x 103 mm.; 274 x 92 mm.; 276 x 76 mm.

We include here a translation of the particularly interesting letter P. Kellis I Gr. 67¹⁴ by Lysimachos (whose name is given in Syriac script on the address) to Theognostos:

To my beloved son Theognostos, from [your father (?)], greetings in God. If your brother Psais is with you, take heed (concerning) your sobriety and ...
(*main text of the letter is lost*)
Greet all by name. Your brothers greet you. I pray that you are well in God, loved ones.
(*second hand*) Send a well-proportioned and nicely executed ten-page notebook for your brother Ision. For he has become a user of Greek and a Syriac reader. (tr) Let the son learn that ... before she was given (?).

---

¹³ Unless we count the expression or exclamation ⲧⲟⲩⲉϣⲧⲉ ⲙ̄ⲡⲛⲟⲩⲧⲉ (see **82**, 16) as a Manichaean 'marker'. Literally it means 'the service of God', but seems to be used simply as 'Praise God!' and to be characteristic of Manichaean authors. See the discussion in P. Kellis V p. 80.

¹⁴ This translation is based on that of K.A. Worp, but follows the readings and suggestions in I. Gardner, 'P. Kellis I 67 revisited', *ZPE* 159, 2007: 223-228. Interesting issues, such as whether Ision was a Syriac *lector* in the Manichaean church, are further discussed there.

P. Kellis Copt. 80

Inv #: P 52G + P 51D

Location: House 3, room 9, deposit 3.

Preservation: An extensive and virtually complete letter, written in Coptic. The papyrus is of good quality and appears to have had no previous use. The document has been reconstructed from eight fragments, and had dimensions of 274 x 103 mm., (with the centre fold at 137 mm., an upper margin of 10 mm.).

Content: Philammon writes to Theognostos, and secondly greets Hor. He has heard of misfortunes and sends words of comfort. It appears that Ision has travelled to the Oasis, and now Theognostos is to return with him to Philammon and other relatives or associates resident in the Nile valley. He is asked to bring some articles with him. Philammon conveys further greetings, and Plousiane adds a short note.

Address:
verso

  κυρίωι μου ἀδελφῶι   X   Θεογνώστωι Φιλάμμων
  To my master brother X Theognostos. (From) Philammon.

Names: Dorothea; Hor; Iena; Ision; Pamour; Papnoute; Pegosh; Philammon; Plousiane; Pshai; Ama Tapshai; Ama Tatou; Ama Theodora; Theognoste/os; Zosime;

Text:

1 ⲡⲁⲥⲁⲛ ⲡⲁϫⲁⲓⲥ ⲡⲁⲙⲉⲣⲓⲧ` ⲛ̄ϣⲟⲩ
2 ⲙⲉⲓⲉ ⲡⲉϯⲙⲉⲓⲉ ⲙ̄ⲙⲁϥ ϩⲛ̄ ⲡⲁϩⲏⲧ`
3 ⲧⲏⲣϥ̄ ⲙⲛ̄ ⲧⲁⲯⲩⲭⲏ ⲧⲏⲣⲥ ⲑⲉⲟⲅⲛⲱⲥⲧⲉ
4 ⲁⲛⲁⲕ ⲡⲉⲕⲥⲁⲛ ⲫⲓⲗⲁⲙⲙⲱⲛ ϯϣⲓⲛⲉ
5 ⲁⲣⲁⲕ ⲧⲟⲛⲟⲩ ϩⲛ̄ ⲡⲭⲁⲓⲥ ⲭⲁⲓⲣⲉ
6 ϩⲁⲑⲏ ⲛ̄ϩⲱⲃ ⲛⲓⲙ ϯϣⲓⲛⲉ ⲁⲣⲁⲕ ⲧⲟⲛⲟⲩ

7 ϯϣⲓⲛⲉ ⲁⲡⲁⲥⲁⲛ [ϩ]ⲱⲣ· ⲉⲩ ϭⲉ ⲡⲉϯⲛⲁⲥⲁϩϥ
8 ⲛⲏⲧⲛ ⲉⲧⲃⲉ ⲡⲛⲁ[ϭ ⲙⲡ]ⲉⲧϩⲁⲩ ⲉⲧⲁϩϣⲱ
9 ⲡⲉ ⲥⲁⲥⲁ ⲡϩ[ⲏⲧ ⲙⲡⲁⲙ]ⲟⲩⲣ ⲙⲛ ⲡⲉϭⲱϣ
10 ⲙⲛⲧⲉ ⲣⲱⲙⲉ ϭⲁⲙ ⲁ[ⲣϩ]ⲱⲃ· ⲡⲛⲟⲩⲧⲉ ⲡⲉⲧ`
11 ⲥⲁⲩⲛⲉ ⲁⲧⲗⲩⲡⲏ ⲉⲧ`ϩ[ⲛ ⲡ]ⲁϩⲏⲧ` ⲛⲧⲱⲧⲛ
12 ⲅⲁⲣ ⲡⲉⲧ`ⲏⲡ ⲁⲥⲥⲱⲗϥ̄ ⲙⲙⲁⲛ ⲧⲛ̄ⲥⲁⲩⲛⲉ
13 ϫⲉ ⲁⲩⲛⲁϭ ⲙⲡⲉⲧ`ϩⲁⲩ ⲉⲓ ⲁϫⲱϥ· ⲁⲩⲱ ⲁⲛ
14 ⲥⲱⲧⲙⲉ ⲁⲛ ϫⲉ ⲁⲧ`ϩⲗⲱ ⲉⲓ ⲁⲃⲁⲗ ϩⲛ ⲥⲱ
15 ⲙⲁ ⲁⲡⲁϩⲏⲧ` ⲛ̄ⲕⲁϩ ⲥⲁⲥⲁ ⲡϩⲏⲧ` ⲛ̄ⲛ̄
16 ⲕⲁⲩⲉ ϩⲱⲟⲩ ⲁⲛ ⲉⲧⲃⲏⲧⲥ̄ ⲁⲓ̈ϫⲟⲥ ⲁⲛ ⲙ̄
17 ⲡⲁⲓ̈ⲱⲧ` ϫⲉ ⲥϩⲉⲓ ⲛ̄ⲥⲁ ⲡⲁⲥⲁⲛ ⲡⲁϫⲉϥ ϫⲉ
18 ⲁⲓ̈ⲟⲩⲱ ⲉⲓ̈ⲥϩ[ⲉ]ⲓ̈ ⲛ̄ⲧⲛ ⲓ̈[ⲥ]ⲓⲱⲛ ϫⲉ ⲉϣϫⲉ
19 ϥⲡⲓⲑⲉ ⲉϥⲛⲁⲉⲓ ⲛⲉⲙⲉϥ· ϯⲛⲟⲩ ⲉⲓⲥ ⲡⲁⲥⲁⲛ
20 ⲓ̈ⲥⲓⲱⲛ ⲁϥⲉⲓ ϣⲁⲣⲁⲕ ⲙ̄ⲡⲣ̄ϭⲱ ⲉⲙⲡⲉⲕ`
21 ⲉⲓ ⲛⲉⲙⲉϥ ⲧⲁⲣⲉⲛⲛⲉⲩ ⲁⲛⲉⲛⲉⲣⲏⲩ ϫⲉ
22 ⲧⲛ̄ⲥⲁⲩⲛⲉ ⲉⲛ ⲁⲡⲃ̄ⲗⲁⲛⲃⲁⲗ ⲉⲧⲛⲁϣⲱⲡⲉ
23 ϯⲛⲟⲩ ⲙ̄ⲡⲱⲣⲕⲁ ⲡⲁϩⲏⲧ` ⲉⲓⲙⲁϫ ⲁⲛⲓ ϯⲟⲩ
24 ⲛⲉⲓⲇⲟⲥ ⲛ̄ϩⲛⲟ ⲛ̄ϩⲁⲙⲧ` ⲛ̄ⲧⲟⲧⲕ` ⲉⲕⲛ̄ⲏⲩ
25 ϩⲛ̄ϩⲱⲃ ⲛⲓⲙ ⲁⲛⲓ ϯⲥⲁⲩϩⲉ ⲛ̄ⲃⲣ̄ⲣⲉ ⲛⲏⲓ̈ ⲙⲛ̄
26 ⲛ̄ⲕⲉⲕⲁⲩⲉ ⲉⲧⲉϩⲛ[ⲉ]ⲕ ⲧⲁⲣⲛ̄ϫⲓ ⲡⲟⲩⲛ̄ⲧⲁⲛ
27 ⲛ̄ϩⲏⲧ` ϩⲱⲛ ⲉⲧⲃⲁ ⲛⲉ[ⲧ]ϭⲁϣⲧ` ⲁⲃⲁⲗ ϩⲛ̄ⲧⲕ̄`
28 ⲙⲛ̄ ⲡⲛ̄ⲥⲁⲛ ⲓ̈ⲥⲓⲱⲛ ϣⲓⲛⲉ ⲁⲛⲉⲛⲥⲛⲏⲩ ⲧⲏⲣⲟⲩ
29 ⲕⲁⲧⲁ ⲡⲟⲩⲣⲉⲛ ϣⲓⲛⲉ ⲁⲡⲁⲥⲁⲛ ⲡϣⲁⲓ̈ ⲙⲛ̄ ⲧⲁⲥⲱ
30 ⲛⲉ ⲙⲛ̄ ⲡⲗⲓⲗⲁⲩⲉ ⲕⲁⲧⲁ ⲡⲟⲩⲣⲉⲛ ⲥⲁⲥⲁ ⲡϩⲏⲧ` ⲙ̄
31 ⲡⲛ̄ⲥⲁⲛ ⲡⲁⲡⲛⲟⲩⲧⲉ ⲉⲧⲉ ⲡⲓⲡⲉⲧ`ϩⲁⲩ ⲉⲧⲁϥϣⲱⲡⲉ
32 ⲛⲉⲧ`ϩⲁⲧ[ⲏ]ⲛ ⲧⲏⲣⲟⲩ ϣⲓⲛⲉ ⲁⲣⲁⲕ ⲙⲁⲗⲓⲥⲧⲁ ⲡⲗⲟⲩⲥⲓⲁⲛⲉ
33 ⲡⲉⲧⲁϥⲥϩⲉⲓ ⲁⲉⲡⲓⲥⲧⲟⲗⲏ ϩⲱⲥⲓⲙⲉ ϣⲓⲛⲉ ⲁⲣⲁⲕ
34 ⲙⲛ̄ ⲁⲙⲁ ⲑⲉⲟⲇⲱⲣⲁ ⲙⲛ̄ ⲇⲱⲣⲟⲑⲉⲁ ⲙⲛ̄ ⲁⲙⲁ ⲧⲁ
35 ⲧⲟⲩ ⲙⲛ̄ ⲁⲙⲁ ⲧⲁⲡϣⲁⲓ̈ ⲙⲛ̄ ⲧⲉⲥϣⲉⲣⲉ ⲙⲛ̄ ⲛⲉⲥ
36 ϣⲏⲣⲉ ⲉⲧϭⲁϣⲧ ⲁⲃⲁⲗ ϩⲛⲧⲕ̄ ⲧⲏⲣⲟⲩ ϫⲉⲕⲛⲁⲧⲁϩⲁⲟⲩ
37 ⲱⲛϩ ⲛ̄ⲕⲟⲩϫⲉⲓⲧⲉ ⲛ̄ⲟⲩⲛⲁϭ ⲛ̄ⲟⲩⲁⲓ̈ϣ ⲕⲁⲧⲁ ⲛⲁϣⲗⲏⲗ·

tr38   ⲁⲛⲁⲕ ⲡⲗⲟⲩⲥⲓⲁⲛⲉ ϯϣⲓⲛⲉ ⲁⲡⲁⲥⲁ[ⲛ] ⲑⲉⲟⲅⲛⲱⲥⲧⲉ ⲧⲟⲛⲟⲩ ϣⲓⲛⲉ ⲁⲓ̈ⲉⲛⲁ ⲙ̄ⲡⲁⲣⲉⲛ
ⲁⲩⲱ ⲙ̄ⲡⲣⲉⲛ ⲙ̄ⲡⲉϥⲥⲁⲛ ⲍⲱⲥⲓⲙⲉ
39   ϣⲓⲛⲉ ⲁⲣⲁϥ ⲁⲛ ⲙ̄ⲡⲣⲉⲛ ⲛ̄ⲫⲓⲗⲁⲙⲙⲱⲛ

---

8 ⲉⲧⲃⲉ: -ⲃ- added by the scribe over the -ⲧ-   17 ⲛ̄ϭⲁ: ⲛ- ex corr.   20 ⲙ̄ⲡ̄ⲣϭⲱ: the split in the papyrus and penetration of ink give the false impression that -ⲡ̄- is duplicated   22 ⲡϭⲁⲛⲃⲁⲗ: -ϭ- ex -ⲗ- corr.   25 ⲛ̄ⲃⲣ̄ⲣⲉ: ⲛ̄- ex corr.   31 ⲉⲧⲉ sic app., read ⲉⲧ‹ⲃ›ⲉ   33 ϣⲓⲛⲉ: ϣ- ex corr.   36 ⲉⲧϭⲁϣⲧ: ⲉ- looks like ⲥ-   37 ⲛ̄ⲟⲩⲁⲓ̈ϣ: ⲛ̄- ex ⲟ- corr.   38 second ϣⲓⲛⲉ: ϣ- ex corr.

My brother, my master, my beloved one whom I love with all my heart and my soul: Theognostos. (It is) I, your brother Philammon. I greet (5) you warmly; in the Lord, - greetings.

Before everything: I greet you warmly. I greet my brother Hor. What indeed will I write to you (pl.) about the great evil that has happened? Comfort the heart of Pamour and Pegosh. (10) Noone can do anything. God knows the grief that is in my heart. For you are the ones who ought to comfort him; surely we know that a great evil has befallen him. And we also heard that the old woman departed the body. (15) My heart grieved. Comfort the heart of the others too on her account.

I also said to my father: "Write for my brother". He said: "I have already written through Ision, if he is persuaded he will come with him". See now, my brother (20) Ision has come to you. Do not stay, not coming with him; so that we can see each other, for we know not what adversity will happen. Now, do not leave my heart grieving. Bring five items, bronze vessels, with you when you come. (25) In any case, bring this new 'egg' for me, and the others that you want; so that we get their benefit ourselves, on account of they who look forward to you and our brother Ision.

Greet all our brothers by name. Greet my brother Pshai and my sister (30) and the children by name. Comfort the heart of our brother Papnoute about this evil that has happened. All they who are with us greet you; especially Plousiane who has written a (?) letter. Zosime greets you; and Ama Theodora and Dorothea and Ama Tatou; (35) and Ama Tapshai and her daughter and her sons, who are all looking forward (to when) you will reach them. Live and be well for a long time according to my prayers.

(tr) I Plousiane, I greet my brother Theognostos warmly. Greet Iena in my name, and the name of his brother Zosime. Greet him also in the name of Philammon.

Commentary:

7-16   This opening section has many of the typical features of letters of condolence, see e.g. J. Chapa, *Letters of Condolence in Greek Papyri*, Firenze 1998.

9-10   Since the misfortune has befallen 'him' (l. 12) rather than 'them', we wonder if the real sense might rather be: 'Comfort the heart of Pamour. Neither Pegosh nor anyone can do anything'.

14   ⲧˋϩⲗⲱ: 'old woman'. There is a connotation of respect here, which is not easily conveyed in English; perhaps rather like the Arabic 'sheikha' (f.), 'matron' or 'old lady'?

17   ⲥϩⲉï ⲛ̄ⲥⲁ ⲡⲁⲥⲁⲛ: Does this mean 'write on behalf of my brother' (i.e. act as his scribe, cf. CD 382b), or 'write for my brother' (i.e. seeking after him)? We have understood the latter, as it makes sense with what follows.

25   ⲥⲁⲩϩⲉ ⲛ̄ⲃⲣ̄ⲣⲉ: 'new egg'; compare **81**, 51 where Philammon writes asking for a ⲥⲁⲟⲩϩⲉ ⲛ̄ϩⲁⲙⲧ 'bronze egg', and similarly CD 374a ⲟⲩⲥⲟⲟⲩϩⲉ ⲛ̄ⲃⲁⲣⲱⲧ. It must be some kind of metal utensil or vessel, presumably oval in shape. Perhaps it is the same as the bronze oven dish (βατέλλιον or small *patella*) of P. Kellis I Gr. 71, 26. Note also **96**, 36 and comm. ad loc.

26-27   ⲡⲟⲩⲙ̄ⲧⲁⲛ ⲛ̄ϩⲏⲧ: lit. 'rest' or 'ease' (CD 194a); here translated rather loosely as 'benefit' according to the evident sense.

33, 38   We have maintained a policy of following the Coptic spelling of names, but presumably this is the familiar male name 'Zosimos'.

34-35   The use of the honorific 'Ama' is otherwise unknown in the archive; whilst the male equivalent 'Apa' is only found for Lysimachos, and on one occasion for Pseke (**90**, 44). We also note that the names Dorothea and Tatou have their sole occurence in this letter, and that the only other Theodora is the giver of *agape* at **44**, 12. Consequently, it may be that the title has a religious connotation, although Ama Tashai certainly seems to have children here. The use of 'Apa' by the Manichaean community is evident from the doxologies in the Coptic Manichaean Psalm-Book (e.g. *PsBk2* 47, 22-23). Cf. CD 13ab.; and especially the recent discussion by M.J. Albarran Martinez, *Ascetismo y monasterios femeninos en el Egipto tardoantiguo*, Barcelona 2011: 115-117.

39   There is some ink further along (after the end of the text), but it may just be smudging.

P. Kellis Copt. 81

Inv #: P 68G

Location: House 3, room 6, deposit 3.

Preservation: A complete and substantial Coptic letter on papyrus. It was found in a single piece, with the only real loss being on the lower right hand side (where a portion seems eaten away and there is some abrasion of the surface). The dimensions are 274 x 92 mm.; with the centre fold at 137 mm., and an upper margin of 10 mm. As with document **80**, the papyrus is of good quality and exhibits no sign of previous usage.

Content: Philammon writes to Theognostos, whom he greets in the letter as Louishai (see further **65**, 3 and the note ad loc.). He adds greetings to Hor. Kapitou (probably the same as Kapiton) has come from the Oasis without a letter from them, and Philammon complains about this. He then starts a complicated narrative of grievance which can not be fully understood, except that the main culprit seems to be the same Kapitou. Another colleague (?) adds his complaint. On the verso, Philammon (?) continues with some further instructions, and requests to be sent some items. Presumably he is still writing to Theognostos, in which case the latter is not actually in Kellis (ll. 50-51). This may explain why (unusually) the letter does not end with greetings to the extended family.

Address:

verso

  κυρίωι μο\υ/ ἀδελφῶι   X   Θεογνῶστωι
               Φιλάμμων

  To my master brother X Theognostos. (From) Philammon.

Names: Apolloni (the man of Siaut); Hor; Kapitou; Louishai; Philammon; Theognostos; -klei

Text:

1. ⲡⲁⲥⲁⲛ ⲡⲁϫⲁⲓⲥ ⲉⲧˋⲧⲁⲓⲁⲓⲧˋ ⲛ̄ⲧⲟⲧ
2. ⲧⲟⲛⲟⲩ ⲗⲟⲩⲓϣⲁⲓ ⲁⲛⲁⲕ
3. ⲫⲓⲗⲁⲙⲙⲱⲛ ⲡⲉⲧˋⲥϩⲉⲓ ⲉⲓϣⲓⲛⲉ
4. ⲁⲣⲁⲕ ϩⲙ̄ ⲡϫⲁⲓⲥˑ ⲭⲁⲓⲣⲉⲓⲛ
5. ϩⲁⲑⲏ ⲛ̄ϩⲱⲃ ⲛⲓⲙ ϯϣⲓⲛⲉ ⲁⲣⲁⲕ ⲧⲟ
6. ⲛⲟⲩ ⲙⲛ̄ ⲡⲁⲥⲁⲛ ϩⲱⲣˋ ϯⲣ̄ⲑⲁⲩⲙⲁ
7. ⲍⲉ ϫⲉ ϩⲁ ⲕⲁⲡⲓⲧⲟⲩ ⲉⲓ ⲃⲁⲗ ϩⲓⲧⲟⲧⲕ
8. ⲙ̄ⲡⲕ̄ϯ ⲟⲩⲉⲡⲓⲥⲧⲟⲗⲏ ⲛⲉϥ ⲁⲛ̄ⲧⲥ̣
9. ⲛⲏⲓ̈ ⲙⲁⲗⲓⲥⲧⲁ ⲁϥⲉⲓ ⲛⲁϫⲉϥ ϫⲉ
10. ⲡⲁⲥⲁⲛ ϩⲱⲣ ϣⲱⲛⲉˑ ⲁⲓ̈ⲣ̄ⲗⲩⲡⲏ
11. ⲧⲟⲛⲟⲩ ϫⲉ ⲙ̄ⲡⲉⲧⲛ̄ⲥϩⲉⲓ ⲛⲏⲓ̈
12. ϫⲉ ⲉϥⲟ ⲛ̄ⲉϣ ⲛ̄ϩⲉˑ ⲧⲉⲧⲛ̄
13. ⲥϩⲉⲓ ⲛⲏⲧⲛ̄ ϫⲉ ⲁⲙⲟⲩ ⲁⲟⲩⲁϩⲉ
14. ⲉⲓ̈ⲛⲏⲩ ⲛ̄ⲉϣ ⲛ̄ϩⲉˑ ⲡⲉϯⲣ̄ⲑⲁⲣⲉ
15. ⲙ̄ⲙⲁϥ ϫⲉ ⲉⲓ̈ⲛⲁⲉⲓ ⲉⲧⲃⲏⲧϥ ϥⲧⲉ
16. ⲛⲏⲓ̈ ⲉⲛ ⲛ̄ⲑⲉ ⲁⲧⲣⲁⲉⲓˋ ⲛ̄ϩⲉⲛⲟⲩϥ
17. ⲉⲧⲁϥⲉⲓ ⲁⲕⲏⲙⲉ ⲁⲓ̈ϯ ϣⲁⲙⲛ̄
18. ⲧⲃⲁ ⲛⲉϥ ⲛ̄ⲧⲓⲙⲏ ⲛ̄ⲕⲏⲙⲉ ⲛ̄ϫⲏϭⲉ
19. ⲁϥⲉⲓ ⲙ̄ⲡϥ̄ϯ ⲗⲁⲩⲉ ⲛⲏⲓ̈ˑ ϯⲛⲟⲩ ⲡⲉ
20. ⲣ̄ⲙⲉⲣ ⲁⲣⲁϥ ⲟⲩⲛ̄ⲧⲉⲓ ⲟⲩⲧⲃⲁ ⲙⲛ̄
21. ϫⲟⲩⲱⲧ ⲛ̄ϣⲉ ⲛ̄ϭⲛ̄ϭⲱⲣ ⲛ̄ⲧⲟⲧϥ
22. ⲙⲁⲣⲉϥⲧⲉⲟⲩ ϩⲁ ϩⲃⲁⲥ ϥⲧⲛ̄ⲛⲁⲩⲥⲟⲩ
23. ⲛⲏⲓ̈ ϯⲣ̄ⲙⲁⲓ̈ϩⲉ ϫⲉ ϥⲛⲟⲩⲁϩⲉ
24. ⲉⲓⲥ ⲟⲩⲏⲣ ⲛ̄ⲟⲩⲁⲓ̈ϣ ⲛⲁⲛ̄ⲕⲉ ⲛ̄ⲧⲟ
25. ⲧϥ̣ ⲙ̄ⲡϥ̄ⲡⲁϭ ⲡⲣⲟⲕⲟⲡⲧⲱⲛ ⲁⲃⲁⲗ
26. ⲁϥⲉⲓ ⲁⲕⲏⲙⲉ ⲛⲁϫⲉϥ ϫⲉ ⲁϥⲉⲓ
27. ⲁⲕⲁ̄ⲗⲉ ⲁϥⲧⲃⲃⲉ ⲡⲣⲟ ⲛ̄ⲧⲣⲓ ϩⲁ
28. ⲁⲡⲟⲗⲗⲱⲛⲓ ⲡⲣⲙ̄ ⲛ̄ⲥⲓⲁⲩⲧˋ ⲁϥⲉⲓ
29. ⲁϥϣⲉⲧˋ ⲛ̄ⲧⲃⲁ ⲥⲛⲉⲩ ⲛ̄ϭⲛ̄ϭⲱⲣ
30. ϯⲛⲟⲩ ⲙⲁⲣⲉϥⲛ̄ⲛⲁⲩ ⲡϯⲟⲩ ⲛ̄

31 ⲛⲥⲁⲓϣ ⲛϩⲃⲁⲥ ⲛⲏⲓ̈ [[.]] ⲥⲉ̄ . . ⲉ
32 ⲧⲉ ϫⲉ ⲧⲣ̄ⲗⲩⲡⲏ ϩⲓ ⲡⲁϩⲏ[ⲧ` . .] . . ⲛ̣
33 ϯϣⲁⲧ` ⲛ̄ⲗⲁⲩⲉ ⲉⲛ` ⲉ . [. . .] . .
34 ⲣⲙ̄ ⲛ̄ⲥⲁⲩⲛⲉ ⲁⲙⲟⲩ ⲛ . [. . . .] . ⲁ̣
35 ϯ ⲧⲣ̄ϩⲏⲙⲉ` ⲁϥⲉⲓ ⲁⲕ̄ⲝ̣[ⲗⲉ .] . . ⲁϥ
36 ⲛⲁϫ ϣⲁⲙⲛ̄ⲧⲃⲁ ⲛ̄ϭⲛ̄[ϭⲱⲣ] ⲟⲩⲉϣ
37 ⲛ̄ⲁⲥⲉ ⲉⲟⲩⲛ†ⲟⲩⲏⲣ ⲁⲛⲁ̣[ⲕ] . . . .
38 ⲕⲗⲉⲓ` ⲛ̄ⲧⲁⲕ ϩⲱⲕ ⲡⲁⲥⲁ[ⲛ .] . . . ⲣ̄
39 ⲙⲉⲣ ⲁⲣⲁϥ ⲙⲁⲣⲉϥⲛ̄ⲛⲁⲩ [ⲡ]ϯⲟⲩ ⲛ̄
40 ⲥⲁⲓ̈ϣ ⲛ̄ϩⲃⲁⲥ ⲛⲏⲓ̈ ϫⲉ ⲕⲥⲁⲩ[ⲛⲉ] ϩⲱⲕ
41 ⲛ̄ⲡ̄ⲁⲥⲉ ⲉⲧⲁϥⲧⲣⲓⲧⲉⲟⲩ` ⲙ̄ⲡϥ†ϣ/ⲗ̄ⲡⲉ
42 ϩⲏⲧ ⲁϥⲱⲡ ϫⲟⲩⲧⲏ ⲛ̄ϣⲉ ⲛ̄ϭⲛ̄ϭⲱⲣ ϩⲁ ⲡⲃⲉ
43 ⲕⲉ ⲛ̄ⲧⲁϣⲧⲏⲛ` ⲱⲛϩ ⲛ̄ⲕⲟⲩϫⲉⲓ̈ⲧⲉ ⲛ̄ⲟⲩⲛⲁ̣ϥ
44 ⲛ̄ⲟⲩⲁⲓ̈ϣ
tr45 ⲉⲣⲉ ⲛⲁϩⲛⲁⲩ ⲟⲩⲛ̄ⲧⲥ̣ ⲧⲣⲉϥⲧ ⲟⲩⲏⲣ ⲛ̄ⲟⲩⲁⲓ̈ϣ ϯⲛⲟⲩ ⲕⲥⲁⲩⲛⲉ ϩⲱⲕ ⲁⲛ ϫⲉ ⲙⲛ̄ϯ ϭⲉⲉⲗⲡⲓⲥ ϩⲛ̄ ⲡⲕⲟⲥⲙⲟⲥ ⲛ̄ⲥⲉⲃⲁⲗⲉⲕ
v46 ⲉϣⲱⲡⲉ ⲕⲥⲁⲩⲛⲉ ϫⲉ ⲟⲩⲛ ⲣⲱⲙⲉ ϩⲁⲧⲏⲕ ⲉϥⲛⲁⲣ̄ ⲡⲁϩⲱⲃ
47 ⲥϩⲉⲓ̈ ⲛⲏⲓ̈ ⲧⲁⲧⲛ̄ⲛⲁⲩ ⲙⲏⲧ ⲛⲉⲕ ⲛ̄ⲙⲛⲁ ⲛ̄ϫⲏϭⲉ ⲕⲧⲉⲟⲩⲁ
48 ⲉⲓⲇⲟⲥ ⲕⲧⲛ̄ⲛⲁⲩⲥⲟⲩ ⲛⲏⲓ̈ ⲉϣⲱⲡⲉ ⲁⲛ ⲙ̄ⲙⲁⲛ ⲥϩⲉⲓ̈ ⲛⲏⲓ̈ ⲡⲛⲟⲩ
49 ⲧⲉ ⲛ̄ⲟⲩⲁⲉⲧϥ ⲡⲉⲧⲥⲁⲩⲛⲉ ⲁⲡⲣⲉϣⲉ ⲉⲧϣⲁϥⲉⲓ ⲁⲡⲁϩⲏⲧ
50 ⲙ̄ⲡⲛⲟ ⲉϯⲛⲁⲥⲱⲧⲙ̄ ⲁⲡⲕ̄ⲟⲩϫⲉⲓ̈ⲧⲉ` ϯⲛⲟⲩ ⲉⲕϣⲁⲃⲱⲕ
51 ⲁϭⲁⲗⲉ ⲡⲓⲕⲟⲩⲓ̈ ⲛ̄ϫⲁⲗⲕⲩ ⲛ̄ⲧⲥⲁⲟⲩϩⲉ ⲛ̄ϩⲁⲙⲧ` ϣⲁⲙⲧ` ⲛ̄ϫⲉⲥⲧⲏⲥ
52 ⲡⲓϩⲓⲛ ⲉⲧϣⲁⲛϣⲓ ⲙ̄ⲙⲁϥ ⲧⲛ̄ⲙⲣⲱϣⲉ ⲡⲓⲕⲟⲩⲓ̈ ⲛ̄ⲁⲥⲕⲁⲩⲗⲉ
53 ⲡⲓⲛ†ϭ ⲛ̄ϩⲏⲧϥ ϣⲓⲛⲉ ⲁⲣⲁⲩ ⲧⲏⲣⲟⲩ ⲛ̄ⲕ̄ⲕⲁⲟⲩ ϩⲓ ⲡϣⲟⲩϣⲧ
54 ⲕⲧⲱⲃⲉ ⲁⲣⲱⲟⲩ ⲙ̄ⲙⲁⲛ ⲁϥⲉⲓ ⲁⲕⲏⲙⲉ ⲙⲁϫⲉϥ ϫⲉ ⲙ̄ⲡⲓϭⲛ̄ⲧⲟⲩ
55 ⲁⲩⲱ ϯⲧⲣ̄ⲥ̄ⲧⲏⲙ

---

5 large initial, covering the margin in front of ll. 4-6   7 ⲕⲁⲡⲓⲧⲟⲩ: -ⲧ- ex corr.   13 ⲛⲏⲧⲛ̄ sic, read ⲛⲏⲓ̈ (cf. **90**, 10)   20 ⲡ̄ ⲙⲉⲣ: ⲡ̄ ex ⲉ- corr.   ⲙⲛ̄: ⲙ- ex corr.   21 ϫⲟⲩⲱⲧ: ϫ- ex corr.   30-31 ⲛ̄|ⲛ̄– dittography   45 ⲛ̣ⲁϩⲛⲁⲩ: ⲛ- ex corr., ⲟⲩⲛ̄ⲧⲥ̣: -ⲛ̄- and -ⲥ ex corr.   46 ϩⲱⲃ: -ⲃ ex corr.   49 ⲛ̄ⲟⲩⲁⲉⲧϥ: -ϥ ex corr.   53 ⲛ̄ϩⲏⲧϥ: -ⲧ- ex corr.

My brother, my master who is greatly honoured by me: Louishai. I, Philammon, am the one who writes greeting you; in the Lord, - greetings.

(5) Before everything: I greet you warmly and my brother Hor. I am surprised that (when) Kapitou came from you, you did not give him a letter to bring to me; especially as he came saying that (10) my brother Hor is sick. I am very distressed that you did not write to me how he is. You write to <me>: "Come to the Oasis". How can I come? The one on whom I rely (15) - so that I could come on his account - does not give me the means to enable me to come! ... (when?) he was in Egypt I paid him 30,000 at Egyptian price for dye. He has come and given me nothing. Now (20) take care of him. I am owed 12,000 talents by him: Let him pay for cloth he sends to me! I am astonished that he has been in the Oasis such a long time, and my things are with (25) him; (and yet) he has not accomplished (any kind of) progress.

(When) he came to Egypt he said that he had been in Kellis and sealed (?) the door of the store for Apolloni, the Assiut man. He came and demanded of me 20,000 talents. (30) Now, let him send me five sets of cloth ... for your grief is in my heart ... I lack for nothing ... someone knowledgeable. Come ... (35) pay your fare. (When) he came to Kellis ... he threw (away) 30,000 talents without cost (to himself?). How much do I have?

(It is) I, -klei: You too my brother ... take care of him. Let him send me five (40) sets of cloth, for you yourself know the costs that he has caused me to pay. He was not ashamed. He reckoned 2,500 talents wages for my tunic! Live and be well for a long time.

(tr 45) ... how much time. Now, you also yourself know that I have no hope in the world except for you.

(v) If you know that there is someone with you who will do my work: Write to me and I will send you 10 *mna* of dye. You produce the items and send them to me. And if not, write to me. God alone knows the joy that comes to my heart (50) any time I hear of your well-being. Now, should you go to Kellis: This small copper, the bronze 'egg'; three *xestai* measures; the *hin* measure that we use; our clay pot; the small *askaule* container; the plant in it. Seek them all and put them in the alcove and seal the openings. For he came to Egypt and said: "I did not find them (55) and I made it shut".

Commentary:

16   ⲛ̄ⲉⲛⲟⲩϥ: We cannot make sense of this as it stands. Here are some (rather speculative) comments:

(1) Both the general context and the following relative perfect would seem to suggest a clause-initial time adverbial (with whatever letter, or none, between ⲛ̄- and ⲛⲟⲩϥ) similar to ⲙ̄ⲡⲛⲉⲩ, ⲛ̄ⲧⲟⲩⲛⲟⲩ, ⲙ̄ⲡ̄ϩⲟⲟⲩ or suchlike. However, no such word is known to exist with -ⲛⲟⲩϥ.

(2) If the reading is indeed ⲛ̄ⲉⲛⲟⲩϥ, one may think of a variant spelling for ⲛⲁⲛⲟⲩϥ 'it is good', perhaps vested with an interrogative ⲛ̄-, so that the meaning might be 'Is it any good? When he came ...'. Apart from the unhelpful vagueness of such an expression, one would also expect an impersonal form ⲛⲁⲛⲟⲩⲥ (or else, ⲡⲉⲧⲛⲁⲛⲟⲩϥ) and ⲉⲧⲁϥ- is unlikely to be a stand-alone temporal in this southern dialect.

(3) Conceivably, (ⲉ)ⲛⲟⲩϥ might be an abbreviated personal name, used to introduce a person other than the one referred to before. In this case, the relative perfect would be only slightly odd. Yet name forms would not usually end like this but rather in -ϭⲉ (such as a short form for ϣⲉⲛⲟⲩϭⲉ; the kind of shortening possibly found in the supposed name ⲛⲟⲩⲧⲉ at **45**, 11) or even in -ϥⲣⲓ (such as the many variant forms of ⲟⲛⲟⲫⲣⲓⲟⲥ: ⲟⲛⲟⲫⲣⲓ, ⲟⲩ(ⲉ)ⲛⲟⲫ(ⲉ)ⲣ, ⲉⲛⲛⲟⲫⲣⲓ, etc.). With the preceding ⲛ̄-, however, this appears most unlikely.

(4) The most obvious interpretation of ⲛⲟⲩϥ as being the suffixed possessive pronoun in the plural, which in this context might be taken to mean 'his relatives', 'his people' instead of the more common 'his belongings', must be discarded because of the singular pronoun in the following ⲉⲧⲁϥ-.

22   ϩⲁ ϩⲃⲁⲥ: 'for cloth' (or clothes?); cf. Philammon again at **82**, 22 + ff.

27   ⲧⲃ̄ⲃⲉ- (inf., prenominal): It is preferable for sense to suppose here a form of ⲧⲱⲃⲉ 'seal' (cf. the noun ⲧⲃ̄ⲃⲉ in dialect *L4*); rather than ⲧⲃ̄ⲃⲟ *S*, ⲧⲟⲩⲃⲟ *L4*, 'purify / cleanse the door of the store'. See also l. 54.

28   ⲥⲓⲁⲩⲧ: The indigenous Egyptian name is given (preserved in the modern Assiut) rather than the Greek Lycopolis.

31, 40   ⲥⲁⲓϣ: lit. 'pair' (?), but see the note and further references at **79**, 20.

37-38 ⲁⲛⲁ[ⲕ] . . . . |ⲕⲗⲉⲓ: '(It is) I, -klei'. It appears that a new writer begins and adds his complaint to reinforce that of Philammon. The ending suggests a name like Heraklei (Herakles); but the traces visible in l. 37 are not very convincing, as they would more obviously read ⲁⲡ . . or ⲁⲣⲧⲁ- vel sim. Indeed, the first letter of l. 38 might itself better be an ⲩ-; (though that would be difficult to reconcile with the line break).

45   We can make no sense of the start of this line. There seem to be a number of corrections, and perhaps some smudging. Presumably Philammon is writing again with his complaint.

51   See further **80**, 25 and note ad loc. for discussion of the bronze 'egg'.

'.. three *xestai* measures': It is not clear to us whether Philammon asks for three separate measures or a single one of this value. Three *xestai* / *sextarii* are half a *chous*, or a sixth of a *keramion* (cf. KAB p. 49).

52   For the *hin* measure see N. Kruit, K.A. Worp, 'Metrological Notes on Measures and Containers of Liquids in Graeco-Roman and Byzantine Egypt', *Archiv für Papyrusforschung*, 45, 1999: 96-127 [121-123 and nn. 35, 40-42].

52-53 ⲡⲓⲕⲟⲩⲓ̈ ⲛ̄ⲁⲥⲕⲁⲩⲗⲉ ⲡⲓⲛ†ϭ ⲛ̄ϩⲏⲧϥ: The small *askaule* must be some kind of container, because it has a plant or herb (cf. ⲛⲧⲏϭ CD 233ab) in it. K.A. Worp suggests that it is an *Ascalonion* jar, for which see N. Kruit, K.A. Worp, 'Geographical Jar Names: Towards a Multi-Disciplinary Approach', *Archiv für Papyrusforschung*, 46, 2000: 65-146 [99-103]; also A. Alcock, 'Coptic Terms for Weights and Measures', *Enchoria*, 23, 1996: 1-7 [1].

53   ϣⲓⲛⲉ ⲁⲣⲁⲩ ⲧⲏⲣⲟⲩ: The normal understanding of the phrase ('Greet them all') would be odd in the middle of things here. Either this is a slip of the pen (ⲁⲣⲁⲩ for ⲛ̄ⲥⲱⲟⲩ) or one may suppose that the basic meaning 'visit' (CD 569a) allows for a nuance '(go and) seek them all out'.

ⲡⲱⲟⲩⲱⲧ: A niche or alcove (CD 608b-609a). The following final comment seems to be another note of mistrust, i.e. that Kapitou will steal the items and try to claim that they were never there. Thus Theognostos is asked to seal it up tight.

55   †ⲧⲣ̄ⲥⲧⲏⲙ: This is an unclear expression, but certainly not what it may look like at first sight: †-ⲧⲣ̄-ⲥⲧⲏⲙ 'I am causing there to be stibium / kohl'. As there is enough talk in the context about stashing away and sealing off things, we have taken the sigma to

belong to the causative infinitive, to be followed by a form of ⲧⲱⲙ 'shut'. That this form should be a stative is surprising, but the most likely interpretation of ϯ-ⲧⲣ̄ⲥ-ⲧⲏⲙ seems to be as an equivalent of ϯⲧⲣⲉⲥⲧⲱⲙ (or ϯⲧⲣⲟ ⲉⲥⲧⲏⲙ) 'I am causing it to be shut'. Whether this is still part of the reported speech, or rather a conclusion of the letter-writer himself, is not clear. Possibly the logic is something like: (Since he said he had not found them) 'now / indeed (ⲁⲩⲱ) I am keeping them shut'.

P. Kellis Copt. 82

Inv #: P 81E (a) + P64A + P69 + P78G + P81B + P93B + P93D

Location: House 3, room 6, deposits 3 + 4.

Preservation: A virtually complete letter in Coptic, now reconstructed from nine fragments; (the lower half remains in one piece, but the upper part above the centre fold has broken up). The document is 276 x 76 mm., with an upper margin of 9 mm. Like the other letters sent by Philammon (**80-81**), it is a very competent production on a fine and new (i.e. not reused) piece of papyrus.

Content: Philammon (in the Nile valley) writes to Loishai (i.e. Theognostos), whom he addresses in the letter simply as Shai. He adds greetings to Hor, and explains that he has not written earlier as he has been ill for three months. He asks that some items be given for Kapiton (in the Oasis) to bring to him, and complains about things not done. Greetings are made to family members, and another colleague adds his own note.

This document provides a number of clear links to other persons central to the broader archive. Pamour is with Philammon in the valley, and their business is going well. Pegosh however is in the Oasis at this point in time. The letter implies that it is Philammon who is the senior figure in their common trading ventures. However, Apa Lysimachos seems to have some overall authority for their movements (see here the discussion in the note to **72**, 35). This latter reference clearly links the group to Makarios and his family. In **21** Lysimachos is placed in Antinoopolis. Although Philammon does not name Makarios, his wife Maria or his sons Matthaios and Piene, he does greet 'my mother Gouria'. If we are right that she is the same as the Kyria of the Makarios family letters, then the fact that she appears here as a matriarch (and without mention of her husband Pshempnoute who is presumably deceased), provides strong evidence that the date of this piece must be somewhat later than the time-frame for those other letters. Conversely, one should compare a letter like **24**, where Makarios ends with greetings to Pamour, Pegosh and Philammon. At that point they are all still in the Oasis.

N.B. This letter was found together with **116**. Although the two pieces have different authors, they clearly relate to the same general context (note especially the references to Kapiton and Egypt in both) and the latter may usefully be read together with **82**.

Address:

verso

κυρίῳ μου ἀδελφῷ   X   ⳓⲱⲓϣⲁⲓ Φιλάμμων

To my master brother X Loishai. (From) Philammon.

Names: A-; Apa Lysimachos; Gouria; Hor; Kapiton; Loishai / Shai (= Theognostos); Pagosh; Pamour; Philammon; Pshai;

Text:

1   [ⲡ]ⲁⲥⲁⲛ ⲙ̄ⲙⲉⲣⲓⲧ ⲉⲧ`ⲧⲁⲓⲁⲉⲓⲧ
2   ⲛ̄ⲧⲟⲧ` ⲧⲟⲛⲟⲩ ⲡⲣⲉⲛ ⲉⲧ`ϩⲁⲗϭ ⲉⲧ`
3   ϩⲛ̄ⲡⲱⲓ ⲛ̄ⲛⲟ ⲛⲓⲙ ⲡⲁⲥⲁⲛ ϣⲁⲓ
4   ⲁⲛⲁⲕ ⲫⲓⲗⲁⲙⲙⲱⲛ ⲡⲉⲧⲥϩⲉⲓ ⲉϥ
5   ϣⲓⲛⲉ ⲁⲣⲁⲕ ϩⲛ̄ ⲡ̄ⲭⲁⲓⲥ ⲭⲁⲓⲣⲉⲓⲛ
6   [ϩ]ⲁⲑⲏ ⲛ̄ϩⲱⲃ ⲛⲓⲙ †ⲱⲓⲛⲉ ⲁⲣⲁ]ⲕ ⲧⲟⲛⲟⲩ
7   ⲉⲓϣⲗⲏⲗ ⲁⲡⲛⲟⲩⲧⲉ [ϫⲉ ⲉⲓⲁ]ⲟⲩⲁϣⲧⲕ̄
8   ⲛ̄ⲕⲉⲥⲁⲡ` ⲛ̄ⲧⲉ ⲡⲁⲣⲉϣⲉ ϫⲱⲕ ⲁⲃⲁⲗ
9   ⲭⲱⲣⲓⲥ ϩⲁϩ ⲛ̄ⲥⲉϫⲉ ⲕⲥⲁⲩⲛⲉ ⲛ̄ⲧⲁ
10 ⲅⲁⲡⲏ ⲉⲧⲛ̄ϩⲏⲧ ϣ[ⲁ]ⲣⲁⲕ` †ϣⲓⲛⲉ

11 ⲧⲟⲛⲟⲩ ⲁⲡⲁⲥⲁⲛ ϩ[ⲱ]ⲣ ⲙⲛ̄ ϣⲁⲓ̈ ⲉⲡⲣ̄

12 ϭⲛⲁⲣⲓⲕⲉ ⲧⲉ ⲁⲣⲁⲓ̈ ϫⲉ ⲙ̄ⲡⲓⲥϩⲉⲓ̈ ⲛⲉⲕ

13 ⲛ̄ⲛⲓϩⲟⲟⲩ ⲡⲛⲟⲩⲧⲉ ⲣ̄ⲙⲛ̄ⲧⲣⲉ ϫⲉ

14 ⲉⲓⲥ ϣⲁⲙⲛ̄ⲧ ⲛ̄ⲉⲃⲁⲧ ϯϣⲱⲛⲉ

15 ⲙ̄ⲡⲓϭⲛ̄ ⲡⲣⲏⲧⲉ ⲛ̄ⲥϩⲉⲓ̈ ⲁⲗⲗⲁ

16 ⲧⲟⲩⲉϣⲧⲉ ⲙ̄ⲡⲛⲟⲩ⟨ⲧⲉ⟩ ⲉⲓⲥⲧⲉ ⲁⲓ̈ⲧⲱ

17 ⲟⲩⲛ ⲉϣⲁⲧⲉ ⲕⲁⲡⲓⲧⲱⲛ ⲉⲓ ⲉϥⲛ̄ⲏⲩ

18 ⲁⲕⲏⲙⲉ † ⲧⲛⲁϭ ⲛ̄ϣⲁϣⲁⲧⲉ ⲛⲉϥ

19 ⲙⲛ̄ ⲡⲁⲕ`ⲕⲓⲁ[.] ϫⲉ ⲉϥⲛ̄ⲏⲩ ⲛⲏⲓ̈

20 ϣⲁⲟⲩⲏⲣ ⲛ̄ⲥⲁⲡ` ϩⲓⲥϩⲉⲓ̈ ⲛⲏⲧⲛ̄ ϫⲉ

21 ⲙⲁⲣⲉ ⲡⲁⲓ̈ⲱⲧ ⲡϣⲁⲓ̈ † ⲛ̄ϩⲁⲙⲧ

22 ⲧⲉⲧⲛ̄ⲧⲉⲟⲩ ϩⲁ ϩⲃⲁⲥ ⲧⲉⲧⲛ̄ⲧⲉⲁⲩ

23 ⲥⲟⲩ ⲙ̄ⲡⲉⲧⲛ̄ⲣ̄ ⲫⲱⲃ ϯⲛⲟⲩ ⲙⲁⲣⲉϥ

24 ⲧⲉⲟⲩ ⲧⲉⲧⲛ̄ⲧⲉⲁⲩⲥⲟⲩ ϫⲉ ϩⲓ† ϩⲛ̄

25 ⲛⲁϭ ϩⲱⲧ ⲛ̄ⲁⲥⲉ ⲁⲡⲥⲛⲓ̈ⲛ ϣⲁ

26 ⲧⲉϥⲑⲉⲣⲁⲡⲉⲩⲉ ⲙ̄ⲙⲁⲓ̈ ϯϣⲓⲛⲉ ⲁⲧⲁ

27 ⲙⲟ ϭⲟⲩⲣⲓⲁ ⲧⲟⲛⲟⲩ ⲙⲛ̄ ⲧⲁⲥⲱⲛⲉ

28 ⲙⲛ̄ ⲡⲥϩⲉⲓ̈ ⲙⲛ̄ ⲧⲉⲥϣⲉⲣⲉ ϯϣⲓ

29 ⲛⲉ ⲁⲡⲁⲥⲁⲛ ϩⲱⲣ ⲙⲛ̄ ⲧϥ̄ϩⲓⲙⲉ ⲙⲛ̄

30 ⲛⲉϥϣⲏⲣⲉ ϯϣⲓⲛⲉ ⲁⲡⲁⲥⲁⲛ ⲡⲁ

31 ϭⲱϣ ⲙⲛ̄ ⲧⲉϥϩⲓⲙⲉ ⲡⲁⲙⲟⲩⲣ

32 ϣⲓⲛⲉ ⲁⲣⲱⲧⲛ̄ ϥϩⲁⲧⲛ̄ⲓ̈ ⲙ̄ⲙⲏⲛⲉ

33 ϥⲣ̄ϣⲉⲩ ϥⲓⲣⲉ ⲙ̄ⲡⲉϥϩⲱⲃ ⲕⲁⲗⲱⲥ

34 ϩⲁ . . ϩⲁⲓ̈ ϫⲉ ϩⲉϣⲥ ⲕⲣ̄ ⲡⲉⲕϩⲱⲃ

35 ϩⲱⲃ ⲛⲓⲙ ⲉⲓ̈ⲉⲓⲣⲉ ⲙ̄ⲙⲁϥ †† ⲁⲥⲉ

36 ⲉⲛ ⲁⲕ`ⲥϩⲉⲓ̈ ϫⲉ ϯⲛ̄ⲏⲩ ⲁⲕⲏⲙⲉ

37 ⲙ̄ⲡⲣ̄ⲉⲓ ϯⲛⲟⲩ ϫⲉ ⲙⲏ ⲧⲁⲭⲁ ⲉⲛⲁ

38 ⲉⲓ ⲛⲉⲛ ⲣϣ ϫⲉ ϩⲓϫⲛⲟⲩ ⲁⲡⲁ ⲗⲩⲥⲓⲙⲁ

39 ϫⲟⲥ ⲙ̣ⲁⲭⲉϥ ϫⲉ ⲛ̄ⲉ

40 ⲛⲁϩⲙⲁⲥ ⲧⲉⲓ̈   ἔρρ(ωσο)

tr41 ⲁⲛ̣ⲁⲕ ⲁ . [. . .] . . ϯϣⲓ̣[ⲛ]ⲉ ⲧⲟⲛⲟⲩ ⲁⲛ̣ⲁ̣ⲥ̣ⲛ̄ⲏⲟⲩ ⲛ̄ⲁϫⲓⲥⲁⲩⲉ ⲉ[ⲧ]ⲉⲙ̄ⲡⲛ̄ⲥϩⲉⲓ̈ ⲛⲏⲧⲛ̄ ⲛ̄ⲛⲓϩⲟⲟⲩⲉ ϫⲉ ⲧⲛ̄ⲥⲁⲩⲛⲉ ⲉⲛ ⲙ̄ⲡⲣⲱⲙⲉ

11 ⲉⲡⲣ̄-, i.e. ⲙ̄ⲡⲣ̄-   34 ⲭⲉ: ⲭ- ex ⳓ- corr., ϩⲉⲱⲥ: -ⲱ- ex corr.

My loved brother, greatly honoured by me, the sweet name in my mouth at all times: My brother Shai. (It is) I, Philammon, who writes (5) greeting you; in the Lord, - greetings.

Before everything: I [greet] you warmly; I am praying to God [that I might] embrace you another time and my joy be complete. Without many words: You know the (10) love that I have for you. I greet warmly my brother Hor, and Shai. And do not find fault with me, that I did not write to you these days. God bears witness that I have been sick for three months. (15) I did not find the means to write; but, praise God, look, I am restored!

When Kapiton sets out to come to Egypt, give him the large cushion and the ..., for he is coming to me. (20) How many times have I written to you (pl.): "Let my father Pshai give the money and you can pay for clothes and send them". You have not done the thing. Now, let him pay and you send them; for I have (25) myself had great costs to the doctor until he healed me.

I greet my mother Gouria warmly, and my sister and her husband and her daughter. I greet my brother Hor and his wife and (30) his sons. I greet my brother Pagosh and his wife. Pamour greets you (pl.). He is with me daily. He is diligent, doing his work well, (so much so) that I said (to him): "As long as you (sg.) perform your work, (35) nothing I do makes a loss".

You wrote: "I am coming to Egypt". Do not come now, for is there any chance we will meet? In that I asked Apa Lysimachos, (and) he said that we might not (40) stay here.

(tr) (It is) I, A-, I greet warmly my brothers, my masters: That we have not written to you these days is because we do not know the man.

Commentary:

7-8   Here again is the familiar prayer formula, an almost exact parallel to **35**, 25-26; **42**, 12-14; **115**, 4-6 (and slightly variant wording elsewhere at **78**, 10-12 etc.). Of course, there are familiar New Testament parallels; but we suspect that the model is Mani's *Epistles*. See further the discussions at **78**, 11-12 and **90**, 7-8.

11   Probably this is not a second person named Shai; rather, he is just repeating himself. In his other letters Philammon greet (Loui)shai / Theognostos first, then afterwards Hor; but noone else until the concluding section.

16   ⲧⲟⲩⲉϣⲧⲉ ⲙ̄ⲡⲛⲟⲩ⟨ⲧⲉ⟩: cf. **71**, 36; **116**, 15; and the references and comments in P. Kellis V at p. 80.

17   More literally: 'If Kapiton comes, he is coming ...'.

18   ⲧⲛⲁϭ ⲛ̄ϣⲁϣⲁⲧⲉ: 'the large cushion'; cf. CD 573b ϣⲛϣⲱⲧⲉ and 609a ϣⲉϣⲟⲧⲉ.

19   ⲡⲁⲕ`ⲕⲓⲁ[ . ]: We suppose that this item goes with the previous 'large cushion'; but the reading is very unclear as it lies across the (broken) centre fold.  As the spelling ⲁⲕ`ⲕ- normally indicates a Greek word in ἀγκ- or ἀγγ-, the best candidates would all seem to be nouns which are feminine in gender, such as ἀγκύλη 'loop' or 'hook', or perhaps ἀγκάλη 'bundle'; (but reading ⲧ- instead of ⲡ- for the article seems difficult here). On the other hand, omicron after iota (to read a form of ἀγγεῖον) is excluded.

38   ⲛⲉⲛ ⲣⲱ: Perhaps one should emend to ⲛⲉ⟨ⲕ⟩, with the following ⲣⲱ as emphatic. Thus: '.. lest perhaps we might rather come to you ...'.

39-40   ⲛ̄ⲉⲛⲁϩⲙⲁⲥ ⲧⲉⲓ̈: In P. Kellis V (p. 31) we referred to this passage, suggesting that it meant: 'Do not save this!'. However, on reflection, we think that that was incorrect and that the verb is ϩⲙⲉⲥⲧ 'sit down' (CD 679a + ff.), rather than ⲛⲟⲩϩⲙⲉ 'save'; which is then followed with the particle ⲧⲉⲓ̈ 'here' (CD 390ab). See W.-P. Funk, 'Negative ⲛ- without ⲁⲛ as a late Survival in southern Coptic?', (paper presented to the Ninth International Congress of Coptic Studies, Cairo, September 2008, to be published in *Lingua Aegyptia*).

41   (Lit.) ' .. we do not know the man': The meaning is probably general rather than specific to any one person. It is a common feature of the papyri to find comments to the effect that the writer has not been able to find any reliable carrier for the letter.

LETTERS FROM THEOGNOSTOS

Theognostos is a central figure in the archive. He is the primary recipient of all three letters by Philammon (**80-82**), and the one in Greek by Lysimachos (P. Kellis I Gr. 67); but he is also frequently greeted by the brothers Pamour and Pegosh, together with others of the same circle such as Pshai. In particular, we find that Theognostos is often mentioned in association with Hor and with Andreas. Whilst it is possible to suppose that there is more than one person of this name in the archive as a whole, it seems most probable that the great majority of references are to the same man. He is also named Louishai or similar, which can itself be abbreviated to Shai (see **65**, 3 note ad loc.).

Despite all this, it is not entirely clear what role Theognostos has, nor his precise relationship to the principal family. P. Kellis I Gr. 71, 9-10 may indicate that Andreas is his son (that is, if one understands it literally), and it could be that Theognostos is related by marriage to the House 3 family. However, it is not apparent to us who would be his wife. It is true that, amongst the women, he is especially linked to Partheni / Heni. In **83** he writes to her directly; and **71**, 2-3 might be taken to indicate that Andreas was her son. In that case she would be Theognostos' wife. However, this line of thinking has to be balanced against similar arguments we have made that Partheni is Pegosh's wife (see e.g. **75**). Perhaps, in fact, Theognostos is Partheni's brother? Probably it is impossible to disentangle the relationships completely given the loose terminology used (especially in Coptic). Document **73** provides another example of the very close relationships between these characters, and (tellingly) discusses how children could be adopted within the larger family group.

Theognostos often appears as part of the general circle of people in Kellis and its surroundings who are written <u>to</u> from the Nile valley; but we do know that he also travelled 'to Egypt'. Thus, in **80** he is to journey there with Ision, bringing items for Philammon. Perhaps such visits give a context to **83** (which may belong with the Pamour - Pegosh - Philammon letters that are generally written from the valley to the Oasis). However, the short periods of time referred to in **84**, ranging from two to five days, means surely that in this second piece Theognostos is writing from quite close by. In **81**, 50-51, the implication is that Theognostos is in the Oasis but elsewhere than Kellis. Incidentally, these letters (**84** by Theognostos and **81** from Philammon to him) were very closely associated in their find site (note their inventory numbers of P 68G and P 68G (a)).

We can be virtually certain that Theognostos was himself a Manichaean, noting especially his connection to Lysimachos; although in **83-84** we do not receive any specific indication about his faith. However, an important issue is the relationship of **84** to a pair of overtly Manichaean letters published in volume 1: **32** and **33**. Although we do not know the author of those pieces, the hand is very similar (see the comments at n. 218 in the earlier volume); and there are also other stylistic similarities noted in the commentary. The only securely-attested name in **33** is Heni. It seems more probable than not that **32**, **33** and **84** were all written by the one scribe; but whether Theognostos himself composed the remarkable Manichaean sentiments in **32** (especially) is an unanswerable question.

P. Kellis Copt. 83

Inv #: A/5/24

SCA #: 1858

Location: House 3, room 6, deposit 1 north-west corner.

Preservation: Part of a well-written letter in Coptic on a wooden board. The dimensions of the surviving piece are 80 x 20-25 (x 3) mm. Side 'A' starts almost immediately with Theognostos greeting Heni, and what follows is perhaps most easily understood as a lengthy postscript to a letter primarily written by another person; this is because what precedes Theognostos' introduction of himself seems to be more than the initial opening formula of a letter. In this case, it would be likely that the text on side 'B' in fact belongs to the earlier part of the letter and that the speaker there is not Theognostos. If this hypothesis is correct, then a good candidate for the lost 'first' author might be Pegosh, given his own close association with Partheni. It can be noted that in P. Kellis I Gr. 72 Theognostos is with Pegosh, though in that instance they seem to be in the Oasis and writing to Pamour in the valley. Support for this hypothesis may also come from **76**, a letter from Pagosh to Partheni, where a Pollon (see l. 10 *infra*) appears. In that piece the Shai of l. 26 might then be Theognostos himself.

Content: If side 'B' in fact precedes 'A', the content of the letter indicates a concern about some item not being sent that is very typical of these pieces. As elsewhere, the precise details of the matter are difficult to determine. Theognostos' postscript is then directed to Heni and the household (in Kellis?), who are sick. He makes an ambiguous if intriguing reference to his location being 'disturbed'.

Address: None preserved, and probably (given that it is a wooden board) one was not written.

Names: Heni; Lauti (= Lautine?); Pini; Pollon; Tagoshe; Theognostos;

Text:

```
            [ . . . . . . . . . . . . . . . . . . . . . . . . . . . . . ⲧⲛ̄ⲛⲁⲩ]
A (x+)1  ⲥⲉ ⲛ̄ⲧⲟⲧϥ . . . . . . . . [ . ] . . [ . . ] . . [ . . . . . ] . [ . . . . . . . . . . . ]
2        ⲧⲁⲙⲟ ⲧⲁϭⲟϣⲉ ⲉⲧⲃⲉ ⲡϩⲱⲃ· vac ⲁⲛⲁⲕ· ⲑⲉⲟⲅⲛⲱⲥⲧⲟⲥ ϯϣⲓⲛⲉ ⲁ
3        ⲣⲟ ⲧⲟⲛⲟⲩ ⲧⲁⲥⲱⲛⲉ ϩⲉⲛⲓ ⲙⲛ̄ ⲛⲉⲧϩⲙ̄ ⲡⲏⲓ̈ ⲧⲏⲣⲟⲩ ⲙⲁⲗⲓⲥⲧⲁ ⲛⲓⲕⲟⲩⲓ̈
4        ⲁⲓ̈ⲣ̄ⲗⲩⲡⲏ ⲧⲟⲛⲟⲩ ⲛ̄ⲧⲁⲣⲉ ⲡⲓⲛⲓ ⲭⲟⲥ ϫⲉ ⲧⲉⲧⲛ̄ϣⲱⲛⲉ ⲁⲗⲗⲁ ⲟⲩⲛ̄ ϭⲁⲙ·
5        ⲙ̄ⲡⲛⲟⲩⲧⲉ ϥϯ ⲡⲟⲩϫⲉⲓ̈ⲧⲉ ⲛⲏⲧⲛ̄· ⲡⲛⲟⲩⲧⲉ ⲡⲉⲧⲣ̄ⲙⲛ̄ⲧⲣⲉ ϫⲉ ⲡⲉⲧⲛ̄ⲣ̄ⲡⲙⲉⲩ
6        ⲉ ϩⲓ ⲡⲛ̄ϩⲏⲧ ⲛ̄ⲛⲟ ⲛⲓⲙ· ⲉⲛⲟⲩⲱϣ ⲉⲓ ⲧⲛ̄ⲛⲟ ⲁⲣⲱⲧⲛ̄· ⲁⲗⲗⲁ ⲉⲛⲛⲁⲣ̄ ⲟ ϫⲉ
7        ⲡⲙⲁ ⲧⲏϩ ϯⲛⲟⲩ ⲧⲛ̄ⲣ̄ϩⲁⲧⲉ ⲙⲛ̄ⲧⲣⲉ ⲟⲩⲡⲉⲑⲁⲩ ϣⲱⲡⲉ ϣⲁⲧⲉ ⲡⲙⲁ ϭⲱ
8        ⲉϥⲧⲏϩ· ⲉϣⲱⲡⲉ ⲉⲛ . . . ⲛ̄ⲧ ⎯ . . . . [ . . . . . . . . ] ⎯ . [ . . . . . . . . ]

B9       . . [ . ] . . . . . . . . [ . ] . . . [ . . ] . [ . . . . ] . [ . . . . ] . [ . . . . . . ] . [ . . . ] ⲉ̣ⲧ[ⲁⲓ̈]
10       ϩⲁⲃⲥ̄ ⲙ̄ⲡⲓ̈ⲱⲧ ⲡⲟⲗⲗⲱⲛ ⲉⲧⲃⲉ ⲡϩⲛⲟ ⲉⲧⲛ̄ⲧⲟⲧϥ̄ ϫⲉ ⲉϥⲁⲙⲁϩⲧⲉ̣
```

```
11    ⲙ̄ⲙⲁϥ ⲛⲉⲩ ⲉⲓϣ`ⲭⲉ ⲙ̄ⲡϥ̄ⲧⲛ̄ⲛⲁⲩϥ· ⲙ̄ⲡⲉϥϩⲉⲓ ⲅⲁⲣ ⲭⲉ ⲁϩⲉ
12    ⲭⲛ̄ ⲙ̄ⲡⲉ . . ⲕⲁⲓ ⲧⲁⲩⲧⲁ ⲣⲱ ⲧⲉⲥⲁⲩⲛⲉ ϩⲱⲉ ⲭⲉ ⲡⲁϩⲏⲧ` ϩⲗⲉⲡ`
13    ⲗⲁⲡⲧ ⲁⲣⲁⲓ ⲉⲧⲃⲏⲧϥ̄ ⲧⲟⲛⲟⲩ ⲭⲉ ⲙ̄ⲡⲓϭⲛ̄ ⲟⲩⲱ ⲙ̄ⲙⲁϥ· ⲙⲛ̄
14    ⲧⲣⲉϥⲟⲩ . ⁻ . ⲗⲁ . . . . ⲛ̄ⲧⲉⲧⲛ̄ ϩⲟⲩ ⲟⲩⲱ ϩⲛ̄ⲗⲁⲩⲉ ⲛ̄ϩⲉ· ϩⲁ
15    [ . . . . . . . . . . . ] . . ϣⲉ ⲭⲟⲥ ⲭⲉ ⲗⲁⲩ† ⲛ̄ⲧⲁⲣⲉϥⲉⲓ ⲛ̄ⲥⲁ ⲡϩⲛⲟ
tr16                         ] . . . [ . ]ϣⲁⲙⲧ̄ ⲙ . [
```

11 ⲙ̄ⲡⲉϥϩⲉⲓ: -ⲉ- ex -ⲕ- corr.

(A) ... send] them by (way of) ... my mother Tagoshe about the matter.

(It is) I, Theognostos: I greet you warmly, my sister Heni; and all who are in the house, especially these little ones. I was very grieved when Pini said that you (pl.) are sick; but (5) God has power to give you health. God is witness that your memory is in our heart at all times, as we wish to come and see you. But what can we do? For the place is disturbed now (and) we are afraid. Let nothing evil happen whilst the place remains disturbed. If we ...

(B) ... which I (?)] (10) sent to father Pollon. As for the item that he has: Is he keeping it for them, if he did not send it? For you (fem.) did not write whether yes (he did) or not, even though you know how my heart is so weary about it. For I have not had any news. Do not let ... and benefit not cease some way. (15) ... Tagoshe (?) said that Lauti, when he came for the item, (tr) ... three ...

Commentary:

4   Pini: The name otherwise only appears in the archive at **41**, 13; but there is no particular reason to associate these two pieces. However, there are a number of very similar names elsewhere, including the Pine of **73**, 18.

7-8   The implications of the area being 'disturbed' (ⲧⲏϩ) are, frustratingly, unknowable. Somewhat similar phrasing, that 'the place is difficult' (ⲡⲙⲁ ⲙⲁⲭϩ̄) is also found at **31**, 47 and **110**, 26. But, whilst that could conceivably mean little more than being in an uncomfortable place (thus CD 163b), Theognostos' meaning here (with its ominous tones about being afraid and an evil happening) must be more serious and widespread. See also the comments and references at **71**, 30.

10   For 'father Pollon' see also **45**, 7 and perhaps **76**, 59. The name 'Heni' is also common to these three documents.

One really has no idea what this 'item' (ϩⲛⲟ 'thing', cf. CD 692b-693a) was; but because the letters were read out in public, perhaps the use of an indefinite term became a way to preserve privacy.

15   Tagoshe (?): It is preferable to suppose that ϫⲟⲥ 'said' is preceded by a proper name ending ϣⲉ-, than to read ⲙⲙⲉ in its place. Obviously, Tagoshe is the likely reading, though it should be noted that the preceding visible traces are not very satisfactory. If this is correct it provides a link to the recurrence of the same name at A, 2.

Lauti: Probably for Lautine, see further the introduction to **58**.

P. Kellis Copt. 84

Inv #: P 68G(a)

Location: House 3, room 6, deposit 3.

Preservation: A complete papyrus letter written by a fluent hand in Coptic, with the brief opening formula in Greek. It is now broken at the centre fold. The dimensions are 264 x 60 mm., with an upper margin of 8 mm. and 5 mm. on the left hand. The lower 36 mm. of papyrus is blank. The piece should be compared to **32** (and **33**).

Content: Theognostos writes to Psais. Most probably the latter is in Kellis and the author elsewhere in the Oasis (compare **81**, 50-51). The principal context for the letter is news of a sick woman, and it is conceivable that she could be Eirene (the recipient of **32**). Still, illness is a common theme in the papyri.

Address:

verso

  κυρίωι μου ἀδελφῶι Ψάϊτι   X   Θεόγνωστος

                       ἀδελφός

  To my master brother Psais.   X   (From) brother Theognostos.

Names: Andreas; Hom; Hor; Kyros; Pshai; Theognostos;

Text:

1 κυρ[ί]ῳ μου ἀδελφῶι Ψάϊτι
2 Θεόγνωστ[ο]ς ἀδελφὸς χαίρειν
3 ϯϣⲓⲛⲉ ⲁⲣⲁⲕ ⲧⲟⲛⲟⲩ ⲙⲛ̄ ⲛⲓⲗⲁⲩ
4 ⲉ ⲁⲩⲥⲁⲡ ⲕⲁⲧⲁ ⲛⲟⲩⲣⲉⲛ ⲛ̄ⲛⲁϭ
5 ⲙⲛ̄ ⲛ̄ⲕⲟⲩⲓ̈ ϯⲣ̄ϣⲡⲏⲣⲉ ⲧⲟⲛⲟⲩ
6 ϫⲉ ⲙ̄ⲡⲉⲧⲛ̄ⲧⲁⲓ̈ⲁⲓ̈ ⲁⲥϩⲉⲓ̈ ⲛⲏⲓ̈
7 ⲟⲩⲧⲉ ⲛ̄ⲧⲛ ϩⲱⲙ ⲟⲩⲧⲉ ⲛ̄ⲧⲛ̄
8 ϩⲱⲣ ⲙⲁⲗⲓⲥⲧⲁ ⲉⲧⲃⲉ ⲧⲥϩⲓⲙⲉ
9 ⲉⲧϣⲱⲛⲉ ϫⲉ ⲉϭⲟ ⲛ̄ⲉϣ
10 ⲛ̄ϩⲉ ϫⲉ ⲁⲣⲁ ⲛⲁⲥϯ ⲁⲡⲟⲩⲭⲉⲓ̈
11 ⲧⲉ ⲭ[ⲛ] ⲙⲡⲉ· ⲁⲓ̈ⲱⲛ̄ ϩⲱⲙ
12 ⲁⲛ ⲡ[ⲉ] ⲡⲁϫⲉϥ ϫⲉ ⲙⲛ̄ ⲛⲁϭ
13 ⲛ̄ϣⲱⲛⲉ ⲛ̄ⲙⲁⲥ· ϩⲟⲙⲱⲥ
14 ϯϥⲓ ⲣⲁⲩϣ ϫⲉ ⲙ̄ⲡⲉⲧⲛ̄ⲥϩⲉⲓ ⲛⲏ
15 ⲓ̈ ϯⲛⲟⲩ ⲉϣⲱⲡⲉ ⲛⲁⲙⲏⲉ ⲉ
16 ⲙⲛ̄ ϩⲟⲩⲟ ϣⲱⲛⲉ ⲛ̄ⲙⲁⲥ ⲉ
17 ⲣⲉ ⲡⲛ̄ϣⲏⲣⲉ ⲁⲛⲇⲣⲉⲁⲥ ⲥⲣⲁϥⲧ
18 ⲛ̄ⲛⲓϩⲟⲟⲩ ⲉⲟⲩⲛ̄ ϣϭⲁⲙ ⲁⲧⲣⲉϥ
19 ⲉⲓ ϩⲱϥ ϥⲣ̄ ϥⲧⲟⲩ ϩⲣⲉⲩ ϩⲁ
20 ⲧⲏⲛ ⲛ̄ⲛⲓⲙⲁ ⲏ ⲛ̄ⲧⲁⲕ ⲫⲩ
21 ⲥⲉⲓ ⲛ̄ⲧ\ⲓⲉ/ ⲙⲁⲣⲉ \ⲡ/ⲟⲩⲉ ⲙ̄ⲙⲱⲧⲛ̄ ϯ
22 ϩⲁⲓ̈ ⲛ̄ⲙⲁϥ ⲉϣⲱⲡⲉ ⲉⲙⲛ
23 ⲟⲩϣⲱⲛⲉ ⲛ̄ⲙⲁⲥ ⲉⲛϣⲁ

24	ⲣ ⲡϩⲟⲟⲩ ⲥ̣ⲛ̣ⲟ ϩⲱⲉ̣ ⲁϥ . . [.] .
25	ⲕⲉ̣ ⲧⲛ̅ⲛⲁϭⲛ̣[ⲧ]ⲛ̣ ⲙⲛ̅ ⲛⲉⲛ̣
26	ⲉⲣⲏ̣ⲩ ⲧⲁⲣⲛ̅ϫⲓ ϩⲏⲧ ⲁ̣ⲛⲉⲛⲉⲣⲏⲩ
27	ϩ̣ⲓ ⲡⲙⲁⲓⲧ ⲛ̅ⲙⲁⲛ ϯⲟⲩⲱϣ
28	ⲉⲓ . ⲉ̣ⲧ ϩⲛ̅ ⲡⲓϯⲟⲩ ⲛ̅ϩⲟⲟⲩ·
29	ⲉϣⲱⲡⲉ ⲇⲉ ⲉⲥϣⲱⲛⲉ ⲛⲁ
30	ⲙ̣ⲏⲉ vac ⲧⲟⲛⲟ̣ⲩ ⲉⲓⲉ
31	ϩⲱⲃ ⲛⲏⲓ̈ ⲧⲁⲭⲩ ⲧⲁⲛⲟ ϫⲉ
32	ⲛ̅ϯⲛⲁϭⲛ̅ ⲣⲱⲙⲉ ⲧⲁⲉⲓ
33	ⲁϩⲣⲏⲓ̈ ⲁ ⲡⲥⲁⲛ ϩⲱϥ ⲁⲛ
34	ⲕⲩⲣⲟⲥ ⲥⲱⲧ ⲁϩⲟⲩⲛ̣ ⲁⲡ
35	ϣⲱⲛⲉ ⲡϥ̅ⲙⲁⲓⲧ ⲡⲉ̣ ⲉⲙ
36	ⲡⲉ̣ϥⲕⲃⲟ· ϩⲱⲃ ⲛⲏⲓ̈
	vac
37	ⲛ̅ⲟⲩⲱ ⲛⲓⲙ· ⲛ̅ⲧⲛ̅ ⲡⲉⲧⲛⲁ
38	ⲛ̅ ϯⲉⲡⲓⲥⲧⲟⲗⲏ ⲛⲏⲧⲛ̅ ἐρ
39	ρῶσθαί σε εὔχο
40	μαι πολλοῖς χρό
41	νοις κύριε ἀδελφέ

---

9 ϣⲱⲛⲉ: written around a pre-existing hole in the papyrus between ϣ- and -ⲱ-?   30 Was the space left due to a fault in the papyrus already at the time of writing?

To my master (and) brother Psais; (from) brother Theognostos, - greetings. I greet you warmly and the children, each one by their name, the large (5) and the small.

I am very astonished that you (pl.) did not honour me (enough) to write to me, either by way of Hom or by Hor; - especially about the woman who is ill, how she is? (10) Whether she was tending towards health or not? I have again asked Hom: He says that there is no great sickness for her. Nevertheless, I am concerned that you did not write to (15) me.

Now, truly, if there is no exceptional sickness for her: Is our son Andreas unoccupied these days? Is it possible for him to come (and) spend four days with (20) us here; or you, naturally? So, let one of you take the trouble; if there is no sickness for her. If we spend the two days ... (25) we will be reunited with one another, so that we take heart (from) one another on the path! Otherwise, I want ... in five days. However, if she is truly very ill, (30) then send to me quickly and I will see whether I can find someone and come up. Also, brother Kyros himself has relapsed into (35) sickness. It is his path as he did not keep cool.

Send me any news by way of the one who will bring you (pl.) this letter. I pray for your health (40) for many years, master brother.

Commentary:

7, 11   Hom: The same name is also found at **39**, 39 and **45**, 4.

17   Here Theognostos terms Andreas 'our son' (ⲡⲡⲱϩⲣⲉ), but their relationship to the other characters in the archive remains a problem. Certainly, P. Kellis I Gr. 71, 8-10 has Προσε[ί]πατε ἡμῖν τ[ὸ]ν κύριον ἀδελφὸν Θεόγνωστον καὶ [τ]ὸν υἱὸν Ἀνδρέαν, which - taken with the present text - suggests that he is indeed our author's son. In **71**, 1-3 Pamour greets 'my sister' Partheni and 'my son' Andreas; in **73**, 4-5 Pegosh greets son Andreas and brother Theognostos; and in **79**, 4-6 he names brother Theognostos and brother Andreas. All of this might suggest that Partheni / Heni is the sister of the two brothers Pamour and Pegosh, that she is married to Theognostos and that the couple have a son Andreas. However, this all has to be balanced by the strong indications that Partheni is in fact Pegosh's wife, especially **75**, 1-6 (where he names her as 'my woman / wife' ⲧⲁⲥϩⲓⲙⲉ). The best solution might be to suggest that Theognostos is Heni's brother, but the problem remains about who might be Andreas' mother.

20-21   This rather casual-seeming use of φύσει ('naturally') recalls **32**, 36. These are the only two instances in the Coptic archive, and the similarity encourages the hypothesis of a common authorship. The meaning is much the same as the English 'of course'.

24   ϩⲱⲉ might be an unusual spelling for ϩⲱ 'suffice it', but the reading is uncertain. It is not clear whether the apodosis answering the conditional should be found already here or rather in l. 25.

26   ⲧⲁⲣⲛ̄ϫⲓ ϩⲏⲧ ⲁⲛⲉⲛⲉⲣⲏⲩ: lit. 'so that we take heart to one another'; perhaps it means something like 'so that we may enjoy each other's company'?

27, 35 Theognostos seems rather fond of a metaphorical use of 'path' (ⲙⲁⲓⲧ). Again, this recalls the allusive style of **32** (though obviously the use of ⲙⲁⲓⲧ in l. 11 there itself is different).

LETTERS FROM AND TO PLOUTOGENES

There is a person named Ploutogenes who belongs to the same main group of characters we have identified as 'Pamour and his circle', and who have dominated the documents in volume 2 to this point. This is apparent from **86** where he writes to Pshai, greets Pegosh and Andreas, and mentions dealings with Kapiton. Letter **85** is also sent from Ploutogenes to Pshai and probably written by the same hand. Interestingly, the two documents have a somewhat different style: Whereas **86** is rather matter-of-fact, **85** is elaborate in its greetings and their style strongly suggests that the author is a Manichaean believer. N.B. On the basis of the hand alone one might suppose that **106** is also by Ploutogenes, but we have not placed it here as there are no other obvious connections and the author is not named.

The relationship of this first pair to the other letters we have included here become more problematic, and the unity of authorship is open to question. There is also an issue about abbreviations of the name. It is necessary to explain our logic in grouping all these pieces and to note the problems. We can start with the important and lengthy piece **90**, in which a certain Psekes writes to Ploutogenes according to the address, whilst the letter itself opens with a greeting to Iena. Consequently, we have supposed that Iena / Gena will be an abbreviation of this name. Further, a reference to a certain 'Soure' in **90**, 39 has encouraged us to restore Ploutogenes' name in the fragment numbered **87**, as Soure appears there also (and nowhere else in the archive). However, whether it is the same person in this second pair of letters (**87, 90**) as the first (**85, 86**) is not secure.

To turn now to **89**, this piece is written by a Piena according to the address, but the author introduces himself as Ploutogenes in the body of the letter. He also greets his brother Plotogenes (presumably this is just a simple writing error or phonetic spelling of the same name) and Hor. This suggests that Piena is a further variant of the name, and also links the name to that of Hor (whilst introducing the problem of there being two characters called Ploutogenes or similar). This then leads to **88**, where a Piena writes to Andreas; this could be same author as the Ploutogenes of **86** who greets Andreas. Finally, we have included here **91**, where an unknown author writes to 'Iena and Hor'.

It is apparent that we could well be dealing with more than one person. The following references should also be taken into account: At **118**, 5 is found 'Pshai and Iena Hor ...' (should it be <and> Hor?), whilst in P. Kellis I Gr. 75 there is a greeting to 'Psais and Ploutogenes and Hor' and in **36**, 10 (a letter written to Psais and Andreas) there is a greeting to the brothers Iena and [Hor (?)]. In **115** Tegoshe writes to Pshai, and at l. 12 greets the children Maria, Piena and Hor; this letter is carried by Andreas. From all this it is apparent that two brothers named Ploutogenes / Iena and Hor are frequently named together, and often found in close association to Pshai and Andreas. Again, in **105** Psais writes to Andreas. Here he sends greetings from Piena and Hor, whilst there are also greetings to (?) a 'father Iena'. One might also note **80**, 38 where Plousiane greets Iena, and **19** where there are a number of references to Gena; but probably in **61**, where the Teacher writes to a Ploutogenios (note spelling), we are dealing with a different person.

We are unable to resolve all these issues to complete satisfaction, but nevertheless have grouped **85-91** together both for convenience of reference and because it is clear that a good proportion of them must belong to the main group of characters that have been made known by the previous letters in this volume. However, we do not think that Piene, the brother of Matthaios and a member of Makarios' family (see volume 1), is the same person.

P. Kellis Copt. 85

Inv #: A/5/1

Location: House 3, room 2, level 1 north-east corner.

Preservation: 1 papyrus fragment from the upper part of a letter, written by a very fine hand in Coptic, and now breaking along the central vertical fold. From the placing of the name on the verso it seems likely that we have a quarter of the original document. The surviving dimensions are 40 x 81 mm.; but the original was probably approximately 160 x 81 mm. The papyrus has been reused, with clear traces of the previous text visible on both the recto and (especially) the verso. The hand is similar to some others; note (e.g.) the very distinctive long ⲉ. In particular, **86** (also from Ploutogenes to Pshai) may well be by the same scribe; and one should also compare **106** (an unknown author to Lammon).

Content: Ploutogenes writes to Pshai and others whose names are not preserved. In **86** he greets Pegosh and Andreas, and it is probable that here too he is addressing a number of the men residing in Kellis whose names are familiar to us from the previous groups of letters by Pamour and his circle (e.g. **65** from Pamour to Pegosh, Pshai, Theognostos and Andreas). In this instance, only the elaborate opening formula of the letter survives, which may be taken as typical of the 'Manichaean' style. We know nothing about the content of the letter, which is now lost.

Address:
verso

        [. . . . . Χ Π]λουτογένης

        [To Pshai (?). X (From)] Ploutogenes.

Names: Ploutogenes; Pshai; Tapshai;

Text:

r1   ⲛⲁⲥⲛⲏⲩ ⲛⲁϫⲓⲥⲁⲩⲉ ⲉⲧⲁⲓ̈ ⲛ̄ⲧⲟⲧ ⲧⲟⲛⲟⲩ

2   ⲛⲉⲧⲉⲣⲉ ⲡⲟⲩⲣ̄ⲡⲙⲉⲩⲉ ⲧⲁⲃⲉ ϩⲛ̄ ⲧⲁⲯⲩⲭⲏ ⲛ̄ⲛⲉⲩ

3   ⲛⲓⲙ· ⲛⲉⲧⲟⲩⲏⲩ ⲙⲉⲛ ⲙ̄ⲙⲁⲓ̈ ϩⲛ̄ ⲡⲥⲱⲙⲁ ⲉⲩ

4   ϩⲏⲛ ⲇⲉ ϩⲛ̄ ⲧⲇⲓⲁⲑⲉⲥⲓⲥ ⲛ̄ⲧⲁⲅⲁⲡⲏ ⲛ̄ⲁⲧϣⲓⲃⲉ

5   ⲁⲛⲏϩⲉ· ⲛ̄ϩⲗⲁϭⲏⲧ ⲛ̄ⲅⲛⲏⲥⲓⲟⲥ ⲙ̄ⲙⲁⲓ̈ⲣⲱⲙⲉ·

6   ⲛ̄ϣⲃⲉⲣ ⲛ̄ⲁⲧⲡⲱⲛⲉ· ⲛⲁⲥⲛⲏⲩ ⲙ̄ⲙⲉⲣⲉⲧⲉ ⲉⲧⲁⲓ̈

7   ⲛ̄[ⲧ]ⲛ̄ [ⲧ]ⲁⲯⲩⲭⲏ ⲡϣ[ⲁ]ⲓ̈ ⲙⲛ̄ . . . .

- - - - -

tr(x +)8   ϣⲓⲛⲉ ⲛⲏⲓ̈ ⲁⲧⲣⲁⲟⲩⲏ [

9   vac   ⲧⲁⲡϣⲁⲓ̈ [

___

4 ⲛ̄ⲁⲧϣⲓⲃⲉ: -ⲧ- ex corr.

___

My brothers, my masters who are very precious to me: They whose memory is sealed in my soul at all times, though they are far from me in the body yet they are near in the state of never changing love; (5) sweet, true, people-loving; the immutable comrades; my beloved brothers who are precious to my soul: Pshai and …

- - - - -

(tr) Greet the neighbourhood for me … Tapshai …

Commentary:

3-4 The recurring theme of being 'far, yet near' is typical of Manichaean letters in the archive (see the references at **63**, 15-16), and may well be derived from Mani's own style (note the quotation from him at **19**, 9-10 and the way it is picked up by Makarios later in that letter at ll. 69-70). In general, Ploutogenes' elaborate greetings recall those of known Manichaean authors such as Matthaios and Piene (thus the openings of **25**, **26** and **29**). Whilst the virtues of ἀγάπη and so on are in a broad sense simply Christian, there is something very distinctive about this epistolary style.

P. Kellis Copt. 86

Inv #: P17Vi

Location: House 3, room 10, level 3. The document was found 'associated with a keg'.

Preservation: This is a fine, complete letter written in Coptic on papyrus. It was recovered in a single piece, with just a small amount of deterioration evident at the top. The centre fold is apparent, and the dimensions are 136 x 60 mm. The hand is very similar to that of **85**, and we think that both the author and the scribe are the same.

Content: In **85** Ploutogenes wrote to Pshai very much in the Manichaean style. This piece is more matter-of-fact, but probably that is simply because it is a brief note to try and sort out an overdue payment to Kapiton for some oil. It is not entirely clear to us whether Pshai is at fault for failing to settle the bill, or Kapiton for failing to provide the goods.

Address:
verso

κυρίῳ μου   X   Ψάϊτι
ἀδελφῷ   ὁ ἀδελφός

To my master brother X Psais. (From) the brother.

Names: Andreas; Pshai; Ploutogenes; Kapiton; Pegosh;

Text:

1 ⲡⲁⲥⲁⲛ ⲡⲁϫⲁⲓⲥ ⲡϣⲁⲓ̈
2 ⲁⲛⲁⲕ ⲡⲗⲟⲩⲧⲟⲅⲉⲛⲏⲥ
3 ϯϣⲓⲛⲉ ⲁⲣⲁⲕ ϩⲛ̄ ⲡϫⲁⲓ̈ⲥ·
4 ϯϣⲓⲛⲉ ⲧⲟⲛⲟⲩ ⲁⲧⲕ̄ⲙⲛ̄ⲧⲥⲁⲛ
5 ⲉⲧⲉⲛⲓⲧ ⲙⲛ̄ⲛ̄ⲥⲱⲥ ϯⲣⲁϩⲓⲟⲩ

6 ⲙ̄ⲙⲁⲕ ⲡⲁⲥⲁⲛ ⲡⲁϫⲁⲓ̈ⲥ ϫⲉⲕⲁ
7 ⲣⲱϣⲉ ⲙⲛ̄ ⲕⲁⲡⲓⲧⲱⲛ ⲉⲧⲃⲉ
8 ⲡⲥⲉϫⲉ ⲙ̄ⲡⲕⲟⲩⲥ ⲥⲛⲉⲩ ⲛ̄
9 ⲛⲏϩ ϫⲉ ⲧⲁⲭⲣⲉⲓⲁ ⲧⲉ ⲧⲟⲛⲟⲩ
10 ⲁⲣⲓⲡⲙⲉⲩⲉ ϫⲉ ⲛ̄ⲧⲁϥϫⲟⲥ
11 ⲛⲏⲓ̈ ϫⲉ ⲧⲟⲛⲟⲩ ⲧⲟⲛⲟⲩ ⲙⲛ̄
12 ⲛ̄ⲥⲁ ϩⲛ̄ⲕⲉⲕⲟⲩⲓ̈ ⲛ̄ϩⲟⲟⲩ ϩⲛ̄
13 ⲡⲡⲁⲥⲭⲁ ϯⲛⲟⲩ ϭⲉ ⲉⲓⲥ ⲕⲉⲉ
14 ⲃⲁⲧ ⲥⲛⲉⲩ· ⲕⲣⲱϣⲉ ⲟⲩⲛ ⲡⲁ
15 ⲙⲉⲣⲓⲧ ⲛⲙ̄ⲙⲉϥ ⲛ̄ϩⲉ ⲛⲓⲙ
16 ⲁⲧⲣⲉϥⲥⲃⲧⲱⲧⲟⲩ ⲛⲏⲓ̈ ϣⲁ
17 ⲥⲟⲩⲉ ⲙ̄ⲡⲁⲁⲡⲉ ⲙ̄ⲛ̄ⲛⲥⲁ ⲡⲓ
18 ϩⲟⲟⲩ ⲥⲛⲉⲩ ϫⲉ ϯⲛ̄ⲏⲩ ⲁϩⲣⲏⲓ̈
19 ⲉⲥϣⲱⲡⲉ ⲙ̄ⲙⲁⲛ ⲟⲩⲛ̄
20 ⲟⲩⲁⲣⲓⲕⲉ ⲛⲁϣⲱⲡⲉ ϣⲓⲛⲉ
21 ⲛⲏⲓ̈ ⲁⲡⲥⲁⲛ ⲡⲉϭⲱϣ ⲧⲟ
22 ⲛⲟⲩ ⲙⲛ̄ ⲁⲛⲇⲣⲉⲁⲥ ἔρρ(ωσο)

---

7 ⲣⲱϣ appears struck out, but erroneously   10 ⲁⲣⲓ: perhaps corrected to ⲉⲣⲓ?

My brother, my master Pshai: I, Ploutogenes, I greet you in the Lord.

I greet your good brotherliness warmly. (5) Further: I beg you, my brother (and) my master, to settle with Kapiton about the matter of the two *choes* of oil; for my need is great. (10) Remember that he said to me: "Yes, yes; a few days after Easter". But now it is already another two months. Can you therefore settle (15) with him, my loved one, in some way; so that he makes them ready for me by the 1st of Paope, two days from now? For I am coming up. If not, it (20) will be at fault.

Greet brother Pegosh warmly for me, and Andreas. Farewell.

Commentary:

13   The reference to Easter is of some interest, presuming that these people are all Manichaeans; but see also **22**, 18 and P. Harr. I 107 for documentary evidence that the festival was celebrated by the community. Augustine (*c. Epist. Fund.* 8) remarks that it was attended only by a few half-hearted worshippers with no special fast prescribed for the hearers. However, he also comments that the *bema* festival was held at the same time.

17   ⲙ̄ⲡⲁⲁⲡⲉ: perhaps read ⲙ̄ⲡⲁⲱⲛⲉ (cf. ll. 13f., time elapsed since Easter?), the tenth month of the year. Paope is the second month, whilst Easter usually falls in the eighth (Parmoute); and thus some emendation seems to be required.

ⲙⲛ̄ⲛ̄ⲥⲁ ⲡⲓϩⲟⲟⲩ ⲥⲛⲉⲩ: lit. 'after these two days'.

19-20   ⲟⲩⲛ̄ ⲟⲩⲁⲣⲓⲕⲉ ⲛⲁϣⲱⲡⲉ: '.. it will be at fault', or perhaps '.. there will be blame'.

P. Kellis Copt. 87

Inv #: P 32

Location: House 3, room 1, deposit 1 south doorway.

Preservation: A small fragment of a letter written in Coptic on papyrus, with the opening formula in Greek. All that remains is a strip from the centre of the first seven lines, and a substantial upper margin is apparent. Our reconstruction of the opening formula suggests that the width of the piece was relatively narrow and the lines short; but a more elaborate text might well be possible. The verso is blank.

Content: Ploutogenes writes to father Soure. Presumably the latter's name (in Greek) was Σύρος. The archive evidences many similar examples of this feature of Coptic texts (e.g. Zosime or Theognoste at **80**, 38), most probably derived from the spoken vocative form.

Address: None preserved.

Names: Ploutogenes; Soure / Syros;

Text:

1   [τῶι δε]σπό[τ]ῃ μ[ου καὶ]
2   [τιμι]ωτάτωι [πατρὶ]
3   [Σύρ]ῳι Πλου[τ]ο[γένης]
4   [vac ἐν] κ(υρί)ῳ χαίρ[ειν]
5   [ⲡⲁⲓ]ⲱⲧ ⲥⲟⲩⲣⲉ . [. . . . .]
6   [. . . .] ⲁⲓⲧⲥⲉⲃ[ⲟ . . . . .]
7   [. . . .] . ⲟⲩⲥ ⲡⲉ[. . . . . .]

To my my master and honoured father Syros; (from) Ploutogenes, - greetings in the Lord.

(5) To my father Soure / Syros: ... I have taught ...

Commentary:

5   Soure (with Ploutogenes) may connect this piece to **90** (see l. 39). This person is not found elsewhere in the Coptic letters from House 3, although there are a number of references to the name Syros in the Greek documents.

P. Kellis Copt. 88

Inv #: P 56C

Location: House 3, room 9, deposit 3 west doorway.

Preservation: There remains a left hand strip from a papyrus letter, written in Coptic by a crude hand. The original would have been about twice the width, but the surviving length may be complete. The address has been written by a different hand. The piece should be compared to **89**.

Content: Piena writes to Andreas. The letter seems to be little more than a series of greetings, many of which are to women. We have included the piece here on the hypothesis that the author is Ploutogenes, corresponding both to the abbreviation of the name Piena in **89** and a tentative reading of his full name in line 5. However, it remains most uncertain as to whether this is the same person as in the previous pieces, and indeed impossible if the fine hand of **85** and **86** is that of the author himself. Still, there is certainly an Andreas amongst his circle.

Address:

verso

  κυρίῳ μου ἀδελφῷ   X   Ἀνδρέᾳ Πϊενα ὁ

             ἀδελφός σου

To my master brother X Andreas. X (From) Piena your brother.

Names: Andreas; Kep[itou] (?); Lio[u-]; Lo; Ol[binos] (?); Philammon; Piena / Ploutogenes (?); -na; -ne;

Text:

1	ⲡⲁⲥⲁⲛ ⲡⲁ[ⲙⲉⲣⲓⲧ ⲉⲧⲁⲓ ⲛ̄]
2	ⲧⲟⲧ ⲧⲟⲛⲟ[ⲩ ⲡϣⲟⲩⲙⲉⲓⲉ]
3	ⲛ̄ⲧⲁϯⲩ[ⲭⲏ ⲙⲛ̄ ⲡⲧⲁⲗⲏⲁ ⲙ̄]
4	ⲡⲁϩⲏⲧ [ⲁⲛⲁⲕ ⲡⲗⲟⲩ]
5	ⲧⲟⲅⲉⲛⲏⲥ [. . . . . . . ϣⲓ]
6	ⲛⲉ ⲁⲕⲉⲡ[ⲓⲧⲟⲩ . . . . . .]
7	ⲧⲁⲭⲁⲓⲥ ⲧⲁ[. . . . .]
8	ⲙⲉⲣⲓⲧ . ⲟⲩ[. . . . .]
9	ⲁⲧⲁⲙⲟ ⲧⲁ[. . . . . . ⲧⲉⲧⲉ]
10	ⲣⲉ ⲡⲉⲥⲣⲉⲛ [ϩⲁⲗⲇ̄ ⲧⲟⲛⲟⲩ ϩⲛ̄]
11	ⲣⲱⲓ ⲛ̄ⲧⲟⲧ [. . . . .]
12	ⲡⲉ . . . . . [. . . . .]
13	ⲧⲁⲙⲟ ⲗⲓⲟ[ⲩ . . . .]
14	ⲛⲁⲧⲁⲗⲁ . [. . . . .]

15	ⲧⲁⲙⲟ ⲗⲟ . [. . . . . ⲱⲏ]
16	ⲣⲉ ⲙ̄ⲛ ⲛ̣[. . . . .]
17	ⲛⲁ ⲙ̄ⲛ [. . . . .]
18	ⲛⲉ ⲙ̄ⲛ ⲫⲓⲗ[ⲁⲙⲙⲱⲛ . . . .]
19	ⲙ̄ⲛ ⲧⲁⲙⲟ ⲧ[. . . . .]
20	ϫⲓ †ϫⲏⲗϭⲉ [. . . . .]
21	ⲥ̣ⲙⲏϩ ⲙ̣ . [.]ⲑ[. . . . .]
22	ⲧⲁⲙⲟ ⲧⲁ[. . . . .]
23	ⲧⲓ ⲁ̣ⲓ̈ⲧⲱⲣϩ̣ [. . . . .]
24	ⲛⲟⲩ̄ⲛ̣ⲁ ⲟⲗ[ⲃⲓⲛⲟⲥ ϣⲓⲛⲉ]
25	ⲁⲣⲱⲧ̄ⲛ ⲧⲟ[ⲛⲟⲩ ϣⲓⲛⲉ ⲧⲁ]
26	ⲙⲟ ⲗⲟ· ⲙ̄ⲛ [. . . . .]
27	[.] . . ⲙ̄ⲛ . [. . . . .]
28	[. . .]ⲁ̣ ⲙ̄ⲛ ⲡⲁ̣[. . . . .]
(tr)29	[. . . .] . . . ⲁ̣ⲃⲁⲗ . . . . ⲛ̄ϣⲁⲧⲛ ⲗⲟ ⲙ̄ⲛ ⲧ̄ⲥ̄ⲥⲱⲛ̣[ⲉ . . . . .]
30	[. . . .] . . . . . ⲛⲟ . ϫⲉ . . . .

―――

17 ⲛⲁ: -ⲁ ex corr.   29 ⲧ̄ⲥ̄ⲥⲱⲛ̣[ⲉ: -ⲥ̄- ex corr.

―――

My brother, my [loved one who is] very [precious] to me, [the beloved] of my soul [and the joy of] my heart. [(It is) I], (5) Ploutogenes, [who greets] Kepitou (?). [I greet] my lady, my loved ... [I greet] my mother ... whose (10) name [is very sweet in] my mouth ... my mother Liou- ... (15) my mother Lo ... her children and her ... -na and ... -ne and Philammon and my mother ...

(20) Take this cloth bag ... it is full of ... my mother ... I have been upright (?) ... Olbinos (?) [greets] (25) you warmly. [Greet my] mother Lo and ... and ... and my ...

(tr) ... except Lo and her sister ...

Commentary:

1-5   The style of the opening has been reconstructed from the typical style of these pieces, but particularly that of **89**. These two letters by Piena should be carefully compared, noting particularly the many women greeted in both.

24   If it is correct to read Olbinos here, it would relate this document to **111**.

P. Kellis Copt. 89

Inv #: P 95B

Location: House 3, room 6, deposit 3.[15]

Preservation: This is a letter written in Coptic on papyrus, which was found complete in one piece (with even the tie intact). The dimensions are 200 x 50 mm. Whilst there is some abrasion and smudging, virtually the entire text is secure. The hand appears rather slow and less confident than many of the professionally written pieces in the archive. The document should be compared to **88**, and it is possible that the two pieces were written by the same scribe.

Content: Piena (= Ploutogenes) writes to Tabes; although in the letter itself he first addresses Shinnoute. As with **88**, the document is little more than a series of greetings and names, many of which are to women. It may well be that the author of this pair of letters is different from that of **85** and **86**. Certainly, the hands contrast markedly.

Address:
verso

  τῇ κυρίᾳ μου μητρὶ   X   Τάβης· Πϊενα

    To my lady mother X Tabes. (From) Piena.

---

[15] There appears to be no individual record for the find site of P 95B. However, the location is presumed to be the same as that of P 95, which is therefore given here.

Names: Hor x 2; Jmsho; Lampe; Martha; Nos, son of Tiola (?); Pena; Philammon; Piena / Ploutogenes; Plotogenes; Shai; Shanona; Shinnoute / Shaino(u)ta / Shennou(te); Tabes; Tahor;

Text:

1	ϩⲓⲑⲏ ⲛ̄ϩⲱⲃ ⲛⲓⲙ ⲧⲓⲥϩⲉⲓ
2	ⲁⲓ̈ϣⲓⲛⲉ ⲁⲡⲁⲥⲁⲛ ⲡⲁ
3	ϫⲁⲓ̈ⲥ ⲙ̄ⲙⲉⲣⲓⲧ ⲉⲧⲁⲓ̈
4	ⲛ̄ⲧⲟⲧ ⲧⲟⲛⲟⲩ ⲡϣⲟⲩⲙⲉⲓ̈
5	ⲛ̄ⲧⲁⲯⲩⲭⲏ ⲡⲟⲩⲣⲁⲧ
6	ⲙ̄ⲡⲁⲡⲛⲉⲩⲙⲁ ⲡⲧⲁ
7	ⲗⲏⲗ ⲙ̄ⲡⲁϩⲏⲧ ⲁⲛⲁⲕ
8	ⲡⲗⲟⲩⲧⲟⲅⲉⲛⲏⲥ ⲡⲉ
9	ⲧⲥϩⲉⲓ ⲙ̄ⲡⲉϥⲥⲁⲛ
10	ϣⲓⲛⲛⲟⲩⲧⲉ ϯϣⲓ
11	ⲛⲉ ⲁⲧⲁⲙⲟ ⲧⲁⲃⲏⲥ
12	ⲙⲛ̄ ⲧⲁⲙⲟ ⲡⲉⲛⲁ
13	ⲙⲛ̄ ⲧⲁⲙⲟ ⲙⲁⲣⲑⲁ
14	ⲙⲛ̄ ⲧⲁϩⲱⲣ ⲙⲛ̄ ⲗⲁⲙ
15	ⲡⲉ ⲙⲛ̄ ϫⲙ̄ϣⲱ
16	ⲙⲛ̄ ⲧⲥⲱⲛⲉ
17	ϯⲥϩⲉⲓ ⲁⲓ̈ϣⲓⲛⲉ
18	ⲁⲡⲁⲥⲁⲛ ⲡⲗⲟⲧⲟ
19	ⲅⲉⲛⲏⲥ ⲙⲛ̄ ϩⲱⲣ
20	ⲙⲛ̄ ⲧⲉϥⲙⲟ ⲙⲛ̄
21	ⲧⲉϥⲥⲱⲛⲉ
22	ϩⲱⲣ ϣⲓⲛⲉ ⲁⲣⲱ
23	ⲧⲛ̄ ⲧⲟⲛⲟⲩ ⲛϩⲟ
24	ⲧⲉⲩⲁⲥⲛϩⲟ ⲡⲁⲥⲁⲛ
25	ϣⲁⲓⲛⲟ̄ⲧⲁ ϣⲓⲛⲉ
26	ⲛⲏⲓ̈ ⲧⲟⲛⲟⲩ ⲁⲡⲁ

27	ⲥⲁⲛ ⲫⲓⲗⲁⲙⲙⲟⲛ
28	ⲙⲛ̄ ⲡⲁⲥⲁⲛ ϣⲁⲓ
29	ⲁⲛⲥⲱⲧⲙ̄ ϭⲉ
30	ϫⲉ ϩⲁⲧⲛ̄ϫⲓ ϩⲛ̄
31	ϭⲟⲩⲓ ⲛ̄ϩⲓⲥⲉ
32	ϩⲁⲛⲥⲱⲧⲙ̄ ⲁⲛ ϫⲉ
33	ϩⲁ ⲧⲁⲙⲟ ⲡⲉⲛⲁ
34	ϫⲓ ϩⲛ̄ϩⲓⲥⲉ ⲧⲏⲣⲟⲩ
35	ϩⲱⲃ ⲅⲁⲣ ⲙⲓⲛ
36	ⲁⲧⲉⲧⲛ̄ⲟⲩⲁϣϥ
37	ⲛ̄ⲛⲓⲙⲁ ϫⲓ †
38	ϫⲏⲗϭⲁ ⲛⲉⲕ
39	ⲡⲁⲥⲁⲛ ϣⲉⲛⲛⲟⲩ
40	ⲛⲧⲟⲧϥ ⲙ̄ⲛⲟϭ
41	ⲛ̄ⲧⲓⲱⲗⲁ †ⲣ̄
42	ϣⲡⲏⲣⲉ ⲅⲁⲣ
43	ϫⲉ ⲉⲧⲃⲉ ⲉⲩ
tr44	ⲙ̄ⲡⲉⲧⲛ̄ⲥϩⲓ ⲛⲏⲓ ⲙ̄ⲡⲉⲧⲛ̄ⲟⲩⲭⲉⲓⲧⲉ ϣⲁⲛⲱⲛⲁ ϣⲓⲛⲉ ⲁⲣⲱⲧⲛ̄ ⲧⲏⲣⲧⲛ̄ ϩⲛ̄ ⲡϫⲁⲓⲥ

---

1 and 35 ⲙⲓⲛ: sic, for ⲛⲓⲙ   38 ϫⲏⲗϭⲁ: -ⲏ- and -ⲁ ex corr.

Before everything: I write greeting my brother, my loved master who is very precious to me, the beloved (5) of my soul, the gladness of my spirit (and) the joy of my heart. (It is) I, Ploutogenes, who writes to his brother (10) Shinnoute. I greet my mother Tabes, and my mother Pena and my mother Martha and Tahor and Lampe (15) and Jmsho and the sister. I write greeting my brother Plotogenes and Hor (20) and his mother and his sister.

Hor greets you (pl.) warmly, face to face (?). My brother (25) Shaino(u)ta: Greet for me warmly my brother Philammon and my brother Shai.

Now, we have heard (30) that you have suffered a few troubles. We also heard that mother Pena has suffered nothing but trouble. (35) For anything you might want from here (just ask). Take this cloth bag for you, my brother Shenou, (40) from Nos (son of?) Tiola. And I wonder why (tr) you did not write to me about your well-being? Shanona greets you all in the Lord.

Commentary:

1   The abrupt start is rather odd, in that this formula ('Before everything') commonly follows the standard opening greetings that conclude with χαίρειν. Here, the letter has begun with what is really the second element.

ⲧⲓⲥϩⲉⲓ: The scribe uses both ⲧⲓ- and ϯ- (ll. 10, 17, etc.).

18-19   Plotogenes: a phonetic spelling variant for Ploutogenes. The coupling of the name with that of Hor reminds one of the various instances of 'Iena and Hor' in the archive (see the introduction to this group of letters). In any case, this seems to be clear evidence that there were at least two persons named Ploutogenes or similar. Given the various possible abbreviations to Piena, Iena or Gena, it is certainly difficult to separate the characters represented.

22-28   It seems that Hor (not the same as in l. 19) now adds his greetings to those of Piena / Ploutogenes. Since he greets Philammon and Shai it is possible that these are the same as the Philammon and Theognostos (= Louishai or Shai) we have met a number of times before in close association with a Hor.

23-24   ⲛϩⲟ|ⲧⲉⲛⲁⲥⲛϩⲟ: This seems to be an abbreviated version of the 'until face greets face' formula (ϣⲁⲧⲉ ϩⲟ ⲟⲩⲱϣⲧ ϩⲟ). Perhaps, if ⲧⲉ is for ⲇⲉ, one could simply translate 'but face to face'? See also *1Keph.* 206: 17 [ⲛ̄]ϩⲟ ⲙⲛ̄ ϩⲟ and 235: 16 ⲛ̄ϩⲟ ϩⲓ ϩⲟ; 2Jo. 12 and 3Jo. 14.

25   ϣⲁⲓⲛⲟ̄ⲧⲁ: It might also be possible to read ϣⲛ̣ⲛ̣ⲟ̄ⲧⲁ. Either way, it is clearly intended to refer to the same person named ϣⲛⲛⲟⲩⲧⲉ in l. 10 and ϣⲉⲛⲛⲟⲩ in l. 39.

34   The use of ⲧⲏⲣⲟⲩ here, with an indefinitely determined noun phrase, must mean something like 'nothing but ..'. There may be a deliberate contrast to the 'few troubles' of l. 31. Here (and in l. 30) we have translated ϫⲓ 'receive' as 'suffer'.

35-37   We imagine that what is intended is the common sentiment: 'Anything you want from here, tell me and I will do it gladly' (e.g. **35**, 48).

39   ϣⲉⲛⲛⲟⲩ: This looks like ⲙ̣ⲉⲛⲛⲟⲩ, but we think that Piena has intended ϣⲉⲛⲛⲟⲩ(ⲧⲉ), i.e. the name of his addressee (cf. l. 10).

40-41 Nos: The name (like a number of others in this letter) is not otherwise found in the Coptic documents from Kellis. However, it does occur in the KAB (ll. 660 etc.). It is unclear whether Tiola is his father's name or a toponym. It is rather strange, presuming that we have read it correctly. There is also a Tola (Τωλα) in the KAB (ll. [[1073]], 1649), though with no obvious connection to Nos. See further the comments at **90**, 5.

P. Kellis Copt. 90

Inv #: P 27A/B + P 64A + P 81D

Location: House 3, room 6, deposits 2 + 3 + 4.

Preservation: This is a lengthy and proficiently written Coptic letter on papyrus. There now remains from the upper part a main fragment and four smaller pieces joining it (in the photograph these are not placed exactly), to the height of 94 mm. The lower half is complete in height from what we imagine to be the central fold to the bottom (128 mm.), although now beginning to break up. This would indicate an original height of 256 mm.; with about 34 mm. missing from the upper half, or approximately 6 lines of text. The document is also lacking a strip all the way down the left hand side, of approximately 2 letters per line. One can calculate an original width with margin of ca. 90 mm., of which up to 84 mm. remains at places. All the fragments certainly belong to the one letter, although in parts the ink has a distinct reddish colour that contrasts with the black elsewhere. Probably this is the result of the conditions of preservation.

Content: Psekes writes to his father Ploutogenes, whom he names as Iena in l. 3. The author is in the Nile valley, probably in Aphrodite (cf. l. 37), from where he is writing to Kellis. Timotheos travels between the locations. The majority of the letter is about the details of some complicated dispute, but includes unusual and interesting terminology. Despite the fact that Pseke seems to make a number of writing errors, his style is educated and he uses Greek words not usually found in these letters.

Address:

verso

    τῶι κυρίωι μου π(ατ)ρὶ   X   Πλουτογένης

                                           Ψεκῆς ὁ υἱός σου

To my lord father X Ploutogenes. (From) Psekes, your son.

Names: Iena / Ploutogenes; Paias; Pseke; Soure; Timotheos;

Text:

1 [ⲡⲁⲓⲱⲧ ⲡⲁ]ϫⲁⲓⲥ ⲉⲧⲁⲓ ⲛ̄ⲧⲟⲧ ⲧⲟⲛⲟⲩ ⲡϣⲟⲩ
2 [ⲙⲉ]ⲓⲉ ⲛ̄ⲧⲁϯⲯⲩⲭⲏ ⲙ̄ⲛ ⲡⲁⲡⲛⲉⲩⲙⲁ ⲡⲁⲓⲱⲧ
3 [ⲡ]ⲁϫⲁⲓⲥ ⲓ̈ⲉⲛⲁ ⲙ̄ⲛ ⲡⲁⲥⲁⲛ ⲙ̄ⲙⲉⲣⲓⲧ ⲡⲁⲓⲁⲥ
4 [ⲁⲛ]ⲁⲕ ϯⲉⲕⲉ ⲡⲉⲧϣⲓⲛⲉ ⲁⲣⲱⲧⲛ̄ ϩⲛ̄ ⲡϫⲁⲓⲥ
5 [ⲛ̄]ⲧⲁⲣⲉ ⲡⲛ̄ⲥⲁⲛ ⲧⲓⲙⲟⲑⲉⲟⲥ ⲉⲓ ϣⲁⲣⲁⲛ ⲁⲛⲣⲉϣⲉ
6 [ⲧ]ⲟⲛⲟⲩ ⲛⲉ ϩⲁⲙⲁⲓ ⲛⲉ ϩⲱⲧⲧⲏⲛⲉ ⲡⲉⲧⲁⲧⲉⲧⲛ̄
7 [ⲉⲓ] ⲁⲕⲏⲙⲉ ⲧⲛ̄ⲟⲩⲱϣ̄ⲧ̄ ⲡⲉⲧⲛ̄ϩⲟ ⲛ̄ⲕⲉⲥⲁⲡ ϩⲛ̄
8 [ⲡ]ϭⲱⲙⲉ ⲕⲁϭⲛ̄ⲧⲥ ϩⲛ̄ ⲡⲁ̄ⲣ̄ⲥ̄ⲥ̄ ⲛ̄ⲉⲡⲓⲥⲧⲟⲗⲏ
9 [ⲁⲓ̈]ⲧⲛ̄ⲛⲁⲩⲥⲟⲩ ⲛⲏⲧⲛⲉ ⲭⲱⲣⲓⲥ ϩⲛⲟ ⲙ̄ⲡⲉⲧⲛ̄ⲥ̄
10 [ϩ]ⲉⲓ̈ ⲛⲏⲧⲛⲉ ⲁⲛⲏϩⲉ ⲁⲩⲱ ⲁⲓ̈ϩⲓⲥⲉ ⲙ̄ⲛ ⲧⲓⲙⲟ
11 [ⲑⲉ]ⲟⲥ ϫⲉ ϥⲓ ⲟⲩⲗⲁⲩⲉ ⲕ̄ϫⲓⲧϥ̄ ⲛⲉⲩⲁϩⲉ· ⲡⲁⲭⲉϥ
12 [ϫ]ⲉ ⲙ̄ⲡⲉ ⲛ̄ⲃⲁⲣⲁϩⲉ ⲁⲡⲧ̄ ⲁϥⲓ· ϯⲥⲁⲩⲛⲉ ⲅⲁⲣ
13 [ⲡⲁ]ⲓ̈ⲱⲧ ⲛ̄ⲧⲕⲙ̄ⲛ̄ⲧ̄ⲧ̄ⲁⲉⲓⲣⲏⲛⲏ ϫⲉ ⲙⲓϣⲉ ⲛⲓⲙ
14 [ⲁⲛ ⲉⲧ]ⲉⲛ̄ⲧⲁⲕⲥⲉ ϣⲁⲕⲑ̄ⲣ̄ⲕⲁⲩ †
15 [. . . . . . .]ⲛⲉⲧⲛ̄ [ⲉⲧ]ⲃⲉ ⲡⲥⲉϫⲉ ⲛ̄[. . .]
16 [. . . . . . .]ⲛ̄ⲥϩⲉⲓ̈ . [. . . . .]

approx. 6 lines missing

23 [. .] . ϩⲁⲣⲁⲓ̈ ⲙ[. . .] . . [. . .] . [. . . . .] ⲉⲓϣϫⲉ .
24 [. .]ⲉⲧⲛ̄ⲙⲉⲓ̈ⲉ ⲛ̄ . . ⲟⲩ . ⲁⲧϥ ⲁⲃⲁⲗ ⲧⲉⲧⲛ̄ⲣⲱϣⲉ
25 [. .]ⲩ ⲙ̄ⲛ ⲟⲩⲥⲓⲁ ϩⲛ̄ ⲧⲛ̄ⲙⲏⲧⲉ̄ ⲁⲙⲓϣⲉ ϩⲓⲱϥ ⲙ̄ⲛ
26 [. .]ⲛ̄ⲭⲣⲓⲁ ⲡⲟⲩⲗⲁⲕ ⲡⲥⲛⲁϥ ⲁϣⲁⲗϥ̄ ⲁⲃⲁⲗ ⲙⲁ
27 [. .]ⲉ ⲛ̄ⲧⲉⲙⲓϣⲉ ⲙⲛ̄ⲛⲉⲩⲉⲣⲏⲩ· ⲉⲓ̈ⲣ ⲁⲣⲛⲉ ⲉⲛ ϫⲉ ⲁⲓ̈
28 [ϫⲓ] ϣⲁⲛⲧⲉ̄ ⲛ̄ϩⲟⲗⲟⲕⲟⲧⲓⲛⲟⲥ ϩⲓⲧⲛ̄ⲧⲏⲛⲉ ϯϭⲏⲗ ⲁⲃⲁⲗ

29 [. .] ⲉⲓϣϫⲉ ⲧⲉⲧⲛ̄ⲟⲩⲱϣ ϩⲱⲛ ⲁⲧϩⲟⲙⲟⲗⲟⲅⲓⲁ ⲉⲧⲁ
30 [ⲧⲉⲧ]ⲛ̄ⲥⲙⲛ̄ⲧⲥ ϩⲱⲛ ϯⲛⲁϯ ⲡⲥⲁⲩ ⲛ̄ϩⲟⲗⲟⲕⲟⲧⲓⲛⲟⲥ
31 [ⲧⲁ]ϫⲓ ⲡⲉϥⲙⲉⲣⲟⲥ ⲁⲥⲱϩⲉ ⲁⲣⲉⲧⲥ̄ ⲛ̄ⲧⲁϥ ϫⲉ ϯ
32 [ⲛⲁ]ϯ ⲡⲥⲁⲩ ⲛ̄ϩⲟⲗⲟⲕⲟⲧⲓⲛⲟⲥ ⲧⲁϫⲓ ⲡⲙⲉⲣⲟⲥ ⲉⲧⲛ̄
33 [ⲧⲉϥ] ϫⲉ ⲁϥ[ⲟ] ⲛⲁⲗⲗⲟⲧⲣⲓⲟⲛ ⲉϣⲱⲡⲉ ⲙⲙⲁⲛ ⲡϣⲟⲩ
34 [ⲙⲉⲓ]ϣ ϥⲛⲁⲧⲉⲉϥ ⲙⲛ ⲛⲉⲛⲉⲣⲏⲩ ⲉϣⲁⲥⲃⲱⲕ ⲁϥⲓⲥ
35 [.]. ⲙ . . . . ⲥ̣[ϩ]ⲓ̣ⲙⲉ ⲛ̄ⲧⲱⲧⲛⲉ ⲡⲉ ⲛⲉⲙⲉⲥ ⲙⲛ̄ⲧⲉ . .
36 [. .]ⲁ̣ⲕ . . . . ⲛ̄ⲛⲓ ϣⲁⲛⲧⲧⲁϭⲛ̄ ϩⲟⲗⲟⲕⲟⲧⲓⲛⲟⲥ ⲉⲁⲓ̈
37 [. .] ⲉ̣ⲓⲥ ϫⲟⲩⲧⲉϥⲧⲉ ⲛ̄ⲣⲁⲙⲡⲉ ϫⲛ̄ⲧⲁⲓ̈ⲉⲓ ⲁⲁϥⲣ
38 [. .] . . . . ⲡⲁϥⲟⲩⲱ ⲙ̣ⲙⲁⲩ ⲁⲛⲏϩⲉ ⲉ̣ⲥ̣ⲧⲱⲛ
39 [. .] ϫⲛ̄ⲧⲁⲡⲁⲥⲁⲛ ϭⲟⲩⲣⲉ ⲉⲓ ⲁⲕⲏⲙⲉ ⲁⲥϥⲓ ⲡⲥⲁⲩ ⲛ̄
40 [ϩⲟⲗ]ⲟⲕⲟⲧⲓⲛⲟⲥ ⲁⲥⲛ̄ ⲡⲥⲁⲩ ⲛ̄ϩⲟⲗⲟⲕⲟⲧⲓⲛⲟⲥ ⲁⲥⲕⲁ
41 [. .]. ⲁ̣ⲛ ⲡⲁϫⲉⲥ ϫⲉ ⲙ̄ⲙⲟ ⲡⲓⲥ̣ⲁⲩ ⲛ̄ϩⲟⲗⲟⲕⲟⲧⲓⲛⲟⲥ ⲕⲁ
42 [ⲧⲁ ⲧϩⲟⲙ]ⲟ̣ⲗⲟⲅⲓⲁ ⲡⲁϫⲉⲥ ⲛⲉϥ ϫⲉ ⲙ̄ⲙⲟ ⲙⲁⲣⲟⲩⲛ̄
43 [ⲧⲟⲩ] ⲛⲏⲓ̈ ⲁⲕⲏⲙⲉ ⲡⲁϫⲉϥ ⲛⲏⲓ̈ ϫⲉ ϯⲟ ⲛ̄ⲁⲗⲗⲟⲧⲣⲓ
44 [ⲟⲛ] ϫⲉ ⲁⲡⲁ ϯⲉⲕⲉ ⲛ̄ⲥⲁⲛϣⲟⲡⲧ̄
45 ⲱⲛϩ ⲛ̄ⲧⲉⲟⲩϫⲉⲓⲧⲉ [. .] . .

---

6 ⲛⲉ ϩⲱⲧⲧⲏⲛⲉ sic; read either ⲛⲉ ⟨ⲛ̄ⲧⲱⲧⲛⲉ⟩ ϩⲱⲧⲧⲏⲛⲉ (omission through homoioteleuton) or ⟨ⲛ̄ⲧⲱⲧ⟩ⲛⲉ ϩⲱⲧⲧⲏⲛⲉ   9 ⲭⲱⲣⲓⲥ: -ⲓ- ex corr.; ϩⲛⲟ: -ⲟ- ex corr.; ⲙ̄ⲡⲉⲧⲛ̄ⲥ[ϩ]ⲉⲓ̈: ⲙ̄- ex corr.   10 ⲛⲏⲧⲛⲉ sic; read ⲛⲏⲓ̈ (cf. 81, 13)   27 ⲛ̄ⲧⲉ- sic; read ⲛ̄ⲥⲉ-   28 ϩⲟⲗⲟⲕⲟⲧⲓⲛⲟⲥ: -ⲓ- ex -ⲟ- corr.   38 ⲉ̣ⲥ̣ⲧⲱⲛ: ⲉⲥ- ex corr. and very uncertain   45 ⲛ̄ⲧⲉ- sic; read (?) ⲛ̄ⲧⲉ⟨ⲧⲛ̄⟩-

---

[My father, my] master who is very precious to me, the beloved of my soul and my spirit: My father, my master, Iena; and my loved brother Paias. I, Pseke, am the one who greets you in the Lord.

(5) When our brother Timotheos came to us, we rejoiced greatly. Would that it had been <you> yourselves who had come to Egypt, that we might adore your face once again in the body. You will find it in the ... letter. I have sent them to you without obligation (?). You did (10) never write to <me>, and I had trouble with Timotheos (when I asked him to) take something and bring it to the Oasis. He said: "The caravan-

drivers did not allow me to carry (anything)". For I know, my father, your peace-making; that any fight you are having you are able to calm down. (15) ... about the matter of ... write ... [... (20) ...]

... me ... if you (pl.) love ... you (pl.) are responsible (25) for them (?). There is no substance between us to fight over. There is no need for a cup of blood to flow! ... and <they> can fight with one another. I am not denying that I have [received] 3 *holokottinoi* from you. I am turned around! If you want to enforce the agreement that (30) you set, (then) demand (it). I will give the 6 *holokottinoi* [and] assume his (?) share. But she is steadfast. For I [will] give the 6 *holokottinoi* and assume the share that is [his (?)], because she is not liable. If (we do) otherwise, beloved one, he will (have to?) pay it (himself) with our friends. Should she go to ... (35) ... woman. It is you (pl.) and her ... until I can find (some?) *holokottinoi*, as I have ...

It is already twenty-four years since I came to Aphr(odite?), ... (n)ever. ... since my brother Soure came to Egypt. She took the 6 (40) *holokottinoi*. She brought (?) the 6 *holokottinoi*. She has ... She said: "Take these 6 *holokottinoi* according to the agreement". She said to him: "Take [them], let them be brought to me in Egypt". He said to me: "I am not liable, since Apa Pseke (will pay for me?)". (45) Live and be well [for me (?)].

Commentary:

Address   The central 'cross' is drawn more elaborately than usual and resembles a flower or similar.

5   The same phrasing about Timotheos occurs in one of the 'Petros' letters at **39**, 5-6. Indeed, there is a general similarity in the language about these two persons, when they are said to come from one place to another (see Petros throughout **38-40**). It is tempting to identify them with the two named Manichaean monks in the KAB (thus P. Kellis IV Gr. 96, ll. 975, 1080 etc.), also a Petros and a Timotheos; especially when one considers the itinerant lifestyle. Support for this might come from the reference to a Nos at **89**, 40-41; given that Timotheos the monk has a brother with that unusual name. However, the Nos and Timotheos of the KAB have a father named Kome. Another way to understand Timotheos' occupation here would be as directly involved in the transport business: When he comes they are glad, because he brings letters and other items. See perhaps **92** for Timotheos and the caravans.

8   ⲡⲁⲣⲅⲥⲥ ⲛ̄ⲉⲡⲓⲥⲧⲟⲗⲏ: Here is found one continuous long supralinear stroke, possibly indicating some sort of abbreviation or encoded insider usage. One way to speculate about the sense of this is to suppose that Pseke is giving a reference or authority

for what he has just said, i.e. that 'we might adore your face once again in the body'. It is reasonable to suppose that the phrase is a quotation or allusion, for very similar phrasing occurs elsewhere (e.g. **35**, 25 and see **82**, 7-8 note ad loc. with further references). Of course, it recalls 2Jo. 12 and 3Jo. 13-14; but the contexts in this archive are Manichaean and so the reference might be to one of Mani's *Epistles*. See perhaps the text quoted in W. Sundermann, 'A Manichaean Collection of Letters and a List of Mani's Letters in Middle Persian', op. cit., 2009: 273 '.. that I myself with corporeal eyes might see'. If this is correct, then it would be most interesting to understand what may here be some kind of abbreviated title. Certainly, there are many Greek words beginning αγ- that might be appropriate; but it is difficult to understand the construction and perhaps the problem needs a different approach. What appears to be a masc. article is strange, but one must compare **19**, 82 where there is a similar problem (and in that instance undoubtedly referring to Mani's *Epistles*). Here, the initial ⲁ- of the abbreviation could otherwise be ⲗ- (to read ⲗ̄ⲅ̄ⲥ̄ⲥ̄).

However, to think about it differently, perhaps more weight should be given to ⲕⲁϭⲛ̄ⲧⲥ as indicating an abrupt transition to more worldly matters, a formula meaning 'Please find attached x' (i.e. rather than referring to the preceding pious sentiment). The prepositional phrase would then hint at some sort of 'epistolary attachment' and this would fit seamlessly with what follows in l. 9. But what was indicated by the abbreviation remains unknown to us.

9   Presuming it is correct to read ϩⲛⲟ, one has to decide whether it refers to a material receptacle for what Pseke has sent, or whether its meaning here is abstract. The translation given reflects the latter. Further, it is unclear what Pseke has in fact sent to Iena. Given our discussion of the previous line *supra*, perhaps it was indeed a volume of Mani's *Epistles*; after all, Makarios requests the same at **19**, 82-83.

26   ⲟⲩⲗⲁⲕ ⲛ̄ⲥⲛⲁϥ 'a cup of blood': The reading is clear enough; presumably it is a kind of colloquial saying equivalent to the English phrase, 'there's no need to spill blood over it'.

29   Soure: i.e. Syros, see further **87**.

29, 30   ϩⲱⲛ: It appears that Pseke repeats the verb ('bid', 'command') to emphasise his point. Our translation is a little loose in order to convey what we think must be the sense here. Literally, 'if you wish / please to bid according to the agreement' etc. It is not quite clear whether the writer offers a choice to the addressees or is urging them: 'Will you please stick to the agreement'. Unfortunately, we do not know whether the agreement they settled upon earlier corresponds to what the writer goes on to stipulate himself or not; but the final imperative of this sentence, 'bid / demand', makes a real conditional ('If ..., then ...') more likely.

31   At this point Pseke seems to introduce another person (female) into the discussion, but we have no idea who she is or her part in the argument.

34   ⲫⲓⲥ: It is unclear if this is a place-name, the start of a name, or something else.

37   ⲉⲓ ⲁⲁⲫ[: 'went to Aphrodite'? The reading is rather uncertain, but see further the address on **77** and the note to **66**, 21-23.

41   It is tempting to read 'Kellis' here, which might make good sense in contrast to 'Egypt' in l. 39; but it is difficult to imagine what would fit in the remaining available space.

43   Probably, when Pseke says 'be brought to me in Egypt', he means himself rather than the woman (i.e. he has confused persons in the use of direct speech).

44   This appears to read ⲛ̄ⲥⲁⲛϣⲟⲣⲡ, but we can make no sense of that and presumably we are seeing it wrongly. What we understand is the conclusion of reported direct speech which brings the whole matter to a close.

45   ⲱⲛϩ ⲛ̄ⲧⲉ⟨ⲧⲛ̄⟩ⲟⲩϫⲉⲓⲧⲉ [.] . . : There is not enough room to complete the standard formula (i.e. with ⲛ̄ⲟⲩⲛⲁϭ ⲛ̄ⲟⲩⲁϣ). Perhaps Pseke simply finished with ⲛⲏⲓ̈ 'for me'.

P. Kellis Copt. 91

Inv #: P 51C(a)

Location: House 3, room 9, deposit 3 east wall.

Preservation: This is a short, mostly complete, Coptic letter. It is written transverse on a 'scrap' piece of papyrus. The dimensions are 38 x 135 mm.

Content: An unknown author writes a short note to the brothers Iena and Hor, (for further references to this pair see the introduction to the Ploutogenes letters). The document is somewhat reminiscent of the 'Petros' letters in both style and format, and also has the same find site. Still, there is no obvious connection in terms of the persons named, nor is it written from a son to his mother (compare **38-41**). Thus we have, rather tentatively, preferred to place it in this group of letters from and to Ploutogenes.

Address: No address. The verso is blank.

Names: Hor; Iena; Papnoute;

Text:

1   ϯϣⲓⲛⲉ ⲁⲣⲱⲧⲛ̄ ⲧⲟⲛⲟⲩ ⲛⲁⲥⲛⲏⲩ ⲙ̄ⲙⲉⲣⲉⲧⲉ ⲓⲉⲛⲁ ⲙⲛ̄ ϩⲱⲣ· ⲉⲓ̈ϣⲗⲏⲗ ⲁⲡⲛⲟⲩⲧⲉ ϫⲉ[ϥⲛⲁ]

2   ⲣ[ⲁⲓ̈ⲥ . .] ⲛ̄ⲛⲉⲩ ⲛⲓⲙ· ϫⲓ ϯⲉⲡⲓⲥⲧⲟⲗⲏ ⲉⲧⲁ ⲡⲁⲥⲁⲛ ⲧⲛ̄ⲛⲁⲩⲥⲉ ⲁⲃⲁⲗ ⲙ̄ⲡⲧⲁϣ· ⲁϥ[ⲧⲛ̄]

3   ⲛⲁⲩⲥⲉ ⲛ̄ⲧⲟⲧϥ̄ ⲙ̄ⲡⲁⲡⲛⲟⲩⲧⲉ ⲉⲓⲥ ⲕⲉ ϯⲟⲩ ϩⲟⲟⲩ ⲙ̄ⲡⲓϭⲛ̄ ⲣⲱⲙⲉ ⲁⲧⲛ̄ⲛⲁⲩ . [. . .]

4   [. . .] . ⲉ ⲉⲙ̄ⲡⲉ ⁒ ⲙⲉ ⲁⲛⲧ̄ ⲁϥⲓ ⲟⲩϩⲛⲟ ⲁⲛ̄ⲧϥ̄ ⲛⲏⲧⲛ̄ ⲙⲁⲗⲓⲥⲧⲁ ϫⲉⲛ̄ⲛⲉ\ⲩ/ⲏⲡ· ϯϣ[. . .]

5   . . . . . ⲛ̣ⲁⲗ . . . . ⲁⲧⲛ̄ⲟⲩ . . . . ⲟⲩⲃⲉ ⲡϩⲟⲟⲩ ⲉⲧⲥ̄ϣⲉ ⲉϣⲁⲧⲉⲧⲛ̄ⲟⲩϣ̣ . [.]

6   [. . . . . .] . . . . . . ⲁϩⲣⲏⲓ̈ ⲧⲛ̄ⲛⲟ ⲁⲡ[. . .] ἔρ(ρωσο)

---

1 ⲁⲣⲱⲧⲛ̄: -ⲱ- ex corr.   2-3 ⲧⲛ̄ⲛⲁⲩⲥⲉ (bis) sic, read ⲧⲛ̄ⲛⲁⲩⲥ   3 read ⟨ⲛ̄⟩ϩⲟⲟⲩ   4 ϫⲉⲛ̄ ⲛⲉ\ⲩ/ⲏⲡ·: -ⲛ̄- ex corr.   5 ⲉϣⲁⲧⲉⲧⲛ̄-: second -ⲧ- ex corr.

I greet you warmly: My brothers Iena and Hor. I am praying to God that [he will guard you] at all times. Receive this letter which my brother has sent from the border. He has sent <it> with Papnoute. It has already been another five days (that) I did not find anyone to send ... since no ... allowed me to carry a vessel and bring it to you; especially since they do not allow ... (5) ... against the day that is fitting. If you are going to ... up and we will see ... Farewell.

Commentary:

2 p[ⲁⲓⲥ . .]: There really is not enough room for the expected ⲁⲣⲱⲧⲛ̄.

ⲡⲧⲁϣ 'the border': cf. **50**, 29-30; **91**, 15. The term can also mean a district or nome. We suppose that it means the entry-point to the Oasis, where there would be official and military control.

4 Perhaps one should somehow read ⲣⲱⲙⲉ here, i.e. '... since no person (with authority) allowed me ..'. However, the traces are problematic.

KYRA / LOIHAT / TIMOTHEOS GROUP

These are two letters that are not obviously linked to the main family archive, and which have a number of names in common that are not found elsewhere: Kyra, Loihat, Theodoros. The first and better preserved letter is sent by a Timotheos, and his name also occurs in the second. However, whilst the name is more common in the Ismant el-Kharab texts, as might be expected, it is found in disparate documents and only Timotheos the monk (see further **90**, 5 note ad loc.) achieves any real identity. The problem then is to find some kind of context for these two pieces.

In **92** Timotheos adds greetings from a certain Plousiane. We find a person of this name adding a note to one of Philammon's letters (**80**), and this would suggest that Timotheos might belong to the latter's circle of acquaintances in the Nile valley writing to Kellis. However, again in **92**, Timotheos sends news of his 'sister' Nonna and her family. Other than an uncertain reading with no context in **98**, this name occurs elsewhere only in **115**, where Tegoshe (clearly in the Oasis and it would seem writing to the valley) states that Nonna's children have died. Of course, we have a number of instances of persons who move between the Oasis and the valley.

In sum, these pieces remain somewhat of a problem, in that their context in terms of the wider archive is not clear. Nevertheless, **92** is a well-preserved document and an excellent example of the fourth-century Coptic letter; whilst **93** has some interesting features of its own that are discussed *infra*.

P. Kellis Copt. 92

Inv #: P 90B

Location: House 3, room 6, deposit 4 west wall.

Preservation: This almost complete Coptic letter on papyrus was recovered in one piece, although it is beginning to break at the central and the vertical folds. In particular, a strip along the left of much of the upper half has broken away; but (due to the generous margin) little of the actual text is lost. The document has been proficiently written in a clear and regular hand, and even utilises basic punctuation marks.

Content: Timotheos (with Loihat) writes to his 'sister' Kyra. He disavows responsibility for some problem to do with goods belonging to her son, and assures her of his proper attention to her business. These kinds of matters, often somewhat obscure (abridged and hard to understand) in our letters, are here expressed with remarkable clarity and subtle sensibility (see, e.g., notes on ll. 23-25 and 28-30). Greetings are sent, and Klaudios adds his own short note. The reference to the border (l. 15 and cf. **91**, 2) suggests that Timotheos is at some distance; possibly he is in the Nile valley and writing to Kellis. If the Plousiane of this piece is the same person as in **80**, it would certainly support that reconstruction.

Address:
verso

  κυρίᾳ μου ἀδελφῇ   X   Κύρᾳ Τιμόθεος
  My lady sister X Kyra. (From) Timotheos.

Names: Andreas; Kyra; Klaudios; Loihat; Nonna; Plousiane; Pshai; Theodoros; Timotheos;

Text:

1. ⲧⲁⲥⲱⲛⲉ ⲙ̄[ⲙⲉ]ⲣⲓ[ⲧ] ⲕⲩⲣⲁ
2. [ⲁ]ⲛⲁⲕ ⲧⲓⲙ[ⲟⲑⲉⲟ]ⲥ ⲙⲛ ⲗⲱϩⲁⲧ
3. [ⲧ]ⲛ̄ϣⲓⲛⲉ ⲁⲣⲟ ⲙⲛ̄ ⲛⲉⲣⲱⲙⲉ ⲧⲏ
4. [ⲣ]ⲟⲩ ⲛⲁϣⲏⲣⲉ ϣⲓⲛⲉ ⲁⲣⲟ ⲙⲛ̄
5. ⲧⲉⲙⲟ ⲙⲛ̄ ⲛⲉⲥⲛⲏⲩ ⲙⲛ̄ ⲛⲟⲩ
6. ϣⲏⲣⲉ ϩⲛ̄ ⲡⲭⲁⲓ̈ⲥ ⲭⲁⲓⲣⲉⲓⲛ
7. ϣⲁⲣⲡ ⲙⲉⲛ ⲉⲓ̈ϣⲓⲛⲉ ⲁⲣⲱⲧⲛ̄ ⲛⲁ
8. ⲙⲉⲣⲉⲧⲉ ⲙⲛ̄ⲛ̄ⲥⲱⲥ †ⲥϩⲉⲓ ⲛⲉ
9. ϫⲉ ⲙ̄ⲡⲣ̄ⲙⲉⲩⲉ ⲁⲣⲁⲓ̈ ϫⲉ ⲛ̄ⲧⲁⲓ̈
10. ⲟⲩⲁϣ ϭⲓ ⲛ̄ⲛ̄ⲕⲉ ⲉⲧⲁⲧⲉⲟⲩ ⲛⲏⲓ̈
11. ⲁⲛ̄ⲧⲟⲩ ⲙ̄ⲡⲉϣⲏⲣⲉ ⲙⲏ ⲅⲉⲛⲟⲓⲧⲟ
12. ⲡⲁϣⲏⲣⲉ ⲅⲁⲣ ϩⲱⲧ ⲡⲉ ⲁⲗⲗⲁ
13. ⲕⲁⲛ ⲁⲟⲩⲁⲙⲉⲗⲓⲁ ϣⲱⲡⲉ· ⲧⲱ
14. ⲓ ⲉⲛ ⲧⲉ ⲧⲁⲡⲃⲁⲣⲱϩ ⲧⲉ ⲉⲧⲁϩ
15. ⲥⲁϫⲡⲟⲩ ⲁⲡⲁϩⲟⲩ ⲙ̄ⲡⲧⲁϣ` ⲉ
16. ϩⲉ ϭⲉ ⲙ̄ⲙⲁⲛ ⲛ̄ⲧⲁⲟ ϣⲱ[ⲡ]ⲉ̣
17. ⲉⲓⲥⲧⲉ ⲁⲛ ⲁⲩⲛ̄ⲧⲟⲩ ⲁⲓ̈ⲧⲉⲟⲩ
18. ⲛⲉϥ ⲕⲁⲗⲏ ⲡⲓⲥⲧⲓⲥ ϥ̄ⲣ̄ϣⲉⲩ
19. ϣⲓⲛⲉ ⲁⲣⲟ ⲛ̄ⲗⲓⲗⲁⲩⲉ ⲁⲩⲥⲁⲡ
20. ϣⲓⲛⲉ ⲁⲣⲟ ⲧⲛ̄ⲥⲱⲛⲉ ⲛ̣ⲟ̣ⲛ̣
21. ⲛⲁ ⲙⲛ̄ ⲛⲉⲥϣⲉⲣⲉ ⲥⲉⲣ̄ϣⲉⲩ
22. ⲧⲏⲣⲟⲩ· ⲕⲁ ⲡⲉϩⲏⲧ` ⲛ̄ⲧⲟ ⲁⲃⲁⲗ
23. ϫⲉ ⲉⲓ ⲕⲁⲛ ⲛⲉϣⲁⲓ̈ⲥⲗⲁϩⲗⲉϩ
24. ⲫⲱⲃ ⲛ̄ⲟⲩⲁⲛ ⲛⲓⲙ ⲡⲱ ⲣⲱ
25. ⲛ̄ⲧⲟ †ⲛⲁⲣ̄ⲁⲙⲉⲗⲉ ⲁⲣⲁϥ ⲉⲛ·
26. ⲡⲛ̄ⲥⲁⲛ ⲁⲛ ⲡⲗⲟⲩⲥⲓⲁⲛⲉ ϣⲓ
27. ⲛⲉ ⲁⲣⲱⲧⲛ̄ ⲁϥⲉⲓ ⲁⲓ̈† ⲛⲉϥ
28. ⲡϣⲁⲧ ⲙⲛ̄ ⲛⲉⲕⲟⲛ· ⲡⲓⲣⲉⲛ
29. ϫⲉ ϩⲏⲙⲉ ⲙ̄ⲡⲓⲛⲟ ⲁⲟⲩⲁⲛ ⲛ̄
30. ⲧⲟⲧϥ̄· ϩⲱⲃ ⲉⲧⲉⲭⲣⲓⲁ ⲙ̄ⲙⲁϥ

31	ⲥϩⲉⲓ ⲛⲏⲓ ϫⲉ ⲁⲣⲱ ⲧⲉⲥϩⲉⲓ ⲛⲏⲓ	
32	ⲉⲛ ϫⲉ ⲕⲁⲗⲱⲥ ⲏ ⲕⲁⲕⲱⲥ	
33	ⲛ̄ⲁⲗⲁⲩⲉ ϣⲓⲛⲉ ⲁⲣⲟ ⲡϣⲁⲓ	
34	ⲡⲡⲣⲉⲥⲃⲩⲧⲉⲣⲟⲥ ⲁⲛⲇⲣⲉⲁⲥ	
35	ⲑⲉⲟⲇⲱⲣⲟⲥ ⲁⲛⲁⲕ ϩⲱⲧ ⲕⲗⲁⲩ	
36	ⲇⲓⲟⲥ ϯϣⲓⲛⲉ ⲁⲣⲟ	ἔρρωσο
37	ϣⲓⲛⲉ ⲁⲣⲁⲩ ⲧⲏⲣⲟⲩ	μοι ἐν
38	ⲛ̄ⲃⲁⲗ ⲙ̄ⲡⲏⲓ	κυρίῳ

My loved sister, Kyra: (It is) I, Timotheos, and Loihat. We greet you and all your people. My children greet you, and (5) your mother and your siblings and their children; in the Lord, - greetings.

First, I am greeting you (pl.), my loved ones. Next, I write to you (fem.): Do not think of me that I (10) wanted to take the things that you gave me to bring to your son. Never! For he is my son too. But even if some negligence has happened, it is not mine; it is that of the caravan-driver who (15) left them behind at the border. Very well then - what happened? They have now (finally) been delivered (and) I have given them to him (i.e. the son) in good faith. He is well (and) greets you. The children all together (20) greet you. Our sister Nonna and her daughters are all well. Do not worry: Even if I were being slack with everyone's business, yours indeed (25) I would not neglect.

Also, our brother Plousiane greets you. He came. I gave him the cushion and the buckets (?). As for that item for freight: I have not seen anything (30) from him.

Whatever you need, write to me. For why do you not write to me whether (things are) good or bad? The children greet you. Pshai the presbyter (?), Andreas, (35) Theodoros. I too, Klaudios, I greet you. Greet all of them outside the house. Be well for me in the Lord.

Commentary:

1 There seems to be no good reason to identify Kyra with that Kyria / Gouria (once ϭⲟⲩⲣⲉ at **20**, 3-4) who is the wife of Pshem(p)noute and a central figure for the Makarios family.

14 ⲡⲃⲁⲣⲱϩ: One must presume that it is not the animal but its keeper that is to blame, cf. CD 44b 'fodderer' and the index to this volume. On the issue of identifying the precise pack-animal see **20**, 54 note ad loc.

15   ⲡⲧⲁϣ 'the border': Perhaps this was a place where the animals were changed, thus explaining the negligence. See further **91**, 2 note ad loc.

15-16   ⲉϩⲉ ϭⲉ ⲛ̄ⲙⲁⲛ: Cf. **64**, 5-6 (note ad loc.); **105**, 46; **108**, 26.

18   '.. in good faith': The adverbial *bona fide* formula is borrowed from the Greek καλῇ πίστει as a whole (although the dative was here 'normalised' into the more commonly known form ⲡⲓⲥⲧⲓⲥ). This adds another lexical item to the small number of loan expressions containing a form of καλός in Coptic (mainly καλῇ προαιρέσει and μετὰ καλοῦ, cf. H. Förster, *Wörterbuch der griechischen Wörter in den koptischen dokumentarischen Texten*, De Gruyter, Berlin / New York, 2002: 370).

23   ⲥⲗⲁϩⲗⲉϩ: perhaps 'to be slack'. See further **106**, 29 note ad loc.

23-25   With ⲉⲓ ⲕⲁⲛ ⲛⲉϥϣⲁⲓ̈- in the protasis and a First Future (preceded by the object in anteposition plus *augentia*) for the apodosis, this is quite an unusual form of a conditional (half *irrealis*) period. The apodosis ('yours indeed ...') is expressively connotated for the author's personal commitment to the addressee, and the use of an unconverted Future seems to stress the reality of this commitment.

28   ⲉⲕⲟⲛ: Probably for ἀγγεῖον. Much less likely would be εἰκών; or ⲁϭⲁⲛ 'stand (for wine-jars)'.

28-30   'As for that item ...': In the topical position of this sentence, instead of the common ⲡⲓⲥⲉϫⲉ '(concerning) this / that matter', the author uses ⲡⲓⲣⲉⲛ 'this / that name', which is the metalinguistic term for 'word' (= ὄνομα), followed by ϫⲉ and a zero-determined noun (lexeme); that is, a full-fledged typical naming construction. This can only be understood as a sarcastic note, expressing the author's annoyance with the matter at issue and the person ('him') connected to it. It may be approximately paraphrased as: 'Oh, (when I hear) this word ...', or 'As for that (cursed) word ...'. In the middle of an otherwise quite trivial exchange of information, this is a strongly marked rhetorical device. In sum, Timotheos is remarking that he has received no payment.

34   It is not entirely certain whether 'the presbyter' refers to Pshai or Andreas, or even to a separate and otherwise unnamed person. Still, the most likely usage of such functional titles should be (as in Greek) after the name. Presumably these persons are all with Timotheos and send their greetings, but it is not entirely clear.

P. Kellis Copt. 93

Inv #: P 92.262

Location: House 3, room 11, deposit 4.

Preservation: This is a very fragile letter written in Coptic on parchment, which is now breaking up badly and in danger of complete disintegration. The recto is the 'hair' side and the verso is the 'flesh'. Comparison of the digital photograph, taken in January 2009, with an older black and white from the mid 1990s, shows significant erosion along the edges. See further the note to l. 20. The three main fragments can be placed so as to give the dimensions of an original document at approximately 90 x 74 mm. There are perhaps ten other small pieces and scraps. There are also traces of an earlier text clearly visible throughout. This was written in Coptic[16] and seems to begin with ⲁⲛⲁ[(i.e. ⲁⲛⲁⲕ?), which suggests that the text was again a letter. One can probably read ⲭⲁⲓⲣⲉⲓⲛ in l. 4.

The only other example of parchment recovered from the site is P. Kellis Syr. / Gr. 1. It is also in extremely poor condition, but is evidently the scant remains of a once fine bilingual production in Greek and Syriac. The use of parchment for a letter is certainly unusual in this period, but there are other instances. Noteworthy are the two Oxyrhynchite examples, letters of commendation, from the archive of bishop (?) Sotas: PSI III 208, IX 1041 (late 3rd century C.E?). See now A. Luijendijk, *Greetings in the Lord: Early Christians and the Oxyrhynchus Papyri*, Cambridge (Mass.) 2008, chapters 4 and 5. She speculates that Sotas was engaged in manuscript production and that the letters were penned on leftover scraps (see pp. 144-151).

Content: The letter is written by a woman to her sister Talou. Apart from the greetings (which are interesting because the commonality of names connects this piece to **92**), all that we can discern about the content is that Kyra is ill. Theodoros adds a short note. It

---

[16] One can certainly read letters such as -ϩ-, -ϫ- and -ϭ-; as well as (e.g.) ⲛ̄ⲧⲟⲧϥ at the start of the last line on the verso.

is unknown where the letter was written. The hand is very fine, with a number of notable flourishes (such as the pointed initial ⲁ-).

Address:

verso

    ἀπ[. .] . ρ[. . . . . α]παμμωνι

    [. . . . .] . ου

    ... [Sara]pammon (?) ...

Names: Eutuchos; Hat; Kyra; Kyrilla; Loihat; [Sara]pammon (?); Talou; Theodoros; Timothe; Tatom (?);

Text:

1	ⲧⲁⲥ[ⲱⲛⲉ ⲉⲧⲁⲓ̈] ⲛ̄ⲧⲟⲧ ⲧⲟⲛⲟⲩ ⲧⲉⲧⲉⲡⲉⲥⲣⲉⲛ
2	ϩⲁⲗ[ϭ ϩⲛ̄ ⲣⲱⲓ̈] ⲧⲁⲥⲱⲛⲉ ⲙ̄ⲙⲉⲣⲓⲧ ⲧⲁⲗⲟⲩ
3	ⲁⲛⲁⲕ [. . . . .]ⲛ ⲧⲉⲧⲥϩⲉⲓ̈ ⲉⲥϣⲓⲛⲉ ⲁⲣⲟ
4	ϩⲛ̄ ⲡⲭⲁⲉⲓ[ⲥ ⲭⲁⲓ]ⲣⲉⲓⲛ vac ϩⲁ[ⲑ]ⲏ ⲛ̄
5	ϩⲱⲃ ⲛⲓⲙ ϯ[ϣⲓⲛⲉ] ⲁⲡⲁⲓ̈ⲱⲧ [. . . . . . .]
6	ⲁⲩⲱ̄ ⲟⲩⲕⲟϩ[. . . . .]
7	ⲥⲱⲧⲙⲉ ⲧⲉ[. . . . .] . . . ⲉϥ[ϣⲁ]
8	ⲛⲟⲩⲉ ⲇⲉ ⲁ . . . [. . . . .] ⲡⲁⲭⲉⲩ ⲭ[ⲉ]
9	ϥⲛ̄ⲛⲟⲩ ϩⲱϥ ⲁⲛ̣ ϯ . . . . . . ⲏⲩ ⲁⲃⲁⲗ
10	ⲛ̄ⲕⲉⲥⲁⲡ ϣⲓⲛⲉ ⲛⲏⲓ̈ ⲧⲟⲛⲟⲩ ⲁⲡⲁϣⲏⲣⲉ ⲉⲩ
11	ⲧⲩⲭⲟⲥ ⲙⲛ̄ ⲡⲉϣⲏ[ⲣ]ⲉ ⲧⲓⲙⲟⲑⲉ ⲛ̄[. . . .]
12	ⲇⲉ ⲁⲣⲁⲓ̈ ⲛ̄ϭⲱⲣϩ̣ ϩⲛ̄ [.] . . . [. . .] . . [. .]
13	ⲕⲩⲣⲁ ϣⲱⲛⲉ . . . [. . . . .]
14	ⲙⲉⲛ ⲛⲏⲓ̈ ⲭⲉ̣ [. . . .]ⲉⲡⲓⲥⲧⲟⲗ[ⲏ . . . .]
15	ⲧ . [. . . . .]ⲟⲩⲭⲉ̣[. . . . . . .]
16	ⲛⲁⲙⲏⲉ ⲉ̣ . . . . ⲁ . . . . [. .]
17	ⲉϥϩⲱⲃ ⲛ̄ⲧⲉ . . . ⲛ̣ⲟ . ⲧ̣ⲕ ⲙ̄ⲙⲏ . . [. .]
18	ⲭⲉ ⲛ̄ⲛⲉⲁⲥⲛ̄ⲧⲁⲛ ⲭⲛ̄ ⲙ̄ⲡⲉ̣ vac . . [. . .]
tr19	ϣⲓⲛⲉ ⲛⲏⲓ̈ ⲁⲧⲁⲙⲟ ⲕⲩⲣⲓⲗⲗⲁ ⲙⲛ̄ ⲧⲁⲥⲱⲛⲉ

20   ϩⲁⲧ ⲙⲛ̄ ⲧⲁϣⲉⲣⲉ ⲗⲱⲓϩⲁⲧ ⲙⲛ̄ ⲧⲁϣⲉⲣⲉ ⲧⲁⲧⲱⲙ
v21   ⲛⲉⲧⲙ̄ⲡⲓⲙⲁ ⲧⲏⲣⲟⲩ ϣⲓⲛⲉ ⲁⲣⲱⲧⲛ̄
22   ⲁⲛⲁⲕ ⲑⲉⲟⲇⲱⲣⲟⲥ ϯϣⲓⲛ[ⲉ . .] . . . [. .]
23   . ⲛ̄ . . . . [. . . . . . . ϣⲓ]
24   ⲛⲉ ⲛⲏⲓ̈ ⲁ . . . . [. . . . .]
25   ⲥⲛⲏⲟⲩ ⲧⲏⲣⲟⲩ ⲕⲁⲧ[ⲁ ⲛⲟⲩⲣⲉⲛ . . . . .]

plus an unplaced fragment with ⲧⲓ]ⲙⲟⲑⲉ[visible

My [sister who is] very [precious] to me, the one whose name is sweet [in my mouth]: My loved sister Talou. I, …, am the one (fem.) who writes greeting you; in the Lord, - greetings.

Before (5) everything I [greet] my father … hear … However, if he is going to … they say that he too is coming … out (10) another time. Greet me warmly to my son Eutuchos and your son Timothe. And … to me at night … Kyra is sick … for me that … letter (15) … truly … he sends … whether she has recovered or not. (tr) Greet me to my mother Kyrilla, and my sister (20) Hat and my daughter Loihat and my daughter Tatom. (v) Everyone here greets you.

I, Theodoros, I greet … (25) all (my?) brothers by [name] …

Commentary:

Address: This almost certainly belongs to the underlying text, i.e. an earlier letter that has now been overwritten. If so, the name (Sarapammon?) may not be relevant to the understanding of the current document.

3   If indeed the author's (female) name ends with a -ⲛ, one could consider something like ⲭⲛ̄ⲓ̈ⲟⲛ (cf. **45**, 9).

6   ⲁⲩⲱ̄: The initial ⲁ is written as the beginning of a new word; and thus it cannot be read as the end of the father's name (e.g. [Orm]auo).

20   In an older photograph (from the mid 1990s) the left-hand border of the document is preserved all the way down to the break between the fragments. Thus the reading provided here: ϩⲁⲧ ⲙⲛ̄ ⲧⲁϣⲉⲣⲉ (now partly lost). Careful comparison of other sections, especially the fragments that remain from the right hand of the recto, evidence further losses. The transcript includes some readings that are no longer possible (such as ⲡⲁϫⲉⲩ at l. 8).

INDIVIDUAL AND UNPLACED DOCUMENTS AND LETTERS

This edition of the Coptic documentary texts from House 3 is completed with the remains of a further twenty-eight letters that are here listed as 'individual or unplaced'. What this simply means is that they do not fit neatly into the categories that have been established, and that there is little to be gained now in introducing a whole further series of groups which will either be ill-defined or composed of single documents. These are all placed together and edited according the sequence of their original inventory numbers; (and thus the following order does not indicate anything of relevance with regards to a piece's relationship to other texts from the House 3 excavations in terms of its content).

It should be emphasised that a good proportion of these letters are, without doubt, written by or to the same family groups already encountered. In some instances it is highly probable that better preservation would have enabled us to place documents into the categories already established, i.e. some of these may well have been written by Pamour or Pegosh or whoever, but we cannot be certain. In other instances, such as **102** (Psais to Partheni) or **105** (Psais to Andreas), it is clear that we are dealing with persons that are already known. However, there are a few pieces that are difficult to place in terms of our general understanding of the background situation and families to whom, it should be emphasised, the great majority of the documents certainly belong.

P. Kellis Copt. 94

Inv #: A/5/163

SCA #: 1871

Location: House Three, room 6, deposit 3.

Preservation: This is a complete personal letter in Coptic, written in a very small script on a wooden board. The dimensions are 130 x 42 mm. Apart from a few minor issues of reading, where the text is rather abraded, the piece is a good example of a fourth century letter, albeit difficult to understand for outsiders. The script is fluent and practised.

Content: Neither the author nor the recipient is named. Greetings are sent to an Iene (amongst others), and perhaps the piece could have been placed in the group of letters sent from or to Ploutogenes (whose name is certainly sometimes abbreviated to Iena). However, a number of the names found here are not represented elsewhere in the House 3 documents, such as Ianou and Pantoni; (although the latter may be the same as Pantonume, cf. **36**, 41-42). The best way to provide a context for the letter could be through 'father Antinou' (l. 8), perhaps the same person as in **79**, 21-22 (and see the 'brother Antinou' of **78**, 40). The latter pair of letters are by Pegosh and closely related to each other. They also feature (Phi)lammon and various financial transactions, as does the present piece. Still, this is all rather tenuous.

The body of the letter is about business, mostly money that is owed and various goods to be purchased or sent. As usual, it is difficult to follow the details without knowing the background to the issues. In this letter, the normal social and family greetings are a relatively minor element compared with the majority of examples in the archive. There is no real indication of where it was written; but the discussion in the final lines about meeting up would suggest that the author and recipient are not too distant from each other. The reference to a man from Mot (i.e. Mothis) in ll. 29-30 points to an Oasis context, although we know that persons from there also dealt with each other in the valley.

Note that, if one takes the 2nd person pronouns seriously, the author addresses a male person (that is, his brother, according to the incipit), mixed in with a few plurals, throughout ll. 3–46 (by extension, 50) and 55 till end; but clearly a female in ll. 51–54 (and possibly in l. 22, but uncertain).

Address: None, and there is no available space as both sides of the board are fully covered by text. Indeed, the use of a wooden board may be taken as indicative of a context where it is not expected that the 'letter' will be sent in the normal way.

Names: Antinou; Blle (from Mot); Hor; Ianou; Iene; Kolouthos; Lammon; Pantoni; Shai, (son) of mother Tnahte;

Text:

A1 κυρίωι μου ἀδελφῶι
2 ὁ ἀδελφὸς χαίρειν
3 ϯϣⲓⲛⲉ ⲁⲣⲁⲕ ⲧⲟⲛⲟⲩ ⲡⲁⲥⲁⲛ
4 ⲙ̄ⲙⲉⲣⲓⲧ ⲙ̄ⲛ ⲛⲓⲡ̄ⲗⲁⲩⲉ ⲉⲩ
5 ⲥⲁⲡ· ⲕⲁⲧⲁ ⲛⲟⲩⲣⲉⲛ ⲙⲁⲗⲓⲥⲧⲁ
6 ϩⲱⲣ ⲡⲁⲓ̈ⲱⲧ [ϯϣⲓ]ⲛⲉ ⲁⲣⲁⲕ
7 ⲧⲟⲛⲟⲩ ⲙ̄ⲛ ⲡⲁⲥⲁⲛ ⲓ̈ⲉⲛⲉ ⲙⲛ
8 ⲡⲁⲓ̈ⲱⲧ ⲁⲛⲧⲓⲛⲟⲩ ⲓ̈ⲁⲛⲟⲩ
9 ϣⲓⲛⲉ ⲁⲣⲁⲕ ⲧⲟⲛⲟⲩ ⲙ̄ⲛ ⲧϥ
10 ⲙⲟ ⲙ̄ⲛ ⲛⲉϥⲥⲛⲏⲩ ⲉⲩⲥⲁⲡ·
11 ⲕⲁⲧⲁ ⲛⲟⲩⲣⲉⲛ· ⲧⲉⲧ̄ⲛ
12 ϭⲛ̄ ⲁⲣⲓⲕⲉ ⲣⲱ ϩⲱϥ ⲁⲣⲁⲓ̈
13 ϩⲓⲉⲩ· vac? ⲉⲧⲃⲉ ⲛ̄ϩⲁⲏⲧ·
14 ϫⲉ ⲙ̄ⲡⲕⲧ̄ⲛⲁⲩⲥⲉ ⲙ̄ⲡⲕ
15 ⲧⲛⲛⲁⲩⲥⲉ ⲟ ⲧⲉ ⲧⲁϭⲁⲙ· ⲛ̄ⲉⲩ
16 ⲟⲩⲏϩ ⲉⲙⲡⲓϭⲛ̄ ⲑⲉ ⲛ̄ⲧⲛ̄ⲛⲁⲩ
17 ⲥⲉ· ⲉⲓⲧⲉ ⲛⲉⲕ· ⲉⲓⲧⲉ ⲛⲉⲥ· ⲁⲗⲗⲁ
18 ⲡⲛⲟⲩⲧⲉ ⲛⲟⲩⲁⲉⲧϥ̄ ⲡⲉⲧⲥⲁⲩⲛⲉ
19 ⲛ̄ⲛⲉϯⲉⲓⲣⲉ ⲙ̄ⲙⲁⲩ ⲙ̄ⲡⲓ̈ⲱⲧ
20 ⲡⲁⲛⲧⲱⲛⲓ ⲙ̄ⲙⲏⲛⲉ ⲁⲩⲱ ⲛ̄
21 ⲡϥ̄ⲣϩⲉ ⲁⲣⲁⲓ̈ ⲁⲛⲏϩⲉ ⲡⲕⲉ †
22 ⲟⲩ ⲛⲉ ⲛ̄ϣⲉ ⲥⲉⲛⲁⲧⲉⲩ ⲛⲏⲓ̈ ⲛ̄
23 ⲣⲉⲥⲧⲁ ⲉⲩϣⲁⲧⲉⲩ ϯⲛⲁⲧⲛ̄ⲛⲁⲩ
24 ⲥⲉ· ⲛⲉⲧⲁⲙⲟ ϩⲱⲥ ⲁⲛ· ⲛⲁ

25	ⲡⲣⲱⲛ ⲉⲓⲥⲧⲉ ⟨ϯ⟩ⲧⲛ̄ⲛⲁⲩ ⲧⲉ
26	ⲙ̄ⲙⲁⲩ ⲕⲟⲩⲓ̈ ⲕⲟⲩⲓ̈ ⲁⲓ̈ⲧⲛ̄ⲛⲁⲩ
27	ϣⲙⲟⲩⲛ ϣⲉ ⲛ̄ⲧⲟⲧϥ̄ ⲛ̄ⲗⲁⲙ`
28	ⲙⲱⲛ ⲕⲉ ϣⲙⲟⲩⲛ ⲛ̄ⲧⲟⲧϥ̄
29	ⲛ̄ⲕⲟⲗⲟⲩⲑⲟⲥ ⲙⲛ̄ ⲃⲁⲗⲉ ⲡⲓⲣⲙ̄
30	ⲙ̄ⲙⲟⲧ` ⲡⲁϫⲉⲩ ϫⲉ ⲧⲛ̄ⲛⲁⲙⲟⲩ
B31	ⲧⲉ ⲁϩⲟⲩⲛ ⲧⲛ̄ⲧⲉⲩ ⲛⲏⲧⲛ̄ ⲗⲟⲓⲡⲉ
32	ⲕⲉ ⲙⲛ̄ⲧⲥⲁϣϥⲉ ⲛ̄ϣⲉ ⲡⲉⲧⲕⲁϥ
33	ⲁⲛ ⲁⲧⲉⲩ ⲙ̄ⲡⲓϩⲟⲟⲩ ⲥⲛⲟ ⲏ ⲁⲧⲁ
34	ϩⲟⲩ ϩⲣⲏⲓ̈ ⲡⲥⲉϫⲉ ⲇⲉ ⲛ̄ⲧϩⲁⲓ̈ⲧⲉ ⟨ⲉ⟩ⲧⲟⲩ
35	ⲛϩ ϣⲁ ϯⲛⲟⲩ ⲙ̄ⲡⲉⲣⲱⲙⲉ ϥⲓⲧⲥ̄
36	ⲡⲁϫⲉⲩ ⲧⲏⲣⲟⲩ ϫⲉ ϣⲁ ⲡϩⲓⲧⲛ̄
37	ⲁⲓ̈ⲉⲓ ⲁⲡϩ . ⲉ ⲁϣⲁⲓ̈ ⲛ̄ⲧⲙⲟ ⲧⲛⲁϩ
38	ⲧⲉ ⲉⲓ ⲁϩⲟⲩⲛ ⲁⲓ̈ⲧⲉⲥ ⲛⲉⲩ ⲁⲧⲣⲉϥⲛ̄ⲧⲥ̄
39	ϩⲣⲏⲓ̈ ⲁϥⲉⲓ ⲇⲉ ⲁϩⲟⲩⲛ ⲛ̄ⲣⲟⲩϩⲉ ⲡⲁ
40	ϫⲉ . . . ϣ ϫⲉ ⲙ̄ⲡϥ̄ⲕⲁ ϭⲉ
41	ⲙⲁ ⲁⲧⲟⲧ` ⲉⲙⲡⲓ vacⲙⲁϣ⁻
42	ⲙ̄ⲡⲟⲩϥⲓⲧⲥ̄ vac ⲡⲁϫⲉⲓ̈
43	ϫⲉ ⲁⲓ̈ϣⲉⲃⲁⲗ vac ⲁⲧϩⲱⲥⲉ
44	ⲛⲙ̄ⲙⲉⲥ` ⲡⲁϫⲉⲩ ϫⲉ ϫⲟⲩⲧⲏ
45	ⲛ̄ϣⲉ ⲁⲡⲙ̄ⲙⲛⲁ ⲁⲓ̈ϫⲟⲥ ⲛⲉϥ
46	ϫⲉ ⲃⲱⲕ ⲕ̄ⲛⲟ ϫⲉ ⲛ̄ⲥⲉⲛⲁ
47	ⲧⲉⲩ ⲧⲏⲣⲟⲩ ϩⲓ ⲟⲩⲥⲁⲡ ⲛ̄ⲟⲩ
48	ⲱⲧ` ⲉϣⲱⲡⲉ ⲥⲉ ⲧⲉⲥ ⲙ̄ⲡⲁ
49	ⲧⲉϥⲉⲓ ⲛⲏⲓ̈ ⲛ̄ⲟⲩⲱ ⲡⲁϫⲉϥ ⲁⲛ
50	ϫⲉ ϯⲛ̄ⲏⲩ ⲛ̄ⲣⲉⲥⲧⲁ ⲉⲓ ⲙⲉⲛ
51	ⲁⲩϥⲓⲧⲥ̄ ⲉⲓⲛⲁⲛ̄ ⲛϩⲁⲙⲧ̄ ⲛⲉ
52	ⲉϣⲱⲡⲉ ⲁⲛ ⲙ̄ⲡⲉ ⲛ̄ϩⲉ ϥⲛⲁ
53	ⲛ̄ⲧⲥ̄ ⲁⲛ ⲛⲉ ⲛ̄ⲧⲉⲙⲛ̄ⲧⲉⲥⲁⲩ
54	ⲛⲉ ϫⲉ ⲥⲉⲛⲁϥⲓⲧⲥ̄ ⲉⲛ ⲛ̄ⲛⲓⲙⲁ
55	ⲉϣⲱⲡⲉ ⲉⲕⲧⲏϣ ⲁⲉⲓ ⲁϩⲣⲏⲓ̈
56	ⲛⲓⲉ ⲁⲙⲟⲩ ⲁⲛ ⲙ̄ⲡⲓϩⲟⲟⲩ ⲥⲛⲟ ⲧⲁ

57	ⲣ̄ⲛⲉⲓ ⲛⲙ̄ⲙⲉⲕ` ⲙ̄ⲧⲣⲉⲕⲉⲓ ϩⲟⲩⲛ
58	ⲁⲛ ϩⲙ̄ ⲡⲛⲟ ⲕⲉⲓ` ⲉϣⲱⲡⲉ ⲁⲛ ⲉⲕⲟⲩ
59	ⲏⲩ ⲁⲛ ⲉⲧⲉⲧⲛ̄ⲟⲩⲱϣ ⲧⲣⲉⲓ ⲛ̄ⲓⲉ
60	ⲥϩⲉⲓ ϯϭⲛ̄ ⲣⲱⲙⲉ ϯⲉⲓ
61	ἔρ(ρωσο)

---

34 There could possibly be a letter prior to -ϩⲟⲩ (thus: . ϩⲟⲩ)   41 ⲙⲁ: -ⲁ ex corr.   45 ⲛⲉϥ: -ϥ ex corr.

(A) To my master brother: (from your) brother, - greetings.

I greet you warmly, my loved brother; and the children (5) altogether, by their names. Especially Hor, my father: I greet you warmly, and my brother Iene, and my father Antinou. Ianou greets you warmly; and his (10) mother and his brothers altogether, by their names.

But now, for what do you find fault with me? About the cash payments? Saying: "You have not sent them, you have not (15) sent them"! What is my capacity (to pay)? Are they sitting (here) and I did not find any way to send them, either to you or to her? But God alone knows what I do for father (20) Pantoni daily; and he was never well-disposed towards me.

The other 500 for you (fem.): They will give them to me tomorrow. Should they pay, I will send them. And for her part, (what about the payments by) my mother, the ones for (25) the cloak? Look, I am sending them little by little. I have sent 800 with Lammon; another 8 (hundred) with Kolouthos and Blle, this man (30) from Mot. They say: "We will call (B) in and give them to you". As for the rest, there is yet another 1700 due to be paid during these two days, or tallied up (?).

And the matter of the robe that is (35) waiting: Until now noone has taken it. They all say: "Until …". I came to ... Shai, (son) of mother Tnahte, came in. I gave it to him so that he could bring it over; and he came in at nightfall. (40) [(N.N.?)] says: "He did not allow any space to me, as I (?) did not … They did not take it". I say: "I went out to the ... with it". They say: "2500 (45) to the *mna*". I told him: "Go, you see if they will pay all at one time". If so, give it (to them). As yet, he has not come to me with news. He also says (50): "I am coming tomorrow". If they take it I will bring the money to you (fem.). And if (there is) no way, he will bring it to you. You (fem.) cannot know whether (or) not they will carry it from here. (55) If you (masc.) are assigned to come up, then come in two days that we may come with you. However, do not come in (to our place) at the moment you arrive. But if you are still far away and want me to come (instead), then (60) write and I will find someone and come. Farewell.

Commentary:

13   'vac?': It appears probable that the scribe has left a space where there is a knot in the wood, though he has not done so in the previous two lines where it was even worse.

'cash payments': lit. coins or monies.

22   '.. for you (fem.)' is uncertain as the position is very unusual for a dative preposition. Alternatively, ⲛⲉ might be the subject pronoun of a Nominal Sentence, literally '.. is it', used here to introduce a new matter. Thus: 'As for the other 500, they will ...'.

33-34   ⲁⲧⲁ|ϩⲟⲩ ϩⲡⲏⲓ̈: The reading is by no means certain, but we think that this must be the verb ⲧⲁϩⲟ with (previously unattested) the adverb ϩⲡⲏⲓ̈. This would provide reasonable sense, i.e. the money is to be paid (†) or tallied up (ⲧⲁϩⲟ + ϩⲡⲏⲓ̈).

36   ϣⲁ ⲡϩⲓⲧⲛ̄: We do not understand this. It seems to be the excuse made by the people who have failed to collect the robe.

41-43   The scribe has written around a knot in the wood.

51   ⲁⲩϥⲓⲧⲥ̄: 'take it' or 'have taken it'. Alternatively, the reading may be ⲁⲩϣⲓⲧⲥ̄: 'If they have measured it ..'.

58   The use of the conjunctive (instead of a relative) is remarkable.

P. Kellis Copt. 95

Inv #: P51B

Location: House 3, room 9, deposit 3 east wall.

Preservation: This is a densely written Coptic letter. It has been written in a fluent, tiny script on one side of a squarish piece of old 'spare' papyrus. It is probably complete (in two joined fragments); but the text is substantially abraded. The dimensions are 72 x 90 mm.

Content: The letter is written by an unknown male author to Partheni. However, he also sends greetings from Kame, and it may be convincing to relate these persons to the two weavers (Kame and Heni) in **44**, 4-5. There is also a weaver named Kame in P. Kellis I Gr. 71, 48; and, of course, (Part)heni often occurs in the main family group (see especially **75** from which we deduce that she is Pegosh's wife). Certainly, this present letter belongs to the main House 3 archive. Here various financial transactions are discussed; but they are particularly difficult to follow due to uncertain readings and the loss of substantial sections of text.

Address: The verso is blank.

Names: Hat; Kame; Louishai (?); Partheni; Pshai (?);

Text:

1   τῇ κυρίᾳ μου ἀδελφῇ Παρθενι vac ὁ ἀδελφὸς χαίρειν
2   [†]ϣine ⲁⲣⲟ ⲧⲟⲛⲟⲩ ⲙⲛ̄ ⲛⲉϥϣⲏⲣⲉ ⲕⲁⲙⲉ ϣⲓⲛⲉ ⲁⲣⲱⲧⲛ̄
3   . . . . ⲓⲱⲧ . . . ϭⲉ ⲉⲧⲁⲓⲉⲓ ⲁⲃⲁⲗ . . . . ⲉ ⲙ̄ⲙⲁⲥ ⲉⲓⲥ ⲡ . ι . ⲉⲁⲓ . . .
4   . . . . ⲁⲓ̈† ⲙⲁⲃϣⲁⲙⲧⲉ ⲛ̄ϣⲉ ⲏ . . . ⲛ̄ϭⲛ̄ϭⲱⲣ ⲛ̄ . . . . ̄
5   . . . . . ⲛ̄ⲛⲓⲙⲁ· . . . †ⲗⲓⲙ . . . †ⲛⲁⲧⲛ̄ⲛⲁⲩϥ ⲛⲉⲕ †ⲛⲁ . ⲉⲓ̈
6   . . . . ⲛ̄ⲧⲁⲓ̈ⲧⲉϥ ⲇⲉ ⲙ̄ⲡⲱⲡ ⲛ̄ϫⲟⲩⲧⲏ ⲛ̄ϣⲉ ⲁⲡⲙ̄ⲙⲛⲁ ⲁ2ⲛ̄ⲃ . ⲁⲛ
7   . . ⲉⲛⲁⲛⲟⲩϥ· ⲉⲁⲙⲛ̄ⲧⲥⲛⲁⲩⲥ ⲙ̄ⲙⲁⲭⲉ . . . . ⲁⲩⲧⲉⲩ ⲛⲉⲛ ⲁⲗⲗⲁ . ⲩ2ⲁ .
8   . . ⲕⲁⲥ ϫⲉ ⲡⲁⲭⲉϥ ϫⲉ ⲙⲏⲧ ⲛ̄ϣⲉ ⲛ̄ϭⲛ̄ϭⲱⲣ ⲥ2ⲉⲓ̈ ⲁⲛ ⲛⲏⲓ̈ ⲉⲧⲃⲉ .
9   . . . . ⲛ̄ⲛ2ⲁⲙⲧ` ⲉⲧⲃⲉ ⲡ2ⲱⲃ ⲁⲛ ⲙ̄ⲡⲓ2ⲟⲟⲩ ⲉⲧ2ⲁⲉⲓ ⲟⲩⲧⲁ . .
10 . . . . . . ⲛ̄ⲥⲁ ⲧⲉⲙⲟ ⲛ̄ⲧⲉⲭⲟⲥ ⲛⲉⲥ ⲙ . . ⲉⲥ ⲁⲙⲏ ⲁⲡⲙⲁ ⲛ̄2ⲁⲧ ⲛ̄ϭ
11 . . . . ⲉⲥϣⲱⲡⲉ ⲉ2ⲁ ⲡ2ⲱⲃ ⲙ̄ⲡⲣⲱⲙⲉ ⲙⲟⲩⲭⲧ̄ . . . . . .
12 . . . . ⲛ̄ⲓ̈ ⲛ̄ⲥⲛ̄ⲧϥ̄ ⲛ̄ϭⲧ . . . . . ⲙⲉⲛⲉⲧ . . . . .
13 . . . . ⲛ̄ⲓ̈ⲉ ⲭⲓ· ⲉϣⲱⲡⲉ ⲁⲛ ⲙ̄ⲙⲁⲛ [. . .]ⲅ̄. ϫⲟⲥ ϫⲉ . ⲁⲩⲥ
14 [. .] . ϣⲁ†ⲉⲓ ⲙ̄ⲛⲱⲡ ⲟⲩⲣⲙ̄ . . ⲟ ⲛ̄ⲛⲉⲛⲙⲁ· vac . . ϭⲓ ⲁⲃⲁⲗ ⲙ̄
15 . . . ⲛⲱ ⲁⲓⲧⲉⲟⲩⲟ ⲡⲥⲉⲭⲉ ⲛⲉ 2ⲙ̄ ⲡ . . ⲉⲑ . . . . . . ⲧ . ϭⲛ̄ⲧ . . [. .]
16 . . . . ⲉⲛⲉⲓ̈ . . ϣⲁⲉⲓ ⲟⲩⲃⲉ ⲡϣⲁⲓ̈ ⲥⲙ̄ⲡ . . ⲧⲟⲩⲟⲩ . . ⲣ . . .
17 . . . . ⲙ̄ⲡⲟⲩⲕⲁⲧ . ⲉⲓ̈ ϣⲓⲛⲉ ⲛⲏⲓ̈ ⲧⲟⲛⲟⲩ ⲁ . . . .

18   vac ⲙⲛ ⲧⲁ . . ϣ︦ⲓ̣[ⲛ]ⲉ̣ . . . ⲁ̣ⲟ̣ⲩ . ϣⲁ̣ⲓ .   ἔρ(ρωσο)

To my lady sister Partheni: (from your) brother; - greetings. I greet you warmly and your children. Kame greets you ...

... came forth ... I paid 3300 talents to ... (5) from here. ... I will send it to you. I will ... And I have paid the account of 2500 to the *mna* for some good quality ... 12 *maje* ... Now, they have given them ... He (?) says: 1000 talents. Write again to me about ... the cash payments. Also, about the work on the day when you came ... (10) ... after your mother; and you tell her ... come to Hat's place and she ... If the work of the man is mixed ... and she brings it and she ... then take it. But if not, ... tell her that ... until I come. Do not reckon a ... man in our places. ... took away (15) ... I have recounted the affair to you (fem.) in the ... if ... comes against Pshai (?). ...

Greet for me warmly ... and ... Greet ... Louishai (?). Farewell.

Commentary:

10   Hat: see also **93**, 20; but probably an abbreviated name for which there are various possibilities. It is tempting to think of Tehat, a woman of importance in the local weaving business (see especially **18**).

18   If it is correct to read here the name Louishai, cf. **65**, 3 ad loc. However, it is very uncertain.

P. Kellis Copt. 96

Inv #: P 51B(a)i

Location: House 3, room 9, deposit 3 east wall.

Preservation: Three poorly preserved fragments survive from a Coptic letter written on papyrus. They can be arranged to reconstruct the remains of what is probably the lower half of the document. The original would have been well written, with regular margins and a confident script. However, the postscript on the verso would seem to have been written by a 'squarer', less fluent hand.

Content: The references to wool and 'cutting' are consistent with the general textile business that is so prevalent in the main House 3 archive. The obvious similarities in style, dialect and personal names make it highly probable that the piece should be associated with all those belonging to the principal family represented by the House 3 Coptic documents. The name Tagoshe (Greek Takysis or Tekysis) occurs a number of times in the archive. K.A. Worp identifies a Tekysis as the wife of Pamour 'I' in his stemma (P. Kellis I p. 51); but we think that that person (first part of the IVth century) is probably too early for the Coptic documents, as these are mostly to be placed two generations later (i.e. at the time of Pamour 'III'). The woman in this present letter may more likely be the same as in (for instance) **78**, a letter by Pegosh that is also concerned with wool and other similar items as found here. See further the note to l. 33 on this.

Address: No address preserved (possibly on the verso of the lost upper half of the letter).

Names: Andreas; Pine (?); Pshai (?); Tagoshe;

Text:

approximately sixteen lines lost

17 . . . [. .] . ⲁ . [. . . . .]

18 ⲧ[ⲁ]ϭⲟϣⲉ ⲧⲉ . [. . . . . . ⲥⲧⲓ]

19 ϫⲁ ⲥⲛ̄ⲧⲉ ⲛ̄ⲧ[. . . . .]

20 ⲉ[.]ⲉ ⲟⲩⲁϫⲟⲩ ⲧ[. . . . .]

21 ⲉⲧⲁⲧⲛ̣ⲛⲁⲩ ⲛ̣[. . . . .]

22 ⲧⲣⲁ̣ . . ⲧⲛ̄ⲛⲁ[ⲩ . . . . .] . [. . .]

23 . . . . [. .] . . ⲧⲉⲥ ⲙ̄ⲡⲣⲱⲙⲉ

24 . . . . [.] . . . ⲛ̣ϩⲉ . . ⲟⲩⲱ ⲧⲟⲛⲟ̣[ⲩ]

25 ⲡⲁⲧⲉ̣[.] . ⲉⲙ . . . ⲁⲡ . ⲁϥ ϣⲓ

26 ⲛⲉ ⲁⲧ[.] . . . . . ⲙ̣ⲛ̣ ⲛⲉ̣ⲥϣⲏⲣⲉ̣

27 ϣⲓ̣ⲛⲉ ⲛⲏⲓ ⲁⲡϣⲁⲓ . . . . ⲧⲟⲛⲟⲩ ⲛ̣

28 ⲛⲉϥϣⲏⲣⲉ ⲙ̣ⲛ̣ ⲧⲣⲉⲟⲩⲏ ⲧ[ⲏⲣⲥ]

29 ⲕⲁⲧⲁ ⲡ[ⲟⲩⲣⲉ]ⲛ̣ ⲱⲛϩ̄ ⲛ̣ⲧⲉⲧⲛ̣

30 [ⲟⲩⲭⲉⲓⲧⲉ ⲛ̄ⲟ]ⲩⲛⲁϭ ⲛ̄ⲟⲩⲁⲓϣ
31 [vac ⲕⲁⲧⲁ ⲛ]ⲉⲛϣⲗⲏⲗ vac
32 [vac?   . . .] . vac

v33 ϫⲓ ⲡⲙⲁⲃ ⲛ̄ⲙ̄ⲛⲁ ⲛ̄ⲥⲁⲣⲧ [. . . . .]
34   ⲛ̄ⲧⲛ̄ ⲁⲛⲇⲣⲉⲁⲥ ⲁⲓ̈ⲙⲁϩϥ ⲛ̄ⲑⲏ[ⲙⲉ . . . .]
35   ⲡⲣⲟⲥ ϣⲉ ⲛ̄ϭⲛ̄ϭⲱⲣ ⲁⲡⲙ̄ⲛⲁ ⲁ[. . . . .]
36   . . . ⲇⲉ ϫⲓ †ϭⲁⲗⲁϩⲧ ⲛ̄ⲥⲁⲩϩⲉ [. . . . .]
37   ⲧⲉ ⲛⲏⲓ̈ ⲙ̄ⲡⲓ[ⲛ]ⲉ ⲟⲩϭⲁⲗⲁϩⲧ ⲣⲱ ⲛ̄ⲧ . [. . . . .]

———

27 end: read ⟨ⲙ⟩ⲛ-

———

(r) ... Tagoshe ... two *sticharia* ... (20) ... cut them ... that you (fem.) sent ... send ... give it to the man ... greatly (25) ...

Greet (your wife?) and her children. Greet for me Pshai (?) ... warmly, ⟨and⟩ his children and all the neighbourhood by name. Live and (30) [be well] for a long time according to our prayers. [Farewell].

(v) Take the 30 *mna* of wool, [less one (?)], from Andreas. I have cleared the freight charge. [You can pay (?)] (35) up to 100 talents to the *mna* ... Take this egg pot ... for me from Pine (?). Indeed, a pot for ...

Commentary:

26   Possibly 'your wife' ⲧ[ⲉⲕ]ⲥϩⲓⲙⲉ, but very uncertain.

27   ⲡϣⲁⲓ: Very uncertain. The initial letter looks more like ⲧ-, but there seems no room to read Tapshai (ⲧ[ⲁⲡ]ϣⲁⲓ).

33   ϫⲓ ⲡⲙⲁⲃ ⲛ̄ⲙ̄ⲛⲁ ⲛ̄ⲥⲁⲣⲧ: Very similar phrasing is found in a pair of letters by Pegosh at **78**, 41-42 and especially **79**, 38; but in those instances '30' is followed by 'less one' (ϣⲁⲧⲛ̄ⲟⲩⲉ), which perhaps could be supposed to fill the lacuna at the end of the line here. The remarkable parallel does suggest that this may be another letter by that author or one of his circle (this postscript is written by a second hand).

36   †ϭⲁⲗⲁϩⲧ ⲛ̄ⲥⲁⲩϩⲉ: It is uncertain whether this is a container full of eggs, or otherwise an earthenware pot with an oval shape like an 'egg'. As regards the latter, cf. **80**, 25 ad loc.

37   It is something of a guess to read the name Pine (ⲡⲓ[ⲛ]ⲉ) here, following **73** (by Pegosh).

P. Kellis Copt. 97

Inv #: P 51B(a)ii

Location: House 3, room 9, deposit 3 east wall.

Preservation: There remains one long, thin strip of papyrus from the centre of a letter written in Coptic. It is possible to restore much of the first fifteen lines following standard formulae and the common style of these documents. The original letter would have been substantial, written in a regular and competent hand.

Content: The only surviving name is that of Piena, who is clearly present with the unknown author of the letter. For this person see the group of letters from and to Ploutogenes; and for the characteristic formula in ll. 10-13 see the note and further references at **90**, 8. The wording here is particularly close to that of Ouales at **35**, 23-26.

Address:
verso

] ἀδελφῷ   X   . . . . . [. . . . .] . . .
  [To my ...] brother X ...

Names: Piena;

Text:

1 [. . . . .]
2 [. . . . .]
3 [. . . . .]
4 [. . .] ⲭⲁⲓⲣⲉⲓⲛ· [ⲁⲑⲏ]
5 [ⲛϩⲱⲃ] ⲛⲓⲙ †ϣⲓⲛ[ⲉ ⲁ]
6 [ⲣⲱⲧⲛ] ⲧⲟⲛⲟⲩ· ⲉⲓ[ϣⲗⲏⲗ]
7 [ϩⲁ ⲡⲉ]ⲧⲛⲟⲩϫⲉⲓⲧ[ⲉ ⲛⲟⲩ]
8 [ⲛⲁϭ ⲛ̄]ⲟⲩⲁⲓϣ ⲡⲛ̣[ⲟⲩⲧⲉ]
9 [ⲉϥⲛⲁ]† ⲡⲓϩⲙⲁⲧ̣ [ⲛⲏⲓ̈ ⲉ]
10 [ⲧⲉ ⲡⲉⲓ̈] ⲡⲉ ⲡⲧⲣⲓⲛ̣[ⲉⲩ ⲁ]
11 [ⲡⲉⲧⲛ̄]ϩⲟ ⲛⲕⲉⲥⲁ̣[ⲡ ϩⲙ̄ ⲡ]
12 [ⲥⲱⲙⲁ] ⲛⲧⲉ ⲡⲁⲣⲉ̣[ϣⲉ ϫⲱⲕ]
13 [ⲁⲃⲁⲗ] ⲡⲓ̈ⲉⲛⲁ ϣ[ⲓⲛⲉ]
14 [ⲁⲣⲱ]ⲧⲛ̄ ⲧⲟⲛⲟⲩ [ϩⲁⲛ]
15 [ⲥⲱ]ⲧⲛ̄ ϭⲉ ϫⲉ [. . . . .]
16 [. . . . .]ⲉ . . ⲟ̣ . . [. . . . . .]
17 [. . . .]ϣⲧⲁ̣ⲣⲧⲣ̄ . [. . . . . .]
18 [. . . . .] . . . [. . . . . .]
19 [. . . . .] . . [. . . . . .]
20 [. . . . .] . . [. . . . . .]
21 [. . . . .]
22 [. . . . .]
23 [. . . . .]
24 [. . . . .]
25 [. . . . .]
26 [. . . .] . . . . [. . . . . . .]
27 [. . . .] . . . ϣⲓⲛ[ⲉ . . . . . .]
28 [. . . .] . . . ⲙ̣ . . [. . . . . .]
29 [. . . . .]
30 [. . . . .]
31 [. . . .] . . ⲓ̣ⲥ ⲉⲧ . [. . . . . .]

32	[. . . .]ṇc̣ . pt2 . [. . . . . .]
33	[. . . .]ω̄ . ṇ . . . [. . . . . .]
34	[. . 2a]ïte c̣ . [. . . . . . .]
35	[. . . .] . [. .] . . . [. . . . . . .]
36	[. . . . . . .] . . . [. . . . . . .]
37	[. . . . .]
38	[. . . . . . .] . †t[. . . . . .]
39	[. . . . . . .]e aïp . [. . . . . .]
40	[. . . . . . .]m̄n̄[. . . . . . .]
41	[. . . . . . .] m̄пe[. . . . . . .]
42	[. . . . . . .] . . [. . . . . . .]
43	[. . . . . . .]x̣eṇa[. . . . . . .]
44	[. . . . .]
45	[. . . . . . .] . . [. . . . . . .]
46	[. . . . . . .]nh[. . . . . . .]
47	[. . . . . to]no[y . . . . . .]
48	[. . . . . . .]ẹịt . [. . . . . .]
49	[. . . . .]
50	[. . . . .]

18-25 some papyrus extant, but hor. fibres mostly gone (same at 29-30 and 34); no papyrus extant at all at extreme upper and lower ends.

(To) ...: (from) ..., - greetings.

[Before] (5) every[thing]: I greet [you] warmly. I am [praying for] your continuing health; (and that) [God will] grant [me] this grace, (10) [which is] to enable me to [see your] face once more [in the body], and my joy will be [complete]. Piena greets you warmly.

Now, [we have] heard that ... disturb(ance) ...
remainder of the letter not translatable

Commentary:

Address   Some traces may belong to a second (lower) line of the address lying to the right of the central cross.

P. Kellis Copt. 98

Inv #: P 51B(a)iii

Location: House 3, room 9, deposit 3 east wall.

Preservation: There remains one poorly preserved papyrus fragment from the lower left hand side of a letter written in Coptic. This placing is made evident by the section of transverse text, and because the remaining traces of the main letter on the recto are consistent with the substance of its content rather than the introductory formulae and greetings. Nevertheless, the length of the lines on the recto (width of the letter) is unknown; and thus also the number of lines lost on the verso.

Content: Nothing is known of the authorship or purpose of the letter, and its interest lies in the wording on the transverse text, apparently something to do with 'good news' (ⲉⲩⲁⲅⲅⲉⲗⲓⲟⲛ). We suppose a broadly Christian or Manichaean context to this.

Address: No address survives. If it was written it would have been on the verso of the lost upper half of the letter.

Names: Nonna; Pshai (?);

Text:

(x +)1   [. . .] . ⲉⲧ[ⲃⲉ . . . .]
2   [.] . ⲥ ⲁⲃⲁⲗ [. . . . .]
3   ⲛⲥⲉⲱⲉⲡ [. . . . .]
4   ⲡⲁⲓ̈ ϫⲉ . [. . . . .]

5   ⲇⲉ ⲁⲛ . [. . . . .]
6   ⲙⲁⲗⲁ[. . . . .]
7   ⲃⲟⲩⲗ . . [. . . . .]
8   ⲇⲉ ϫ . . [. . . . .]
9   ⲛ̄ⲟⲩⲁⲛ . [. . . . ⲡⲛⲟⲩⲧⲉ]
10 ⲡⲉⲧⲣ̄ⲙ[ⲛ̄ⲧⲣⲉ . . . . . .]
11 ⲛⲗⲁ . . [. . . . .]
12 . . . . [. . . . .]
13 [. . . . .]
14 [. . . . .]
15 [. . . . .]

tr(x+)21 [. . . . .]ⲉⲩⲁⲅ`ⲅⲉⲗⲓⲟⲛ ⲟⲩⲃⲉ ⲡⲓ[. . . . .]
22 [. . . . . ⲥ]ϩⲉⲓ̈ ⲛⲏⲓ̈ ⲙ̄ⲡⲟⲩⲱ ⲛ̄ⲧ . [. . . . .]

v(x+)23 [. . . . .] . . . . [. . . . .]
24 [. . . . .] . ⲉⲣⲓⲙⲉⲣ` ⲁ . ⲁ . . . . [. . . . .]
25 [. . . . .] . . . . ⲁⲛⲟⲛⲛⲁ` ⲉⲕ . [. . . . .]
26 [. . . . .] ϣⲓⲛⲉ ⲛⲏⲓ̈ ⲧⲟⲛⲟⲩ ⲁⲧⲁ[. . . . .]
27 [. . . . .]ⲣⲟ . . . ϣⲓⲛⲉ ⲛⲏⲓ̈ ⲧⲟⲛⲟⲩ ⲁⲧ . [. . . . .]
28 [. . . . .] . . . . [. . .] ⲙ̄ⲡⲁⲥⲁⲛ ⲡϣⲁ[ⲓ̈ . . . .]
29 [

line numbers only for purpose of reference

introduction and unknown amount of text is lost

... and they give thanks (?) ... (5) ... [God] (10) bears witness ... (15) ... (20) .... (tr) ... good news against (?) ... write to me news of ... (v) ... Have a care for ... (25) ... Nonna (?) ...

Greet me warmly to my ... Greet me warmly to ... of my brother Pshai (?) ...

Commentary:

3   Possibly one can presume the common construction of ϣⲉⲡ- (ϣⲱⲡ) + ϩⲙⲁⲧ 'give thanks'.

21 One supposes that εὐαγγέλιον here has a Christian or Manichaean religious meaning, but nothing remains to give us a clue about the context. The following preposition ⲟⲩⲃⲉ could be in the sense of 'against' or 'towards' or even 'according to'.

25 The reading of the name 'Nonna' is not entirely secure; but see (for the same) **92**, 20-21 and **115**, 17-18, 30. Of course, another possibility would be to understand ἀννῶνα; but we regard that as less likely.

28 The reading of the name 'Pshai' is very uncertain.

P. Kellis Copt. 99

Inv #: P 51D

Location: House 3, room 9, deposit 3 east wall.

Preservation: This is a mostly complete letter written in Coptic on papyrus. However, the text is heavily abraded, with large sections lost or unreadable. The script is confident and practised, with well-formed letters. Dimensions are 270 x 60 mm.

Content: There is little real sense to be derived, beyond a number of characteristic phrases and formulae.

Address:
verso
    ἀπ(όδος) κυρίῳ μου [. . . . .]ι traces
    Deliver to my master ...

Names: Lamou; Pshai;

Text:
1   ⲡⲁⲓⲱⲧ ⲙ̄ⲙ[ⲉⲣⲓ]ⲧ . . . [ⲉⲧ]
2   ⲧⲉⲓⲁⲓⲧ ⲛ̄ⲧ[ⲟ]ⲧ̀ ⲧⲟ[ⲛ]ⲟⲩ
3   ⲡⲣⲉⲛ [ⲉⲧ]ⲟⲁ[ⲗ]ϭ ϩⲛ̄ [ⲣ]ⲱⲓ ⲛ̄

4   [ⲛ]ⲉⲩ ⲛⲓ[ⲙ] ⲡⲁ[ⲓ̈]ϣ[ⲧ] . . . . .
5   ⲁⲛⲁⲕ . [.] . [. ⲡⲉⲧ]ⲥ̣[ϩ]ⲉ̣ⲓ̈
6   ⲛⲉⲕ` ϩⲙ̄ ⲡϫ[ⲁⲓ̈ⲥ ⲭⲁⲓⲣ]ⲉⲓⲛ
7   ϩⲓⲑⲏ ⲛ̄[ϩ]ⲱ[ⲃ ⲛⲓⲙ] ϯϣⲓ
8   ⲛⲉ ⲁⲣⲁⲕ ⲧⲟⲛ̣[ⲟⲩ . . .]
9   ⲁ . ⲙ̣ⲛ̣ . . . . [. . . . . .]
10 ϩ̣ⲧ . ⲕ ⲁ . . . [. . . .] .
11 . . ⲁⲥⲧ . ⲧ̄ⲛ̄ⲛⲁ̣[ⲩ . . . . .] .
12 . ⲏⲛⲉ . . . [. . . . .]
13 ⲛ̣ⲉ ϣⲁⲕⲧⲣ . . . .
14 ⲥ̣ⲁⲛ ⲡϣⲁⲓ̈ † . . . . . .
15 . . ⲛ̄ . . [. . . .] . . . . .
16 ⲙ̄ⲙⲉⲣⲓⲧ` ⲛ . . . . . ⲛⲁⲩ
17 ⲱϣⲥ` ⲉⲁ[. . . .] . . . . .
18 ⲙ̣ⲏ . . ⲭⲉ . . [.]ⲉⲥ` . . .
19 ⲕ . ⲁⲉⲓ ⲁⲧ̣ . ⲉ[.] . ⲣⲁ . ⲛ̣
20 ⲧⲁ ⲁⲣⲁ̣ⲕ . [. . .] . . . ⲉ̣ ⲛ̄ .
21 ⲡⲉ ⲡⲕⲁⲧ` . . . . . . ⲉ
22 ⲉⲓ ⲁⲡ†ⲙⲉ̣ [.]ⲁ̣ . [.] ⲣ̄̄ ⲧ
23 ⲁⲛⲁⲅ`ⲕⲏ ⲁⲣⲁⲓ̈ †[ⲛⲟ]ⲩ
24 ⲁⲧⲣⲁⲥⲁ̣ⲩⲛⲉ [.] . ⲉⲛ . . . . ⲟⲩ/ ⲭⲉ̣ .
25 \ⲙⲙⲁⲛ/ . . † . . ⲛⲏⲓ̈ . . . . . .
26 . [.] . [. . . . . .] . . . ⲉ
27 . . . ⲡ̣ⲓ̣ⲕⲉⲙⲏⲧ ⲛ̄ϩⲟⲟⲩⲉ̣
28 . . . ̄ †ⲥⲁⲩ[ⲛⲉ] ⲅⲁⲣ ⲛ̄
29 [. . .] . ⲛ[. . . .]ⲛ̣ⲁⲛⲧ`
30 [. . .] . . . . [. . .] . ⲛ̄ . ⲧⲏⲥ
31 ⲙ . . . . . [. .] . . ⲟ̣ⲩ .
32 †ϣⲓⲛⲉ . . [. .] . . . ⲧⲕ
33 . . ⲩ ⲛⲏ̣ⲓ̈ . [. . .] . . [. . .]
34 . . . . [. . .]ⲁⲡ . .
35 . . . . . . [. . .]ⲏⲥ̣ ⲛ̄ⲧⲁ

36	......[...]ⲡ̣` ⲛⲉⲩ
37	ϥⲁ....[...]....
38	ⲝⲉ.....[...]ⲏ̣ï̈
39	ⲡⲧ.....[..]..ⲉ..
40	ⲁⲛ ⲉ....[..]...[..]
41	ϯϣⲟⲩ........ⲙ̣ⲉ
42	ⲣⲓⲧ` ⲙ̄ⲡ...ⲉⲧⲁ...ï̈
43	ⲁⲃⲁⲗ..[...]...[.]ⲅ̄.[.]
44	ⲡⲕⲁⲓⲣ[ⲟ]ⲥ̣ [.]........
45	ⲁ̣ⲛ̣ⲁⲕ....ⲧⲛ̣ⲛ̣ⲁⲩ
46	ⲥⲉ ⲛⲉ..[..].ⲝⲉ...
47	ⲡⲟⲩ..[...]...[..]
48	ϩⲱ[ⲧ]ⲛ̄ [.].[......]ⲉ
49	ⲙⲛ̄[.]ⲥ.....[ⲁ]ⲧⲣⲉ̣[. ⲡ̄]
50	ⲡⲕⲱⲧⲉ.[...]ⲛ̣ⲟⲩ ⲁ̣ⲛ̣
51	ϩⲱⲃ ⲉ̣..[...].......
52	ⲉⲛⲏ̣.[......].[..]...
53	ⲧⲉ ⲛ̣[.].[....].ⲁⲉ̣[..]
tr54	ⲙ̄ⲡⲣ̄ϭⲱ ϭⲉ ⲉⲙ̄ⲡⲕ̄ϩⲃ ⲡⲁⲥⲁⲛ ⲗⲁⲙⲟⲩ ⲛⲏï̈ ⲛ̄[.].ⲥ̣....vac [.....]ⲝ̣ ⲉⲧⲝ̣.......

---

24 Both in-line and above-line text utterly unclear, but the insertion in 24 may be connected to that of ⲙ̄ⲙⲁⲛ in 25 (and ⲝⲉ go with ⲥⲁⲩⲛⲉ)   35-39 line beginnings: assuming that the left hand margin is not quite straight; otherwise each preceded by [.]

(To) my loved father ..., who is greatly honoured by me; the sweet name in my mouth at all times, my father ... (5) (It is) I, ..., who writes to you in the Lord, - greetings.

Before everything: I greet you warmly ... (10) ... brother Pshai. I ... (15) ... beloved ... (20) ... come to the village ... do the necessity for me now so that I may know ... (25) ... even these ten days ... For I know ... merciful. (30) ... I greet (?) ... (35) ... (40) ... beloved ... come forth (?) ... the season ... (45) ... send them to ... so that [you / he may make] (50) the trip ...

(v) Now, do not remain without you sending my brother Lamou to me ...

Commentary:

Address   The traces are faint and uncertain.

19-20 Although the traces are not encouraging, it is perhaps not impossible to read ⲡⲁⲡⲁⲛⲧⲁ ⲁⲣⲁⲕ '(and) meet you' after 'to come to ..'. Also, ⲡⲕⲁⲧ' (l. 21) might mean 'the voyage', 'the visit'.

54   Lamou: This is probably an abbreviation for the name '(Phi)lammon', see the note at **66**, 42.

P. Kellis Copt. 100

Inv #: P 51D(b)i

Location: House 3, room 9, deposit 3 east wall.

Preservation: This is a small fragment of papyrus with Coptic text on both sides. The script is well formed and rather similar to that of **31**, although this piece can not belong there. If one uses that other document as a model, one can suppose that the side with ⲧⲛⲟⲩ is the verso[17] (cf. l. '5'), and that this is the final word written at the end of a long penultimate line of the postscript; which must itself finish part-way along line '6' (since it is followed by papyrus devoid of script). In this case, line '1' must be the line immediately below the centre fold of the letter (presuming it is such) on the recto. Consequently, the entire upper half is lost.

Content: Nothing can be said about the content. We presume that this is the scant remains of a well-executed letter similar to **31**.

Address: None preserved.

---

[17] If this is correct, the photographs are wrongly designated as (r) and (v).

Names: None.

Text:

```
(x+)1     . . . . . ⲧⲛ̄ⲛ]ⲁ̣ⲩⲥ ⲕⲁⲧⲁ ⲡ[ . . . . .
2         . . . . . . . ⲡ]ⲱ̣ⲱ̣ ⲛ̄ϩⲏⲧ` ⲁ[ . . . . .
3         . . . . . . . . ⲉⲧ]ⲙ̄ⲙⲟ ⲕⲁⲛ ⲉⲛ̣[ . . . .

v(x+)4    [ . . . . . . . . . . . . . . . . . . . . . . . . . . . . . . ] .
5         [ . . . . . . . . . . . . . . . . . . . . . . . . . ]ⲁ̣ ϯⲛⲟⲩ
6         [ . . . . . . . . . . . . . ]
```

(r) ... send it (?) according to the ... heartbreak ... that [place (?)], even though we ... (5) ... now ...

(v) ... (5) ... Now, ...

Commentary:

1-3   It is impossible to situate the text with reference to the margins, or to know how long were the lines, before or after what has been preserved.

P. Kellis Copt. 101

Inv #: P 51D(b)ii

Location: House 3, room 9, deposit 3 east wall.

Preservation: A single small fragment of papyrus. Parts of the lower three lines of Coptic text from the document are preserved. It is presumed to be the remnant of a letter, given the predominance of such amongst the archive, and because there is no obvious 'literary' quality.

Content: Report of comments made by a woman.

Address: None preserved.

Names: None.

Text:

(x+)1 . . . .] . . . . [. . . . . . .

2 . . . . . . ⲡ]ⲁϫⲉⲥ ϫⲉ ⲉϣ[ⲱⲡⲉ . . . .

3 . . . . . ⲡ]ⲁϫⲉⲥ ϫⲉ ⲉⲕⲧⲙ̄[. . . . . . .

... she says: "If ...". She says: "If you (masc.) do not ...". ...

Commentary:

1-3   It is impossible to situate the text with reference to the side margins, or to know how long were the lines, before or after what has been preserved.

P. Kellis Copt. 102

Inv #: P 52Ci

Location: House 3, room 9, deposit 3.

Preservation: This a virtually complete short letter or note, 100 x 40 mm., written in Coptic on papyrus. It is now breaking along the vertical folds. Indeed, the left hand strip has separated, and a few letters have been lost where the papyrus has worn away along the break. The hand is very clear and competent. The papyrus has been cleaned and reused, with traces of the previous text still visible.

Content: This document differs from the typical letters found so abundantly in House 3. Although it includes some greetings and the barest elements of epistolary formulae and conventional style, it is really a note about one specific matter. Apparently Pamoun has failed in his duty to pass on some message or suchlike, and has now gone missing. Psais writes to Partheni to explain this, and to ask whether he has turned up at her place. From this scenario, one may presume that the document was written close by to Kellis and within the Oasis. The names Partheni and Chares (i.e. Charis) are common in the archive, see e.g. **71**. We have tentatively identified these women as the wives of Pegosh and Philammon, matriarchs in the larger family group and resident in Kellis whilst their menfolk are away. Thus Psais writes to Partheni in this piece.

Address:

verso

   ἀπ(όδος) Παρθενι   X   Ψάϊς

   Deliver to Partheni. X (From) Psais.

Names: Chares; Pamoun; Partheni; Psais;

Text:

1	ϯϣⲓⲛⲉ ⲁⲣⲱⲧⲛ̄ ⲧⲟⲛⲟⲩ·
2	ⲛⲓⲕⲟⲩⲓ̈ ϣⲓⲛⲉ ⲁⲣⲱⲧⲛ̄
3	ⲧⲟⲛⲟⲩ· ⲛ̄ⲧⲁⲣⲉ ⲡⲁⲙⲟⲩⲛ ϭⲉ
4	ⲉⲓ ϣⲁⲣⲁⲓ̈· ⲁϥⲧⲉⲟⲩⲉ ⲡⲥⲉϫⲉ
5	ⲛⲏⲓ̈ ⲉⲧϩⲁϩⲁⲃϥ̄ ⲙ̄ⲙⲁϥ· ⲙ̄ⲡϥ̄
6	ⲣ̄⟨ⲗ⟩ⲁⲩⲉ ⲛ̄ϩⲱⲃ· ⲛ̄ⲥⲁ ϩⲓ ⲣⲟⲩϩⲉ
7	ⲙ̄ⲡ[ϩ]ⲟⲟⲩ ⲉⲧⲙ̄ⲙⲉⲩ· ⲉⲧⲁϥⲉⲓ ⲁϥ
8	ϫⲟⲥ ⲛⲏⲓ̈ ⲡⲁϩⲉⲓ ϫⲉ ⲟⲩⲱ ⲛⲓⲙ
9	ⲙⲁ[ⲣ]ⲓⲛⲟ ⲁⲣⲁⲕ· ⲛ̄ⲣⲉⲥⲧⲉ· ⲁϥ
10	ⲃⲱⲕ· ⲙ̄ⲡⲓϣⲁϭⲉϥ· ⲙ̄ⲡⲓ̈ⲁⲣϩϥ̄·
11	ⲕⲁϭⲛ̄ⲧⲥ̄ ⲁⲓ̈ϫⲁⲩ ⲛ̄ⲉⲙⲏⲧ` ⲛ̄ⲥⲁⲡ
12	ⲉⲓ̈ⲕⲱⲧⲉ ⲛ̄ⲥⲱϥ· ⲙ̄ⲡⲟⲩϭⲛ̄ⲧϥ̄·
13	ⲙⲛ̄ϩⲱⲃ ⲛ̄ⲧⲟⲧϥ̄· ⲛ̄ⲛⲁⲣⲉ ⲙⲛ̄ ⲡⲥⲉ
14	ϫⲉ ⲣⲱ ⲛ̄ⲧⲟⲧϥ̄· ⲭⲛ̄ ⲙ̄ⲡⲓⲟⲩⲉ ⲥⲁⲡ·
15	ϣⲓⲛⲉ ϩⲁⲧⲏ ⲛ̄ⲧⲉⲛⲟ· ϫⲉ ⲟⲩⲛ̄
16	ⲣⲱⲙⲉ ϣⲓⲛⲉ ⲛ̄ⲥⲉⲟⲩⲁⲛ ⲛ̄
17	ⲑⲉ [ⲉ]ⲧⲙ̄ⲙⲉⲩ· ⲉϣⲱⲡⲉ ⲁⲥⲉ

18	ⲧⲉ[ⲥ]ϩⲉⲓ ⲛⲏⲓ ⲙ̄ⲡⲟⲩⲱ ⲧⲉⲭⲩ·
19	ϣ[ⲓⲛ]ⲉ ⲁⲛⲓⲛ̄ⲗⲁⲩⲉ ⲉⲩⲥⲁⲡ ⲕⲁ
20	ⲧⲁ [ⲛⲟ]ⲩⲣⲉⲛ ⲙⲁⲗⲓⲥⲧⲁ ⲧⲙⲟ ⲭⲁ
21	ⲣⲏ[ⲥ] ⲙⲛ̄ ⲛⲉⲥⲱ[ⲛ]ⲉ ἔρρ(ωσο)
tr22	ϩⲁⲡⲗⲱⲥ ⲥϩⲉⲓ ⲛⲏⲓ ⲙ̄ⲡⲟⲩⲱ ϩⲟⲥⲟⲛ ϯ ⲛ̄ⲛⲓⲙⲁ· ϫⲉ
23	ⲉⲓϣϫⲉ ⲥⲉ· ⲛ̄ⲓⲉ ϯⲧⲣⲉ ⲡⲣⲱⲙⲉ ϯ ⲡϩⲛⲟ· ⲧⲁⲛ̄ⲧϥ̄ ⲉⲓ̈ⲛ̄ⲏⲩ
v24	ⲉϣⲱⲡⲉ ⲁⲛ ⲙ̄ⲙⲁⲛ· ⲛ̄ⲓⲉ ϯⲕⲁⲑⲏ ⲁⲃⲁⲗ

---

6 p̄⟨ⲗ⟩ⲁⲩⲉ: perhaps p̄ⲁ[ⲗ]ⲩⲉ (sic)   24 There is ink (?) of unknown significance above ⲕⲁⲑⲏ

I greet you (pl.) warmly. The little ones greet you warmly.

Now, when Pamoun came to me, he recounted to me the message (5) you (fem.) had sent to him. He did nothing (about it); except in the evening of that day, when he came and told me. I said: "Any news? Let me see you tomorrow". He (10) went. I did not strike him. I did not see him. You will find (that) I sent about ten times, searching for him. He was not to be found. There is nothing from him. Indeed, there has been no word from him since this one time. (15) Search at your place, and see whether there is anyone. Seek after someone like that. If yes, you write to me the news quickly.

Greet the children, altogether (and) by (20) their name; especially mother Chares and your sisters. Farewell.

(tr) Just write me the news whilst I am here, for if (it is) yes then I can make the man pay (his) debt; and I can bring it when I come. (v) And if not, then I am stuck!

Commentary:

3   The name Pamoun is also found at **45**, 1.

4   ⲡⲥⲉϫⲉ: lit. 'the word' or perhaps 'lesson' or 'matter'. We have translated it as 'message'.

5   ϩⲁϩⲁⲃϥ̄ ⲙ̄ⲙⲁϥ: 'you had sent to him'; perhaps the meaning is that Pamoun has been asked to pass the message on to Psais (thus 'sent via him')?

8   'Any news?': Alternatively, ⲟⲩⲱ ⲛⲓⲙ may be an adverbial in anteposition. Thus: 'Whatever the news (= in any event?), let me ..'.

10   ⲙ̄ⲡⲓⲁⲣϩϥ̄: 'I did not see him'; probably Psais means that he did not see him again (i.e. Pamoun did not return in the morning as promised).

11   ⲕⲁϭⲛ̄ⲧⲥ̄: The 2nd masc., being neither the 2nd plural found here nor the 2nd fem. of the addressee, is really the 'general' person so often found in expressions with ϭⲓⲛⲉ. Its purpose is to assert the veracity of the following statement and might be translated more freely, e.g. 'Truly, I sent ..'.

13   ⲙⲛ̄[ϩ]ⲱⲃ ⲛ̄ⲧⲟⲧϥ: 'There is nothing from him'; perhaps 'there is no message from him'?

13   ⲛ̄ⲛⲁⲣⲉ: We do not understand this. One can speculate about a scribal error. Psais might have meant something like: 'Believe me'.

21   ⲛⲉⲥⲱ[ⲛ]ⲉ: 'your sisters' or ⲛⲉ‹ⲥ›ⲥⲱ[ⲛ]ⲉ 'her sisters'? If the former, it would provide an important indication of the relationship between Partheni and the other senior women. However, one should not suppose that they were necessarily biological siblings.

23   † ⲡϩⲛⲟ: lit. 'give the thing'. We suppose the meaning here to be abstract and have interpreted it as 'pay (his) debt' in the translation.

P. Kellis Copt. 103

Inv #: P 56B + P 56C/E

Location: House 3, room 9, deposit 3 west doorway.

Preservation: A mostly complete and substantial letter written in Coptic on papyrus. The dimensions are 260 x 70 mm. It is beginning to break along the vertical folds, and the section down the lower right hand side of the document has been lost, (and an upper right hand strip has detached). The hand is exceptionally clear to read. It has been professionally written, utilises some punctuation, and has preserved narrow but regular margins.

Content: An unnamed brother writes to Pegosh. Since he greets his father first, together with 'our brother' (l. 2), it seems probable that they are real siblings. The most obvious identification of the author would thus be Pamour, and the unnamed father as Psais 'II' following K.A. Worp's stemma. The 'Lo' of l. 38 would then be the brothers' mother Tapollos, and the 'Pshai' of l. 31 another brother (named after their father). One can compare, e.g., **64** for the same persons. If all of this is correct, the piece should certainly be read together with the earlier letters by the two brothers (**64-79**). However, we have been somewhat cautious and not placed this piece with those, partly because the author is not named, and partly because the letter lacks Pamour's usual many greetings and the regular postscript by his wife Maria.

The letter contains valuable information about the textile business, both the cutting of garments and about dye. The completeness of the document, its many details and the relative ease of reading, make it an important addition to the archive. It is also notable for the business-like style and general absence of those formulaic and conventional elements that take up such a great proportion of the majority of the letters from House 3.

Address:

verso

  κυρίωι μου ἀδελφῶι X πεϭωϣ ὁ ἀδελφός

  To my master brother X Pegosh. (From your) brother.

Names: Lo; Masour; Pegosh; Pshai;

Text:

1 κυρίωι μου πατρὶ ὁ υἱὸς χαίρειν
2 ϯϣⲓⲛⲉ ⲁⲣⲁⲕ ⲧⲟⲛⲟⲩ ⲙⲛ̄ ⲡⲛ̄ⲥⲁⲛ
3 ⲉⲧϩⲁⲧⲏⲕ· ⲁⲩⲱ ϯⲣ̄ϣⲡⲏⲣⲉ ϫⲉ
4 ⲙ̄ⲡⲉⲧⲛ̄ⲡⲱⲗϭ ⲁⲃⲁⲗ ⲁⲉⲓ ϣⲁⲣⲁⲛ
5 ϯϣⲓⲛⲉ ⲁⲡⲁⲥⲁⲛ ⲡⲉϭ[ⲱ]ϣ ⲙⲛ̄
6 ⲛⲉϥϣⲏⲣⲉ· ⲛ̄ⲧⲁⲕ ⲇⲉ [ⲁⲛ] ⲡⲁ

7 ⲥⲁⲛ ⲡⲉϭⲱϣ· ⲙ̅ⲙⲉ ϫⲉ ϩⲁⲩⲛ̅
8 ⲧⲕⲉⲙ̅ⲛⲁ ⲛ̅ϫⲏϭⲉ ⲛ̅ⲥⲧⲏⲙ
9 ⲛⲏⲓ̈ ⲛ̅ⲁⲛⲁⲅⲕⲁⲓⲟⲛ ⲉⲛⲁⲛⲟⲩϥ
10 ⲧⲟⲛⲟⲩ· ⲉⲣⲉⲙ̅ⲡⲓⲧ̅ⲛⲁⲩⲥ †
11 ⲛⲟⲩ ϫⲉ ⲛ̅ⲧⲁⲓ̈ⲕⲁⲥ ⲁϩⲉⲥⲧ̅ⲥ̅ ⲛ̅ⲛⲓ
12 ⲙⲁ· ϫⲉ ⲛ̅ⲛⲉⲕϭⲁⲩϣⲕ` ⲁϣⲓ
13 ⲛⲉ ⲛ̅ⲥⲁ ⲟⲩⲁⲛ ϩⲁⲧⲏⲕ· ⲙⲏⲡⲱⲥ
14 ⲕⲛⲁϭⲓⲛⲉ ⲉⲛ ⲉⲛⲁⲛⲟⲩϥ· ⲛ̅ⲑⲉ ⲙ̅
15 ⲡⲉⲓ̈ ⲁⲩⲱ ⲉⲡⲓⲇⲏ ⲁⲓ̈ϫⲟⲥ ⲛⲉⲕ
16 ϫⲉ ϥⲓⲧ̅ⲥ̅ ⲙ̅ⲡⲉⲧⲟⲩⲏϩ· ⲕⲟⲩⲁϫⲉ
17 ⲛ̅ϣⲁⲧ· ϣⲁⲧⲟⲩⲛ̅ⲧⲥ̅· ⲧⲛ̅ⲟⲩⲁϩⲥ̅
18 ⲁⲡⲥ̅ⲙⲁ· ϩⲁⲣⲏϩ· ⲙ̅ⲡⲣ̅ϫⲱϩ
19 ⲁⲟⲩⲁⲛ· ϣⲁⲧⲟⲩ[[ⲛ̅]]ϩⲉⲥⲧⲉⲓ̈ ⲧⲁ
20 ⲧⲛ̅ⲛⲁⲩⲥ ⲛⲉⲕ· ⲕⲟⲩⲁϫⲟⲩ ⲛⲏⲓ̈
21 ⲛ̅ⲧⲕϭⲓϫ· ⲉϣⲱⲡⲉ ϭⲉ ⲉⲕ
22 ⲛⲁϣⲧⲁ ⲛ̅ⲛⲉⲕⲁ ⲙⲏⲧ ⲙ̅
23 ⲙⲁⲥⲟⲩⲣ· ⲁⲡⲗⲁⲥⲓⲛ· ⲧⲁⲣⲉ[ϥ]
24 ⲧⲉϥ ⲛ̅ϫⲏϭⲉ· ⲧⲕⲥⲡⲟⲩ[ⲇⲏ]
25 ϩⲱⲕ ⲧⲉ ⲧⲉⲓ̈ ⲙⲛ̅ ⲧⲕⲙ̅[. . . .]
26 ⲉⲧⲕⲛⲁⲟⲩⲁⲛϩ̅ ⲁⲃⲁⲗ ⲁ̣[. . . .]
27 ⲣⲁ . . ⲙⲟⲛⲟⲛ ⲙ̅ⲡⲣ̅ⲧⲱϣ [ⲁⲧⲣⲟⲩ]
28 ⲧⲉⲗⲁⲩ ϣⲁ†ⲧⲣⲟⲩϩⲉⲥⲧ̅ⲥ̅ [ⲧⲁⲧ]
29 ⲛ̅ⲛⲁⲩⲥ ⲛⲉⲕ· ⲕⲟⲩⲁ[ϫⲉⲥ]
30 ⲛⲏⲓ̈ ⲛ̅ⲧⲕϭⲓϫ· ⲛ̅ⲧⲁⲕ ϩ̣[ⲱⲕ ⲡⲁ]
31 ⲥⲁⲛ ⲡϣⲁⲓ̈ ⲙ̅ⲙⲉ ϫⲉ [. . . .]
32 ⲁⲛⲁⲕ ⲡⲉⲧⲛⲁⲡⲱϭ [ⲙⲛ̅]
33 ⲛⲉⲛⲉⲣⲏⲩ ⲡⲁⲣⲁ ⲙⲉⲣ[ⲟⲥ ⲛ̅]
34 ⲧⲉ ⲡⲥⲉϫⲉ ⲛ̅ⲧⲕⲉⲙⲛ[ⲁ ⲛ̅]
35 ϫⲏϭⲉ ⲟⲩⲱ· ϫⲉ ⲁⲛⲁⲣ[ⲱⲙⲉ]
36 ⲧⲁϩ[. .]ⲧⲁⲩⲥ· ϣⲁⲧⲛ̅ⲣ̅[ⲁⲡⲁⲛ]
37 ⲧⲁ ⲁⲛⲉⲛⲉⲣⲏⲩ· ⲧⲛ̅ⲙⲙ[ⲉ ⲧⲛ̅ⲣ̅]
38 ⲡⲛ̅ϣⲡ· ⲁⲣⲓⲙⲉⲣ` ⲁⲗⲟ [. . . .]

39 ⲡϩⲁⲙ ⲧⲁⲭⲁ ϥⲥⲙⲛ̄ [ⲟⲩⲕⲟⲗ]
40 ⲗⲁⲣⲓⲟⲛ ⲛⲏⲓ̈ ⲧⲁⲙⲁϥ [ⲁⲣⲁϥ]
41 †ⲛⲁⲩⲁⲥⲙⲁϩϥ̄ ⲛ̄ⲥⲟⲩⲛ̄ⲧ[ϥ̄ . . .]
42 ⲙⲛ̄ⲧⲣⲉϥⲥⲛⲉⲧ· ϥⲧⲙⲛ̄[. . . ϥ]
43 ⲥⲙⲛ̄ⲧϥ̄ ϩⲁⲣⲏϩ ⲟⲩⲛ ⲱ[. . ⲡⲁ]
44 ⲥⲁⲛ ⲡⲉϭⲱϣ· ⲙ̄ⲡⲣ̄ⲧⲱϣ [. . . .]
45 ⲁϥⲓ ⲭⲏϭⲉ ⲛ̄ⲧⲉⲕ ⲁ† ⲁⲛϣ[. . . .]
46 ϫⲉ †ⲟⲩⲁϣϥ̄ ⲉⲛ· ⲟⲩⲧⲉ . [. . . .]
47 ⲛⲁⲛⲩⲁⲥⲟⲩϥ ⲉⲛ ⲛ̄ⲑⲉ ⲙ̄ⲡ[ⲉⲓ̈ ⲉ]
48 ⲧⲁⲩ[[ⲉⲓ]]ⲩⲁⲥⲛ̄ⲧϥ̄ ⲛⲏⲓ̈ ⲕⲏ[ⲡ]
49 ϩⲱⲕ ⲛ̄ⲛⲉⲩ ⲁⲣⲁϥ ἐρ[ρῶ]
50   σθαί \σε/ εὔχομαι πολλο[ῖς]
51   χρόνοις κύριε πάτερ

———

8 ⲥⲧⲏ̣ⲙ: -ⲏ- ex corr.   22 ⲛ̄ⲛⲉⲕⲁ: i.e. ⲛ̄ⲛⲉⲕⲕⲁ   26 ⲉ̣ⲧⲕⲛⲁⲟⲩⲁⲛϩⲥ: -ⲧ- ex corr.   47 ⲛ̄ⲑⲉ: ⲛ- ex corr.

———

To my master father; (from your) son, - greetings.

I greet you warmly, and our brother who is with you; yet I am astonished that you (pl.) did not decide to come to us. (5) I greet my brother Pegosh and his children. And you, my brother Pegosh: Know that they have brought me the necessary other *mna* of dye (made from) antimony, which is excellent quality. (10) I did not send it now because I have put it (aside) to be spun here, so that you would not be troubled to search for something at your place; you will never find (stuff) as good as (15) this. Now, as (to what) I told you (earlier): "Take it from what is available and cut the cushions so that they may bring it and we can put it in its place" - be sure not to touch a thing until this has been spun (here) and I (20) send it to you and you cut them for me by your own hand.

Now, if you are in need, do not allow ten to Masour for the rough cloth and (instead) make him give it for dye. This is your own haste (25) and your ... which you will display ... Just do not appoint them to set up (the loom) until I get it spun and sent to you; and you cut it (30) for me by your own hand.

For your part, you, my brother Pshai: Know that ... I am the one who will settle (things) among ourselves, and the matter of the other *mna* of (35) dye will disappear, for my people (?) ... have bought it, - until we meet with one another and know (more precisely) and do our accounts. Take care of Lo ... the craftsman: Perhaps he (can) repair a (40) *collarium* for me? Instruct him about it. I will pay its cost ... Do not let him pass by without ... -ing [and] repairing it.

Now, be careful: ... my brother Pegosh. Do not appoint ... (45) to carry the dye for you (or) to give ..., because I do not want it and ... is not as good as the one that they brought to me. You ought to see it yourself!

(50) I pray for your health for many years, master father.

Commentary:

Address   Note that the Coptic form of the name 'Pegosh' is written within the Greek address (rather than Pekysis).

1   The author starts by greeting his father as a matter of respect (similarly in the closing formula at l. 51); but the letter is really written to his brother Pegosh, whom he starts to address from l. 5.

4   ⲡⲱⲗϭ ⲁⲃⲁⲗ: lit. 'reach conclusion' or 'settle'; here translated somewhat loosely.

8   ϫⲏϭⲉ ⲛ̄ⲥⲧⲏⲙ: 'antimony-dye'; perhaps a dark blue-black like kohl (which is made of powdered antimony sulphide).

8-11   Given that the author has put it aside to be spun, we wonder if the author actually means a *mna* of dyed wool (but has failed to include the word ⲥⲁⲣⲧ whether by error or because he thought it unnecessary).

12   '.. be troubled': ϭⲁⲩϣⲕ appears to be a suffix form of an infinitive not hitherto attested as such, *ϭⲱⲟⲩϣ. It may or may not be identical with the transitive verb ϭⲱⲟⲩϭ 'bend', 'twist' (CD 836ab). A reflexive expression such as 'bend oneself' may stand for 'make extraordinary efforts (to ..)'.

23   The name 'Masour' is not otherwise attested in the archive, but ⲙⲁⲥⲟⲩⲁⲣ is listed in Hasitzka's *Namen* (and a Μασυρᾶς at http://www.trismegistos.org/nam).

34-35   Is this the same *mna* of dye or dyed wool that the author has been discussing with Pegosh (l. 8)? If so, it would seem that one brother is responsible for the weaving and the other for the financial accounts, presuming that that is what the author is now organising with Pshai.

38-40 Perhaps this should be translated less literally, something like: 'Give a gentle reminder to Lo about the tailor - perhaps he has repaired my *collarium*?'. The tense for the verb ϥⲥⲙⲛ̄ could be past (<ⲁ>ϥⲥⲙⲛ̄), i.e. 'he has repaired'. Of course, the translation 'tailor' supposes that the *collarium* is a fabric collar or neckband of some sort.

P. Kellis Copt. 104

Inv #: P 56C(a)iii

Location: House 3, room 9, deposit 3 west doorway.

Preservation: A single small strip of papyrus with well-preserved and written Coptic text. It is presumed to be from a letter; but there can be no certainty about that, nor is there any indication (such as margins) about where the fragment should be placed within a document. The script is fluent and professional.

Content: Perhaps from the 'business' content of a letter.

Address: There is nothing visible on the verso.

Names: None preserved.

Text:

(x +)1 . . . .] . [. .]ⲡ[. . . . .
2   . . . . .]ẋⲁⲩⲥⲉ· ⲙ̄ⲡⲣ̄ẋⲁⲩⲥⲉ ⲇẹ [. . . . .
3   . . . ẋⲁ]ⲩⲥⲉ ⲁⲛ ⲥⲉⲕⲁⲩ ⲛ̄ϩⲟ ·̇· [. . . . .

... send them. However, do not send them ... send (?) them again and they will be placed on sight (?) ...

Commentary:

3   ⲛ̄ϩⲟ: This looks like an adverbial use of ϩⲟ, cf. CD 647a.

P. Kellis Copt. 105

Inv #: P 56Ci (ex P56C + P57B + P51B + P51D)

Location: House 3, room 9, deposit 3 west and north doorway.

Preservation: Nineteen fragments of a papyrus letter, written in Coptic with a very small script, have been joined or placed in position. Two further fragments probably belong, but can not be placed. It is calculated from the centre crease that the original document must have been approximately 274 x 75 mm. It has broken along the vertical folds and now a number of sections are lost. However, there remains substantial text from this remarkable letter.

Content: Pshai writes to Andreas. Most of the persons named in the letter are familiar and belong to the main family group resident at House 3 or working in Egypt. The comments about wanting to come to the Oasis (thus l. 44) indicate that this is one of the documents written from the valley, and indeed there are references to 'Egyptians' at ll. 67-68. A matter of especial interest is that this is the only Coptic piece to mention an Eirene, other than the striking Manichaean letter **32**. The letter contains a number of intriguing and unique features, discussed in the commentary; and ends with high emotion: 'I have written this letter, my tears flowing over it'. It is a personal and deeply-felt piece, where Pshai is evidently in distress.

Address:

verso

κυρίῳ μου ἀδε[λφῷ] X ᾿Αγδρέᾳ Ψάϊς ὁ ἀδελφός

σου

To my master brother X Andreas. (From) your brother Psais.

Names: Andreas; Charis; Eirene; Hor; Iena; Piena; Pine (?); Pshai (x 2);

Text:

1 [ⲛⲁϫⲁⲓⲥ] ⲛⲁⲥⲛⲏⲟⲩ ⲉⲧⲁⲓⲁⲓ̣[ⲧ]
2 [ⲧⲟⲛⲟ]ⲩ ϩⲛ̄ ⲧⲁ[ϯ]ⲩⲭⲏ ⲙⲛ̄ ⲡⲁⲡ[ⲛ̄ⲁ]
3 [. . . . .]· ⲛⲉⲧⲉⲣⲉ̣ ⲡⲟⲩⲣⲉⲛ ϩⲁⲗϭ
4 [ϩⲛ̄ ⲣⲱⲓ̈ ⲛ̄]ⲛⲉⲩ ⲛⲓⲙ ⲁⲛⲇⲣⲉⲁⲥ ⲙⲛ̄
5 [. . . . .] . \ⲙⲛ̄ ⲡⲓⲛⲉ̣/ ⲁⲛⲁⲕ` ⲡⲉⲧⲛ̄ⲥⲁⲛ ⲡϣⲁⲓ̈
6 [ⲡⲉⲧⲥϩⲉ]ⲓ̈ ⲛⲏⲧⲛ ϩⲙ̄ ⲡⲭⲁⲓ̈ⲥ ⲭⲁⲓⲣⲉⲓⲛ̣
7 [ϩⲁⲑⲏ ⲛ̄ϩ]ⲱⲃ ⲛⲓⲙ ϯϣⲓⲛⲉ ⲁⲣⲱⲧⲛ̄
8 [ⲧⲟⲛⲟⲩ ⲉⲓ̈]ϣⲗⲏⲗ ϩⲁ ⲡⲉⲧⲛ̄ⲟⲩϫⲉⲓ̈ⲧⲉ̣
9 [ⲡⲉⲓ̈ ⲉⲧⲛ̄]ⲧⲟⲧ ⲡⲁⲣⲁ ϩⲱⲃ ⲛⲓⲙ
10 [ⲡⲓⲉⲛⲁ ⲙ]ⲛ̄ ϩⲱⲣ ϣⲓⲛⲉ ⲁⲣⲱⲧⲛ̄
11 [. . . . . ⲛⲟ]ⲩϣ[ⲏⲣ]ⲉ ⲉⲧⲣⲁ̣[ⲩⲧ . . .]
12 [. . . . .] . . . . . [. . . . .]
13 [. . . . .] . . . . . [. . . . .]
14 [. . . . .]ⲩⲁⲙⲁϩⲧⲉ ⲙ̄ⲙⲁϥ vac
15 [. . . . . . .] . . ϯⲛⲟⲩ ϭⲉ ⲙ̄ⲡⲣ̄ϭⲛ̄ ⲁⲣⲓⲕⲉ ⲁ
16 [ⲣⲁⲓ̈ ϫⲉ] ⲙ̄ⲡⲓⲧⲛ̄ⲛⲁⲩ ⲟⲩⲗⲁⲟⲩⲉ ⲛⲏⲧⲛ̄
17 [ϫⲉ ⲙ̄ⲡⲓ]ϣⲥⲛ̄ ⲡⲙⲁ ⲁⲃⲁⲗ ⲁϣⲉ ⲁ
18 [. . . . .]ϣⲧⲏⲛ ⲉⲧⲃⲉ ⲡⲓϩⲱⲃ· ⲁⲩϩⲁ
19 [ⲃⲧ̄ (ⲛ̄)ⲟⲩⲏ]ⲣ ⲛ̄ⲥⲁⲡ ⲭⲛ̄ⲛ̄ ⲁⲓ̣ϩⲱⲧⲡ· ⲟⲩ
20 [ⲧⲉ ⲙⲛ̄ϯ] ⲧϭⲣⲏϭⲉ· ⲙ̄ⲡⲓϣⲥⲛ̄ ⲡⲙⲁ ⲁⲃⲁⲗ
21 [. . . . .] . ⲉ ⲙ̄ⲡⲙⲁ ⲛⲁϩⲣⲁⲕ` ⲡⲛⲟⲩⲧⲉ
22 [ⲡⲉⲧⲣ̄ⲙ̄]ⲛ̄ⲧⲣⲉ ⲁϫⲱⲓ̈ ϫⲉ ⲟⲩⲛ̄ ⲟⲩⲛⲁϭ
23 [ⲛ̄ⲗⲩⲡⲏ] ⲛ̣̄ⲙ̄ⲙⲏⲓ̈ ⲙⲛ̄ ⲟⲩⲛⲁϭ ⲙ̄ⲡⲱϣ
24 [ⲛ̄ϩⲏⲧ·] ϫⲉ ⲙ̄ⲡⲉ ⲗⲁⲩⲉ ϫⲓ ⲛ̄ⲧⲟⲧ` ⲁⲧⲛ̄
25 [ⲛⲁⲩ ⲛ]ⲏ̣ⲧⲛ̄ ⲁⲓ̈ϩⲓⲥⲉ ⲉⲓ̈ⲕⲱⲧⲉ ⲙⲛ̄ ⲛⲁ
26 [ⲥⲛⲏⲟⲩ] ⲁⲟⲩⲁϩⲟⲩ ⲛ̄ⲉ̣ⲟⲩⲱ· ⲧⲁⲭⲁ ϯϭⲛ̄
27 [ϩⲟⲗⲟⲕ]ⲟⲧⲓ ⲛ̄ ϩⲛ̄ϩⲁⲙⲧ̄· ⲡϣⲉⲩ ⲛ̄ϯⲟⲩ
28 [ⲙ̄ⲙ̄ⲛⲁ] ⲛ̄ⲥⲁⲣⲧ` ⲙ̄ⲙⲉⲧⲉ· ⲙ̄ⲡⲉ ⲣⲱⲙⲉ

29 [ⲉⲓ ⲁⲧⲉ]ⲓ̈ⲧⲟⲩ ⲡⲟ[ⲩ]ⲉ ⲡⲟⲩⲉ ⲡⲁϫⲉⲩ ϫⲉ
30 [ⲧⲛ̅ϣⲟⲡ] ⲟⲩⲛ ϩⲛ̅ ⲟⲩⲥⲕⲁⲙⲙⲁ· ⲁⲛⲟⲩⲱ
31 [ⲉⲛϯ ⲙ̅]ⲙⲁⲩ ⲛ̅ⲛⲉⲧⲁϩⲱⲛ̅ⲧⲛ̅ ϩⲱⲛ
32 [ⲁⲣⲁⲩ ⲙ̅]ⲡⲓϭⲛ̅ ⲡⲕⲉⲓ̈ⲱⲧ` ⲡϣⲁⲓ̈ ⲉϥⲁϩⲉ
33 [. . . . .]ⲓ̈ⲧ` ⲛ̅ϣⲁ[ⲙ]ⲧ` ⲛ̅ⲧⲃⲁ ⲛ̅ϩⲁⲙⲧ`
34 [. . . . .] ⲛ̅ϫⲟⲩⲱⲧ ⲛ̅ϣⲉ ⲛ̅ϭⲛ̅ϭⲱⲣ
35 [. . . . .] ⲭⲱⲣⲓⲥ ⲡ[ϩ]ⲙⲉⲥⲛⲁⲩⲥ ⲛ̅[ϣⲉ]
36 [. . . . .]ⲩ ⲛⲉⲩ ⲛ̅ⲟⲩⲁ[ϩ]ⲉ· ⲡⲁϫⲉⲩ [ϫⲉ ⲕ]
37 [ⲛⲁⲟⲩⲁ]ϣⲣⲉ ⲣⲱ ⲁⲣⲁⲕ` ⲁⲛⲉⲓ̈ ϫ[. . . .]
38 ⲡⲉ· ⲛⲉ ⲙ̅ⲙⲁⲛ ⲛⲉ ⲕⲉⲟⲩⲉ ⲡⲉ . [. . . .]
39 ϣⲉⲧϥ̅ ⲛ̅ϩⲟⲩⲟ· ⲛ̅ⲧⲁⲓ̈ϥ[ⲓ] ⲡⲁⲡⲣⲏϣ [. . . .]
40 ⲙ̅ⲙⲁⲩ· ϣⲁϯϭⲛ̅ⲧⲟⲩ· ⲧⲟⲧⲉ ⲛ . [. . ϩⲁ]
41 ⲡⲗⲱⲥ ⲡⲉⲓ ⲡⲉⲧⲛ̅ⲧⲱϣ` ϩⲱⲧ`ⲧ[ⲏⲛⲉ ⲉⲧ]
42 ⲃⲉ ⲡⲧⲣⲉϥⲃⲁⲗ ⲕⲃⲁⲃ ⲛ̅ⲟⲩϣⲏⲙ· ⲧ̄[. . .]
43 ⲉⲃⲁⲗ· ϫⲉ ⲁⲛⲁⲕ` ⲣⲱ ⲛⲁⲥ‹ⲛ›ⲏⲩ ϯ[ⲟⲩⲱ]
44 ϣ ⲉⲓ ⲁⲟⲩⲁϩⲉ ⲛ̅ⲛⲓⲟⲩⲁⲓ̈ϣ` ⲣⲱ· ⲉϣ[ⲁⲧⲉ]
45 ⲧⲛ̅ⲡⲱϩ ϩⲁ ⲃⲣ̅ⲣⲉ· ⲧⲁⲣⲡⲱⲃϣ̅· ⲛ̅[ⲡⲁϯ]
46 ⲙⲉ· ⲁϩⲉ ϭⲉ ⲙ̅ⲙⲁⲛ ⲉⲓⲥⲧⲉ ϯⲡⲏⲧ` ϭ[ⲱϣⲧ̅]
47 ⲁⲃⲁⲗ ϩⲏⲧϥ̅ ⲛ̅ⲁⲛ . . ⲛ̅ϣⲧⲁ· ⲙⲛ̅ϯ [. . .]
48 ⲁⲛⲏϩⲉ· ⲉ[. . . . . . ⲟ]ⲩⲗⲁⲩⲉ ⲛ[. . .]
49 ϩ[ⲏ]ⲧϥ̅ ⳺· [. . . . .] . [. . . . . .]
50 ⲁⲣⲁϥ [. . . . .]
51 ϫⲛ̅ⲛⲕ[. . . . .]
52 ⲉⲓⲧⲉ ⲛ[. . . . .]
53 ⲃⲁⲗ` ⲛ̅[. . . . .]
54 ϣⲏϣ [. . . . .]
55 ⲉⲩⲡⲓⲑⲉ [. . . . .] ⲁⲃⲁⲗ [. . . .]
56 ⲁⲙⲟⲩ ⲁ[. . .]ⲉⲓ . . [. . .] . . ⲟⲩ . . . [. . . .]
57 ⲛⲉⲕ` ⲙⲛ̅[. .] . . . . [. . .]ⲑⲉ ⲛⲟ[. . . .]
58 ⲧⲉⲧⲛ̅ . [. .] . . . . . [.] . . ⲥⲁⲩ . [. . . .]
59 [. . . . . . .]ⲟⲩ· ⲉⲓⲧⲉ . [.] . ⲥⲁⲩⲛⲉ[. . . .]
60 [. . . . .]ⲥⲁⲩⲛⲉ ⲉⲛ [ϫ]ⲉ ⲡⲕ̅ⲣⲉⲛ . [. . .]

61 [. . . . . ⲡ]ⲙⲁ ⲧⲏⲣϥ̅ . [.] . ⲧⲛ̅ⲛⲁⲩ . [. . .]
62 [. . . . . .]ⲉⲩⲙⲉⲩⲉ· . . ⲛ̅ⲧⲁⲕ` ⲉⲓ[. . .]
63 [. . . . ⲧⲁ]ⲙⲁⲓ ϫⲉ ⲡⲉⲧⲕ`ⲟⲩⲁϣϥ̅ [. . .]
64 [. . . . . .]ϫⲓⲧϥ` ⲛ̅ϥⲉⲓ· ⲛ̅ϥⲥϩⲉⲓ̈ [. . .]
65 [. . . . . .] . ⲡⲓⲥ . ‾ . ⲡ . . . . . [. . . . . . .]
66 [. . . . ⲟⲩϫ]ⲉⲓ̈ⲧⲉ ⲛ . [. . . . .]

(tr)67 [(+/- 60?)] . . . [. . . . . ⲉⲓⲥ] ⲭⲁⲣⲓⲥ ⲁⲥⲧⲉⲓ̈ ⲁⲟⲩⲉ ⲛ̅ⲣⲙ̅ⲛ̅ⲕⲏ[ⲙⲉ . . . . .]
68 [. . . . . .] ⲙⲟⲛⲟⲛ ⲙ̅ⲡ̅ⲣ̅ϭⲱ ⲉⲙ[ⲡⲉⲕ (+/- 60?) ⲙⲛ̅ⲧ]ⲧⲁⲓ̈ⲉⲓⲣ[ⲏ]ⲛⲏ ⲁⲣⲙ̅ⲛ̅ⲕⲏⲙⲉ ⲙⲛ̅ [. . . . .]
]

(v) *about five lines lost*
74 . . . . [. . . .]
75 ⲙⲛ̅ ⲛⲉϥϣⲏⲣⲉ ⲙⲛ̅ ⲧ[. . . . .] ⲙⲛ̅ ⲧϣⲱⲉⲣⲉ· ⲙⲛ̅ ⲛⲉⲑⲛ̅ ⲡⲟⲩⲏⲓ̈ ⲧⲏⲣⲟⲩ
76 ⲕⲁⲧⲁ ⲛⲟⲩⲣⲉⲛ· ⲁⲣⲓⲙⲉⲣ . [. . . . . ⲧ]ⲁⲣϥ̅ⲧⲛ̅ⲛⲁⲩ ⲧϭⲛ̅ⲧⲉ ϭⲉⲡ· ⲛⲏⲓ̈ ϣⲓⲛⲉ ⲛⲏⲓ̈
77 ⲧⲟⲛⲟⲩ ⲁⲡⲁⲥⲁⲛ . . . [. . . . .] . ⲡⲉ ⲙⲛ̅ ⲛⲓⲕⲉⲕⲟⲩⲓ̈ ⲡⲓⲉⲛⲁ ⲙⲛ̅ ϩⲱⲣ ϣⲓ
78 ⲛⲉ ⲁⲣⲱⲧⲛ̅ ⲧⲏⲣⲧⲛ̅ . . . . [. . . . . .]ⲅ· ϣⲓⲛⲉ ⲛⲏⲓ̈ ⲁⲣⲁⲩ ⲧⲟⲛⲟⲩ ⲛ̅ . . . . . .
79 ⲓⲱⲧ ⲓⲉⲛⲁ· ⲙⲛ̅ . . ⲓ̈ . ⲣⲙ[. . . .] . . . ⲣⲱⲙⲉ ⲡⲛⲟⲩⲧⲉ ⲡⲉⲧⲣ̅ⲙⲛ̅ⲧⲣⲉ ⲁ
80 ϫⲱⲓ̈ ϫⲉ ⲛ̅ⲧⲁⲓ̈ⲥϩⲉⲓ̈ ϯⲉⲡⲓⲥⲧⲟⲗ[ⲏ ⲉⲛ]ⲁⲣⲙ̅ⲓ̈ⲁⲩⲉ ϣⲟⲩⲟ ⲁϫⲱⲥ·
81 ϣⲓⲛⲉ ⲛⲏⲓ̈ ⲁ . . . . [. . . . ⲙ]ⲛ̅ ⲉⲓⲣⲏⲛⲏ ⲧⲉϯⲉⲓⲣⲉ ⲙ̅ⲡⲉⲥⲣ̅ⲡⲙⲉⲩⲉ
82 ⲛ̅ⲛⲉⲩ ⲛⲓⲙ· ⲉⲓ̈ϣⲗⲏⲗ ⲁ[ⲡⲛⲟⲩⲧⲉ] vac

83 (between 80 / 81)   ἔρρ(ωσο)

(unplaced fragment a)

Traces of six lines, reading on the third ⲉ]ⲡⲓⲥⲧⲟⲗⲏ 'letter'

(unplaced fragment b)

Traces of seven lines, reading on the fourth] . ⲛ̅ⲙⲉ[; on the fifth ⲛ̅ⲛⲟⲩⲃ 'golden' (?, probably not ⲛ̅ⲛⲟⲩⲃⲥ); and on the sixth . ⲣ̅ⲁⲛⲁ . . [.

---

28 ⲣⲱⲙⲉ: -ⲱ- ex corr.

[(To) my masters], my brothers who are very honoured by me in my soul and my spirit ...; the ones whose name is sweet [in my mouth at] all times: Andreas and (5) ... \and Pine (?)/. I am your (pl.) brother Pshai, [who is writing] to you in the Lord, - greetings.

[Before] everything: I greet you [warmly, I am] praying for your well-being [which] I esteem more than everything. (10) [Piena] and Hor greet you; (together with) their children (?), who are flourishing ... they master it.

(15) ... So, now, do not blame [me for] not having sent anything to you; [in that I was not] able to pass by the place to go to ... tunic because of this matter. How many times have I been posted (?) since I joined; nor (20) [do I have] the dowry. I was not able to pass by the place ... the place before you. God can testify for me, that I have a great [sadness] and a great heartbreak that no one has received (anything) from me to send (25) to you.

I have struggled, going around with my [brothers (?)] to set them for surety. Perhaps I can find some *holokottinos* or money, the worth of 5 [*mna*] of wool only! No people have [come to pay]. One by one they say that (30) now [we are] in a pit! We have already [given] them to those who asked us personally [about them]. I have not even found father Pshai, as he is set ... for 30 myriads of bronze ... 2000 talents (35) ... less the 4200 (that were paid?) for them in the Oasis. They say: "[Will you] indeed be content with these (payments)?". ... another one ... demanded more. I took my blanket ... (40) until I found them. Then ... simply, this is your own assignment on account of ... a little ... so that, indeed, I, my brothers, I want to come to the Oasis for these very seasons; if you (45) reach (me) anew and I forget my village!

Very well then: See I am running! Watch out for (many?) faults! I never have ... anything ... (50) to him ... since you (sing.) ... either ... is equal ... (55) they are persuaded ... come ... for you ... either ... know ... (60) ... does not know that your name ... the whole place ... send ... they think.

... instruct me: whatever you want ... receive it; and he comes and he writes ... (65) ... Be well (for a long time).

(tr) ... Charis is here. A certain Egyptian ... Just do not remain without ... spreading peace to the Egyptians and ...

(v) ... (Greet for me) ... (75) and his sons, and ... and her daughter, and everyone in their house by name. Take care ... so that he sends the two measures (?) to me. Greet me warmly to my brother ... and the other children. Piena and Hor greet you all ... Greet me to them warmly, and ... father Iena and ... people. God can testify (80) for me, that I have written this letter, my tears flowing over it. Greet for me ... and Eirene, (she is) the one I remember at every hour. I am praying to God. Farewell.

Commentary:

5   The reading of 'Pine' here is rather uncertain.   If it is correct, see **73**, 18 and perhaps **83**, 4. However, one might also consider reading, e.g., \?] . . ⲛⲏⲓ ⲛ . . / .

10   The name 'Piena' is read here following l. 77.

17-18 Perhaps this tunic is what Pshai wanted to purchase and send as a gift; or otherwise could it indicate the workshop from which items were forwarded on to the Oasis? Anyway, something has prevented him.

18-19 ⲁⲩϩⲁ[ⲃⲧ̄: If we are correct in this restoration from the verb ϩⲱⲃ 'send', then the implication must be that Pshai has constantly been sent on tasks elsewhere and thus been unable to do what he had wanted. Thus our translation of 'posted'. A clue to the meaning should lie in the second verb ϩⲱⲧⲡ 'join' or 'reconcile'; but, again, without a context we do not really know what stands behind this.

26   [ⲥⲛⲏⲟⲩ]: 'brothers'; but the restoration is just a guess, and perhaps Pshai indicated some goods that he has attempted to pawn.

38   ⲛⲉ ⲙⲙⲁⲛ ⲛⲉ: The meaning is obscure.

42   ⲡⲧⲣⲉϥⲃⲁⲗ ⲕⲃⲁⲃ ⲛ̄ⲟⲩϣⲏⲙ: The meaning is obscure, although the reading is mostly certain. ⲃⲁⲗ must be 'loosen' or similar; whilst ⲕⲃⲟ (CD 100a) means to 'become cool', (e.g. it is used for the passing or dying down of a fever).

45   ϩⲁ ⲃ̄ⲣ̄ⲣⲉ: 'anew'? It could be a place-name (cf. CD 43b for similar), but we do not think that that is the meaning here. Pshai is complaining about something and wants to return to Kellis. Still, its meaning with the verb ⲡⲱϩ ('reach' or 'attain') is not clear.

46   ⲁϩⲉ ϭⲉ ⲛ̄ⲙⲁⲛ: Cf. **64**, 5-6 (note ad loc.); **92**, 15-16; **108**, 26.

68   The meaning is probably: 'Just do not remain without your coming' or '.. writing'.

76   ϭⲉⲡ: Perhaps a measure for corn or other commodities (CD 113b s.v. ⲕⲁⲡ).

P. Kellis Copt. 106

Inv #: P 56D(a)

Location: House 3, room 9, deposit 3.

Preservation: This is an almost complete and well-preserved letter, written in Coptic on a thin strip of papyrus. It is now broken in two at the centre fold, and some small sections have been lost from the upper right hand where the papyrus has cracked along the vertical creases. The dimensions are 278 x 41 mm. The hand is practised. Its style and extravagant flourishes strongly recall that of two documents sent by Ploutogenes (**85** and **86**). The author's occasional turn-of-phrase and use of some less-common Greek terms may suggest a level of education beyond that indicated by the highly-repetitive style of many of these letters.

Content: It is somewhat unusual (although there are a number of other instances in this archive) that the author does not name himself. However, since the handwriting is especially close to that of **86**, we think that he ('the brother') may be Ploutogenes. Note especially the extended and angular style of letters such as -ϵ- and -ϭ-; compare the -ⳉ- (**86**, 5 and **106**, 18); also the rather odd and shaky -ⲡ- (e.g. the initial letters of **86**, 1 with **106**, 13). The name of the recipient (Lammon) could, of course, be the same as Philammon. As regards the actual content of the piece, the apparent reference to some gossip or scandal is intriguing but not explained. Otherwise, there are the fairly typical references to the need for news and certain items. There is no real indication of where the letter was written; but the phrase about Lammon having 'gone up' to somewhere may suggest local travel within the Oasis (see the references in the note to ll. 10-11). If this is correct, then one should be cautious about identifying this recipient with the author (Philammon) of **80-82**, who is clearly in the Nile valley.

Address:

verso

τῶι ἀγαπητῶι ἀδελφῶι Λάμμωνι ὁ ἀδελφός

To my loved brother Lammon. (From your) brother.

Names: Lammon; Shai;

Text:

1 τῶι ἀγαπη[τῶι]
2 ἀδελφῶι [μου]
3 Λάμμωνι [?]
4 ὁ ἀδελφός [σου]
5 ϯϣⲓⲛⲉ ⲁⲣⲁⲕ
6 ⲧⲟⲛⲟⲩ· ⲛⲉⲡⲁ
7 ϩⲏⲧ ⲇⲓⲥⲧⲁⲍⲉ
8 ⲉⲧⲃⲏⲧⲕ ϫⲉ ⲙ̄
9 ⲡⲓⲥⲱⲧⲙ̄ ⲉⲧⲃ[ⲏ]
10 ⲧⲕ̄ ϫⲛ̄ⲧⲁⲕⲃⲱⲕ
11 ⲁϩⲣⲏⲓ̈ ⲙⲏⲡⲱⲥ
12 ⲉⲁⲗⲉⲥⲭⲏ ϣⲱ
13 ⲡⲉ ⲛⲉⲕ· ϯⲛⲟⲩ ⲙ̄
14 ⲡⲣ̄ϭⲱ ⲉⲙ̄ⲡⲕⲥϩⲉⲓ
15 ⲛⲏⲓ̈ ⲧⲁⲭⲩ ⲙ̄ⲡⲟⲩ
16 ⲱ ⲛ̄ϩⲱⲃ ⲛⲓⲙ
17 ⲁⲩⲱ ⲧⲁⲭⲩ ⲕⲥⲃ̄
18 ⲧⲉ ⲛ̄ϩⲁⲗⲍ ϫⲉ ⲁ
19 ⲡⲣⲱⲙⲉ ⲧⲱϣ
20 ⲁⲡϩⲱⲃ· ⲙ̄ⲡⲣⲁ
21 ⲙⲉⲗⲉ ⲁⲗⲁⲩⲉ ⲛ̄
22 ϩⲱⲃ· ⲁⲩⲱ ⲁ
23 ⲧⲣⲉⲕⲥϩⲉⲓ ⲛⲏⲓ̈ ϫⲉ
24 ⲉϣ ⲧⲉ ⲑⲉ ⲉⲧⲁⲕ

25 ⲧⲱϣ ⲁⲉⲥ·
26 ⲁⲩⲱ ⲙ̄ⲡⲣ̄ⲧⲛ̄
27 ⲛⲁⲩ ⲉⲡⲓ[[ⲥ]]vacⲥⲧⲟⲗⲏ
28 ⲛ̄ⲧⲛ ⲣⲱⲙⲉ ⲉϥ
29 ⲥ̣ⲗⲁϩⲗⲁϩ̄· ⲁⲗⲗⲁ
30 ⲉϣⲱⲡⲉ ⲉⲟⲩⲛ̄
31 ϭⲁⲙ` ⲁⲡⲧⲏⲣϥ̄
32 ⲧⲁϩⲟⲩ· ⲉⲕϣⲁⲛⲓ̈
33 ⲉⲕϣⲓⲛⲉ ⲁⲡ̄ⲣⲧⲁⲃ
34 ⲛ̄ϫⲁï̈ⲧ ⲕⲧⲉϥ ⲁⲩ
35 ϩⲛⲟ ⲕⲧⲁⲃⲉϥ ⲕⲧⲛ
36 ⲛⲁⲩⲥⲉ· ϣⲓⲛⲉ
37 ⲛⲏï̈ ⲁⲡⲥⲁⲛ ϣⲁï̈
38 ⲉϣⲁⲧⲉ ⲉⲩⲕⲁⲓⲣⲓⲁ
39 ϣⲱⲡⲉ ⲧⲛ̄
40 ⲛⲁⲩ ⲛ̄ϭⲁϭⲉ
41 ϫⲉ ⲛ̄ⲛⲟⲩⲧⲉⲕⲟ·
42 † †ⲟⲩ ⲏⲓ̈ ⲛ̄ϩⲏⲧⲟⲩ
43 ⲙ̄ⲡⲥⲁⲛ ϣⲁï̈ ἔρ(ρωσο)

---

5 †ϣⲓⲛⲉ: -†- ex corr. or smudged?   27 ⲉⲡⲓ[[ⲥ]]vacⲥⲧⲟⲗⲏ: the scribe has had to write around a flaw in the papyrus, repeating the -ⲥ- after a space   29 ⲥ̣ⲗⲁϩⲗⲁϩ̄: second -ϩ- ex corr.

To [my] loved brother Lammon; [(from) your] brother.

(5) I greet you warmly. I have been worried on your account, for I did not hear about (10) you since you went up - perhaps some gossip had arisen (against) you? Now, do not remain not having written (15) quickly to me the news about everything; and quickly prepare the ..., for someone has been assigned (20) to the work. Do not neglect any (aspect) of the matter, and you must write to me how you have (25) decided to do it. And do not send (any) letter by a slack (?) person. However, (30) if at all possible, secure them.

If you are going to ask about the *artab* of olives: You can put it in a (35) vessel, seal it and send them.

Greet for me brother Shai. Should opportunity arise: (40) Send baked goods so that they do not perish. Give five pairs (?) from them to brother Shai. Farewell.

Commentary:

Address: Although there are some visible ink traces below the right hand part of the address, the name of the sender does not seem to have been written.

3   The name of the sender might be expected here after that of the recipient; but there is scarcely room for more than a couple of letters in the lost fragment and we doubt that it was included.

6-8   'I have been worried on your account': lit. 'my heart was hesitating ..'. We have supposed that the author is expressing fear for Lammon's welfare rather than doubt about his actions or motivations. Still, it is difficult to reconstruct the situation and the reasons for the potential scandal or gossip (l. 12 λέσχη).

10-11   ⲃⲱⲕ ⲁϩⲣⲏⲓ: Lammon is said to have 'gone up'. The parallel phrase, to 'come up' (ⲉⲓ ⲁϩⲣⲏⲓ), is found elsewhere. At **94**, 55 (a document that also features a Lammon) it probably refers to travel <u>within</u> the Oasis; similarly (in-so-far as one can tell) at **32**, 27-28; **40**, 10; **84**, 32-33.

18   ϩⲁⲗϫ: The term is unknown to us, but probably the same as ϩⲁⲗⲕⲥ at **39**, 43 (a letter that also mentions a Lammon).

29   ⲥⲗⲁϩⲗⲁϩⲧ: We prefer an initial ⲥ- to an ⲉ- (and cf. **92**, 23). From the context of these two instances we think the meaning of the verb must be something like 'to be slack' (i.e. 'lazy' or 'neglectful'); but it could have a more active connotation such as 'dishonest'. Compare CD 149b ⲗⲁϩⲗⲁϩ 'be tall' (or 'proud'); 139a ⲗⲟⲩⲕⲗⲁⲕ 'wicked' (*B*) and 333b-334a ⲥⲗⲟϭⲗϭ 'be smooth' (noting Gen. 27: 11 where it has the connotation of slyness).

32   ⲧⲁϫⲟⲩ: We think that the author is still worried about the letters, and understand here the verb ⲧⲱⲕⲥ (CD 406b-407a) 'pierce' in the sense of something firmly fixed, perhaps even 'sealed'.

40   ϭⲁϭⲉ: cf. CD 843b 'baked loaf' or 'cake'.

42   ϯⲟⲩ ⲏⲓ: 'five pairs'. Compare **76**, 32 (ⲉⲓ), and the analogous use of ⲥⲁⲓⲱ (thus **79**, 20 note ad loc.). These two Coptic terms, both meaning a 'pair', may better be

rendered as 'sets' or similar. Note also the Greek ζεῦγος, which can be used for pairs of bread loaves (or 'double-loaves'?); e.g. P. Prag. Varcl. II 6, 107-124.

P. Kellis Copt. 107

Inv #: P 56D(b) + P52A + P56H

Location: House 3, room 9, deposit 3.

Preservation: Three fragments can be placed to reconstruct an almost complete letter written in Coptic on papyrus, although it is now rather faded and difficult to read in parts. The upper half is in one piece; but the document has broken apart at the centre fold some time in the past, and the two lower portions are particularly poor with a distinctly different colour to the upper (indicating rather different conditions of preservation). The original dimensions were 264 x 60 mm. The hand appears a little crude compared with many from the archive; but it is competent enough and includes both opening and closing formulae in Greek.

Content: A certain Dorotheos writes to his 'son' Andreas. There are no other instances of the sender's name in the Coptic archive, and it is difficult to relate this piece to any of the known characters from House 3 (although the name Andreas is common enough). The content is remarkably personal. Unfortunately, the connotations are difficult to understand without context; especially given the author's brevity and allusiveness, combined with the difficulty of reading parts of the lower text. In general, the document strikes one as unusual in its style, and different in its concerns to the majority of the letters. It may also evidence some variant features as regards dialect; (though these could be idiosyncracies of the scribe). It is a shame that we do not understand the text better.

Address: No visible address.

Names: Andreas; Dorotheos;

Text:

1 τῷ τιμιωτάτῳ υἱῷ
2 [μο]υ̣ Ἀνδρεαντι [?]
3 Δορόθεος χαίρειν
4 ϩⲁⲑⲏ ⲛ̄ϩⲱⲃ ⲛⲓⲙ ϯϣⲓ
5 ⲛⲉ ⲁⲧⲉⲕⲙⲛ̄ⲧϣⲏⲣⲉ
6 ⲉⲧⲁⲓⲁⲓⲧ ⲛ̄ⲧⲟⲧ ⲧⲟⲛⲟⲩ
7 ⲡⲉⲧⲣ̄ⲁⲛⲏⲓ̈ ϩⲱⲧ
8 ϩⲛ̄ ⲧⲁ[ⲯⲩ]ⲭⲏ ⲉⲓ̈ϣⲁ
9 ⲟⲩⲱϣ[ⲉ] ⲙⲉⲛ ⲉⲧⲁⲟⲩⲟ
10 ⲁⲣⲁⲕ ⲛ̄ⲛⲉⲧϩⲛ ⲡⲁϩⲏⲧ
11 ϯⲛⲁϣ[ϭⲛ̄] ⲑⲉ ⲉⲛ ϩⲛ ⲡ
12 ⲥϩⲉⲓ̈ ⲁⲛⲁⲕ [ⲉⲧ]ϫⲱ ⲙ̄ⲙⲁⲥ
13 ϫⲉ ⲕⲣ̄ⲁⲓⲥⲑⲁⲛⲉ ⲁⲣⲁⲩ
14 ⲁⲗⲗⲁ ⲉⲡⲓⲇⲏ ⲁⲩⲱⲧⲣⲉ
15 ⲡϩⲱⲃ ⲉⲧⲛ̄ⲧⲛ̄ⲙⲏⲧⲉ
16 ϯⲛⲟⲩ ϭⲉ ϯⲧⲉⲟⲩⲟ ⲡⲥⲉ
17 ϫⲉ ϩⲛ̄ ⲟⲩⲥⲩⲛⲧⲟⲙⲓⲁ
18 ⲡϩ̣[ⲱⲃ ⲁⲛ] ⲉⲧⲁⲕⲥϩⲉⲓ
19 ⲛⲏⲓ [ⲉⲧ]ⲃⲏⲧϥ̄ ⲙⲛ̄
20 ϣϭⲁ[ⲙ . . .] ⲛ̄ⲗⲁⲩⲉ
21 ⲉⲓⲙⲏⲧⲓ ⲁⲧⲛ̄ⲟⲩⲉⲓⲉ
22 ϫⲉ ⲡⲥⲉϫⲉ ⲡⲉ ⲙ̄ⲡ
23 ⲥⲙⲁⲧ ⲙ̄ⲙⲉⲧⲉ ϫⲉ
24 ϩⲁⲓ̈ⲟⲣⲱ ⲉⲓ̄ⲣ ⲁⲛⲁϣ
25 ϩⲛ̄ ⲟⲩⲛⲁϭ ⲛ̄ⲱⲣⲕ
26 ⲉⲧⲁϭⲛ̄ ⲕⲉϩⲱⲃ ⲉϣⲱ
27 ⲡⲉ ϯϯ[. .] . . ϣⲁϫ ⲥ
28 ϣⲟⲡ ϯⲛ . . ⲟ ⲉⲧⲟⲧ ⲁⲣⲁϥ
29 ⲥⲧⲁⲙⲉ ⲁⲧⲉⲟⲩⲟ ⲧⲙⲏ
30 ⲉ ⲁ[ⲣ]ⲁⲕ ⲡ[ⲁ]ϣⲏⲣⲉ

31 ⲉⲛ[ⲁ]ⲛⲟⲩ[ϥ] ἐρρῶσθαί
32 σε εὔχομαι
33 πολλοῖς χρόνοις

———

6 ⲉⲧⲁⲓⲁⲓⲧ for ⲉⲧ-ⲧⲁⲓⲁⲓⲧ   14 it may be possible to read -ⲉⲓ in ligature at the close of the line   16 read †ⲧⲉⲟⲩⲟ ‹ⲛ̄›ⲡⲥⲉϫⲉ (or is †- conjunctive?)

———

To my most honoured son Andreas; (from) Dorotheos, - greetings.

Before everything: I greet (5) your sonship, greatly honoured by me; the one who also pleases me in my soul. Indeed, though I should love to tell (10) you the things in my heart, I will not be able to [find] the way in the letter. I am saying that you perceive them; but, since (15) the matter between us has been fixed, therefore I am now recounting the affair in brief. [Again], the matter about which you wrote to me: There is no (20) possibility [to do] anything, except to go away; in that the affair is only of such a kind that I have already pledged (25) with a great oath to resist (?) another matter. If ... occurs ... to him, it is appropriate to tell the truth (30) to you, my good child.

I pray for your health for many years.

Commentary:

Address: Although there is no apparent address, there are some ink traces on the verso. They do not appear to be text, but one should view the digital photograph.

2   Ἀνδρεαυτι [?]: Given that this is a most irregular form of the dative (as if the word were ἀνδριάς?), and the possibility that there is lost text following (see the photograph), perhaps one should better read: Ἀνδρεα . . ι . . . [.]? It is possible that the top layer of papyrus has stripped away, noting what may be a downward stroke reaching the final -ν on the following line.

26   ⲧⲁϭⲛ: If the reading is correct and the verb is ⲧⲱϭⲛⲉ (cf. CD 466ab), then one has to decide on the appropriate sense for the context from the basic meanings of 'push' and 'repel'. However, otherwise, since the initial ⲉ- seems to stand here for the preposition ⲁ-, it could also be the verb ϭⲛ- 'find' after a form ⲧⲁ- of the causative

infinitive (for ⲁⲧⲣⲁ-): '(oath) that I shall find another thing'. Either way, in this section of the text it is unclear to us whether Dorotheos is talking about some actual legal matter.

P. Kellis Copt. 108

Inv #: P56G + P56C + P56I

Location: House 3, room 9, deposit 3 west doorway.

Preservation: Six fragments of inscribed papyrus can be arranged to provide the remnants of a letter written in Coptic. Three form parts of the upper half (calculated to 72 x 58 mm.), and three form almost the entire lower half (also 72 x 58 mm.). Approximately four lines can be supposed to be completely missing from the centre, with the original height calculated as ca. 165 mm. The script is proficiently written and clear to read. The initial ϩ- of l. 6 is slightly indented and writ large, indicating a concern for format and clarity that is also apparent in the punctuation signs. The hand and formatting are quite similar to the same in **31**; compare (e.g.) the ⲭⲁⲓⲣⲉⲓⲛ.

Content: Pshai writes to Pegosh. The context is certainly that of the circle of Pamour, whose letters dominate the earlier sections of this volume. Consequently, Kapidon is surely the same as Kapiton; Lo is Tapollos; Philammon may well be the same as the author of **80-82**; and the letter must be read with those written by Pegosh himself (**73-79**). As we saw previously, the adult men were generally working in the Nile valley (some together with their wives), from where they sent letters and items back to the extended family in the Oasis. In this instance, it seems that Pshai is in Kellis (ll. 26-27), from where he writes to Pegosh; and thus we are seeing the other half of the correspondence. Compare, e.g. **73**.

Address: The verso is blank, (and there is probably not enough room in the lost section for what one would expect to be written).

Names: Hapia; Kapidon; Lo; Pegosh; Philammon; Pshai (x 2?);

Text:

1	ⲡ[ⲁϫⲁⲓⲥ] ⲡⲁϭⲁⲛ ⲙ̄ⲙⲉ
2	ⲣⲓⲧ [ⲉⲧⲧⲁ]ⲓ̈ⲁⲓ̈ⲧ ⲛ̄ⲧⲟⲧ`
3	ⲧⲟ[ⲛⲟⲩ ⲡⲉϭ]ⲱϣ` ⲁⲛⲁⲕ
4	ⲡⲉ[ⲕⲥⲁⲛ ⲡ]ϣⲁⲓ̈ ⲡⲉⲧⲥϩⲉⲓ̈
5	ⲛⲉ[ⲕ ϩⲙ̄ ⲡⲭ]ⲁⲓ̈ⲥ ⲭⲁⲓⲣⲉⲓⲛ`
6	ϩⲓ[ⲑⲏ ⲛ̄ϩⲱⲃ ⲛⲓ]ⲙ ϯϣⲓⲛⲉ
7	ⲁ[ⲡⲁⲥⲁⲛ ⲧⲟⲛⲟ]ⲩ` ⲉⲓ̈ϣⲗⲏⲗ
8	ⲁ[ⲡⲛⲟⲩⲧⲉ] ⲛ̄ⲛⲉⲩ ⲛⲓⲙ ϩⲁ
9	[ⲡⲕⲟⲩϫⲉⲓ̈ⲧ]ⲉ vac . . . ⲛ̣ . ϭ̣ . ⲥ
10	[. . . . . . .] . [. . .]ϭⲛ̄[. . .] .
11	[. . . . . .] . . . .
12	[. . . . . .] . . . . ⲉ
13	[. . . . .] . . . . ⲛⲑⲉ .
14	[. . . . .] . . . [.]
15	[. . . . .]
16	[. . . . .]
17	[. . . . .]
18	[. . . . .]
19	[.] . . . . . [. . . . .]
20	[ⲡ]ϣⲁⲓ̈ ⲙⲛ̄ ϩⲁⲡⲓⲁ ⲁⲓ̈
21	ϫⲓ ⲡⲥϩⲉⲓ̈ ⲛⲉϥ` ⲁⲓ̈ϫⲟⲥ
22	ⲁⲣⲁϥ ⲉⲧⲃⲉ ⲛⲁⲟⲩⲛ̣ⲟⲩⲉ`
23	ⲡⲁϫⲉϥ ϫⲉ ⲁϥⲧⲉⲛⲉ ⲟⲩ
24	ⲉⲡⲓⲥⲧⲟⲗⲏ ϩⲱⲧ` ⲛⲏⲓ̈ ⲉ
25	ⲧⲃⲉ ⲕⲉⲛ̣ⲙⲁ ⲙ̄ⲙⲏϭⲉ`
26	ⲁϩⲉ ϭⲉ ⲙ̄ⲙⲁⲛ` ⲁϥⲉⲓ
27	ⲁϭⲏⲗⲏ ⲁϥⲛ̄ⲧⲟⲩ` ⲡⲁ
28	ϫⲉϥ ϫⲉ ⲟⲩϭⲓⲥ ⲧⲃⲁ ⲛ̄
29	ϩⲁⲙⲧ` ⲡⲁϫⲉⲛ ϫⲉ ϣⲁ

```
30  ⲧϥ̄ⲉⲓ ⲁⲟⲩⲁϩⲉ· ⲛⲓⲛ̄ⲗⲁⲩⲉ
31  ⲧⲏⲣⲟⲩ ⲉⲩⲥⲁⲡ· ϣⲓⲛⲉ ⲁ
32  ⲣⲁⲕ ⲧⲟⲛⲟⲩ· ϣⲓⲛⲉ ⲛⲉⲛ
33  ⲧⲟⲛⲟⲩ ⲁⲫⲓⲗⲁⲙⲙⲱⲛ·
34  ⲙⲛ̄ ⲧϥ̄ⲥϩⲓⲙⲉ· ἐρρῶσθαί
35  σε εὔχ[ομ]αι πολ[λ]οῖς χρόνοις

(tr)36  ⲕⲁⲡⲓⲇⲱⲛ ⲙⲛ̄ ⲧϥ̄ⲥϩⲓⲙⲉ· ⲙⲛ̄ [ⲛⲉϥϣⲏⲣⲉ ϣⲓ]ⲛⲉ ⲁⲣⲁⲕ ⲧⲟⲛⲟⲩ· ⲡⲁϫⲉ ⲗⲟ ϫⲉ ϯⲣⲁϩ̣ⲓ
37  ⲟⲩ ⲙ̄ⲙⲁⲕ . [ . . . . . . . . ] . ⲉϥ ⲙⲁⲣϥ̄ⲧⲛ̄ⲛⲁⲩ ⲟⲩⲗⲉϯⲉ ⲛⲏⲓ̈ ⲛ̄ϫⲏⲛϭⲉ·
```

(To) [my master], my loved brother who is very honoured by me, Pegosh. (It is) I, [your brother] Pshai, who writes (5) to [you in the] Lord, - greetings!

Before every[thing]: I greet [my brother] warmly; I am praying to [God] every hour for [your well-being] ... (10) ... (15) ... (20) Pshai and Hapia. I have taken the letter to him. I have spoken to him about my hours (?). He says that he has drawn up a letter for me too, (25) concerning another *mna* (?) for interest. Very well then! He came to Kellis and brought (?) them. He says: "Half a myriad of bronze". We say: "Until (30) he comes to the Oasis".

All the little ones, every one, greet you warmly. Greet warmly for us Philammon and his wife. (35) I pray for your health for many years. (tr) Kapidon and his wife and [his children] greet you warmly. Lo says: "I beg you ... Let him send me a small portion of dye".

Commentary:

4, 7   ⲥⲁⲛ: The restoration of 'brother' is based on the probable reading of the same in l. 1. Also, compare **73**, 1-2.

20   This Pshai (or Shai?) is probably a different person to the author. For Hapia see **77**, 20.

22   ⲟⲩⲛ̣ⲟⲩⲉ: We have supposed a strange plural form or error instead of the expected ⲟⲩⲛⲁ(ⲟ)ⲩⲉ, but perhaps it is a different word. The idea of 'work hours' seems suspiciously anachronistic; but (e.g.) well-usage was measured in time, cf. O. Trim. 19.

25   ⲕⲉⲛ̣ⲙⲁ̣ ⲙ̄ⲙⲏⲥⲉ: We have understood this as 'another *mna* for interest'. Obviously, it requires reading ⲛ̣ⲙⲁ̣ as an error for ⲙⲛⲁ. The idea of providing extra

weight (i.e. quantity of some commodity) for delayed supply seems plausible; but it is quite possible that we are misunderstanding the clause. In particular, what we have read as a -ⲛ- is poorly formed; but no possible alternatives (such as -ⲏ- or even -ⲁⲓ-) make any better sense to us.

26 ⲁϩⲉ ϭⲉ ⲙⲙⲁⲛ: Cf. **64**, 5-6 (note ad loc.); **92**, 15-16; **105**, 46.

27 ⲁϥⲛ̄ⲧⲟⲩ: lit. 'he brought them'. The reading seems correct, but does not make good sense. We wonder whether it would be better to read ⲁϣⲛ̄ⲧⲟⲩ. The meaning would then be: 'He came to Kellis to ask for them'.

28-29 'Half a myriad of bronze': or perhaps better, '5000 cash'.

29-30 'Until he comes ..' : The meaning is probably, 'wait until ..'.

36 'Kapidon and his wife and [his children]': similarly e.g. **72**, 25-26; **77**, 5-6. On this person and his relationship to Pegosh, see particularly the introductory comments to the latter piece.

P. Kellis Copt. 109

Inv #: P 59A(i) + P 59B/F + P 60D + P 64A + P 93B

Location: House 3, room 3, deposit 3; room 6, deposits 3 + 4; room 9, deposit 4.

Preservation: There remain seven papyrus fragments of what was probably a single letter, written in Coptic with a distinctive large script. They can be arranged to restore portions of the document, the dimensions of which would have been 266 x 86 mm. It has broken at the folds, perhaps already in antiquity (as indicated by the varied find-sites and differing states of preservation of the extant fragments). Most of the right-hand side is missing.

Content: The letter is poorly preserved and little of value can be ascertained about its contents. The piece is of some interest for its script; also the terminology at ll. 30-32 (discussed below) which again relates to the textile business.

Address:

verso

ἀπ(όδος) τῇ συνβίᾳ   vac   Τεϻογις

παρὰ Καπιτος

Deliver to my wife Tegsogis (?). From Kapitos (?)

Names: Kapitos; Pegosh; Pishai; Psounte- (?); Tahom (?); Tegsogis (?);

Text:

1   ⲧⲁⲥⲱⲛⲉ [. . . . .]
2   ⲁⲛⲁⲕ ⲧⲉ . [. . . ϯϣⲓⲛⲉ ⲁⲣⲟ ⲧⲟ]
3   ⲛⲟⲩ ⲙⲛ̄ ⲧⲁ[. . . . .]
4   vac   [ⲭⲁⲓⲣⲉⲓⲛ]
5   ϩⲁⲑⲏ ⲛ̄ϩⲱ[ⲃ ⲛⲓⲙ ϯϣⲓⲛⲉ ⲁⲣⲟ]
6   ⲧⲟⲛⲟⲩ [ⲉⲓ̈ϣⲗⲏⲗ ⲁⲡⲛⲟⲩⲧⲉ]
7   ϫⲉϥⲁⲣ[ⲁⲓ̈ⲥ ⲁⲣⲟ . . . .]
8   ⲁⲣⲁⲓ̈ ϣⲁ[. . . . .]
9   ⲉⲣⲏⲩ ⲛ̄[. . . . .]
10   ⲧⲛ̄ⲛⲁ[ⲩ . . . .]
11   ⲛ̄ϯⲧϭ[. . . . .]
12   ⲛϥ̄ⲛ̄ⲧϥ̄ . [. . . . .]
13   ⲙⲛⲁ ⲥⲛⲉⲩ ⲛ̄[. . . . .]
14   ϯⲛⲁⲙⲁϩϥ̄ ⲛ̄[. . . . .]
15   ⲡⲓⲙⲁ . . [. . . . .]
16   ⲡⲥⲟⲕ . . . . [. . . . . . .]
17   ⲁⲣⲟ ⲙ̄ⲙⲁϥ ⲧ[. . . . .]
18   ⲉⲩⲡ̄ϣⲉⲩ ⲛ̄ⲧⲉ . [. . . . .]
19   [ⲉ]ⲧⲃⲉ ⲉⲩ ϭⲉ ⲁ[. . . . .]
20   ⲡⲓϩⲁⲗⲟⲕⲟⲧⲓⲛ[ⲟⲥ . . . .]
21   ⲧⲁϩⲱⲙ ⲛ̄ϥ[. . . . .]
22   . ϣⲛⲉⲧⲙ̄ⲙ[. . . . .]
23   ϩⲁⲧⲏⲥ̄ . ⲁⲓ̈ⲛ[. . . . .]

24	. . ϩⲛ̄ ⲕⲏⲙⲉ [. . . . .]
25	ϩⲱⲃ ⲛⲓⲙ ⲉ[. . . . .]
26	[. .] . . ϭ . [. . . . .]
27	[. . . . .]
28	[. . . . . .]ⲧⲉϥ ⲛ̄ⲧⲉⲃⲱⲕ
29	ϣ . . ⲁ . [.] . ⲙ[ⲡ]ⲓⲙⲁ ϣⲁⲡⲟⲉ
30	ⲉⲧⲃⲉ ⲡⲓϩⲟⲗⲟⲕⲟⲧⲓⲛⲟⲥ ⲟⲩⲛ̄
31	ⲧⲉ ⲡⲉϭⲱϣ ⲟⲩⲥⲁⲣⲧ` ⲛ̄ⲣⲱϥ ⲙ̄
32	ⲡⲥⲟⲩⲛ̄ⲧⲉ[. ⲙ]ⲛ̄ ⲧⲉ[ϥ]ϩⲓⲙⲉ ϯⲡⲗ̄ϭⲉ
33	ⲛ̄ϩⲁⲓ̈ⲧⲉ [. .] . ⲧ . [. .]ⲙ̄ⲙⲉⲥ ⲡϣ̄ⲧ
tr34	vac ⲓ̈ⲥ ⲗⲁⲃⲏⲥ ⲛⲉ ϯⲛⲁ[.] . . . ⲙ̄ . . . [.] . . . . [. .] . . . . ⲧ . [. . . .] . . ⲏⲩⲉ
	ⲙ̄ⲡⲓϣⲁⲓ̈
v35	ϣⲓ ⲙⲏⲧ ⲛ̄ⲛⲙ̄ⲛ[ⲁ . . . .]
36	ⲧⲉⲧ[ⲟ]ⲩ ⲙ̄ⲡⲥ̣ . . [. . . . .]
37	ϩⲁ ⲛⲏϩ vac

34 ⲗⲁⲃⲏⲥ: -ⲁ- ex -ⲉ- corr.

(To) my sister ... (It is) I, your ... [I greet you] warmly, and ..., - [greetings (?)].

(5) Before [every]thing: [I greet you] warmly. [I am praying to God] that he will [guard you] ... to me until (we can greet) one another (again).

... (10) send ... and he brings it ... two *mna* of ... I will pay him ... (15) here ... to you ... they are useful ... Now, why ... (20) this *holokottinos* ... Tahom (?); and he ... in Egypt ... (25) everything ... and you go to ... (from?) this place ... (30) on account of this *holokottinos*. Pegosh has a ... fleece from (?) Psounte- [and (?)] his wife. This torn robe ... the warp.

(tr) Here is a trap (of fish?) for you. I will ... from Pishai. (v35) Measure ten *mna* ... give them to ... for oil.

Commentary:

Address: It would appear that the name of the recipient is written with a Coptic -ϭ- in the midst of her name, which is otherwise given a Greek form. Whilst one might expect some form of ⲧⲁϭⲟϣⲉ / Τεκυσις, this does not seem to be the case. However, one should note that the initial τε- seems separated from what follows, as if it were not part of the same word. Perhaps a better reading or interpretation of the address can be suggested.

2 It would appear that the author is another woman. Perhaps read: ⲧⲉⲥ[ⲱⲛⲉ.

3 ⲧⲁ[: This could be another woman's name or a term of relationship ('my mother / daughter' / etc.).

8-9 As a restoration, *exempli gratia*, ϣⲁ[ⲧⲡⲣⲁⲡⲁⲛⲧⲁ ⲁⲛⲉⲛ]ⲉⲣⲏⲩ (cf. **32**, 38; **103**, 36f.).

29 ϣⲁⲡⲟⲉ: The reading is clear, but meaningless to us. Perhaps one should read ϣⲁ ⲡⲟ<ⲩ>ⲉ?

30-31 ⲟⲩⲥⲁⲣⲧ` ⲛ̄ⲣⲱϥ: This looks like 'mouth-fleece', but what that might mean we have no idea.

32 Psounte-: Cf. the many spellings listed under ⲡⲉⲥⲩⲛⲑⲓⲟⲥ in Hasitzka's *Namen*.

32-33 †ⲡⲗ̄ϭⲉ ⲛ̄ϩⲁⲓ̈ⲧⲉ: See the references in CD 262b.

34 λαβης: 'trap' or otherwise 'kettle' (of fish?); cf. **76**, 31 note ad loc.

P. Kellis Copt. 110

Inv #: P 61G/1 + P 65E/F/G/J

Location: House 3, room 8, deposits 3 + 4.

Preservation: A number of papyrus fragments can be placed to reconstruct the major part of a letter written in Coptic. It has broken along the horizontal folds into four main sections, and the fibre has begun to disintegrate so that sections only retain a structure like 'lace'. The document was written in a practised and flowing hand, with characteristic features such as an -ⲉ- written in two loops (see l. 11). The opening lines are particularly poorly preserved, and the final lines of the recto (and verso) almost entirely lost.

Content: Psais writes to his sons. He names first Pamour (whose name is given on the address), and then probably Pagosh and other members of the family. If this is correct, the piece is an important addition to the archive, written from Psais 'II' (following Worp's stemma) to Pamour 'III'. It may well indicate that Pamour is the eldest son. The letter must be read together with the many others belonging to the brothers and their circle. Unfortunately, much of the text is difficult to read and the contents hard to follow. Mostly, Psais seems to be dealing with business matters. At l. 26 he relates a comment that 'the place is difficult' (ⲡⲙⲁ ⲙⲁⲭϩ, cf. **31**, 47); but the connotation is unclear.

Address:

verso

$$\tau\hat{\omega}\iota\ \delta\epsilon\sigma\pi\acute{o}\tau\eta\ \mu o\upsilon\ \upsilon\acute{\iota}\hat{\omega}\iota\quad X\quad \Pi\alpha\mu o\hat{\upsilon}\rho\iota$$
$$\Psi\acute{\alpha}\ddot{\iota}\varsigma$$

To my master son X Pamour. (From) Psais.

Names: Kapitou; Pagosh; Pamour; Pottes (?); Psais; Shai;

Text:

1   [ⲛⲁ]ϫⲓⲥⲁⲩⲉ ⲙ̄ⲙⲉⲣⲉⲧⲉ ⲉⲧⲧⲁⲓⲁⲓⲧ
2   [ⲛ̄ⲧⲟ]ⲧ ⲧⲟⲛⲟⲩ [ⲡⲁ]ⲙⲟⲩⲣ ⲙⲛ̄ ⲡⲁ
3   [ϭⲱϣ] . . . . ⲛ̄[. . . .] . ⲙⲛ̄
4   [. .] . . ⲡⲣ . . [.]ⲁ . . . . . . [ϩⲁ]
5   [ⲑⲏ] ⲛ̄ϩⲱⲃ ⲛ[ⲓⲙ] †ⲣ̄ϣ[ⲡⲏ]ⲣ[ⲉ ⲡ]ϣ[ⲥ ⲛ̄]
6   [ⲧⲁ]ⲕ ⲡⲁϭⲱ[ϣ] ⲛⲛⲉϣⲁⲣⲉ[ⲕ] .
7   [. .] ⲙ̄ⲡⲣⲱⲙⲉ . . . ⲡⲁ . . . . . . ⲛ
8   [. .] . ⲛⲉⲧⲟⲩ . . . . ⲣⲱ ⲉⲓ̈ⲥϩⲉⲓ [ⲛ]ⲉⲕ
9   [ϫⲉ ⲙ̄]ⲡⲣ̄† ⲛⲉϥ ⲛ̄ⲛⲟⲩⲙϭ ⲙ̄ⲡⲃⲉ
10 [ⲕ]ⲉ ⲡⲙ̄ⲛ̄ⲧⲥ̄ⲛⲁⲩⲥ ⲛ̄ϣⲉ ⲛ̄ϭⲛ̄ϭⲱⲣ
11 . . . ϭⲉ ⲁⲛ ⲛⲏⲧⲛ ϫⲉ ϩⲓⲡⲱϣ
12 . . . ϩⲛ̄ⲡⲱⲗϭ̄ ⲙⲛ̄ ⲛⲉⲛⲉⲣⲏⲩ
13 ⲁⲛ[ⲁ]ⲕ ⲙⲛ̄ ⲡⲣⲱⲙⲉ ⲁⲡⲟⲩⲉ
14 ⲡⲟ[ⲩ]ⲉ ϩⲡϥ̄ⲙⲉⲣⲟⲥ ⲁⲃ[ⲁ]ⲗ ⲛⲉ[.]

15 ⲙⲛ̄ [. . . .]ⲉϥ . ϩⲛ̄ϩⲃ ⲛ̄ⲛ . . ⲥ̣
16 ⲛⲉ[. . . .]ⲡϣⲗϭ ⲙ̄ⲡⲣ̄ⲣ . . .
17 ⲁⲛ[ⲉⲧ]ⲛ̣ⲉⲣⲏⲩ ⲉⲧϩⲁⲧⲛ̄ⲧ . . . . . .
18 ⲡⲣ[. . . .] . . . . ⲉⲓⲙⲟⲩⲭⲧ̄ ⲛⲏ̣
19 ⲧⲛ . ⲓⲙ̣ⲁ ⲉⲧⲉⲧⲛ̄ⲧⲉⲕⲟ ϩⲱⲧⲧⲏ̣ⲛⲉ
20 ⲛ̄ⲛⲉⲧⲛ̄ⲟⲩⲁϩⲉ ϩⲛ̄ⲧⲁϩ ⲥ̣ⲛ̄ⲧⲉ
21 ⲙ̄ⲡⲓⲉ ϩⲛ̄ⲧⲉⲧⲛ̄ⲡⲓⲙⲁ ⲛ̄ⲉ̣ϣⲁ .
22 ⲧⲉ̣ ⲙ̄ . . ⲉ̣ ⲡⲣⲱⲙⲉ ⲧⲛⲟⲩ ϭⲉ
23 ⲙⲛ̄ⲛⲁⲥⲧⲣⲉⲧⲛ̄ϫⲟⲟϥ ϫⲉ̣
24 ϩⲓⲡ̄ⲁⲛⲁⲥⲙⲉⲗⲏ ⲁⲧⲣⲟⲩⲧ[ⲛ̄]ⲛ̣ⲁⲩⲥⲉ̣
25 ⲙ̄ⲡⲗⲁⲟⲩ ⲡⲁϫⲉϥ ⲇⲉ ⲙ̄ⲡϩⲟⲟⲩ
26 ⲡⲟⲟⲩ ϫⲉ ⲡⲙⲁ ⲛⲁϫ̄ϩ̄ ⲟⲩⲧⲉ
27 ⲛⲉⲧⲁ . ϥ . . ⲙ ⲛⲉⲓⲛⲁϫⲓⲧⲟⲩ ⲣ̣ⲁⲓ̈
28 . ⲉⲧⲡ . ⲛⲁϫⲓ ⲟⲩϣⲏⲙ ⲛ̄ϩⲙ . .
29 ⲁⲣⲁϥ ϫⲉϥⲛⲁⲙⲟⲩⲭⲧ̄ ϩⲁⲧⲛ̄ⲥϩ[ⲉ]ⲓ̈
30 ϭⲉ [ⲛⲏ]ⲓ̈ ⲉⲧⲃⲉ̣ ⲡⲥⲉϫⲉ ⲙ̄ⲡⲕⲉ̣
31 ⲣ . [.] . . ϩⲱⲃ ⲛⲓⲙ ⲉϥⲛⲁϣ
32 [. . .] . . ⲧⲏⲛⲉ ⲥϩⲉⲓ̈ ⲛⲏⲓ̈ ϣⲁ
33 [. . .] . . ⲛⲧ ⲧ̄ⲛⲁⲧ̄ ⲡⲉⲣⲟⲥ . .
34 [. . .] . ⲉⲧⲙ̄ⲟ̣ ⲉⲣⲉ̣ . . . . .
35 [. . . .] ⲛ̄ⲉⲡⲓⲥⲧⲟⲗⲏ ⲧ̄[ⲥ]ϩⲉⲓ̈ ⲛⲏ[ⲧⲛ̄]
36 . . . .
37 . . . .
38 [. . . .]ϫⲓ ⲛ̄ⲧ̄ . . . . . [. . . . .]
39 . . . .
40 . . . .
41 . . . .
42 . . . .
43 . . . .
tr44 [. . . . . ⲡ]ⲁ̣ⲙⲟⲩⲣ ϥⲓ ⲡⲣⲁⲩϣ ⲛ̄ⲛ\ⲉⲕ/ⲥⲛⲏⲩ ⲉⲧϩⲁⲧⲏⲕ ⲙ̄ⲡⲣ̄ϥⲓ ⲣⲁⲩϣ ⲛⲏⲧⲛ̄ ϩⲁ ⲡⲉⲧⲙ̄ⲡϥⲙ . [. . . . .]
v45 ⲛ̄ . . . . ϥ ⲁⲡ . . . ⲧⲣⲟⲩ ⲛ̄ϩⲏⲧⲟⲩ ⲛ̣[ⲏ]ⲓ̈ ⲟⲩⲃⲉ̣ ⲡ . . . .

46 .. [. . . .] . . . .
47 [. . .] . ⲓ̈ⲧⲏ . . . †[ⲉ]ⲡⲓⲥ̣ⲧⲟⲗⲏ [ⲉ]ⲧⲛⲁⲧⲉϩⲁⲧⲏⲛⲉ̣ ⲙ̄ⲡⲣ̄ϩⲱ
48 [. . . . .] . . . ⲙ̣ⲡⲉϩⲟⲟⲩ ⲡⲉⲧⲉⲣⲉ ⲡⲟⲧ̣ⲧⲏⲥ̣ ⲛⲁⲡⲁϩⲛ̄ ⲧⲉ
49 [ⲧⲛⲁ . . . . .] . . . . . ⲓ̈ †ⲧⲉ ⲛ̄ⲱⲁⲧⲥ̄ ⲛ̄ⲧⲃ̄ⲧ ⲝⲓⲧⲟⲩ ⲛⲏⲧⲛ̄
50 [. . . . .]ⲛ̣ⲱ̣ⲁⲓ̈ ⲙ̄ⲡⲉⲟⲩⲁⲩⲛⲉ †ⲱⲓⲛⲉ ⲁⲕⲁⲡⲓⲧⲟⲩ
51 [. . . . .] . . . . ⲏⲩ
52 . . . .
53 . . . .
54 . . . . [ⲟⲩⲭ]ⲉⲓ̈ⲧⲉ . .
55 [. . . . .]ⲉⲝⲉⲁⲣ . . . .

There are also a number of other unplaced and poorly preserved fragments and scraps (visible on the digital photograph). On the best of these one can read (lowest of four lines)]ⲙ̄ⲙ . . ⲧⲛ[.

---

14 ϩⲡϥⲙⲉⲣⲟⲥ: assimilated, for ϩ(ⲃ)-ⲡϥ- 19 . ⲓ̣ⲙⲁ: initial letter hardly formed, but the scribe must have intended (ⲙ̄)ⲡⲓⲙⲁ (compare l. 21) 25 ⲙ̄ⲡϩⲟⲟⲩ sic; read ⲙ̄ⲡ‹ⲉ› ⲙ̄ⲡ›ϩⲟⲟⲩ 26 ⲡⲟⲟⲩ: second -ⲟ- ex -ⲩ- corr.

(To) [my] loved masters, who are greatly honoured by me: Pamour and Pagosh (?) ...

[Before (5) every]thing: I am astonished [why you], Pagosh, should ... the man ... So, I am writing to you (sg.): Do not give him the *nummi* for (his) wage, (10) the 1200 talents. Indeed, also, (I must tell) you (pl.) that I have divided ... (and) we have settled with one another. I and the (other) man have, each one, sent his share to ... (15) and ... We have sent the ... (and now it is) settled. Do not (make any payment?) to the fellows whom you have ...

The ... I am mixing for you here, as you are yourselves destroying (20) the ones that are in the Oasis. We have ... two cells with what is here ... the person. So, now, you have no cause to say that I have neglected to get them to send them (?) (25) to the boy. However, he says from day to day (?) that the place is difficult, and not (?) ... I would have received them. ... will receive a little ... to him so that he may mix.

Now, you (pl.) have written (30) to me about the matter of the ... everything he will ... Write to me ... I will give ... that ..., while ... (35) letter. I am writing to you ... (40) ...

(tr) ... Pamour: Take care of your brothers who are with you. Do not care about the one who has not ... (v 45) ... in them to me against the ... this letter which will reach you. Do not ... day, the one when Pottes (?) will reach us, the ... these five portions of fish. Take them for you (50) ... Shai of Peouaune. I greet Kapitou ... Be well (55) (for a long time) ...

Commentary:

2-3   The reading is very uncertain, but probably this is written to both Pamour and Pagosh, from their father Psais. Thus, one should read: [ⲡⲁ]ⲙⲟⲩⲣ ⲙⲛ̄ ⲡⲁϭ|[ⲱϣ .].

18, 29   ⲙⲟⲩⲝⲧ̄: 'mix'. At **32**, 32 the term is used for 'mix the warp'; but the process alluded to here is probably something different.

19   ⲧⲉⲕⲟ: 'destroy'. One supposes that Pshai is being critical.

20-21   ϩⲛ̄ⲧⲁϩ ⲥⲛ̄ⲧⲉ | ⲛ̄ⲣⲓⲉ: Probably one should read 'two cells', even though the number usually follows the noun. The preceding verb (ⲧⲁϩ . , or possibly ⲧⲁϫ .) is problematic. If Pshai's following comment about not have neglected to do something 'for the boy' relates to this, then maybe it is about supplying (work)rooms. But this is highly speculative. In any case, the meaning of ⲣⲓ(ⲉ) 'room' or 'cell' should be considered along with the other instances in the House 3 archive: **39**, 35; **44**, 7, 23; **81**, 27; **120**, 21. We think it probably means a 'workroom' here.

24   ⲧ[ⲛ̄]ⲛⲁⲩⲥⲉ: The reading is very uncertain.

25-26   ⲙ̄ⲡϩⲟⲟⲩ | ⲡⲟⲟⲩ: 'from day to day', or simply an emphatic form for 'today' or 'this very day' (cf. CD 731a). Still, it is unclear to us what exactly this means. Is the situation particularly bad today, or is this something that is said daily? Does it mean that the 'place' is getting progressively worse, or perhaps it is 'difficult' on a day-to-day basis? For ⲡⲙⲁ ⲙⲁⲭϩ̄ ('the place is difficult'), cf. **31**, 47. Presumably this is presented as the reason for delay; but of course we do not understand in what way it is difficult.

29   ⲟⲩϣⲏⲙ ⲛ̄ϩⲙ . . : 'a little ...'. Again, it is frustrating not to be able to read a word that might help to explain the process that he is discussing. Perhaps it is 'salt' (ϩⲙⲟⲩ); but it seems an odd statement and the reading is very uncertain. Anyway, whatever it is is being sent to the boy to 'mix'.

50   ϣⲁⲓ ⲙ̄ⲡⲉⲟⲩⲁⲩⲛⲉ: probably 'Peouaune' is a geographical rather than personal name; compare 'Peiaune' at **77**, 14, 17 (and see the note ad loc.).

P. Kellis Copt. 111

Inv #: P 61J

Location: House 3, room 8, deposit 4.

Preservation: This Coptic letter has been preserved complete on a single piece of papyrus. The dimensions are 162 x 52 mm. The ink is abraded in parts, but virtually the entire text can be read or reconstructed with confidence. It has been professionally written in a clear, rather square hand. The starts of lines 5 and 15 have been indented; and there is some basic punctuation.

Content: This is really a 'double' letter: The first 14 lines are from Pebo; the remainder by Olbinos, who even starts with a standard greeting and χαιρειν formula of his own. The contents are mostly about business matters, written in a straightforward and concise (even terse?) style. There are no greetings to women or children. Pebo is concerned about some 'tetrads' (see further the commentary), and Olbinos about items needed for textile manufacture. However, there are also interesting comments about persons and places; these are discussed below. It is difficult to place the persons involved here with any certainty. However, if these 'tetrads' are the same as in **35**, this could be the same Pshai (and also Andreas) as in the pair of letters **35-36**, and perhaps **37** and **59**. The name 'Olbinos' may occur at **88**, 24 (rather uncertain); but is not otherwise found in the House 3 archive. The general context of the letter is the Oasis, rather than the Nile valley (see further the note to l. 32).

Address:

verso

τῶι ἀγαπητῶι   X   Ψάϊτι
ἀδελφῶι   Πέβος

To the beloved brother X Psais. (From) Pebos.

Names: Andreas; Hor; Olbinos; Pebo; Pshai;

Text:

1 ⲡⲁϭⲁⲛ ⲙ̄ⲙⲉⲣⲓⲧ ⲉⲧⲧⲁⲓⲁⲉⲓⲧ
2 ⲛ̄ⲧⲟⲧ ⲧⲟⲛⲟⲩ ⲡϣⲁⲓ ⲁⲛⲁⲕ
3 ⲡⲉⲕⲥⲁⲛ ⲡⲉⲃⲟ ϯϣⲓⲛⲉ ⲁⲣⲁⲕ
4 ⲧⲟⲛⲟⲩ ϩⲛ̄ ⲡϫⲁⲉⲓⲥ ⲭⲁⲓⲣⲉⲓⲛ /
5 ⲉⲡⲓⲇⲏ ϩⲁⲓ̈ϫⲟⲥ ⲛⲉⲕ ϫⲉ ⲁⲛⲓ
6 ⲙⲏⲧ[ⲉ] ⲛ̄ⲧⲉⲧⲣⲁⲥ ⲛ̄ϩⲏⲧ ⲛ̄ⲧϣⲁ
7 ⲧⲥ̄ ϩⲁⲓ̈ⲉⲓ ⲁⲣⲏⲥ ⲁⲓ̈ϣⲓⲛⲉ ⲛ̄
8 ⲟⲗ[ⲃⲓ]ⲛⲟⲥ ⲡⲁⲭⲉϥ ϫⲉ ⲛ̄ⲟⲩⲱϣ
9 ⲛⲉⲓ̈ ⲉⲛ ⲧⲏⲣⲟⲩ ⲡⲁⲭⲉⲓ̈ ϫⲉ ⲙ̄
10 ⲙⲁⲛ ⲁϩⲣⲁⲛ ⲁⲧⲉⲕⲟ ⲛⲓϩⲛⲟ
11 ⲧⲏⲣⲟⲩ ϯⲛⲟⲩ ⲡⲉ ⲟⲩⲁϣⲣⲉ
12 ⲁⲥϩⲉ[ⲓ̈] ⲛ̄ⲧⲉⲧⲣⲁⲥ· ϩⲱⲃ ⲁⲛ
13 ⲛⲓⲙ [ⲉⲧ]ⲁⲓ̈ϫⲟⲥ ⲛⲉⲕ ⲉⲧⲃⲏⲧϥ̄
14 ⲙ̄ⲡ[ⲱ]ⲣ̄ⲁⲙⲉⲗⲉⲓ ⲁⲣⲁϥ /
15 ⲁⲛⲁⲕ ⲟⲗⲃⲓⲛⲟⲥ ⲡⲉⲧϣⲓⲛⲉ ⲁ
16 ⲡⲁϭⲁⲛ ⲙ̄ⲙⲉⲣⲓⲧ ⲉⲧⲧⲁⲓⲁⲉⲓⲧ
17 ⲛ̄ⲧⲟⲧ ⲧⲟⲛⲟⲩ ⲡϣⲁⲓ ϩⲛ̄ ⲡ
18 ⲭⲁⲉⲓⲥ ⲭⲁⲓⲣⲉⲓⲛ / ϩⲁⲑⲏ ⲛ̄
19 ϩⲱⲃ ⲛⲓⲙ ϯϣⲓⲛⲉ ⲁⲣⲁⲕ ⲧⲟ
20 ⲛ̄[ⲟ]ⲩ ⲙⲛ̄ⲛ̄ⲥⲱⲥ ⲉⲧⲃⲉ ⲛ̄
21 [ⲕⲉⲕ]ⲁⲩⲉ ⲉⲧⲁⲓ̈ⲧⲁⲃϩⲕ ⲙ̄ⲙⲁⲩ
22 ⲁⲣⲓ[ⲡ]ⲙⲉⲩⲉ ⲛ̄ⲡϩⲛⲟ ⲉⲧⲁⲓ̈
23 ⲛ̄[ⲧϥ̄] ⲛⲉⲕ ϫⲉ ϫⲓⲧϥ̄ ⲛ̄ⲧⲟⲧⲥ̄
24 [ⲛ̄ⲧⲁ]ⲙⲟ ⲙ̄ⲡⲣⲟⲩⲁⲣϩⲥ̄ ⲁⲃⲁⲗ
25 [ϣⲁⲧ]ⲥⲧⲉϥ ⲛⲉⲕ ⲙⲛ̄ ⲡⲓ
26 ϣ[ϯ]ⲧ ⲛ̄ⲧⲉ ⲡⲁϭⲁⲛ ⲡϣⲁⲓ
27 ⲉⲧⲁϩⲉⲓ ⲁ[ⲃ]ⲁⲗ ϩⲛ̄ ⲥⲱⲙⲁ
28 ϩ[ⲁⲓ̈ⲥ]ϩⲉⲓ̈ ⲙⲉⲛ ⲛ̄ⲁⲛⲇⲣⲉⲁⲥ

29	ⲉ[ⲧ]ⲃⲏⲧϥ̄ ⲁⲗⲗⲁ ⲛ̄ⲧⲁⲕ ⲁⲣⲓ
30	[. .] . [.] . . ⲙ̄ⲙⲁⲕ` ⲛ̄ⲕ̄ⲃⲱⲕ
31	[ⲛ̄ⲕ̄ⲭ]ⲓ̣ⲧⲟⲩ ⲛ̄ⲧⲟⲧⲥ̄ ⲛ̄ⲕⲏ̄
32	ⲧⲟ̣ⲩ ⲛⲏⲓ̈ ⲛ̄ⲧⲟⲧⲕ ⲁϩⲏⲃ ⲉ
33	ⲕⲛⲁⲉ ⲁⲕⲏⲙⲉ ⲉⲡⲓⲇⲏ ϩⲁ
34	ⲡⲁⲥⲁⲛ ⲡⲁⲃⲟ ϫⲟⲥ ⲛⲏⲓ̈ ϫⲉ ⲕ̄ⲛ̄
35	ⲏⲩ ⲁ̣ϩⲏⲃ ⲛ̄ϩⲟⲩⲟ ⲇⲉ ⲛ̄ϩⲟⲩⲟ
36	ⲙ̣ⲡ̣[ⲣ̄]ⲣ̣ⲁⲙⲉⲗⲉⲓ ⲁⲧⲕⲗⲱⲥⲧⲣⲁ
37	ⲛ̄ⲕϥ̣ⲓ̣ⲧⲥ ⲛ̄ⲧⲟⲧⲥ̣
tr38	vac vac vac ⲁⲡⲥ̄ ϫⲉⲕⲛⲁⲟⲩⲁϫⲟⲩ ⲉⲕϩⲙⲁⲥⲧ ϣⲁⲛⲧⲕ̄ⲧⲣⲟⲩⲧⲁⲛⲁⲥ
39	vac vac vac ⲁⲩⲱ ϯⲛⲁⲙ̄ⲙⲉ ⲁⲡⲉⲕϩⲙⲁⲧ
v40	ϣⲓⲛⲉ ⲁⲡⲁⲥⲁⲛ ⲁⲛⲇⲣⲉ̣ⲁⲥ
41	ⲧⲟⲛⲟⲩ ⲙⲛ̄ ϩⲱⲣ ϯⲣⲁϣⲓ
42	ⲟⲩ ⲙ̄ⲙⲱⲧⲛ̄ ⟦ⲉ⟧ⲛ̣[ⲁ̣]ⲥⲛⲏⲩ ⲛⲁ
43	ϫⲓⲥⲁⲩⲉ ϫⲉ ⲉⲣⲉⲧⲛ̄ⲁ̣ⲣ̄ ⲉⲡⲓⲅⲉⲛⲙ̄
44	ⲛ̄ϥ̄ⲣ̄ ⟦ⲁⲛⲁ⟧ ⲛⲓϩⲃⲏⲩⲉ ⲛⲏⲓ̈

―――

1 ⲉⲧⲧⲁⲓ̈ⲁⲉⲓⲧ: the scribe may in error have written ⲉϣⲁⲓ̈ⲁⲉⲓⲧ (see ϣⲁⲓ̈ in the following line)

34 ⲡⲁⲃⲟ: -ⲃ- ex -ϫ- corr.; ϫⲉ: -ϫ- ex corr.   36 ⲕⲗⲱⲥⲧⲣⲁ: -ⲣ- ex corr.

―――

(To) my loved brother, who is greatly honoured by me, Pshai. (It is) I, your brother Pebo. I greet you warmly in the Lord, - greetings.

(5) Since I told you: "Bring 10 tetrads north of the ditch" - I have come south. I asked Olbinos. He said: "We do not want all these". I said: (10) "Surely (not), why would we want to destroy all these things?". Is it now to stop writing the tetrads? Also, everything I have spoken to you about: Do not neglect it!

(15) I, Olbinos, am the one who greets my loved brother, who is very honoured by me, Pshai; in the Lord, - greetings.

Before everything, I greet you (20) warmly. Next, concerning the other things for which I implored you: Remember the item which I brought for you? Get it from my mother. Do not quit (25) until she gives it to you; and the warp from my brother Pshai, who has just died. I have now written to Andreas about it. But, you, do (30) ... to you, and you go and get them from her, and bring them to me with you to Hibis; if you are going to Egypt. For my brother Pabo has told me that you are (35) coming to Hibis. But, most of all, do not neglect the thread (?); and you carry it from her. (tr) Be sure to cut them whilst sitting (or: 'remaining there'?) so that you get it made; and I will understand your (good) grace.

(v 40) Greet my brother Andreas warmly, and Hor. I ask you (pl.), my brothers, my masters, that you will take on (this) burden and do these things for me.

Commentary:

Address: It is difficult to see whether the scribe has really indicated the final -ι at the end of τῶι and ἀγαπητῶι. Equally, what we suppose to be the final -ς for Πεβος (which usually would be spelt Πεβῶς) is oddly formed. There may be further ink-traces (from previous usage?) below this. Interestingly, the central X of the address has clearly been written after a strip of papyrus has peeled off. It also has a more elaborate form than the majority of examples in this archive. One may compare that at **20**; the design of **25** is the most elaborate example amongst the Coptic letters.

6, 12   ⲧⲉⲧⲣⲁⲥ: 'tetrad'. The term is also found at **35**, 37, where it clearly refers to something written (ⲥϩⲉⲓ); although one should also compare the occurrence of ⲧⲉⲧⲣⲁ at **19**, 27 in the midst of discussion about textiles. There, it obviously refers to some kind of physical object, or a standard measure or shape (e.g. 'square'?) of a known commodity. One might think about the use of 'pair' (ⲥⲁⲓⲱ or ⲏⲓ) in these texts (see further the notes at **79**, 20 and **106**, 42). The crucial question is whether we are correct in our reading of ⲥϩⲉ[ⲓ] at the start of l. 12. If so, then perhaps ⲧⲉⲧⲣⲁⲥ means 'quaternio' (of parchment or papyrus), and one should certainly compare the usage in **35**.

6-7   ⲁⲛⲓ ... ⲛ̄ϩⲏⲧ ⲛ̄ⲧϣⲁⲧⲥ̄: 'Bring ... north of the ditch'. It is not entirely clear whether Pshai was supposed to bring the tetrads to or from the north. Presumably, Pebo gave these instructions in a previous letter (is the ἐπειδή of l. 5 temporal or causal?); but now he writes again to say that he has himself 'come south'. For usage of ⲛ̄ϩⲏⲧ and ⲁⲡⲏⲥ, compare **25**, 44 and 49. For 'the ditch' (CD 593b) as a (natural or man-made?) feature of the local landscape see also **15**, 25: 'Pakous is south of the ditch, harvesting'. In any case, are we to understand that Pshai failed to do what he was asked, and consequently

Pebo has had to come looking for them? See further the note below about Hibis (ll. 32, 35) for a discussion of the geography.

7-8 ⲁⲓϣⲓⲛⲉ ⲛ̄|ⲟⲗ[ⲃⲓ]ⲛⲟⲥ: 'I asked Olbinos'. However, although the papyrus looks blank after ⲛ̄ at the end of l. 7, there is in fact an ink-trace further on. We wonder whether to read ⲁⲓϣⲓⲛⲉ ⲛ̄[ⲥ]ⲁ 'I sought after' or 'enquired for'.

27 '.. who has just died': lit. '.. who has come forth from (his) body'.

30 The missing clause must have been something like: '.. make a real effort'.

32, 35 ϩⲏⲃ: Heb, i.e. Hibis. In the Coptic texts from House 3 the only other reference is at **118**, 7; but both the city and the nome are named in a number of the Greek documents. The letter seems to imply that Olbinos and Pebo are actually in Hibis, from where (one supposes) they are writing to Kellis. Pshai would pass through on his way to the Nile valley. This might suggest that Pebo, having come south, has himself come from there. Does this suggest that the 'ditch' of ll. 6-7 refers to some feature of the road between what we now think of as the two separate oases of Dakhleh and Khargeh (but in antiquity were both part of the Great Oasis)? However, although Hibis is clearly south of where the desert road reaches the valley (nowadays in the vicinity of Siaut / Assyut cf. **81**, 28), it is due east of Kellis.

34 We presume that this Pabo is the same as the Pebo who wrote the first part of the letter.

36 ⲧⲕⲗⲱⲥⲧⲣⲁ: This must either be from the Greek κλωστήρ ('thread' or 'spindle'), or the Latin *claustra* ('key'?); see also **17**, 36 note ad loc. We prefer the former, given the reference to warp at l. 26.

37 The repeated references to 'her' in Olbinos' letter, who is probably the same as 'my mother' (l. 24), and the discussion of items needed for weaving, suggest that this woman could be Tehat. She is very much involved in the textile business (see especially **18** and possibly **58**). One notes that the only other references in the archive to ⲧⲕⲗⲱⲥⲧⲣⲁ ('thread' l. 36) and to ⲧϣⲁⲧⲥ̄ ('the ditch' ll. 6-7) are in letters by Orion, who is the author of **18**.

38-39 It is noticeable that Olbinos writes this extra text only down the side of his own 'letter', as if anxious not to intrude on what Pebo has said. Note that the verb ⲧⲁⲛⲟ 'make' is always specifically used about tailoring in this archive, thus **18**, 4; **19**, 36; **44**, 1, 6, 25; **58**, 19.

39   ⲁⲩⲱ ϯⲛⲁⲙⲙⲉ ⲁⲡⲉⲕϩⲙⲁⲧ: lit. ' and I will understand your grace'; but it probably just means 'and I will be obliged to you'.

43   ⲉⲡⲓⲅⲉⲙ̄: presumably ἐπιγεμίζω, or otherwise ἐπιγέμισις. Perhaps the author is asking his recipients to 'apply some pressure' on his behalf?

P. Kellis Copt. 112

Inv #: P 61S + P 61V/W + P63A + P65D/G

Location: House 3, room 8, deposits 3 + 4.

Preservation: This is a very faded and partly erased letter written in Coptic on papyrus, sent by a certain Pshai (= Psais) to an unknown recipient. The piece is mostly complete (as reconstructed from nine fragments), though now broken along the centre and vertical folds. The original dimensions were 140 x 102 mm.

An unrelated Greek text (edited and published by K.A. Worp as P. Kellis I Gr. 50) has been written on the verso, where traces of the letter's address (i.e. text **112**) can also be discerned. On the recto, and over the right hand ends of the lines of Coptic, this Greek document is titled as: 'Receipt of Psais Tryphanes on behalf of Psais son of Kele, grandson of Patsire'. According to its introduction (ll. 1-2) the receipt was given by Psais Tryphanes to a Psais son of Pamour. Although K.A. Worp expressed uncertainty as to which piece was written first, it seems to us that the Greek has been written over the Coptic, and that there may well have been some deliberate attempt to erase the earlier text. In that case, one might suppose that the Coptic letter had been sent to Psais Tryphanes (or someone close to him), who then reused it when in need of something on which to make the receipt. However, that is most speculative; especially as the Greek document states that it was actually written on the author's behalf by Aurelius Titherios son of Horpatos. On the problems of the name 'Tryphanes' see the note and references at **78**, 35-36.

Content: The Coptic text is difficult to read, but typical of the style found throughout the House 3 letters. Although there is little of obvious value to be derived from the remaining text, it is certain that we are here dealing with characters found elsewhere in the archive. Compare e.g. the Tryphanes and Toni of **50**, or the Psais Tryphanes of P. Kellis I Gr. 71 and 73; though indeed it is difficult to disentangle all the persons with common names.

Address: Some unreadable traces only, under the Greek text on the verso.

Names: Pollon; Pshai; Toni;

Text:

1	ⲡⲁϭⲁⲛ ⲙ̄ⲙⲉⲣⲓⲧ ⲉⲧⲧⲁⲓ̈ⲁⲓⲧ ⲛ̄ⲧⲟⲧ ⲧⲟⲛⲟⲩ
2	ⲡ . . . . ⲉⲧⲉ[ⲡ]ϥ[ⲣⲉ]ⲛ
3	ϩⲁⲗϭ ϩⲛ ⲣⲱⲓ̈ . . . .
4	ⲁⲛⲁⲕ ⲡϣⲁⲓ̈ {†}†ϣⲓⲛⲉ ⲁⲣⲁⲕ ⲧⲟ[ⲛⲟⲩ ϩⲙ̄ ⲡⲭⲁⲓ̈ⲥ]
5	[ⲭ]ⲁⲓⲣⲉⲓⲛ ϩⲁⲑⲏ ⲛ̄ϩⲱⲃ [ⲛⲓⲙ †ϣⲓ]
6	ⲛⲉ ⲁⲣⲁⲕ ⲧⲟⲛⲟⲩ ⲉⲓ̈ϣⲗⲏⲗ ⲁⲡ[ⲛⲟⲩⲧⲉ ϩⲁ ⲡⲕ]
7	ⲟⲩⲭⲉⲉⲓⲧⲉ vac ⲁⲣⲓ[. . . .] . . . . [. . . . .]
8	ϫⲉ ϩⲁⲕⲣ̄ ⲡϩ . . . . . [. . . . .] . . ⲉⲡⲁ . [. .] . .
9	ⲛⲏⲓ̈ ⲉⲧⲃⲉ ⲧⲙⲁϫ[ⲉ ⲥ]ⲛ̄[ⲧⲉ] ⲛ . ⲁⲣⲁ[.] . . .
10	ⲁⲣⲁⲕ ϫⲓⲧⲟⲩ ⲛ̄ . [. .] . . [.]ⲱⲡⲉ [. . .] . . . .
11	†ⲛⲟⲩ ⲁⲛ . ⲉⲧⲃ[.] . . . .
12	[. .] ⲙ̄ⲙⲏ . . . ⲙⲡ . . [.]ⲛ . ⲛ̄ⲧ . . . .
13	ⲣ . ⲙⲛⲁϫⲓⲧϥ̄ [. . . . .] . . . ⲛ̄ϭⲗⲁⲙ †ⲛⲟⲩ
14	ⲇⲉ ⲁⲛ ⲁⲣⲓ ⲡⲁⲙ[ⲉⲩⲉ] ϩⲛ ⲟⲩⲁⲅⲁⲡ[ⲏ] . . . . .
15	ⲛ̄ⲟⲩⲱϣⲛ̄ . . . [. . .]ⲏⲉⲓ ⲉ . [. .] . . . . [. . .]
16	ⲉⲛ . . ⲟⲩⲛ̄ⲧ . . ⲛ̄ . [.] . . ⲛ . . . . . . ⲫ[. . .]
17	†ϣⲓⲛⲉ ⲁⲣⲁⲕ . . . . [. . . †]

18   ⲱⲓⲛⲉ ⲁ . . . ⲙⲛ̄ . . ⲱⲏⲣⲉ ⲙⲛ̄ [. . . . †]
19   ⲱⲓⲛⲉ ⲁⲛⲉⲧϩⲁⲧⲏⲕ ⲧⲏⲣⲟⲩ ⲕⲁⲧ[ⲁ ⲛⲟⲩⲣⲉⲛ]
20   ἐρρῶσθαί σε εὔχομαι πολ[λοῖς χ]ρόν[οι]ς

(tr)21   ⲱⲓⲛⲉ ⲁⲡⲓⲱⲧ ⲧⲱⲛⲓ ⲧⲟⲛⲟⲩ ⲙⲛ ⲧⲁⲙⲟ ⲙⲛ̄ ⲛⲉⲕⲥⲛⲏⲟⲩ
22   ⲙⲛ ⲡⲟⲗⲗⲱⲛ ⲙⲛ ⲧϥ̄ϩⲓⲙⲉ ⲙⲛ ⲛⲉϥϣⲏⲣⲉ

―――

22 ⲧϥ̄ϩⲓⲙⲉ: -ϩ- ex -ⲥ- corr?

―――

(To) my loved brother, who is greatly honoured by me; ... whose name is sweet in my mouth ... (It is) I, Pshai. I greet you warmly [in the Lord]; (5) - greetings.

Before [every]thing: [I] greet you warmly. I am praying to [God for your] well-being. Be ... , for you have made ... for me, on account of the 2 *maje* (?) ... (10) to you. Take them ... Now, ... receive it ... quickly. So, now again, remember me with love (?) ... (15) without ...

I greet you ... [I] greet ... and ... children and ... [I] greet all who are with you, each by [their name]. (20) I pray for your health for many years.

(tr) Greet father Toni warmly, and my mother and your brothers; and Pollon and his wife and his children.

Commentary:

3   The text almost certainly continues after ϩⲛ ⲣⲱⲓ̈ with ⲛ̄ⲛⲟ ⲛⲓⲙ vel sim. ('all the time'), and then the recipient's name ('my brother N.N.'). However, the traces are unreadable.

8   ϩⲁⲕⲣ̄ ⲡϩ . . . : perhaps ϩⲁⲕⲣ̄ ⲡϩⲃⲁⲥ? However, ϩⲃⲁⲥ 'clothes' is not otherwise found with the masc. sg. article in these texts.

9   ⲧⲙⲁϫ[ⲉ ⲥ]ⲛ[ⲧⲉ] ⲛ . ⲁⲣⲁ[.]: Perhaps one should read ⲛ̄ⲕⲁⲣⲁ[ⲩ] (i.e. '2 *maje* of nuts'); compare **44**, 21. Still, the whole section is very uncertain.

19   ⲱⲓⲛⲉ ⲁⲛⲉⲧϩⲁⲧⲏⲕ: The reading is a little difficult, as it looks more like ⲱⲓⲛⲁⲛⲉ . ⲉⲧϩⲁⲧⲏⲕ. Perhaps a correction is necessary.

P. Kellis Copt. 113

Inv #: P 78A

Location: House 3, room 6, deposit 3.

Preservation: Here are two fragments of a letter written in Coptic on papyrus, plus one unplaced scrap. The hand is rather coarse and distinctive, with the letters large and sometimes crudely-formed. The exact extent of missing text between the left and right sides of the column is difficult to determine, but it cannot be very much. Thus, presuming that one must read some form of the name Hermopolis at l. 8, followed by a link to the next clause (at minimum perhaps ⲙⲛ̄] ⲕⲉ ⲥⲛ̄ⲧⲉ 'and another two'), then one can restore ⲟⲩⲛⲧ[ⲏⲉⲓ ϥ]ⲧⲟⲉ ⲙⲁϫⲉ 'I have 4 *maje*' at l. 6. In l. 7 it can not simply be ⲑⲓⲙⲉ ⲛ̄ⲓⲉⲣϩ 'the wife of Ierx ..'. We have provided an approximate estimate of the probable line lengths.

Content: The surviving text concerns small-scale business dealings involving women, such as are typical of many pieces in the archive. No names are preserved, but the reading of 'Hermopolis' is of interest.

Address:
verso

        τῷ] κυρίῳ μ[ου

        ] . ωτης [

To my master ...

Names: Ierx (Hierax?).

Text:

(x +)1   [. . . .] . ⲃⲉⳉ . [. . . . .]

2   ⲙ̄ⲡⲣ̄ⲣⲁⲙⲉⲗⲓ [. . . . .]

3   [.]ⲉ ⲁ . . ⲓⲧⲉ . [. . . . . ⲁⲓ]
4   ϫⲟⲥ ⲛⲉⲕ ϣⲓⲛⲉ [ⲛ̄ⲥⲁ . .] . . . [. . .]
5   ⲛ̣ⲟ̣ⲩ ⲕϣⲉⲧⲟⲩ [. . . . .] . ⲉ . . . ⲁ̣ⲕ
6   ϫⲟⲥ ϫⲉ ⲟⲩⲛⲧ[ⲏⲉⲓ ϥ]ⲧⲟⲉ ⲙ̣ⲁϫⲉ
7   ⲛ̄ⲧⲟⲧⲥ̄ ⲛ̄ⲑⲓⲙ[ⲉ . . . .]ⲉ ⲛ̄ⲓⲉⲣϧ ⲛ̄
8   ⲧⲉⲣⲙⲟⲩⲡ[ⲟⲗⲓⲥ . . .]ⲕⲉ ⲥⲛ̄ⲧⲉ ⲛ̄
9   ⲧⲛ̄ ⲧⲥ̄ϣⲉⲣ[ⲉ . . . .] ⲙ̄ⲡⲣ̄ⲣⲁ
10   ⲙⲉⲗⲓ ⲁϣⲉⲧ[ⲟⲩ . . . . . .]ⲩ ⲙⲛ̄ⲁⲣⲕ
11   vac? ⲥⲓⲧⲉⲃⲁⲗ[. . . . .] .
12   . [. . . . .]

tr(x +)13   [+/- 20] . ⲑ̣ⲟ̣ⲛ vac ἐρρῶσθαί σε̣ εὔχο[μαι πολλοῖς χρόνοις

———

1 -ϫ̣-: ex corr?   13 σε̣: or <σε>?

———

... Do not neglect ... [I] told you: Ask [after] ... (5) you demand from them ... You said: 'I have 4 *maje* from the wife ... Ierx of Hermopolis; (and there are?) another 2 from her daughter ...'. Do not (10) neglect to demand from them ... cast out ...

(tr) ... I pray for your health [for many years (... ?)].

Commentary:

6-7   On the construction ⲟⲩⲛⲧⲉ- ... ⲛ̄ⲧⲟⲧ= see the comments on p. 60 of P. Kellis V.

7   ⲛ̄ⲓⲉⲣϧ ⲛ̄|: One might suppose a rather poorly formed *hori* and understand the preposition ϩⲛ̄ 'in'; but we prefer to read the penultimate letter as -ϧ. Indeed, it would be difficult to understand ⲛ̄ⲓⲉⲣ in isolation. Probably Ierx is for the familiar name Hierax. Nevertheless, what comes before is a problem, as (explained *supra*) it seems one cannot read straight across from (ⲥ)ϩⲓⲙⲉ ('.. the wife of Ierax of Hermopolis').

11   ⲙⲛ̄ⲁⲣⲕ: This is rather obscure, especially if followed by a vacant space at the start of l. 12. One could otherwise take the *kappa* with the following verb ('.. you cast out'); but that still does not explain what precedes.

P. Kellis Copt. 114

Inv #: P 78Ji + P93B

Location: House 3, room 6, deposit 3.

Preservation: The remains of the upper part (?) of a document written in Coptic on papyrus, restored from two fragments. The original dimensions and extent of lost text is unknown, but (judging from the abbreviated nature of the contents as preserved) the piece may not have been very large. Indeed, it is possible that the document is complete, as the lower lines have become badly abraded and difficult to read. The text appears to have been written on a spare rectangle of papyrus, and the whole construction reminds one of such pieces as **41**, **49** and **117**.

Content: Although it is written in epistolary form, this document is a reminder of financial transactions, amounts paid and owed. It is not possible to identify the persons named with any security.

Address: No address or title is preserved (the verso is blank), and may well not have been written.

Names: Philammon; Pshai;

Text:

1   ⲧϣⲓⲛⲉ ⲁⲡⲁϭⲁⲛ ⲫⲓⲗⲁⲙⲙⲱⲛ ⲁϫⲟⲟϥ ⲛⲉⲕ
2   ϫⲉ ⲁⲣⲉ ⲟⲩⲛⲧⲉⲕ ⲛⲓϩⲁⲙⲧ ⲁⲣⲁï ϩⲁⲉⲩ ⲙⲁϫⲉ ⲡⲓ
3   ⲱⲧ ⲡϣⲁï ϫⲉ . ⲁ . . . ⲉ̣ ⲉⲓ ⲛⲏï ϫⲉ ⲟⲩⲛⲧⲉï ⲡⲁ
4   [ⲱⲡ . .]ϩⲓⲧⲃ̣ . ⲟⲧϥ̄ ⲧϣⲛⲉ ϫⲉ ϩⲓϫⲓ ⲛ̄ϩⲁⲙⲧ
5   [. . .]ⲟ . ⲟⲧϥ̄ ⲙⲛ̄ ⲡⲁϣⲡ ⲛⲉⲙⲙⲏï ⲕⲓⲣⲉ ⲙ̄
6   [. . . .]ⲟⲩⲉⲧⲁⲣⲓ . [.] . ϥϫⲉ ⲟⲩⲱϣ ⲁⲧⲣⲁ

7 [. . . .] ⲙⲛ̅ ⲡⲓⲱ̣ⲧ ⲡϣⲁⲓ̈ . . . [.] . ϣ . . ⲙ̅ⲙⲁⲓ

ⲁⲡⲁⲥ̣ⲁ̣ⲛ: looks more like ⲁⲡⲁⲡ̣ⲁⲛ? 3 ⲟⲩⲛⲧⲉⲓ̈: -ⲉ- ex corr.

I am greeting my brother Philammon to say: "For what do I owe you these monies?". Father Pshai says that (N.N?) came to me, (saying) that I have (am owed?) my [account] ... the sister, in that I received the money (5) ... and the account with me. You make ... want to cause ... and father Pshai ... me.

Commentary:

1   ϯϣⲓⲛⲉ ... ⲁ̣ϫⲟⲟϥ ⲛⲉⲕ: lit. 'I greet ..'. The syntax seems somewhat unusual.

2   ⲙⲁϫⲉ: This is another clear instance of an initial ⲙ- for the common word ⲡⲁϫⲉ- '(N.N.) says ..'. See the note at **73**, 9,11 and compare other examples at **70**, 32; **77**, 14; **81**, 9,26,54; **82**, 39.

2-3   ⲟⲩⲛⲧⲉ-: These are interesting instances of the construction discussed at p. 60 of P. Kellis V, although one would expect it to be followed by ⲛ̅ⲧⲟⲧ⸗. It must indicate some kind of debt or credit. Literally one reads here (in the first instance of l. 2): '.. you have these monies to me for what?'. Perhaps one might translate: '.. why are you holding these monies against me?'. The sense may well be that Philammon is holding up payment to the author against some supposed debt; but the whole scenario behind the document is difficult to reconstruct with so many uncertain readings.

4-5   Probably the same construction ending -ⲟⲧϥ̄ is repeated; but it does not seem possible to read e.g. ϩⲓⲧⲟⲟⲧϥ̄ or ⲛ̅ⲧⲟⲧϥ̄ in either instance.

P. Kellis Copt. 115

Inv #: P 80A + P 81A

Location: House 3, room 6, deposit 4 south wall.

Preservation: This is an almost entirely complete and well-preserved letter, written in Coptic on papyrus. One detached fragment has been added to the mid left-hand margin (section of l. 44 reading ⲛⲁⲣ̄ⲙⲛⲧⲣⲉ ⲛⲉⲕ). It is written in a fluent, attractive and practised hand; with extravagant flourishes at times. New sentences are indicated with enlarged initials (e.g. l. 9 ϩⲓⲑⲏ, l. 13 ⲭⲟⲥ). The formulaic farewell has been carefully indented, as with other professionally written pieces (e.g. **25, 36**); but note that it is written in Coptic not Greek. The dimensions are 272 x 65 mm.; and the centre fold is apparent but unbroken. There is some smudging of the ink.

Content: Tegoshe writes a sorrowful letter to Pshai, detailing deaths and a sense of abandonment. The piece manages to rise above the stock phrases of so many others, to be an affecting and personal document. Contrary to the common situation in these letters, it appears that the author is in the Oasis (ll. 25-26) and writing to Egypt. Presumably Pshai brought the letter back to Kellis at some future time, from where it has now been recovered.

Many of the names found here are common to other documents in the archive, but it is somewhat difficult to identify the situation in this piece exactly. Our best hypothesis is that the author is that same Tagoshe who is the sister of the brothers Pamour and Pegosh, and the estranged wife of Kapiton / -ou; see **75**, 37-38 and the general discussion of **77**. However, this is by no means certain.

Address:
verso

τῶι δεσπότῃ μου ἀδελφῶι   X   Ψαΐωι Τεκύσι ἡ ἀδελφή σ
                                                                             ου

To my master brother X Psais. (From) Tekysis, your sister.

Names: Ammon; Andreas; Hor; Maria (x 2); Nonna; Piena; Pshai; Tapshai; Tegoshe; Tsh(e)nbes;

Text:

1 ⲡⲁϫⲁⲓⲥ ⲡⲁⲥⲁⲛ ⲙ̄ⲙⲉⲣⲓⲧ`
2 ⲉⲧ`ⲧⲁⲓ̈ⲁⲓ̈ⲧ` ⲛ̄ⲧⲟⲧ` ⲧⲟⲛⲟⲩ` ⲡⲉⲧⲉ
3 ⲡⲩⲣⲉⲛ ϩⲁⲗⲇ̄ ϩⲛ̄ ⲧⲁⲧⲁⲡⲣⲟ ⲛ̄ⲛⲟ
4 ⲛⲓⲙ` ⲉⲓ̈ϣⲗⲏⲗ ⲁⲟⲩⲁϣⲧϥ̄ ϩⲛ̄
5 ⲡⲥⲱⲙⲁ ⲛ̄ⲧⲉ ⲡⲁⲣⲉϣⲉ ϫⲱⲕ
6 ⲁⲃⲁⲗ ⲡⲁⲥⲁⲛ ⲡϣⲁⲓ̈ ⲁⲛⲁⲕ
7 ⲧⲉⲕⲥⲱⲛⲉ ⲧⲉϭⲟϣⲉ ⲧⲉⲧⲥϩⲉⲓ̈
8 ⲛⲉⲕ` ϩⲛ̄ ⲡϫⲁⲓ̈ⲥ ⲭⲁⲓⲣⲉⲓⲛ
9 ϩⲓⲑⲏ ⲛ̄ϩⲱⲃ ⲛⲓⲙ` ϯϣⲓⲛⲉ ⲧⲟ
10 ⲛⲟⲩ ⲁⲧⲕⲙⲛ̄ⲧⲥⲁⲛ ⲉⲧⲛⲁⲛⲟⲩⲥ
11 ⲙⲛ̄ ⲛⲁϫⲓⲥⲁⲩⲉ ⲛⲁϣⲏⲣⲉ
12 ⲙⲁⲣⲓⲁ ⲡⲓⲉⲛⲁ ⲙⲛ̄ ϩⲱⲣ
13 ϫⲟⲥ ⲇⲉ ⲛⲏⲓ̈ ⲛ̄ⲧⲁϣⲉⲣⲉ
14 ⲙⲁⲣⲓⲁ ϫⲉ ⲙ̄ⲡⲣ̄ⲧⲁⲣⲟ ⲡⲉϩⲛ̄ⲧ
15 ⲛ̄ⲧⲟⲧ` ϫⲉ ⲙ̄ⲡⲣⲉⲓ ⲁⲟⲩⲁⲣⲡⲉ ⲁ
16 ⲃⲁⲗ ⲉⲡⲉⲓⲇⲏ ⲛ̄ⲧⲁⲓ̈ⲟⲩⲱϩ ⲁ
17 ⲡϣⲧⲟ ⲁ ⲛ̄ϣⲏⲣ[ⲉ] ⲛ̄ⲛⲟⲛ
18 ⲛⲁ ϣⲱⲛⲉ ⲁⲩⲙⲟⲩ ⲁⲓ̈ⲣ ⲓ̈ⲁ
19 ⲃⲉ ϩⲱⲧ` ⲙ̄ⲡ⟨ⲓ⟩ϭⲛ̄ ⲑⲉ ⲛ̄ⲉⲓ
20 ⲛ̄ⲧⲁⲕ` ⲇⲉ ⲡⲁⲥⲁⲛ ⲙ̄ⲡⲣ̄ⲣ̄ ⲡⲁ
21 ⲱⲃϣ ⲁⲗⲗⲁ ⲑⲉ ⲉⲧⲉⲛⲉⲕ`ϭⲓ
22 ⲙ̄ⲡⲁⲣⲁⲩϣ` ⲛ̄ⲛⲓⲙⲁ ⲙ̄ⲡⲣ̄
23 ⲕⲁⲧ ⲁⲛ ⲛ̄ⲥⲱⲕ vac ϣⲓⲛⲉ ⲛⲏⲓ̈
24 ⲧⲟⲛⲟⲩ ⲁⲧⲁϫⲁⲓ̈ⲥ ⲧⲁⲥⲱⲛⲉ ⲧⲁ
25 ⲡϣⲁⲓ̈ ϫⲟⲥ ⲛⲉⲥ ϫⲉ ⲛⲉⲓ̈ⲧⲛ̄ϣ
26 ⲁⲉⲓ ⲁⲕⲏⲙⲉ ⲁⲛⲁⲕ` ⲙⲛ̄ ⲧⲕⲟⲩⲓ̈
27 ⲁ ⲡⲙⲟⲩ ϭⲉ ϫⲓⲧ ⲛ̄ϫⲛⲁϩ ⲁϥϥⲓ
28 ⲧⲥ̄ ⲛ̄ⲧⲟⲧ` ⲉⲩ ⲧⲉ ⲧⲁϭⲁⲙ` ⲙⲛ ⲉⲣⲉ ⲛ̄
29 ⲧⲁⲥ ⲡⲉ ⲛ̄ⲟⲩⲁϩⲧⲥ̄ ⲁⲗⲗⲁ ⲛ̄ⲕⲉϣⲏ
30 ⲣⲉ ⲛ̄ⲛⲟⲛⲛⲁ ⲁⲩⲙⲟⲩ ϩⲱⲟⲩ ⲁⲛ
31 ⲁⲓ̈ϫⲓ ⲧϫⲏⲗϭⲉ ⲛ̄ⲧⲟⲧϥ ⲛ̄ⲁⲙ

32	ⲙⲱⲛ ⲛ̄ⲣⲟϩⲁ ⲡⲉⲧⲁⲕⲧⲛ̄ⲛⲁ\ⲩ[ϥ]/
33	ⲧⲏⲣϥ̄ ⲁⲓ̈ϫⲓⲧϥ̄ ⲙⲡⲣ̄ⲣ ⲡⲁϣⲃϣ
34	ⲧⲁⲭⲁ ϩⲱⲧ ϯϭⲛ̄ ⲑⲉ ⲙ̄ⲡⲱϩ [ⲁ]
35	ⲣⲱⲧⲛ̄ ⲉϣⲱⲡⲉ ⲡⲉ ⲡⲉⲓ̈ ⲁⲓ̈
36	ⲛⲁϭⲱ ⲉⲓ̈ⲥⲙⲁⲛⲧ ϣⲓⲛ[ⲉ]
37	ⲛⲛⲓ̈ ⲧⲟⲛⲟⲩ ⲁⲧⲁⲥⲱⲛⲉ ⲙⲁⲣⲓⲁ
38	ⲙⲛ̄ ⲛⲉⲥϣⲏⲣⲉ ⲙⲛ̄ ⲧⲁⲥⲱ
39	ⲛⲉ ⲧϣⲛ̄ⲃⲏⲥ ⲙⲛ̄ ⲛⲉⲥϣⲏ
40	ⲣⲉ ⲙⲛ̄ ⲟⲩⲁⲛ ⲛⲓⲙ` ⲉϥϯ ⲙ̄ⲧⲁⲛ
41	ⲛⲉⲕ ⲱⲛϩ̄ ⲛ̄ⲕⲟⲩϫⲉⲓ̈ⲧⲉ ⲛ
42	ⲟⲩⲛⲁϭ ⲛ̄ⲟⲩⲁⲓ̈ϣ ⲡⲁϫⲁⲓ[ⲥ]
43	ⲡⲁⲥⲁⲛ

tr44 ⲡⲁϣⲏⲣⲉ ⲇⲉ ⲁⲛⲇⲣⲉⲁⲥ ⲛⲁⲣⲙⲛⲧⲣⲉ ⲛⲉⲕ ⲛ̄ⲟⲩⲱ ⲛⲓⲙ` ⲙⲛ̄ ⲑⲉ ⲧⲏⲣⲥ` ⲉϯϣⲟⲡ ⲙ̄ⲙⲁⲥ ⲛ̄ϥ̄ⲧⲉⲟⲩⲟ ⲁⲣⲁⲕ ⲉⲧⲃⲉ ⲡⲁⲕⲁⲧ ⲛ̄ⲱⲛϩ̄

---

15 ⲟⲩⲁⲣⲡⲉ: -ⲡ- ex corr.   22 ⲙ̄ⲡⲣ̄ pap.   44 ⲱⲛϩ̄ pap.

(To) my master, my loved brother who is greatly honoured by me: The one whose name is sweet in my mouth at all times; while I am praying to embrace him in (5) the body, and my joy will be complete. My brother Pshai: I, your sister Tegoshe, am writing to you in the Lord; - greetings.

Before everything: I greet (10) warmly your good brotherliness; and my masters, my children Maria, Piena and Hor. Now, say for me to my daughter Maria: "Do not force your heart (15) for me, do not be about to launch forth" - just because I am laid low. The children of Nonna fell ill and died. I, myself, developed pus; (and) I have not been able to come. (20) But, you, my brother: Do not forget me. Rather, just as you were taking care of me here (before), do not abandon me now.

Greet me warmly to my lady, my sister (25) Tapshai. Tell her that I was set to come to Egypt, myself and the little girl. Then death forced itself on me (and) carried her away. I am powerless. It is not only her; but (30) Nonna's children also have died.

I received the cloth bag from Ammon of Roha (?). All that you have sent I have received. Do not forget me; and perhaps I can find a way to reach (35) you (pl.). If this happens I will stay being all right.

Greet me warmly to my sister Maria and her children, and my sister Tshenbes and her children, (40) and everyone who gives rest to you. Live and be well for a long time, my master, my brother. (tr) And my son Andreas will bear witness to you (sg.) of all the news and the state I am in, and he will tell you about my life's course.

Commentary:

Address   The dative Ψάϊωι (rather than Ψάϊτι) would indicate a form of the name as Ψάϊος. See, similarly, **64**, **70** and **72**. However, we doubt that this has any significance. No variation is made in the Coptic form Pshai; and we have continued to transcribe it as Psais.

It appears that the address was written when the letter had already been folded in half. Thus, the scribe has written ἡ ἀδελφη σ, and (having run out of room) then completes σ|ου on the following line.

12   For the pair of brothers Piena and Hor see the introduction to the Ploutogenes letters.

14-17   Tegoshe's message to Maria sounds like the caricature lament of an old lady: 'Don't put yourself out on my behalf'. We have translated the passage rather freely. The noun ⲡⲱⲧⲟ must be derived from ⲭⲧⲟ 'lie down' (CD 792ab); literally the phrase with ⲟⲩⲱϩ would mean something like 'I have settled to the lying-down', i.e. succumbed to sickness. However, note that our understanding of this passage can not be applied to the occurrence of ⲡⲱⲧⲟ at **120**, 23; where it seems to be a toponym. The two instances might be reconciled if the word refers to some kind of place for convalescence, such as (perhaps rather anachronistic) a sanatorium or quarantine area. If so, Tegoshe's lament here would be better translated in a more material fashion as: '.. because I have been put in the sickness place'.

17, 30   Nonna: Perhaps the same as at **92**, 20-21 (where it is stated that she and her daughters are doing well).

23   ⲁⲛ: This could be translated 'again' or 'also'; but we have preferred a more neutral rendering as 'now'.

27   ⲡⲙⲟⲩ: One wonders if 'the death' here might indicate plague (cf. CD 159b)?

28   'I am powerless': lit. 'What is my power?'. The following ⲙⲛ- and ⲉⲣⲉ- are both syntactically most remarkable. Since the context clearly demands the clause to be

negated and there is no other negation here, the element ⲙⲛ- can, as far as our familiar inventory of Coptic grammar goes, only be the negative existential; but it is used here to precede a focalising ⲉⲡⲉ-, which in itself is quite unusual for a Nominal Sentence structure. Put another way, one may recognise in this usage one of the basic functional components of ⲙⲛ-, negating the existence (not of entities but) of entire states-of-affairs, as a reduced proclitic form of ⲙ̄ⲙⲁⲛ 'no', in a construction that may also very well be resolved as: 'Not that it is her alone (but ..)'. And, incidentally, it is interesting to see how a matter of life and death, and the desperation of loss, brings out the most extraordinary examples of rhetorical syntax.

32 Roha: Probably a toponym. It could, of course, be the name of Ammon's father; but there is nothing similar recorded in Hasitzka's *Namen*. Either way, there are a number of figures named Ammon in these texts, and it is difficult to identify / distinguish them.

37 This must be a different Maria to the daughter that Tegoshe made her complaint to earlier. If our hypothesis is correct that the author is Pamour's sister, then this Maria would most likely be the latter's wife.

40-41 Note the repeated use of the term ϯ ⲙ̄ⲧⲁⲛ 'give rest' in both the Orion and Ouales letters of volume one (P. Kellis V); especially the references and discussion there at p. 53. This is the only other instance in the archive, and the question remains whether it has some specific communal meaning (the other groups of letters have a clear Manichaean context). For translation, perhaps one might prefer something like 'brings calm to you' or 'sets you at peace'; or, even, a much freer 'everyone who pleases you'.

44 Presumably Andreas has carried the letter with him to the Nile valley.

P. Kellis Copt. 116

Inv #: P 81E + P93B

Location: House 3, room 6, deposit 4 south wall.

Preservation: Three fragments of inscribed papyrus can be joined to reconstruct a substantial section from the lower part of a letter written in Coptic. The original document may well have broken on the centre fold, with the upper half now entirely missing. Since what remains is 134 x 91 mm., this suggests an original height of approximately 268 mm.; which would be similar to a good number of the other larger letters: e.g. **80** (274 mm.), **82** (276 mm), **105** (274 mm.), **106** (270 mm.). Many of these pieces are not as wide as **116** (which must have originally exceeded 100 mm.); but compare **80** (274 x 103 mm.) and imagine a left hand strip missing from the centre fold down. However, in contrast to that piece, this scribe has filled the entire available space with his distinctive small and slanted (to the right) script.

Content: The major part of this document (P81E) was found together with the major part of **82** = P81E(a). Although the letters have different authors (**82** was written by Philammon to Loishai, i.e. Theognostos), the two pieces clearly stem from the same context in the Nile valley. In the other piece Kapiton is about to come to Egypt from the Oasis; here he has already visited and left for Antinoou. The latter city also features in the Makarios family letters (cf. **19**, **21**, **25**), which are clearly linked to those of Philammon through the figure of Lysimachos. Note also the reference to doing business there at P. Kellis Gr. I 71, 16. Thus, this letter belongs to those characters and events that are central to the House 3 archive. The author may indeed be the same as that Tapshai in Egypt greeted in the previous letter (**115**, 24-26), as well as a number by Makarios and his son Matthaios (**19**, **25**, **26**) and also by Pamour and Maria (**65**, **67**, **68**). However, there could very well have been more than one person of this name (see the repetition at **65**, 44 and 48). Pshai, the recipient of this letter, may be the author's husband (note **67**, 34-35). However, in the text Tapshai is mostly addressing a woman, perhaps Tegoshe (see the note to l. 5). In that case, the address to Pshai would simply be the usual practice in a patriarchal society, where he is the husband or male 'guardian' of the recipient (compare **115** for these persons). Alternatively, it may be because a substantial part from the start of the letter is lost, and in that first half Tapshai has addressed Pshai.

Address:

verso

κυρί]ῳ μο\υ/ ἀδελφῶι   X   Ψάϊτι ἡ ἀδελφή σου Τεψάϊ[ς]

To my master brother X Psais. (From) your sister Tepsais.

Names: Eni; Jmpnoute; Kapiton; Lammon; Maria; Pshai; Tabes; Tepsais; Titoue;

Text:

x + 1   [. . . . .] . [. .] . [. . . . .] . [. . . . . . .] . [.]

2   [. . . . .]ⲉ ⲛⲙ̄ⲙⲉϥ ⲟⲩⲱ ⲉϥⲙ̄ⲙⲉ ⲁⲡⲥⲉϫⲉ· ⲉⲓ̈ⲥⲁⲩⲛⲉ ⲁⲛ

3   [. . . . . ⲟⲩ]ⲛⲟⲩ ⲙ̄ⲙⲁϥ· ⲧⲙ̄ⲙⲛ̄ⲧϣⲃⲏⲣ` ⲛⲁⲕⲛ̄ⲧϥ̄ ⲉⲛ ⲁⲃⲁⲗ ⲁ

4   [. . . . .]ⲉ †ⲣϣⲡⲏⲣⲉ ⲧⲟⲛⲟⲩ ⲙⲛ̄ {ⲙ}ⲛ̄ⲥⲉϫⲉ ⲉⲧⲉⲛⲉⲣⲉⲧⲉⲟⲩ

5   [ⲟ ⲙ̄ⲙⲁⲩ . . . . . .]ⲙⲟⲩⲛ ⲛ̄ⲥⲉϫⲉ ⲙ̄ⲡⲣ̄ϭⲱ ⲉⲙⲡⲉⲉⲓ ⲁⲃⲁⲗ ⲧⲉⲛ̄ ⲧⲕⲟⲩ

6   [ⲓ̈ . . . .] ⲉⲧⲃⲏⲧⲛ̄ ⲕⲁⲛ ⲁⲙⲏ ⲉⲧⲃⲉ ⲡⲕⲟⲩⲓ̈ ϫⲉ ϥⲧⲉⲟⲩⲟ ⲙ̄ⲡⲉⲣⲉⲛ

7   [. . . . .]ⲛ̣ ⲁⲣⲁⲛ †ⲛⲟⲩ· ⲉⲙⲡⲁⲧⲉ ⲡϥ̄ⲓ̈ⲱⲧ ⲃⲱⲕ ⲁⲙ[ⲁ] ⲉϥⲟⲩⲛⲟⲩ

8   [. . . . .]ⲅ̄· ⲧⲣⲁⲙⲡⲉ· ϥ̄2ⲏⲛ ⲁⲣⲁⲛ· ⲉϣⲱⲡⲉ ⲉⲩⲛⲁϥⲓ ⲛ̄ϣⲁⲧ` ϩⲁ

9   [. . . . . ⲛ̄]ⲏⲧⲛ̄ ϥⲕⲏ ⲁϩⲣⲏⲓ̈ ⲭⲛ̄ ⲙ̄ⲡⲟⲩⲁⲓ̈ⲱ ⲉⲧⲁⲛⲉⲓ ⲁⲕⲏⲙⲉ· ⲉ

10   [. . . . .] · ϩⲁⲡⲗⲱⲥ [.] . [.]ϫⲉ ⲧⲉⲉⲓ ⲑⲉ ⲉⲧⲉⲣⲉ ⲡⲛⲟⲩⲧⲉ ⲛⲁⲥⲃⲧⲱ

11   [ⲧⲥ̄ . . . . ⲡ]ⲁⲥⲁⲛ ⲕⲁ̣ⲡⲓⲧ[ⲱⲛ] ϣⲓⲛⲉ ⲁⲣⲱⲧⲛ̄· ⲛ̄ⲧⲁϥⲃⲱⲕ ⲁⲁⲛⲧⲓⲛⲟⲟⲩ

12   [. . . . .]ⲉ †ϣⲓⲛⲉ ⲁ̣[ⲧⲁⲙⲟ] ⲙⲁⲣⲓⲁ ⲙⲛ̄ ⲉ̄ⲛⲓ ⲙⲛ̄ ⲛⲉⲥϣⲏⲣⲉ

13   [. . . . .]ϣⲓⲛⲉ ⲁⲡⲁⲓ̈[ⲱⲧ ††]ⲟⲩⲉ ⲙⲛ̄ ⲗⲁⲙⲙⲱⲛ· †ϣⲓⲛⲉ ⲁⲧⲁⲃⲏⲥ·

14   [. . . . .] . ⲧ . . [. . . ⲉϣⲱ]ⲡⲉ ⲉⲩⲛⲁϭⲛ̄ ⲑⲉ ⲛ̄ⲛ̄ⲧϥ̄· ⲛ̄ⲓ̈ⲉ ⲙ̄ⲡⲣ̄ϭⲱ

15   [ⲉⲙⲡⲉ . . . . . .]ⲧⲟⲩ[. . . . . †]ϣⲁⲧ ⲛ̄ⲗⲁⲩⲉ ⲉⲛ· ⲧⲟⲩⲉϣⲧⲉ ⲙ̄ⲡⲓⲛⲟⲩ

16   [ⲧⲉ . . . .] . ⲁⲣⲱⲧⲛ̄ ⲉⲛ· ⲛ̄ⲧⲁⲕ ⲇⲉ ⲡⲁⲥⲁⲛ

17   [. . . . .]ⲁ̣ⲥⲱ ϫⲉⲕⲉ̄ⲓ̣ ⲛⲙ̄ⲙⲉⲩ ⲧⲛ̄ⲛⲟ ⲁⲣⲱⲧⲛ̄

18   [. . . . .]ϫⲙ̄ⲡⲛⲟⲩⲧⲉ ⲙⲛ̄ ⲛⲉⲥϣⲏⲣⲉ· ⲕⲟ ⲛ[

19   [. . . . .] . ⲉⲛ ⲁⲥⲉⲓ̈ ⲛⲏⲧⲛ̄·   ἐρρῶσθαί σε

20   vac   εὔχομαι πολλοῖς

21   χ[ρ]ό[νο]ις κύριέ μου

———

address ἡ: ῆ pap.   16 ⲁⲣⲱⲧⲛ̄:-ⲛ ex corr.

———

... with him ceases, as he understands the matter. I also know ... [being far away (?)] from him. Our friendship will [never (?)] fail him ... I am very surprised at the words that you (fem.) were uttering (5) ... word. Do not delay your coming out, and bring the little girl [with you; if not] on our account, at least come because of the boy, for he is uttering your name. ... to us now, before his father goes to a distant place ... year. He is near to us.

If they will take the cushions for ... to you (pl.). It has been laid down since the time we came to Egypt. (10) ... In short, ... and you (fem.) come, the way that God will provide ...

My brother Kapiton greets you (pl.). He has gone to Antinoou ... I greet [my mother] Maria, and Heni and her children ... greet my father Titoue and Lammon. I greet Tabes ... If they can find a way to bring him, then do not delay (15) ... [I] lack for nothing. Praise God! ... not to you. But, you, my brother, ... that you (masc. sg.) come with them and we see you (pl.) ... Jmpnoute and her children. You are ... she came to you. I pray for your health (20) for many years, my master.

Commentary:

3   ⲕⲛ̄ⲧϥ̄: cf. comm. ad **77**, 11.

3-4   It would be attractive to read here ⲁ|[ⲛⲏϩ]ⲉ 'ever'; but the sequence of words elsewhere (e.g. the following ll. 4-5) suggests that there must be rather more lost at the start of each line.

5   One wonders whether this is the same little girl who has died in **115**, 23-26; in which case the woman that Tepshai is here addressing should be Tegoshe.

5-6   One might restore, *exempli gratia*, ⲧⲕⲟⲩ|[ⲓ̈ ⲛⲙ̄ⲙⲉ ⲉⲓⲙⲏⲧⲓ].

8   It may be no coincidence that there is a discussion of a 'large cushion' ⲧⲛⲁϭ ⲛ̄ϣⲁϣⲁⲧⲉ at **82**, 18.

12   ⲉ̄ⲛⲓ: What is typified in the transcription as a stroke above the epsilon is actually a bow-shaped breathing, just as above the Greek article (ῆ) in the address.

15-16   ⲧⲟⲩⲉϣⲧⲉ ⲙ̄ⲡⲛⲟⲩ[ⲧⲉ: cf. comm. ad **82**, 16.

P. Kellis Copt. 117

Inv #: P 91B

Location: House 3, room 6, deposit 5.

Preservation: This is a 'spare' rectangular strip of papyrus (43 x 94 mm.), with Coptic text written across the fibres. It seems to be mostly complete in one piece; although some small edge fragments are breaking away, and the lower left hand corner is lost (but was probably not inscribed). However, it is possible that a further fragment of inscribed papyrus has been lost from the right hand side, which could explain some of the textual difficulties (see below). One should compare **114** and the other pieces referenced there.

Content: This is a brief note rather than a letter, but still with a number of problems. In particular, what is the meaning (and indeed syntax) of the initial governing construction ⲛ̄ⲧⲟⲩⲙⲏⲥⲉ? Whilst the reading itself is not entirely clear, we have supposed ⲙⲏⲥⲉ (CD 186a) and translated 'their offspring'; but this still leaves the function of the initial ⲛ- somewhat problematic ('To ..'?). Is it conceivable that there could be some connotation such as: 'On their birthday' (though this should rather be ϩⲟⲩⲙⲓⲥⲉ CD 185ab and masc.). Alternatively, the ⲙⲏⲥⲉ might refer to financial interest; or could it even be possible that Toumese is in fact a third name to go with Senapollo and Gena (cf. Τμεσιῶς under ⲙⲉⲥⲓⲱ 'midwife' CD 186b). For the lexical range of the words ⲙⲓⲥⲉ and ⲙⲏⲥⲉ see CD 184b-186b.

Further to those problems, it remains unclear who actually is being greeted (ϣⲓⲛⲉ) and by whom. Presuming that the initial ⲧⲟⲩ- is the possessive 'their', and fem. to agree with ⲙⲏⲥⲉ; it must still be noted that the latter is singular. Again, why is 'her sister' mentioned twice; and is Partheni the name of a second sister, or in fact the sender of the piece with her name subscribed at the close?

Finally, one must reckon with the possibility that some text has been lost at the end of both lines 1 and 2. We take the unusual step of providing some alternative ways of understanding the text.

Address: The verso is blank and there would have been no address.

Names: Gena; Partheni; Senapollo; (Toumese?);

Text:

1   ⲛ̄ⲧⲟⲩⲙⲏϭⲉ ⲥⲉⲛⲁⲡⲟⲗⲗⲱ ⲙⲛ̄ ⲅⲉⲛⲁ
2   ⲧϣⲓⲛⲉ ⲁⲧⲥ̄ⲥⲱⲛⲉ ⲙⲛ̄ ⲧⲥ̄ⲙⲟ ⲙⲛ̄ ⲧⲥ̄
3   ⲥⲱ[ⲛ]ⲉ ⲡⲁⲣⲑⲉⲛⲓ

---

   2 ⲧϣⲓⲛⲉ: for ⲉⲧ-, or perhaps for ⲧ<ⲓ> / ϯ- or even ⲧ<ⲛ>-?

(It is) their offspring, Senapollo and Gena, who greet her (i.e. Senapollo's?) sister and her mother, and her sister Partheni.
or perhaps: On (this?) birthday: Senapollo and Gena greet her sister and mother and sister Partheni.
or even: For Toumese, Senapollo and Gema. I greet her (i.e. my) sister and mother and sister. (From) Partheni.
or, presuming some lost text: To their offspring: Senapollo and Gena ... greets her sister and her mother and her ... sister Partheni.

Commentary:

1   Senapollo: cf. Jnapllo at **64**, 32. There are a number of names in the archive constructed in this familiar fashion (i.e. Tse- or ϫⲉ- for ⲧϣⲉ(ⲣⲉ) 'the daughter of ..').

   Gena: Probably the same name as found elsewhere in the archive (i.e. a form of Piena / Iena), in which case it is masc.; or possibly one could read Gema.

2   ⲧϣⲓⲛⲉ: It is difficult to know whether this - presumably erroneous - text was intended to continue what had gone before (i.e. a relative construction 'Senapollo and

Gena who greet ..'), or marked the start of a new sentence (i.e. a first present tense 'I / We greet ..').

P. Kellis Copt. 118

Inv #: P 92.1

Location: House 3, room 4, floor surface.

Preservation: A papyrus fragment preserving the upper portion of a letter written in Coptic (and Greek) in a tiny script; now 24 x 49 mm. The original dimensions are unknown, but the width is probably completely preserved (although the right hand edge of the recto is eroded in places). Exceptionally, the 'recto' is the side with vertical fibre; the 'verso' with horizontal.

N.B. There are four other small fragments glassed with this piece at P92.1, also in tiny script. They appear to be from a number of other texts (at least two) and can not be joined with **118**. Consequently, they have not been edited here; but there remains a small possibility that some could belong to this document. It may be noted that one of them preserves part of the address on the verso: It was evidently written to Psais (read Ψάϊτι) from Andreas.

Content: There is little text preserved, but the piece is of interest for a number of reasons. Firstly, there is the remarkable small, fluent script; and the way that the bilingual scribe switches from the formulaic Greek opening into Coptic, but then forgets himself by writing ⲡⲁⲛⲧⲱⲛ for ⲧⲏⲣⲟⲩ ('all of them') in l. 4. In l. 7 the form ⲁⲙⲙⲱⲛⲓ would also seem to betray a Greek form. Secondly, as regards content, readable text on the verso ends with a rare reference (in the Coptic material) to the Roman administration. Prosopographical cross-referencing (cf. the note to l. 6) suggests that this piece could belong with the Ouales letters (**35**, **36**, **59**); which are all themselves distinguished by a fluent use of Greek.

Address: None preserved.

Names: Ammon; Bale (i.e. Ouales or Belle?); Bo (?); Hor; Iena; Pshai;

Text:

1 κυρίωι μου ἀδελφῶι ὁ ἀδελφὸς
2 χαίρειν ϩιθη ⲛϩⲱⲃ ⲛⲓⲙ` ϯϣⲓⲛⲉ
3 ⲁⲣⲁⲕ ⲧⲟⲛⲟⲩ ⲙⲛ̄ ⲡⲁⲭⲁⲓⲥ ⲡⲁⲓⲱⲧ ⲙⲛ̄
4 ⲛ̄ⲕⲉⲥⲛⲏⲩ ⲉⲑⲁⲧⲏⲕ ⲡⲁⲛⲧⲱⲛ ⲕⲟⲩⲓ ⲛⲁϭ
5 ⲙⲛ̄ [ⲡ]ϣⲁⲓ ⲙⲛ̄ ⲓⲉⲛⲁ ϩⲱⲣ ⲙⲛ̄ . [. . .]

-----

v(x +)6 ϩⲁ ⲃⲟ . . ⲩ . ⲓ̈ ⲧⲛ̄ϫⲟⲥ ⲙ̄ⲡⲓ̈ⲱⲧ ⲃⲁⲗⲉ ⲙⲙⲁⲛ
7 ⲣⲱ ⲁⲙⲙⲱⲛⲓ ⲁϥⲃⲱⲕ ⲁⲛ ⲁϩⲏⲃ
8 ϩⲁ ⲡⲧⲣⲓⲃⲟⲩⲛⲟⲥ . . . ⲣ . . . .
9 traces

---

6 ⲧⲛ̄ϫⲟⲥ: right hand upright of the -ⲛ- overwritten by the following -ϫ-; ⲓ̈ⲱⲧ: ⲓ̈- looks like ϩ̄-

---

To my master brother. (From) the brother; - greetings.

Before everything: I greet you warmly; and my master, my father; and the other brothers who are with you, all of them, young and old; (5) and Pshai and Iena (and) Hor and ...

(v) on account of Bo (?) ... and we will tell father Bale: "No indeed". Ammoni has also gone to Hibis on account of (?) the tribune ...

Commentary:

4 ⲡⲁⲛⲧⲱⲛ: The bilingual scribe / author has slipped into Greek, when for 'all of them' he should have given the Coptic ⲧⲏⲣⲟⲩ.

5   It is better to presume that Iena and Hor are two persons (rather than a single name Ienahor), for reasons discussed in the introduction to the Ploutogenes group of letters.

6   Bo may be a name, as the same occurs in the KAB (ll. 600, 901, 1306, etc.). This is probably an abbreviated form of Pebo, which occurs a number of times in the House 3 archive. However, we do not understand the complex following 'Bo', and perhaps another solution can be found. We have transcribed ϩⲁ ⲃⲟ . . ⲩ . ï, but this is difficult to explain. At the start one might try an -ⲩ- ligatured with some other letter; in which case it could be ϩⲁⲃ- 'send' plus the indefinite article ⲟⲩ. But, again, one can make no sense of what follows. A rather ambitious alternative could be ϩⲁ ⲃⲟⲩⲗ . . . . or even ϩⲁ ⲃⲟⲩⲗⲉⲩ . ⲛ̄ⲧⲛ̄ϫⲟⲥ (reading ⲛ̄- for the following conjunctive rather than a final -ï). Obviously, Greek words beginning βουλ- suggest a number of interesting possibilities, especially if the construction is set in parallel to the ϩⲁ ⲡⲧⲣⲓⲃⲟⲩⲛⲟⲥ of l. 8. But this is very speculative, and does require a scribe who switches between Coptic and Greek without thinking.

Bale is a better reading than Blle; but could be same name as Belle(s), which is spelt in various ways in the Coptic texts. Interestingly, these two name (Pebo and Belle) mean, respectively, 'dumb' and 'blind' in Coptic; see CD 38a and 178ab. Alternatively, Bale could be for Vales. Although this name is spelt Ouales in **35** and **36** (and restored in **59**), in each instance it occurs only in the Greek address or opening formula; i.e. we have no Coptic spelling of the name from the Kellis texts. Interestingly, at **36**, 10 we should probably read 'Iena and [Hor]'. Given that the Ammon of **37** is a probable associate of that Ouales, this correspondence of names could well indicate that **118** belonged to the same circle. Ouales was almost certainly a professional scribe and of Manichaean belief; and the group of letters associated with him is particularly interesting.

7   ⲁⲙⲙⲱⲛⲓ: Perhaps read 'Ammoni(os)'?

8   ⲧⲣⲓⲃⲟⲩⲛⲟⲥ: The reading is convincing, and must be for τριβοῦνος / *tribunus* (cf. LSJ supp. 295b). We think it is unlikely to be a personal name, because of the preceding definite article; although otherwise the word can be used as such (cf. *Namen*). It is not clear exactly what force the preceding preposition ϩⲁ has, given that we do not know the context; it could mean 'at', 'by reason of', 'for', 'under', 'on behalf of', or even 'against'.

P. Kellis Copt. 119

Inv #: P92.15B

Location: House 3, room 1, deposit 1.

Preservation: Here are four fragments of inscribed papyrus, which probably belong to a single letter written in Coptic. Two fragments can be joined to read the start of three lines of transverse text down the margin; and thus probably belong to the upper left-hand corner of the document (compare e.g. the published plate of **25**). The verso is not inscribed, and the address was probably written on this half of the original letter (now almost entirely lost). The other two fragments preserve the beginning and end of lines on the verso, and thus belong to the lower half of the original document (again compare **25**). In fact, where these lines end on the verso one can see the centre fold. So, whilst these factors give a general idea of the placing of the four fragments in terms of the original document, we still do not know exactly how long any of the lines were or the actual dimensions. Line lengths given in the edition below are purely illustrative of the probable range. The line numbers are simply for the purpose of reference, although we have made an assumption that the document may have been similar in proportions to a letter such as **31** (which the hand in some ways resembles). This gives about 50 lines of text on the recto. Therefore l. 25 is the number given to the line immediately above the centre fold; and l. 50 here is the one at the foot of the page, followed directly by the first line in the margin.

This reconstruction makes good sense, but there is one anomaly. It means that the scribe must have added a transverse final line of text on the verso (i.e. l. 66); perhaps greetings to 'all, great and small'. This is unusual, but the alternative of trying to reverse the fragment, so that the transverse text corresponds to the end of a line in the margin of the recto, is simply too problematic.

House 3   251

Content: There is little sense to be made of what is preserved, apart from the usual extensive greetings and a reference to coming to the Oasis (but it is uncertain whether the author is there or in the Nile valley).

Address: No address is preserved.

Names: Loutou; -a;

Text:

1	ⲡ̣[. . . . .]
2	[. . . . .]
3	. [. . . . .]
4	ⲡ[. . . . .]
5	ϩ . [. . . . .]
6	. [. . . . .]
7	⸢ⲣ⸣ọ[. . . . .]
8	ⲥ . [. . . . .]
9	ⲁṇ[. . . . .]
10	ⲧⲟ[. . . . .]
	unknown number of lines lost
23	[. . . . .]ⲙ̣ⲡ̣ⲉ . . . . [. . . . .]
24	[. . . .]ⲉ̣ⲙⲁⲩ ⲛ̄ϩⲟⲩⲟ [. . . . . .]
25	[. . . . .]ⲡⲕⲉϩⲟⲗⲟⲕ[ⲟⲧⲓⲛⲟⲥ]
26	[. . . ⲉⲧ]ⲁⲕⲧⲉϥ ⲛⲉϥ [. . . . . .]
27	[. . . . . .] ⲁⲛⲥⲁϩⲩ̄ ⲛ[. . . . . .]
28	[. . . . . . .]ⲩ· ϫⲉ ϩⲁϩ [. . . . .]
29	[. . . . . . .] . · ⲁⲛⲁⲛ . [. . . . . .]
30	[. . . . .] . [. . . . .]
	unknown number of lines lost
44	[. . . . .] . . ⲁⲗ ⲛ̄ⲟⲩⲁⲧ[. . . . .]
45	[. . . . . ⲧ]ⲏⲛⲉ· ⲛ̄ ⲡ . [. . . . . .]
46	[. . . . .] ⲙ̣ⲙⲁⲩ ⲉⲛ· ⲉⲩ[. . . . .]

47   [. . . . ⲧ]ⲉⲥϭⲁⲙ· ⲟⲩⲧ[. . . . . .]

48   [. . . . .]ⲧ ϯⲛⲟⲩ . [.] . [. . . . . .]

49   [. . . . .] . ⲁⲛ ⲕⲁⲧⲁ ⲡⲛⲁ̣[. . . . .]

50   vac?   ⲛ̄ⲟⲩⲛⲁϭ ⲛ̄ⲟⲩ[ⲁⲓϣ vac?]

(tr)51   ϯⲛⲟⲩ ϭⲉ ⲉⲥⲛ̄ⲥⲱⲕ· . [. . . . .]

52   ⲉⲓ ⲁⲟⲩⲁϩⲉ· ⲁⲓϭⲛ̄ⲧⲥ̄ ⲁ̣ⲕ[. . . . .]

53   ⲁⲓⲥϩⲉⲓ̈ ⲁⲓ̈ⲧⲁⲙⲁⲕ [. . . . .]

about five lines lost?

(v)59   ⲙⲛ̄ ⲛⲉϥϣ[ⲏⲣⲉ . . . .] ⲙ̣ⲛ̣̄ ⲧ̣[ⲥ̄]

60   ϭ̣ϩⲓⲙⲉ· ⲙⲛ̄ [. . . . .] . ⲁ ⲙⲛ̄ ⲧⲥ̄

61   ϣⲉⲣⲉ ϣⲓⲛ[ⲉ . . . . ⲙ]ⲛ̄ ⲛⲟⲩⲱⲏ

62   ⲣⲉ ϣⲓⲛⲉ ⲁⲣⲱ[ⲧⲛ̄ . . . .]ⲉ ⲛ̄ⲗⲟⲩⲧⲟⲩ

63   [. .]ⲛⲡⲓⲑⲉ ⲙ̣[. . . . .] . . ⲉ

a small number of lines lost?

(tr)66   [. . . . .]ⲕⲟⲩⲓ̈   vac

(To) ... (5) ... (10) ... (15) ... (20) ... more ... (25) ... the other *holokottinos* [that] you paid him ... We have written it to (you?) ...; in that many ... We (?) ... (30) ... (35) ... (40) ... (45) you (pl.), or ... not, as they ... its / her power, nor (?) ... Now ... according to ... (50) for a long time.

(tr) Now, then, it depends on you (masc. sg.) ... come to the Oasis. I found it, you ... I have written, I have informed you ...

(v) ... (55) ... (I greet warmly) ... and his sons ... (I greet warmly) ... and his (60) wife and ... -a and her daughter. Greet ... and their sons greet you (pl.) ... from / son of (?) Loutou; and we (?) are persuaded ... (65) ... (tr) [Greet everyone there by name, old and (?)] young.

Commentary:

9   The initial ⲁ- looks like it may be writ large and thus the start of a new sentence; possibly ⲁⲛ[ⲁⲕ].

50   Here there is clearly a form of the common final formula, preceded almost certainly by 'be well for me (ⲟⲩϫⲉⲓ̈ⲧⲉ ⲛⲏⲓ̈)' or similar, and perhaps followed by 'according to my prayers'. However, the author then continues in the margin and overleaf, as in many other examples (e.g. **31**).

60   There is almost certainly a woman's name here ending in -ⲁ, or quite possibly -ⲓⲁ. The obvious candidate would be Maria, but there are other possibilities.

62   There is a Loutou at **47**, 15, 17; but there is no particular reason to suggest that this is the same person.

P. Kellis Copt. 120

Inv #: P 92.17

Location: House 3, room 11, deposit 2.

Preservation: This is a complete letter, written in Coptic on papyrus, and recovered in one piece. The dimensions are 176 x 56 mm. The hand is regular and clear to read. The text is almost entirely complete; despite some erosion of the papyrus down the right-hand edge, and a number of small holes in the fabric. Nevertheless, a few words (although clear to read) remain problematic.

Content: There is a particular interest in the reference to various Christian or Manichaean books at the start of the letter. Unfortunately, the context of the document is most uncertain. Most obviously, one wonders if this is another letter by Pegosh to his brother Pamour; but the spelling of the author's name as 'Pekos' makes this debateable. Somehow, the style of the letter is rather different from the majority of House 3 letters in Coptic. There are strange spellings and oddities, but it is difficult to speculate about the cause on such meagre evidence.

Address:
verso

α . . Παμοῦρ   X   Πεκῶς

(Deliver to?) Pamour. X (From) Pekos.

Names: Lamon; Pabo; Pamour; Pebo; Pekos; Psemnouthes; Tagoshe;

Text:

1 ϯϣⲓⲛⲉ ⲁⲣⲁⲕ ⲧⲟⲛⲟⲩ
2 ⲡⲓϫⲱⲙ ⲉⲧⲛⲧⲟⲧϥ̄ ⲛ
3 ⲗⲁⲙⲱⲛ ⲧⲁⲣⲉ ⲛⲓⲡⲣⲁ
4 ⲝⲉⲓⲥ ϩⲣⲓϥ ⲛ̄ⲧⲁϥ ⲡⲉⲩ
5 ⲁⲅ`ⲅⲉⲗⲓⲟⲛ ⲧⲣⲟⲩⲛ̄
6 ⲧϥ ⲛⲏⲓ̈ ⲛ̄ⲧⲟⲧϥ ⲙ̄ⲡⲓ
7 ⲱⲧ vac ⲡⲁⲃⲟ
8 ⲏ̈ⲧⲉ ⲙ̄ⲙⲁϩⲉ ⲛ̄ⲕⲛ
9 ⲧⲉ ο . [.] . ⲩ ⲁϯⲙⲁⲡⲧ[.]
10 ⲕⲧⲣⲟⲩⲛ̄ⲧⲥ̄ ⲛⲏⲓ̈ ⲛⲕⲁ
11 ⲕⲉⲩⲉ ⲛⲉ ⲁⲗⲁⲕ ⲁⲣⲁⲕ
12 ϣⲁϯϩⲁϥⲟⲩ ⲛⲉⲕ
13 ⲉϣⲱⲡⲉ ⲉⲙⲡⲭⲓ ϯⲉ
14 ⲡⲓⲥⲧⲟvacⲗⲏ ⲧⲧⲁⲃ̄ ϫⲁⲩ ⲁ
15 ⲡⲏⲓ̈ ⲙ̄ⲡⲓⲱⲧ ⲡⲉⲃⲟ ⲛ̄
16 ⲥⲱⲥ ⲥϩⲉⲓ̈ ⲛⲏⲓ̈ ⲛ̄
17 ⲟⲩⲱϩ ⲛⲓⲙ ⲙ̄ⲡⲓϩⲟⲟⲩ
18 ⲥⲛⲟ ⲛⲓϣⲟⲩ ⲟⲩⲁⲛ
19 ⲧⲟⲩⲏϩⲧ` ⲛ̄ⲧⲡⲉ ϥⲓ
20 ⲧⲟⲩ ⲁⲛ ⲁⲡⲓⲧⲛ̄ ⲕⲁⲩ ⲛ̄
21 ϩⲟⲩⲛ̄ⲧⲣⲓⲉ ⲙ̄ⲡⲣ̄
22 ϭⲱ ⲁⲙⲡⲕϣⲉ
23 ⲁⲡϣⲧⲟ ⲁⲛⲟⲩ ⲁⲡⲣⲱ
24 ⲙⲉ ϫⲉ ϩⲁⲩⲃⲱⲕ ⲛ̄
25 ⲥⲁ ⲡⲓⲱⲧ ⲡϯⲉⲛⲛⲟⲩ
26 ⲑⲏⲥ ⲇⲉ ⲉⲕϣⲁⲛⲥⲱⲧⲙ
27 ⲕⲉⲓ ⲕⲛⲟ ⲁⲣⲁϥ ⲁⲣⲓ
28 ⲙⲉⲣ ⲛⲏⲓ̈ ⲁⲡⲓⲱⲧ ⲡⲉ
29 ⲃⲟ ⲉⲧⲃⲉ ⲡⲧⲟⲩ̣
30 ϫⲉ ϩⲁⲓ̈ϫⲟⲥ ⲁⲣⲁϥ

31   ⲙⲁⲣⲉ ⲧⲁϭⲟϣⲉ

32   † ⲡϣⲉ ⲛⲉⲕ ⲛ̄ϭⲛ

33   ϭⲱⲣ ⲕⲧⲣⲟⲩⲛ̄ⲧⲟⲩ

34   ⲛⲏⲓ̈

v35   ϫⲟⲩ ⲙⲏⲧ ⲁⲛ ⲙ̄ⲡⲕⲟⲩⲓ̈

———

     2 ϫⲱⲙ: read ϫⲱⲙ<ⲉ>   13 ⲉⲙⲡϫⲓ- sic, read ⲉⲙⲡ<ⲕ>ϫⲓ-   15 ⲙ̄ⲡⲓⲱⲧ: ⲙ̄- ex ⲁ- corr.   17 read ⲟⲩⲱ ⲛⲓⲙ   18 ⲛⲓϣⲟⲩ: -ⲩ ex corr?   30 ⲁⲣⲁϥ: -ⲣ- ex corr.   33 ⲛ̄ⲧⲟⲩ: final -ⲩ- very poorly formed

———

I greet you warmly. (About) this book that Lamon has: Let the *Acts* be copied. But the (5) *Gospel*: Let them bring it to me from father Pabo.

These 5 *maje* of figs ... (10) you let them bring it to me. (As for) the other ones: Wait until I send them to you. If <you> did not receive this letter, make him give (it) and send (it) to (15) the house of father Pebo.

Next, write to me any news of these two days. These ... above: Take (20) them down again (and) put them inside the cell. Do not delay to go to the place for convalescence (?) to see the man, for they have gone (25) after the father. But, (as for) Psemnouthes: If you should hear (about him), you come (and) see him. Do remind father Pebo for me about the repayment (?); (30) for I said to him: "Let Tagoshe give you the 100 talents (and) you have them brought to me". (v35) Also, send 10 to the boy.

Commentary:

Address: The traces preceding Pamour's name are not very convincing for the expected ἀπ(όδος) 'Deliver to ..'. There may also be some ink traces after the central cross preceding 'Pekos'.

3, 5   The causative conjunctive (l. 3) and the causative infinitive (l. 5) both seem to be used here as imperatives; i.e. instead of ⲙⲁⲣⲉ-.

3-5   The 'Acts' and the 'Gospel' could obviously be Christian works, but are more likely in this context to be Manichaean. The 'great' or 'living' *Gospel* was one of Mani's chief works, but is now not extant. The opening is preserved in both Greek and Middle Iranian (see I. Gardner, S.N.C. Lieu, *Manichaean Texts from the Roman Empire*, Cambridge, 2004: 156-159). The Manichaean community also circulated copies of the so-called 'Leucian' Acts, and a text related to the *Acts of John* was found in House 3 (cf. P. Kellis VI Gr. 97). On this see now also O. Zwierlein, 'Die Datierung der Acta Iohannis und der Papyrus Kellis Gr. Fragm. A.I', *ZPE*, 174, 2010: 65-84.

4 ϩⲣⲓϥ: We understand ϫⲓ ϩⲣⲃ 'take a likeness', i.e. 'copy'; cf. CD 701b.

9 We can make no sense of the text here.

13-14 ϯⲉⲡⲓⲥⲧⲟⲗⲏ 'this letter': This can not be the letter that we are reading here. Given the clear reference to actual books in the opening lines, it is possible that it refers not to a personal letter but to Mani's (book of) *Epistles*; or conceivably Paul. We know that both of these circulated in the community at ancient Kellis, because remnants of such codices were found in House 3 (**6**, **53** and perhaps **54**); and indeed they are referred to explicitly at **19**, 82-83.

14 ⲧⲧⲁⲃ̄: We have understood the verb ⲧⲧⲟ 'make give' or 'require', and thus read 'make him give (it)'. However, the -ⲃ̄ is strange (for -ϥ), and one might prefer to understand ⲉⲧ(ⲧ)ⲁⲃⲉ 'which is sealed'. If ⲧⲟⲩⲏϩⲧ in l. 19 is understood as <ⲉ>ⲧⲟⲩⲏϩ (see below), then one could well-argue that the scribe regularly omitted the initial ⲉ- of a relative construction. Thus here one could read 'the sealed letter'. Although it would seem most unlikely, it should be noted that the last *Epistle* Mani wrote in prison was known as *The Seal Letter*. Fragments of this important text have been recovered from Central Asia, see e.g. C. Reck, 'A Sogdian Version of Mani's *Letter of the Seal*', in J.D. BeDuhn (ed.), *New Light on Manichaeism*, Leiden-Boston 2009: 225-239. However, it can be supposed that it also circulated in fourth-century Egypt, and indeed the name is preserved on a leaf of the *Kephalaia* codex held at the Chester Beatty Library in Dublin (i.e. *The Chapters of the Wisdom of my Lord Manichaios*). There is currently a major project by I. Gardner, J. BeDuhn and P. Dilley working to edit the codex. It reads ⲧⲉⲡⲓⲥⲧⲟⲗⲏ ⲛ̄ⲧⲥⲫⲣⲁⲅⲓⲥ; and the passage can be viewed in the facsimile edition published by S. Giversen, *The Manichaean Coptic Papyri in the Chester Beatty Library. Vol. I Kephalaia*, Genève 1986, pl. 326: 6. Coptic ⲧⲱⲃⲉ is the usual equivalent to σφραγίζειν.

15 It may well be that this 'father Pebo' is the same as the 'father Pabo' of l. 7; and see also ll. 28-29.

18-19 ⲛⲓϣⲟⲩ ⲟⲩⲁⲛ ⲧⲟⲩⲏϩⲧ`: This complex is incomprehensible to us as it stands. We have separated the elements corresponding to apparent divisions made by the scribe; but this may not be correct. One could try ⲛⲓϣⲟⲩⲟⲩ ⲁⲛ ⲧⲟⲩⲏϩⲧ: 'Also, these ϣⲟⲩⲟⲩ (a plural noun) which are set above (i.e. understanding here <ⲉ>ⲧⲟⲩⲏϩ with the final -ⲧ either as an error or an unattested form)'. The following clause suggests that the author is talking about some items that are hung or otherwise placed high up for some reason; e.g. wall-hangings or something put up to dry? But these are little more than guesses.

21 As elsewhere in these texts, the precise implications of the ⲣⲓⲉ 'cell' are impossible to gauge ('monastic' or 'prison' cell, 'room' in a house, 'storeroom'?). Cf. CD 287b-288a for the range of meanings.

23 ⲡϣⲧⲟ: 'place for convalescence (?)'. For this interpretation, see **115**, 14-17 note ad loc.; but perhaps one should just read 'Pshto'. See also perhaps the end of **41**, 16 (where it may be that the same should be read or restored); and perhaps **43**, 5 (destroyed context).

24-25 There is no way to know who has 'gone after' the father, or what the implication might have been.

25-26 The use of the Greek form of the name Psemnouthes (rather than Pshemnoute) is surprising. One wonders if the author or scribe was not a native speaker of Egyptian. It is possible that this is intended as a vocative: 'But, Psemnouthes, if you should hear ...'.

29 ⲡⲧⲟⲩⲟ: We have supposed in the translation that this is for ⲧⲟⲩⲓⲟ 'repayment'; but that is a guess based on the sense of the passage. It is possible that further letters were originally written; but the following lines suggest that from here on the scribe finished his lines rather earlier than he had done previously. Perhaps the fragment of papyrus that is now lost was already deteriorated at the time of writing.

P. Kellis Copt. 121

Inv #: P92.20

Location: House 3, room 14, deposit 3.

Preservation: A fragment of what is almost certainly a letter written in Coptic on papyrus. This is another example of a very tiny script (cf. e.g. **105, 118**). The right hand margin is probably preserved; but otherwise we can not know the dimensions of the letter or the length of the lines. The line lengths given are only illustrative. The reading of ⲉϥϫⲱ at l. 2 suggests that a further fragment of papyrus must have been lost when the digital photograph was taken in early 2009.

Content: Nothing can be determined about the content. The dialect is typical of these pieces, and the main interest of the piece is the reading preserved at l. 5.

Address: None preserved (the verso is blank).

Names: None preserved.

Text:

(x+)1 [. . . . .] . vac ⲁⲛⲁⲕ ⲙⲉⲛ ⲛⲙⲙⲉⲕ ⲛⲉ ⲁⲛ .
2   [. . . . .] . ⲉϥϫⲱ ⲙⲙⲁⲥ ϫⲉ . . . ⲁ
3   [. . . . .]̄. ⲟⲩϣⲏⲣⲉ` ⲡϣⲁⲣ . . . ϫⲉ
4   [. . . . . .] . . ⲙⲟⲩⲛ . . ⲃ . . . . . . ϣⲁⲛ . ⲟⲩⲉ . . ⲁⲓⲟⲩ . . ̄ⲙⲙ . .
5   [. . . . . .]ϣⲁⲏⲗ ϩⲁⲧⲏⲕ` ⲙ̄ⲡⲣ̄ⲧϩⲣⲟⲡⲟⲩϩⲡ[.] . . . ϫ . . . . .
6   [. . . . . .] . ̄. . . ⲉⲛⲧ/ϣⲁ ⲛ̄ⲟⲩⲁ . . . . . [. . . . .]

As for me and you (masc. sg.), we have ... with him saying: ... their (?) son(s)?. ... (5) ... pray (?) for you. Do not make ... worthy (?) ...

Commentary:

5   ⲙ̄ⲡⲣ̄ⲧϩⲣⲟⲡⲟⲩϩⲡ[: This is the most interesting feature of an otherwise poorly preserved fragment. One must read a negative imperative with a previously unattested causative verb. The reading is mostly secure. From which root base this causative may actually be derived remains unclear for the time being. Apart from any of the known or unknown consonantal stems containing /hr/ or /rh/, one might perhaps think of simply

another variant form for ⲧⲣⲟ *L4* ('cause', 'force', 'constrain'), for which the archive already presents the unusual variant ⲧⲁⲣⲟ- (at **115**, 14). In this case one would be tempted to read ⲡⲟⲩϩⲏ[ⲧ for what follows (cf. **115**, 14 ⲙ̄ⲡ̄ⲣ̄-ⲧⲁⲣⲟ-ⲡⲉϩⲏⲧ, probably not ⲧϩⲣⲟ-); but ⲏ is not particularly likely. On the whole, it is more probable that ⲧϩⲣⲟ is the causative of a base that in fact contained some fricative /h/, and that we have to wait for new attestation to see it more clearly.

LIST OF OTHER (NOT EDITED) COPTIC FRAGMENTS FROM HOUSE 3

This concludes the edition of Coptic documentary texts from House 3 at Ismant el-Kharab. However, the excavations there during the 1990-91 and 1991-92 archaeological seasons, directed by C.A. Hope, also recovered many other small fragments (mostly inscribed papyrus) with Coptic text. As far as can be known, almost all of these were from personal and business letters, similar to the many such documents edited in CDTI and II. Here follows a brief record of these fragments, which may be useful in any attempt to calculate the original number of discrete documents found at the site, and perhaps the proportions of Coptic material or different genres of texts within the total find. Apart from such purposes, the decision of the present editors is that the following fragments are too small for useful publication at this time.

In the following list, the inventory numbers refer to glass frames, some of which contain a good number of different pieces (on occasion both Greek and Coptic). Some description and occasional Coptic text is recorded, but these have not been systematically checked and their inclusion here is only to aid in any future attempt to identify the fragments in storage. It is probable that the list is not complete. There are a great many small scraps of papyrus, some of which may belong together and some of which continue to break apart. For the smallest and worst preserved pieces it is not always clear even whether they were written in Coptic. Consequently, it has proved impossible to record an absolute total.

A/5/217	Small frg. Coptic.
P4	At least two other Coptic frgs. apart from those published as **62**. Read: ⲡⲉ]ⲕⲡⲛⲁ.
P12	Small frg. Coptic?
P17DD	Small frg. Coptic.
P17Zi	Three small frgs. Coptic; at least two from the same text.
P26	Small frg. Coptic.
P35D	Small frg. Coptic.
P38	Small frg. of Coptic letter.
P39	Very small frg. of Coptic letter.
P43	Small frg. of Coptic letter.
P44	Small frg. of Coptic letter, tiny script. 5 lines. Starts:]ϥϫⲱ ⲙ̄ⲙⲁⲥ ⲛⲓ[.
P47	Small frg. Coptic.
P48	Small frg. Coptic.
P50	Top left-hand corner. Start of Coptic letter with first 2 lines in Greek.
P51B(a)iv	Frg. with tr. text.
P51C(b)	Three poorly preserved frgs. of a single (?) Coptic letter, with first 2 lines in Greek.
P52B	Poor frg. of Coptic letter.
P52Cii	Two frgs. of Coptic letter. Also three frgs. of another Coptic letter, written on both sides.
P53	Small frg. of Coptic letter. [ⲡⲉ]ϭⲱϣ?
P54	Small frg. Coptic?
P55	Small frg. Coptic?
P56B(a)	Three small frgs. from Coptic letters.
P56C(a)iv	Small scrap:]ⲡⲁⲥⲁ[ⲛ?
P56C(a)v	Thin vertical strip from 11 lines, Coptic.
P56Ci	In addition to the twenty-one frgs. of the letter published as **105**, a small frg. from the top of a Coptic letter. Also here, a Coptic frg. with 5 line starts and 2 of tr. text.
P56F	Tiny frg. of Coptic letter and perhaps others.

P56H	Small frg. of Coptic letter.
P57B	Two small frgs. from Coptic letters.
P59B	Small frg. of Coptic letter.
P59C	Small frg. of Coptic letter. Read: ⲙⲛ̄ ⲧϭⲁϭⲉ; ⲁⲅⲁⲑⲟⲛ.
P61V	Two small frgs. of Coptic.
P77B	Two small frgs. of Coptic.
P78A	Small frg. Coptic.
P78G	Small frg. of Coptic letter, ⲧⲁⲙⲟ ⲭⲁⲣⲓⲥ on r. and Greek address on v.
P81D	Pieces from multiple documents. Three frgs. from one Coptic letter including ⲗⲁⲙⲙⲱⲛ; ⲡϫⲱⲧ ϣⲁⲓ̈. Four frgs. from various other letters inscribed on both sides, including names: ⲑⲉⲟⲅⲛⲱⲥⲧⲟⲥ; ⲭⲙ̄ⲡⲛⲟⲩ[ⲧⲉ; ⲡϣⲁⲓ̈. Perhaps more Coptic here also.
P82B	Frgs. of Coptic.
P85D	Two frgs. of Coptic letters? Read: ⲕⲁⲣⲡⲟⲥ. Not dissimilar to **22** and **23** (also from P85).
P89B	Small frg. Coptic.
P92B	Small frg. of Coptic letter.
P93B	Various small frgs. Coptic?
P92.1	Four frgs. of Coptic letters all written in very tiny script. Three have been taken from P92.5 and one from P92.37. They are glassed here together with **118** in order to compare with it; but they probably derive from other documents. It is difficult to determine how many different texts are represented in total.
P92.4(a)	Two small frgs. of one letter, written in Coptic on both sides. The script is similar to **32**, **33**, and **84**; but probably not the same. Read the name ⲧⲓⲃⲉⲣⲓ; also ⲧⲥⲉⲃⲁⲩ, ⲕⲟⲥⲙⲟⲥ, ⲛ̄ϩⲏⲛⲉ.
P92.6	One frg. of a letter, very poor preservation and difficult to determine if written in Greek or Coptic. The address is the same as **74** (Π]εκῦσις Ψάϊς ὁ ἀδελ|φός).
P92.9	Small frg. Coptic.

P92.13	One frg. of a Coptic letter, written in a crude hand (and spelling). Text from 20 lines. Read from near the start (lines x+3-8):]ϣηρε μη̄ [πaϣηρ]ε μ̄μερι[τ ανδ]ρεαc ϩμ̄ [πχαϊ]c χερειν ϩαθη ν̄ϩω[β νιμ] †ρ̄ϣπηρε etc. Different hand on v (not sure if Greek or Coptic). Also other frgs. of Coptic letters here.
P92.15A	One small edge frg. with Coptic script.
P92.16	Three frgs. from different Coptic letters. One reads ϣηρ]ε ανδ[ρεαc; another πκ̄ογχει[τε; another ϩαλϭ.
P92.17(a)	Very faded frgs., difficult to determine if Greek or Coptic.
P92.18	Small frg. Coptic.
P92.29	Two frgs. with Coptic text on both sides.
P92.35Gi(a)	Two small frgs. join, and perhaps Coptic, from top centre of a letter.
P92.42	One small frg. Coptic in a plastic bag. Read: χε †νηγ αβαλ.
P92.46	Two small frgs. Coptic.
P92.48	Small frg. Coptic.
P92.50	One frg. Coptic. Read †ϣαηλ.

HOUSE 4

The archaeological excavations in House 4 took place during the 1992-93 field-season, and these texts were all found early in 1993. The excavation of the structure was never completed, as the site came to be considered unsafe and likely to collapse. The principal interest, as regards the study of Coptic documents from ancient Kellis, is that this material provides an important contrast to the much greater quantity of such recovered from House 3. Indeed, Houses 1, 2 and the 'North Building' are all contiguous with House 3 on the northern side of Area A at Ismant el-Kharab; and, whilst all the inscribed material from those structures can not properly be termed a single archive, it does (with minor exceptions) evidence a certain homogeneity in terms of Coptic dialect, styles of writing, socio-economic factors and so on. A great many of the texts published in CDT I and II belonged to the one extended family group and their associates from the second half of the fourth century.

In contrast, House 4 was in good part selected for excavation as it is architecturally somewhat different (it is on two levels for a start), and several hundred metres away to the south-west (more precisely WSW). Nevertheless, it was also a domestic structure inhabited during the fourth century. Although there was nothing like the same quantity of inscribed material recovered here as in House 3, there are a number of important Coptic texts edited and published here as **122-126**. Mention must also be made of the previously published Coptic literary text from House 4 (T. Kellis II Copt. 7), if only because it was a Manichaean psalm written in dialect *L4* (the same as the Medinet Madi Manichaean codices). This is especially interesting because it demonstrates that two of the characteristic features of the Coptic texts from House 3 and contiguous structures, Manichaean belief and use of this dialect family, were not somehow specific to one corner of the village or one small group of its inhabitants. However, the wooden board with the psalm was found near the surface of House 4, and may not have belonged to the inhabitants of the building.

As regards the Coptic documents edited here, none of them provides any evidence of Manichaean belief. In fact, the letter **124** and the invocation **126** are probably the first Coptic texts recovered by the excavations at Ismant el-Kharab that should be classified as clearly Christian and certainly not Manichaean. Of course, there are a number of pieces that could be either; and this is particularly true of many of the personal and business letters from House 3. It is also true of **122** and **123**. But here in House 4, with **124** and **126**, we find unambiguous evidence of Christian belief and practice.

As regards dialect the inscribed material in Coptic from House 4 may be less homogenous than that in House 3 (although the small numbers of texts make this dubious statistically). Whilst the Manichaean psalm, and the letter **122** (on which see further below), belong to the dialect family *L*; document **123** and the Christian letter **124** are typical examples of 'southern' (regional, modified) Sahidic. Whether there is any link between social-cultural group and dialect choice is impossible to state on this evidence; but there is reason to think that the Christian community promoted Sahidic whilst all Manichaean texts ever yet found in Egypt can be grouped in (the admittedly somewhat artificial) dialect family *L*.

Finally, there is the important but unresolved question of dating. None of the Coptic documents from House 4 provide any evidence by which we could attempt to date them, beyond the general parameters of the fourth century, and probably from the second half. This can be said due to the archaeological record, and on general principles regarding the spread and use of Coptic. But it is not specific. This is unfortunate, as one would like to know more about the spread of new religions (i.e. Christianity and Manichaeism) in the village, and the development of Coptic and its dialects. Also, **123** provides a very interesting reference to 'father Shoi from the monastery'; and one would certainly like to know more about the nature and development of monasticism in the Oasis.

LETTERS

P. Kellis Copt. 122

Inv #: P 93.44 + 93.40A

Location: House 4, room 1B, deposit 2.

Preservation: This is a complete letter written in Coptic on papyrus. It was found in 3 portions, where it had broken along the folds; but these can easily be joined and virtually all the text is preserved (apart from a little abrasion on the upper left-side of the recto). The restored document has dimensions of 134 x 107 mm. The papyrus has been reused, as clear ink-traces (and even the occasional letter) of an earlier text can easily be seen. The hand is strong, distinctive and professional.

Somewhat surprisingly, this professional writing ductus goes along with a certain looseness of dictional style (of which the lack of consistency in the use of grammatical persons is only one example) as well as a number of linguistic forms which are highly unusual. While the language of this piece can not be expected to be in agreement with any of the known *literary* dialects of Coptic, it is also seen to be only in partial agreement with what is known from the majority of the letters found in Houses 2 and 3 (the variety of southern Coptic that we preliminarily dubbed *L**). The tendency to spell ⲁ instead of ⲉ here goes much farther than anywhere else: ⲁ- and ⲁⲧⲁ- for ⲉ- and ⲉⲧⲉ- (the circumstantial and relative converters), ⲁⲧⲃⲁ- for ⲉⲧⲃⲉ-, ⲉⲧⲁⲡⲁ- and ⲁⲧⲁⲧⲛ̄- for ⲉⲧⲉⲣⲉ- and ⲉⲧⲉⲧⲛ̄- (converted Present), ⲙⲛ̄ⲧⲁⲧⲛ̄- for ⲙⲛ̄ⲧⲉⲧⲛ̄-, ⲉϣⲁⲛⲧⲁ- for ⲉϣⲁⲛⲧⲉ-, ϫⲁ for ϫⲉ, etc. It is difficult to determine whether this is merely a matter of spelling and orthography; or whether actual phonological (and thus 'dialectal') peculiarities are behind this phenomenon, and if so, which. The brevity and uniqueness of this piece of writing will probably preclude any such determinations even for some time in the future, especially since there are only few distinct morphosyntactic features to be found here. One such feature is the use, exclusive as it seems, of the base ϩ// for the

Affirm. Perfect (ϩⲓ- l. 30 and an implicit ϩⲕ- l. 20), which links this piece with the more distinctly 'local' documents **44–48** (and / or with the very peculiar no. **50**). Another characteristic trait, clearly limited to the level of orthography but in stark contrast to the normal usage in the *L** corpus as well as the local documents, is the spelling of ⲉⲓ for the front glide in postvocalic position (normally spelt ï), which is quite consistent, as it seems, in ⲥϩⲉⲉⲓ and ⲟⲩⲭⲉⲉⲓⲧⲉ (but ⲕⲟⲩï and ⲡⲁⲓⲥ), cf. also ⲁⲉⲓ- (for ⲉï- / ⲁï- Sec. Pres.), ⲟⲉⲓ (stative of ⲉⲓⲣⲉ). The morphology of this latter form (no matter whether ⲟⲉⲓ or ⲟï) would also appear unusual for *L**, where it is normally ⲟ.

Content: On the recto Pshai and Masi have written a rather formal letter of filial piety to their father (and mother). One might suppose that this is complete in itself; but on the verso we find a rather more interesting, plaintive and personal set of appeals to the parents. The brothers are friendless and eager for news and a visit. They send a number of small gifts. See further the commentary on the problematic lines at the bottom of the recto and the top of the verso, and the issue of how to connect the two sides of the letter.

Address: None. Both recto and verso are covered in text.

Names: Chares; Lammon; Masi; Pakous; Papnoute; Philammon; Pshai; Sarapa; Sarapi;

Text:

1   ⲡⲁⲓⲱⲧ ⲡⲁⲙⲉⲣⲓⲧ ⲡⲁⲡⲣⲉⲛ ⲉⲑⲁⲗϭ
2   ϩⲛ ⲣⲱï ⲛⲛⲟ ⲛⲓⲙ ⲡⲁⲓⲱⲧ ⲛⲁⲅⲁⲡⲏⲧⲟⲥ
3   ⲥⲁⲣⲁⲡⲁ ⲁⲛⲁⲕ ⲡϣⲁï ⲙⲛ ⲙⲁⲥⲓ ⲛⲉⲕ
4   ϣⲏⲣⲉ ⲁⲛⲥϩⲉⲉⲓ ⲛⲉⲕ ϩⲛ ⲡⲭⲁⲓⲥ ⲭⲁⲓⲣⲉⲓⲛ
5   ϣⲁⲣⲡ ⲛϩⲱⲃ ⲛⲓⲙ ⲧⲛϣⲓⲛⲉ ⲁⲧⲕⲙⲛⲧ
6   ⲓⲱⲧ ⲉⲧⲛⲁⲛⲟⲩⲥ ⲧⲁⲧⲁⲙⲡⲟⲩⲁⲛ ⲛⲧϭϩⲉ
7   ϩⲁⲛϣⲁⲏⲗ ⲛⲡⲛⲟⲩⲧⲉ ϩⲁ ⲡⲕⲟⲩⲭⲉⲉⲓⲧⲉ
8   ⲭⲁϥⲛⲁⲣⲁⲓⲥ ⲁⲣⲁⲕ ⲛⲉⲛ ⲛⲟⲩⲛⲁϭ ⲛⲟⲩ
9   ⲁ⟨ⲓ⟩ϣ ⲙⲛ ⲧⲁⲙⲉⲩ ⲧⲁⲭⲁⲓⲥ ⲁⲧⲁⲧⲛϣⲟⲡ
10 ⲛⲉⲛ ⲛⲥⲁⲃⲧ ⲛⲛⲁϣⲧⲉ ⲁⲛⲑⲁⲣⲣⲉ ⲛⲙⲙⲁ

11 ⲙ̄ⲙⲁ ⲛⲓⲙ ⲁⲧⲁⲧⲛ̄ϣⲟⲡ ⲛ̄ϩⲏⲧϥ ⲉⲓⲧⲉ

12 ϩⲛ̄ ⲟⲩⲁϩⲁ ⲉⲓⲧⲉ ϩⲛ̄ ⲕⲏⲙⲉ ⲁⲛ̄ϣⲗⲏⲗ

13 ⲙ̄ⲙⲉⲧⲉ ⲁⲡⲉⲧⲛ̄ⲟⲩⲭⲉⲉⲓⲧⲉ ⲙⲛ̄ ⲛⲁ

14 ⲥⲛⲏⲩ ⲛⲁϫⲓⲥⲁⲩⲉ ⲕⲁⲧⲁ ⲡⲟⲩⲣⲉⲛ ⲕⲟⲩⲓ ⲛⲁϭ

15 ⲙⲁⲗⲓⲥⲧⲁ ⲡⲁⲙⲉⲣⲓⲧ ⲛ̄ⲥⲁⲛ ⲥⲁⲣⲁⲡⲓ ⲙⲛ̄ ⲧⲁ

16 ⲕⲟⲩⲓ ⲛ̄ϣⲉⲣⲉ ⲧⲉⲧⲁⲣⲁ ⲡⲛⲟⲩⲧⲉ ⲛⲁⲣⲁⲓⲥ ⲁⲣⲁⲥ

17 vac ⲁϩⲉ ⲙⲛ̄ ⲡⲁⲙⲉⲣⲓⲧ

tr18 ϣⲉⲛ̄ ⲧⲏⲣϥ̄ vac ⲁⲛⲓ ⲕⲟⲩⲥ ⲥⲛⲟ ⲛⲏϩ

v19 ⲙⲛ̄ⲧⲁⲧⲛⲁϩϭⲱ ϩⲁⲣⲉⲧϥ ⲛ̄ⲡⲃⲁⲣⲃⲁⲣⲁⲥ ϯϣⲓⲛⲉ ⲧⲟⲛⲟⲩ

20 ⲁⲡⲁⲙⲉⲣⲓⲧ ⲛ̄ⲥⲁⲛ ⲡⲁⲡⲛⲟⲩⲧⲉ ϯⲣ̄ⲑⲁⲩⲙⲁⲍⲏ ϫⲛⲑⲕ

21 ⲕⲛ̄ⲧⲛ̄ ⲁⲃⲁⲗ ⲛ̄ⲡⲕⲥϩⲉⲉⲓ ⲛⲉⲛ ⲁⲧⲃⲁ ⲡⲕⲟⲩⲭⲉⲉⲓⲧⲉ ⲟⲩⲧⲉ ϩⲕ̄

22 ϫⲟⲥ ⲁⲛ ϫⲁ ϯⲛⲁⲛ̄ ⲛⲓⲕⲟⲩⲓ ⲁⲃⲁⲗ ⲛ̄ⲙⲙⲏⲓ ⲙ̄ⲡⲕⲉⲓⲣⲉ

23 ⲧⲛ̄ⲣⲉϣⲉ ⲧⲟⲛⲟⲩ ⲧⲛⲉⲓⲁⲣⲙ̄ ⲁⲃⲁⲗ ϩⲏⲧⲧⲏⲛⲉ ϫⲁ ⲧⲛⲟⲉⲓ ⲛ̄ⲁⲧ

24 ⲣⲱⲙⲉ ⲙ̄ⲛⲓⲙⲁ ⲉⲓ ⲙⲉⲛ ⲙⲛ̄ⲧⲁⲧⲛ̄ⲛⲏⲩ ⲥϩⲉⲉⲓ ⲛⲉⲛ ⲛ̄ⲡⲉ

25 ⲧⲛ̄ⲟⲩⲭⲉⲉⲓⲧⲉ ⲉϣⲁⲛⲧⲁ ⲛⲓⲃⲁⲣⲁϩⲓ ⲟⲩⲁϣⲃⲉⲧ ⲁϥⲓ ⲟⲩⲗⲁⲩⲉ

26 ϯⲛⲁⲧⲛ̄ⲛⲁⲩϥ̄ ϭⲛ ⲟⲩⲧⲁⲟⲩ ⲁⲛⲁⲛⲟⲩϥ ⲧⲁⲛ̄ⲧϥ ⲛⲏⲓ ⲧⲁⲙⲟ

27 ⲁⲛⲁⲕ ⲙⲁⲥⲓ ⲧⲥϩⲉⲉⲓ ⲛⲉ ⲙⲛ̄ ⲟⲩⲉ ⲛ̄ⲡⲟⲩϣⲏⲣⲉ ⲥⲁⲣⲁⲡⲁ

28 ϫⲁ ⲙⲁϥⲕⲓⲙ ⲁϥϫⲱ ⲧⲟⲩϩⲙⲏ ⲛⲉ ϫⲓ ϯⲕⲟⲩⲓ ⲛ̄ⲃⲉⲣⲉ

29 ⲛⲏⲧⲛ̄ ⲧⲟⲧϥ ⲛ̄ⲡⲁⲕⲟⲩⲥ ⲁⲣⲁⲡⲓⲧⲛ ⲛⲏⲧⲛ̄ ⲧⲟⲛⲟⲩ ϩⲛ̄

30 ⲡⲁϩⲛ̄ⲧ ⲙⲛ̄ⲧⲣⲁⲧⲛ̄ϫⲟⲥ ϫⲁ ϩⲓⲣⲁⲙⲉⲗⲓ ⲁⲉⲓϫⲱ ⲙⲁⲥ

31 ϫⲁ ⲙⲏ ⲥⲉⲛⲁⲧⲁϩⲱⲧⲛ̄ ⲛ̄ϩⲟⲩⲛ ⲙⲛ̄ⲧⲣⲁⲧⲛ̄ϭⲛ ⲁⲣⲓⲕⲉ

32 ϫⲓ ϯⲭⲁⲃⲉ ⲛⲉ ⲧⲟ ⲧⲁⲙⲟ ⲛ̄ⲧⲟⲧϥ ⲛ̄ⲗⲁⲙⲙⲱⲛ ⲁⲥⲙⲏϩ ⲛⲁⲣ

33 ϣⲓⲛ ⲟⲩⲛ ϣⲙⲟⲩⲛⲉ ϣⲁⲧⲉ ⲧⲃⲧ ⲛ̄ϩⲏⲧⲥ ⲙⲛ̄ ⲟⲩⲕⲁⲑⲁ

34 ⲣⲟⲛ ϫⲁ ⲡⲁⲡⲁⲕⲟⲩⲥ ⲙⲛ̄ ⲭⲁⲣⲏⲥ ⲟⲩⲁϣⲃⲉⲧ ⲁϥⲓ ⲗⲁⲩⲉ

35 ⲁⲣⲁ ϫⲓ ⲧⲭⲁⲃⲉ ⲧⲟⲧϥ ⲡⲁⲕⲟⲩⲥ ϫⲁ ⲡⲁⲫⲓⲗⲁⲙⲙⲱⲛ

36 ⲁϩⲉ

---

4 ⲛⲉⲕ: ⲛ- ex corr. 24 ⲙⲛ̄ⲧⲁⲧⲛ̄ⲛⲏⲩ sic! 27 ⲛ̄ⲡⲟⲩ- sic, read ⲛ̄ⲛⲟⲩ- 28 ⲁϥϫⲱ ⲧⲟⲩϩⲙⲏ, i.e. ⲉϥϫⲟ ⲛ̄ⲧⲟⲩϩⲙⲏ 33 i.e. ⲟⲩⲛ ϣⲙⲟⲩⲛⲉ ⲛ̄ϣⲁⲧⲉ ⲛ̄ⲧⲃⲧ 35 i.e. (ⲛ̄)ⲧⲟⲧϥ ⲛ̄ⲡⲁⲕⲟⲩⲥ; read ⲡⲁⲫⲓⲗⲁⲙⲙⲱⲛ ⟨ⲡⲉ⟩?

(To) my father, my loved one, he of the name that is sweet in my mouth at all times; my beloved father Sarapa. I, Pshai, and Masi, your sons; we are writing to you in the Lord, - greetings.

(5) First of everything: We salute your good fatherhood, which is without equal. We have prayed to God for your well-being: That he will guard you (sing.) for us a long time - and my mother, my lady - as you (pl.) are (10) for us a wall of protection; (and) we are confident with you (fem. sg.) (?), wherever you (pl.) are, whether in the Oasis or in Egypt. We are praying only for your (pl.) well-being; and (that of) my brothers, my masters, each by name, young and old, (15) especially my loved brother Sarapi and my little daughter, the one whom God will guard. Stay with my beloved (brother?).

(tr) Receive all <the ...> (?). Bring 2 *choes* of oil.

(v) You (pl.) can not remain under the foreigner. I greet warmly (20) my loved brother Papnoute. I am amazed that, since you (sg.) moved away, you have not written to us about your health. And nor have you told us: "I will bring the little ones with me". You did not do (that). (Nevertheless?), we are overjoyed and looking out for you (pl.); for we know noone here. Even if you can not come, write to us of (25) your health. When those pack-animals (i.e. the caravan) answer me (and) carry something, I will send it. (Can you please) find a good pair of shoes and bring (them) for me, my mother.

(It is) I, Masi, who writes to you (fem.), together with one of your (?) sons, Sarapa, for he can not move. He sends your (?) fare to you (fem.). Receive this small basket (?) for you (pl.) from Pakous. I am yours from the bottom of (30) my heart. Do not say that I have been neglectful. I am asking: "Will they reach you at home?". Do not find fault. Receive this cloth bag for yourself, my mother, from Lammon. It is full of lentils. There are eight portions of fish in it and some fine white bread; for Pakous and Chares did not answer me to (say that they would?) carry something. (35) So, receive this cloth bag from Pakous; for that of Philammon is wanting (?).

Commentary:

3   The name 'Masi' only occurs in this one letter amongst all the Kellis documents; but it is known from elsewhere. It is derived from the word for a young animal; cf. CD 186a. In contrast, various forms of the name Sarapa are found in a good number of Greek documents; but, again, nowhere else in the Coptic material.

5   We have here translated ϣⲓⲛⲉ 'greet' as 'salute', as you can not really greet an abstract quality.

10   ⲁⲛⲑⲁⲣⲣⲉ ⲛⲙⲙⲁ: We have supposed that the construction of ⲑⲁⲣⲣⲉ (θαρρεῖν) plus ⲙⲛ̅ (ⲛⲙ̅ⲙⲉ//) 'with' must here mean that the writers feel themselves to be confident because of the parents' care. This makes sense following the previous clause about the latter being 'a wall of protection'. Still, the suffix to ⲛⲙ̅ⲙⲉ// must be fem. sg., applying therefore to the mother alone; and this is slightly odd. One might consider instead whether here is intended ⲛ̅ⲙⲁ//, the normal preposition after this verb; although in that case the vowel (ⲛ̅ⲙⲁ for ⲛ̅ⲙⲟ) is more unexpected than the spelling ⲛⲙ̅ⲙⲁ for ⲛⲙ̅ⲙⲉ (i.e. 2nd fem.). Another interpretation would be to suppose that the brothers feel confident about the parents' protection, wherever they go, following their prayer to God to guard them. This would also make sense, but in this case ⲛⲙ̅ⲙⲁ must be interpreted differently. One could conjecture some error here in view of the following word ⲛ̅ⲙⲁ.

17   ⲁϩⲉ ⲙⲛ̅ ⲡⲁⲙⲉⲣⲓⲧ: The meaning of this final line is problematic. It appears to be (as here translated) a brief additional sentence, perhaps an injunction to the little girl to stay with her uncle Sarapa, termed ⲡⲁⲙⲉⲣⲓⲧ in l. 15. Nevertheless, the use of ⲁϩⲉ (from ⲱϩⲉ 'stand') strikes one as rather odd; and then there is the question of who is being addressed and why 'the beloved' is not named. On the latter question, there is evident some ink-traces below. One partial solution would be to suppose that some following text was written, perhaps a name; though if one compares the verso it is hard to imagine that papyrus has been lost at this point. Is it conceivable that the scribe wrote an extra line, not noticing that the surface for this document had finished? If so, is the strange beginning of the transverse text (l. 18) somehow related to this?

18   ϣⲉⲡ̅ ⲧⲏⲣⲥ̅: The meaning of this, which seems to stand alone at the start of the marginal text, is obscure. One solution might be to connect it somehow to the ending of l. 17 (surely not the name of 'the beloved'?); on which see the note above. However, as it stands, it looks like the verb ϣⲱⲡ 'receive' or 'accept', with ⲧⲏⲣ// 'all'. This is how it has been translated, though it is entirely unclear as to what it would refer (perhaps a feminine definite noun has been omitted by mistake?).

19   The start of the text on the verso appears very strange. However, it may be best to read this as a continuation of what was being said in l. 17: 'Stay with my beloved N.N. - you can not remain with the foreigner'. If this is correct, then the injunction of l. 17 ('stay') has been made not just to the daughter, but to the family members (plural) to

whom the letter has been written. Of course, the way that the scribe keeps switching between persons, singular to plural and male to female, is confusing; and a real feature of the text. But at least this makes some sense and helps to connect the text on the verso to the recto, which can now be read as one continuous letter. Admittedly, it would mean that the margin text (l. 18) must have been added after the verso was completed. Finally, there is the problem, probably unanswerable, about what or who is actually meant by the βάρβαρος; here translated rather neutrally as 'foreigner'. Obviously, the author is writing in Coptic rather than Greek; and one would therefore suppose that the term refers to a true outsider, such as the Libyan of **50**, 27-28 or perhaps a Nubian. Alternatively, although the date may be rather early for this, perhaps the term is being used summarily and without ethnic meaning? Already in Shenoute (only a few years later) it has currency with a very pejorative connotation for all kinds of misbehaving contemporaries.

ⲁϩϭⲱ: Perhaps a compound expression (not hitherto attested to our knowledge), made as a construct of ⲁϩ(ⲉ) and ϭⲱ; although such a compound may be of doubtful standing, since quasi-synonyms are not usually compounded (as are antonyms, reversatives, consecutives and the like), but rather pleonastically coupled in circumstantial constructions (as are sometimes ϭⲱ and ⲙⲏⲛ ⲉⲃⲟⲗ). It might be conceivable as a means of intensification, such as 'stay forever'; or perhaps it is a kind of 'hesitation duplicate'. At any rate, ⲁϩ- can not be the participial prefix since this would need a pronominal determiner after ⲙⲛⲧⲁⲧⲛ-. Thus, we seem to have an instance of an 'autonomous' ⲙⲛⲧⲁ// followed by an infinitive. This is attested otherwise only with the prenominal ⲙⲛⲧⲉ- (plus ⲗⲁⲁⲩ ⲛ-) or a generic ⲙⲛⲧⲟⲩ- (*Pistis Sophia* 268: 19; 269: 17 etc.); in which case the meaning is always 'can not' or 'it is impossible for ... to'.

24 The combination of ⲙⲛⲧⲁⲧⲛ-, if this is a variant spelling of ⲙⲛⲧⲉⲧⲛ- (as it seems), with the stative ⲛⲏⲩ, appears to be incompatible with anything we know about Coptic syntax. However, the use of the negative existential ⲙⲛ- in front of a definite Present preformative ⲧⲉⲧⲛ- (where ⲛⲏⲩ belongs) would be no less unusual.

25 On the nature of the pack-animals, cf. **20**, 54 note ad loc; but here one might better understand reference to the drivers themselves. We assume that the Conditional (ⲉϣⲁⲛⲧⲁ-) is used with the common function of a future temporal. Alternatively, the writer may have had real doubts about their ever answering, in which case: 'If ...'.

26   'I will send it': It is not at all clear to what this refers.

ⲧⲁⲟⲩⲁ: Our best suggestion is to understand ⲧⲟⲟⲩⲉ, (pair of) shoes; cf. CD 443b. Alternatively, one might try ⲧⲟⲩⲁ 'door-post'; but it seems less-likely for sense.

27   When Masi writes ⲙⲛ̄ '(together) with' it is uncertain whether the sender or recipient is intended; but we think the latter. One should note that Pshai has already addressed the father Sarapa in l. 3 and a brother Sarapi in l. 15; and it is most economical to suppose that Masi now refers again to the second of these.

27-28 ⲡⲟⲩϣⲏⲣⲉ / ⲧⲟⲩϩⲙⲙⲓ: In the context of most other documents from Kellis this would certainly be 'their', but the idiolect of **122** remains to be explored. For these two occurrences of a possessive article with -ⲟⲩ the text makes easier reading if they are understood as referring to 2nd person fem., as they would be in Sahidic and the Middle-Egyptian dialects. Of course, there is also the problem of the inappropriate singular (surely one should read ⲛⲟⲩϣⲏⲣⲉ?).

28   †ⲕⲟⲩⲓ̈ ⲛ̄ⲃⲉⲣⲉ: 'this small basket (?)'. We understand ⲃⲓⲣ (CD 41b-42a); though one might consider ⲃⲡⲡⲉ 'young' and thus translate 'this young girl', or ⲉⲃⲣⲁ 'seed' and translate 'this small amount of seed'. The last is least likely, because it should be masculine. Gender would favour the second interpretation; but we prefer the first for sense, noting that Crum gives examples of the noun as fem.

29-30 This is a tentative free translation of a rather unusual and difficult sentence. Apparently, the dative ⲛⲏⲧⲛ̄ functions as an adverbial predicate, which resembles the structure of 'cheer formulas' in which a verbal element like ⲉϥⲉϣⲱⲡⲉ or ⲉϥⲛⲁϣⲱⲡⲉ, preceding the dative, is most often omitted. Thus, ⲁⲡⲁ- is read as Second Present, and a good literal rendering of the sentence might be: 'The ground be to you very much in my heart'. Otherwise, an entirely different interpretation of ⲡⲓⲧⲛ ⲛⲏⲧⲛ̄ might be that of a verbal form of † (the 'pre-dative' ⲧⲛ-); in which case ⲁⲡⲁ would be one of the Greek particles and ⲡⲓ- would have to stand for ⲙ̄ⲡⲓ- Neg. Perf.: 'Have I not given you very much in my heart?'. However, we consider it very unlikely that the sentimental reinforcer adverb ⲧⲟⲛⲟⲩ would ever be used with an actional predicate such as 'give'; even when it is somehow connected with the 'heart'.

31   Perhaps the 'they' refers to the messengers; or otherwise understand: 'Will you be reached at home?'. We have glossed the adverb ⲛϩⲟⲩⲛ as 'at home', but it could just be a phrasal reinforcer rather like the colloquial English: 'Will they catch you in?'.

32   ⲛⲉ ⲧⲟ: presumably for ⲛⲉ ⲛ̄ⲧⲟ, with the *augens* reinforcing personal reference.

33-34   ⲕⲁⲑⲁⲣⲟⲛ: '(fine) white bread'; cf. LSJ 850b. Thus e.g. a καθαρουργός is a baker of fine bread.

36   ⲁϩⲁⲉ: apparently an adverbial predicate, but unknown as such. Although it seems to contain a form of ϩⲁⲉ 'last', it can hardly be a nominal construction. In this context (replacement of one thing for another?), and because of its predicate function, it can not fail to remind one of the pandialectal verb ⲣ̄-ϩⲁⲉ 'be wanting' (CD 636a), for which it may be an adverbial Present equivalent.

P. Kellis Copt. 123

Inv #: P 93.85 + P93.89

Location: House 4, room 6, deposit 14.

Preservation: This is a mostly complete document, written in Coptic on a narrow strip of papyrus, and with dimensions of 270 x 65 mm. It is now broken into three pieces at the upper and lower horizontal folds; and there has been some loss of the basic fabric. It was rather coarsely written, with thick strokes and a large script. The dialect is a variety of southern regional Sahidic.

Content: This is essentially a loan receipt and an agreement to repay in kind (sometimes called a 'sale in advance'); although it is written in epistolary form. As such it makes a useful addition to the mass of personal letters that dominate the Coptic documents from Kellis. According to the terms of the loan agreement the *holokottinos* / *solidus* will be repaid not in cash but by its value in oil. Oil was typically 40 *sextarii* to the *solidus*, perhaps even cheaper in Dakhleh than the Nile valley. Since 20 *choes* are 120 *sextarii*, the amount to be repaid is very high, i.e. about triple the value of the loan.

The religious context for the document can not be known for certain, but is most likely to be Christian. The following letter (**124**) also features a Besas, and thus the two pieces could conceivably be associated. That text is certainly Christian.

Address:

verso

          [κυρί]ῳι μου . .   Χ   . . . .

          . . . . . . ωρος

          To my master ... Χ (From) ...

Names: Ioseph son of Besas; Louioros; Shoei;

Text:

1	τ[ῶι ἀγα]πητῷι ἀ-
2	δε[λφῶ]ι Ἰωσηφ
3	Βησᾶτος Λ[ου]ιωρος
4	ἐν̄ κ(υρί)ῳ χαίρειν
5	†[ⲣ̄]ϩⲟⲙⲟⲗⲟⲅⲓ
6	ⲭⲉ ϩⲓⲭⲓ ⲛ̄ⲧⲟ
7	[ⲧⲕ̄] ⲛ̄ⲡⲓϩⲟⲗⲟ
8	ⲅⲟⲧⲓⲛⲟⲥ ⲉⲧⲉ
9	ⲭⲣⲓⲁ ⲁⲩⲱ ⲉ
10	ⲡⲉϥⲛ̄ⲡϣⲁ ⲭⲉ
11	ⲛ̄ⲕⲁⲁⲥ ⲉⲉⲓ
12	ⲛⲁ† ⲛⲁⲕ ⲛ̄
13	ⲡⲓⲭⲟⲩⲱⲧ ⲛ̄
14	ⲕⲟ[ⲩ]ⲥ ⲛ̄ⲛⲏϩ
15	ⲙ̄ⲡⲓⲕⲟⲩⲥ ⲛ̄
16	ⲡⲁⲉⲓⲱⲧ ϣⲟⲉⲓ
17	ⲛ̄ⲑⲁⲛⲉⲧⲁ
18	ⲉⲙⲛ̄ⲧⲟⲩ ⲗⲁⲩⲉ

19	ⲛ̄ⲁⲛⲧⲓⲗⲟⲅⲓⲁ
20	†ⲧⲁⲛⲟ ⲛⲁⲕ ⲛ̄
21	†ⲉⲡⲓⲥⲧⲟⲗⲏ ⲉⲩ
22	ⲱⲣⲝ` ⲟⲩⲭⲁⲉ̣ⲓ̣
23	ϩⲛ̄ ⲡϫⲟⲉⲓⲥ . ⲉ
24	ⲁⲅⲁⲡⲏⲧⲟⲥ ⲛ̄
25	ⲥ̣ⲟ̣ⲛ ⲉⲧⲧⲁ . \ . /ⲏ
26	ⲟⲩ ⲁⲩⲱ ⲉⲧⲥ̣ⲟ̣ⲉ̣ⲓ̣

---

9 punctuation mark after ⲭⲣⲓⲁ?   11 punctuation mark after ⲕⲁⲁⲥ?

To my loved brother Ioseph son of Besas. (From) Louioros; in the Lord, - greetings.

(5) I acknowledge that I have received from [you] this *holokottinos* for my need and (10) its worth, so that I will pay you these twenty *choes* of oil (15) per the *chous* (-measure) of my father Shoei of the monastery; for they are not disputed. (20) I am drawing up this letter for you as a deed of security.

Be well in the Lord my (?) beloved (25) brother, who is honoured (?) and ...

Commentary:

Address: The traces are faint and any reading is very uncertain.

2-3   If we have understood the sequence of names correctly, the letter is written from a Ioseph son of Besas to a Louioros; the latter name rendering what would be in Coptic 'Louihor'. Compare Λωιωρ, which is common in the KAB.

10-11   ϫⲉⲛ̄ⲕⲁⲁⲥ: an unusual variant for ϫⲉⲕⲁⲁⲥ 'in order that'.

13   The letter evidently accompanies the payment ('.. these twenty'), which therefore is thought to be present in the situation of both sender and receiver.

17   ⲑⲁⲛⲉⲧⲁ: This is most obviously the word for 'monastery', i.e. ϩⲉⲛⲉⲧⲉ (with fem. article). The word is also found at **12**, 6 (connected to a 'father Pebok'). The modern village of Teneida, at the eastern entrance to the Dakhleh Oasis, may be supposed to derive its name from the same. The question arises as to whether these occurrences refer to a functioning monastery in the vicinity of Kellis, or to a village with the same

etymology. It is worth noting that in both instances (i.e. in **12** and **123**) the word is associated with a 'father N.N.'; and we suppose that an actual monastery is meant. The term μοναστήριον is found in two Greek texts from Kellis: P. Kellis I Gr. 12, 18-19; and an unpublished piece from the Temple Area (P 96.31, 9).

18-19 ⲉⲙⲡⲟⲩ ⲗⲁⲩⲉ ⲛⲁⲛⲧⲓⲗⲟⲅⲓⲁ: '.. for they are not disputed'. We understand the meaning to be that father Shoei's measure is a commonly accepted standard, beyond dispute. However, alternatively, in Greek contracts of this period the term ἀντιλογία is commonly used to assert that the loan will be returned at a certain date 'without protest'; compare e.g. P. Kellis I Gr. 45, 17, a loan of money from 386 C.E. and referring to the *chous*-measure of Hibis. In this case one might simply translate '.. without any dispute'.

24 Whilst the reading of ⲁⲅⲁⲡⲏⲧⲟⲥ is certain, the text around it is most unclear. Most obviously, one would imagine that it was preceded by ⲡⲉ- 'my' (for ⲡⲁ-); but the reading is not very satisfactory.

25-26 ⲉⲧⲧⲁ . \ . /ⲏⲟⲩ: This looks like the scribe intended to write ⲉⲧⲧⲁⲉⲓⲏⲟⲩ 'honoured'. There appears to have been a correction. We do not understand the conclusion to l. 26.

P. Kellis Copt. 124

Inv #: P 93.89 + P93.54 + P93.77 + P93.109

Location: House 4, room 6, deposit 14; room 4, deposits 1A and 6.

Preservation: Here are fragments of a letter, written in Coptic on papyrus, which has broken at the centre fold and is in the process of disintegration. Much of the lower half can be joined together, and portions of the upper half, to reconstruct (an original) document of approximately 270 x 85 mm. The script is rather square and not particularly fluent. There is one fragment glassed here (visible only on the photograph of the verso and placed separate to the others) which probably does not belong.

The dialect is a form of southern regional Sahidic (similarly see **123**). It is comparable to the language of NHC II, both with regard to its use of some local non-Sahidic vocalisations (especially in everyday expressions) and the occasional 'hyper-Sahidicism'. As such, it contrasts strongly with the language of the great majority of Coptic documents recovered from Ismant el-Kharab, certainly those from House 3 and associated structures.

Content: The author was certainly a Christian; as evidenced by the rather florid style and biblical references typical of Coptic literature, as well as the postscript by Hor the ὑποδιάκονος (surely here as an ecclesiastical role) and the naming of the sender(s?) as priest(s) on the address. Unfortunately, there is no way to date the piece with any exactitude; but one may presume that it is contemporary with the many Manichaean-styled documents of House 3. This makes **124** an important addition to our understanding of the religious situation in Kellis during the second half of the IVth century C.E. An unpublished Greek document from House 4 (P 93.38) refers to an ἀρχιδιάκονος.

Address:
verso

  ⲧⲁⲁⲥ ⲡⲉⲛⲁⲅⲁⲡⲏ[ⲧⲟⲥ] Ⳁ ϩⲓⲧⲛ ⲁⲡⲁ ⲃⲏⲥⲁⲥ . [. . .] ⲙ̄ⲛ

  ⲥⲧⲉⲫⲁⲛⲟⲥ ⲑ ⲑ [. .]   ⲁⲅⲁⲑⲏⲙⲉⲣⲟⲥ ⲡⲣ/

Give it to our beloved Stephanos. ... Ⳁ From Apa Besas ... and Agathemeros, presbyters.

Names: Agathemeros; Besas; Hor; Stephanos;

Text:

1 ⲃⲏⲥⲁ[ⲥ ⲡⲡ]ⲣⲉⲥⲃⲩ[ⲧⲉⲣⲟⲥ]
2 ⲙⲛ ⲁⲅⲁⲑⲏⲙⲉⲣⲟ[ⲥ . .]
3 ⲡⲉⲧⲥϩⲉⲓ ⲡ[ⲉϥ]ⲉⲓⲱⲧ ⲥ . . . [.]
4 ϩⲙ ⲡⲭⲟⲉ[ⲓ]ⲥ ⲭⲁⲓⲣⲉⲓⲛ
5 ϩⲁⲑⲏ ⲛ̄ϩ[ⲱ]ⲃ ⲛⲓⲙ ⲧⲛϣ̣ⲓ
6 ⲛⲉ ⲉⲣⲟⲕ ⲧⲛϣⲓⲛⲉ ⲉⲛⲉⲧⲛ̣

7 ⲛⲙ̄ⲙⲁⲕ ⲧⲏⲣⲟⲩ ⲕⲁⲧⲁ
8 ⲡⲟⲩⲣⲁⲛ ⲛⲉⲧⲛⲛⲙ̄ⲙⲟⲛ
9 ⲧⲏⲣⲟⲩ ϣ[ⲓⲛⲉ ⲉⲣⲟⲕ ⲧⲛ̄]
10 ⲣ̄ⲗⲩⲡⲏ ⲉⲧ[ⲃⲉ . . . . ϣⲱ]
11 ⲡⲉ ⲧⲛ̄ⲥⲟⲟ[ⲩⲛ . . . . . .]
12 ⲁⲅⲁⲑⲟⲥ . [. . . . .]
13 ⲧⲉⲕⲙⲛ̄[ⲧ . . . . . . ⲙⲛ̄]
14 ⲧⲉⲕⲁⲅ[ⲁⲡⲏ . . . . . .]
15 [. . . . .]
16 [. . . . .]
17 [. . . . .]
18 [. . . . .]
19 [. . . . .]
20 . [.] . ⲙⲉ[.] . . ϣⲁⲣⲟⲛ
21 ⲧⲛ̄ϣⲡⲏⲣⲉ ⲙⲟⲕ ϫⲉ ⲙ
22 ⲡⲉⲕⲉⲓ ϣⲁⲣⲟⲛ ϣⲁ
23 ⲡⲟⲟⲩⲉ ⲛ̄ϩⲟⲟⲩ ⲉⲛϭⲱ
24 ϣⲧ̄ ⲛ̄ⲑⲉ ⲛⲟⲩⲕⲁϩ ⲉϥⲁⲓ
25 ⲃⲉ ⲉϥϭⲁϣⲧϥ ⲉⲃⲟⲗ
26 ⲙ̄ⲡⲙ[ⲟ]ⲩ ⲛ̄ϩⲟⲩ ⲁⲩⲱ
27 ⲛ̄ⲑⲉ ⲛⲟ[ⲩ]ⲁⲅⲅⲉⲗⲟⲥ
28 [ⲉ]ϥ[.] . . ⲉⲡⲛⲟⲩⲧⲉ ⲡⲉⲧ
29 ϭⲱϣⲧϥ \ⲉⲃⲟⲗ/ ϩⲏⲧϥ ϣⲁⲣⲉ
30 ⲟⲩϣⲱⲥ ⲉⲛⲁⲛⲟⲩϥ
31 ϣⲛ ϩⲧⲏϥ ϩⲁⲛⲉϥ\ⲉ/ⲥⲟⲟⲩ
32 [. . .] ϭⲉ ⲱ ⲡⲙⲁⲕⲁ
33 [ⲣⲓⲟ]ⲥ ⲛⲓⲱⲧ ϣⲛ̄
34 [ϩⲧⲏ]ⲕ ϣⲁⲣⲟⲛ ⲛⲕⲉ
35 ⲛ[.] . . [. . . . .] . ⲛⲉ
36 ⲕ[. . . . .]ϩⲱⲃ ⲉⲕⲟⲩ
37 ⲱϣ . . ⲉϩⲉⲓ . . . ϯⲛⲁ
38 ⲁϥ . [.] . [. . . . ⲟ]ⲩϫⲉⲓⲧⲉ

tr39	ϩⲙ ⲡϫⲟⲉⲓⲥ ⲡⲉⲛⲟⲩⲧⲉ [. . . . .] . ⲟⲩ . . .
v40	ⲁⲛⲁⲕ ϩⲱⲣ ⲡϩⲩⲡⲟⲇⲓⲁⲕⲟⲛⲟⲥ
41	ⲛϭⲉⲗⲏ ϯϣⲓⲛⲉ ⲉⲣⲟⲕ vac . . . ϣ .
42	ϣⲓⲛⲉ ⲉⲣⲟⲕ ⲡⲁⲅⲁⲡⲏⲧⲟⲥ

Address read <ⲙ>ⲡⲉⲛⲁⲅⲁⲡⲏ[ⲧⲟⲥ (?) 3 the entire line has been squeezed in after the following had been written; read <ⲙ>ⲡ[ⲉϥ]ⲉⲓⲱⲧ (?) 21 read ⲧⲛ̄<ⲣ̄>ϣⲡⲏⲣⲉ 24-25 ⲉϥⲁⲓⲃⲉ sic? read ⲉϥⲁⲃⲉ 25 ⲉϥϭⲁϣⲧϥ sic? read ⲉϥϭⲁϣⲧ 29 ϭⲱϣⲧϥ sic? read ϭⲱϣⲧ 31 ϣⲛ ex corr.

Besas the presbyter, and Agathemeros [presbyter (?)], the one who writes to [his] father Stephanos; in the Lord, - greetings.

(5) Before everything: We greet you (and) we greet all they who are with you by their name. All who are with us [greet you. We are] (10) distressed about [what has] happened. We know your good[ness] and your ...-ness and your love ... (15) ... (20) ... to us. We are astonished at you (sing.), that you did not come to us until today. We do look (forward to your visit) just as parched earth (25) looks forward to rain, and like an angel who is [close to] God looks forward to him. (30) A good shepherd has pity for his sheep. So, [now], o blessed father, have pity towards us for another (35) ... Anything you want, write ... and I will [gladly] do it. Be well (tr) in the Lord, our God ...

(v40) (It is) I, Hor, the sub-deacon of Kellis (?). I greet you. ... greets you, the beloved one.

Commentary:
Address: ⲑ ⲑ after the name of Stephanos might be understood as a date, i.e. ⲑ[ⲱ]ⲑ followed by a number (now lost). However, there is scant room for any (lost) -ⲱ-, and perhaps one should consider instead a Christian symbol.

We take the final ⲡⲣ/ (the abbreviation mark appears struck through both letters) to indicate that the senders were priests; i.e. for πρ(εσβύτερος). This itself might well only refer to Agathemeros; but we note that there is also some (lost) text after the name of Besas, and that l. 1 in the letter can well be restored to read 'Besas the presbyter'. The latter is titled 'Apa' on the address.

There is an ink trace above and to the right of the final -ⲛ on the upper line, which may indicate that there was further text above.

2   There may be room for ⲡⲣ/ at the end of the line (as on the address).

3   ⟨ⲙ⟩ⲡ[ⲉϥ]ⲉⲓⲱⲧ (?): or otherwise ⲡ[ⲉⲛ]-, ⲡ[ⲉⲩ]- or ⲡ[ⲟⲩ]-. We have supposed that both here and in the address ⲛ̄- has been omitted, noting that this scribe shows a certain lack of carefulness elsewhere (cf. ⟨ⲣ̄⟩ϣⲡⲏⲣⲉ in l. 21 or the redundant -ϥ in l. 25). However, it is true that the syllabic entity of this preposition can be totally assimilated to a following ⲡ-, as can be observed elsewhere especially in non-literary documents. A similar 'economic' spelling of the initial can be observed in ⲙⲟⲕ (for ⲛ̄ⲙⲟⲕ) in l. 21, which may indicate that it is not in fact an error.

The name at the end of the line is presumably Stephanos. Whilst there appears to be scant space, the entire l. 3 has in fact been added into the document and squeezed between ll. 2 and 4. Probably one should read ⲥⲧⲉⲫⲁ[ⲛⲟⲥ].

6-7   There is no need to emend the double-ⲛ in ⲛⲛⲛ̄ⲙⲁⲕ, nor to assume dittography. The repeated occurrence in l. 8 suggests that the double spelling is a regular feature of the writer's dialect. Although the same is exceptionally also found in Biblical Sahidic manuscripts (but mainly after ⲉⲧ-, where it may be purely phonetic), our best witness for this as a grammatical phenomenon is NHC II. In that codex, all occurrences of ⲛⲛ̄ⲙⲁ// are spelt with initial syllabic ⲛ when used as predicate in the Bipartite Pattern (and not only after ⲉⲧ-), whereas outside this predicative usage it never has the additional syllable.

10   ⲉⲧ[ⲃⲉ . . . . ϣⲱ]|ⲡⲉ: A nominalised Perfect relative must be restored, but we do not know the form that the scribe would have used (ⲡⲉⲧⲁϥ-, ⲡⲉⲛⲧⲁϥ-, or even with one of the participial prefixes ⲉⲣ- and ⲁϩ-).

11   ⲧⲛ̄-: The notation here above the -ⲛ- (and indeed elsewhere in this letter) is not really a superlinear stroke but rather a simple dot. Unfortunately, the font being used for the edition does not render the different signs very satisfactorily, so they have all been indicated in a uniform way. See further **127**, 2 ad loc.

22-23   ϣⲁ ⲡⲟⲟⲩⲉ ⲛ̄ϩⲟⲟⲩ: expressed with the insisting formula ('today's day'), i.e. 'this very day'.

24-26   The same image is found elsewhere in Coptic documents (perhaps cf. Job 29:23); e.g. W.E. Crum, *Varia Coptica*, Aberdeen, 1939 no. 54: 'God knoweth, like a thirsty land that longeth for water, even so have I thirsted for thy holiness ..'.

29   ϭⲱϣⲧϥ: It is true that the final letter (-ϥ) is uncertain and (given that it is impossible) might better be transcribed as ϭⲱϣⲧ{ . } (= unidentifiable trace). However, it is the most likely reading and the same oddity is certainly found in l. 25.

32   Perhaps [ⲧⲟⲧⲉ] ϭⲉ.

36-38   The text is badly destroyed, but enough remains to identify the familiar promise: '... anything you wish I will do it joyfully' (vel sim.). Cf. **35**, 48; **36**, 37-39; **128**, 46-47. The shift to the sing. ('I') from pl. ('we') is surprising, and may indicate that this has been added in a rather formulaic manner.

39   ⲡⲉⲛⲟⲩⲧⲉ: for ⲡⲉⲛ-ⲛⲟⲩⲧⲉ.

41   ⲛϭⲉⲗⲏ: The reading is very uncertain. Another possibility is simply ⲕⲉⲗⲗⲏ.

42   This final line is very uncertain. If we have understood it correctly there should be another name at the end of l. 41.

INVENTORY

P. Kellis Copt. 125

Inv #: A/6/34

SCA #: 2326

Location: House 4, room 1B, deposit 2. Excavated 11/1/93.

Preservation: This is a wooden board inscribed in Coptic. It is probably complete, but the board may well have been cut down from previous usage (the lower edge is markedly coarser). The drill-hole, and possible 'ordering' mark on the right side of side A, suggest that the board was originally part of a primitive codex. But the fabric has deteriorated and cracked, and this piece has finally been used for a rather basic list. The text is badly abraded in places. The dimensions are 127 x 71-81 (x 1.5-3 mm. thick).

Content: A list of commodities, with many 'ticked' (as e.g. in the KAB). There are no recognisable prices, dates or persons; but l. 4 may well refer to Trimithis.

Text:

(Ai)1	/ ⲛ̄ϩⲃⲁⲥ	(ii)18	/ ⲛⲟⲃⲥ
2	/ . ⲡⲣⲁ .	19	/ ⲁⲗⲁⲗⲁ
3	ⲛ̇ϩⲉ . . ⲧⲟⲩ	20	/ ϫⲓⲧ`ⲁⲙ . .
4	/ . . . ⲏ . . ⲛ̄ⲧⲣⲓⲙⲓ\ⲧ/	21	/ ϫⲓⲧ`ⲕⲁ . . . .
5	/ ⲛⲓⲛ	22	/ ϣⲟⲟⲩϣ̄
6	// ⲛⲓⲕⲟⲩï ⲛ̄ⲉⲓⲗⲟⲥ	23	/ . . . ⲛ̇ⲃⲉⲣⲉ
7	/ . . . ⲧⲏⲛ	24	/ ⲕⲛ̄ⲧⲉ ϣⲱⲟⲩ
8	traces	25	/ ⲟⲩⲁⲣⲁ .
9	/ traces	26	/ ⲃⲛ̇ ϫϩⲉ
10	. . . . . . ⲡϣⲉ	27	/ ϩ . ⲏⲛⲉ .
11	. . . . ϭⲁ . . ⲉϥ	28	ϩⲁⲗⲱⲙ`
12	traces	29	/ ⲕⲟⲣϣ .
13	/ ⲧ . ⲏⲣⲉ . `ⲃⲉⲣⲉ	30	/ ⲗⲁⲙ . .
14	/ ⲛⲓⲧⲟⲟⲩⲉ ⲛ̄ . . . ⲡ	31	/ ⲧⲕ . . . . . . ⲩⲥⲓⲥ
15	ⲛⲉϥϩⲗϭⲉ	32	/ ⲛⲓⲛⲟϭ ⲛ̄ϩⲁⲙⲧ`
16	ⲡ . . . ⲁ	33	ⲧϭ . ⲡϣⲡ` ⲛ̄ⲧⲟⲧϥ
17	traces	34	/ ⲛⲓ . . . ⲉ
		35	ⲉⲙⲡⲗ . .
		36	ⲛⲓⲕ . . . . .
		37	ϫ . . . .

(B)38	// ⲛⲓⲏ . . . . . ϩ
39	ⲛⲓⲁⲕⲟⲛ ⲛ̄ⲛ̇ⲏϩ
40	ⲛⲓϩⲉⲧ
	vac
41	ⲧⲥⲟⲩⲥⲏⲙⲏ

42	ⲧⲕⲟⲩⲓ̈ ⲛ̄ⲡⲏⲣⲉ
43	ⲛⲓϩⲟⲣ`
44	ⲧⲥⲓⲣⲁ
45	ⲡⲙⲉⲗⲁ

---

21 ⲕ̄- ex corr.   26 ⲃ- ex corr.

(Ai)1	The garments		(ii)18	Jujubes.
2	...		19	Grapes.
3	...		20	... olives.
4	... of Trimith(is)		21	Black (?) olives.
5	...		22	Dried (olives?).
6	These small items		23	Fresh (?) ...
7	...		24	Dried figs.
8	...		25	...
9	...		26	... dates (?).
10	...		27	...
11	...		28	Cheese.
12	...		29	...
13	Fresh (?) ...		30	...
14	These shoes (?) of ...		31	...
15	His sweet (ones)?		32	These large coppers (?).
16	...		33	... from him (?).
17	...		34	...
			35	...
			36	...
			37	...

(B)38	...
39	These *akon* of oil.
40	These silver (vessels?).
	vac
41	The sesame.
42	The small quail.
43	These keys (?).

44   The butter.
45   ...

Commentary:

1   It is difficult to know whether to read ϩⲃⲱⲥ, ϩⲃⲁⲥ, ϩⲃⲥⲱ (et al.); the traces are very faint. The first looks to be the easiest, but the latter two are preferable for dialect. In any case, the meaning is much the same in all instances, 'linen' or 'garments'; cf. CD 659b-660a.

4   The raised final -ⲧ surely indicates an abbreviation for Trimith(is). Compare the KAB ll. 1215, 1407 (though with a -θ) and **50**, 19. At the start of the line one could possibly read ⲡⲣⲏϣ 'mat'; but the letters would be rather spread out and it is not very convincing.

5   This looks at first like a long horizontal line and we wondered whether it was an erasure (or even a foreign script). But we think that this is something of an illusion, and that there is Coptic text here beginning ⲛⲓ- 'these' or ϫⲓ 'receive'.

7   Perhaps ϣⲧⲏⲛ 'garment' or 'tunic'.

13-15 The script is reasonably clear in this section, and it is frustrating not to be able to make more sense. ⲃⲉⲣⲉ is either 'new' (probably as an adjective) or for ⲉⲃⲣⲁ 'seed'. ϩⲏⲗϭⲉ looks like the word for 'sweetness' (CD 673b); but its meaning here escapes us, unless it be for 'sweet wine' (cf. γλεῦκος, also in the KAB).

19   ⲁⲗⲁⲗⲁ: If the reading is correct, this must be for ⲉⲗⲁⲗⲉ (cf. CD 54b). This would indicate that we are dealing with a rather extreme alpha-vocalisation, as found in a good number of the Kellis documents.

20-21 These must be different kinds of olives or olive products (cf. CD 790b-791a). It is very tempting to think of 'black olives' at l. 21, which could be ϫⲓⲧˊⲕⲁⲙⲉ vel sim. (compare ⲥϯⲕⲉⲙⲉ 'black cumin').

22   We suppose a partly misspelt abbreviation for (ⲉϥ)ϣⲟⲩⲱⲟⲩ 'dried' or another form of ϣⲟⲩⲟ 'dry'. See also l. 24. The word ⲃⲉⲣⲉ (ll. 13, 23?) may well be the opposite, i.e. 'new' or 'fresh'.

24   ⲕⲛ̄ⲧⲉ ϣϣⲟⲩ(ⲉ): 'dried figs', cf. CD 40b ⲃⲛϣⲟⲟⲩⲉ 'dried dates'; also ἰσχάδιον in the KAB.

32 ϩⲁⲙⲧ`: If the reading is correct, it is still unclear what is meant. The term may be used of money (copper coins); but here is more likely to be some kind of vessel. Compare l. 40.

39 ⲁⲕⲟⲛ: probably for ἀγγεῖον; see also **15**, 14; **17**, 10, 19; **22**, 12.

40 ⲛⲓϩⲉⲧ 'these silvers': Presumably for silver vessels rather than money; there is a similar issue at l. 32.

41 We believe that this must be for σησαμῆ. If this is correct, then it is a good illustration of the problems involved in reading this list.

42 The reading is clear enough, though ⲡⲏⲣⲉ 'quail' is supposed to be masc.

43 ϩⲟⲣ`: This must be for ϩⲟⲩⲣ 'ring' or 'key'. The apparent superlinear, which we have rendered as (`), could be for the -ⲩ-; but it would be oddly placed.

44 Again, the reading is clear enough, but ⲥⲉⲓⲣⲉ 'butter' (CD 353a) is also supposed to be masc.

45 ⲛⲉⲗⲁ: Obviously, there are all sorts of possibilities, including words formed with the Greek μέλας 'black' or 'dark'. One should also consider μέλι 'honey'; and Coptic words such as ⲛⲉⲗϩ 'salt'. However, there are too many variables (especially in what we do and do not know about the scribe's spelling) to make a reasonable decision about what is most likely.

INVOCATION

P. Kellis Copt. 126

Inv #: P93.13A + P93.19

Location: House 4, room 1, deposit 1; room 1B, deposit 1.

Preservation: Here are found multiple small fragments of papyrus, which can be partly arranged to show the remains of two texts. The first to have been written is presumed to be the large and impressive official document in Latin, some of which is visible on what is here termed the 'verso'. No attempt has been made to edit this text, which is only partially preserved. On the 'recto' there are columns of a Coptic invocation. We have ordered the two sides in this way under the presumption that the original Latin document has been reused to write the Coptic text. On the 'verso' there are the remains of two further columns of the Coptic invocation.

Nevertheless, it is difficult to know the sequence in which the columns of Coptic should be read; and the placing of some fragments remains uncertain. Here they are edited beginning at the upper left of the 'recto'; but noting that these terms should not be accorded any absolute value. In the translation each column is treated separately and numbered r(ecto)i, ii, etc. Line numbers are purely for reference purposes, as it is impossible to know the extent of the original Coptic text. Thus, 'ri' is a narrow column of text marked by repetition of the phrase: 'Have mercy on me!' (ⲛⲁⲁ ⲛⲏⲓ). Beside it is found 'rii', which (quoting from Psalm 145) is rather more expansive in both format and style. The relationship of 'riii' (calling on the name of the saviour) and 'riv' (where is found a repetitive design) to the previous two columns is unknown. In 'vi' the author calls upon the name of the Lord God (parallel to riii); whilst beside it there are minimal traces of column 'vii'.

Content: This Coptic invocation is presumed to be Christian, calling upon the 'name' of the Lord God and of the saviour. The hand is fluent and practised. The dialect is southern regional Sahidic (remarkably involving a few local forms that are mainly known from *A* and *I* dialects, such as ϣⲁⲣⲉϥ- Affirm. Aorist, ⲙⲙⲟ 'there' and ϩⲟⲩ 'day').

Text:

(ri) 1   ] . . ⲉⲣ .
2   ⲛⲙ̄ⲡⲁ
3   ⁻ . ⲉⲓⲛⲁ
4   [. . .] . ⲛ̄ⲁⲁ
5   [ⲛⲏⲓ] ⲛⲁⲁ ⲛⲏⲓ
6   [. . .] ⲛⲁⲁ ⲛⲏⲓ
7   [ⲡ]ⲉⲕϭⲁⲩⲁⲛ

8   [ⲡ]ϣⲏⲣⲉ ⲛ̄
9   [. . .]ⲭⲥ̄[

and probably more

(rii)10   ϣⲁⲣⲉϥⲕⲁⲧϥ
11   ⲛ⟨ϥ⟩ⲥⲟⲩⲱⲛⲅ ⲁ̣[ⲡ]ϥ
12   ⲕⲁϩ/ ⲉϥⲱⲟⲩ
13   ⲉⲧⲙⲙⲟ ⲥⲉⲛⲁⲧⲁ
14   ⲕⲟ ⲛϭⲓ ⲛⲟ⟨ⲩ⟩ⲙⲉⲩⲉ
15   [ⲧ]ⲏⲣⲟⲩ/ ⲛⲁⲓ̈ⲁⲧϥ
16   ⲙ̄ⲡⲉ̣ⲧⲉⲣⲉ ⲡⲉϥ

and more

(riii)17   ⲁⲩⲱ ⲡⲣⲁⲛ [ⲛⲡ]
18   ⲥⲱⲧⲏⲣ ⲧⲁ
19   ⲉⲡⲓⲕⲁⲗⲓ ⲙⲙ̣[ⲁϥ]
20   ⲛⲏⲓ̈ ⲡⲭⲟ[ⲉⲓⲥ]
21   ⲡⲁⲛⲟⲩⲧⲁ
22   ϫⲉ ⲁⲛⲟⲕ` ⲡ[ⲉ]
23   ⲁⲛⲁⲕ` ⲡⲉ ⲡ[. . .]
24   ⲧⲁ ⲡⲉⲕϭⲁⲩ[ⲁⲛ ⲛ]
25   ⲧⲟⲕ` ⲡⲭⲟⲉⲓ[ⲥ . .]
26   vac   ⲁⲉⲓ ⲛ̣[. . .]

and more?

(riv)27   ⲡⲉⲧⲁ . [
28   design

(vi)29   ⲡⲣⲁⲛ̣
30   ⲛ̣ⲡⲭⲟ
31   ⲉⲓⲥ ⲡⲁ
32   ⲛⲟⲩⲧⲉ
33   ⲧⲁⲉⲓ ⲛ[ⲧⲁ]

34   ⲚⲞⲨⲦⲈ

35   [Ⲙ]ⲘⲀϤ drawing

(vii)37   . ẹ . ẹ

---

32 ⲚⲞⲨⲦⲈ: -ⲉ ex -ⲁ corr.

(ri) ... Have mercy (5) [on me]! Have mercy on me! ... Have mercy on me! Your servant, the son of ...

(rii10) He shall return and know you on his earth. On that day all their thoughts (or: 'plans') will perish. (15) Blessed is he whose [helper] ...

(riii) And the name [of the] saviour, let me invoke it (20) o Lord my God: "I am". I am ... your servant. (25) You are (?) the Lord ...

(riv) The one who ...

(vi) The name (30) of the Lord my God, let me come and invoke it.

(vii) ...

Commentary:

1   It is unclear whether there is here really text or some design element. Notably the ink begins to the left of the column edge apparent in ll. 2-3; and also does not continue across to the right. At the same time, it is difficult to understand how the text can properly start in l. 2, or what is the meaning of these initial lines.

4   It is not certain whether this is really a superlinear above the ⲛ̄. Possibly one should read, preceding it and starting in l. 3, ⲚⲀ[ⲀⲚⲎ]Ï. Thus the call for mercy would be made four times.

8   Either the 'son' refers to the author (i.e. God's 'servant') or to the saviour.

9   ⲭ̄ⲥ̄: It is very uncertain whether this is really an abbreviation for ⲭ(ⲞⲈⲒ)Ⲥ 'Lord'.

10-16 This part of the text ('rii') quotes Psalm 145:4f. LXX from the end of verse 4a to at least the beginning of verse 5. Compare the Sahidic of 4b ed. Budge: ϩⲙ ⲡⲉϩⲟⲟⲩ ⲉⲧⲙ̄ⲙⲁⲩ ⲥⲉⲛⲁⲧⲁⲕⲟ ⲛ̄ϭⲓ ⲛⲉⲩⲙⲉⲉⲩⲉ ⲧⲏⲣⲟⲩ. A division of *stichoi* is made visible by diagonal strokes in the manuscript (this device is not found in other parts of **126**).

11 ⲛⲥⲟⲩⲱⲛⲅ obviously intrudes between ϣⲁⲣⲉϥⲕⲁⲧϥ and what must be ⲁⲡϥⲕⲁϩ 'he shall return to his earth'; it has no place in the Psalms quotation. The easiest way to construct it, following the Affirm. Aorist, would be a conjunctive; but this necessitates assuming the omission of <ϥ> after ⲛ. This is what we have recorded. Less likely is an interpretation as ⲛ-inf. 'to know you', since infinitives after reflexive ⲕⲱⲧⲉ are constructed with ⲉ- / ⲁ- and used only after a negated ⲕⲁⲧ//, not in the Affirmative. Either way, the original destination of return (ⲁⲡϥⲕⲁϩ 'to his earth') is irretrievably obfuscated by this intrusion and altered into a simple locative.

16 If this reading of ⲉⲧⲉⲣⲉ- is correct, the presumed continuation of the quote must once again have deviated from the standard Psalms text, where the phrase 'whose helper is the God of Jacob' necessitates a Nominal Sentence in Coptic and would be converted by the simple ⲉⲧⲉ-; not a Relative Present or Future.

17 The initial ⲁ- is stylised to indicate the start of a new section.

18, 33 The verb form ⲧⲁ- is a 1st person Conjunctive without antecedent, which expresses a kind of auto-induced action of the speaker, self-encouragement or promise.

21-22 There could be space for further letters at the end of these two lines, but we have assumed not in our transcription and understanding of the text.

ⲡⲁⲛⲟⲩⲧⲁ: The final -ⲁ is especially notable, and compare l. 32 where the same seems to have been corrected. In the following ll. 22-23 the scribe writes first ⲁⲛⲟⲕ, and then ⲁⲛⲁⲕ. These details give the impression that it is a struggle to achieve something close to standard Sahidic orthography, and that the scribe tends naturally to the characteristic alpha-vocalisation of many other Kellis documents.

We suppose that the first ⲁⲛⲟⲕ ⲡⲉ, which after ϫⲉ gives the impression of actually being the called-for name, may well be an allusion to the famous "I-am-who-I-am" name of Ex. 3:14.

23-26 This small fragment is slightly mis-aligned on the photograph. It should be shifted the width of one full letter to the left.

28   This looks like a closing design, but may be a succession of vowels (6 or 7 x ⲉ followed by the same of ⲩ?) as is common in many 'magical' texts.

35   This looks like a drawing of a bird.

LIST OF OTHER (NOT EDITED) COPTIC FRAGMENTS FROM HOUSE 4

We can find no records of further Coptic fragments recovered from House 4 (1993 season), other than the one scrap glassed together with those published as **124**. However, there probably were some other small pieces. One would need to search all the frames in the P93 sequence.

TEMPLE ENCLOSURE

The final texts published in this volume were all recovered in early 1996 or early 1997, during two seasons of excavation in the Temple area. It is not surprising that no Coptic texts have been found that can be associated with the Temple itself; but it appears that the pagan cult ceased about 335 C.E. (cf. P. Kellis I Gr. 13, 14 and comm. ad loc.) and some of the area was then used for domestic purposes, storage and indeed rubbish. It is with this final half-century of occupation and reuse that the following documents (other than **129**) should be associated. We may suppose, although there are no specific dating criteria, that they were all written in the second half of the IVth century, contemporary with the other documents published in CDT I and II. Apart than this, we have no real context for these pieces and each should be treated as a discrete find. **127, 128** and **131** were recovered from D/8, a domestic unit built after the outer *temenos* of the Tutu Temple had been removed. **130** was found in D/2 (Shrine I).

The one exception to the above summary is the ostracon **129**. This fascinating find provides the only clear evidence from Ismant el-Kharab for the development and use of Coptic prior to its maturity as a script, as evident from the many documents published here and dating to the later IVth century. The ostracon has been the subject of especial interest, and may best be dated to the second half of the IIIrd century. It was recovered in the area of wells and storage chambers at the north-west corner of the inner *temenos* of the Tutu Temple.

LETTERS

P. Kellis Copt. 127

Inv #: P 96.2(i) + P 96.4 + P 96.16 + P 96.24

Location: Temple area, room 1, deposits 2 west and south + 5; room 3, deposit 4; recovered 1996.

Preservation: Here are found many small fragments of papyrus that can be joined or arranged to reconstruct remains from the lower half of a document written in Coptic. This is presumed to be a letter from the second half of the fourth century. Twenty-one fragments are from P 96.2, four from P 96.4, and one from P 96.24. The unplaced edge fragment, which appears to come from the upper half of the same letter, is from P 96.16. The hand is rather square and awkward. The scribe uses a greater range of diacritical marks than are commonly found in the Coptic texts recovered from Ismant el-Kharab; see comm. ad l. 2. It may be that a new scribe began at l. 34, or at the very least the scribe utilised a new pen. N.B. A number of readings in the transcript are based on small fragments that seem to have disintegrated or been lost by the time the digital photograph was taken in 2009; see e.g. comm. ad l. 25.

Content: It is very difficult to make any sense of the overall content or purpose of the text. Nevertheless, there is some interesting terminology. The dialect is again Sahidic, as with a number of the pieces from House 4; and this encourages one to suppose a Christian context. Some passages might well imply religious instruction, perhaps from a superior.

Address: None preserved, although - if it existed - it may have been written on the (lost) upper half of the letter.

Names: -shampe (?);

Text:

r(x +)1 [. . . . .] . ϩⲏ

2 [. . . . . Ⲧ]ⲉϩⲓⲙ̄

3 [. . . . .] . ⲉ

4 [. . . . .]ⲥ̣

5 [. . . . .] ⲙ̄

6 [. . . . .]ⲉ̣ⲧ

r(x +)7 [. . . . .] .

8 [. . . . .]ⲏ̣ ⲉⲁⲕ

9 ϣⲱⲡⲉ̣ ⲛ̣ⲟⲩⲥⲱϫ[ⲡ] ⲛ̄ⲧⲅⲉ

10 ⲛⲉⲁ ⲛ̄ⲧⲉ ⲛⲉⲕ̣̄ . [. . . . .]

11 ⲉⲩⲛⲁⲁ̣[. .] . ⲙⲁⲍⲉ̣ [. . . .]

12 ⲛ̄ⲛⲉⲕ . [. .] . ϩⲓⲧ . [. . . .]

13 ⲁⲩⲱ ⲛ̄ . . ⲧⲏⲣⲟⲩ . [. . . .]

14 ⲙ̄ⲡⲉⲟⲟⲩ ⲛ̄ⲛ . ⲧⲉⲩ[. . . .]

15 ϫⲉⲕⲁⲥ ⲛ̄[. . .]ⲩ̣ⲥϣ[. . . .]

16 ⲑ[. . .] . [. . . . .]ⲉ̣ⲛ[. . . .]

17 ⲉⲓⲥⲁⲩϣ[. . . .]ⲧⲙ[. . . .]

18 ⲛ̄ⲛⲟⲙⲟ[ⲥ] ⲛ̄ⲧⲉ ⲛⲉ[. . . .]

19 ⲕ . . . ⲉϣⲱⲡⲉ ⲉⲡ[. . .]

20 ⲡⲉ ⲁⲣⲓ ⲧⲁⲅⲁⲡⲏ ⲛ̄ . [. . .]

21 ⲁⲡⲟⲥⲧⲟⲗ[ⲟⲥ] ⲛⲁⲛ ⲛ̄[. . .]

22 ⲛⲉⲓ̈ⲕⲟⲩⲉⲓ̣ [ⲧⲏ]ⲣⲟⲩ ⲁⲩ[ⲧⲛ]

23 ⲛⲁⲩϥ ⲙ̣[.] . . ⲙ̄ⲙⲟⲛ̣ [. .]

24 ⲓ̣ⲧⲟⲙⲛ̄ ⲙ̄ⲙ[ⲟ]ⲛ̣ ⲙ̣ⲛ̄ ⲧ̣[. . .]

25 . . . ⲇⲉ ⲟ̣[ⲩ]ϫⲁⲓ̈[. . . . .]

(v)26 [. . . .] . ⲩ

27 [. . . .]

28 [. . . .] .

29 [. . . .] .

30   [. . .] . ⲡⲉ̣ ⲧⲛ̄ϣⲓⲛⲉ . [.]ϣⲁⲙⲡⲉ ⲙⲛ ⲡⲉϥⲏⲉ̣[ⲓ]
31   ⲙ̄ⲡⲉⲣⲁⲙⲉⲗⲓ ϭⲉ ⲉⲧⲃ⟨ⲉ⟩ ⲡⲟⲩⲁ ⲛ̄ⲛ̄ⲭⲱ
32   ⲱⲙⲉ ⲉⲧⲛⲛⲁⲩϥ [. . . . .] ⲛ̄ⲧⲉ̣ . . [.] . ⲧ̣ . ⲟⲥ̣
33   ⲁⲩⲱ [. . .]ⲛ̄ⲛⲁⲛ̣[. . . . .]ⲩⲁⲥ̣[. . . .]
34   . . . . [. . .] . ⲟⲛ̣[. . . . .]ϣⲁ
35   ⲣⲟⲛ ϩⲱⲥ ⲉⲛⲧⲁⲩⲡ[ⲗ]ⲣⲁⲍⲉ ⲙⲙⲟϥ ϩⲓ ⲧⲉ
36   ϩⲓⲏ ⟦ . ⟧ ⲭⲉⲕⲁ[ⲥ] ϭⲉ [ⲉⲩ]ⲛⲁϭⲱϣⲧ ⲉⲣⲟϥ
37   ϩⲓⲛⲁⲥ ⲭⲉ ⲛ̄ⲛⲉ ⲡⲉⲡⲣⲉ̣ⲡⲟⲥⲓ ⲉⲣ ⲗⲁⲩ ⲛ̄
38   ⲡⲉⲑⲟⲟⲩ ⲛⲁϥ

---

35 ⲉⲛⲧⲁⲩⲡ[ⲗ]ⲣⲁⲍⲉ: initial ⲉ- ex corr.   37 ⲭⲉ: ⲭ- ex corr.

... the road ... (5) ... since (?) you (masc. sg.) came to be a remainder from the generation (10) of your ..., as they will be ... your ... and all the ... of glory ... (15) so that ... the laws of ... (20) Be good enough to [send (?) the] *Apostolos* for us ... all these little ones. They have sent it ... us ... us ... (25) ... Be well (and live for a long time?).

(v) ... (30) ... We (?) greet -shampe (?) and his household. Now, do not neglect about (this particular) one of the books, to send it ... and ... to (35) us. Since he has (already) been attacked on the road, (let us make sure) now that he will be looked after, lest the commander do any evil to him.

Commentary:

2   ϩⲓⲛ̄: The notation above the -ⲛ resembles a *djinkim* point, and close examination of the text throughout shows that the scribe uses a sophisticated system of diacritics quite unlike anything found in the majority of *L* texts recovered from Ismant el-Kharab. Compare again the final -ⲛ and the following ⲙ- at l. 24, or the ⲛⲛ- at l. 31. Unfortunately, the font being used here for the edition does not render the different signs very satisfactorily, so they have all been indicated with a uniform superlinear stroke (although clearly there are a number of very different functions that deserve careful study).

11   It is difficult to read e.g. ⲁⲧⲓⲙⲁⲍⲉ (ἀτιμάζειν).

21   The *Apostolos* here is probably the Pauline letters, or used in the general sense (as opposed to the *Gospel*); but Mani can not be entirely excluded. The same work may very well be 'the (particular) one of the books' that the recipient is reminded to send in ll. 31-32. Thus we are inclined to restore the verb 'send' at the end of l. 20, though it could equally be 'copy' or similar.

23-24   Naturally, one thinks of a word like ἐπιτομή; but the sense of the text escapes us.

25   ο̣[υ]ϫⲁϊ̈[: This is found on earlier photographs (and in our notes), but the relevant fragment of text must have been lost by the time the digital photograph was taken in 2009. It strongly suggests the standard farewell formula at the close of the recto, before the author has continued with further messages on the verso.

30   Here one understands the familiar epistolary greetings to -shampe and his household; in which case one should probably restore ⲧⲛ̄ϣⲓⲛⲉ ⲉ[ⲡ]ϣⲁⲙⲡⲉ (Pshampe, lit. 'son of heaven'?). Normally, one would expect ⲡⲉϥⲏⲉ̣[ⲓ] to be followed by ⲧⲏⲣϥ̄, but there is no room.

35-36   ⲧⲉϩⲓⲏ: the 'way' or 'road'. The reference at l. 2 may refer to the same episode, but has no surviving context. Concerning the translation of ⲡⲓⲣⲁⲍⲉ, although LSJ 1354b has only one reference for the meaning 'attack', πειράζειν was almost a technical term in Hellenistic military language as can be seen e.g. from the entry in the *Polybios-Lexicon*. This was obviously a serious matter and required renewed caution.

37   ⲡⲉⲡⲣ̣ⲉ̣ⲡⲟⲥⲓ: 'the πραιπόσιτος (Latin *praepositus*)'. On this military title see also the comments of K. A. Worp at P. Kellis I Gr. 27, 3; but here there is not sufficient detail to know his exact function or the territory under command, nor indeed why exactly he should be feared.

P. Kellis Copt. 128

Inv #: P 97.15 + P96.98 + P96.108

Location: Temple area, room 7, deposit 2; room 8, deposit 3 on 4; recovered 1996 and 1997.

Preservation: Here are many fragments from a substantial letter written in Coptic on papyrus. In 1996 there was found a strip from the upper left-hand edge of the document (P 96.108); this is all that remains of the upper quarter (ll. 1-11). There were also found a series of strips from the lowest quarter (P 96.98), evidencing parts of the final four lines (ll. 46-49) and a substantial body of blank papyrus below. Then in 1997 (P 97.15) many fragments from the central part of the letter (i.e. the second and third quarters) were recovered from the adjacent room 8, level 3 on 4. It is clear that these all belong to the same document as one can read across l. 46 by combining the lowest line of P 97.15 with the uppermost of P 96.8. However, it must be noted that this has only been done on the basis of the photographs. The join became apparent to us during editorial work, but we have subsequently been unable to find the glass frame containing P 96.98 and P 96.108. Therefore, the upper and lower quarter of the document do not appear in the digital photograph taken in 2009, and can only be viewed on the much earlier photograph reproduced in the plates. Indeed, the fragments from 1996 and 1997 have never been physically joined in a single frame.

The letter is written in virtually standard Sahidic with a distinctive square script. The language is also marked by a large number of Greek loan words. As with **124** and **127** there may be a greater range of diacritical marks than found in any of the documents from House 3, see comm. ad l. 26 and **127**, 2. Our supposition is that the author was a Christian of substantial education. Without any specific dating criteria (beyond the general archaeological context) we presume that the piece was written in the second half of the fourth century.

The papyrus is very brittle, and shows a marked deterioration since it was first recovered (it is now breaking into ever smaller fragments). The width of the document is 65 mm. The second and third 'quarters' are each 80 mm. in length; but the total may have been less than 4 x 80 = 320 mm., if the uppermost and lowest 'quarters' were in fact rather shorter than the others (as appears from the extant remains). The original document has broken along both vertical and horizontal folds.

Content: It is difficult to gain a proper sense of the purpose and content of this letter. However, it is marked by an educated style and frequent pious phrases. The probable Christian context is in marked contrast to the great mass of letters from House 3.

Address:

verso

      [. . . . .]   X   ϣⲁⲓ̈

[To ...] X (From) Shai.

Names: Ammon; Shai;

Text:

1   ⲧ . [. . . . .]

2   . . [. . . . .]

3   vac   [ⲭⲁⲓⲣⲉⲓⲛ]

4   ⲛ̄ⲧ[. . . . .]

5   ⲣⲙ̄ ⲛ̄[. . . . .]

6   ϣⲉ . [. . . . .]

7   ⲧⲉⲡ[. . . . .]

8   ⲡⲙⲉ[. . . . .]

9   ⲟⲛⲁⲉ[. . . . .]

10   ⲣⲟⲩⲥ . [. . . . .]

11   . [. . . . .]

12   . . [. . .] . [. . . . .] . . [.]

13   ⲙⲁⲗⲓⲥⲧⲁ ⲉⲙⲛ . . . . [. . ⲣ]ⲱⲙⲉ

14   ⲉϥⲟ ⲛ̄ⲁⲝⲓⲟⲥ ⲙ̄ⲡⲉ[. . .] . . . .
15   ⲉⲛⲉ ⲛ̄ⲧⲁⲕϩⲁⲓ̈ ⲉ[ⲣⲟⲓ̈ ⲛ̄]ⲟⲩⲉⲡⲓ
16   ⲥⲧⲟⲗ[ⲏ] ⲛⲉⲉⲓⲛⲁⲣϣ[ϣⲉ . .] . . ⲣ\. / . .
17   ⲡⲁⲗⲓⲟⲛ ϫⲉ ϯϣⲡ ϩⲙ[ⲟⲧ ⲛ̄]ⲧⲛ̄
18   ⲡⲛⲟ[ⲩ]ⲧⲉ . [. ⲉ]ⲅⲭⲟⲣⲏⲓ[ⲁ .] . ϥⲉⲛⲓ
19   ⲙⲉⲧⲉⲱⲣ[ⲟ]ⲥ ϫⲓ ⲙⲕⲁϩ . [.]ⲉⲛⲧⲁϥ
20   ⲭⲁⲣ[ⲓ]ⲍⲉ ⲛⲁⲛ̄ [.]ⲉⲅⲭⲟⲣⲏⲓⲁ ⲙ̄
21   ⲙⲡ . [.]ⲉⲛⲁ ⲉ[. .] . ⲟⲩ ⲡⲁⲓ̈ ⲉⲧϯ ⲟⲩ
22   ⲟⲉⲓ ϩ[.] . ⲟⲩⲅⲉⲛⲉⲁ [ⲛ̄]ⲉⲧϩⲱ[ⲧ]ⲡ ⲉⲛⲉⲩ
23   ⲁⲣⲏ[ⲩ ⲙ]ⲛ̄ ⲛⲉⲧϣⲓ]ⲛⲉ ⲛ̄ⲥⲱ[ϥ] ⲙ̄ⲡⲉⲩ
24   ϩⲏⲧ [.] . ϥ . . ⲛ̄ϩⲩⲡⲟⲕⲣⲓ[ⲥⲓ]ⲥ ϫⲉ
25   ⲉⲃⲟⲗ [ⲟ]ⲛ ϩⲓⲧⲛ̄ ⲧⲉⲉⲓⲡⲣⲟⲫⲁⲥⲓⲥ
26   ⲁϥⲧⲁ[ⲁ]ⲥ ⲛⲁⲛ̄ ⲉⲡⲧⲣⲉⲛⲁⲥⲡⲁⲍⲉ
27   ⲛ̄ⲛⲉⲛ[ⲁ]ⲣⲏⲩ ϩⲙ̄ ⲡⲉⲧϩⲏⲡ ⲙⲉⲛ
28   ϩⲓⲧⲛ̄ [. . . .]ⲩⲙⲙ . ⲡⲁⲓⲁ[ⲥⲧ]ⲏⲙⲁ
29   ⲉⲧⲟⲩ[ⲧ]ⲱⲛ ⲙⲛ̄ ⲛⲉⲛⲉⲣⲏ[ⲩ] ⲙ̄ⲡϭ
30   ⲱⲗⲡ ⲇⲉⲃⲟⲗ ⁻ . [. . . . . .] . . [.]
31   ⲟⲩⲟ ⲛ̄[.] . ⲛ ⲉϩⲟⲩⲛ ⲁ . [. . ⲛ̄]ⲉ[ⲛⲉ]
32   ⲣⲏⲩ ⲑ[. .] . . ⲉ ⲇⲉ ⲉⲉⲓⲙⲟ[ⲩⲧⲉ ⲉ]ⲣⲟⲥ
33   ⲉⲫⲱ[ⲃ ⲉⲃⲟⲗ] ϩⲓⲧⲛ ⲡⲙⲁⲕⲁⲣⲓⲟⲥ
34   ⲛ̄ⲓ̈ⲱⲧ [ⲉⲯⲁ]ⲩⲧⲁⲉⲓⲟⲩ ⲡⲉⲡⲓⲥⲕⲟ
35   ⲡⲟⲥ ⲛ̄[ⲧⲟϥ ⲛ̄]ⲧⲁϥⲥϩⲁⲓ̈ ⲛⲁⲥ ⲉⲧⲙⲧⲣⲉ
36   ⲗⲁⲁⲩ . [. . .]ⲗⲉⲓⲛ ⲥⲉⲛⲁⲧⲁⲙⲟ[ⲥ
37   ϭⲉ ⲉⲡ[. . . .] . ⲉ ϩⲛ̄ . [.] . . . [.]ⲧⲁ
38   ⲡ . . [. . . . . . .]ⲛ̄ ⲁⲣⲟⲕ [. .] ϯⲥϩⲁⲓ̈
39   ϭⲉ ⲉⲣ[ⲟⲕ ϫⲉ ϯⲉⲓⲙ]ⲉ ⲉ[ⲧⲉⲕ]ⲙⲛ̄ⲧ
40   ⲙⲁⲓ̈ⲥ[ⲟⲛ . . . . .] . . ϭ . . [.] . ϩⲩⲡⲟ
41   ⲕⲣⲓⲥⲓ[ⲥ . . . . .] . . ϩ[ⲛ̄] ⲧⲉⲕⲙⲛ̄ⲧ
42   ⲉⲩⲉ[ⲣ]ⲅⲉ[ⲧⲏⲥ ϯϣⲓⲛⲉ ⲉⲛⲉⲧⲙⲛ[[.]]
43   ⲙⲁⲕ ⲧⲏⲣⲟⲩ ⲕⲁⲧⲁ ⲛⲉⲩⲣⲁⲛ ☩
44   ϣⲓⲛⲉ ⲉⲣⲟⲕ ⲁⲛⲟⲕ ⲁⲙⲙⲱⲛ
45   ⲡⲉⲕ[.] . . . . ⲉ . ⲉ . . . . . .

46   [ϩ]ωβ [ε]κογαϣ[ϥ] cϩαï ναï †
47   ναλαϥ εειραϣ[ε ογχαï ϩⲙ]
48   ⲡϫⲟⲉⲓⲥ ⲡⲙⲉⲣⲓⲧ ⲛⲥⲟⲛ ⲉⲧ
49   ⲉⲓⲣⲉ ⲛⲛⲉⲧⲣ ⲁⲛⲁϥ vac

---

16 ⲡⲁⲗⲓⲟⲛ, i.e. ⲡⲁⲗⲓⲛ ⲟⲛ   29-30 the line break in ⲙⲡϭ|ⲱⲗⲡ is very unusual; ⲁⲉⲃⲟⲗ, i.e. ⲁⲉ ⲉⲃⲟⲗ   42 traces at end of the line may be an erasure; a possible reading is ⲉⲛⲉⲧⲏⲛ|ⲙⲁⲕ (writing ⲛⲛⲙⲁⲕ for ⲛⲙⲙⲁⲕ)

..., - [greetings].

... (5) ... (10) ... especially if there is no ... person who is worthy ... (15) If you had written [me] a letter, I would have been content ...

Something else: I give thanks to God [for the] possibility (that he can make?) these haughty ones suffer ... he has (20) gracefully accorded us [the] possibility of ... This one (i.e. God) who searches [through (?)] a generation (for?) they who are reconciled to one another, and they who seek after [him] in their heart (without any?) hypocrisy. For (25) also from this motive he has given us cause to cordially greet one another. On the one hand, in a hidden way, from ... they understand (?) the difference which is between us and our comrades; on the other hand in (30) openness ... one another. As for ... (fem.), when I spoke to her about the matter by way of the blessed [and] honoured father, the bishop (35) [himself] wrote to her to make sure that no one ... Thus she will be informed about the ... Nonetheless, I am writing to [you, in that I know your] (40) brotherly love ... (without) hypocrisy ... in your beneficence.

I greet all they who are with you according to their names. I greet you, I Ammon, (45) your ... Anything that you want: Write to me, I will gladly do it. [Farewell in] the Lord, the loved brother who (should) do what he pleases.

Commentary:

18, 20 ἐγχωρία: the term is fairly ambiguous (and rarely used in Coptic). We suppose 'possibility' or perhaps 'permission'; but some talk of 'custom' or 'tradition' can not be excluded in this lacunous context.

19   μετέωρος: cf. LSJ 1120b, 2Kings 22:28 and Isaiah 2:12 LXX.

26   ⲛⲁⲛ: ink above final -ⲛ could be accidental as this notation is not generally apparent in the document, unless the same in l. 20? Compare **127** and note the comments there at l. 2.

27, 31   Since the scribe certainly writes ⲁⲣⲏⲩ in l. 23, and probably ⲉⲣⲏⲩ in l. 29, it can not be determined which spelling he used in these lacunas. A similar ambivalence is apparent elsewhere, perhaps ⲁⲣⲟⲕ in l. 38 and ⲉⲣ[ⲟⲕ in l. 39.

32   ⲑ[. .] . . ⲉ: Perhaps a woman's name (possibly read ⲑ[. .] . ⲣⲉ?).

43ff   This may be a postscript written by Ammon (starting ϯ|ϣⲓⲛⲉ from the very end of l. 43), as the author of the letter itself, according to the address, is Shai.

46-47   'Anything you wish ... I will do it rejoicing': cf. **35**, 48; **36**, 37-39; **124**, 36-38.

VARIA

P. Kellis Copt. 129

Inv #: D/1/234 (drawing sheet no. 97/79a)

SCA #: 2547

Location: Temple area, zone 20, deposit 12 surface (recovered 22 / 01 / 1997).

Preservation: Here is found an ostracon inscribed with an early form of Coptic script on the concave side. The text is probably to be dated to the second half of the third century C.E. (based on the decoration on the exterior, the jar type, and the archaeological context); and the piece was then used as a chinking sherd during the construction of the vault of a storage chamber. The dimensions are 148 x 80 mm., with the lower 25 mm. blank. There is a break at the top which could indicate that the start of the text has been lost; but this is uncertain as the first line as preserved would make a coherent start to the message. Some letters are rather faint and can not be read with certainty.

Content: This piece was first published by I. Gardner, 'An Old Coptic Ostracon from Ismant el-Kharab?', *ZPE*, 125, 1999: 195 - 200. It has attracted substantial interest, and in particular R. S. Bagnall challenged the designation 'Old Coptic' in his 'Linguistic Change and Religious Change: Thinking about the Temples of the Fayoum in the Roman Period', *Christianity and Monasticism in the Fayoum Oasis*, ed. G. Gabra, Cairo / New York, 2005: 11-19. The importance of the piece lies in the fact that the text evidences a writing system that differs from that which came to prevail in standard forms of Coptic. In particular, the letters derived from Demotic are closer to their earlier shapes than in later orthography. Further, there is evidence of differences in the lexicon compared to the mass of fourth century Coptic texts recovered from Ismant el-Kharab (noting especially the word ϣⲣⲱⲧ 'child' at ll. 3 and 5, see CD 631ab). Given the probable later third century date, and thus approximately seventy-plus years prior to the great majority of Coptic documents from the site, the piece clearly is important for an understanding of the development of Coptic as a writing system. For further discussion see the papers by Gardner and Bagnall. Note that the non-Greek characters are represented by their corresponding equivalents in a standard Coptic typeface (the photograph and the *ed. princ.* by Gardner should be consulted).

Names: Hout; Imouthes; Moni; Ps-;

Text:

1   ⲧⲓϣⲓⲛⲁ ⲁϯⲉ
2   . . ⲙⲛ̄ ⲛϥ̄
3   ϣⲣⲱⲧ
4   ⲙⲛ̄ ϩⲟⲩⲧ
5   ⲙⲛ̄ ⲛϥ̄ϣⲣⲱⲧ
6   ⲧⲓϣⲓⲛⲁ ⲁ
7   ⲙⲟⲛⲓ ⲙⲛ̄ ⲛϥ̄
8   ϭⲣⲁⲛⲉ ⲁ
9   ⲓⲙⲟⲩⲑⲏⲥ
10 ⲧⲥϣⲁⲉⲓ
11 ⲛⲉⲧⲛ̄ ⲭⲁ

12   ⲭ̄ⲛ̄ⲧⲏⲡ . . .

———

8 ϭⲃⲁⲛⲉ: ϭ- ex corr?   11 ⲛⲉⲧⲛ̄: -ⲧ- ex corr.

———

I greet Pse- and his children, and Hout (5) and his children. I greet Moni and his servants (?). (I greet) Imouthes (10). I am writing to you because ...

Commentary:

1   ⲧⲓϣⲓⲛⲁ: The writing system appears to lack any single character for the sequence tau + iota. Of course, whilst this feature has sometimes been seen as a mark of early Coptic, many texts even several centuries later and especially from the south do not use -ϯ-. For some tentative comments on 'dialect' see Gardner 1999: 198f.

3, 5   ϣⲣⲱⲧ: This term for 'child' is never used in *L* or Sahidic, where one always finds ϣⲏⲣⲉ (or ⲁⲗⲟⲩ). Note also that, whilst *L* and Sahidic resolve various Egyptian consonants as -ϩ-, this writing system utilises at least two distinct letters (as does Bohairic and some other dialects). See further Gardner 1999: 198.

7   Moni: One might prefer to read <ⲁ>moni; or it is even possible that there is an additional (very faint) ⲁ- at the end of l. 6.

8   ϭⲃⲁⲛⲉ: The initial and somewhat unclear character has been resolved as ϭ-, in order to render some sense to the text by reading here a form of ϭⲁⲩⲟⲛⲉ 'servant' (pl.), see CD 835b. However, one should note that the letter may have been corrected and that its intended shape is uncertain. One might also consider ⲕ- (but still rendering the same meaning).

10   ⲧⲥϭⲁⲉⲓ: In the *ed. princ.* this was resolved as ⲧ<ⲛ>ⲥϭⲁⲉⲓ 'we'; but after discussion the editors have agreed that the emendation is not sufficiently justified to be included here.

11-12   ⲭⲁ|ⲭ̄ⲛ̄ⲧⲏⲡ . . . : We can not resolve this sequence, but presumably it is here that the author sends some kind of message (i.e. the purpose of the piece, which otherwise is only greetings). Various possibilities may be considered. In the *ed. princ.* it was supposed that ⲭⲁ stood for ⲭⲉ; but (for instance) could there be a further faint letter such as ι at the end of l. 11, to read ϫ(ⲉ)- + ⲁⲓ-? Or else might one understand ϫ(ⲉ)- + ⲁϫⲛ- (prep.)? These possibilities could yield meaning such as: 'I am writing to you because I have done ..'; or 'I am writing to you because (I have been?) without our / your ..'.

The latter part of l. 12 (ⲡ . . .) looks rather like ⲡⲓⲉ . , with the final letter as -ϯ or -ϩ. We can make no sense of these readings.

P. Kellis Copt. 130

Inv #: D/2/4

SCA #: 2446

Location: Temple area, Shrine I (the *mammisi*), room 1, deposit 6.

Preservation: Here is found an ostracon inscribed with Coptic text on the concave side. It was recovered in a single piece, but has now broken into three fragments during storage. The script is rather coarse and some parts are very faint. It is not certain whether the text is complete.

Content: The interpretation is problematic, but it may be an agreement to pay for the use of land. The date of the text is unknown, but presumed to be fourth century. N.b. *solidi* are not found in the papyri until the reign of Constantine.

Text:

1   ϩⲁ ⲛⲟⲩⲁⲓⲉ ⲡ
2   ⲉⲥ̣ⲧⲁⲧⲟⲩ ϯϫⲱⲣⲁ
3   ⲉϥⲉⲓ ⲁⲟⲩ2ⲁ ⲉϥ
4   ϣⲓⲧⲃ ⲛᵒ ⲗⲉ
5   ⲁⲧⲩⲣⲏⲧ ⲁ̣ . . . ⲩ .
6   . .

3 ⲟⲩ2ⲁ: understand ⲟⲩⲁ2ⲁ

The cultivators have made an agreement for this place (?). When he comes to the Oasis he will demand from him 35 *nomismatia* (5) for ...

Commentary:

1-2 The interpretation of the first two lines is very uncertain. We have presumed that (ⲉ)ⲣ at the end of l. 1 is for ⲣ̄ plus a Greek verb. In this case the initial 2ⲁ- would be the Affirmative Perfect base, and ⲉⲥⲧⲁⲧⲟⲩ could represent a form of ἵστημι. Alternatively, the verb may be a form of (ⲧ)ⲥⲧⲟ 'pay back'. Whilst this might make grammatical sense, the use of χώρα strikes one as oddly vague for some kind of agreement of this sort. One would also expect the subject of l. 3, the owner, to be named somewhere.

5-6 We can make no sense of these lines.

P. Kellis Copt. 131

Inv #: D/8/111

Location: Temple area, room 8, deposit 3; recovered 22 / 01 / 1997.

Preservation: This is a fragment of a wooden board inscribed with Coptic text. The hand is fluent and practised. On side A is found the starts of eighteen lines, the third of which seems to be indented. The left hand margin is 9 mm. On side B only the upper portion is inscribed; there are traces from probably five lines. The dimensions of the extant portion are 135 x 34 x 3 mm. The straight cut at the bottom suggests that this may be the lower part of the original board. Whilst it is impossible to know the dimensions of that, one can compare e.g. T. Kellis Copt 2 (approx. 195 x 70 mm.) or the KAB (335 x 107 mm.). Thus the width of the lines may have been in the region of 2-3 times what survives. Line lengths in the edition below are purely indicative of this sort of range and have no absolute value.

Content: The genre of this text is unknown. It is not obviously a letter, nor any kind of list or financial document. It may in fact be a literary or sub-literary text; but we are not able to suggest any identification. The dialect is non-Sahidic, in so far as one can tell from the scant remains. We have not attempted a translation, as there are simply too many uncertainties.

Text:

A(x +)1	[. . .] . . . [. . . . .]
2	[. .]ϫⲟⲥ ϫ[ⲉ . . . .]
3	. . ⲧ` ⲧⲉⲟⲩⲉ . [. . . . .]
4	ⲛⲏⲓ̈ ϩⲁⲉ[. . . . . ⲙⲛ̄ⲛ̄]
5	ⲥⲱⲥ ⲡⲅⲣⲁ[. . . . .]
6	ⲧⲣⲉⲓ̈ϯ ⲡⲃⲁ[. . . . .]
7	ⲡⲗⲏ ⲛ̄ⲧⲛ̄ . [. . . . .]
8	ⲁϩⲣⲁⲩ ⲛ̄ⲧ[. . . . .]
9	ⲁϩⲣⲏⲓ̈ ϩⲛ̄ . [. . . . . ⲁ]
10	ϩⲣⲉ ⲡϩⲣϩ[. . . . .]
11	ⲛ̄ⲅ̄ϭⲓⲛⲥ ⲛ̄[. . . . .]
12	ⲛ̄ⲥⲁⲃⲁⲗ ⲁ[. . . . .]
13	ⲧⲉ ⲉⲛ ⲉⲧⲉ . [. . . . .]
14	ϩⲱⲉ . . [. . . . .]
15	ϣⲱⲧ[. . . . .]
16	ϫⲁⲩⲧⲁ[. . . . .]
17	. ϩⲱ . [. . . . .]
18	. . . . [. . . . .]
B(x +)19	[. . . . .] . [. . . . .]
20	[. . . . .] . . . . [. . .]
21	[. . . . .] . ⲛ[ⲟ]ⲩⲧⲉ . .
22	[. . . . .] . . . . .

23 [. . . . .] . . .

Commentary:

3 The start appears to be indented, and one imagines that the initial letter was writ large. It could be a ⲧ-; but unfortunately what follows is most uncertain. It is not clear whether one should read . . ⲧ` ⲧⲉⲟⲩⲉ . , or perhaps . . ⲧⲥⲧⲉⲟⲩⲉ . ?

6 Probably a causative precedes the verb ϯ.

LIST OF OTHER (NOT EDITED) COPTIC FRAGMENTS FROM THE TEMPLE ENCLOSURE

Here are listed those other pieces of inscribed material in Coptic that were recovered from the Temple Enclosure by the archaeological excavations of 1996 and 1997. All are on papyrus except D/8/75. Their preservation is poor and they have not been edited. Nevertheless, they are recorded here in order to complete the publication of the Coptic texts from Ismant el-Kharab (i.e. in the four volumes KLTI and II, CDTI and II). There may have been other small frgs.; but this exhausts our records.

D/8/75	Vertical strip from the middle of a wooden board. Coated and inscribed on both sides. Side A: perhaps letters or traces from 10 lines? Side B: perhaps letters or traces from 13 lines? The genre of the text is unknown. Read on B: ρ]ωχϩ̄.
P96.10	Remnants from the middle of perhaps 9 lines of Coptic. No margins. Curious punctuation signs (or decoration?) seem to divide some clauses. The text could be literary, but uncertain. At l. 4 read:]ⲁⲃⲉ ⲡⲉⲛⲧⲁϩⲁϥ . [.
P96.20	Three Coptic frgs.; two with margins.
P96.29	One Coptic frg.?
P96.48	One edge frg. from a Coptic letter with margin. Read: ⲙⲡ̄ⲕⲣ̄ ⲁⲙⲉⲗⲉ.
P96.109	Two poorly preserved Coptic frgs.
P96.114	One frg. inscribed on both sides in Coptic.
P96.116	One Coptic frg.
P96.146	The start of a letter written in Coptic. Read (ll. 1-3): ⲡⲁϫⲁⲓⲥ [. . . . .]| ⲙⲉⲣⲓⲧ ⲉⲧ[ⲧⲁⲓⲁⲓⲧ ⲛ̄]|ⲧⲟⲧ ⲧⲟⲛ[ⲟⲩ . . . . . .].
P97.16	Three or four frgs. of Coptic; very poor preservation.
P97.53	Corner from a personal letter written in Coptic. Read on v: ⲧⲓⲙⲟⲑ[ⲉⲟⲥ.

INDICES

Native words*

ⲁ-, ⲁⲣⲁ⸗ prep. ⲁ- **57**.14; **58**.14,22,30,32,33,36,37; **60**.3; **62**.7; **64**.18,20,26; **65**.8,28,29,37,39,41,43,44,45,47; **66**.11,22,31,35,39,42,43; **67**.2,4,6,16,33,34,40; **68**.8,10,13,29,37,47; **69**.3; **70**.11,12,41,43,45; **71**.2,5,12,27,28,31,31; **72**.4,6,7,19,23,24,24,25,30,32,35; **73**.5,17,20,24,24; **75**.2,4,33,41; **76**.2,39,47; **77**.5,6,10,35; **78**.6,12; **79**.9,27,39,45; **80**.7,11,21,22,28,29,33,38,38; **81**.13,17,26,27,35,37,49,49,50,51,54; **82**.7,11,18,25,26,29,30,36,41; **84**.10,26,34; **85**.8; **86**.4,21; **88**.6,9; **89**.2,11,18,26; **90**.7,29,34,37,39,43; **91**.1,6; **92**.29; **93**.5,10,19; **94**.37,43,45; **95**.6,10,17; **96**.26,27,35; **98**.26,27; **99**.19,22; **102**.19; **103**.5,18,19,37,38; **105**.37,44,68,77,82; **106**.20,21,33,34,37; **107**.5; **108**.7,27,30,33; **110**.17,50; **111**.15,32,33,35,36,39,40; **112**.6,19,21; **114**.1; **115**.10,16,24,26,37; **116**.2,7,9,11,12,13,13; **117**.2; **118**.7; **119**.52; **120**.14,23,23,28; **122**.5,13,20; **126**.11; **129**.1,6,8; **130**.3   ⲉ- **72**.8

see also adverbs *s.v.* ⲃⲁⲗ, ⲙⲁ, ⲙⲉⲩ, ⲡⲁϩⲟⲩ, ⲣⲏⲥ, ⲣⲉⲧ⸗, ⲥⲁⲡ, ϩⲁⲉ, ϩⲟⲩⲛ, ϩⲣⲏï; compound prepositions ⲁⲣⲛ-, ⲁⲧⲛ-, ⲁϫⲛ-

ⲁⲣⲁ⸗: ⲁⲣⲁï **58**.27; **66**.29; **69**.3; **70**.40; **82**.12; **83**.13; **92**.9; **93**.12; **94**.12,21; **99**.23,54; **105**.15; **109**.8; **114**.2   ⲁⲣⲁⲕ **57**.4; **62**.10; **64**.30; **66**.4; **68**.7; **70**.4,36; **72**.36; **73**.2,21; **74**.1; **76**.44; **77**.3; **78**.5,7,11; **79**.10; **80**.5,6,32,33; **81**.4,5; **82**.5,6; **84**.3; **86**.3; **94**.3,6,9; **99**.8,20; **102**.9; **103**.2; **105**.37; **106**.5; **107**.10,30; **108**.31,36; **111**.3,19; **112**.4,6,10,17; **115**.44; **118**.3; **120**.1,11; **122**.8   ⲁⲣⲟ **66**.30; **75**.39; **76**.34; **83**.2; **92**.3,4,19,20,33,36; **93**.3; **95**.2; **109**.17   ⲁⲣⲁϥ **58**.31,34; **66**.39; **71**.11,14; **79**.39; **80**.39; **81**.20,39; **92**.25; **103**.49; **105**.50; **107**.28; **108**.22; **110**.29; **111**.14; **120**.27,30   ⲁⲣⲁⲥ **72**.20; **122**.16   ⲁⲣⲁⲛ **116**.7,8   ⲁⲣⲱⲧⲛ **58**.23; **61**.11; **65**.5; **67**.5,50; **70**.7; **71**.3,24,25,26; **72**.3,9,10,15,16,17,31; **75**.36; **76**.6,8; **78**.49; **79**.7; **82**.32; **83**.6; **88**.25; **89**.22,44; **90**.4; **91**.1; **92**.7,27; **93**.21; **95**.2; **97**.14; **102**.1,2; **105**.7,10,78; **115**.34; **116**.11,16,17; **119**.62   ⲁⲣⲱⲧⲛⲉ **66**.37; **77**.35   ⲁⲣⲁⲩ **64**.8; **65**.35; **71**.18; **75**.26; **81**.53; **92**.37; **105**.78; **107**.13

ⲣⲁ⸗: ⲣⲁï **110**.27   ⲣⲱⲧⲛⲉ **66**.34   ⲣⲁⲩ **70**.43

(Sah.:) ⲉ- **123**.8,9,21; **124**.6,28; **126**.12; **128**.22,26,33,37,39,42

ⲉⲣⲟ⸗: ⲉⲣⲟï **128**.15   ⲉⲣⲟⲕ **124**.6,41,42; **128**.39,44   ⲁⲣⲟⲕ **128**.38   ⲉⲣⲟϥ **127**.36   ⲉⲣⲟⲥ **128**.32

ⲁ- preceding infinitive **58**.22,23,26; **64**.28; **65**.35; **67**.48; **70**.41,43; **71**.15,20,30; **72**.18,21; **73**.16; **76**.52; **77**.15,27; **78**.46; **80**.10,12; **81**.8,34; **84**.6;

---

* The alphabetical order of entries is that of Westendorf 1965/1977. The grammatical gender of nouns is indicated only when attested in the corpus. The occasional indicator "(Sah.:)" refers to the group of (quasi-)Sahidic texts, not necessarily to the particular forms.

90.12,25,26; 91.3,4,4; 92.11; 94.33,33,55; 99.19; 103.4,11,12,23,45,45; 105.17,24,26; 106.25; 107.29; 111.10,12; 113.10; 114.1; 115.4,15,26; 120.23; 122.25,34   ⲉ- 107.9,26; 127.32

with caus inf.: ⲁ- 58.22; 59.8; 76.52; 79.9; 81.16; 84.18; 86.16; 94.38; 99.24; 106.22; 107.21; 110.24; 114.6   ⲉ- 128.35

ⲁ- *about* (with quantifiers) 65.26   ⲉ- 102.11

(ⲁⲓⲟ) *verily, come* ⲁⲉⲓ 126.26   ⲁⲓ̈ 71.36

(ⲁⲓ̈ⲉⲩ) *be great* :
stat. ⲁⲓ̈ 63.2; 65.1; 73.1,23; 85.1,6; [88.1]; 89.3; 90.1; 93.1

(ⲁⲕⲉ) *sesame* ⲁⲕⲁ 65.27

ⲁⲙⲟⲩ imp. *come* 72.28; 81.13,34; 94.56; 105.56
f. ⲁⲙⲏ 71.29; 95.10; 116.6

ⲁⲙⲁϩⲧⲉ *seize, restrain* 79.16; 83.10; 105.14

ⲁⲛ *again, also* 58.14,20,24,26; 64.10,14,18,31; 67.60; 68.32; 72.20; 75.32,43; 76.28,29,30,37; 79.12; 80.14,16,16,39; 81.45,48; 84.12,33; 89.32; 92.17,26; 93.9; 94.24,33,49,52,53,56,58,58,59; 95.8,9,13; 99.40,50; 102.24; 104.3; 110.11; 111.12; 112.14; 115.23,30; 116.2; 118.7; 120.20,35; 122.22

(Sah.:) ⲟⲛ 128.17,25

(ⲁⲛⲉⲓ̈) *be pleasant, good* :
stat. ⲉⲛⲓⲧ 86.5

ⲁⲛⲁⲕ etc. (augens, independent pronoun) ⲁⲛⲁⲕ 57.2; 65.39; 66.21; 71.1; 75.1; 76.44; 78.48; 80.4,38; 81.37; 82.41; 83.2; 86.2; 92.2,35; 93.22; 99.45; 105.43; 109.2; 110.13; 111.2; 112.4; 115.26; 122.3   ⲛⲧⲁⲕ 64.25; 65.51; 67.28,29; 72.21; 78.47; 79.30,42; 81.38; 84.20; 103.6,30; 105.62; 110.5; 111.29; 115.20; 116.16   ⲛⲧⲟ 64.28; 71.29; 92.22,25   ⲧⲟ 122.32   ⲛⲧⲁϥ 79.45   ⲁⲛⲁⲛ 119.29   ⲛⲧⲱⲧⲛ 58.24; 61.12,27; 75.25

(Sah.:) ⲁⲛⲟⲕ 128.44   ⲁⲛⲁⲕ 124.40   ⲛⲧⲟⲕ 126.24   ⲛⲧⲟϥ 128.35

functioning as predicate: ⲁⲛⲁⲕ 60.1; 64.19; 65.4; 66.3,42; 67.1; 69.1; 70.3; 71.26,27; 73.2; 76.1,9; 79.6; 81.2; 82.4; 89.7; 90.4; 93.3; 99.5; 103.32; 105.5; 107.12; 108.3; 111.15; 115.6; 121.1; 122.27   ⲛⲧⲁϥ 63.31; 72.8   ⲛⲧⲁⲥ 115.28   ⲛⲧⲱⲧⲛ 64.15; 80.11   ⲛⲧⲱⲧⲛⲉ 90.35

(Sah.:) ⲁⲛⲟⲕ 126.22   ⲁⲛⲁⲕ 126.23

ⲁⲛⲁϣ *oath* :
ⲣ-ⲁⲛⲁϣ *pledge* 107.24

ⲁⲛⲏϩⲉ *eternity* :
adv. ϣⲁ-ⲁⲛⲏϩⲉ *for ever* 73.23
adv. ⲁⲛⲏϩⲉ *ever* (adneg.) 58.34; 61.16; 85.5; 90.10,38; 94.21; 105.48

ⲁⲣⲓⲕⲉ *blame* 86.20
ϭⲛ-ⲁⲣⲓⲕⲉ *find fault, blame* 70.40; 82.12; 86.20; 94.12; 105.15; 122.31

ⲁⲣⲛ-, ⲁⲣⲱ⸗ prep.: ⲁⲣⲱⲟⲩ 81.54

ⲁⲣϣⲓⲛ *lentil* 122.32

ⲁⲥⲉ *loss, damage* 81.37,41; 82.25
†-ⲁⲥⲉ *suffer loss* 82.35

ⲁⲥⲕⲁⲩⲗⲉ (a container, *Ascalonion* jar ?) 81.52 (see comm. ad loc.)

Indices: Native words

ⲁⲧ- priv. prefix: with infinitive, see ⲗⲁϭⲉ, ⲡⲱⲛⲉ, ϣⲓⲃⲉ
   with noun, see ⲣⲱⲙⲉ

ⲁⲧⲛ-, ⲁⲧⲟ(ⲟ)ⲧ⸗ prep.: ⲁⲧⲟⲧ **94**.41   ⲉⲧⲟⲧ **107**.28   ⲁⲧⲟⲧⲕ **69**.10 (comm.); **72**.13   ⲁⲧⲟⲧⲧⲏⲛⲉ **70**.16
   ⲉⲧⲛ- **72**.11 (for ⲁϫⲛ-?)

(ⲁⲟⲩⲱ) f. *pledge, surety*: ⲉⲟⲩⲱ **105**.26

ⲁⲩⲱ *and, indeed* etc. **62**.7; **70**.25; **73**.14,17,22; **76**.7,11,22; **80**.13,38; **81**.55; **90**.10; **93**.6; **94**.20; **103**.3,15; **106**.17,22,26; **111**.39; **123**.9,26; **124**.26; **126**.17; **127**.13,33

ⲁϩ- perfect participle:
   ⲉⲧⲁϩ- **80**.8; **92**.14; **105**.31; **111**.27

ⲁϩⲣⲁ⸗ *why...?*: ⲁϩⲣⲁⲛ **111**.10   ⲁϩⲣⲁⲩ **131**.8   ⲁⲣⲱ (2nd fem.) **92**.31

ⲁϫⲛ-, ⲁϫⲱ⸗ prep. *(up)on* etc.:
   ⲁϫⲱ⸗: ⲁϫⲱï **105**.22,79   ⲁϫⲱϥ **80**.13   ⲁϫⲱⲥ **105**.80

ⲃⲉⲕⲉ m. *wage, reward* **77**.32; **81**.42; **110**.9
   ⲃⲉⲕⲉ-ⲥⲱϩⲉ m. *weaving wage* **58**.27

ⲃⲱⲕ *go* **58**.22; **69**.3; **70**.36; **71**.23; **72**.16,16; **78**.24; **81**.50; **90**.34; **94**.46; **102**.10; **106**.10; **109**.28; **111**.30; **116**.7,11; **118**.7; **120**.24

ⲃⲁⲗ *outside*:
   adv. ⲁⲃⲁⲗ **58**.2; **62**.15; **63**.20; **64**.5,30; **65**.36,51; **66**.7,27,41; **68**.33; **70**.20; **71**.8,15,19,22,29,30,34; **72**.8,14,28,29; **73**.19; **77**.11; **78**.12,44; **79**.19,26; **80**.14,27,36; **81**.25; **82**.8; **88**.29; **90**.24,26,28; **91**.2; **92**.22; **93**.9; **95**.3,14; **98**.2; **99**.43; **102**.24; **103**.4,26; **105**.17,20,47,55; **110**.14; **111**.24,27; **115**.6,15; **116**.3,5; **122**.21,22,23   ⲉⲃⲁⲗ **105**.43
   (Sah.:) ⲉⲃⲟⲗ **124**.25,29; **128**.25,30
   adv. ⲛⲃⲁⲗ **92**.38
   -ⲃⲁⲗ (in compound, for ⲁⲃⲁⲗ or ⲛⲃⲁⲗ): ⲉⲓⲃⲁⲗ **67**.19 **75**.27 **81**.7   ⲛⲏⲩ ⲃⲁⲗ **78**.36   ⲥⲓⲧⲉⲃⲁⲗ **113**.11   ϣⲉⲃⲁⲗ **94**.43   ⲟⲩⲉⲃⲁⲗ **58**.26
   adv. ⲛⲥⲁⲃⲁⲗ **131**.12
   ...]ⲃⲁⲗ **65**.12 (possibly ⲡ-ⲃⲁⲗ *escape*)

(ⲃⲱⲗ) *loosen, free up*:
   ⲃⲁⲗ- **105**.42

ⲃⲱⲗⲕ *be wroth* **71**.24

(ⲃⲱⲱⲛ) *bad* (adjunct): ⲃⲱⲛⲉ **71**.9

(ⲃⲛⲛⲉ) *(fruit of) date palm*:
   ⲃⲛ- **125**.26 (uncertain)

ⲃⲁⲛⲓⲡⲉ *iron* **65**.24

(ⲃⲉⲉⲣ) *basket (?), scoop (?)*: ⲃⲉⲣⲉ **122**.28

ⲃⲣⲣⲉ *new, young* **80**.25   ⲃⲉⲣⲉ **125**.13,23
   adv. ϩⲁⲃⲣⲣⲉ *anew* **105**.45

ⲃⲁⲣⲱϩ m. *caravan (driver)* **71**.16; **92**.14   ⲃⲁⲣⲱϩⲉ **71**.15,[[16]]
   pl. ⲃⲁⲣⲁϩⲉ **90**.12   ⲃⲁⲣⲁϩⲓ **122**.25

ⲉ- circumstantial converter
   with nominal sentence: **127**.19
   with adjective verbs: **58**.1,15; **71**.6; **75**.15; **95**.7; **103**.9,14; **107**.31; **124**.30   ⲁ- **122**.26
   with existential expressions: **79**.20; **81**.37; **84**.15,22; **106**.30; **123**.18; **128**.13
   see also conjugations (ⲁ- see Circumst. Present, Affirm. Perfect, Neg. Perfect)
   converter as focus marker, outside conjugation: ⲉ- **84**.18   ⲉⲣⲉ- **81**.45; **115**.28 (negated by ⲙⲛ-)   ⲁ- **103**.35   ⲁⲣⲉ- **102**.13

ⲉⲃⲁⲧ *month* **72**.33; **82**.14; **86**.13

ⲉⲓⲉ see ⲉⲓⲉ

(ⲉⲗⲁⲗⲉ) *grape* : ⲁⲗⲁⲗⲁ **125**.19

ⲉⲛ negative particle **58**.29; **64**.6; **71**.20; **72**.10,18; **78**.31; **79**.14,28,34; **80**.22; **81**.16,33; **82**.36,41; **90**.27; **92**.14,25,32; **94**.54; **103**.14,46,47; **105**.60; **107**.11; **111**.9; **116**.3,15,16; **119**.46 **131**.13
   ⲛ-... ⲉⲛ **79**.33

(ⲉⲛⲉ-) interrogative : ⲛⲛⲉ- **93**.18; **110**.6   ⲛⲉ- **105**.38   ⲛ- **58**.15,17; **70**.44; **78**.50; **84**.32; **94**.15,46   ⲛⲛ- **78**.33

ⲉⲛⲉ- remote condition **128**.15

ⲉⲛⲉ⸗ *(be) pleasant to* :
   ⲡ-ⲉⲛⲉ⸗ : ⲡ-ⲉⲛⲉ **77**.24 (2nd fem.)   ⲡ-ⲉⲛⲉϥ **79**.39
   ⲡ-ⲁⲛⲉ⸗ : ⲡ-ⲁⲛⲏⲓ **107**.7   ⲡ-ⲁⲛⲁϥ **128**.49

ⲉⲣⲏⲩ *fellows* (reciprocity) **62**.13,17, frg; **64**.4; **69**.6; **80**.21; **84**.26,26; **90**.27,34; **103**.33,37; **109**.9; **110**.12,17; **128**.29,31   ⲉⲣⲏⲟⲩ **77**.26   ⲁⲣⲏⲩ **128**.23,27

(ⲉⲥⲁⲩ) *sheep* :
   (Sah.:) ⲉⲥⲟⲟⲩ **124**.31

ⲉⲧⲉ- relative converter (see also conjugations)
   with nominal sentence: **64**.9; **79**.39; **80**.26
   with existentials: **72**.5; **90**.14   ⲁⲧⲁ- **122**.6
   ⲉⲧ- **91**.5 (-ϣⲉ)   with adjective verbs: **115**.10; **122**.6

ⲉⲧⲃⲉ-, ⲉⲧⲃⲏⲧ⸗ prep. *about, because of* etc.
   ⲉⲧⲃⲉ- **58**.13; **64**.15; **65**.25,31,32; **68**.36; **70**.20; **73**.22; **75**.43; **76**.40; **77**.13,17,20; **78**.17,32,47; **79**.13; **80**.8,31; **83**.2,10; **84**.8; **86**.7; **89**.43; **90**.15; **94**.13; **95**.8,9; **98**.1; **105**.18,41; **108**.22,24; **109**.19,30; **110**.30; **111**.20; **112**.9; **115**.44; **116**.6; **120**.29; **124**.10; **127**.31   ⲉⲓⲉⲧⲃⲉ- (in ⲉⲓⲉⲧⲃⲉ-ⲉⲩ) **77**.12,16   ⲉⲧⲃⲁ- **80**.27   ⲁⲧⲃⲁ- **122**.21
   ⲉⲧⲃⲏⲧ⸗ : ⲉⲧⲃⲏⲧ **75**.28   ⲉⲧⲃⲏⲧⲕ **106**.8,9   ⲉⲧⲃⲏⲧϥ **64**.2; **71**.10; **72**.21; **81**.15; **83**.13; **107**.19; **111**.13,29   ⲉⲧⲃⲏⲧⲥ **63**.25; **80**.16   ⲉⲧⲃⲏⲧⲛ **116**.6   ⲉⲧⲃⲏⲧⲟⲩ **69**.11

ⲉⲩ *what?* **65**.31; **71**.24; **77**.12,16; **80**.7; **89**.43; **94**.13; **109**.19; **114**.2; **115**.28   ⲟ **72**.22; **83**.6; **92**.16; **94**.15   ⲟⲩ **78**.47
   ϫⲉ-ⲟ *what for? why?* **77**.19,20

ⲉⲁⲩ m. *glory* :
   ϯ-ⲉⲁⲩ *glorify* **58**.33
   (Sah.:) ⲉⲟⲟⲩ **127**.14

(ⲉⲟⲩⲉⲛ) m. *colour* ⲁⲟⲩⲉⲛ **58**.17

ⲉϣ *what (kind of ...)?* **60**.7; **73**.7; **79**.44; **81**.12,14,36; **84**.9; **106**.24

ⲉϣⲱⲡⲉ *if (it happens that)* **58**.11; **64**.31; **65**.51; **70**.21,31; **72**.18,19,28; **75**.28,31,42,42; **76**.21,27,28; **77**.15,24; **78**.37,48; **79**.42; **81**.46,48; **83**.8; **84**.15,22,29; **90**.33; **94**.48,52,55,58; **95**.13; **101**.2; **102**.17,24; **103**.21; **106**.30; **107**.26; **115**.35; **116**.8,14; **120**.13; **127**.19   ⲉⲥϣⲱⲡⲉ **86**.19; **95**.11   ⲁϣⲱⲡⲉ **58**.2,28; **72**.26

ⲉϣϫⲉ see ⲉⲓϣϫⲉ

ⲉϩⲉ *yes, indeed* **64**.5; **71**.12; **76**.36; **92**.15   ⲁϩⲉ **83**.11; **105**.46; **108**.26

ⲏⲓ̈ m. *house* **60**.4; **66**.33; **67**.42; **77**.11; **83**.3; **92**.38; **105**.75; **120**.15   ⲏⲉⲓ **127**.30

ⲏⲓ̈ m. *pair, couple* **106**.42   ⲉⲓ **76**.31 (read <ⲏ>ⲉⲓ)

ⲉⲓ *come* **59**.8; **65**.34; **71**.14; **72**.19; **77**.15; **80**.13,19,20,21; **81**.9,15,16,17,19,26, 26,28,35,49,54; **82**.17,37; **83**.6,15; **84**.19,28; **90**.5,7,37,39; **92**.27; **94**.37,49,57,58,59,60; **95**.9,14,16; **99**.19,22; **102**.4,7; **103**.4; **105**.29,44,64; **108**.26,30; **111**.7; **115**.15,19,26; **116**.9,10,17,19; **119**.52; **120**.27; **124**.22; **126**.33; **130**.3   ⲓ̈ **58**.21,22; **71**.13; **72**.21; **99**.42; **106**.32

   ⲉⲓ ⲛⲉ⸗ refl. **82**.38

   ⲉⲓ ⲁϩⲣⲏⲓ̈ *come up* **84**.32; **94**.55

   ⲉⲓ ⲁⲃⲁⲗ *come forth, come out* **64**.30; **71**.22; **72**.28; **80**.14; **111**.27; **116**.5

   ⲉⲓ ⲁϩⲟⲩⲛ *come in, enter* **61**.15; **69**.3; **94**.38,39

   as compounds : ⲉⲓⲃⲁⲗ *come forth, depart* **67**.19; **75**.27; **81**.7

      ⲉⲓϩⲟⲩⲛ *enter, come here* **69**.11; **94**.57

ⲉⲓⲉ, ⲛⲓ̈ⲉ, ϩⲓⲉ etc. (various particles)

   apodotic: ⲉⲓⲉ **71**.13; **75**.31; **77**.16,24; **79**.43; **84**.30   ⲉⲓ̈ⲉ **72**.21,27   ϩⲓⲉ **64**.8   ⲛⲓ̈ⲉ **70**.32; **73**.18; **75**.32; **76**.28; **84**.21; **94**.52,56,59; **95**.13; **102**.23,24; **116**.14   ⲛⲓ̈ⲁ **78**.39

   interrogative: ⲉⲓⲉ **72**.13; **79**.33

(ⲉⲓⲃⲉ) *be thirsty*

   stat. ⲁ{ⲓ}ⲃⲉ **124**.24

(ⲓ̈ⲁⲁⲃⲉ *pus, decay*)

   ⲣ-ⲓ̈ⲁⲃⲉ *develop pus* **115**.18

(ⲉⲓⲛⲉ) *bring, lead* :

   ⲛ- **73**.18; **76**.30; **84**.38; **90**.40; **94**.51; **103**.7; **116**.5; **122**.22

   ⲛⲧ⸗ : ⲛⲧⲉ **71**.15   ⲛⲧϥ **58**.7; **76**.15; **91**.4; **95**.12; **102**.23; **103**.48; **109**.12; **111**.23; **116**.14; **120**.5; **122**.26   ⲛⲧⲥ **64**.28; **73**.19; **76**.38; **81**.8; **94**.38,53; **103**.17; **120**.10   ⲛⲧⲟⲩ **90**.42; **92**.11,17; **108**.27; **111**.31; **120**.33

   imp.: ⲁⲛⲓ- **67**.58; **71**.22; **80**.23,25; **111**.5; **122**.18   ⲁⲛⲉ- **77**.36

      ⲁⲛⲓ⸗ : ⲁⲛⲓϥ **67**.31

ⲉⲓⲣⲉ *do* [**61**.7]; **66**.16; **76**.62; **78**.42; **82**.35; **94**.19; **105**.81; **122**.22; **128**.49   ⲓ̈ⲣⲉ **58**.32   ⲓⲣⲉ **82**.33; **114**.5

   ⲣ- **57**.17; **58**.28; **73**.16; **76**.25; **78**.47; **81**.46; **82**.23,34; **83**.6; **84**.19,24; **99**.22; **102**.6; **103**.37; **111**.44   ⲉⲣ- **127**.37

ⲣ-ⲛⲥⲱ⸗ *be after, take care of* (?) **77**.19
for compounds and phraseologies see ⲁⲛⲁϣ, ⲉⲛⲉ⸗, ⲓⲁⲁⲃⲉ, ⲙⲁⲓ̈ϩⲉ, ⲙⲛⲧⲣⲉ, ⲙⲉⲩⲉ, ⲱⲃϣ, ϣⲡⲏⲣⲉ, ϣⲉⲩ, ϩⲱⲃ, ϩⲁⲡ, ϩⲁⲧⲉ

ⲣ- with Greek verbs: **57**.18; **58**.14,30; **67**.7,58; **68**.36; **70**.34; **75**.19; **76**.52; **78**.18; **79**.14,39; **81**.6,10,14,20,38; **83**.4; **86**.5; **90**.27; **92**.25; **99**.19; **103**.36; **107**.13; **108**.36; **110**.24; **111**.14,36,41,43; **113**.2,9; **122**.20,30; **124**.10; **130**.1

ⲉ(ⲉ)⸗: ⲉϥ **76**.46   ⲉⲥ **73**.16; **106**.25   ⲉⲩ **71**.25   ⲉⲟⲩ **58**.10; **76**.17
(Sah.:) ⲁⲁϥ **128**.47   ⲁϥ **124**.38

imp. ⲁⲣⲓ- **67**.8; **103**.38; **105**.76; **111**.29; **112**.7,14; **120**.27; **127**.20   ⲉⲣⲓ- **98**.24

stat. ⲟ **69**.8; **81**.12; **84**.9; **90**.33,43; **116**.18; **128**.14   ⲟⲉⲓ **122**.23

(ⲓ̈ⲱⲣⲙ) *gaze* :
stat. ⲉⲓⲁⲣⲙ **122**.23

(ⲓ̈ⲱⲣϩ) *see, perceive* :
ⲓⲁⲣϩ⸗ : ⲓⲁⲣϩϥ **102**.10

ⲉⲓⲥ- deictic existential **58**.16; **64**.26; **72**.33; **80**.19; **81**.24; **82**.14; **86**.13; **90**.37; **91**.3; **95**.3   ⲓⲥ- **67**.46; **109**.34

ⲉⲓⲥϩⲏⲡⲉ *behold!* **72**.27

ⲉⲓⲥϩⲏⲧⲉ *behold!* **64**.11   ⲉⲓⲥⲏⲧⲉ **77**.25

ⲉⲓⲥⲧⲉ *behold!* **82**.16; **92**.17; **94**.25; **105**.46

see also ϩⲏⲧⲉ

ⲓⲱⲧ m. *father* **57**.1; **60**.4; **64**.2,7,27,32; **65**.8,28,45; **66**.17,32,35,42,43; **69**.6; **70**.14,33; **71**.5,17,31,37; **72**.4,23; **73**.14,24,26; **75**.2,41; **76**.44; **77**.22,28; **78**.35; **79**.1,3,21,45; **80**.17; **82**.21; **83**.10; **87**.5; **90**.1,2,13; **93**.5; **94**.6,8,19; **95**.3; **99**.1,4; **105**.32,79; **112**.21; **114**.2,7; **116**.7,13; **118**.3,6; **120**.6,15,25,28; **122**.1,2; **124**.33; **128**.34   ⲉⲓⲱⲧ **123**.16; **124**.3

ⲙⲛⲧⲓⲱⲧ f. *fatherhood* **122**.5/6

ϣⲏⲣⲓⲱⲧ m. *half-brother* **70**.12

ⲓⲱⲧ m. *barley* **78**.47

(ⲉⲓⲧⲛ) m. *ground, bottom* : ⲓⲧⲛ (in uncertain phraseology) **122**.29
adv. ⲁⲡⲓⲧⲛ *down* **120**.20

(ⲉⲓϣⲉ) *hang, suspend* :
ⲉϣⲧ⸗ : ⲉϣⲧϥ **76**.41

ⲉⲓϣⲡⲉ see ⲉⲓϣϫⲉ

ⲉⲓϣϫⲉ *if (it is true that)* **83**.11; **90**.23,29; **102**.23   ⲓ̈ϣϫⲉ **73**.14,18   ⲉϣϫⲉ **80**.18

ⲉⲓϣⲡⲉ **76**.36   ϣⲡⲉ **64**.6,13; **65**.26

(ⲕⲉ) *other* : ⲕⲉ- **58**.12,15; **64**.9; **65**.4; **70**.7; **76**.30; **77**.15; **79**.17,25,32,44; **86**.12,13; **91**.3; **94**.21,28,32; **99**.27; **103**.8,34; **105**.32,38,77; **107**.26; **108**.25; **110**.30; **113**.8; **115**.29; **118**.4; **119**.25   ϭⲉ- **78**.24; **81**.45; **94**.40

pl. ⲕⲁⲩⲉ **80**.16   ⲕⲉⲕⲁⲩⲉ **80**.26; **111**.21   ⲕⲁⲕⲉⲩⲉ **61**.4,28; **120**.10

(ⲕⲱ) *put, let, leave* ⲕⲁ- **71**.21; **73**.8; **78**.24; **80**.23; **90**.40; **92**.22; **94**.40; **103**.22

ⲕⲁ(ⲁ)⸗ : ⲕⲁⲧ **115**.23   ⲕⲁⲉ **71**.13   ⲕⲁⲥ **58**.3; **73**.10   ⲕⲁⲩ **71**.20; **104**.3; **120**.20   ⲕⲁⲟⲩ **81**.53

    stat. ⲕⲏ **116**.9

    + 2nd vb *let, permit* ⲕⲁⲉ **71**.29   ⲕⲁϥ **79**.39   ⲕⲁⲥ **72**.21; **103**.11

    ⲕⲱ ⲁⲃⲁⲗ *remove, release* ⲕⲁⲩ **71**.19

ⲕⲃⲟ *be cool, recover* **84**.36

    ⲕⲃⲁⲃ (unclear) **105**.42

(ⲕⲱⲃⲉ) *compel, force*

    stat. (?) ⲕⲁϥ *be due* (?) **94**.32

ⲕⲟⲩⲓ̈ *small, little* **64**.31; **65**.52; **70**.7; **71**.18; **73**.7,22; **77**.15; **78**.14; **81**.51,52; **83**.3; **84**.5; **86**.12; **102**.2; **105**.77; **115**.26; **116**.5,6; **118**.4; **119**.66; **120**.35; **122**.16,22,28; **125**.6,42   ⲕⲟⲩⲓ̈ ⲛⲁϭ *young and old* **122**.14   ⲕⲟⲩⲉⲓ **127**.22   ϭⲟⲩⲓ̈ **89**.31

    adv. ⲕⲟⲩⲓ̈ ⲕⲟⲩⲓ̈ *little by little* **94**.26

ⲕⲗⲉϥⲧ f. *hood, cowl* **58**.1,21

ⲕⲁⲙⲉ *black* **125**.21

ⲕⲓⲙ *move* : (neg. + Circ. Pres. *not cease to*) **78**.22; **122**.28

(ⲕⲙⲏⲙⲉ) *(very) dark* ⲕⲙⲉⲓⲙ **72**.11

ⲕⲛ-, ⲕⲛⲧ⸗ ⲁⲃⲁⲗ (vb of uncertain meaning:) *leave* (?) : ⲕⲛⲧϥ **116**.3   ⲕⲛⲧⲛ **122**.21   ⲕⲛ-ⲑⲏⲛⲉ **77**.11

ⲕⲛⲧⲉ *fig* **120**.8; **125**.24

ⲕⲣⲁϥ *guile* **72**.5

(ϫⲟⲩⲣ) *(finger-)ring* : ϫⲟⲣ (pl.?) **125**.43

ⲕⲁⲧ m. *motion, direction, course* **115**.44

ⲕⲱⲧⲉ *turn, return* **105**.25

    ⲕⲁⲧ⸗ : ⲕⲁⲧϥ **126**.10

    ⲕⲱⲧⲉ ⲛⲥⲁ- *go after, seek* **58**.19; **102**.12

    ⲕⲱⲧⲉ nn. m. *surroundings, region* **66**.16; **99**.50

ⲕⲁϩ m. *land, earth* **124**.24; **126**.12

ⲗⲟ *cease, be healed* etc. **72**.34

    imp. ⲁⲗⲁⲕ **120**.11

ⲗⲁⲕ *bowl, cup* **90**.26

ⲗⲉⲕⲙⲉ f. *piece, fragment* **64**.9

ⲗⲓⲗⲟⲩ *youth, child* **110**.25

    pl. ⲗⲓⲗⲁⲩⲉ **80**.30; **92**.19,33   ⲗⲁⲩⲉ **84**.3   ⲛⲗⲁⲩⲉ **94**.4; **102**.19; **108**.30

ⲗⲉⲯⲉ *small portion* **66**.14; **70**.31(m.),38(m.); **78**.41(f.); **108**.37   ⲗⲉⲡⲥⲉ **71**.34(f.); **77**.27; **79**.43(f.),44(f.)

ⲗⲁⲩⲉ *little bit* **71**.39; **76**.50; **90**.11; **105**.48; **122**.25   ⲗⲁⲟⲩⲉ **105**.16

ⲗⲁⲩⲉ indef. pronoun **58**.29,33; **63**.23; **64**.8; **72**.6,15; **77**.21; **81**.19,33; **83**.14; **102**.6; **105**.24 **106**.21; **107**.20; **116**.15; **122**.34; **123**.18   ⲗⲁⲁⲩ **128**.36   ⲗⲁⲩ **127**.37

(ⲗⲁϭⲉ) *cease* :

    ⲁⲧ-ⲗⲁⲕⲉ *unceasing, endless* (?) **71**.26

ⲙⲁ m. *place* **71.**30; **72.**26,29; **83.**7,7; **94.**41; **95.**10,14; **103.**18; **105.**17,20,21,61; **109.**15 **110.**21,26; **116.**7; **122.**11
    ⲙⲁⲛ- **71.**9   see also ⲣⲏⲥ
    ⲙⲁ ⲙⲁ *every place* **72.**16
    demonstr. adverbials *here* : ⲁⲡⲓⲙⲁ **71.**14   ⲙⲡⲓⲙⲁ **58.**20,26; **70.**6; **79.**28,34,38; **93.**21; **109.**29   ⲛⲛⲓⲙⲁ **64.**11; **70.**18; **71.**11; **75.**35; **84.**20; **89.**37; **94.**54; **95.**5; **102.**22; **103.**11; **115.**22; **122.**24   ⲛⲓⲙⲁ **72.**31
ⲙⲏⲉ f. *truth* **62.**8; **65.**8; **71.**5; **72.**4; **78.**33; **107.**29
    ⲣⲙⲙⲙ[ⲓ]ⲉ *truthful, honest* **58.**30
    adv. ⲛⲁⲙⲏⲉ *truly* **64.**13; **71.**12; **72.**19; **76.**35; **78.**32; **84.**15,29; **93.**16
(ⲙⲟ) *take!* ⲙⲙⲟ **90.**41,42
ⲙⲟⲩ *die* **73.**8; **115.**18,30
    ⲙⲟⲩ nn. m. *death* **115.**27
(ⲙⲁⲁⲃⲉ) *thirty* ⲙⲁⲃ **78.**41; **79.**38; **96.**33
    ⲙⲁⲃ- **95.**4
    ⲗ (in ⲗⲉ *35* for money) **130.**4
ⲙⲉⲓⲉ *love* **80.**2; **90.**24
    ⲙⲉⲓⲉ nn. m. *love* **72.**8
    ϣⲟⲩ-ⲙⲉⲓⲉ *lovable, endearing* **80.**1/2; [**88.**2]; **90.**1/[2],33/[34]   ϣⲟⲩⲙⲉⲓ **89.**4
    p.c. ⲙⲁⲓ- : ⲙⲁⲓⲥⲟⲛ **128.**40; see also ⲣⲱⲙⲉ
ⲙⲁⲓⲧ m. *road, way* **84.**27,35
ⲙⲁⲓϩⲉ *wonder* :
    ⲣ-ⲙⲁⲓϩⲉ *be astonished* **67.**18,26; **68.**9; <**73.**15>; **81.**23
(ⲙⲁⲕⲙⲉⲕ) *consider, intend* : ⲁⲙⲕⲉⲙⲉⲕ **77.**31 (here?)
ⲙⲕⲁϩ *be in pain, grieved* **80.**15
    stat. ⲙⲁⲭ **80.**23   ⲙⲁⲭϩ **110.**26
    ⲙⲕⲁϩ nn. m. *pain* **128.**19
(ⲙⲟⲩⲕϩ) *cause pain* : ⲙⲁϩⲕ- **72.**14
ⲙⲁⲗⲓⲙⲙⲉ m. (meaning unknown) **78.**45
ⲙⲙⲉ *know, understand* **72.**18; **77.**9; **78.**31; **103.**7,31,37; **111.**39; **116.**2
    (Sah.:) ⲉⲓⲙⲉ [**128.**39]
ⲙⲙⲁⲛ *no, otherwise* **58.**28; **75.**32,32; **78.**18,35; **81.**48; **84.**27; **86.**19; **90.**33; **95.**13; **99.**25; **102.**24; **111.**9; **118.**6
ⲙⲙⲁⲛ various particles :
    ⲙⲙⲁⲛ *indeed; for* **64.**4,6,29; **80.**12; **81.**54
    in ⲏ ⲙⲙⲁⲛ *or else* **58.**3
    in ⲁϩⲉ/ⲉϩⲉ ϭⲉ ⲙⲙⲁⲛ *well then* (?) **64.**6; **92.**16; **105.**46; **108.**26
    (unclear) **105.**38
ⲙⲙⲏⲛⲉ adv. *daily* **82.**32; **94.**20
ⲙⲙⲉⲧⲉ adv. *only* **64.**9; **105.**28; **107.**23   ⲛⲙⲉⲧⲉ **122.**13
ⲙⲛ- neg. existential **58.**8,10,31; **72.**5,5; **75.**43; **84.**12,16,22; **90.**25,25; **102.**13,13; **107.**19; **122.**6
    preceding ⲉⲡⲉ- + Nominal Sentence **115.**28

Indices: Native words

ⲙⲛ-, ⲛⲉⲙⲉ⸗ prep. *with, and*
    ⲙⲛ- **58.**21,24,25,27,32,36; **60.**4; **61.**1,4,4,8,28; **63.**6,30; **64.**4,19,21,21,21,22,22, 23,23,23,24,26,32; **65.**2,2,4,13,28,38,38,40,42,43,44,45,46,48; **66.**12,14,18,23, 32,35,37,42,42,43,44; **67.**7,17,18,28,35,38,39,41,47; **68.**21,22,28,30; **69.**6; **70.**5,6,7,10,11,14,15,34; **71.**2,6,9,27; **72.**24,25,30,35; **75.**3,5,10,41,41; **76.**3,27,31,34; **77.**3,4,5,5,6,7,10,26,35,35,35; **78.**9,13,14,14,15,42,43,43; **79.**4, 5,5,11,22,24,24,28,29,40,41,45; **80.**3,9,25,28,29,30,34,34,34,35,35,35; **81.**6,20; **82.**11,19,27,28,28,29,29,31; **83.**3; **84.**3,5,25; **85.**7; **86.**7,22; **88.**16,17,18, 19,26,27,28,29; **89.**12,13,14,14,15,16,19,20,20,28; **90.**2,3,10,27,34; **91.**1; **92.**2,3,4,5,5,21,28; **93.**11,19,20,20; **94.**4,7,7,9,10,29; **95.**2,18; **96.**26,28; **102.**21; **103.**2,5,25; **105.**2,4,5,10,23,25,75,75,75,75,77,77,79,81; **108.**20,34, 36,36; **109.**3; **110.**2,3,12,13; **111.**25,41; **112.**18,21,21,22,22,22; **114.**5,7; **115.**11,12,26,38,38,39,40,44; **116.**12,12,13,18; **117.**1,2,2; **118.**3,3,5,5,5; **119.**59,59,60,60,61; **122.**3,9,13,15,17,27,33,34; **124.**address,2; **127.**30; **128.**23,29; **129.**2,4,5,7
    ⲛⲉⲙⲉ⸗: ⲛⲉⲙⲉϥ **80.**19,21   ⲛⲉⲙⲉⲥ **90.**35
    ⲛⲙⲙⲉ⸗: ⲛⲙⲙⲏⲓ̈ **61.**1; **105.**23; **122.**22   ⲛⲉⲙⲙⲏⲓ̈ **114.**5   ⲛⲙⲙⲉⲕ **73.**22; **94.**57; **121.**1   ⲛⲙⲙⲉ **71.**22   ⲛⲙⲙⲉϥ **86.**15; **116.**2   ⲛⲙⲙⲉⲥ **94.**44 ⲛⲙⲙⲉⲩ **116.**17
    (Sah.:) as predicate in Bipartite Pattern:
        ⲛⲛⲙⲙⲁ⸗: ⲛⲛⲙⲙⲁⲕ **124.**6   ⲛⲛⲙⲙⲟⲛ **124.**8
        ⲙⲛⲙⲁⲕ **128.**42

ⲙⲟⲩⲛ ⲁⲃⲁⲗ *remain, last* **66.**40
ⲙⲛⲛⲥⲁ-, ⲙⲛⲛⲥⲱ⸗ prep. *after*
    ⲙⲛⲛⲥⲁ- **79.**12; **86.**11,17
    ⲙⲛⲛⲥⲱⲥ *thereafter, next* **60.**5; **76.**34; **86.**5; **92.**8; **111.**20; **131.**4
ⲙⲛⲧ- nominal abstract **124.**13; and see ⲓ̈ⲱⲧ, (ⲙⲁⲓ̈)ⲣⲱⲙⲉ, ⲥⲁⲛ, ϣⲃⲏⲣ, ϣⲏⲣⲉ, ϩⲁϭⲏⲧ; εἰρήνη, εὐεργέτης
ⲙⲛⲧⲉ-, ⲙⲛⲧⲉ⸗ *not have* : ⲙⲛⲧⲉ- **80.**10
    ⲙⲛⲧⲉ⸗: (only construct forms:) ⲙⲛ†- **81.**45; **105.**20,47   ⲙⲛⲧⲉⲧⲛ- **58.**5 ⲙⲛⲧⲁⲧⲛ- (sic) **122.**24   ⲙⲛⲧⲟⲩ- **76.**42; **123.**18
    ⲙⲛⲧⲉ⸗ + vb *cannot* : ⲙⲛⲧⲉ- (2nd fem.) **94.**53   ⲙⲛⲧⲁⲧⲛ- **122.**19
ⲙⲛⲧⲣⲉ *witness* :
    ⲣ-ⲙⲛⲧⲣⲉ *bear witness* **82.**13; **83.**5; [**98.**10]; **105.**22,79; **115.**44
ⲙⲡⲉ *no, not* **77.**18,22; **78.**50; **83.**12; **84.**11; **93.**18; **94.**52
ⲙⲡⲱⲣ *no, don't* **71.**20
ⲙⲡϣⲁ *be worthy* **121.**6
    ⲙⲡϣⲁ nn. m. **123.**10
ⲙⲉⲣⲓⲧ *beloved* **57.**1; **60.**1; **63.**1,4,[50]; **64.**20; **65.**1; **66.**1,19,22; **70.**[1],43; **71.**1; **73.**1,6; **76.**2; **79.**4; **80.**1; **82.**1; **86.**15; **88.**[1],8; **89.**3; **90.**3; **92.**1; **93.**2; **94.**4; **99.**1,16,41; **108.**1; **111.**1,16; **112.**1; **115.**1; **122.**1,15,17,20; **128.**48
    pl. ⲙⲉⲣⲉⲧⲉ **61.**3; **85.**6; **91.**1; **92.**8; **110.**1
ⲙⲣⲱϣⲉ *clay pot* (?) **81.**52
ⲙⲏⲥⲉ *offspring, generation* **117.**1 (? - unclear)

ⲘⲎⲤⲈ *usury, interest* **108.**25
ⲘⲎⲦ *ten* **99.**27; **65.**26; **75.**10; **78.**26,44; **79.**38; **81.**47; **95.**8; **102.**11; **103.**22; **109.**35; **120.**35
    f. ⲘⲎⲦⲈ **68.**46; **111.**6
    ⲘⲚⲦ- **58.**3,7,25; **76.**27; **78.**21,26,28; **94.**32; **95.**7; **110.**10
ⲘⲎⲦⲈ f. *middle* **90.**25; **107.**15
ⲘⲞⲨⲦⲈ *call* **94.**30; **126.**34; **128.**32
ⲘⲦⲀⲚ *rest* **79.**18; **93.**18
    ⲘⲦⲀⲚ nn. m. *rest* **61.**27
    ⲘⲦⲀⲚ ⲚϨⲎⲦ nn. m. *satisfaction* **80.**26
    †-ⲘⲦⲀⲚ *set at ease* **115.**40
ⲘⲞⲨⲦⲚⲈ *set at rest* :
    stat. ⲘⲀⲦⲚ **72.**26   ⲘⲀⲦⲚⲈ **77.**36
(ⲘⲀⲨ) m. *water* :
    ⲘⲞⲨⲚϨⲰⲞⲨ *rain water* **124.**26
ⲘⲈⲨ f. *mother* **65.**39; **71.**27; **122.**9   ⲘⲞ **60.**1; **64.**20,23,26,29; **65.**48; **68.**19, 23,23,29,[30]; **76.**47; **77.**35; **78.**15; **82.**27; **83.**2; **88.**9,13,15,19,22,26; **89.**11,12,13,20,33; **92.**5; **93.**19; **94.**10,24,37; **95.**10; **102.**20; **111.**24; **112.**21; [**116.**12]; **117.**2; **122.**26,32   ⲘⲀ (sic) **70.**14
ⲘⲈⲨ *that place* :
    adv. ⲀⲘⲈⲨ **58.**22
    adv. ⲘⲘⲈⲨ **71.**23; **102.**7,17   ⲘⲘⲞ **58.**5; **100.**3; **110.**34; **126.**13
ⲘⲈⲨⲈ *think* **92.**9
    ⲘⲈⲨⲈ nn. m. *thought* **105.**62; **126.**14
    ⲢⲠⲘⲈⲨⲈ *remember* **70.**23
    imp. ⲀⲢⲒⲠⲘⲈⲨⲈ **86.**10; **111.**22 (ⲠⲀ-); **112.**14
    ⲢⲠⲘⲈⲨⲈ nn. m. *remembrance, memory* **61.**7; **83.**5; **85.**2; **105.**81
ⲘⲀϢⲈ *go!* **61.**14
ⲘⲒϢⲈ *fight* **71.**23; **77.**25; **90.**25,27
    ⲘⲒϢⲈ nn. m. *fight, quarrel* **90.**13
ⲘⲞⲨϨ *fill, pay* :
    ⲘⲀϨ≠ : ⲘⲀϨϤ **75.**17; **79.**38; **96.**34; **103.**41; **109.**14   ⲘⲀϨⲤ **64.**27   ⲘⲀϨ≠? **68.**33
    stat. ⲘⲎϨ **76.**12; **77.**18; **88.**21; **122.**32
    p.c. ⲘⲀϨ- **77.**7
ⲘⲀϪⲈ (measure of capacity) **95.**7; **112.**9; **113.**6; **120.**8
ⲘⲞⲨϪⲦ *mix* **95.**11; **110.**18,29

Ⲛ- negation: see ⲈⲚ
    as sole negator (?) **79.**33
Ⲛ- attributive **57.**15; **58.**4,4,8,25,25,25,33; **64.**10,10; **65.**9,26; **66.**14,24,44,44,45; **67.**6; **68.**46; **69.**2,7; **70.**8,17,31; **71.**6,24,34,35; **72.**11,34; **73.**8,23; **75.**8,9, 11,41; **76.**22,31,31,31,63; **77.**36; **78.**21,21,26,27,28,28,40,41,42,43,44,48; **79.**10,24,29,32,37,38,38,41,41,43,44; **80.**1,24,24,24,25,37; **81.**12,14,18,18,21, 21,24,29,30,31,36,37,39,40,42,42,44,45,47,47,51,51,51,51,52; **82.**9,14,18,20,25;

Indices: Native words

83.14; 84.10,13,28; 85.4,6; 86.8,12; 89.31; 90.26,28,30,32,37,39,40,41; 94.22,32,45,47; 95.4,4,6,8,8; 96.30,33,33,35,36; 99.27; 102.6,11; 103.8,8; 105.33,33,34,34,35,35,67; 106.21,34; 107.25; 108.28,37; 109.33; 110.10,10,21,28,49,49; 111.6,12; 112.9; 115.42,44; 116.5; 119.50; 120.8,32; 122.2,8,10,15,16,18,20,28; 123.13,14,19,24; 124.23,33 125.6,32,39,42; 128.34,48   ⲚⲚ- 72.33; 109.35   Ⲙ- 57.1; 63.1,4,50; 64.20; 65.1,24; 66.1,19,22; 70.1,43; 71.1; 73.1,6; 76.2; 79.4; 80.13; 82.1; 85.6; 89.3; 90.3; 91.1; 92.1; 93.2; 99.1; 94.4; 95.7; 105.23; 108.1,25; 110.1; 111.1,16; 112.1; 113.6; 115.1; 120.8; 127.37   ⲚⲘ- 78.41

Ⲛ- with infinitive 64.14; 71.34; 79.35; 82.15; 94.16; 103.49; 115.19; 116.14   Ⲙ- 115.34

Ⲛ- identity 58.23; 66.46; 75.14,41; 78.41; 79.38; 89.40; 90.33,43; 94.27,29; 113.7; 115.31; 120.2; 122.10,19,23,29,32; 126.16; 127.9; 128.14   Ⲙ- 66.45 69.8; 75.13,42; 76.45; 77.12; 91.3; 120.6

Ⲛ-, ⲘⲘⲁ⸗ prep. of object (trans. verbs)   Ⲛ- 57.13; 66.7,44; 73.11; 78.42; 81.16; 82.9; 84.37; 89.44; 90.13; 94.19; 98.22; 99.28; 107.10; 110.20; 111.7; 120.16; 122.24; 123.7,20 128.49   Ⲙ- 62.15; 76.45; 82.33,41; 102.18,22; 105.81; 106.15; 115.22; 116.6; 123.12   ⲘⲚ- 77.19

ⲘⲘⲁ⸗ : ⲘⲘⲁⲕ 73.6; 79.13   ⲘⲘⲁϥ 78.34; 80.2; 81.52; 82.35   ⲘⲘⲁⲥ 71.12; 78.20; 79.17; 107.12; 121.2   Ⲙⲁⲥ 122.30   ⲘⲘⲱⲧⲚ 70.19 ⲘⲘⲁⲩ 64.14; 76.62; 79.18; 94.19; 105.31

Ⲛ-, ⲘⲘⲁ⸗ other kinds of relationship   Ⲛ- 58.1,9,18; 60.3,7; 61.6,7,8,9; 65.7,12,32,33,34; 66.32; 67.4,5; 68.6; 70.14,23,24; 71.4,5,8,9,10,35; 72.3,14; 73.4,12,12,12,17; 75.18,19; 76.6,62; 77.3,17,18,19,20,30; 78.4,8,36,36,41; 79.3,8,10,13,16,19,38,44;   80.6,15,37;   81.5,12,14,18,23,27,29,33,41,43,43; 82.3,6,13,41; 83.6; 84.9,18; 85.2,4; 86.15; 88.3; 89.1,5,23,24; 90.2,26; 91.2; 92.24; 93.4; 94.34,37,49; 95.6; 96.34; 99.3,7; 102.11; 103.9,21,24,30,34,41; 105.26,27,36,42,44,45,82; 106.16; 107.4,15; 108.8; 109.5; 110.5,20,21,44; 111.6,18,22;   112.5;   115.3,9,17,30,32,41,44;   116.15;   118.2;   119.50; 122.2,5,6,8,11,27,32;   123.15,17 124.5,24,27,41;   126.30;   127.31;   128.27   ⲚⲚ- 66.41; 72.34; 79.36   Ⲙ- 58.4,15,17; 61.8; 66.16; 67.46; 70.35,38; 76.36; 77.10,14,17; 78.44; 80.30,38,38,38,39,39; 83.5; 86.8,17; 89.6,7; 91.2; 92.15,38; 94.33,56; 95.6,9,11; 102.7; 103.14,16,47; 109.34; 110.9,25,30,50; 120.15,17; 123.15; 127.14; 128.14,29   ⲘⲚ- 116.4

ⲘⲘⲁ⸗ : ⲘⲘⲁⲓ̈ 72.10; 82.26; 85.3   ⲘⲘⲁⲕ 86.6; 108.37; 111.30   ⲘⲘⲁϥ 58.10,30; 79.39; 81.15; 83.11,13; 84.22; 92.30; 102.5; 105.14; 109.17; 116.3; 126.19,35   ⲘⲘⲁⲥ 84.13,16,23; 115.44   ⲘⲘⲱⲧⲚ 58.14,34; 59.4,6; 67.8; 84.21; 111.42   ⲘⲘⲁⲩ 94.26; 111.21

(Sah.:) ⲘⲞⲔ 124.21   ⲘⲘⲞϥ 127.35

Ⲛ-, Ⲛⲉ⸗ prep. of dative Ⲛ- 58.5,19,19; 64.32; 65.36; 66.46; 75.38; 76.29,32; 77.29; 79.38; 105.31; 111.28; 115.13; 117.1; 122.7; 127.9   Ⲙ- 64.27; 66.15; 69.1,10; 71.21,32,36; 73.13; 76.13; 80.16; 82.16; 83.10; 89.9; 92.11; 94.19; 96.23; 106.43; 110.25; 116.15; 118.6; 120.35

ⲚⲈ⸗ : ⲚⲎⲒ 57.11,15; 58.2,6,11,32; 60.6; 61.11; 64.3,11,12,17,29,31; 65.16,34; 66.11,31,43; 67.20,60; 70.17,19,33,39; 71.5,10,18,29,33,35; 72.22,23,26,27, 32,34; 73.10,19,19; 75.17,22,42,43; 76.14,19,23,40,50,52; 77.4,6,13,14,17, 21,36; 78.12,17,25,27,29,45,46,47; 79.31,32,38; 80.25; 81.9,11,16,19,23, 31,40,47,48,48; 82.19; 84.6,14,31,36; 85.8; 86.11,16,21; 89.26,44; 90.43,43; 92.10,31,31; 93.10,14,19,24; 94.22,49; 95.8,17; 96.27,37; 98.22,26,27; 99.25,33,54; 102.5,8,18,22; 103.9,20,30,40,48; 105.76,76,78,81; 106.15,23,37; 107.19; 108.24,37; 110.30,32,45; 111.32,34,44; 112.9; 114.3; 115.13,23,37; 120.6,10,16,28; 120.34; 122.26; 126.5,6,20; 131.4   ⲚⲈⲔ 58.3,7; 65.31; 66.9,20,44; 67.27; 69.4,9; 71.21; 72.11,23,28; 76.28,30; 78.47; 79.12,15,15,21,36; 81.47; 82.12; 89.38; 94.17; 95.5; 99.6; 103.15,20,29; 105.57; 106.13; 108.5; 110.8; 111.5,13,23,25; 113.4; 114.1; 115.8,41,44; 120.12,32; 122.4   -ⲚⲔ- (in ⲦⲚⲔ-) 76.50   ⲚⲈ 60.2; 66.24; 71.34; 75.41; 90.11; 92.8; 94.22,51,53; 95.15; 109.34; 122.27,28,32   ⲚⲈϤ 64.12; 71.16; 73.9,13; 77.18; 79.39; 81.8,18; 82.18; 90.42; 92.18,27; 94.38,45; 108.21; 110.9; 119.26   ⲚⲈⲤ 76.36; 77.23; 94.17; 95.10; 115.25   ⲚⲈⲚ 58.20; 65.25,33; 68.39; 69.5; 82.38; 108.32; 122.8,10,21,24   ⲚⲎⲦⲚ 58.4,6,13,16,26,28,33; 64.18,28; 70.24,30,32; 75.30; 76.10; 78.35; 80.8; 81.13 (but read ⲚⲎⲒ); 82.20,41; 83.5; 84.38; 91.4; 94.31; 105.6,16,25; 110.11,18,35,44,49; 116.9; 116.19; 122.29,29   ⲚⲎⲦⲚⲈ 73.10; 90.9,10   ⲚⲈⲦⲚ 129.11   ⲚⲈⲨ 64.13; 71.12; 76.49; 83.11; 105.36

(Sah.:) ⲚⲀⲔ 123.12,20   ⲚⲀϤ 127.38   ⲚⲀⲤ 128.35   ⲚⲀⲚ 127.21; 128.26

(ⲚⲀ) *be going* : ⲚⲀⲈ 111.33

ⲚⲀ- instans, after nominal subject : **86.**20; **110.**48; **115.**44; **116.**3,10; **122.**16   ⲚⲈ- **71.**20; **78.**44

for pronominal subjects, see conjugations

(ⲚⲀⲈ) *have mercy* : ⲚⲀⲀ **126.**4,5,6

ⲚⲈ- preterite converter **71.**17 (possibly Imperfect); **90.**6,6

for Imperfect forms, see conjugations

ⲚⲞⲨⲈ *be about to* **91.**5; **93.**8

ⲚⲞⲨⲂ m. *gold* **70.**29; **75.**43; **78.**32

ⲚⲞⲨⲂⲤ *jujube* **77.**36   ⲚⲞⲂⲤ **125.**18

ⲚⲒⲈ see ⲈⲒⲈ

(ⲚⲈⲒⲈⲦ⸗) *be blessed* :

(Sah.:) ⲚⲀⲒⲀⲦϤ **126.**15

ⲚⲔⲈ *thing* **81.**24; **92.**10

ⲚⲒⲘ *each, every* **58.**9,11,35; **60.**3; **61.**9,12; **62.**6,9; **63.**10,27; **64.**17; **67.**4; **68.**6; **69.**5; **71.**4,14,15; **72.**3; **73.**4,21; **76.**6,12; **77.**3,13; **78.**4,8; **79.**3,9; **80.**6,25; **81.**5; **82.**3,6,35; **83.**6; **84.**37; **85.**3; **86.**15; **90.**13; **91.**2; **92.**24; **93.**5; **97.**5; **99.**4; **102.**8; **105.**4,7,9,82; **106.**16; **107.**4; **108.**6,8; **109.**25; **110.**5,31; **111.**13,19; **115.**4,9,40,44; **118.**2; **120.**17; **122.**2,5,11; **124.**5   ⲘⲒⲚ **89.**1,35

(ⲚⲀⲚⲞⲨ-,) ⲚⲀⲚⲞⲨ⸗ *be good* ⲚⲀⲚⲞⲨϤ **75.**15; **95.**7; **103.**9,14,47; **107.**31; **122.**26; **124.**30   ⲚⲀⲚⲞⲨⲤ **115.**10; **122.**6   ⲚⲀⲚⲞⲨⲞⲨ **58.**15   ⲚⲀⲚⲞⲨ **58.**1

ⲛⲥⲁ-, ⲛⲥⲱ⸗ prep. *behind* etc. ⲛⲥⲁ- **64**.4,6,9; **80**.17; **83**.15; **95**.10; **103**.13; **120**.24
ⲛⲥⲉ- **58**.20; **71**.11; **102**.16
ⲛⲥⲱ⸗ : ⲛⲥⲱⲓ̈ **77**.19 (in ⲡ-ⲛⲥⲱ⸗ *be after* ...) ⲛⲥⲱⲕ **115**.23; **119**.51
ⲛⲥⲱϥ **102**.12; **128**.23 ⲛⲥⲱⲥ **120**.15
ⲛⲥⲁ- *except* **77**.12; **102**.6
(ⲛⲥⲁⲃⲗⲗⲉ-,) ⲛⲥⲁⲃⲗⲗⲉ⸗ prep. *except* ⲛⲥⲉⲃⲗⲗⲉⲕ **81**.45
ⲛⲧⲉ-, ⲛⲧⲉ⸗ prep.: ⲛⲧⲉ- **70**.42; **71**.5,9; **72**.4; **111**.26; **127**.10,18
ⲛⲧⲉ⸗ : ⲛⲧⲉⲕ **103**.45 ⲛⲧⲉϥ [**90**.32]; **120**.4 ⲛⲧⲉⲛ **69**.7
(with 2nd suffix:) ⲛⲧⲁⲕⲥⲉ **90**.14
ⲛⲁϩⲧ *merciful* **99**.29
ⲛⲟⲩⲧⲉ m. *god* **62**.8; [**65**.8]; **66**.5; **67**.4; **71**.4,5,36; **72**.4,7,33; **76**.7; **78**.6; **79**.8,9; **80**.10; **81**.48; **82**.7,13,16; **83**.5,5; **91**.1; **94**.18; **97**.8; [**98**.9]; **105**.21,79,[82]; [**108**.8]; [**109**.6]; [**112**.6]; **116**.10,15; **122**.7,16; **124**.28,39; **126**.32; **128**.18
ⲛⲟⲩⲧⲁ **126**.21
ⲛⲧⲛ-, ⲛⲧⲟ(ⲟ)ⲧ⸗ prep.: ⲛⲧⲛ- **61**.12; **70**.26; **78**.29,40; **80**.18; **84**.7,7,37; **85**.7; **96**.34; **106**.28; **113**.8 **128**.17
ⲛⲧⲟ(ⲟ)ⲧ⸗ : ⲛⲧⲟⲧ **57**.1; **63**.2; **66**.2; **71**.1; **76**.3; **79**.1; **81**.1; **82**.2; **85**.1; **88**.1,11; **89**.4; **90**.1; **93**.1; **99**.2; **105**.9,24; **107**.6; **108**.2; **110**.2; **111**.2,17; **112**.1; **115**.2,15,28 ⲛⲧⲟⲟⲧ **65**.1 ⲛⲧⲟⲧⲕ **67**.28; **80**.24; **111**.32; **123**.6 ⲛⲧⲟⲧϥ **58**.8; **66**.25,45,46; **71**.[[16]],32,33; **75**.42; **76**.21,44; **77**.12; **78**.41; **79**.38; **81**.21,24; **83**.1,10; **89**.40; **91**.3; **92**.29; **94**.27,28; **102**.13,14; **115**.31; **120**.2,6; **122**.32; **125**.33 ⲧⲟⲧϥ **75**.12; **122**.29,35 ⲛⲧⲟⲧⲥ **77**.21; **111**.23,31,37; **113**.7 ⲛⲧⲟⲧⲑⲛⲉ **76**.35 ⲛⲧⲟⲧⲟⲩ **75**.22
ⲛⲧⲁϥ (invariable) **58**.17; **64**.7; **90**.31 (see also ⲁⲛⲁⲕ)
(ⲛⲧϩϭ) *herb, weed* ⲛϯϭ **81**.53
ⲛⲉⲩ *see* **66**.38; **71**.23; **72**.9,10; **80**.21; **97**.10; **103**.49 ⲛⲟ **58**.23; **64**.30; **75**.26,33; **78**.10,22; **83**.6; **84**.31; **91**.6; **92**.29; **94**.46; **102**.9,15; **116**.17; **120**.27 ⲛⲟⲩ **120**.23
imp. ⲁⲛⲉⲩ **77**.30 ⲁⲛⲟ **58**.15; **71**.18
ⲛⲉⲩ *hour, time* **63**.10; **85**.2; **91**.2; **99**.4; **105**.4,82; **108**.8 ⲛⲟ **82**.3; **83**.6; **94**.58; **115**.3; **122**.2
relative adverbials *when* ⲡⲛⲉⲩ **71**.33 ⲡⲛⲟ **79**.35 ⲙⲡⲛⲟ **81**.50
ⲛⲏⲩ stat. *be coming* **65**.51; **71**.29; **72**.13; **78**.36; **80**.24; **81**.14; **82**.17,19,36; **86**.18; **94**.50; **102**.23; **111**.34; **122**.24 (after ⲙⲛⲧⲁⲧⲛ-) ⲛⲏⲟⲩ **93**.9 ⲉⲛⲏⲩ **66**.27
(ⲛⲁϣⲉ-), ⲛⲁϣⲱ⸗ *be numerous* : ⲛⲁϣⲱϥ **71**.6
ⲛⲁϣⲧⲉ *protection, defence* **122**.10
ⲛⲟⲩϥⲉ *good* (adjunct) see ⲥⲧⲁⲓ̈
ⲛⲏϩ m. *oil* **70**.17,17,21; **86**.9; **109**.37; **122**.18; **123**.14; **125**.39
(ⲛⲁϩⲣⲛ-, ⲛⲁϩⲣⲉ⸗) prep. *in the face of* : ⲛⲁϩⲣⲁⲕ **105**.21
ⲛⲁϩⲧⲉ *trust, believe* :
ⲛⲁϩⲧⲉ nn. m. *faith* **61**.9; **63**.20,30
(ⲛϫⲓ-) *subject marker* :
(Sah.:) ⲛϭⲓ- **126**.14
(ⲛⲟⲩϫⲉ) *throw* :

ⲛⲁϫ- **81**.36
    stat. ⲛⲏϫ **70**.20
ⲛⲁϭ *great* **57**.14; **58**.25; **63**.34; [**65**.9]; **66**.41; **67**.6; **71**.6,24,35; **72**.34; **79**.10,36; **80**.8,13,37; **81**.43; **82**.18,25; **84**.4,12; **96**.30; **105**.22,23; **107**.25; **115**.42; **118**.4; **119**.50; **122**.8   ⲕⲟⲩⲓ̈ ⲛⲁϭ *young and old* **122**.14
    (Sah.:) ⲛⲟϭ **125**.32

ⲡⲉ *textual marker (background)* **81**.19; **84**.12; **111**.11
    for the subject (copular) pronoun see Triadic pronominals
ⲡⲗϭⲉ *torn cloth, rag* **109**.32
ⲡⲱⲗϭ *settle* **103**.32; **110**.12,16   ⲡⲗϭ- **58**.34; **78**.44; **81**.25
    ⲡⲱⲗϭ ⲁⲃⲁⲗ ⲁ- *inf. decide to (do)* **103**.4
ⲡⲱⲛⲉ *change, displace* :
    ⲁⲧⲡⲱⲛⲉ *unchanging, immutable* **85**.6
ⲡⲁⲁⲡⲉ *(name of 2nd month)* **86**.17
ⲡⲏⲣⲉ f. *quail* **125**.42
(ⲡⲱⲣⲥ) *extend, apply* : ⲡⲣⲥ- **72**.17
ⲡⲣⲏϣ m. *mat, blanket* **76**.52; **79**.28; **105**.39
(ⲡⲱⲣϫ) *separate* :
    stat. ⲡⲁⲣϫ **66**.45
ⲡⲉⲧ- (invariable) **67**.30
    see also *s.v.* ϩⲁⲩ
(ⲡⲱⲧ) *run, flee* :
    stat. ⲡⲏⲧ **105**.46
(ⲡⲱϣⲉ) *divide* : ⲡⲱϣ- **110**.11
    ⲡⲱϣ ⲛϩⲏⲧ *nn. m. heartbreak, distress* [**100**.2]; **105**.23
ⲡⲁϩⲟⲩ *hinder part, back* :
    adv. ⲁⲡⲁϩⲟⲩ **92**.15
ⲡⲱϩ *reach* **105**.45; **115**.34   ⲡϩ- **73**.23
    ⲡⲁϩ⸗ : ⲡⲁϩⲛ **110**.48
ⲡⲁϫⲉ-, ⲡⲁϫⲉ⸗ *said* :
    ⲡⲁϫⲉ- **77**.22; **94**.39; **108**.36
    ⲡⲁϫⲉ⸗ : ⲡⲁϫⲉⲓ̈ **58**.8; **94**.42; **102**.8; **111**.9   ⲡⲁϫⲉϥ **58**.31; **75**.36; **78**.30; **80**.17; **84**.12; **90**.11,43; **94**.49; **95**.8; **108**.23,27; **110**.25; **111**.8   ⲡⲁϫⲉⲥ **90**.41,42; **101**.2,3   ⲡⲁϫⲉⲛ **108**.29   ⲡⲁϫⲉⲧⲏⲛⲉ **77**.23   ⲡⲁϫⲉⲩ **57**.11; **64**.5; **93**.8; **94**.30,36,44; **105**.29,36
    ⲙⲁϫⲉ- **70**.32; **114**.2   ⲙⲁϫⲓ- **77**.14
    ⲙⲁϫⲉ⸗ : ⲙⲁϫⲉϥ **73**.9,11; **81**.9,26,54; **82**.39

ⲣⲁ *state, matter* :
    adv. ϩⲁⲡⲣⲁ (ⲛ-) *on the matter (of), concerning* **71**.10
ⲣⲓ f. *cell, room* **81**.27   ⲣⲓⲉ **110**.21; **120**.21
ⲣⲟ m. *door* **81**.27

Indices: Native words

ⲣⲱ⸗ *mouth*: ⲣⲱⲓ̈ **63.**3; [**70.**2]; **82.**3; **88.**11; [**93.**2]; **99.**3; **112.**3; **122.**2 ⲣⲱϥ **109.**31

ⲣⲱ *particle* **70.**44; **71.**24; **76.**63; **82.**38; **83.**12; **92.**24; **94.**12; **96.**37; **102.**14; **105.**37,43,44; **110.**8; **118.**7

ⲣⲁⲓ̈ⲥ *watch, guard* **62.**10; **67.**5; **76.**8; **78.**7; **79.**10; [**91.**2]; **109.**7; **122.**8,16

ⲣⲓⲙⲉ *weep* **67.**15

ⲣⲱⲙⲉ *man, human* **58.**29; **63.**22; **66.**15; **67.**47; **75.**20,42; **76.**45; **80.**10; **81.**46; **82.**41; **84.**32; **91.**3; **94.**35,60; **95.**11; **96.**23; **102.**16,23; **103.**35; **105.**28,79; **106.**19,28; **110.**7; **110.**13,22; **120.**23; **128.**13

    (with poss.) *relative* **92.**3

  ⲁⲧⲣⲱⲙⲉ *without people* **122.**23/24

  ⲙⲁⲓ̈ⲣⲱⲙⲉ *loving people, benevolent* **57.**13(ⲙⲛⲧ-); **85.**5

  ⲣⲙ(ⲛ)- **128.**5; see also *s.v.* ⲙⲏⲉ, ⲣⲉⲟⲩⲏ, ⲥⲁⲩⲛⲉ; ⲕⲏⲙⲉ, ⲙⲟⲟⲧ, ⲙⲱⲛⲱ, ⲥⲓⲁⲩⲧ, ⲧⲁⲛⲁⲓ̈ⲉⲧⲟⲩ

(ⲣⲙⲓ̈ⲏ) *tear, weeping*:

  pl. ⲣⲙⲓ̈ⲁⲩⲉ **105.**80

ⲣⲁⲙⲡⲉ f. *year* **70.**18; **77.**22,23; **90.**37; **116.**8

ⲣⲉⲛ m. *name* **60.**5; **61.**5; **63.**2; **64.**24; **65.**30,47; **66.**13; **70.**1,10,34,45; **71.**2,32; **72.**32; **75.**7; **76.**4,44; **78.**16; **79.**2; **80.**29,30,38,38,39; **82.**2; **84.**4; **88.**10; **92.**28; **93.**1,25; **94.**5,11; **96.**29; **99.**3; **102.**20; **105.**3,60,76; **112.**2,[19]; **115.**3; **116.**6; **122.**1,14

  (Sah.:) ⲣⲁⲛ **124.**8; **126.**17,29; **128.**43

ⲣⲏⲥ *south*:

  adv. ⲁⲣⲏⲥ *southward* **111.**7

  ⲙⲁⲣⲏⲥ *southern country, Upper Egypt* **79.**27,34

ⲣⲉⲥⲧⲉ *morrow*:

  adv. ⲛⲣⲉⲥⲧⲉ *tomorrow* **102.**9   ⲛⲣⲉⲥⲧⲁ **94.**22,50

ⲣⲉⲧ⸗ *foot*: (compound prepositions)

  ⲁⲣⲉⲧ⸗: ⲁⲣⲉⲧⲥ **90.**31 (ⲱϩⲉ ~)

  ϩⲁⲣⲉⲧ⸗: ϩⲁⲣⲉⲧϥ **122.**19

  ϩⲓⲣⲉⲧ⸗: ϩⲓⲣⲉⲧⲥ **77.**15

ⲣⲏⲧⲉ m. *manner* **82.**15

ⲣⲧⲁⲃ m. *artaba* **77.**36; **106.**33

ⲣⲉⲟⲩⲏ f. *quarter, neighbourhood* **77.**4; **96.**28   ⲣⲁⲟⲩⲏ **85.**8

  ⲣⲙ-ⲣⲉⲟⲩⲏⲧⲟⲩ (sic? involving correction) *people of neighbourhood* **71.**31

ⲣⲁⲩϣ m. *care* (in phraseology with ϥⲓ) **73.**11; **110.**44,44; **115.**22

  ϥⲓ-ⲣⲁⲩϣ *take care* **84.**14

ⲣⲉϣⲉ *be glad, rejoice* **76.**46; **77.**9; **90.**5; **122.**23

  (Sah.:) ⲣⲁϣⲉ **128.**47

  ⲣⲉϣⲉ nn. m. *gladness, joy* **78.**11; **81.**49; **82.**8; **97.**12; **115.**5

ⲣⲱϣⲉ *be sufficient (for)* **128.**16

  take charge, be responsible **58.**9; **90.**24

  (+ ⲙⲛ-) *deal with* **86.**7,14

ⲣϣⲱⲛ m. *cloak, covering* **58.**24,24,25; **94.**25

ⲣϩⲉ *be willing* **94.**21

ⲣⲟⲩϩⲉ *evening* :
    adv. ⲛⲣⲟⲩϩⲉ **94.**39
    adv. ϩⲓⲣⲟⲩϩⲉ **102.**6

ⲥⲁ m. *side, part* : ⲥⲁⲛ- see ⲃⲁⲗ, ⲉⲓⲧⲛ
ⲥⲉ *yes* **94.**48; **102.**23   ⲉⲥⲉ **58.**11   ⲁⲥⲉ **102.**17
ⲥⲁⲃⲧ *wall* **122.**10
ⲥⲁⲃⲧⲉ *make ready* **71.**20
    ⲥⲃⲧⲉ- **106.**17
    ⲥⲃⲧⲱⲧ⸗ : ⲥⲃⲧⲱⲧⲥ **116.**10   ⲥⲃⲧⲱⲧⲟⲩ **86.**16
ⲥⲉⲓⲛⲉ *physician* : ⲥⲏⲓⲛ m. **82.**25
(ⲥⲉⲓⲡⲉ) *butter* : ⲥⲓⲡⲁ f. **125.**44
ⲥⲁⲓⲧ m. *fame, report* **78.**33
ⲥⲁⲓϣ m. *pair, twofold* **78.**25,40,47; **79.**20; **81.**31,40
(ⲥⲁⲗⲥⲗ) *comfort, encourage* : ⲥⲗⲥⲗ- **80.**9,15,30
    ⲥⲗⲥⲱⲗ⸗ : ⲥⲗⲥⲱⲗϥ **80.**12
ⲥⲗⲁϩⲗⲉϩ (meaning uncertain) *neglect* (?) **92.**23
    stat. ⲥⲗⲁϩⲗⲁϩⲧ **106.**29
(ⲥⲙⲓⲛⲉ) *fix, set right, repair* : ⲥⲙⲛ- **103.**39
    ⲥⲙⲛⲧ⸗ : ⲥⲙⲛⲧϥ **103.**43   ⲥⲙⲛⲧⲥ **90.**30   ⲥⲙⲛⲧⲟⲩ **58.**23
    stat. ⲥⲙⲁⲛⲧ **115.**36   ⲥⲙⲛⲧ **75.**43
ⲥⲙⲁⲧ *sort, kind* :
    adv. ⲙⲡⲥⲙⲁⲧ *of such kind* **107.**22
ⲥⲁⲛ m. *brother* **58.**21; **64.**25,26,30; **65.**1,3,4,37,41; **66.**1,2,3,8,39; **67.**2,6,7,17, [34],40,46; **68.**7,8,38; **69.**2; **70.**1,5,11,15,15,45; **71.**12,17,21; **72.**12,25,35,36; **73.**1,5,[6],20,20; **76.**2,25; **77.**5; **78.**13,14,40,47; **79.**4,5,5, 6,30,42,45; **80.**1,4,7,17,19,28,29,31,38,38; **81.**1,6,10,38; **82.**1,3,11,29,30; **84.**33; **86.**1,6,21; **88.**1; **89.**2,9,18,24,27,28,39; **90.**3,5,39; **91.**2; **92.**26; **94.**3,7; **98.**28; **99.**14,54; **103.**2,5,7,31,44; **105.**5,77; **106.**37,43; **108.**1,[4,7]; **111.**1,3,16,26,34,40; **112.**1; **114.**1; **115.**1,6,20,43; **116.**11,16; **122.**15,20
    pl. ⲥⲛⲏⲩ **58.**5; **61.**1; **67.**57; **70.**8; **72.**32; **75.**3,41; **78.**15; **80.**28; **85.**1,6; **91.**1; **92.**5; **94.**10; <**105.**43>; **110.**44; **111.**42; **118.**4; **122.**14   ⲥⲛⲏⲟⲩ **82.**41; **93.**25; **105.**1,[26]; **112.**21
    ⲙⲛⲧⲥⲁⲛ f. *brotherhood, fraternity* **70.**23; **72.**5; **86.**4; **115.**10
    (Sah.:) ⲥⲟⲛ **123.**25; **128.**40 (ⲙⲁⲓ-),48
ⲥⲓⲛⲉ *pass by* : ⲥⲛ- **105.**17,20
    ⲥⲉⲛ⸗ : ⲥⲛⲉⲧ (for ⲥⲉⲛⲧ) **103.**42
ⲥⲱⲛⲉ f. *sister* **64.**21; **65.**42; **66.**22,31; **68.**22,37; **70.**[9],43; **71.**1,2,28; **72.**15; **73.**8; **80.**29; **82.**27; **83.**3; **88.**29; **89.**16,21; **92.**1,20; **93.**1,2,19; **102.**21; **109.**1; **114.**4; **115.**7,24,37,38 **117.**2,3
ⲥⲛⲉⲩ *two* **72.**36; **73.**12; **78.**43,43,48; **81.**29; **86.**8,14,18; **109.**13   ⲥⲛⲟ **58.**24; **77.**36; **79.**32,41; **84.**24; **94.**33,56; **120.**18; **122.**18
    f. ⲥⲛⲧⲉ **58.**15; **65.**53; **66.**45; **73.**8; **96.**19; **105.**76; **110.**20; [**112.**9]; **113.**8

Indices: Native words

ⲥⲛⲁⲩⲥ **58.**8; **78.**21; **95.**7; **105.**35; **110.**10
    adv. ⲙⲡⲥⲛⲟ **71.**21
ⲥⲛⲁϥ *blood* **90.**26
ⲥⲁⲡ m. *occasion, time* **73.**12; **82.**20; **102.**11,14; **105.**19
    relative adverbial: ⲡⲥⲁⲡ **75.**23
    indefinite adverbials: ⲁⲩⲥⲁⲡ **77.**4; **84.**4; **92.**19   ⲉⲩⲥⲁⲡ **76.**4; **78.**15; **94.**4,10; **102.**19; **108.**31
        ϩⲓⲟⲩⲥⲁⲡ **61.**28; **94.**47 (+ ⲛⲟⲩⲱⲧ)
        ⲛⲕⲉⲥⲁⲡ **76.**8; **78.**11; **82.**8; **90.**7; **93.**10; **97.**11
ⲥⲱⲣ *spread, scatter* **78.**34
ⲥⲱⲣⲙⲉ *lead astray* **64.**29
ⲥⲁⲣⲧ f. *wool* **58.**17,20; **71.**34; **75.**9,41; **76.**21,23,26; **78.**41,42; **79.**31,33,38; **96.**33; **105.**28; **109.**31
(ⲥⲣϥⲉ) *be at leisure*
    stat. ⲥⲣⲁϥⲧ **84.**17
ⲥⲓⲧⲉ *throw, sow*: ⲥⲓⲧⲉⲃⲁⲗ **113.**11
ⲥⲱⲧ *return, repeat*: ⲥⲱⲧ ⲁϩⲟⲩⲛ *relapse* **84.**34
(ⲥⲧⲁï) *smell*: ⲥϯ-ⲛⲟⲩϥⲉ *good smell, fragrance* **61.**11
ⲥⲧⲏⲙ *antimony* **103.**8
ⲥⲱⲧⲙⲉ *hear* **71.**11; **73.**7,9,25; **80.**14; **93.**7   ⲥⲱⲧⲙ **81.**50; **89.**29,32; **97.**15; **106.**9; **120.**26
(ⲥⲱⲧⲡ) *choose*:
    ⲥⲁⲧⲡ⸗: ⲥⲁⲧⲡⲟⲩ **76.**25; **79.**39
ⲥⲁⲧⲉⲣⲉ *stater* **58.**25
ⲥⲁⲩ *six* **66.**24; **75.**8; **90.**30,32,39,40,41
    -ⲉⲥⲉ **75.**10; **78.**26; **79.**24
ⲥⲏⲩ *time, season* **61.**9; [**62.**9]; **78.**8
    ⲥⲟⲩ- *day (of month)*: ⲥⲟⲩⲉ *day one* **86.**17
ⲥⲟⲩⲛ⸗ *price, value*: ⲥⲟⲩⲛⲧϥ **103.**41   ⲥⲟⲩⲛⲧⲥ **58.**6; **64.**18
ⲥⲁⲩⲛⲉ *be acquainted with, know* **57.**12; **64.**15; **72.**6,8,20; **79.**33; **80.**11,12,22; **81.**40,45,46,49; **82.**9,41; **83.**12; **90.**12; **94.**18,53; **99.**24,28; **105.**59,60; **116.**2
    ⲥⲁⲩⲛⲉ nn. m. *knowledge* [**63.**30]
    ⲣⲙⲛ-ⲥⲁⲩⲛⲉ *knowledgeable* **81.**34
    (Sah.:) ⲥⲟⲟⲩⲛ **124.**11
        ⲥⲟⲩⲱⲛ⸗: ⲥⲟⲩⲱⲛⲅ **126.**11
ⲥⲁⲩϩⲉ f. *egg* **80.**25; **96.**36   ⲥⲁⲟⲩϩⲉ **81.**51
ⲥϣⲉ *it behoves* [**67.**30 comm.]; **91.**5
(ⲥⲁϣϥ) *seven*:
    f. ⲥⲁϣϥⲉ **76.**22; **94.**32   ⲥⲁϣⲃⲉ **66.**44; **78.**42
ⲥⲁϩ m. *teacher* **61.**1
ⲥⲱϩⲉ *weave* **58.**27 (in ⲃⲉⲕⲉ-ⲥⲱϩⲉ *weaving wage*)
ⲥϩⲉï *write* **58.**2,4,20,22; **60.**2; **64.**20; **65.**[5],25,33,36; **66.**9; **67.**1,60; **69.**1,4; **70.**[3],33,44; **71.**26,28,29; **72.**10,22,26,27,28; **73.**9,13; **75.**38,42,43; **76.**1,10,23,40; **77.**13,17,21; **78.**5,16,23,27,34,49; **79.**7,12,30; **80.**17,18,33;

81.3,11,13,47,48; 82.4,12,15,20,36,41; 83.11; 84.6,14; 89.1,9,17; 90.9,16; 92.8,31,31; 93.3; 94.60; 95.8; 98.22; 99.5; 102.18,22; 105.6,64; 106.14,23; 107.18; 108.4; 110.8,29,32,35; 111.28; 115.7; 119.53; 120.16; 124.3,37
  ⲥϩⲉⲉⲓ 122.4,21,24,27
  (Sah.:) ⲥϩⲁⲓ̈ 128.15,35,38,46
  ⲥⳁⲁⲉⲓ 129.10
ⲥϩⲉⲓ̈- 105.80; 111.12   ⲥϩⲓ- (+ dat.) 89.44
ⲥⲁϩ⸗ : ⲥⲁϩϥ 80.7; 119.27   ⲥⲁϩⲟⲩ 71.10
ⲥϩⲉⲓ̈ nn. m. *letter, document* 72.11; 107.12; 108.21
ⲥϩⲓⲙⲉ f. *woman, female* [70.9]; 75.5; 77.5; 78.38; 84.8; 90.35; 108.34,36; 119.60
  ⲥϩⲉⲓⲙⲉ 72.25,30
  ϩⲓⲙⲉ f. *wife* 65.38,[46]; 66.12,42,43; 67.17,38; 70.11,13; 72.24; 74.2; 77.35; 82.29,31; 109.32; 112.22   with art. ⲑⲓⲙⲉ 113.7
ⲥϩⲟⲛⲉ *woman, female* (?) 58.19 (precise meaning unknown, cf. P. Kell. V, p. 171, note ad 20.50)
ⲥⲉϫⲉ *speak* 73.21
  ⲥⲉϫⲉ nn. m. *word* 58.8; 71.10; 75.43; 79.13; 82.9; 86.8; 90.15; 94.34; 95.15; 102.4,13; 103.34; 107.16,22; 110.30; 116.2,4,5   ϣⲉϫⲉ 70.38
ⲥⲱϫⲡ *leave over, behind*
  ⲥⲁϫⲡ⸗ : ⲥⲁϫⲡⲟⲩ 92.15
  ⲥⲱϫⲡ nn. m. *remainder* 127.9
ⲥⲱϭ *be paralysed* 70.37

ϯ *give* 64.14; 78.30,31; 79.18; 84.10; 103.45; [105.31]
  pre-dat.: ϯ- 58.11; 92.27; 110.9; 123.12   ⲧⲉ- 81.15   ⲧ(ⲛ)- 76.50 (ⲧⲛⲕ-)
  prenom.: ϯ- 58.6; 60.6; 64.32; 70.31; 71.15,21; 72.22; 77.15; 78.25; 79.38; 81.8,17,19,35; 82.18,21; 83.5; 90.30,32; 95.4; 97.9; 102.23; 106.42; 110.33; 120.8,32; 128.21; 131.6   ⲧⲓ- 79.17
  ⲧⲉ(ⲉ)⸗ : ⲧⲉϥ 58.28; 70.32,39; 75.30; 77.18; 95.6; 103.24; 106.34; 111.25; 119.26   ⲧⲉⲉϥ 72.21; 90.34   ⲧⲉⲥ 57.11; 58.31; 64.12,13,27; 69.10; 76.29,30,32,36; 77.16,33; 94.38,48; 96.23   ⲧⲉⲉⲥ 58.5   ⲧⲉⲟⲩ 58.12; 66.26; 76.12,13; 79.26; 81.22,41; 82.22,24; 92.10,17   ⲧⲉⲩ 66.46; 69.10; 72.13; 94.22,23,31,33,47; 95.7   but ⲧⲉⲧⲟⲩ 109.36   ⲧⲉⲓ̈ⲧⲟⲩ 64.5; 65.33,34,36; 78.29; 105.29

  ϯ- and p.c. ⲧⲁⲓ̈-: for compounds see ⲉⲓⲣⲏⲛⲏ, ⲁⲥⲉ, ⲉⲁⲩ, ⲙⲧⲁⲛ, ⲱⲡ, ϩⲁⲓ̈
  (Sah.:) ⲧⲁⲁⲥ 124.address; 128.26
ⲧⲃⲁ *myriad, ten thousand* 81.20,29; 105.33; 108.28
  ϣⲁⲙⲛⲧⲃⲁ *thirty thousand* 81.17,36
ⲧⲱⲃⲉ *seal, stamp* 81.54
  ⲧⲃⲃⲉ- 81.27
  ⲧⲁⲃⲉ⸗ : ⲧⲁⲃⲉϥ 106.35
  stat. ⲧⲁⲃⲉ 85.2
ⲧⲃⲧ *fish* 66.44; 76.31; 79.41; 110.49; 122.33   ⲧⲏⲃⲧ 78.43
ⲧⲱⲃϩ *entreat, implore* 67.4

ⲧⲁⲃϩ⸗ : ⲧⲁⲃϩⲕ **111.**21
(ⲧⲁⲓⲟ) *honour, praise* :
   ⲧⲁⲓⲁ⸗ : ⲧⲁⲓⲁⲓ **84.**6
      stat. ⲧⲁⲓⲁⲓⲧ **57.**1; **61.**12; **62.**1; [**63.**37]; **71.**1; **76.**2; **81.**1; **108.**2; **110.**1; **112.**1; **115.**2   in rel. ⲉⲧⲁⲓⲁⲓⲧ [**66.**1]; **79.**1; **105.**1; **107.**6   ⲧⲁⲓⲁⲉⲓⲧ **82.**1; **111.**1,16   ⲧⲉⲓⲁⲓⲧ **99.**2
   (Sah.:) ⲧⲁⲉⲓⲟϥ **128.**34   stat. ⲧⲁⲉⲓⲏⲟⲩ (? uncertain, scribal correction) **123.**25
ⲧⲉⲓ adv. *here* **82.**40; **105.**67
(ⲧⲟⲩⲓⲟ) *repay, reward* : ⲧⲟⲩⲟ **120.**29
ⲧⲉⲕⲟ *ruin, destroy* **65.**35; **106.**41; **110.**19
   ⲧⲉⲕⲟ- **111.**10
   (Sah.:) ⲧⲁⲕⲟ **126.**13
(ⲧⲉⲗⲟ) *set up (on loom), weave* :
   ⲧⲉⲗⲁ⸗ : ⲧⲉⲗⲁⲩ **103.**28
ⲧⲁⲗⲏⲗ *be glad, rejoice* **65.**11; **71.**7; **79.**11
   ⲧⲁⲗⲏⲗ nn. m. *gladness, joy* [**88.**3]; **89.**6
ⲧⲙ- (negation of infinitive) **69.**8; **83.**14; **101.**3; **128.**35   ⲧⲙⲛ- **103.**42
ⲧⲁⲙⲟ *inform, instruct* **79.**13
   ⲧⲁⲙⲁ⸗ : ⲧⲁⲙⲁⲓ **64.**14; **105.**63   ⲧⲁⲙⲁⲕ **119.**53   ⲧⲁⲙⲁϥ **103.**40
   (Sah.:) ⲧⲁⲙⲟⲥ **128.**36
†ⲙⲉ *village, town* **99.**22; **105.**45
(ⲧⲱⲙ) *shut* :
   stat. ⲧⲏⲙ **81.**55
(ⲧⲱⲙⲉ) *join* :
   stat. ⲧⲁⲙⲉ *be fitting* **107.**29
ⲧⲁⲛⲟ *make, create* **123.**20
   ⲧⲉⲛⲉ- **108.**23
   ⲧⲁⲛⲁ⸗ : ⲧⲁⲛⲁⲥ **111.**38   ⲧⲁⲛⲁⲩ **58.**19
-ⲧⲏⲛⲉ (suffix pronoun) **70.**16; **72.**9; **75.**27; **76.**35; **77.**11,23; **78.**46; **90.**6,28; **105.**41; **110.**19,32,47; **119.**45; **122.**23
†ⲛⲟⲩ *now* **58.**9; **64.**15; **65.**33,36; **67.**37; **69.**4; **71.**10,14; **72.**12,17,27; **73.**6; **79.**16; **80.**19,23; **81.**19,30,45,50; **82.**23,37; **83.**7; **84.**15; **86.**13; **99.**23; **100.**5; **103.**10; **105.**15; **106.**13; **107.**16; **110.**22; **111.**11; **112.**11,13; **116.**7; **119.**48,51
   ϣⲁ†ⲛⲟⲩ *until now* **94.**35
ⲧⲟⲛⲟⲩ *very much* **57.**2,4; **58.**18; **63.**2,33; **66.**2,11,30; **67.**2,8; **68.**9,29; **70.**1,4,18,44; **71.**1; **72.**3,32,35; **73.**3,5,19; **76.**3,6,47; **77.**3,4,9; **78.**5,49; **79.**2,39,40,45; **80.**5,6,38; **81.**2,5,11; **82.**2,6,11,27,41; **83.**3,4,13; **84.**3,5,30; **85.**1; **86.**4,9,21; **88.**2,25; **89.**4,23,26; **90.**1,6; **91.**1; **93.**1,10; **94.**3,7,9; **95.**2,17; **96.**24,27; **97.**6,14,47; **98.**26,27; **99.**2,8; **102.**1,3; **103.**2,10; **105.**2,77,78; **106.**6; **107.**6; **108.**3,7,32,33,36; **109.**2,6; **110.**2; **111.**2,4,17,19,41; **112.**1,4,6,21; **115.**2,9,24,37; **116.**4; **118.**3; **120.**1; **122.**19,23,29   ⲧⲟⲛⲉ **65.**2,28,37,40
   ⲧⲟⲛⲟⲩ ⲧⲟⲛⲟⲩ **58.**22; **86.**11

ⲧⲛⲛⲁⲩ *send* **58.**13; **64.**12; **65.**15; **70.**19; **94.**25; **96.**21,22; **99.**11; **105.**24
 ⲧⲛⲛⲁⲩ- **58.**35; **64.**17,29,31; **65.**31; **66.**20,28; **69.**9; **70.**17; **73.**9; **75.**21; **76.**52; **77.**27; **78.**46; **79.**31,43; **81.**30,39,47; **91.**3; **94.**26; **105.**16,61,76; **106.**26,39; **108.**37; **109.**10
 ⲧⲛⲛⲁⲩ⸗ : ⲧⲛⲛⲁⲩϥ **58.**16; **64.**2; **65.**27; **70.**22,24; **72.**22; **75.**16,41,41; **76.**50,53; **83.**11; **95.**5; **115.**32; **122.**26; **127.**22,32   ⲧⲛⲛⲁⲩⲥ **58.**2,26; **64.**10,17,32; **68.**15; **76.**26,29,38; **78.**39; **79.**35,44; [**100.**1]; **103.**10,20,28   ⲧⲛⲛⲁⲩⲥ{ⲉ} **91.**2,2   ⲧⲛⲛⲁⲩⲥⲉ **67.**47; **76.**24; **78.**46,48; **79.**14,15,21; **83.**[0/1]; **94.**14,15,16,23; **99.**45; **106.**35; **110.**24   ⲧⲛⲛⲁⲩⲥⲟⲩ **77.**36; **81.**22,48; **90.**9   ⲧⲛⲁⲩⲥⲟⲩ **71.**33   ⲧⲉⲛⲁⲩⲥⲟⲩ **82.**22,24

ⲧⲡⲉ *upper part* :
 adv. ⲛⲧⲡⲉ *above* **120.**19
ⲧⲁⲡⲣⲟ f. *mouth* **79.**3; **115.**3
ⲧⲣⲟ *force, constrain* : ⲧⲁⲣⲟ- **115.**14
 ⲧⲣ(ⲉ)⸗ : ⲧⲣⲥ- **81.**55 (?)
 ⲧⲣ(ⲉ)⸗ (in conjugation) *cause to (do)* : ⲧⲣⲟⲩ- **58.**18; **71.**34; **76.**30,38; **103.**28; **111.**38; **120.**5,10,33
ⲧⲏⲣ⸗ (augens): ⲧⲏⲣϥ **69.**8; **77.**11; **80.**3; **105.**61; **115.**33   ⲧⲏⲣⲥ **77.**4; **80.**3; **96.**28; **115.**44; **122.**18   ⲧⲏⲣⲛⲉ **68.**32   ⲧⲏⲣⲧⲛ **89.**44; **105.**78   ⲧⲏⲣⲧⲛⲉ **67.**50   ⲧⲏⲣⲟⲩ **60.**4; **61.**2,4; **65.**30; **66.**33; **67.**42; **70.**45; **71.**8,10; **80.**28,32,36; **81.**53; **83.**3; **89.**34; **92.**3,22,37; **93.**21,25; **94.**36,47; **105.**75; **108.**31; **111.**9,11; **112.**19; **124.**7,9; **126.**15; **127.**13,22; **128.**43
 adv. ⲁⲡⲧⲏⲣϥ *in any way* **106.**31
(ⲧⲱⲣⲉ) *hand, spade* :
 ⲧⲟⲧ⸗ : ⲧⲟⲧ **79.**16
(ⲧⲁⲣⲧⲣ) *thrust, penetrate* :
 stat. ⲧⲣⲧⲁⲣⲧ **72.**6
ⲧⲱⲣϩ *be alert, sober* **88.**23
ⲧⲥⲉⲃⲟ *make wise, teach* **87.**6
(ⲧⲧⲟ) *make give, make pay, require* :
 ⲧⲁ- **72.**16
 ⲧ(ⲧ)ⲁ⸗ : ⲧⲧⲁⲃ **120.**14
(ⲧⲧⲁⲩ) *buy* :
 ⲧⲁⲩ⸗ : ⲧⲁⲩⲥ **79.**19; **103.**36
ⲧⲉⲟⲩⲟ *utter, proclaim, tell* **107.**16; **115.**44; **116.**4,6   ⲧⲁⲟⲩⲟ **107.**9
 ⲧⲉⲟⲩⲟ- **95.**15; **107.**29   ⲧⲉⲩⲟ- **73.**21   ⲧⲉⲟⲩⲁ- **81.**47   ⲧⲉⲟⲩⲉ- **102.**4
 ⲧⲉⲟⲩⲁ⸗ : ⲧⲉⲟⲩⲁϥ **71.**17   ⲧⲉⲟⲩⲁⲩ **71.**11
ϯⲟⲩ *five* **72.**33; **78.**43; **79.**41; **80.**23; **81.**30,39; **84.**28; **91.**3; **94.**21; **105.**27; **106.**42
 f. ϯⲉ **110.**49; **120.**8
 -(ⲧ)ⲏ (after tens) **76.**27; **78.**28; **81.**42; **94.**44; **95.**6
 ⲉ (in ⲗⲉ *35* for money) **130.**4
ⲧⲟⲟⲩⲉ *shoe* **125.**14
 ⲧⲁⲟⲩⲁ *pair of shoes* (?) **122.**26
ⲧⲱⲟⲩⲛ *raise* **82.**16

Indices: Native words

ⲧⲁϣ m. *boundary, district* **91**.2; **92**.15

ⲧⲱϣ *define, appoint* **77**.14; **103**.27,44; **106**.19,25
    stat. ⲧⲏϣ **94**.55; **115**.25
    ⲧⲱϣ nn. m. *assignment* **105**.41

ⲧⲉϩⲟ *reach, befall* :
    (ⲧⲉϩⲁ-) ⲧⲉϩⲁⲧⲏⲛⲉ **110**.47
    ⲧⲁϩⲁ⸗ : ⲧⲁϩⲱⲧⲛ **122**.31   ⲧⲁϩⲁⲟⲩ **80**.36

ⲧⲱϩ *stir up, mix* :
    ⲧⲁϩ⸗ : ⲧⲁϩⲟⲩ **94**.33
    stat. ⲧⲏϩ **83**.7,8

ⲧϩⲣⲟ (meaning unknown) **121**.5

(ⲑⲣⲕⲟ) *quieten* :
    ⲑⲣⲕⲁ⸗ : ⲑⲣⲕⲁⲩ **90**.14

ⲧⲁϫⲣⲟ *fasten, strengthen* :
    ⲧⲁϫⲣⲟ nn. m. *strength, firmness* **61**.8

(ⲧⲱϭⲛⲉ) *push, repel* :
    ⲧⲁϭⲛ- **107**.26 (?)

ⲧⲱϭⲥ *pierce, fasten, secure* :
    (ⲧⲁϭⲥ⸗) : ⲧⲁϫⲟⲩ **106**.32

ⲧⲱϭⲥ *tread, pound* (so *dye* ?)
    ⲧⲱϭⲥ nn. m. *dye* (?) **58**.30

ⲟⲩ-, ϩⲛ- (indef. art.): ⲟⲩ- **58**.25,27,30; **62**.12; **63**.34; **64**.26,29,32; **66**.13,14,28,41;
    67.5,8,30; **70**.17; **71**.5,6,35,39; **72**.34; **73**.12,12; **75**.21; **76**.25,26,50;
    77.22,23,23,27; **78**.33; **79**.10,23,36; **80**.37; **81**.8,20,36,43; **83**.7; **84**.23; **86**.20;
    90.11,26; **91**.4; **92**.13; **93**.6; **94**.47; **95**.14; **96**.30,37; **105**.16,22,23,30,42,48;
    107.17,25; **108**.23,28,37; **109**.31; **110**.28; **112**.14; **115**.42; **119**.50;
    122.8,25,26,33; **124**.24,27,30; **127**.9; **128**.15,22   -ⲩ- **57**.14; **80**.13; **106**.34;
    123.21
    pl. ϩⲛ- **58**.23; **77**.15; **82**.24; **86**.12; **89**.30,34; **105**.27

ⲟⲩⲉ *one* **58**.15,26; **59**.4; **64**.27; **71**.21,21,22; **78**.42; **79**.38,41; **84**.21; **102**.14;
    105.38,67; **122**.27   -ⲩⲟⲩⲉ **65**.34
    (in ⲥⲟⲩⲉ *day one*) **86**.17
    f. ⲟⲩⲓ̈ⲉ **73**.10   ⲟⲩⲓ̈ **76**.30
    ⲡⲟⲩⲉ ⲡⲟⲩⲉ *each one* **61**.17; **65**.30,46; **70**.22; **105**.29; **110**.13
    (Sah.:) ⲟⲩⲁ **127**.31

ⲟⲩⲱ *finish, cease* **83**.14; **103**.35
    as auxiliary of Affirm. Completive: **80**.18; **105**.30; **107**.24; **116**.2

ⲟⲩⲱ m. *news, report* **58**.6,11; **83**.13; **84**.37; **94**.49; **98**.22; **102**.8,18,22; **106**.15;
    115.44   ⲟⲩⲱϩ **120**.17

ⲟⲩⲃⲉ- prep. *against* **69**.9; **71**.18; **91**.5; **95**.16; **98**.21; **110**.45

(ⲟⲩⲁⲓ̈) *rush, course* :
    (Sah.:) ϯ-ⲟⲩⲟⲉⲓ *search* (?) **128**.21

(ⲟⲩⲁⲓ̈ⲉ) *husbandman, peasant* : ⲟⲩⲉⲓⲉ (uncertain) **130**.1

ⲟⲩⲉⲓⲉ *be distant* **107**.21
    stat. ⲟⲩⲏⲟⲩ **116**.3,7   ⲟⲩⲏⲩ **61**.6; **72**.10; **85**.3; **94**.58
ⲟⲩⲁⲓϣ m. *time* **61**.6; **65**.9; **67**.6; **71**.6,35; **72**.34; **76**.11; **79**.10,37; **80**.37; **81**.24,44,45; **96**.30; **97**.8; **105**.44; **115**.42; **116**.9; **119**.50   ⲟⲩⲁⲉⲓϣ **63**.26
    ⲟⲩⲁϣ **122**.8
ⲟⲩⲛ- affirm. existential **64**.31; **65**.27; **71**.39; **72**.20; **76**.30; **78**.41,48; **81**.46; **83**.4; **84**.18; **86**.19; **102**.15; **105**.22; **106**.30; **122**.33   ⲟⲩ- **79**.20
(ⲟⲩⲛⲟⲩ) *hour* :
    pl. (?) ⲟⲩⲛⲟⲩⲉ (?) **108**.22
ⲟⲩⲁⲛ *someone, something* **76**.21; **78**.30,48; **92**.29; **98**.9; **102**.16; **103**.13,19; **122**.6
    ⲟⲩⲁⲛ ⲛⲓⲙ **61**.12; **64**.16; **92**.24; **115**.40
ⲟⲩⲉⲛ *open* **65**.35
ⲟⲩⲛⲧⲉ-, ⲟⲩⲛⲧⲉ⸗ *have* :
    ⲟⲩⲛⲧⲉ- **109**.30
    ⲟⲩⲛⲧⲉ⸗ : ⲟⲩⲛⲧⲉⲓ **81**.20; **114**.3   ⲟⲩⲛⲑⲉⲓ **113**.6   ⲟⲩⲛⲧⲉⲕ **114**.2
    (reduced form) ⲟⲩⲛϯ- **76**.26; **81**.37
ⲟⲩⲱⲛϩ *make known* **71**.12
    ⲟⲩⲁⲛϩ⸗ : ⲟⲩⲁⲛϩⲥ **103**.26
ⲟⲩⲏⲣ *how much? how many?* **65**.33; **70**.27; **81**.24,37,45; **82**.20; **105**.19
ⲟⲩⲱⲣⲡ *send* **78**.38
    ⲟⲩⲁⲣⲡ⸗ : ⲟⲩⲁⲣⲡⲉ **115**.15
ⲟⲩⲣⲁⲧ *be fresh, ready, glad* :
    stat. ⲣⲁⲩⲧ **71**.7; **105**.11
    ⲟⲩⲣⲁⲧ nn. m. *gladness* **89**.5
(ⲟⲩⲱⲣϩ) *set free* :
    ⲟⲩⲁⲣϩ⸗ : ⲟⲩⲁⲣϩⲥ **111**.24
(ⲟⲩⲧⲉ-), ⲟⲩⲧⲱ⸗ prep. *between*
    ⲟⲩⲧⲱⲓ **69**.4,11   ⲟⲩⲧⲱⲛ **69**.5; **128**.29
ⲟⲩⲁⲉⲧ⸗ (augens) :
    ⲛ̄ⲟⲩⲁⲉⲧ⸗ : ⲛ̄ⲟⲩⲁⲉⲧϥ **72**.7; **81**.49; **94**.18   ⲛ̄ⲟⲩⲁⲉⲧⲥ **115**.29
ⲟⲩⲏⲧⲉ *remit, waive (claim)* **64**.8
ⲟⲩⲱⲧ *single, same* **94**.47
(ⲟⲩⲱϣ) *gap* :
    ⲛⲟⲩⲱϣⲛ- prep. *without* **112**.15
ⲟⲩⲱϣⲉ *desire* **72**.19; **107**.9   ⲟⲩⲱϣ **114**.6; **124**.36
    ⲟⲩⲱϣ-inf. **58**.19,23; **64**.12; **67**.32; **72**.9,28; **76**.28; **78**.38; **83**.6; **84**.27; **90**.29; **94**.59; **105**.43; **111**.8   ⲟⲩⲁϣ-inf. **79**.39; **92**.10
    ⲟⲩⲁϣ⸗ : ⲟⲩⲁϣϥ **58**.7 **76**.46 **89**.36; **103**.46; **105**.63; **128**.46   ⲟⲩⲁϣⲥ **58**.3; **63**.5; **76**.27
    in interlocutive phraseology, *please do* : ⲟⲩⲱϣⲉ ⲁ-inf. **65**.15   ⲟⲩⲁϣ-inf. **67**.60
(ⲟⲩⲱϣⲃⲉ) *answer* :
    ⲟⲩⲁϣⲃ(ⲉ)⸗ : ⲟⲩⲁϣⲃⲉⲧ **122**.25,34
ⲟⲩⲁϣⲣⲉ *cease, fail* **105**.37; **111**.11
ⲟⲩⲱϣⲥ *make wide, broad* : -ⲩⲱϣⲥ **99**.16

stat. ⲟⲩⲁϣⲥ **73**.16
ⲟⲩⲉϣⲧⲉ f. *reverence, praise (be to ...)*:
 (in formula ⲧⲟⲩⲉϣⲧⲉ ⲙ̄ⲡⲛⲟⲩⲧⲉ *God be praised*) **71**.36; **82**.16; **116**.15
ⲟⲩⲱϣⲧ *worship* **72**.12; **90**.7
 ⲟⲩⲁϣⲧ⸗: ⲟⲩⲁϣⲧⲕ **82**.7   ⲟⲩⲁϣⲧϥ **115**.4   ⲟⲩⲁϣⲧⲛⲉ **62**.11
ⲟⲩⲁϩⲉ *Oasis* (without article, as if proper noun) **58**.22,32; **65**.37; **68**.11; **81**.13,23; **105**.36,44; **108**.30; **110**.20; **119**.52   -ⲩⲁϩⲉ **90**.11   ⲟⲩⲁϩⲁ **122**.12 ⲟⲩϩⲁ **130**.3
ⲟⲩⲱϩ *place, dwell* **115**.16
 ⲟⲩⲁϩ⸗: ⲟⲩⲁϩⲥ **103**.17   ⲟⲩⲁϩⲟⲩ **105**.26
 stat. ⲟⲩⲏϩ **94**.16,34; **103**.16   ⲟⲩⲉϩ <**69**.3>
(ⲟⲩⲱϫⲉ) *cut, tailor*:
 ⲟⲩⲁϫⲉ- **58**.26; **103**.16
 ⲟⲩⲁϫ(ⲉ)⸗: ⲟⲩⲁϫⲉϥ **75**.41   ⲟⲩⲁϫϥ **75**.14   ⲟⲩⲁϫⲉⲥ **76**.29,37; **103**.29 ⲟⲩⲁϫⲟⲩ **58**.24; **78**.45; **96**.20; **103**.20; **111**.38
ⲟⲩϫⲉⲓ(ⲧⲉ) *be safe, healthy*: ⲟⲩϫⲉⲓ **67**.43   ⲟⲩϫⲉⲓⲧⲉ [**96**.30]; [**110**.54]; **71**.35; **72**.34; **76**.43; **79**.36; **80**.37; **81**.43; **90**.45; [**105**.66]; **115**.41; **124**.38
 (Sah.:) ⲟⲩϫⲁⲉⲓ **123**.22   ⲟⲩϫⲁⲓ **127**.25
 stat. ⲟⲩϫⲁϫ **65**.[10],11; **71**.6,8; **78**.7
 ⲟⲩϫⲉⲓⲧⲉ nn. m. *health* [**62**.8]; **72**.5; **77**.10,10; **81**.50; **83**.5; **84**.10; **89**.44; **97**.7; **105**.8; **108**.9   ⲟⲩϫⲉⲉⲓⲧⲉ **112**.7; **122**.7,13,21,25

ⲱⲃϣ *forget*:
 ⲣ-ⲡ(⸗)ⲱⲃϣ **105**.45; **115**.20/21,33
(ⲱⲕ ⲛϩⲏⲧ) *be pleased*:
 stat. ⲏⲕ ⲛϩⲏⲧ **73**.14
ⲱⲛϩ *live* **65**.9; **66**.40; **67**.43; **71**.5,35; **72**.34; **76**.43; **79**.36; **80**.37; **81**.43; **90**.45; **96**.29; **115**.41
 ⲱⲛϩ nn. m. *life* **73**.23; **115**.44
ⲱⲡ *count, reckon* **57**.5; **81**.42; **95**.14
  ⲏⲡ- (thus apparently) **91**.4
  ⲁⲡ⸗: ⲁⲡⲥ **62**.16; **75**.25; **111**.38
  ⲱⲡ nn. m. *account* **95**.6; **103**.38; **114**.5
   ϯ-ⲱⲡ *give account* **67**.46
  modal usage *suppose (to do)*: ⲁⲡ⸗: ⲁⲡⲧ **70**.41,43; **90**.12; **91**.4
  stat. ⲏⲡ **64**.14; **72**.18; **80**.12; **103**.48
ⲱⲣⲕ *swear* **107**.25
ⲱⲣϫ *fasten, ascertain*:
 ⲱⲣϫ nn. m. *security* **123**.22
ⲱⲧⲡ *load*:
 ⲁⲧⲡ⸗: ⲁⲧⲡϥ **71**.15,16
 ⲱⲧⲡ nn. m. *burden* **73**.17
ⲱϩⲉ *stand, stay*: ⲁϩⲉ **73**.13; **122**.17
 stat. ⲁϩⲉ **105**.32; **124**.28

ⲱϩⲉ ⲁⲣⲉⲧ⸗ *make a stand, be steadfast* **90**.31
 ⲁϩ-6ⲱ ϩⲁⲣⲉⲧ⸗ *remain* (?) **122**.19

ϣ- *be able to* : with inf. **58**.10; **72**.10; **105**.17,20; **107**.11; **110**.31
 in modal ⲟⲩⲛ-/ⲙⲛ-ϣ-6ⲁⲙ : **84**.18; **107**.20
ϣⲁ-, ϣⲁⲣⲁ⸗ prep.:
 ϣⲁ- **61**.2,10; **62**.16; **82**.20; **86**.16; **94**.36; **124**.22
  ϣⲁⲣⲁ⸗ : ϣⲁⲣⲁⲓ̈ **78**.39; **102**.4   ϣⲁⲣⲁⲕ **80**.20; **82**.10   ϣⲁⲣⲁⲛ **90**.5;
   103.4 ϣⲁⲣⲱⲧⲛ **72**.7
 (Sah.) ϣⲁⲣⲟⲛ **124**.20,22,34; **127**.34
ϣⲉ *go* **67**.48; **105**.17; **120**.22
 ϣⲉⲃⲁⲗ *go out* **94**.43
ϣⲉ *hundred* **58**.4,8; **65**.26; **76**.22,63; **78**.21,26,28; **79**.20; **81**.21,42; **94**.22,27,32,45;
 95.4,6,8; **96**.35; **105**.34,35; **110**.10; **120**.32
ϣⲓ *measure* **81**.52   ϣⲓ- **109**.35
ϣⲓⲃⲉ *change* :
 ⲁⲧϣⲓⲃⲉ *unchanging, immutable* **85**.4
ϣⲃⲱⲛ *cereals* (?) **78**.46; **79**.29
ϣⲃⲏⲣ *companion, friend* :
 pl. ϣⲃⲉⲣ **85**.6
 ⲙⲛⲧϣⲃⲏⲣ nn. f. *friendship* **116**.3
(ϣⲱⲗ) *shed, make flow* :
 ϣⲁⲗ⸗ : ϣⲁⲗϥ **90**.26
ϣⲗⲏⲗ *pray* **61**.9; **62**.7; **65**.7; **67**.53; **71**.4; **72**.4; **76**.7; **78**.6; **79**.9; **82**.7; **91**.1;
 97.6; **105**.8,82; **108**.7; [**109**.6]; **112**.6; **115**.4; **121**.5; **122**.7,12
 ϣⲗⲏⲗ nn. m. *prayer* **63**.11; **79**.37; **80**.37; **96**.31
(ϣⲙⲁ) *be fine, subtle* :
 stat. ϣⲙⲁⲧ **58**.16,18
ϣⲏⲙ *small, little* **75**.41; **105**.42; **110**.28
ϣⲙⲟⲩⲛ *eight* **94**.27,28
 f. ϣⲙⲟⲩⲛⲉ **122**.33
ϣⲁⲙⲧ *three* **76**.31; **81**.51; **82**.14; **83**.16; **105**.33
 f. ϣⲁⲙⲧⲉ **58**.4; **90**.28; **95**.4
 ϣⲁⲙⲛⲧⲃⲁ *thirty thousand* **81**.17,36
ϣⲙϣⲉ *serve, worship* :
 ϣⲙϣⲉ nn. m. *worship* **73**.16
ϣⲓⲛⲉ *ask, question* **106**.33; **111**.7   ϣⲛ- **84**.11
 ϣⲛⲧ⸗ : ϣⲛⲧϥ **75**.35   ϣⲛⲧⲛ **105**.31
 ϣⲓⲛⲉ ⲛⲥⲁ- *ask for, seek* **64**.4,6,8; **102**.15,16; **103**.12; **113**.4; **128**.23
 ϣⲓⲛⲉ ⲁ- *visit, greet* **57**.4,7; **58**.36,36,37; **60**.3; **61**.29; **62**.6; **64**.18,20;
  65.[5],28,29,37,39,41,43,43,45,47;   **66**.4,11,17,21,29,30,30,34,34,36,39,42,43;
  67.2,6,25,33,34,40,[42],50,56;   **68**.7,8,[12],16,37;   **70**.[4],6,10,12,33,43,45;
  71.2,3,26,28,31,31;   **72**.3,23,24,29,31,32,35,36;   **73**.2,4,5,6,19,24,24;   **74**.1;
  75.2,4,39,41;   **76**.1,6,34,39,44,47,63;   **77**.3,4,6,35,35;   **78**.5,12,49;   **79**.7,39,45;

80.4,6,7,28,29,32,33,38,38,39; 81.3,5,53; 82.5,[6],10,26,28,30,32,41; 83.2; 84.3; 85.8; 86.3,4,20; 88.5,[24,25]; 89.2,10,17,22,25,44; 90.4; 91.1; 92.3,4,7,19,20,26,33,36,37; 93.3,[5],10,19,21,22,23; 94.3,6,9; 95.2,2,17,18; 96.25,27; 97.5,13,27; 98.26,27; 99.7,32; 102.1,2,19; 103.2,5; 105.7,10,76,77,78,81; 106.5,36; 107.4; 108.6,31,32,36; [109.2,5]; 110.50; 111.3,15,19,40; 112.4,5,17,18,19,21; 114.1; 115.9,23,36; 116.11,12,13,13; 117.2; 118.2; 119.61,62 120.1; 122.5,19; 124.5,6,9,41,42; 127.30; 128.42,44

ϣⲓⲛⲁ 129.1,6

ϣⲓⲛⲉ nn. *news, report* 72.11,11

ϣⲱⲛⲉ *be ill* 64.31; 71.39; 72.33; 81.10; 82.14; 83.4; 84.9,29; 93.13; 115.18

   ϣⲱⲛⲉ nn. m. *illness, disease* 84.13,16,23,35

(ϣⲛϩⲧ) *have mercy* :

   (Sah.:) ϣⲛϩⲧ⸗ : ϣⲛϩⲧⲕ 124.33   ϣⲛϩⲧϥ 124.31

(ϣⲱⲛⲉ) *exclude, deprive* :

   ϣⲁⲛⲉ⸗ : ϣⲁⲛⲉⲧ 64.7,13

ϣⲡⲉ see ⲉⲓϣϫⲉ

ϣⲓⲡⲉ *be ashamed* :

   †-ϣⲓⲡⲉ *shame* 81.41

ϣⲱⲡ *receive, buy* etc.: ϣⲉⲡ(-) (unclear) 122.18

   (in phraseology with ϩⲙⲁⲧ *give thanks*) ϣⲱⲡ 76.45   ϣⲉⲡ- 128.17

   stat. ϣⲏⲡ 72.33

ϣⲱⲡⲉ *be, become, happen* 64.3; 77.16,24; 80.8,22,31; 83.7; 86.20; 92.13,16; 106.12,39 124.10; 127.9

   stat. ϣⲟⲡ 69.5; 70.44; 78.48; [105.30]; 107.28; 115.44; 122.9,11

   ϣⲟⲡ in unclear construction 90.44

ϣⲡⲏⲣⲉ *wonder* :

   ⲣ-ϣⲡⲏⲣⲉ *be astonished* [60.5 comm.]; 70.16,25,44; 84.5; 89.42; 103.3; 110.5; 116.4 124.21

ϣⲡⲧⲱⲣⲉ *be surety* :

   adv. in ϫⲓⲧ⸗ ϣⲡⲧⲱⲣⲉ 71.13

ϣⲉⲣⲉ f. *daughter* 63.1,4,50; 64.21,22,23; 65.40,43; 66.23,38; 67.40; 71.27; 73.8,11,12,25; 77.36; 80.35; 82.28; 92.21; 93.20,20; 105.75; 113.9; 115.13; 119.61; 122.16

ϣⲏⲣⲉ m. *son, child* 58.11; 60.1; 61.3; 63.51; 64.19,22,24; 65.29,38,42,44,46; 66.12,29,32,36,42,44; 67.10,18,35,39; 68.27,31; 70.8,[10,34]; 71.2,3; 72.24,26,30,31; 73.4; 75.6; 76.3,34,39,41,44; 77.4,6,6,35; 80.36; 82.30; 84.17; 88.15; 92.4,6,11,12; 93.10,11; 95.2; 96.26,28; 103.6; 105.11,75; 107.30; [108.36]; 112.18,22; 115.11,17,29,38,39,44; 116.12,18; 119.59,61; 121.3; 122.4,27; 126.8

   ϣⲏⲣ-ⲓⲱⲧ m. *half-brother* 70.12

   ⲙⲛⲧϣⲏⲣⲉ f. *sonship* 61.8; 107.5

ϣⲁⲣⲡ *first* :

   adv. ϣⲁⲣⲡ 92.7; 122.5   ⲛϣⲁⲣⲡ 58.35

ϣⲱⲥ *shepherd* 124.30

ϣⲧⲁ *be in need, have defect* **103.**22
 ϣⲧⲁ nn. m. *fault, defect* **105.**47
ϣⲁⲧ m. *pillow, cushion* **79.**42; **92.**28; **103.**17; **116.**8
ϣⲁⲧⲉ f. *portion* (of fish, cf. also ϣⲁⲧⲥ) **122.**33
(ϣⲓⲧⲉ) *demand, make give* :
 ϣⲉⲧ⸗ : ϣⲉⲧ **81.**29 ϣⲉⲧⲕ **70.**35 ϣⲉⲧϥ **105.**39 ϣⲓⲧⲃ (here?) **130.**4
  ϣⲉⲧⲟⲩ **113.**5,10
ϣⲱⲱⲧ *cut (off)* :
 stat. ϣⲁⲧ *be in need (of)* **81.**33; **116.**15
 stat. ϣⲏⲧ ⲁⲃⲁⲗ (unclear) *cut off* (?) **71.**30
 prep. ϣⲁⲧⲛ- *except, minus* **78.**42; **79.**38 ⲛϣⲁⲧⲛ- **88.**29
ϣⲧⲏⲛ f. *tunic* **81.**43; **105.**18
(ϣⲱⲧⲡ) *urge, hasten* :
 ϣⲁⲧⲡ⸗ refl. + circ. *hasten to* : ϣⲁⲧⲡⲧ **66.**9
ϣⲧⲁⲣⲧⲣ *disturb, trouble* **78.**40; **97.**17
 ϣⲧⲣⲧⲣ-ⲑⲏⲛⲉ **78.**46
ϣⲁⲧⲥ f. *portion* (of fish, cf. also ϣⲁⲧⲉ) **66.**44,45; **68.**46; **110.**49
ϣⲁⲧⲥ f. *cutting, ditch* **111.**6
ϣⲧⲧ m. *warp* **58.**25; **109.**33; **111.**26 ϣⲧⲓⲧ **79.**32
ϣⲟⲩⲟ *pour, flow* **105.**80
ϣⲉⲩ *use, value* :
 ⲣ-ϣⲉⲩ *be useful, be well* **67.**45; **71.**30; **75.**33,37; **78.**45; **82.**33; **92.**18,21; **109.**18
 ϣⲟⲩ- see ⲙⲉⲓⲉ
ϣⲉⲩ m. *measure, extent* **105.**27
(ϣⲉⲟⲩⲉ) *be dry* : uncertain readings (adjunct?) ϣⲟⲟⲩⲱ **125.**22 ϣⲱⲟⲩ **125.**24
ϣⲁϣ *jar* **64.**29
(ϣⲱϣ) *make level, compare* :
 stat. ϣⲏϣ **105.**54 (here? - no context)
ϣⲁϣⲁⲧⲉ f. *cushion* (?) **82.**18
ϣⲟⲩϣⲧ m. *niche, alcove* **81.**53
(ϣⲱϭⲉ) *strike, wound* :
 ϣⲁϭⲉ⸗ : ϣⲁϭⲉϥ **102.**10

ϥⲓ *take (off), carry* **90.**12; **95.**14
 ϥⲓ- **76.**21; **78.**23; **90.**11,39; **91.**4; **92.**10; **103.**45; **105.**39; **116.**8; **122.**25,34
 ϥⲓⲧ⸗ : ϥⲓⲧⲥ **70.**41,43; **76.**28; **94.**35,42,51,54; **103.**16; **111.**37; **115.**27 ϥⲓⲧⲟⲩ **76.**63; **120.**19
 in phraseology with ⲣⲁⲩϣ *take care (of)* : ϥⲓ ⲙ-ⲡ⸗ⲣ. **115.**21 ϥⲓ-ⲡ⸗ⲣ. **73.**11
  ϥⲓ-ⲡⲣ. ⲛ- **110.**44
 compound ϥⲓ-ⲣ. (+ ⲭⲉ) **84.**14 (+ dat. refl. + ϩⲁ-) **110.**44
ϥⲧⲁ m. (apparently so, of unknown meaning) **71.**25
(ϥⲧⲁⲩ) *four* :
 f. ϥⲧⲟⲉ **113.**6

ϥⲧⲟⲩ- **84.**19
-ⲉϥⲧⲉ **90.**37

ϩⲁ-, ϩⲁⲣⲁ⸗ prep. *under* etc.: ϩⲁ- **58.**12; **62.**8; **67.**53; **69.**6; **70.**27; **71.**17; **72.**4; **75.**30; **78.**26,30; **79.**20; **81.**22,27,42; **82.**22; **105.**8; **108.**8; **109.**37; **110.**44; **114.**2; **118.**8; **122.**7; **124.**31
    see also ⲣⲁ, ⲣⲉⲧ⸗, ϩⲏ, ϩⲁ(ϩ)ⲧⲛ-
ϩⲁⲣⲁ⸗ : ϩⲁⲣⲁï **90.**23   ϩⲁⲣⲁϥ **64.**8   ϩⲁⲣⲁⲥ **70.**44; **72.**22
ϩⲁ⸗ *said* : ϩⲁï **82.**34
ϩⲁⲉ *last* :
    adv. (?) ⲁϩⲁⲉ **122.**36
ϩⲁⲏ f. *end* : (with art. ⲑⲁⲏ) **62.**16
ϩⲉ f. *manner* **58.**9; **79.**44; **81.**12,14; **83.**14; **84.**10; **86.**15; **122.**6
    (with art. ⲑⲉ) **73.**7; **81.**16; **94.**16; **106.**24; **107.**11; **115.**19,34,44; **116.**14
    demonstrative adverbial: ⲛ︦ϯϩⲉ **72.**18
    relative adverbials: ⲧϩⲉ **79.**39   ⲑⲉ **115.**21; **116.**10   ⲛⲑⲉ **58.**1,18; **73.**11; **102.**16; **103.**14,47; **108.**13; **124.**24,27   ⲕⲁⲧⲁ ⲧⲑⲉ (sic) **67.**23
ϩⲏ f. *fore part, beginning* :
    adv. ϩⲁⲑⲏ **65.**7; **67.**4; **68.**6; **70.**4; **71.**4; **72.**3; **73.**4; **76.**6; **77.**3; **78.**4; **79.**8; **80.**6; **81.**5; **82.**6; **93.**4; **107.**4; **109.**5; **111.**18; **112.**5; **124.**5
    adv. ϩⲓⲑⲏ **78.**20; **89.**1; **99.**7; **108.**6; **115.**9; **118.**2
    prep. ϩⲏⲧ⸗ : ϩⲏⲧ **81.**42   ϩⲏⲧⲕ **80.**27,36   ϩⲏⲧϥ **105.**47; **124.**29   ϩⲏⲧⲧⲏⲛⲉ **72.**8 **122.**23

ϩⲓ-, ϩⲓⲱⲱ⸗ prep. *on*
    ϩⲓ- **63.**40; **68.**34; **81.**32,53; **83.**6; **84.**27; **94.**13,47; **102.**6; **127.**35
    see also ⲣⲉⲧ⸗, ⲣⲟⲩϩⲉ, ⲥⲁⲡ, ϩⲏ; ϩⲓⲧⲛ-
ϩⲓⲱ(ⲱ)⸗ : ϩⲓⲱϥ **90.**25   ϩⲓⲱⲥ **76.**27   ϩⲓⲱⲱⲥ **64.**17
ϩⲟ m. *face* **72.**12,12; **90.**7; **97.**11; **104.**3
    in phraseology ϩⲟ ... ϩⲟ **89.**23
(ϩⲱ) *suffice it* : ϩⲱⲉ **84.**24 (uncertain)
ϩⲱ(ⲱ)⸗ augens: ϩⲱⲧ **64.**14; **67.**60; **73.**15; **82.**25; **92.**12,35; **107.**7; **108.**24; **115.**19,34   ϩⲱⲕ **65.**51; **81.**38,40,45; **103.**25,30,49   ϩⲱⲉ **64.**28; **83.**12; **131.**14   ϩⲱϥ **84.**19,33; **93.**9   ϩⲱⲥ **94.**24   ϩⲱⲛ **80.**27; **105.**31   ϩⲱⲧⲧⲏⲛⲉ [**61.**27]; **90.**6; **105.**41; **110.**19   ϩⲱⲟⲩ **80.**16; **115.**30
    ϩⲱϥ (invariable) **94.**12
ϩⲱⲃ *send* **67.**16; **78.**40; **84.**31,36; **93.**17
  cstr.: ϩⲱⲃ- **64.**2   ϩⲱϥ- **76.**20   ϩⲁⲃ- **66.**13 **78.**47   ϩⲃ- **99.**54; **110.**15   ϩⲡ- **110.**14
  ϩⲁⲃ⸗ : ϩⲁⲃⲧ [**105.**18]   ϩⲁⲃϥ **102.**5   ϩⲁⲃⲥ **83.**10   ϩⲁϥⲟⲩ **120.**12
ϩⲱⲃ m. *thing (done), matter, task* **57.**17; **58.**13,28,33; **60.**6; **67.**44,60; **71.**20; **73.**14,23; **76.**46; **81.**46; **82.**33,34; **83.**2; **92.**30; **95.**9,11; **99.**51; **102.**6,13; **105.**18; **106.**20,22; **107.**15,18,26; [**108.**6]; **124.**36; **128.**46   with art. ⲫⲱⲃ **77.**20; **82.**23; **92.**24; **128.**33
    pl. ϩⲃⲏⲩⲉ **72.**13; **111.**44   ϩⲃⲏⲩⲟⲩⲉ **71.**24 (ditt. at line break)

ϨⲰⲂ ⲚⲒⲘ *everything* **58**.34; **60**.3; **62**.6; [**65**.7]; **67**.4; **68**.6; [**70**.4]; **71**.4,14,15; **72**.3; **73**.4,21; **76**.6; **77**.3,13; **78**.4; **79**.9; **80**.6,25; **81**.5; **82**.6,35; **89**.1,35; **93**.5; **97**.5; **99**.7; **105**.7,9; **106**.16; **107**.4; **109**.5,25; **110**.5,31; **111**.12,19; **112**.5; **115**.9; **118**.2; **122**.5; **124**.5

 Ⲣ-ϨⲰⲂ *work* **72**.18; [**80**.10]

ϨⲂⲀⲤ *linen, clothes* **75**.30; **81**.22,31,40; **82**.22; **125**.1   ϨⲘⲀⲤ **78**.48

ϨⲒⲈ see ⲈⲒⲈ

ϨⲒⲎ f. *road, path* **127**.2,36

ϨⲀⲒ *trouble, endeavour* :

 Ϯ-ϨⲀⲒ ⲘⲘⲀ⸗ refl. *take trouble, endeavour* **84**.22

ϨⲈⲒ m. *husband* **64**.32; **82**.28

ϨⲀⲒⲦⲈ f. *robe* **58**.35; **71**.32; **79**.29; **94**.34; **97**.34; **109**.33

ϨⲀⲖⲈⲔ *ring, disc* [**65**.23]

ϨⲀⲖϪ (meaning unknown, cf. ϨⲀⲖⲔⲤ **39**.43) **106**.18

ϨⲀⲖⲞ *old person* **68**.47

 f. ϨⲀⲰ **80**.14

ϨⲀⲖⲰⲘ *cheese* **125**.28

(ϨⲖⲀⲘⲖⲀⲘ) *entangle* :

 ϨⲖⲀⲘⲖⲈⲘ nn. m. *complication* **64**.3

(ϨⲖⲀⲠⲖⲈⲠ) *be weary, despondent* :

 stat. ϨⲖⲈⲠⲖⲀⲠⲦ **83**.12

(ϨⲖⲀϬ) *be sweet* :

 stat. ϨⲖⲀϬ **63**.3; **70**.2; **79**.2; **82**.2; [**88**.10]; **93**.2; **99**.3; **105**.3; **112**.3; **115**.3; **122**.1 (in rel. ⲈⲐⲀⲖϬ)

ϨⲚⲖϬⲈ *(something) sweet* (?) **125**.15

ϨⲖϬⲎⲦ *gentle, kind* **85**.5   ϨⲈⲖϬⲎⲦ **58**.22

 ⲘⲚⲦϨⲈⲖϬⲎⲦ f. *kindness* **61**.7

ϨⲘⲈ *forty* **76**.26,31

 ϨⲘⲈ- **76**.22; **105**.35

ϨⲀⲘ m. *craftsman* **103**.39

ϨⲎⲘⲈ f. *fare, freight* **58**.30; **75**.18; **79**.38,39; **81**.35; **92**.29; **96**.34   ϨⲎⲘⲎ **122**.28

ϨⲒⲘⲈ see ⲤϨⲒⲘⲈ

ϨⲀⲘⲀⲒ *would (that ...)!* **90**.6

ϨⲘⲀⲤ(Ⲧ) *sit, stay, remain* : ϨⲘⲀⲤ **82**.40

 stat. ϨⲘⲀⲤⲦ **76**.37 (of things); **111**.38

ϨⲘⲀⲦ m. *grace, gift* **97**.9; **111**.39

 in phraseology with ϢⲰⲠ / ϢⲎⲠ *give thanks* : **72**.33; **76**.45

 (Sah.:) ϨⲘⲞⲦ [**128**.17]

ϨⲀⲘⲦ *copper, bronze, money* **58**.12; **64**.10; **69**.7; **80**.24; **81**.51; **82**.21; **94**.13,51; **95**.9; **105**.27,33; **108**.29; **114**.2,4; **125**.32

ϨⲚ-, ⲚϨⲎⲦ⸗ prep. *in, by* etc.

 ϨⲚ- **61**.11; **62**.13,14,17; **63**.3,20; **65**.12,36; **68**.11; **71**.3,7,7,8; **72**.6,11,15; **73**.3; **76**.25; **79**.3,7,11,42; **80**.2,5,11,14,25; **81**.45; **82**.3,5; **83**.14; **84**.28; **85**.2,3,4; **86**.3,12; **89**.44; **90**.4,7,25; **92**.6; **93**.4; **99**.3; **105**.2,30; **107**.8,10,11,17,25;

109.24; 110.21; 111.4,17,27; 112.3,14; 115.3; 122.2,4,12,12,29; 123.23; 128.41; 131.9 (in rel. ⲉⲑⲛ-) 105.75 ⲍⲙ- 57.3; 60.2,4; 63.15; 65.6; 78.8; 81.4; 83.3; 90.8; 94.58; 95.15; 99.6; 105.6; 115.4,8; 124.4,39; 128.27 ⲛϩⲏⲧ⸗: ⲛϩⲏⲧ 82.10 ⲛϩⲏⲧϥ 76.11; 79.29; 81.53; 122.11 ⲛϩⲏⲧⲥ 72.5; 76.32; 77.10; 78.43; 79.23,23,25; 122.33 ⲛϩⲏⲧⲟⲩ 73.10; 106.42; 110.45

ϩⲛⲉ⸗ *be willing* : ϩⲛⲉⲕ 80.26   ϩⲛⲉϥ 79.39

ϩⲛⲟ m. *vessel, thing* 57.15; 64.10; 69.5,7; 75.42; 76.53; 80.24; 83.10,15; 90.9; 91.4; 102.23; 106.35; 111.10,22   ϩⲛⲉⲩ 65.25; 72.20
    pl. ϩⲛⲁⲩⲉ 64.4; 69.9; 79.25   ϩⲛⲁⲟⲩ 69.2   ϩⲛⲁⲩ 81.45

ϩⲏⲛⲉ f. *cloth, fabric* (?) 58.15,21,23; 70.31

ϩⲓⲛ m. *vessel, cup* (liquid measure) 81.52

ϩⲟⲩⲛ *inside* :
    ⲉⲓ-ϩⲟⲩⲛ *come in* 69.11; 94.57
    adv. ⲁϩⲟⲩⲛ 61.15; 69.4; 84.34; 94.31,38,39   ⲉϩⲟⲩⲛ 128.31
    adv. ⲛϩⲟⲩⲛ 120.20; 122.31

(ϩⲱⲛ) *approach, be near* :
    stat. ϩⲏⲛ 61.7; 63.16; 85.4; 116.8

ϩⲱⲛ *bid, order* 70.16; 90.29,30

(ϩⲉⲛⲉⲧⲉ) f. *monastery* :
    (with art.) ⲑⲁⲛⲉⲧⲁ 123.17 (here? see also at "Geographical names")

ϩⲉⲡ m. *judgment* 73.18

(ϩⲱⲡ) *hide* :
    stat. ϩⲏⲡ 128.27

ϩⲣⲏⲓ *upper part* :
    adv. ϩⲣⲏⲓ *above* (but in verbal idioms) 94.34,39
    adv. ⲁϩⲣⲏⲓ 84.33; 86.18; 91.6; 94.55; 106.11; 116.9; 131.9

ϩⲣⲕⲏⲧ *calm, quiet* 62.2

(ϩⲣⲱⲧ) *child, offspring* :
    ϧⲣⲱⲧ 129.3,5

ϩⲣⲓϥ *take shape* (?) 120.4

ϩⲁⲣⲉϩ *keep, guard* [61.10]; 103.18,43

ϩⲉⲥ m. *dung* 72.17

ϩⲓⲥⲉ *weary, trouble* 58.27; 70.[19],36,40; 90.10; 105.25
    ϩⲓⲥⲉ nn. m. *trouble* 89.31,34

(ϩⲓⲥⲉ) *spin* : ϩⲉⲥ- 103.19
    ϩⲉⲥⲧ⸗: ϩⲉⲥⲧⲥ 103.11,28   ϩⲉⲥⲧⲟⲩ 58.18

ϩⲁⲧⲉ *fear* :
    ⲣ-ϩⲁⲧⲉ *be afraid* 83.7

ϩⲁⲧⲉ *moment* 79.3

ϩⲉⲧ *silver* 125.40

ϩⲏⲧ m. *heart* 63.6; 72.7,14; 80.2,9,11,15,15,23,30; 81.32,49; 83.6,12; 88.4; 89.7; 92.22; 106.7; 107.10; 115.14; 122.30; 128.24
    ϫⲓ-ϩⲏⲧ *take courage* 84.26
    adv. ⲛϩⲏⲧ see ⲙⲧⲁⲛ, ⲡⲱϣⲉ, ⲱⲕ

ϩⲏⲧ *north* :
    adv. ⲛϩⲏⲧ **111.**6

ϩⲏⲧⲉ (for ⲉⲓⲥϩⲏⲧⲉ) **66.**15

ϩⲓⲧⲛ m. (meaning unknown) **94.**36 (cf.? ϩⲓⲧ **46.**2,6)

ϩⲓⲧⲛ-, ϩⲓⲧⲟⲧ⸗ prep. *by* :
    ϩⲓⲧⲛ- **58.**29; **66.**8; **124.**address; **128.**25,28,33
    ϩⲓⲧⲟⲧ⸗ : ϩⲓⲧⲟⲧ **72.**14   ϩⲓⲧⲟⲧⲕ **81.**7
    2nd pl.: ϩⲓⲧⲟⲧⲧⲏⲛⲉ **75.**27   ϩⲓⲧⲛⲧⲏⲛⲉ **90.**28

ϩⲱⲧⲡ *attune, reconcile* **105.**19; **128.**22

(ϩⲱⲧⲣⲉ) *join, fix* : ⲱⲧⲣⲉ- **107.**14

ϩⲟⲩⲟ m. *surplus* **70.**35
    indef. ϩⲟⲩⲟ- *more* **84.**16
    adv. ⲛϩⲟⲩⲟ **105.**39; **119.**24   iterated: **111.**35

ϩⲁⲩ stat. *be bad* **76.**24
    ⲡⲉⲧϩⲁⲩ nn. *evil* **80.**8,13,31   ⲡⲉⲑⲁⲩ **83.**7
    (Sah.:) ⲡⲉⲑⲟⲟⲩ **127.**38

(ϩⲏⲩ) *profit, advantage* : ϩⲏⲟⲩ **83.**14

ϩⲟⲟⲩ m. *day* **58.**5; **63.**43; **75.**26; **77.**16,30; **78.**37; **82.**13; **84.**18,24,28; **86.**12,18; **91.**3,5; **94.**33,56; **95.**9; **102.**7; **110.**25,48; **120.**17; **124.**23   ϩⲱⲟⲩ (with art. ⲫⲱⲟⲩ) **126.**12   ϩⲟⲟⲩⲉ **65.**34; **79.**17; **82.**41; **99.**27
    pl. ϩⲣⲉⲩ **84.**19
    adv. ⲙⲡⲟⲟⲩ *today* **78.**20   ⲡⲟⲟⲩ **110.**26   ⲡⲟⲟⲩⲉ **124.**23

ϩⲱⲟⲩ *rain* :
    ⲙⲟⲩⲛϩⲱⲟⲩ m. *rain water* **124.**26

ϩⲁⲩⲧ *male* **70.**9

ϩⲁϩ (ⲛ-) *much, many* **69.**2; **82.**9; **119.**28

ϩⲁ(ϩ)ⲧⲛ-, ϩⲁ(ϩ)ⲧⲏ⸗ prep. *by the side of, near* :
    ϩⲁⲧⲏⲓ **72.**31; **82.**32   ϩⲁⲧⲏⲕ **65.**29 (with rel. ⲉⲑ.) **71.**21; **81.**46; **103.**3,13; **110.**44; **112.**19; **118.**4 (ⲉⲑ.); **121.**5   ϩⲁⲧⲏ **102.**15   ϩⲁⲧⲏⲛ **80.**32; **84.**19   ϩⲁⲧⲏⲧⲛ **58.**36   ϩⲁⲧⲛⲧⲏⲛⲉ **61.**29

ϫⲉ various conjunctions:
    causal: **57.**11,19; **58.**27; **63.**17,21,31; **64.**32; **67.**18,26; **68.**9,38; **70.**17,44; **71.**24,39; **76.**15,24; **77.**9,14,15,19,22; **79.**16,39; **80.**18,21; **81.**7,11,23,32,40; **82.**12,19,24,37,38,41; **83.**6,13; **84.**14; **86.**9,18; **89.**43; **90.**13,33,44; **92.**23,31; **102.**22; **103.**3,11,46; **105.**24,43; **106.**8,18; **107.**22,23; **110.**11,26; **114.**3,4; **116.**6; **119.**28; **120.**24,30; **124.**21; **126.**22; **128.**24   ϫ- **122.**20   ϫⲁ **122.**23,28,34,35

    discourse introductory (and sim.) **57.**11; **58.**2,5,7,8,15,17,31; **64.**5; **65.**33,34,36; **67.**20; **69.**5; **70.**16,25,36,44; **71.**13,13,18,19,20,23,25,29,32; **72.**14,15,20,22, 26; **73.**8,9,13,15,25; **75.**37; **76.**23,50; **77.**14,18,21,22,23,24; **78.**18,20,22,27, 31,33,50; **79.**14,18,26,31,31,33; **80.**13,14,17,17; **81.**9,12,13,15,26,45,46,54; **82.**13,20,34,36,39; **83.**4,5,10,11,12,15; **84.**6,9,10,12,31; **86.**10,11; **89.**30,32; **90.**11,12,27,31,41,42,43; **92.**9,9,29,32; **93.**8,18; **94.**14,30,36,40,43,44,46,

46,50,54; **95.**8,13; **97.**15; **101.**2,3; **102.**8,15; **103.**7,16,31; **105.**22,29,60,63,80; **106.**23; **107.**13; **108.**23,28,29,36; **110.**23; **111.**5,8,9,23,34; **113.**6; **114.**2; **115.**14,15,25; **121.**2; **123.**6; **128.**17; **131.**2   ⲭⲁ **122.**22,30,31; **129.**11

purpose: **61.**10; **63.**13,46; **64.**7; **73.**23; **91.**4; **103.**12,35; **106.**41; **111.**43; **114.**3; **127.**37   ϫ(ⲉ)- in coalescence with initial ⲉ- **57.**13; **61.**21; **64.**27; **65.**8; **67.**5; **70.**32; **71.**5; **73.**16; **76.**7; **78.**7; **80.**36; **86.**6; **91.**1; **109.**7; **110.**29; **111.**38; **116.**17; **122.**8

ϫⲓ *take, receive* **66.**44; **77.**19; **95.**13; **105.**24; **110.**38; **123.**6

ϫⲓ- **58.**8; **64.**7; **66.**23,45; **70.**30; **71.**32; **72.**11; **75.**7,24,42; **76.**23,35,44; **77.**9,11,21; **78.**28,40,41,50; **79.**28,31,38,41,43; **80.**26; **88.**20; **89.**30,34,37; **90.**[28],31,32; **91.**2; **96.**33,36; **108.**21; **110.**28; **114.**4; **115.**31; **120.**13; **122.**28,32,35

ϫⲓⲧ⸗ : ϫⲓⲧ **115.**27   ϫⲓⲧⲉ **71.**13   ϫⲓⲧϥ **58.**28; **71.**15; **90.**11; **105.**64; **111.**23; **115.**33   ϫⲓⲧⲥ **112.**13   ϫⲓⲧⲟⲩ **58.**13; **71.**33; **75.**12; **79.**27; **110.**27,49; **111.**31; **112.**10

for compounds see ⲙⲕⲁϩ, ϩⲏⲧ

ϫⲟ *send, put forth* : ϫⲱ **122.**28

ϫⲱ *say* **71.**12; **78.**19; **107.**12; **121.**2; **122.**30

ϫⲉ- **114.**6

ϫⲟ(ⲟ)⸗ : ϫⲟϥ **110.**23   ϫⲟⲟϥ **114.**1   ϫⲟⲥ **57.**12; **58.**6; **67.**20; **71.**18,19,20,25,32; **72.**15; **73.**12; **77.**14,23,29; **78.**18; **79.**25,31; **80.**16; **83.**4,15; **86.**10; **94.**45; **95.**10,13; **102.**8; **103.**15; **108.**21; **111.**5,13,34; **113.**4,6; **115.**13,25; **118.**6; **120.**30; **122.**22,30; **131.**2

imp. ⲁϫⲟⲥ **76.**49

(ϫⲱ⸗) *head* :

adv. (ⲛⲥⲁϫⲱ⸗ *headlong?*): ⲛⲥⲁϫⲟ **73.**16

ϫⲁⲃⲁ(ⲁ)ⲧ stat. *be hard* : ϫⲁⲃⲁⲧ **73.**17

ϫⲁïⲥ m. *lord* **57.**3; **60.**2; **61.**5; **64.**25; **65.**1,[6]; **66.**5; **68.**8; **69.**8,10; **70.**2,33; **71.**3; **73.**3; **79.**1,7; **80.**1,5; **81.**1,4; **82.**5; **86.**1,3,6; **89.**3,44; **90.**1,3,4; **92.**6; [**99.**6]; **105.**1,6; **108.**1,5; [**112.**4]; **115.**1,8,42; **118.**3; **122.**4   ϫⲁⲉⲓⲥ **93.**4; **111.**4,18

f. *lady* **65.**40; **71.**28; **88.**7; **115.**24; **122.**9

pl. ϫⲓⲥⲁⲩⲉ **82.**41; **85.**1; **110.**1; **111.**43; **115.**11; **122.**14

(Sah.:) ϫⲟⲉⲓⲥ **123.**23; **124.**4,39; **126.**20,25,30; **128.**48

ϫⲁïⲧ m. *olive* **106.**34

ϫⲓⲧ- (specifier unidentified) **125.**20,21

ϫⲱⲕ *complete, accomplish* **62.**15; **78.**12; **82.**8; **97.**12; **115.**5

ϫⲉⲕⲁⲥ *in order that* **62.**9; **127.**15,36   ϫⲉⲛⲕⲁⲁⲥ **123.**10

ϫⲗⲃⲉ f. (*thing sewn*, so) *cloth bag* (?) **64.**26,30; **70.**30; **76.**44; **77.**19; **79.**19; **122.**32,35   ϫⲏⲗⲃⲉ **88.**20; **115.**31   ϫⲏⲗⲃⲁ **89.**38

(ϫⲱⲙⲉ) m. *book* : ϫⲱⲙ **120.**2 (read ϫⲱⲙ<ⲉ>?)   ϫⲱⲱⲙⲉ **127.**31

ϫⲛ- *or, whether ... or* **83.**12; **84.**11; **93.**18   ϩⲛ- **77.**18,21; **78.**50

ϫⲛ(ⲛ)- prep. *since, from* : ϫⲛ- **72.**35   ϫⲛⲙ- **102.**14; **116.**9   ϫⲛⲛ- (+ clause) **105.**19

(ϫⲛⲟⲩ) *interrogate* : ϫⲛⲟⲩ- **82.**38

ϫⲛⲟⲩ⸗ : ϫⲛⲟⲩϥ **79.**39
ϫⲛⲁϩ *forearm, violence* :
    adv. ⲛϫⲛⲁϩ *violently* **115.**27
(ϫⲧⲟ) *lay low, throw down* :
    ϣⲧⲟ nn. m. *place to lay down* (?) **115.**17; **120.**23
ϫⲁⲩ *send* **102.**11; **120.**14
    ϫⲟⲩ- **120.**35
    ϫⲁⲩ⸗ : ϫⲁⲩϥ **58.**27   ϫⲁⲩⲥ **58.**32; **79.**34   ϫⲁⲩⲥⲉ **104.**2,2,3   ϫⲁⲩⲥⲟⲩ **79.**26
    ϫⲁⲩ ⲁⲃⲁⲗ **71.**34
ϫⲟⲩⲱⲧ *twenty* **76.**62; **81.**21; **105.**34; **123.**13
    ϫⲟⲩⲧ- **79.**24; **81.**42; **90.**37; **94.**44; **95.**6
(ϫⲟⲩϥ) *be costly, rare* :
    stat. ϫⲏϥ **78.**19; **79.**16,19
ϫⲱϩ *touch* **103.**18
ϫⲏϭⲉ *purple (dye)* **66.**15,24; **77.**18; **79.**43; **81.**18,47; **103.**8,24,35,45; **108.**37

ϭⲉ particle (consecutive, adversative) **58.**4,9,21; **64.**5,26; **67.**37; **69.**4; **71.**10,27,29; **72.**12; **73.**6; **77.**9,15; **78.**17,47; **79.**30; **80.**7; **86.**13; **89.**29; **92.**16; **95.**3; **97.**15; **102.**3; **103.**21; **105.**15,46; **107.**16; **108.**26; **109.**19; **110.**22,30; **115.**27; **119.**51; **124.**32; **127.**31,36; **128.**37,39
    adnegative *(not) any more* **99.**54
ϭⲱ *stay, remain* **122.**19
    with Circ. Pres. **83.**7; **115.**36
    (in Neg. Imp.) followed by Circ. Neg. Perf. *(do not) remain without (doing)* **64.**30; **80.**20; **99.**54; **105.**68; **106.**14; **116.**5,14; **120.**22
(ϭⲱⲗ) *roll back, turn down* :
    stat. ϭⲏⲗ **90.**28
ϭⲗⲁⲙ *hasten* :
    adv. ⲛϭⲗⲁⲙ *quickly* **72.**23; **112.**13
ϭⲁⲗⲙ *dry sticks, twigs* **66.**24
ϭⲗⲁⲛⲃⲁⲗ m. *adversity, disaster* **63.**27; **65.**14; **80.**22   ϭⲗⲙⲃⲁⲗ **71.**9
ϭⲱⲗⲡ *disclose, reveal* :
    ϭⲱⲗⲡ ⲉⲃⲁⲗ nn. m. *disclosure, openness* **128.**29
ϭⲁⲗⲁϩⲧ f. *pot* **96.**36,37
ϭⲁⲙ f. *power* **80.**10; **94.**15; **115.**28; **119.**47
    (after ⲟⲩⲛ-/ⲙⲛ-) *possibility* **64.**31; **83.**4; **84.**18; **106.**31; **107.**20
ϭⲁⲛ *low, hollow place* (?) **76.**25
ϭⲓⲛⲉ *find* **66.**7; **103.**14
    ϭⲛ- **58.**15,17; **75.**29; **79.**23,33; **82.**15; **83.**13; **84.**32; **90.**36; **91.**3; **94.**16,60; **105.**26,32; [**107.**11]; **115.**19,34; **116.**14; **122.**26
        for compound see ⲁⲣⲓⲕⲉ
        ϭⲛⲧ⸗ : ϭⲛⲧϥ **102.**12   ϭⲛⲧⲥ **65.**35; **79.**35; **90.**8; **102.**11; **119.**52   ϭⲛⲧⲛ **84.**25   ϭⲛⲧⲟⲩ **58.**10; **81.**54; **105.**40

ϭⲛϭⲱⲣ m. *talent* **58**.4; **78**.21,28; **81**.21,29,36,42; **95**.4,8; **96**.35; **105**.34,35; **110**.10; **120**.32

ϭⲉⲡ (measure of corn?) **105**.76

ϭⲱⲣϩ *night* :
    adv. ⲛϭⲱⲣϩ *at night* **93**.12

ϭⲣⲏϭⲉ f. *dowry* **105**.20

ϭⲁⲥ *half* **77**.23   ⲕⲁⲥ **76**.37
    ϭⲓⲥ- **108**.28

ϭⲁⲟⲩⲁⲛ m. *slave* :
    (Sah.:) ϭⲁⲩⲁⲛ **126**.7,24
    pl. ϭⲃⲁⲛⲉ **129**.8

ϭⲱⲟⲩϣ *trouble* (?) :
    ϭⲁⲩϣ⸗ (refl.): ϭⲁⲩϣⲕ **103**.12

ϭⲱϣⲧ *look* **124**.23; **127**.36
    ϭⲱϣⲧ ⲁⲃⲁⲗ (ϩⲏⲧ⸗) *look out, watch out* [**105**.46]; **124**.29
    stat. ϭⲁϣⲧ **72**.8; **80**.27,36; **124**.25 (ϭⲁϣⲧ{ϥ})

ϭⲓϫ f. *hand* **79**.29; **103**.21,30

ϭⲁϭⲉ *baked loaf, cake* **106**.40

Loan words

ἀγαθός : ⲁⲅⲁⲑⲟⲛ nn. **63**.12
    [ⲙⲛⲧ]ⲁⲅⲁⲑⲟⲥ f. **124**.12

ἀγάπη ⲁⲅⲁⲡⲏ f. <**72**.6>; **82**.9; **85**.4; **112**.14; **124**.14; **127**.20

ἀγαπητός ⲁⲅⲁⲡⲏⲧⲟⲥ m. **122**.2; **123**.24; **124**.42

ἄγγελος ⲁⲅⲅⲉⲗⲟⲥ **124**.27

ἀγγεῖον ⲁⲕⲟⲛ **125**.39   ⲉⲕⲟⲛ **92**.28

(αἰσθάνεσθαι) ⲣ-ⲁⲓⲥⲑⲁⲛⲉ **107**.13

ἀκριβῶς ⲁⲕⲣⲓⲃⲱⲥ [**58**.32]

ἀλλά ⲁⲗⲗⲁ **63**.39; **70**.37,39; **72**.9; **78**.19; **82**.15; **83**.4,6; **92**.12; **94**.17; **106**.29; **107**.14; **111**.29; **115**.21,29

ἀλλότριος *not liable* ⲁⲗⲗⲟⲧⲣⲓⲟⲛ **90**.33,43

ἀμέλεια ⲁⲙⲉⲗⲓⲁ **92**.13

(ἀμελεῖν) *neglect* ⲣ-ⲁⲙⲉⲗⲉⲓ **57**.18; **111**.14,36   (ⲣ-)ⲁⲙⲉⲗⲓ **58**.30,33,34; **76**.52; **78**.18; **79**.14; **113**.2,9; **122**.30; **127**.31   ⲣ-ⲁⲙⲉⲗⲏ **110**.24   (ⲣ-)ⲁⲙⲉⲗⲉ **92**.25; **106**.20

ἀναγκαῖος attr. ⲁⲛⲁⲅⲕⲁⲓⲟⲛ **103**.9

ἀνάγκη ⲁⲛⲁⲅⲕⲏ **99**.23

ἀντιλογία ⲁⲛⲧⲓⲗⲟⲅⲓⲁ **123**.19

ἄξιος ⲁⲝⲓⲟⲥ **128**.14

(ἀξιοῦν) ⲣ-ⲁⲝⲓⲟⲩ **58**.14; **67**.8; **86**.5; **108**.36; **111**.41
(ἀπαντᾶν) ⲣ-ⲁⲡⲁⲛⲧⲁ (+ ⲁ-) *meet, encounter* **99**.19 (comm.); [**103**.36]
ἁπλῶς adv. ϩⲁⲡⲗⲱⲥ **102**.22; **105**.40; **116**.10
ἀπόστολος ⲁⲡⲟⲥⲧⲟⲗⲟⲥ **127**.21
ἀπόφασις ⲁⲡⲟⲫⲁⲥⲓⲥ **76**.42
ἄρα (consequent) ⲁⲣⲁ **122**.35
ἆρα (interrogative) ⲁⲣⲁ **84**.10   ⲁⲣⲉ **114**.2
(ἀρνεῖσθαι) ⲣ-ⲁⲣⲛⲉ **90**.27
(ἀρτάβη) see ⲣⲧⲁⲃ ("Native words")
(ἀσπάζεσθαι) ⲁⲥⲡⲁⲍⲉ **128**.26

βάρβαρος ⲃⲁⲣⲃⲁⲣⲁⲥ **122**.19

γάρ ⲅⲁⲣ **57**.12; **71**.23,25; **72**.6; **75**.23; **77**.13; **78**.20; **80**.12; **83**.11; **89**.35,42; **90**.12; **92**.12; **99**.28
γενεά ⲅⲉⲛⲉⲁ **127**.9; **128**.22
(γίνομαι) μὴ γένοιτο *by no means, God forbid* ⲙⲏ ⲅⲉⲛⲟⲓⲧⲟ **92**.11
γνήσιος ⲅⲛⲏⲥⲓⲟⲥ **85**.5

δέ ⲇⲉ **58**.29; **69**.1; **70**.31,38; **75**.34; **79**.15,42; **84**.29; **85**.4; **93**.8,12; **94**.34,39; **95**.6; **96**.36; **98**.5,8; **103**.6; **104**.2; **110**.25; **111**.35; **112**.14; **115**.13,20,44; **116**.16; **120**.26 **127**.25; **128**.30,32   ⲧⲉ **94**.25; **82**.12; **89**.24
δεῖγμα †ⲕⲙⲁ **58**.16
διάβολος ⲇⲓⲁⲃⲟⲗⲟⲥ **65**.13
διάθεσις ⲇⲓⲁⲑⲉⲥⲓⲥ **85**.4
διάκονος ⲇⲓⲁⲕⲱⲛ **72**.36
διάστημα ⲇⲓⲁⲥⲧⲏⲙⲁ **128**.28
(διστάζειν) ⲇⲓⲥⲧⲁⲍⲉ **106**.7

(ἐγχώριος) ἐγχωρία *possibility (?), custom (?)* ⲉⲅⲭⲟⲣⲏⲓⲁ **128**.18,20
εἰ ⲉⲓ ⲕⲁⲛ **92**.23   ⲉⲓ ⲙⲉⲛ **94**.50; **122**.24
εἰ μήτι ⲉⲓⲙⲏⲧⲓ **72**.7; **79**.34; **107**.21
εἶδος *figure (?), item (?)* ⲉⲓⲇⲟⲥ **70**.24; **80**.24; **81**.48; **125**.6
εἰρήνη ⲉⲓⲣⲏⲛⲏ **62**.12
    ⲙⲛⲧ-ⲧⲁ(ⲓ̈)-ⲉⲓⲣⲏⲛⲏ nn. f. *peace-making (character)* **90**.13; **105**.68
εἴτε ⲉⲓⲧⲉ ... ⲉⲓⲧⲉ **63**.35; **69**.7; **70**.8; **94**.17; **105**.52,59; **122**.11/12
ἐκκλησία ⲉⲕⲕⲗⲏⲥⲓⲁ **62**.14; **73**.17
ἐλπίς ⲉⲗⲡⲓⲥ **81**.45
ἐπειδή ⲉⲡⲉⲓⲇⲏ **115**.16   ⲉⲡⲓⲇⲏ **69**.2; **72**.9; **73**.[7],15; **103**.15; **107**.14; **111**.5,33
(ἐπιβουλή) pl. ⲉⲡⲓⲃⲟⲗⲗⲁⲅⲉ **65**.12
(ἐπιγεμίζειν) ⲣ-ⲉⲡⲓⲅⲉⲙ̅ **111**.43
(ἐπικαλεῖν) ⲉⲡⲓⲕⲁⲗⲓ **126**.19
ἐπίσκοπος ⲉⲡⲓⲥⲕⲟⲡⲟⲥ **128**.34

ἐπιστολή ⲉⲡⲓⲥⲧⲟⲗⲏ 66.28; 75.21,24; 77.9,11; 80.33; 81.8; 84.38; 90.8; 91.2;
   93.14 105.80; 106.27; 108.24; 110.35,47; 120.13; 123.21; 128.15
   pl. ⲉⲡⲓⲥⲧⲟⲗⲁⲩⲉ [67.13]
εὐαγγέλιον ⲉⲩⲁⲅⲅⲉⲗⲓⲟⲛ 98.21; 120.4
εὐεργέτης in ⲙⲛⲧ-ⲉⲩⲉⲣⲅⲉⲧⲏⲥ *beneficence* 128.41/42
εὐκαιρία ⲉⲩⲕⲁⲓⲣⲓⲁ 106.38
εὐχή ⲉⲩⲭⲏ 66.7
ἕως ϩⲉⲱⲥ 82.34

ζιζουλά (cf. ζίζυφον) *jujube* ⲥⲓⲥⲟⲩⲡⲉ 65.32

ἤ ⲏ 58.3,17; 70.44; 78.35; 84.20; 92.32; 94.33; 105.27; 119.45
ἠλακάτη *distaff* ϩⲁⲗⲁⲕⲁⲧⲓ 58.27

(θαρσεῖν / θαρρεῖν) *be confident* ⲑⲁⲣⲣⲉ 122.10   ⲣ-ⲑⲁⲣⲉ 81.14
(θαυμάζειν) *be astonished* ⲣ-ⲑⲁⲩⲙⲁⲍⲉ 75.19; 81.6   ⲣ-ⲑⲁⲩⲙⲁⲍⲏ 122.20
(θεραπεύειν) ⲑⲉⲣⲁⲡⲉⲩⲉ 82.26
θώραξ ⲑⲱⲣⲁⲝ 58.23

ἵνα ϩⲓⲛⲁⲥ 127.37
(ἱστάναι?) ⲉⲥⲧⲁⲧⲟⲩ 130.2 (unclear)

(καθαρὸς ἄρτος) *(fine) white bread* ⲕⲁⲑⲁⲣⲟⲛ 122.33
(καθιέναι) ⲕⲁⲑⲏ ⲁⲃⲁⲗ 102.24
καὶ ταῦτα *although* ⲕⲁⲓⲧⲁⲩⲧⲁ 83.12   ⲉϭⲉⲧⲁⲩⲧⲉ 76.24
καιρός ⲕⲁⲓⲣⲟⲥ 71.6; 99.44
κακῶς adv. ⲕⲁⲕⲱⲥ 92.32
κάλαθος *(wicker band) basket* ⲕⲁⲗⲁⲧⲟⲩⲥ 78.43
κάλαμος *reed(s), reed-pipe* ⲕⲁⲗⲁⲙⲟⲛ 79.20
(καλός in formula καλῇ πίστει) ⲕⲁⲗⲏ ⲡⲓⲥⲧⲓⲥ *in good faith* 92.18
καλῶς adv. ⲕⲁⲗⲱⲥ 75.31; 82.33; 92.32
κἄν (protatic inconditional) *even if* ⲕⲁⲛ 70.37; 92.13,23; 100.3
   (apodotic) *at least* ⲕⲁⲛ 116.6
καρύα / κάρυον *nut* ⲕⲁⲣⲁⲩ 112.9 (comm.)
κατά ⲕⲁⲧⲁ 60.4; 61.5,12; 64.1,24; 65.30,47; 66.12; 70.34,45; 71.2,31; 72.32;
   75.6; 76.4,44; 78.16; 79.37; 80.29,30,37; 84.4; 90.41; 93.25; 94.5,11; 96.29;
   100.1; 102.19; 105.76; 112.19; 119.49; 122.14; 124.7; 128.43
(κλωστήρ) *thread, yarn* ⲕⲗⲱⲥⲧⲣⲁ 111.36
κολλάριον (Latin *collarium*) ⲕⲟⲗⲗⲁⲣⲓⲟⲛ 103.39
κόσμος ⲕⲟⲥⲙⲟⲥ 81.45
*κοῦς see χοῦς

(λαβίς / λαβή) *trap* (?), *catch* (?) (always *of fish*, see comm. ad **76.31**) ⲗⲁⲃⲏⲥ 76.31;
   78.43; 79.41; 109.34

λάσιον *rough cloth* ⲗⲁⲥⲓⲛ **103**.23

λέσχη *gossip, scandal* ⲗⲉⲥⲭⲏ **106**.12

(λοιπόν / τὰ λοιπά) *remainder* (or adv.) ⲗⲟⲓⲡⲉ **94**.31

(λυπεῖσθαι) ⲣ-ⲗⲩⲡⲏ **68**.36; **70**.34; **79**.39; **81**.10; **83**.4; **124**.10

λύπη f. ⲗⲩⲡⲏ **63**.29; **80**.11; **81**.32; [**105**.23]

μακάριος ⲙⲁⲕⲁⲣⲓⲟⲥ **124**.32; **128**.33

μάλιστα adv. *most of all, especially* ⲙⲁⲗⲓⲥⲧⲁ **64**.25; **71**.3; **80**.32; **81**.9; **83**.3; **84**.8; **91**.4; **94**.5; **102**.20; **122**.15; **128**.13

(μέλαν / μελάνιον) *ink* ⲙⲉⲗⲁ **79**.41   ⲙⲉⲗⲁⲛⲓⲟⲛ **78**.42

μέν ⲙⲉⲛ **72**.3; **76**.16; **78**.4; **85**.3; **92**.7; **93**.14; **94**.50; **95**.7; **107**.9; **111**.28; **121**.1; **122**.24; **128**.27

(μεριμνᾶν) (ⲣ-)ⲙⲉⲣ **81**.20,39; **98**.24; **103**.38; **105**.76; **120**.28

μέρος *portion, share* ⲙⲉⲣⲟⲥ **90**.31,32; **103**.33; **110**.14

μετέωρος *haughty, proud* ⲙⲉⲧⲉⲱⲣⲟⲥ **128**.19

μή ⲙⲏ (interrogative) **82**.37; **122**.31

   in ⲙⲏ ⲅⲉⲛⲟⲓⲧⲟ **92**.11

μήπως conjunction/adverb

   ⲙⲏⲡⲱⲥ + Conjunctive *lest* **61**.21

   ⲙⲏⲡⲱⲥ + negated clause *never* **103**.13

   ⲙⲏⲡⲱⲥ + Circumst. Aff. Perf. *perhaps* **106**.11

μνᾶ (measure) ⲙⲛⲁ **58**.24,25; **81**.47; **96**.33,35; **103**.8,34; **109**.13,35   ⲙⲙⲛⲁ **75**.8; **78**.42,44; **79**.32,38; **94**.45; **95**.6; [**105**.28]   ⲛⲙⲁ (here?) **108**.25

μόνον adv. ⲙⲟⲛⲟⲛ *just, only* (preceding imp.) **103**.27; **105**.68

νεᾶνις *girl, female servant* ⲛⲉⲁ f. **69**.9

νομισμάτιον (coin) ⲛⲟⲙⲓⲥⲙⲁⲧⲓⲟⲛ m. **78**.50   N° **130**.4

νόμος *law* ⲛⲟⲙⲟⲥ **77**.16; **127**.18

νοῦμμος (L. *nummus*) ⲛⲟⲩⲙⲟⲥ **79**.24   ⲛⲟⲩⲙⲓⲥ **78**.27   ⲛⲟⲩⲙⲥ **110**.9

ξέστης (measure) ⳉⲉⲥⲧⲏⲥ **81**.51

ὁλοκοττινος ϩⲟⲗⲟⲕⲟⲧⲓⲛⲟⲥ **90**.28,30,32,36,40,40,41; **109**.30; **119**.25
   ϩⲟⲗⲟⲕⲟⲧⲓ **105**.27   ϩⲟⲗⲟⲅⲟⲧⲓⲛⲟⲥ **123**.7   ϩⲁⲗⲟⲕⲟⲧⲓⲛⲟⲥ **109**.20

ὅλως adv. ⲟⲗⲱⲥ **70**.26,44

ὁμολογεῖν [ⲣ-]ϩⲟⲙⲟⲗⲟⲅⲓ **123**.5

ὁμολογία *agreement* ϩⲟⲙⲟⲗⲟⲅⲓⲁ f. **90**.29,42

ὅμως *nevertheless* ϩⲟⲙⲱⲥ **84**.13

ὅσον *while* ϩⲟⲥⲟⲛ **102**.22

οὐδέ / οὔτε ⲟⲩⲧⲉ **58**.29; **70**.29; **84**.7,7; **103**.46; **105**.19; **122**.21

οὖν ⲟⲩⲛ **64**.3; **86**.14; **103**.43; **105**.30

οὐσία *substance (of quarrel)* ⲟⲩⲥⲓⲁ **90**.25

πάλιν (+ ⲟⲛ S) ⲡⲁⲗⲓⲛ **128**.17

παρά **ⲡⲁⲣⲁ-** **105**.9
   with bare noun (for **ⲕⲁⲧⲁ-**?) **103**.33
(πᾶς) **ⲡⲁⲛⲧⲱⲛ** (as modifier) **118**.4
πάσχα **ⲡⲁⲥⲭⲁ** m. **86**.13
(πείθειν) **ⲡⲓⲑⲉ** **73**.13; **119**.63
(πείθεσθαι) **ⲡⲓⲑⲉ** **73**.15,18; **78**.24; **80**.19; **105**.55
(πειράζειν) **ⲡⲓⲣⲁⲍⲉ** **127**.35
πειρασμός **ⲡⲓⲣⲉⲥⲙⲟⲥ** **71**.8
πίστις (in formula καλῇ πίστει) **ⲕⲁⲗⲏ ⲡⲓⲥⲧⲓⲥ** *in good faith* **92**.18
πλεκτή (twisted material) **ⲡⲗⲉⲧⲓ** **75**.11
πλήν **ⲡⲗⲏⲛ** **70**.21
πνεῦμα **ⲡⲛⲉⲩⲙⲁ** [**65**.11]; **78**.10; **89**.6; **90**.2   (π. = π-π.) **71**.8
   ⲡ̄ⲛ̄ⲁ **79**.12; **105**.2
πολιτεία **ⲡⲟⲗⲓⲧⲓⲁ** **61**.13
πραιπόσιτος (L. *praepositus*) **ⲡⲣⲉⲡⲟⲥⲓ** **127**.37
πρᾶξις (in book title of *Acts*) **ⲛⲓⲡⲣⲁⲝⲉⲓⲥ** **120**.3
πρεσβύτερος **ⲡⲣⲉⲥⲃⲩⲧⲉⲣⲟⲥ** **61**.2; **92**.34; **124**.1   **ⲡⲣ** **124**.address
(προκοπή / προκόπτων) *progress* **ⲡⲣⲟⲕⲟⲡⲧⲱⲛ** **81**.25
πρός **ⲡⲣⲟⲥ-** **96**.35
πρόφασις **ⲡⲣⲟⲫⲁⲥⲓⲥ** **128**.25
πῶς **ⲡⲱⲥ** [**60**.6 comm.]; **70**.16,25; **110**.5

(σησαμῆ / σήσαμον) *(cake made of?) sesame* **ⲥⲟⲩⲥⲏⲙⲏ** f. **125**.41
σκέμμα *problem, speculation* **ⲥⲕⲁⲙⲙⲁ** **105**.30
σπουδή **ⲥⲡⲟⲩⲇⲏ** **58**.32; **103**.24
(στιχάριον) **ⲥⲧⲓⲭⲁ** **75**.14,41; **78**.45; [**96**.18]
συντομία **ⲥⲩⲛⲧⲟⲙⲓⲁ** **107**.17
σῶμα **ⲥⲱⲙⲁ** **63**.15; **65**.10; **71**.7; **78**.9; **80**.14; **85**.3; **97**.12; **111**.27; **115**.5
   ⲥⲱⲙⲉ **90**.8
σωτήρ **ⲥⲱⲧⲏⲣ** **126**.18

τάχα *perhaps* **ⲧⲁⲭⲁ** **82**.37; **103**.39; **105**.26; **115**.34
(τάχα / ταχύς) ταχύ adv. *quickly* **ⲧⲁⲭⲩ** **78**.46; **84**.31; **106**.15,17   **ⲧⲉⲭⲩ** **102**.18
τετράς *quaternio* (?) **ⲧⲉⲧⲣⲁⲥ** **111**.6,12
τιμή *price* **ⲧⲓⲙⲏ** **65**.32; **81**.18
τότε **ⲧⲟⲧⲉ** **105**.40
τριβοῦνος (L. *tribunus*) **ⲧⲣⲓⲃⲟⲩⲛⲟⲥ** **118**.8

ὑποδιάκονος **ϩⲩⲡⲟⲇⲓⲁⲕⲟⲛⲟⲥ** **124**.40
ὑπόκρισις **ϩⲩⲡⲟⲕⲣⲓⲥⲓⲥ** **128**.24,40

(φύσις) φύσει adv. **ⲫⲩⲥⲉⲓ** **84**.20

χαίρειν ⲭⲁⲓⲣⲉⲓⲛ 57.3; 60.2; 61.5; 62.5; [65.6]; 66.6; 67.3; 68.5; 70.3; 71.4; 73.3; 76.5; 79.8; 81.4; 82.5; 92.6; 93.4; 97.4; 99.6; 105.6; 108.5; 111.4,18; 112.5; 115.8; 122.4; 124.4; [128.3]   ⲭⲁⲓⲣⲉ 80.5
χαλκεῖον *caldron* ⲭⲁⲗⲕⲩ 81.51
(χαρίζεσθαι) ⲭⲁⲣⲓⲍⲉ 128.20
χάρτης *papyrus (sheet)* ⲭⲁⲣⲧⲏⲥ 78.17,40; 79.13
(χοῦς) (liquid measure) ⲕⲟⲩⲥ 70.17; 86.8; 122.18; 123.14,15
χρεία ⲭⲣⲉⲓⲁ 86.9   ⲭⲣⲓⲁ 58.9,12; 90.26; 123.9
    (verbal usage:) *be short of, need* ⲭⲣⲓⲁ 57.19; 92.30   ⲣ-ⲭⲣⲓⲁ 67.58
χώρα ⲭⲱⲣⲁ 130.2
χωρίς ⲭⲱⲣⲓⲥ 82.9; 90.9; 105.35

ψυχή ⲯⲩⲭⲏ 63.44; [65.12]; 71.7; 78.9; 79.11; 80.3; 85.2,7; 88.3; 89.5; 90.2; 105.2; 107.8

ὦ (vocative) ⲱ 124.32
ὡς ϩⲱⲥ (+ circ.) 77.36; 127.35

Greek words in Greek context

ἀγαπητός **106**.address,1; **111**.address; **123**.1; **124**.address
ἀδελφή **71**.address; **75**.address; **92**.address; **95**.1; **115**.address; **116**.address
ἀδελφός **59**.address,1; **64**.address (*bis*); **66**.address (*bis*); **72**.1; **73**.address; **74**.address; **77**.address,2; **80**.address; **81**.address; **82**.address; **84**.address (*bis*),1,2,41; **86**.address (*bis*); **88**.address (*bis*); **94**.1,2; **95**.1; **97**.address; **103**.address (*bis*); **105**.address (*bis*); **106**.address (*bis*),2,4; **111**.address; **115**.address; **116**.address; **118**.1,1; **123**.1
ἀπό **77**.address
ἀποδίδωμι (in address: *deliver to*) απ´ **65**.address; **67**.address; **68**.address; **71**.address; **76**.address; **93**.address (?); **99**.address; **102**.address; **109**.address

δεσπότης **72**.address,1; **79**.address; **87**.1; **110**.address; **115**.address

ἐγώ **59**.address; **60**.address; **66**.address (*bis*); **71**.address; **72**.address,1; **75**.address,44; **77**.1; **78**.address,1; **79**.address; **80**.address; **81**.address; **82**.address; **84**.address; **84**.1; **86**.address; **87**.1; **88**.address; **89**.address; **90**.address; **92**.address,40; **94**.1; **95**.1; **99**.address; **103**.address,1; **105**.address; **107**.2; **110**.address; **113**.address; **115**.address; **116**.address,21; **118**.1; **123**.address
εἰς **73**.address
ἐν **72**.2; **77**.2; **78**.3; **92**.40; **123**.4
εὔχομαι **65**.49; **75**.44; **84**.39; **103**.50; **107**.32; **108**.35; **112**.20; **113**.13; **116**.20

θεός (in ἐν θεῷ) θω̄ **72**.2

καί **61**.address; **72**.1; **78**.address
κυρία **71**.address; **75**.address,44; **89**.address; **92**.address; **95**.1
κύριος **59**.address,1; **78**.1; **80**.address; **81**.address; **84**.41; **90**.address; **94**.1; **99**.address; **66**.address; **77**.address,1; **78**.address; **82**.address; **84**.address,1; **86**.address; **88**.address; **92**.41; **103**.address,1,51; **105**.address; **113**.address; **116**.address,21; **118**.1; **123**.address
   κω̄ **77**.2; **87**.4; **123**.4   κω̄ι **78**.3

μήτηρ **60**.address; **89**.address

ὁ **59**.address,1; **60**.address; **64**.address; **66**.address; **71**.address; **72**.address,1; **73**.address; **74**.address; **77**.1 (*bis*),2; **78**.address,1; **79**.address; **86**.address; **88**.address; **89**.address; **90**.address (*bis*); **94**.2; **95**.1 (*bis*); **103**.address,1; **105**.address; **106**.address (*bis*),1,4; **107**.1; **109**.address; **110**.address; **111**.address; **115**.address (*bis*); **116**.address; **118**.1; **123**.1

παρά **109**.address
πατήρ **78**.address,2; **79**.address; **87**.2; **90**.address; **103**.1,51
πολύς (πολλός) **65**.49; **75**.44; **84**.40; **103**.50; **107**.33; **108**.35; **112**.20; **116**.20

ῥώννυμι (ἐρρῶσθαι) **65**.48; **75**.43; **84**.38; **92**.39; **103**.49; **107**.31; **108**.34; **112**.20; **113**.13; **116**.19
   abbr. ερρ/ **58**.20; **75**.40; **82**.40; **86**.22; **102**.21; **105**.83   ερ/ **91**.6; **94**.61; **95**.18; **106**.43

σύ **60**.address; **64**.address; **65**.49; **66**.address; **74**.address; **75**.44; **77**.2; **84**.39; **88**.address; **90**.address; **103**.50; **105**.address; **107**.32; **108**.35; **112**.20; **113**.13; **115**.address; **116**.address,19
συμβία **109**.address (συν-)

τίμιος (τιμιώτατος) **60**.address; **73**.address; **78**.address; **87**.2; **107**.1

υἱός **60**.address; **90**.address; **103**.1; **107**.1; **110**.address

χαίρω (χαίρειν) **59**.3; **72**.2; **77**.2; **78**.3; **84**.2; **87**.4; **94**.2; **95**.1; **103**.1; **107**.3; **118**.2; **123**.4

χρόνος **65**.50; **75**.44; **84**.40; **103**.51; **107**.33; **108**.35; **112**.20; **116**.21

ψυχή **77**.1

Personal names*

Ἀγαθήμερος **124.**address,2
ⲁⲙⲁ see ⲑⲉⲟⲇⲱⲣⲁ, ⲧⲁⲡϣⲁⲓ̈, ⲧⲁⲧⲟⲩ
ⲁⲙⲙⲱⲛ **115.**31; **128.**44   ⲁⲙⲙⲱⲛⲓ **118.**7   (ⲁ)ⲙⲟⲛⲓ **129.**6
ⲁⲛⲇⲣⲉⲁⲥ **65.**4; **71.**3; **73.**4; **78.**41; **79.**6; **84.**17; **86.**22; **92.**34; **96.**34; **105.**4;
    111.28,40; **115.**44; (**118.** frg, see "Preservation")   ⲁⲛⲇⲣⲉⲁⲛⲧⲓ **107.**2
    ⲁⲛⲇⲣⲉⲁ **59.**2; **88.**address; **105.**address
ⲁⲛⲧⲓⲛⲟⲩ **78.**40; **79.**22; **94.**8
ⲁⲡⲁ see Βησᾶς, Λυσίμαχος, ⲯⲉⲕⲉ
(Ἀπόλλων) ⲁⲡⲟⲗⲗⲱⲛⲓ **81.**28   ⲡⲟⲗⲗⲱⲛ **76.**59; **83.**10; **112.**22
(Ἀσκλήπιος) ⲁⲥⲕⲗⲏⲡⲓ **77.**19

(Βελλῆς) ⲃⲁⲗⲉ **94.**29; **118.**6
ⲃⲏⲥ **71.**33
Βησᾶς **123.**3 (-ατος); **124.**1
    ⲁⲡⲁ ⲃⲏⲥⲁⲥ **124.**address

ⲅⲉⲛⲁ **117.**1   ⲓⲉⲛⲁ **80.**38; **90.**3; **91.**1; **105.**79; **118.**5   ⲓⲉⲛⲉ **94.**7

ⲇⲣⲟⲩⲥⲓⲟⲥ **61.**29
ⲇⲱⲣⲟⲑⲉⲁ **80.**34
(Δωρόθεος) ⲇⲟⲣⲟⲑⲉⲟⲥ **107.**3

ⲉⲓⲣⲏⲛⲏ **105.**81
ⲉⲩⲧⲩⲭⲟⲥ **93.**10

(Ζώσιμος) ⲍⲱⲥⲓⲙⲉ **80.**33,38

(Ἡρακλῆς) ⲏⲣⲁⲕⲗⲉⲓ **58.**22; [**81.**37 (? see comm.)]

ⲑⲁⲣⲣⲏ **58.**18
ⲑⲉⲟⲅⲛⲱⲥⲧⲟⲥ **70.**5; **73.**5; **78.**13; **79.**4; **83.**2   ⲑⲉⲟⲅⲛⲱⲥⲧⲉ **80.**3,38
    ⲑⲉⲟⲅⲛⲱⲥ **65.**3; **73.**20   ⲑⲉⲟⲅⲛⲟⲥ **67.**7
    Θεόγνωστος **84.**address,2   Θεογνώστωι **72.**2; **80.**address; **81.**address
ⲑⲉⲟⲇⲱⲣⲁ : ⲁⲙⲁ ⲑⲉⲟⲇⲱⲣⲁ **80.**34
ⲑⲉⲟⲇⲱⲣⲟⲥ **92.**35; **93.**22

ⲓⲉⲛⲁ see ⲅⲉⲛⲁ
(Ἱέραξ) ⲓⲉⲣⲝ **113.**7
ⲓ̈ⲟ **66.**36
ⲓⲁⲛⲟⲩ **94.**8
ⲓⲏⲥⲟⲩⲥ **61.**10
ⲓⲙⲟⲩⲑⲏⲥ **129.**9
ⲓⲥⲓⲱⲛ **80.**18,20,28

---

* Name forms in Greek script stand for occurrences in Greek context (mainly addresses).

ⲓⲱⲥⲏⲫ 123.2

ⲕⲁⲙⲏ 95.2

Καπίτων : Καπιτωνι **77**.address,[1]   Καπιτος **109**.address
  ⲕⲁⲡⲓⲧⲱⲛ **70**.15; **72**.25; **77**.5,29; **82**.17; **86**.7; **116**.11   ⲕⲁⲡⲓⲇⲱⲛ **108**.36
  ⲕⲁⲡⲓⲧⲟⲩ **65**.31,37; **75**.37; **81**.7; **110**.50   ⲕⲉⲡⲓⲧⲟⲩ **88**.6

ⲕⲗⲁⲩⲇⲓⲟⲥ 92.35

ⲕⲟⲗⲟⲩⲑⲟⲥ 94.29

Κυρα **92**.address   ⲕⲩⲣⲁ **92**.1; **93**.13

(Κυρία) ⲃⲟⲩⲣⲓⲁ **68**.30; **82**.27

ⲕⲩⲣⲓⲗⲗⲁ 93.19

ⲕⲩⲣⲟⲥ 84.34

Λάμμων : Λαμμωνι **106**.address,3
  ⲗⲁⲙⲙⲱⲛ **72**.30; **77**.6; **78**.44; **94**.27; **116**.13; **122**.32   ⲗⲁⲙⲱⲛ **65**.47; **120**.3
  ⲗⲁⲙⲟⲩ **99**.54   see also Φιλλάμμων

ⲗⲁⲙⲡⲟⲩ 79.38   ⲗⲁⲙⲡⲉ 89.14

(Λαύτινος) ⲗⲁⲩ† **58**.6; **83**.15

ⲗⲟ (probably short for Ταπολλῶς) **64**.23; **65**.43; **70**.42,44; **88**.15,26,29; **103**.38; **108**.36

ⲗⲟⲅⲓϣⲁⲓ **95**.18; **81**.2   ⲗⲓⲟⲩϣⲁⲓ **65**.3   ⲗⲱⲓϣⲁⲓ **82**.address

Λουιωρος **123**.3 (and cf. address)

ⲗⲟⲩⲧⲟⲩ 119.62

Λυσίμαχος : ⲁⲡⲁ ⲗⲩⲥⲓⲙⲁⲭⲟⲥ **82**.38
  ⲁⲡⲁ ⲗ/ **72**.35 (see comm.)

ⲗⲱⲓⲍⲁⲧ 92.2; 93.20

ⲙⲁⲣⲑⲁ 68.22; 89.13

ⲙⲁⲣⲓⲁ 65.39; 66.21,42; 70.14; 71.26,27; 76.47; 77.35; 115.12,14,37; 116.12
  ⲙⲁⲣⲓⲉ 64.19

ⲙⲁⲥⲓ 122.3,27

ⲙⲁⲥⲟⲩⲣ 103.23

ⲛⲟⲉ 71.22

ⲛⲟⲛⲛⲁ 92.20; 98.25; 115.17,30

ⲛⲟⲥ 89.40

ⲟⲗⲃⲓⲛⲟⲥ 88.24; 111.8,15

Οὐάλης [**59**.2]

ⲡⲁⲓⲁⲥ 90.3

ⲡⲁⲕⲟⲩⲥ 77.12; 122.29,34,35

ⲡⲁⲙⲟⲩⲛ 102.3

Παμοῦρ(ις) :   Παμοῦρ **64**.address; **66**.address; **67**.address; **70**.[address]; **72**.address,2; **75**.address; **120**.address   Παμοῦρι **110**.address
  ⲡⲁⲙⲟⲩⲣ **65**.5; **66**.4; **67**.1; **69**.1; **70**.[3]; **71**.1; **76**.44,47; **77**.13,35; **80**.9; **82**.31; **110**.2,44

ⲠⲀⲚⲦⲰⲚⲒ **94.**20
ⲠⲀⲠⲚⲞⲨⲦⲈ **78.**49; **79.**38; **80.**31; **91.**3; **122.**20
ⲠⲀⲢⲐⲈⲚⲒ **70.**9; **71.**2,28,32; **95.**1; **117.**3   ⲠⲀⲢⲐⲈⲚⲈ **64.**18
   Παρθενι **76.**address; **102.**address   Παρθενει **71.**address   Παρθενε **75.**address,[44]
see also ϨⲈⲚⲒ
ⲠⲀⲦⲨⲤⲈ **70.**15
ⲠⲀⲨⲎⲤⲈ **78.**29
ⲠⲈⲂⲞ **61.**4; **66.**8,10,25,45,46; **111.**3; **120.**15,28   ⲠⲀⲂⲞ **111.**34; **120.**7
   (Πεβῶς) Πεβος **111.**address   Πεβο **61.**address
ⲠⲈⲚⲀ **89.**12,33
ⲠⲈϬⲰϢ **65.**2,41,51; **66.**3; **73.**2; **75.**1,41; **79.**6; **80.**9; **86.**21; **103.**address,5,7, 44;
   108.3; **109.**31   ⲠⲀϬⲰϢ **67.**2,17,28,46; **68.**24; **69.**1; **76.**address,1,45;
   82.30; **110.**[2],6
   Πεκῦσις **74.**address; **75.**address; **77.**address,2; **78.**address,3   Πεκυσι **66.**address
     Πακυσι **67.**address   Πεκυσιος **79.**address   Πεκως **120.**address
ⲠⲒⲈⲚⲀ **97.**13; **105.**[10],77; **115.**12
   Πιενα **88.**address; **89.**address
ⲠⲒⲚⲈ **73.**18; **96.**37; **105.**5   ⲠⲒⲚⲒ **83.**4
ⲠⲒϢⲀⲒ **109.**34
(Πλουσίανος) ⲠⲖⲞⲨⲤⲒⲀⲚⲈ **67.**29; **80.**32,38; **92.**26
Πλουτογένης **85.**address; **90.**address
   ⲠⲖⲞⲨⲦⲞⲄⲈⲚⲎⲤ **86.**2; **87.**3; **88.**4; **89.**8   ⲠⲖⲞⲦⲞⲄⲈⲚⲎⲤ **89.**18
Πλουτογένιος : Πλουτογενιωι **61.**address
   ⲠⲖⲞⲨⲦⲞⲄⲈⲚⲒⲞⲤ **61.**3
ⲠⲀⲚⲈ **75.**13
ⲠⲞⲖⲖⲰⲚ see Ἀπόλλων
ⲠⲞⲦⲦⲎⲤ (?) **110.**48 (uncertain reading)
ⲠϢⲀⲒ **57.**3; **62.**22; **64.**2,25,26,30; **65.**2,28; **66.**18,35; **67.**7; **70.**2,33; **71.**17,19,31;
   72.12,24,35; **73.**2; **77.**7,29; **78.**47; **79.**5,30,42; **80.**29; **82.**21; **85.**7; **86.**1;
   92.33; **95.**16; **96.**27; **98.**28; **99.**14; **103.**31; **105.**5,32; **108.**4,20; **111.**2,17,26;
   112.4; **114.**3,7; **115.**6; **118.**5; **122.**3
   Ψάϊς **74.**address; **75.**address; **78.**14; **102.**address; **105.**address; **110.**address
     dat.: Ψάϊτι **59.**2; **84.**address,1; **86.**address; **111.**address; **116.**address; (**118.** frg,
       see "Preservation")   Ψαϊω **64.**address; **70.**address; **72.**address,1; **115.**address
ⲠϢⲀⲘⲠⲈ (?) **127.**30 (see comm.)
ⲠϢⲘⲚⲞⲨⲦⲈ see Ψεμνούθης
ⲠϤⲒϨⲀⲘ (?) **73.**20

ⲤⲀⲢⲀⲠⲀ **122.**3,27   ⲤⲀⲢⲀⲠⲒ **122.**15
Σαραπάμμων (?) : [Σαρα]παμμωνι **93.**address
ⲤⲀⲢⲎⲚ **58.**21
ⲤⲀⲦⲀⲚⲀⲤ : ⲠⲤⲀⲦⲀⲚⲀⲤ **65.**14   ⲠⲤⲀⲢⲦⲀⲚⲀⲤ **71.**9
ⲤⲦⲈⲪⲀⲚⲞⲤ **124.**address
Σύρος : Σύρωι [**87.**3]

ⲥⲟⲩⲣⲉ **87.**5; **90.**39

ⲧⲁⲃⲏⲥ **116.**13
    Ταβης **89.**address,11
ⲧⲁⲗⲁⲫⲁⲛⲧⲓ **58.**19
ⲧⲁⲗⲟⲩ **93.**2
(Ταπολλῶς) see ⲗⲟ
ⲧⲁⲡϣⲁⲓ̈ **65.**44,48; **67.**34; **68.**28,29; **85.**9; **115.**24
    ⲁⲙⲁ ⲧⲁⲡϣⲁⲓ̈ **80.**35
    Τεψαϊς **116.**address
ⲧⲁⲧⲟⲩ : ⲁⲙⲁ ⲧⲁⲧⲟⲩ **80.**34
ⲧⲁⲧⲱⲙ (thus?) **93.**20
ⲧⲁϩⲱⲙ **109.**21
ⲧⲁϩⲱⲣ **89.**14
ⲧⲁϭⲟϣⲉ **64.**22; **67.**33; **75.**38; **78.**44,49; **83.**2; **96.**18; **120.**31
    ⲧⲉϭⲟϣⲉ **115.**7
    Τεκυσι **115.**address   (here?) ⲧⲉϭⲥⲟⲅⲓⲥ (uncertain reading) **109.**address
Τεκῦσις see ⲧⲁϭⲟϣⲉ
Τεψαϊς see ⲧⲁⲡϣⲁⲓ̈
(Τιβέριος) ⲧⲓⲃⲉⲣⲓ **76.**41
ⲧⲓⲙⲟⲑⲉⲟⲥ **90.**5,10; **92.**address,2
    ⲧⲓⲙⲟⲑⲉ **93.**11,[frg]
†ⲧⲟⲩⲉ **70.**43; **72.**31; **77.**14,17; **116.**13
ⲧⲓⲱⲗⲁ (uncertain, possibly toponym) **89.**41
ⲧⲛⲁϩⲧⲉ **94.**37
(Τρυφάνης) ⲧⲣⲟⲩⲫⲁⲛⲏ **78.**36
ⲧⲱⲛⲓ **112.**21   ⲧⲱⲛⲉ **78.**41
ⲧⲱϣⲛⲃⲏⲥ **115.**39

Φιλάμμων **80.**address; **81.**address; **82.**address
    ⲫⲓⲗⲁⲙⲙⲱⲛ **64.**28,32; **65.**45; **73.**24; **77.**28; **78.**23; **79.**44; **80.**4,39; **81.**3; **82.**4;
        88.18; **108.**33; **114.**1; **122.**35   ⲫⲓⲗⲁⲙⲙⲟⲛ **89.**27   ⲫⲓⲗⲁⲙⲟⲩ **66.**42
    see also Λάμμων
ⲫⲓⲗⲁⲥ **67.**28 (to former? see comm. ad loc.)

ⲭⲁⲣⲏⲥ **64.**23; **66.**46; **67.**22; **70.**26; **76.**32,44; **102.**20; **122.**34   ⲭⲁⲣⲓⲥ **105.**67
(Χριστός) ⲡⲉⲭ̅ⲣ̅ⲥ̅ **61.**10

Ψάϊς see ⲡϣⲁⲓ̈
ⲯⲉⲕⲉ **90.**4   ⲯⲉϭⲉ **129.**1
    ⲁⲡⲁ ⲯⲉⲕⲉ **90.**44
    Ψεκῆς **90.**address
Ψεμνούθης **120.**25
    ⲡϣⲙⲛⲟⲩⲧⲉ **66.**43

Ὧρος : Ὧρωι **78**.address,2; **79**.address
ϩⲱⲣ **72**.35; **76**.3; **79**.4,45; **80**.7; **81**.6,10; **82**.11,29; **84**.8; **89**.19,22; **91**.1; **94**.6; **105**.10,77; **111**.41; **115**.12; **118**.5; **124**.40

ϣⲁⲓ̈ **67**.34; **76**.26; **77**.22; **78**.35; **82**.3,11; **89**.28; **94**.37; **106**.37,43; **110**.50; **128**.address
(Sah.:) ϣⲟⲉⲓ **123**.16
see also ⲡϣⲁⲓ̈

ϣⲁⲛⲱⲛⲁ (?) **89**.44 (uncertain reading)
(ϣⲉⲛⲟⲩⲧⲉ ?) ϣⲁⲓⲛⲟⲧⲁ **89**.25   ϣⲉⲛⲛⲟⲩ **89**.39   ϣⲓⲛⲛⲟⲩⲧⲉ **89**.10

ϩⲁⲡⲓⲁ **77**.20; **108**.20
ϩⲁⲧ **93**.20; **95**.10
ϩⲉⲛⲓ **76**.29; **83**.3   ⲉ̄ⲛⲓ **116**.12
see also ⲡⲁⲣⲑⲉⲛⲓ
ϩⲱⲙ **84**.7,11
ϩⲟⲩⲧ **129**.4

ϫⲙⲡⲛⲟⲩⲧⲉ **116**.18   ϫⲛⲡⲛⲟⲩⲧⲉ **71**.27; **72**.35   ϫⲉⲙⲛⲟⲩⲧⲉ **65**.40
ϫⲙϣⲱ **89**.15
(ϫⲛⲁⲡⲟⲗⲗⲱ) : ϫⲛ̄ⲁⲡⲗ̄ⲟ **64**.32   ⲥⲉⲛⲁⲡⲟⲗⲗⲱ **117**.1

ϭⲟⲩⲣⲓⲁ see Κυρία

Geographical names (and provenances)

(ⲁⲛⲧⲓⲛⲟⲟⲩ) ⲁⲛⲧⲓⲛⲟⲩ **116**.11
Ἀφροδίτη ⲁⲫⲣⲟⲇⲓⲧⲏ **90**.37
    Ἀφροδείτης (nome) **77**.address

(Ἑρμοῦ πόλις) ⲉⲣⲙⲟⲩⲡⲟⲗⲓⲥ **113**.8

ⲑⲁⲛⲉⲧⲁ **123**.17 (see also ϩⲉⲛⲉⲧⲉ)

(Ἶβις) ϩⲏⲃ **111**.32,35; **118**.7

(Κέλλις) Κέλλιν **73**.address
    ⲕⲗⲗⲉ **81**.27,35   ϭⲗⲗⲉ **81**.51   ϭⲉⲗⲏ **124**.41   ϭⲏⲗⲏ **108**.27   ϭⲏⲗⲉ **74**.11
ⲕⲏⲙⲉ *Egypt* **68**.10; **69**.3; **72**.19; **81**.17,18,26,54; **82**.18,36; **90**.7,39,43; **105**.67,68; **109**.24 **111**.33 **115**.26 **116**.9; **122**.12

ⲙⲁⲣⲏⲥ *Upper Egypt* see *s.v.* ⲣⲏⲥ
(Μῶθις ⲙⲟⲟⲧ) : ⲣⲙⲙ-ⲙⲟⲧ **94**.30
ⲙⲱⲛⲱ (unclear) in ⲣⲙⲙ-ⲙⲱⲛⲱ **75**.34

ⲟⲩⲁϩⲉ *Oasis* see "Native words"

ⲡⲉⲓⲁⲩⲛⲉ (uncertain toponym) **77**.14,17   (sim.:) ⲡⲉⲟⲩⲁⲩⲛⲉ **110**.50

ⲣⲟϩⲁ (uncertain) **115**.32

ⲥⲓⲁⲩⲧ : ⲣⲙⲛ-ⲥⲓⲁⲩⲧ **81**.28

ⲧⲁⲛⲁⲓⲉⲧⲟⲩ : ⲣⲙ-ⲧⲁⲛⲁⲓⲉⲧⲟⲩ **72**.35

ⲧⲓⲱⲗⲁ (uncertain, possibly personal) **89**.41

(Τριμῖθις ⲧⲣⲓⲙϩⲓⲧⲉ) : ⲧⲣⲓⲙⲓ$^\mathrm{T}$ **125**.4

Conjugations*

First Present

ϯ- **57**.7,12,19; **58**.14; **60**.3,5; **61**.16,29; **62**.6,7; **64**.18; **65**.28,29,39,41,47; **66**.16,21,36; **67**.4,6,7,18,25,26,31,50,56; **68**.8,9,12; **69**.4; **70**.10,25,34,43,44,45; **71**.2,3,4,12,29,39; **72**.3,4,28,33; **73**.2,4,5,6,15,24; **75**.2,4,19,41; **76**.6,7,34,44,45,47,63; **77**.3; **78**.5,5,6,49; **79**.9,12,39; **80**.4,6,7,38; **81**.5,6,23,33; **82**.6,10,14,26,28,30,35,36,41; **83**.2; **84**.3,5,14,27; **86**.3,4,5,18; **89**.10,17,41; **90**.12,28,43; **91**.1; **92**.8,36; **93**.5,22; **94**.3,50; **97**.5; **99**.7,28,32; **102**.1,22; **103**.2,3,5,46; **105**.7,43,46; **106**.5; **107**.4,16; **108**.6,36; **110**.5,35,50; **111**.3,19,41; **112**.4,17; **114**.1; **115**.9; **116**.4,12,13; **118**.2; **120**.1; **122**.19,20; **123**.5,20; **124**.41; **128**.17,38,42,43   ⲧⲓ- **89**.1; **129**.1,6   ⲧ- **129**.10

ⲕ- **69**.8; **73**.14,15,18; **79**.33; **81**.40,45,46; **82**.9; **103**.48; **107**.13; **111**.34; **114**.5; **116**.18

ⲧⲉ- **83**.12; **92**.31

ϥ- **58**.23; **71**.30; **72**.31; **80**.19; **81**.15,23; **82**.32,33,33; **92**.18,19; **93**.9; **116**.6,8,9

ⲥ- **70**.44; **81**.55; **107**.27,29

ⲧⲛ- **63**.16; **64**.6,8; **68**.36; **80**.12,22; **82**.41; **83**.7; **92**.3; **122**.5,23,23,23; **124**.5,6,11,21; **127**.30   ⲛ- **111**.8

ⲧⲉⲧⲛ- **58**.19,30; **70**.21; **72**.9,17; **75**.37; **78**.37; **81**.12; **83**.4; **90**.24,29; **94**.11

ⲥⲉ- **67**.45; **76**.24; **79**.16,18; **92**.21   ⲥⲟⲩ- **61**.28

First Future

ϯⲛⲁ- **58**.6,7,13; **70**.24; **71**.19,34; **72**.10,22; **73**.11; **76**.20,25,38,46; **78**.31,34; **79**.14,20,33,38; **84**.32; **90**.30,31; **92**.25; **94**.23; **95**.5,5; **103**.41; **107**.11; **109**.14,34; **110**.33; **111**.39; **122**.22,26; **124**.37; **128**.46   ⲧⲛⲁ- **71**.15,29

ⲕⲛⲁ- **73**.13; **103**.14

ⲕⲁ- **90**.8; **102**.11

ϥⲛⲁ- **73**.21,21,25; **90**.34; **94**.52

---

* (c) after reference means: ⲉ of a relative form in coalescence with copular ⲡⲉ.

ⲥⲁ- **78.**42

ⲧⲛⲛⲁ- **84.**25; **94.**30

ⲧⲉⲧⲛⲁ- **58.**9,15,17,28,29; **71.**23; **73.**18; **110.**48

ⲥⲉⲛⲁ- **79.**27; **94.**22,46,54; **122.**31; **126.**13; **128.**36

Circumstantial Present: ⲉⲣⲉ- **84.**16

ⲉ⸗ : ⲉⲓ **66.**4,9,42; **67.**15; **70.**20; **72.**8,9; **76.**46; **80.**18,23; **81.**3; **82.**35; **97.**6; **102.**12,23; **105.**25,82; **107.**24; **108.**7; **110.**8,18; **112.**6; **115.**4,36 ⲉⲉⲓ **61.**6; **79.**12,16; **128.**32,47 ⲉⲕ **58.**3; **65.**51,51; **67.**30; **72.**13,20; **78.**7,23; **79.**11; **80.**24; **94.**55,58; **106.**33 **111.**32,38; **124.**36; **128.**46 ⲉⲧⲉ **92.**30 ⲉϥ **69.**5; **75.**39; **76.**12; **78.**45; **82.**4,17,19; **83.**8,10; **93.**17; **105.**32; **106.**28; **115.**40; **116.**2,7; **121.**2; **124.**24,25,28; **128.**14 ⲉⲥ **71.**26,28; **72.**19; **84.**29; **93.**3 ⲉⲛ **83.**8; **124.**23 ⲉⲧⲉⲧⲛ **64.**14,31; **65.**10,10,11; **94.**59; **110.**19 ⲉⲧⲛ **66.**29 ⲉⲣⲉⲧⲛ **71.**6,7 ⲉⲩ **58.**16,18; **66.**45; **77.**36; **78.**19; **79.**19; **85.**3; **105.**55; **109.**18

ⲁ⸗ : ⲁⲓ **89.**2,17 ⲁⲉⲓ **61.**6 ⲁϥ **122.**28 ⲁⲛ **122.**4 ⲁⲧⲉⲧⲛ **89.**36 ⲁⲣⲉⲧⲛ **61.**11; **71.**7,8 ⲁⲧⲁⲧⲛ **122.**9

Second Present:

ⲉ⸗ : ⲉⲓ **72.**10; **81.**14; **82.**7; **90.**27; **91.**1; **92.**7; **116.**2 ⲉϥ **69.**5; **73.**15; **77.**18; **81.**12 ⲉⲥ **84.**9; **119.**51 ⲉⲛ **64.**8; **83.**6 ⲉⲣⲉⲧⲛ **71.**22 ⲉⲩ **94.**15

(ⲁⲣⲉ-) : ⲁⲣⲁ- **122.**29 ⲁ- **78.**35

ⲁ⸗ : ⲁⲉⲓ **61.**9; **122.**30 ⲁⲥ **90.**31,33; **105.**67; **122.**32 ⲁⲛ **78.**47; **122.**10,12 ⲁⲣⲟⲩ **78.**19

Converted Future forms

Circumstantial : ⲉⲕⲛⲁ- **103.**21 ⲉϥⲛⲁ- **58.**21; **110.**31 ⲉⲧⲉⲧⲛⲁ- **75.**28 ⲉⲩⲛⲁ- **116.**8,14

Focalising or promise : ⲉⲓⲛⲁ- **81.**15; **94.**51 ⲉⲉⲓⲛⲁ- **79.**26 ⲁⲓⲛⲁ- **115.**35 ⲉϥⲛⲁ- **58.**26 ⲉⲛⲁ- **79.**35; **82.**37,39 ⲉⲛⲛⲁ- **83.**6 ⲉⲩⲛⲁ- **127.**11

Modal (optative) : ⲉ- **78.**44 ⲉϥⲛⲁ- **80.**19; **81.**46

Forms following ϫ(ⲉ) or ϫⲉⲕⲁⲥ : ⲉⲓⲛⲁ- **64.**27 ⲉⲉⲓⲛⲁ- **123.**11 ⲉⲕⲛⲁ- **80.**36; **111.**38 ⲉⲕⲁ- **57.**13; **86.**6 ⲉϥⲛⲁ- **61.**10; **67.**5; **78.**7; [**91.**1]; **110.**29 ⲉϥⲁ- **70.**32; **76.**7; **109.**7 ⲁϥⲛⲁ- **122.**8 ⲉⲛⲁ- **61.**21; **73.**23 ⲉⲧⲉⲧⲛⲁ- **65.**8; **71.**5 ⲉⲧⲛⲁ- **73.**16 ⲉⲣⲉⲧⲛⲁ- **111.**43 ⲉⲩⲛⲁ- **127.**36

Relative Present : ⲉⲧⲉⲣⲉ- **79.**2; **85.**2; **88.**9; **105.**3; **126.**16 ⲉⲧⲉ- **93.**1; **112.**2; **115.**2

ⲉⲧ(ⲉ)⸗ : ⲉϯ **63.**5; **67.**58; **80.**2; **81.**14; **94.**19; **105.**81; **115.**44 ⲉⲧⲕ **105.**63 ⲉⲧⲉⲕ **58.**7 ⲉⲧⲉⲧⲛ **58.**32; **64.**11,16 ⲁⲧⲁⲧⲛ **122.**11 ⲉⲧⲟⲩ **78.**34

ⲉⲧ- (rectus) : with infinitive: **64.**15(c),20(c),20; **67.**1(c); **69.**1(c); **71.**26(c),28(c); **72.**8,11; **75.**33,38(c); **76.**1(c),1,10; **79.**7(c),7; **80.**10(c); **81.**3(c),49(c); **82.**4(c); **83.**5(c); **84.**9; **89.**8(c); **90.**4(c); **93.**3(c); **94.**18(c),32(c); **98.**10(c); **105.**79(c);

107.7,15;   **108**.4(c);   **111**.15(c);   **115**.7(c);   **124**.3(c),28(c);   **128**.21,22,48,49 ⲧ⸗ **117**.2; **122**.27

with stative: **57**.1; **65**.1; **66**.1,26(c); **70**.2; **71**.1; **72**.6; **73**.1,23; **76**.2,37; **79**.1; **80**.12(c),27,36; **81**.1; **82**.1,2; **85**.1,3,6; **86**.5; **89**.3; **90**.1; **103**.16; **105**.1,11; **107**.6; **110**.1 **111**.1,16; **112**.1; **115**.2; **123**.25,26; **128**.27   ⲉⲑ (= ⲉⲧ-ϩ...) **122**.1

with locative: **58**.5; **60**.4; **61**.1,29; **69**.7; **79**.22,25,29; **80**.11,32; **82**.2,10; **83**.3,10; **90**.32; **93**.21; **102**.7,17; **103**.3; **107**.10; **110**.20,21,34,44; **112**.19; **120**.2; **124**.6,8; **126**.13; **128**.29,42   ⲉⲑ (= ⲉⲧ-ϩ...) **65**.29; **105**.75; **118**.4

Relative Future : ⲉⲧⲉⲣⲉ-... ⲛⲁ- **110**.48; **116**.10   ⲉⲧⲁⲣⲁ-... ⲛⲁ- **122**.16   ⲉϯⲛⲁ- **80**.7(c); **81**.50   ⲉⲧⲕⲛⲁ- **103**.26   ⲉⲧⲉⲧⲛⲁ- **58**.10

ⲉⲧⲛⲁ- (rectus) **58**.24; **75**.29; **80**.22; **84**.37; **103**.32(c); **110**.47

Imperfect : ⲛⲉ- **106**.6   ⲛⲉⲓ **115**.25   ⲛⲉⲧⲉⲧⲛ **64**.14   ⲛⲁ⸗ : ⲛⲁⲥ **84**.10
   Relative: ⲉⲧⲉⲛⲉⲣⲉ- **116**.4   ⲉⲧⲉⲛⲉⲕ **115**.21
   Future Imperfect : ⲛⲉⲓⲛⲁ- **110**.27   ⲛⲉϥⲉⲓⲛⲁ- **128**.16

Affirmative Perfect, base ⲁ-

ⲁ- **64**.29; **65**.34; **71**.19,29; **73**.7,8; **77**.13; **80**.13,14,15; **84**.33; **92**.13; **94**.37; **105**.67; **106**.18; **110**.13; **115**.17,27

ⲁ⸗ : ⲁⲓ **57**.5; **58**.16; **64**.4,27; **66**.9; **69**.3; **70**.16; **71**.20,25,32,33; **72**.15,22,34; **73**.13,13,25; **75**.17; **76**.44; **77**.9,9,9,33; **78**.23,24; **80**.16,18; **81**.10,17; **82**.16; **83**.4; **84**.11; **87**.6; **88**.23; **90**.10,27; **92**.17,27; **94**.26,37,38,43,45; **95**.4,15; **96**.34; **97**.39; **102**.11; **103**.15; **105**.19,25; **108**.20,21; **111**.7; **115**.18,31,33; **119**.52,53,53   ⲁⲉⲓ **65**.35; **79**.28,31   ⲁⲕ **66**.13; **67**.20; **70**.37; **72**.26; **77**.18; **79**.30,31,42; **82**.36; **113**.5   ⲁϥ **64**.13; **65**.31; **69**.3; **71**.18; **73**.9,12; **80**.20; **81**.9,19,26,26,27,28,29,35,35,42,54; **91**.2; **92**.27; **94**.39; **102**.4,7,9; **108**.23,26,27; **115**.27; **118**.7 **128**.26   ⲁⲥ **73**.8; **90**.39,40,40; **93**.18; **116**.19   ⲁⲛ **64**.32; **80**.13; **89**.29; **90**.5; **105**.30; **119**.27   ⲁⲧⲉⲧⲛ **64**.5   ⲁⲧⲛ **77**.21   ⲁⲩ **66**.26; **77**.14,15; **92**.17; **94**.51 (here?); **95**.7; **105**.18; **107**.14; **115**.18,30; **127**.22

Circumstantial: ⲉⲁ- **95**.7; **106**.12   ⲉⲁⲓ **90**.36   ⲉⲁⲕ **127**.8   ⲉⲁϥ **71**.17   ⲉⲁⲩ **65**.35

Relative: ⲉⲧⲁ- **66**.25; **91**.2; **92**.10; **96**.21

ⲉⲧⲁ⸗ : ⲉⲧⲁⲓ **64**.1; **69**.10; **71**.11; **72**.13; **76**.17; **83**.9; **95**.3; **111**.13,21,22   ⲉⲧⲁⲕ **69**.11; **79**.25; **106**.24; **107**.18; **115**.32; **119**.26   ⲉⲧⲁⲣⲉ **71**.10   ⲉⲧⲁ **66**.25; **92**.10; **96**.21   ⲉⲧⲁϥ **76**.14; **80**.31,33; **81**.17,41; **102**.7   ⲉⲧⲁⲛ **116**.9   ⲉⲧⲁⲧⲉⲧⲛ **58**.1; **64**.10; **90**.6(c),29   ⲉⲧⲉⲧⲛ **71**.25   ⲉⲧⲁⲩ **103**.47

(Sah.:) ⲉⲛⲧⲁϥ **128**.19   ⲉⲛⲧⲁⲩ **127**.35

Second Perfect: ⲛⲧⲁ- **64**.7; **92**.16   ⲛⲧⲁ⸗ : ⲛⲧⲁⲓ **92**.9; **95**.6; **103**.11; **105**.39,80; **115**.16   ⲛⲧⲁⲕ **128**.15   ⲛⲧⲁϥ **86**.10; **116**.11; **128**.35   ⲛⲧⲁⲩ **70**.39   ⲧⲁⲩ **71**.24

ϫⲛⲧⲁ- **90**.39   ϫⲛⲧⲁ⸗ : ϫⲛⲧⲁⲓ **77**.11; **90**.37   ϫⲛⲧⲁⲕ **106**.10   ϫⲛⲧⲛ **129**.12

Affirmative Perfect, base ⲁ-, ⲁ⸗

 ⲁ- 58.6; 75.42; 76.41; 81.7; 89.33; 111.33; 130.1

 ⲁ⸗: ⲁⲓ 58.4,5; 107.24; 111.5,7,28; 120.30   ⲁⲕ 76.22; 78.16,27; 112.8
  ⲁⲛ 89.32; 122.7   ⲁⲧⲛ 58.2; 72.16,17; 76.21; 89.30   ⲁⲧⲉⲧⲛ
  65.24   ⲁⲩ 103.7; 120.24

 Circumstantial: ⲉⲁ- 95.11

 Relative: ⲉⲑⲁ 71.33   ⲉⲧⲁ 95.9; 102.5 (all 2nd fem.)   ⲉⲧⲁⲧⲛ 110.17

Affirmative Perfect, base ϩⲁ-, ϩ(ⲁ)⸗

 ϩ(ⲁ)⸗: ϩⲓ 70.40; 75.33,35; 76.12,12,26,32; 78.18,47; 79.23; 82.20,24,38;
  110.11,24; 114.4; 122.30; 123.6   ϩⲕ 122.21   ϩⲛ 110.12,15,20   ϩⲁⲧⲛ
  110.29

 Circumstantial: ⲁϩⲁ- 70.31 (circ.?)   ⲉϩⲓ 76.24   ⲉϩⲟⲩ 70.35

 Relative: ⲉⲧϩⲓ 76.23   ⲧϩⲓ 75.27,41

 (ϫⲛⲧϩ⸗): ϫⲛⲑⲕ 122.20

Negative Perfect

 ⲙⲡⲉ- 90.12; 94.35; 105.24,28

 ⲙⲡ(ⲉ)⸗: ⲙⲡⲓ 58.8,28; 77.11,19; 81.54; 82.12,15; 83.13; 91.3; 92.29;
  102.10,10; 105.16,20,32; 106.8; 115.19   ⲙⲡⲕ 77.17; 81.8; 83.11; 94.14,14
  ⲙⲡⲉⲕ 65.32; 78.22; 124.21   ⲙⲡⲉ 66.27; 75.43   ⲙⲡϥ 81.19,25,41;
  83.11; 94.20,40; 102.5   ⲙⲡⲉϥ 58.31; 76.15; 78.30   ⲙⲡⲛ 78.24
  ⲙⲡⲉⲛ 76.35   ⲙⲡⲉⲧⲛ 60.6; 67.19; 70.18,44; 76.53; 77.13,20; 78.40;
  81.11; 82.23; 84.6,14; 89.44; 90.9; 103.4   ⲙⲡⲟⲩ 57.11; 70.41; 76.23;
  94.42; 95.17; 102.12

 ⲛⲡ(ⲉ)⸗: ⲛⲡⲕ 122.21,22

 ⲡⲁ- 122.34

 ⲡ(ⲉ)⸗: ⲡⲉⲧⲛ <58.30>

 Circumstantial:

 ⲉⲙⲡⲉ- 91.4

 ⲉⲙⲡ(ⲉ)⸗: ⲉⲙⲡⲓ 79.14; 94.16,41   ⲉⲙⲡⲕ 99.54; 106.14; 120.13   ⲉⲙⲡⲉⲕ
  64.30; 80.20; 105.68   ⲉⲙⲡⲉ (2nd fem.) 116.5   ⲉⲙⲡⲉϥ 84.35
  ⲉⲙⲡⲟⲩ 72.20

 ⲁⲙⲡ(ⲉ)⸗: ⲁⲙⲡⲕ 120.22

 Relative:

 ⲉⲧⲉⲙⲡ(ⲉ)⸗: ⲉⲧⲉⲙⲡⲓ 79.15   ⲉⲧⲉⲙⲡⲉ (2nd fem.) 75.20   ⲉⲧⲙⲡϥ 110.44
  ⲉⲧⲉⲙⲡⲛ 82.41

 Focalising (?): ⲉⲣⲉⲙ̄ⲡⲓ 103.10

Affirmative Completive, see *s.v.* ⲟⲩⲱ

Negative Completive

 ⲙⲡⲁⲧ(ⲉ)⸗: ⲙⲡⲁⲧⲉϥ 94.48   ⲙⲡⲁⲧⲟⲩ 76.63

 Circumstantial: ⲉⲙⲡⲁⲧⲉ- 116.7

Affirmative Aorist

 ϣⲁⲣⲉ- 76.18; 124.29

ϣⲁ⸗ : ϣⲁⲕ 90.14; 99.13
ϣⲁⲣ(ⲉ)⸗ : ϣⲁⲣⲉⲕ 110.6   ϣⲁⲣⲉϥ 126.10
Circumstantial:
ⲉϣⲁ⸗ : ⲉϣⲁⲥ 90.34   ⲉϣⲁⲩ 63.18; 128.34
Relative:
ⲉⲧⲉϣⲁ(ⲣⲉ)- : ⲉⲧⲉϣⲁ- 58.18
ⲉⲧϣⲁ(ⲣⲉ)- : ⲉⲧϣⲁⲓ̈ 75.23   ⲉⲧϣⲁϥ 81.49   ⲉⲧϣⲁⲛ 81.52
ⲉϣⲁⲣ(ⲉ)⸗ : ⲉϣⲁⲣⲓ 75.25(c)
Preterite:
ⲛⲉϣⲁ⸗ : ⲛⲉϣⲁⲓ̈ 92.23

Negative Aorist
 ⲙⲁ⸗ : ⲙⲁϥ 122.28   ⲙⲁⲥ 58.34   ⲙⲁⲛ 65.34

Negative Energetic Future
 ⲛⲛⲉ- 127.37
 ⲛⲛ(ⲉ)⸗ : ⲛⲛⲉⲕ 103.12,22   ⲛⲛⲉ 63.13   ⲛⲛⲉⲩ 91.4   ⲛⲛⲟⲩ 106.41
 ⲛⲉ⸗ : ⲛⲓ 64.7   ⲛⲉⲧⲛ 61.15

Negative Imperative
 ⲙⲡⲱⲣ- 57.18; 64.30; 79.39; 80.23; 111.14
 ⲙⲡⲣ- 63.19; 70.36; 72.14,15; 76.52; 78.40,46; 79.39; 80.20; 82.37; 92.9; 99.54; 103.18,27,44; 104.2; 105.15,68; 106.13,20,26; 110.9,16,44,47; 111.24,36; 113.2,9; 115.14,15,20,22,33; 116.5,14; 120.21; 121.5   ⲙⲡⲉⲣ- 127.31   ⲉⲡⲣ- 82.11
 ⲙⲛ- 95.14

Affirmative Causative Imperative
 ⲙⲁⲣⲉ- 70.22; 78.49; 82.21; 84.21; 120.31
 ⲙⲁⲣ(ⲉ)⸗ : ⲙⲁⲣⲓ 102.9   ⲙⲁⲣϥ 108.37   ⲙⲁⲣⲉϥ 81.22,30,39; 82.23   ⲙⲁⲣⲥ 76.37   ⲙⲁⲣⲟⲩ 71.13; 76.50; 77.24; 90.42

Negative Causative Imperative
 ⲙⲛⲧⲣⲉ- 63.22; 83.7
 ⲙⲛⲧⲣⲉ⸗ : ⲙⲛⲧⲣⲉⲕ 78.17; 94.57   ⲙⲛⲧⲣⲉϥ 83.13; 103.42   ⲙⲛⲧⲣⲉⲧⲛ 110.23   ⲙⲛⲧⲣⲁⲧⲛ 122.30,31
 ⲙⲡⲱⲣⲧⲉ- 64.3

Causative Infinitive
 ⲧⲣⲉ- 102.23; 128.35
 ⲧⲣ(ⲉ)⸗ (99.49) : ⲧⲣⲁ 81.16; 99.24; 114.6   ⲧⲣⲓ 71.34; 79.35; 81.41; 94.59; 97.10   ⲧⲣⲉⲓ̈ 131.6   ⲧⲣⲉⲕ 106.23   ⲧⲣⲉϥ 76.20; 79.9; 84.18; 86.16; 94.38   ⲧⲣⲉⲥ 105.42   ⲧⲣⲛ 59.8   ⲧⲣⲉⲛ 128.26   ⲧⲣⲟⲩ 58.22; 110.24
 ⲧ(ⲉ)⸗ : ⲧⲁ 58.9,10,34   ⲧⲛ 76.52; 107.21

Conjunctive
 ⲛⲧⲉ- 82.8; 83.14; {90.27}; 97.12; 103.33; 115.5

pronominal with ⲛ-: ⲛⲧⲁ 58.23; 71.13; 73.10; 79.34; 126.33 ⲛⲅ 131.11 ⲛⲕ 71.21; 72.18,22,34; 76.50; 80.37; 81.43,53; 111.30,31,37; 115.41 ⲛⲧⲉ 66.40; 76.36; 90.45; 95.10; 102.15; 109.28 ⲛϥ 73.9,19; 105.64,64; 109.12,21; 111.44; 115.44; <126.11> ⲛⲥ 95.12,12 ⲛⲧⲛ 68.32 ⲛⲧⲉⲧⲛ 58.12,17; 61.14,22; 66.46; 71.23,35; 77.36; 79.36; 96.29 ⲛⲥⲉ <90.27>; 98.3

(for ⲧⲉ-) ⲧⲁ- 78.11

pronominal without ⲛ-: ⲧⲁ 58.22; 64.12,17; 73.14; 79.44; 81.47; 84.31,32; 90.32; 102.23; 103.19; 105.45; 122.26; 126.18,33 † 71.15; 76.30; 81.55; 94.60,60; 102.23,24; 105.26; 115.34 ⲕ 78.29; 81.47,48,54; 82.34; 86.14; 90.11; 94.46,58; 103.16,20,29; 106.17,34,35,35; 113.5; 120.10,27,27,33 ⲧⲉ 75.16,41; 102.18; 116.5,10 ϥ 81.22; 83.5; 84.19; 103.39,42 ⲥ 76.29,38; 78.50 ⲧⲛ 64.30; 77.25; 79.17; 83.6; 90.7; 91.6; 94.31; 103.17,37; 116.17; 118.6 ⲧⲉⲧⲛ 72.16; 78.45,45; 82.22,22,24 ⲥⲉ 104.3

Causative (or Future) Conjunctive
ⲧⲁⲣⲉ- 120.3

ⲧⲁⲣ(ⲉ)⸗: ⲧⲁⲣϥ 105.76   ⲧⲁⲣⲉϥ 103.23   ⲧⲁⲣⲛ 80.26; 84.26; 94.56 ⲧⲁⲣⲉⲛ 80.21

Temporal
ⲛⲧⲁⲣⲉ- 83.4; 90.5; 102.3

ⲛⲧⲁⲣ(ⲉ)⸗: ⲛⲧⲁⲣⲓ 66.7; 78.22   ⲛⲧⲁⲣⲉϥ 83.15

Limitative
ϣⲁⲛⲧ(ⲉ)⸗: ϣⲁⲛⲧⲧⲁ (1st sing.) 90.36   ϣⲁⲛⲧⲕ 111.38

ϣⲁⲧⲉ- 72.12; 83.7

ϣⲁⲧ(ⲉ)⸗: ϣⲁ† 78.10; 95.14; 103.28; 105.40; 120.12   ϣⲁⲧⲉ (1st sing) 58.28   ϣⲁⲧⲉⲕ 57.12   ϣⲁⲧϥ 108.29   ϣⲁⲧⲉϥ 82.25   ϣⲁⲧⲥ 111.25   ϣⲁⲧⲛ 103.36; [109.8 comm.]   ϣⲁⲧⲟⲩ 78.25; 79.18; 103.17,19

Conditional
ⲉϣⲁⲛⲧⲉ- 71.22   ⲉϣⲁⲛⲧⲁ- 122.25   ⲉϣⲁⲧⲉ- 71.14; 82.17; 106.38 ⲉⲣϣⲁ- 70.43

2nd fem.: ⲉϣⲁⲛⲧⲁ 71.14   2nd pl.: ⲉϣⲁⲧⲉⲧⲛ 66.38; 91.5; 105.44

ⲉ⸗ϣⲁ(ⲛ)-: ⲉⲓϣⲁⲛ 71.37; 78.31   ⲉⲓϣⲁ 71.11; 107.8   ⲉⲕϣⲁⲛ 106.32; 120.26   ⲉⲕϣⲁ 81.50   ⲉϥϣⲁ 93.7   ⲉⲛϣⲁ 84.23   ⲉⲩϣⲁ 94.23

Conditional without -ϣⲁⲛ-
ⲉ⸗: ⲉⲓ 69.8   ⲉⲕ 72.28; 76.27,28; 101.3   ⲉϥ 130.3   ⲉⲧⲉⲧⲛ 67.60   ⲉⲣⲟⲩ 71.13

ⲁ- 77.15

Apodotic
ⲉ⸗: ⲉϥ 130.3

Triadic pronominals (*PTN*)

Demonstr. pronoun
    ⲡⲉⲓ̈ 70.20; **103**.15,47; **105**.41; **115**.35
    ⲧⲉⲓ̈ 77.12; **103**.19,25
    ⲛⲉⲓ̈ 64.6; **65**.36; **66**.26; **72**.13; **76**.35; **77**.24; **79**.12; **111**.9
    (Sah.:) ⲡⲁⲓ̈ **128**.21   ⲛⲁⲓ̈ **128**.46

Demonstr. article
    ⲡⲓ- 58.13,15,25; **61**.11; **66**.23; **70**.35; **75**.8,41; **78**.25,28; **79**.41,41; **80**.31; **81**.51,52,52,53; **84**.28; **86**.17; **90**.41; **92**.28; **94**.29,33,56; **95**.9; **97**.9; **99**.27; **102**.14; **105**.18; **109**.15,20,30; **111**.25; **120**.2,17   ⲡⲉⲓ- **73**.17
    ϯ- 64.31; **66**.44,45; **70**.18,30; **78**.41; **80**.25; **84**.38; **88**.20; **89**.37; **91**.2; **96**.36; **105**.80; **109**.32; **110**.47,49; **120**.13; **122**.28,32; **130**.2
    ⲛⲓ- 58.21,21; **65**.34; **69**.9; **71**.24; **73**.11; **75**.20; **76**.41; **77**.16,30; **78**.37; **82**.13,41; **83**.3; **84**.3,18; **94**.4; **102**.2,19; **105**.44,77; **108**.30; **111**.10,44; **114**.2; **120**.3,18; **122**.22,25   ⲛⲉⲓ- **72**.11
    see also *s.v.* ⲙⲁ
    (Sah.:) ⲡⲓ- **123**.7,13
        ⲧⲉⲉⲓ- **128**.25   ϯ- **123**.21
        ⲛⲉⲓ̈- **127**.22   ⲛⲓ- **125**.5,6,14,32,36,38,39,40,43; **128**.18

Subject pronoun (copular)
    ⲡⲉ 63.31; **67**.30; **78**.33; **84**.35; **90**.35; **92**.12; **97**.10; **107**.22; **115**.29,35; **126**.22,23; **127**.20
    ⲧⲉ 73.7; **86**.9; **92**.14,14; **94**.15; **103**.25; **106**.24; **115**.28
    ⲛⲉ 58.21; **71**.24; **72**.13; **73**.12; **120**.11
(in Cleft Sentence:)
    ⲡⲉ 64.15,20; **67**.1; **69**.1; **75**.38; **76**.1,10; **79**.7; **80**.7,10,12; **81**.3,49; **82**.4; **83**.5; **89**.8; **90**.4,6; **94**.18,32; **98**.10; **103**.32; **105**.38,79; **108**.4; **111**.15; **124**.3,28
    ⲧⲉ 71.26,28; **93**.3; **115**.7
    ⲛⲉ 66.26; **75**.25; **121**.1

Definite article
    ⲡ- 57.3,17; **58**.5,16,27,28; **60**.2,4; **61**.1,5,8; **63**.15,22,30; **64**.2; **65**.6,8; **66**.5,32; **67**.4,46; **70**.1,17,24,29,31,38,38; **71**.3,4,5,5,7,8,9,9,15,17,20,21,21,22,30,36,37; **72**.4,4,7,8,14,17,26,29,33,33,36; **73**.3,7,14,16,18,23,23; **75**.2,26,34,42,42,43; **76**.7,53; **77**.7,10,11,22,28; **78**.6,14,32,33,35,40,40,47,50; **79**.7,8,9,13,20,21,27,28,38,42; **80**.5,8,9,10,15,22,30,38,39; **81**.4,27,28,30,42,45,48,49,53; **82**.2,5,7,13,15,16,19,25,41; **83**.2,3,5,5,5,7,7,10,10,15; **84**.10,21,24,27,33,34; **85**.3; **86**.3,8,8,13,21; **89**.4,5,6,44; **90**.1,4,8,15,30,32,32,33,39,40; **91**.1,2,5; **92**.6,14,15,28,34,38; **93**.4; **94**.18,19,21,25,34,36,45,58; **95**.6,6,9,10,11,11,15; **96**.23,33,35; **97**.8,10; **98**.22; **99**.3,6,21,22,39,44,50; **102**.4,7,13,18,22,23,23;

103.23,34,39; **105**.6,17,20,21,21,27,32,35,42,45,79; **106**.15,19,20,33,37,43; **107**.11,15,16,18,22; **108**.21; **109**.33; **110**.7,9,10,13,22,25,25,26,30,30,44; **111**.4,17,22; **112**.6,21; **114**.2,7; **115**.5,8,17,27; **116**.2,6,9,10,15; **118**.6,8; **119**.25; **120**.4,6,15,15,23,23,25,28,29,32,35 **122**.1,4,7,16,19,29; **123**.15,23; **124**.4,26,28,32,39,40,42; **125**.45; **126**.17,20,25,29,30; **127**.14,31 **128**.18,26, 29,33,34,48,48; **131**.5,6,10

(preceding ϨϹ…) ⲫ **77**.20; **82**.23; **92**.24; **126**.12; **128**.33

ⲡⲉ- **110**.48; **127**.37

see also ⲈⲒⲦⲚⲈ, ⲘⲈⲨⲈ, ⲚⲈⲨ *hour*, ⲦⲎⲢ⸗

ⲧ- **58**.30,32,35; **61**.7; **63**.29; **64**.9; **65**.12,32; **66**.7; **67**.17; **68**.46; **69**.9; **70**.23; **71**.5,7,34,36; **72**.4,6,35; **73**.17,22; **76**.44; **77**.4,15,19; **78**.38; **79**.19,29,31,43,44; **80**.11,14; **81**.27,51; **82**.9,16,18; **84**.8; **85**.4,4,8; **90**.29; **94**.34,37,43; **96**.28; **99**.22; **102**.20; **103**.8,34; **105**.20,76; **107**.29; **111**.6,36; **112**.9; **113**.8; **114**.4; **115**.26,31; **116**.5,8,15,21; **122**.35; **125**.41,42,44; **127**.9,20

(preceding Ϩ…) ⲑ **62**.16; **73**.7; **81**.16; **94**.16; **96**.34; **106**.24; **107**.11; **113**.7; **115**.19,34,44; **116**.14; 123;17; see also ϨⲈ, ϨⲎ

(Sah.:) ⲧⲉ- **123**.8; **127**.2,35

ⲛ- **58**.5,12,19,23,29; **61**.1,28; **64**.4; **65**.12,25,32; **69**.7; **71**.8,9,18; **72**.13; **76**.18,23; **78**.17; **79**.13,25,28; **80**.15,26,30; **81**.41; **82**.21; **84**.4,5; **85**.5,5,6; **90**.12; **92**.10,19,28,33; **94**.13,51; **95**.9; **103**.17; **106**.18,40; **110**.9,15; **111**.20; **114**.4; **115**.17,29; **116**.4,8; **118**.4; **120**.10; **125**.1; **127**.31; **130**.1 ⲙ- **61**.2; **85**.5 ⲛⲛ- **65**.14

Determiner preceding relative

ⲡ- **58**.7; **63**.17; **64**.9,11; **69**.7; **75**.29,33; **79**.2,22,25; **80**.2,33; **81**.14; **84**.37; **103**.16; **105**.63; **107**.7; **110**.44,48; **115**.2,32; **126**.16,27; **128**.27

see also ⲡⲉⲧ- (invariable) *s.v.* ϨⲀⲨ

ⲧ- **58**.1; **63**.5; **93**.1; **105**.81; **110**.21; **122**.6,16

ⲛ- **58**.18; **60**.4; **65**.29; **66**.25; **71**.11,33; **72**.11; **80**.27,32; **83**.3; **85**.2,3; **93**.21; **94**.19; **105**.3,31,75; **107**.10; **110**.20; **112**.19; **124**.6,8; **128**.42,49

Possessive pronoun

ⲡⲀ- **122**.1,35

ⲦⲀ- **92**.14

ⲚⲀ- **66**.33; **67**.42; **72**.35; **75**.41; **94**.24 ⲚⲈ- **58**.21; **94**.24

ⲠⲰ⸗ : ⲠⲰⲒ **64**.29 ⲠⲰ **92**.24 ⲠⲰⲚ **64**.9

ⲦⲰ⸗ : ⲦⲰⲒ **92**.13

Possessive article

Ⲡ(Ⲉ)⸗ : ⲠⲀ- **57**.1; **60**.3; **63**.6,51; **64**.7,25,25,26,27,30,32; **65**.1,1,3,4,28,37,41; **66**.2,8,17,35,39,42,43; **67**.2,6,7,17,34,40; **68**.7,8,8; **69**.2; **70**.1,11,12,15, 33,33,45; **71**.3,12,17,21,31; **72**.6,12,23,24,30,31,35; **73**.1,5,6,13,24,24; **75**.41; **76**.2,25,39,44; **77**.5,6,36; **78**.11,13,14,47; **79**.1,1,3,4,5,5,30,42; **80**.1,1,1,2,7,11, 15,17,17,19,23,29,38,38; **81**.1,1,6,10,32,38,46,49; **82**.1,3,8,11,21,29,30; **83**.12;

Indices: Triadic pronominals 359

86.1,1,6,6,14; 88.1,1,4; 89.2,2,6,7,18,24,26,28,39; 90.2,2,3,3,39; 91.2; 92.12; 93.5,10; 94.3,6,7,8; 97.12; 98.28; 99.1,4,54; 103.5,6; 105.2,39,77; 106.6; 107.10,30; 108.1,1; 111.1,16,26,34,40; 112.1,14; 114.1,5; 115.1,1,5,6,20, 20,22,33,42,43,44,44; 116.11,13,16; 118.3,3; 122.1,1,2,15,17,20,30; 123.16 126.21,31   ⲡⲉⲕ-   60.1; 66.3; 76.45; 78.8,10; 79.11; 80.4; 82.34; 108.4; 111.3,39; 126.7,24; 128.45   ⲡⲕ-   62.8; 77.10,32; 81.50; 105.60; 122.7,21 ⲡⲉ-   63.20; 92.11,22; 93.11; 115.14; 116.6; 123.23   ⲡⲉϥ-   65.47; 66.16; 79.2,45,45; 80.38; 82.33; 89.9; 90.31; 123.10; [124.3]; 126.16; 127.30 ⲡϥ-   58.30; 69.8; 78.44; 84.35; 110.14,21; 112.2; 115.3; 116.7; 126.11 ⲡⲉⲥ-   88.10; 93.1; 105.81   ⲡⲥ-   68.47; 72.36; 73.11; 82.28; 103.18 ⲡⲉⲛ-   124.address,39   ⲡⲛ-   58.21; 66.33; 67.42; 68.38; 69.6; 73.20,20; 80.28,31; 83.6; 84.17; 90.5; 92.26; 103.2,38   ⲡⲉⲧⲛ-   61.9; 62.15; 72.4; 79.6; 83.5; 89.44; 90.7; 97.7; 105.5,8,41; 122.13,24   ⲡⲉⲩ-   105.62; 128.23   ⲡⲟⲩ-   58.17,24; 64.24; 65.30; 66.13; 69.10; 70.34,45; 71.2; 75.7; 76.4,44; 78.16; 80.26,29,30; 85.2; 96.29; 105.3,75; 121.5; 122.14; 124.8

ⲧ(ⲉ)⸗: ⲧⲁ-   63.50; 64.21,23,26,29; 65.39,39,40; 65.42,48; 66.23,31; 68.13,34; 70.14,43; 71.2,27,28,28; 73.25; 75.4; 76.47; 79.3; 80.3,29; 81.43; 82.26,27; 83.2,3; 85.2,7; 86.9; 88.3,7,7,9,9,13,15,19,22; 89.5,11,12,13,33; 90.2; 92.1; 93.1,2,19,19,20,20; 94.15,24; 98.26; 105.2; 107.8; 109.1; 112.21; 115.3,13,24,24,28,37,38; 122.9,9,15,26,32   ⲧⲉ- (still 1st sing.) 66.22 ⲧⲉⲕ-   66.11; 77.9; 78.9; 79.11; 107.5; 115.7; 124.13,14; 128.41   ⲧⲕ- 57.13; 72.14; 81.32,35; 86.4; 90.13; 103.21,24,25,30; 115.10; 122.5   ⲧⲉ- (2nd fem.) 63.44; 92.5; 95.10   ⲧⲉϥ-   65.38,45; 75.18; 78.15; 82.31; 89.20,21; 109.32   ⲧϥ-   62.14,17; 66.42,43; 67.38; 72.24,25,30; 73.8; 77.5,35; 79.38; 82.29; 94.9; 108.34,36; 112.22   ⲧⲉⲥ-   64.20; 65.43; 71.27; 80.35; 82.28; 119.47   ⲧⲥ-   64.21,22,23; 66.37; 77.35; 88.29; 89.16; 105.75; 113.9; 117.2; 117.2,2; 119.59,60; 122.6   ⲧⲛ-   68.29,37; 81.52; 90.25; 92.20; 107;15; 116.3   ⲧⲉⲧⲛ-   72.5; 75.24   ⲧⲟⲩ-   117.1; 122.28

ⲛ(ⲉ)⸗: ⲛⲁ-   58.11; 61.2,3; 63.11; 66.29; 72.32; 75.3; 76.34; 80.37; 81.24,45; 82.41,41; 85.1,1,6; 91.1; 92.4,7; 103.35; 105.1,43,80; 108.22; 111.42,42; 115.11,11   122.13,14   ⲛⲉⲕ-   66.12; 76.3,44; 77.3; 110.44; 112.21; 122.3; 127.12   ⲛⲉ-   71.32; 92.3,5; 95.2; 102.21   ⲛⲉϥ-   58.12; 65.29,38,46; 66.36,42,44; 67.18; 70.11,34; 72.24,25; 75.41; 77.35; 78.15; 79.40; 82.30; 94.10; 96.28; 103.6; 105.75; 112.22; 119.59; 124.31; 125.15   ⲛϥ- 129.2,5,7   ⲛⲉⲥ-   64.19,21,24; 65.44; 66.32; 68.31; 70.7,10; 71.2; 75.5; 80.35; 92.21; 96.26; 115.38,39; 116.12,18   ⲛⲥ-   77.36   ⲛⲉⲛ-   62.13; 69.6; 79.37; 80.21,28; 84.25,26; 90.34; 95.14; 96.31; 103.33,37; 110.12; 128.27,29,31   ⲛⲛ-   64.4; 77.26   ⲛⲉⲧⲛ-   110.17   ⲛⲉⲩ-   90.27; 128.22,43   ⲛⲟⲩ-   67.35,57; 71.32; 72.32; 84.4; 92.5; 94.5,11; 102.20; 105.11,76; 119.61 122.27; 126.14

Subject index

Commodities:
    for **food** see "Native words", *s.v.* ⲁⲕⲉ *sesame*, ⲁⲣϣⲓⲛ *lentil*, ⲃⲛⲛⲉ *date*, ⲉⲗⲁⲗⲉ *grape*, ⲓⲱⲧ *barley*, ⲕⲛⲧⲉ *fig*, ⲛⲟⲩⲃⲥ *jujube*, ⲛⲏϩ *oil*, ϣⲃⲱⲛ *herb*, ϫⲁⲉⲓⲧ *olive*
        see "Loan words", *s.v.* ζιζουλά, καθαρός, καρύα, σησαμή
    for **clothing** see "Native words", *s.v.* ⲕⲗⲉϥⲧ *cowl*, ⲡⲣⲏϣ *blanket*, ⲧⲟⲟⲩⲉ *shoe*, ϣⲁⲧ *cushion*, ϣⲧⲏⲛ *tunic*; (generic:) ϩⲃⲁⲥ, ϩⲁⲓ̈ⲧⲉ
        see "Loan words", *s.v.* θώραξ, κολλάριον, στιχάριον
    for **books** and **documents**, see "Native words", *s.v.* ⲥϩⲉⲓ̈ *letter*, ϫⲱⲙⲉ *book*
        see "Loan words", *s.v.* ἐπιστολή, εὐαγγέλιον, μέλαν, πρᾶξις, τετράς
    for **containers** see "Native words", *s.v.* ⲁⲥⲕⲁⲩⲗⲉ, ⲃⲉⲉⲣ *basket*, ⲗⲁⲕ *bowl*, ⲙⲣⲱϣⲉ *clay pot*, ϫⲗϭⲉ *cloth bag* (?)
        see "Loan words", *s.v.* ἀγγεῖον, κάλαθος, λαβίς, χαλκεῖον
    other materials : see "Native words", *s.v.* ⲛⲟⲩⲃ *gold*, ⲥⲧⲏⲙ *antimony*
        see "Loan words", *s.v.* κάλαμος, κλωστήρ (?) *thread*, πλεκτή (*twisted material*), χάρτης

Measures, weights, and quantities:
    see "Native words", *s.v.* ⲙⲁϫⲉ, ⲣⲧⲁⲃ, ⲥⲁⲧⲉⲣⲉ, ϣⲁⲧⲥ *portion*
    see "Loan words", *s.v.* λαβίς (?), μέρος, μνᾶ, ξέστης, χοῦς

Money:
    see "Native words", *s.v.* ϩⲁⲙⲧ *bronze*, ϭⲛϭⲱⲣ *talent*
    see "Loan words", *s.v.* νομισμάτιον, νοῦμμος, ὁλοκόττινος, τιμή (*at Egyptian price* **81.**18)

Personal names: see above, pp. 346–350

Place-names: see above, pp. 350f. ("Geographical names and provenances")

Textile production:
    see "Native words", *s.v.* ⲃⲉⲕⲉ *wages*, ⲉⲟⲩⲉⲛ *colour*, ⲙⲟⲩϫⲧ *mix*, ⲥⲱϩⲉ *weave*, ⲧⲉⲗⲟ *set up (on loom)*, ϩⲓⲥⲉ *spin*
    see "Loan words", *s.v.* ἠλακάτη *distaff*, κλωστήρ (?), λάσιον

Transport and destinations:
    see "Native words", *s.v.* ⲃⲁⲣⲱϩ *caravan (driver)*, ϩⲏⲙⲉ *fare, freight*
    "travel / come to Egypt" **69.**3; **72.**19; **81.**17,26,54; **82.**18,36; **90.**7,39; **111.**33; **115.**26; **116.**9; "travel to Antinoou" **116.**11; "travel to Aphrodite" **90.**37
    "travel / come to the Oasis" **58.**22; **81.**13; **105.**44; **108.**30; **119.**32; **130.**3; "travel south" **111.**7; "travel / come to Kellis" **81.**26,35,50; **108.**26; "come to the village" **99.**22; "travel to Hibis" **118.**7
    "stay in the Oasis" **81.**23; **122.**12
    "take to / sell in the Oasis" **65.**37; **90.**11; "bring to Egypt" **90.**43
    "send (back) to Upper Egypt" **79.**27,34

INVENTORY NUMBERS

As in previous volumes, the movement of fragments has been tracked and a listing is provided. A close study of the various deposits, within which fragments from specific documents or groups of such were recovered during the excavations, has proved to be of value for the difficult task of reconstructing such fragments or groups. Further, it has potential for understanding the history of the persons who lived within these structures, their relationship to each other, and their association with the other kinds of texts (whether dated Greek contracts, horoscopes or Manichaean psalms) as found especially in House 3. The following list does not include fragments or documents from House 4 and the Temple Area, nor fragments that have not been edited.

House 3, 1990-91 archaeological season:

A/5/1	>		**85**
A/5/24	>		**83**
A/5/163	>		**94**
A/5/260	>		A/5/280
A/5/280	>		**57**
P 4	>		**62**
P 7 + 7A	>		P 4
P 8	>		P 27B
P 9	>		**64**
P 14	>		**63**
P 17EE	>		**58**
P 17V	>	P 17Vi	**86**
P 21	>		P 45
P 22	>		P 14
P 27A/B	>		**90**
P 27B	>		**61**
P 32	>		**87**
P 36	>		P 45
P 40	>		**59**
P 43	>		P 45

P 45	>		**65**
P 47	>		P 45
P 51B	>		P 56Ci
P 51B	>		**95**
P 51B	>	P 51B(a)i	**96**
P 51B	>	P 51B(a)ii	**97**
P 51B	>	P 51B(a)iii	**98**
P 51C	>		P 14
P 51C	>	P 51C(a)	**91**
P 51D	>		P 52G
P 51D	>		P 56Ci
P 51D	>		**99**
P 51D	>	P 51D(b)i	**100**
P 51D	>	P 51D(b)ii	**101**
P 52A	>		P 56D(b)
P 52C	>	P 52Ci	**102**
P 52G	>		**80**
P 52J	>		**73**
P 56B	>		**103**
P 56C	>		P 45
P 56C	>		P 56B
P 56C	>		P 56G
P 56C	>		**88**
P 56C	>	P 56C(a)i	**74**
P 56C	>	P 56C(a)ii	**60**
P 56C	>	P 56C(a)iii	**104**
P 56C	>	P 56Ci	**105**
P 56D	>		**75**
P 56D	>	P 56D(a)	**106**
P 56D	>	P 56D(b)	**107**
P 56E	>		P 56B
P 56E	>		**76**
P 56G	>		**108**
P 56H	>		P 56D(b)
P 56I	>		P 56G
P 57B	>		P 56Ci
P 59A	>		**66**

P 59A	>	P 59A(i)	**109**
P 59B	>		P 59A
P 59B	>		P 59A(i)
P 59C	>		P 59A
P 59E	>		P 78J
P 59F	>		P 59A(i)
P 59F	>		P 78J
P 60D	>		P 59A(i)
P 60D	>		**67**
P 61CC	>		**68**
P 61G	>	P 61G/I	**110**
P 61J	>		**111**
P 61S	>		**112**
P 61V	>		P 61S
P 61W	>		P 61S
P 62	>		P 14
P 63A	>		P 61S
P 64A	>		P 81E(a)
P 64A	>		P 27A/B
P 64A	>		P 59A(i)
P 65D	>		P 61S
P 65E	>		P 61G/I
P 65F	>		P 61G/I
P 65G	>		P 61G/I
P 65G	>		P 61S
P 65J	>		P 61G/I
P 67	>		P 78J
P 68D	>		P 81F/1
P 68G	>		**81**
P 68G	>	P 68G(a)	**84**
P 69	>		P 81E(a)
P 78A	>		**113**
P 78G	>		P 81E(a)
P 78H	>	P 78Hi	**69**
P 78J	>		**70**
P 78J	>	P 78Ji	**114**
P 80A	>		**115**

P 81A	>		P 80A
P 81B	>		P 81E(a)
P 81C	>		**71**
P 81D	>		P 27A/B
P 81E	>		**116**
P 81E	>	P 81E(a)	**82**
P 81F	>	P 81F/1	**77**
P 90B	>		**92**
P 91A/B	>		**72**
P 91B	>		**117**
P 93B	>		P 59A(i)
P 93B	>		P 78Ji
P 93B	>		P 81E
P 93B	>		P 81E(a)
P 93D	>		P 81C
P 93D	>		P 81E(a)
P 95B	>		**89**

House 3, 1991-92 archaeological season:

P 92.1	>		**118**
P 92.15B	>		**119**
P 92.17	>		**120**
P 92.19	>		**78**
P 92.20	>		**121**
P 92.22	>		P 92.19
P 92.22	>		P 92.35G(i)
P 92.35G	>	P 92.35G(i)	**79**
P 92.262	>		**93**

PHOTOGRAPHS

Digital photographs of the texts are provided on the accompanying disc. They were all taken by Jay Johnston in the SCA magazine in the Dakhleh Oasis during January 2009. There are the following exceptions:

61(v), **70**(v), **71**(v): not processed (only the address is found);

63(v), **69**(v), **87**(v), **91**(v), **95**(v), **101**(v), **104**(v), **108**(v), **114**(v), **117**(v), **121**(v): not processed (the papyrus is not inscribed);

128: the glass frame containing the fragments from P 96.98 and P 96.108 could not be found in the magazine in 2009, but a photograph of them from 1997 is provided in the volume as a plate;

130(convex): not processed (convex side of the ostracon not inscribed);

131: this wooden board could not be found in the magazine in 2009, but a photograph from 1997 is provided in the volume as a plate.

A small selection of other photographs taken in earlier seasons is also provided in the volume as plates.

P. KELLIS ADDENDA AND CORRIGENDA

19, 21   Read ⲁⲛⲓ ⲡⲉⲕⲥⲙⲓⲁⲛ ⲥⲛⲟ ⲙⲉⲗⲁ, with ⲥⲙⲓⲁⲛ for σμιλίον '(little) scalpel, penknife', also attested in Greek papyri as σμιλίν. To be translated probably 'Bring your two ink scrapers', if ⲙⲉⲗⲁ represents μέλαν 'ink'. Alternatively, but less likely, it might stand for μέλας 'black'; in which case the meaning would seem to be 'Bring your two black penknives'. The reading ⲥⲙⲓⲁⲛ, along with its interpretation, was first suggested to us by Geneviève Favrelle (Issy-les-Moulineaux, France; personal letter to WPF, 28-11-2001).

19, 33   Instead of ⲉⲧⲛ̄ⲧⲟⲧⲥ̄, read ⲉⲧⲛ̄ⲧⲟⲧⲉ̄; i.e. '.. the coins that you (f.) have'.

19, 47   Instead of ⲛ̄ⲧⲉ, read ⲛ̄ⲥⲉ; i.e. 'I inquired about my son Andreas'.

19, 72   Instead of ⲧⲥ̣ⲙ̣ϣⲁⲓ, read ⲧⲱⲛ̄ϣⲁⲓ.

33, 9f.   Read ⲡ̄ⲙⲉⲣ ⲁ[. . .] . ⲛⲉ ⲕⲧⲉϥ|ⲥⲙ̄ⲛ̄; i.e. '.. take care of (N.N.) and make him (10) fix (or: 'set up') for us the warp' etc. Delete commentary on l. 9; cf. imperative usage of ⲡ̄ⲙⲉⲣ at **81**, 20,39 (equals ⲁⲣⲓⲙⲉⲣ **103**, 38; **105**, 71; **108**, 28).

39, 10   Read probably ⲉⲧⲁⲛ[ⲟⲩ]ⲁϩϥ (either ⲉⲧⲁⲛ- or ⲉⲧⲁⲓ̈-); i.e. '.. the thing which we (or: 'I') have set (aside) for the man'.

39, 20   Translate: '.. not to mention our brother Petros' (A. Shisha-Halevy, 'An Emerging New Dialect of Coptic', *Orientalia* 71, 2002: 306).

39, 30-31   In the translation, these two 'transverse' lines are to be set off as a separate subtext.

43, 37   Read perhaps ⲣⲱ ϩⲓⲛⲉⲩ[ϩ]ⲏⲧ to translate (ll. 36-38): 'Who is it really that takes care of them and their anxiety (?) in their hearts? For, are there any others for them?'.

43, 40   Read ⲡⲁⲭⲉⲩ; i.e. 'They said he did not give it to you'.

46,1,4f.,6,11f. Instead of 'I have ... from him', translate 'He owes me ...'; in ll. 2 and 5f. followed by 'He is to pay them to me ...' (ⲁⲡϩⲓⲧ still unclear). See the explanations in CDT I, p. 60; and also A. Shisha-Halevy, op. cit., 2002: 307 (with some confusion).

47, 27f.   Read ⲡⲉⲧϥⲟⲩⲱ|[ϣ]ⲉ [ⲁ]ⲉϥ; i.e. 'Whatever he wishes [to] do with my children - he is responsible'.

47, 29f.   Translate: 'I owe Mother Partheni 2500 talents - give them to her'.

48, 37f.   Translate: 'I owe you another 400 talents and eight jujubes' ('jujubes' apparently corrected from *nummi*: ⲛⲟⲙⲥ before correction).

P. Kellis Copt. 61 (r)

P. Kellis Copt. 65 (r)

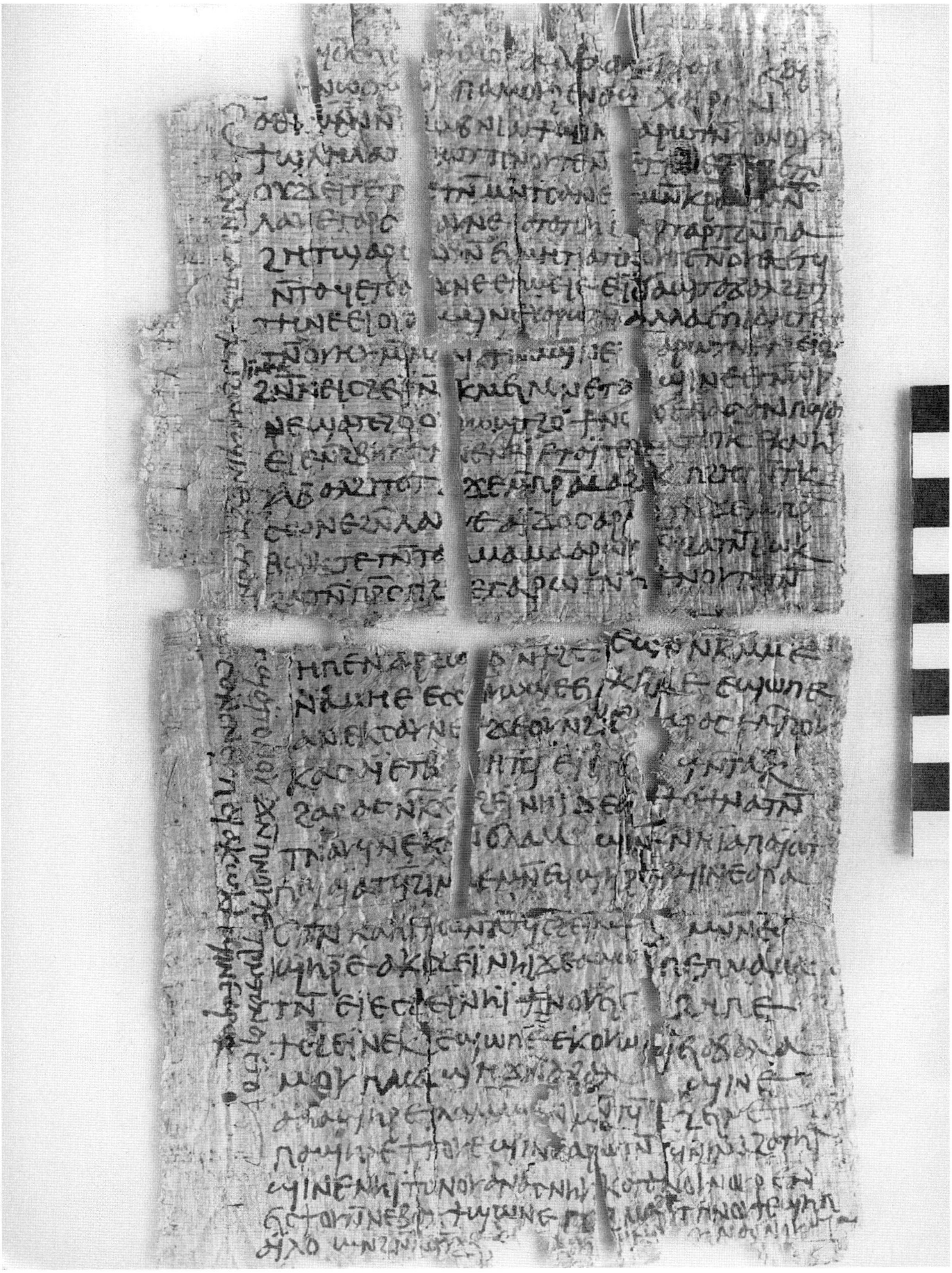

P. Kellis Copt. 72 (r)

P. Kellis Copt. 78 (r)

P. Kellis Copt. 78 (v)

P. Kellis Copt. 80 (r)

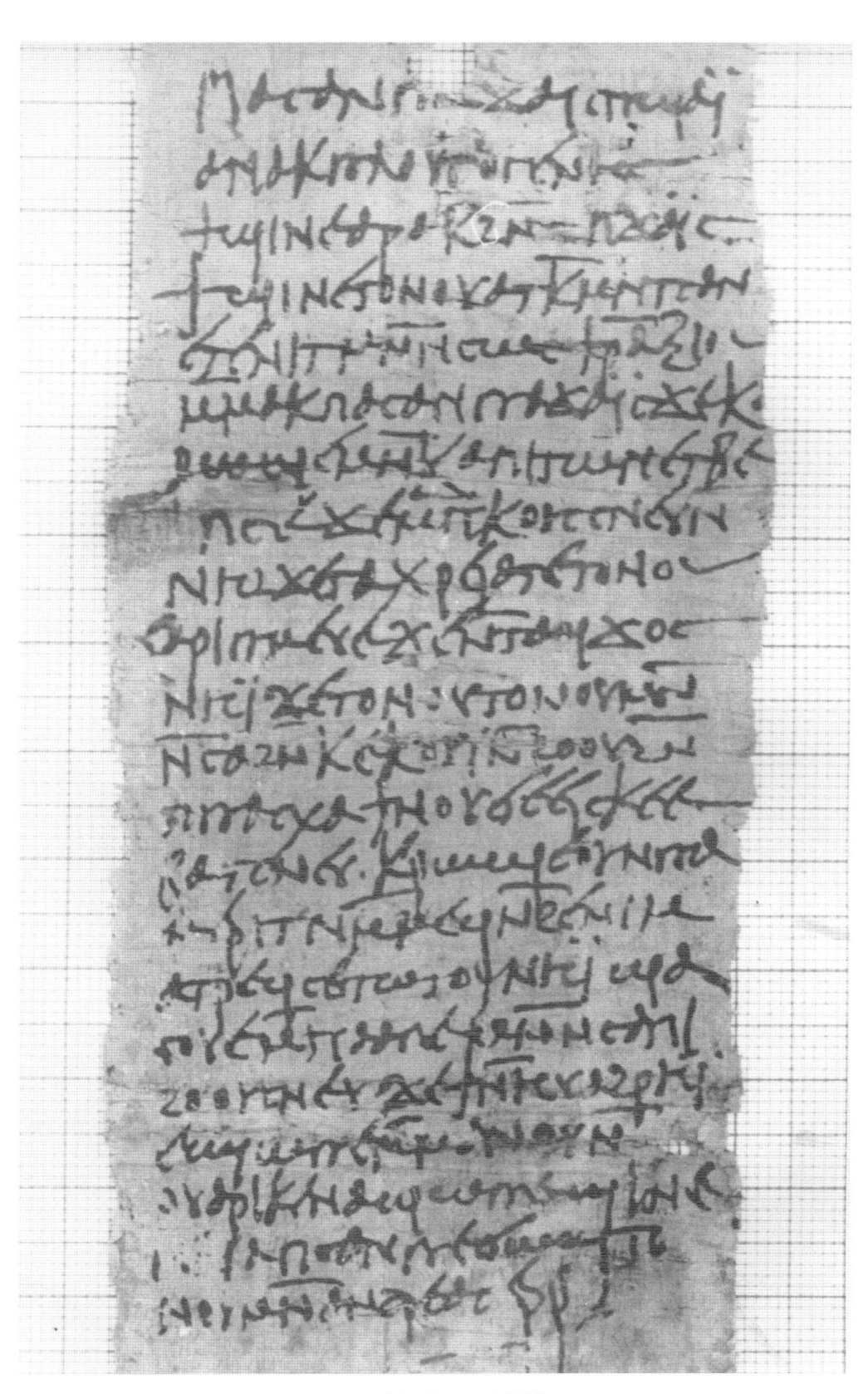

P. Kellis Copt. 86 (r)

P. Kellis Copt. 93 (r)

P. Kellis Copt. 94 (A)

P. Kellis Copt. 94 (B)

P. Kellis Copt. 122 (r)

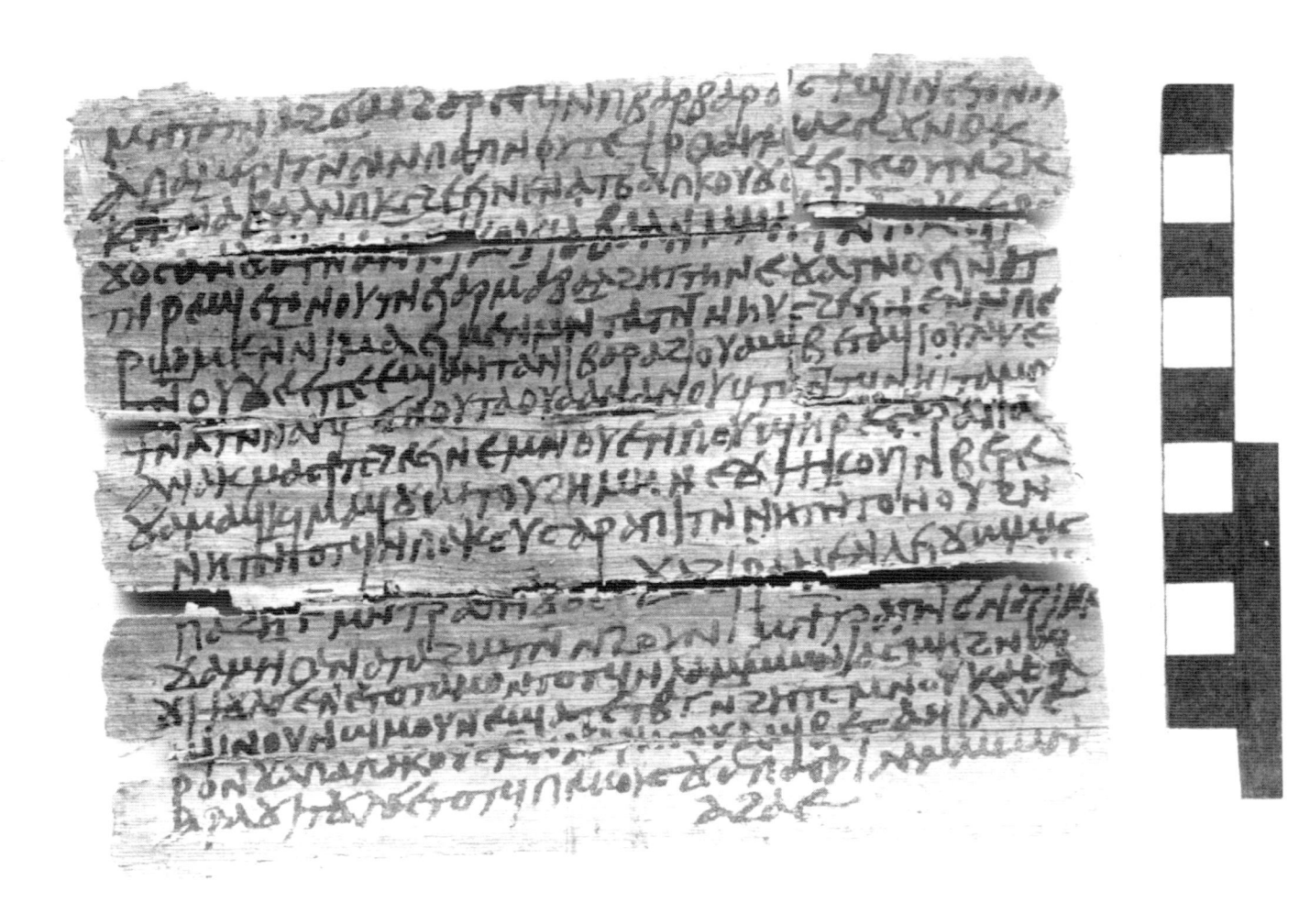

P. Kellis Copt. 122 (v)

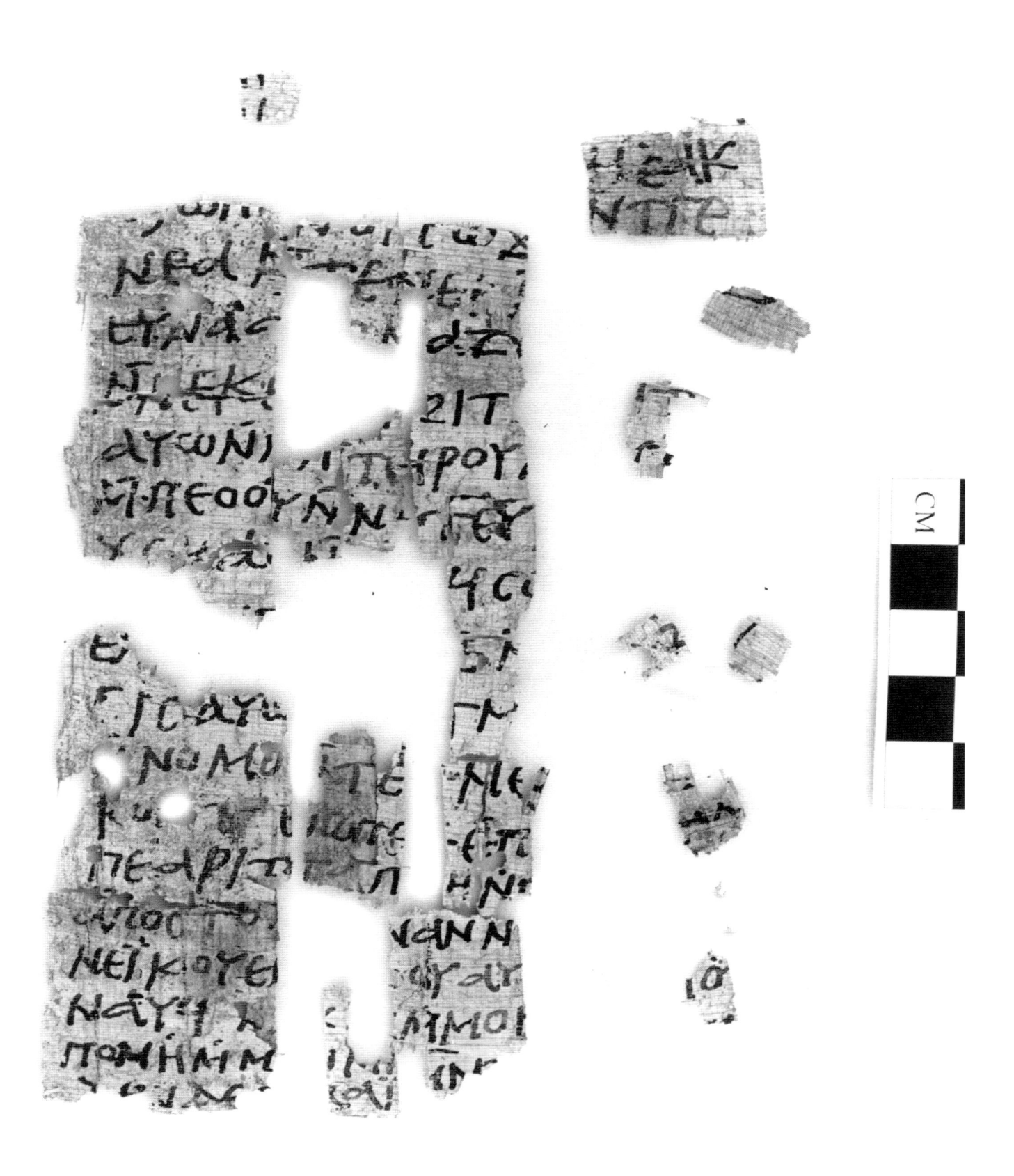

P. Kellis Copt. 127 (r)

P. Kellis Copt. 127 (v)

P. Kellis Copt. 128 (ex P96.98 + P96.108)

P. Kellis Copt. 128 (ex P97.15)

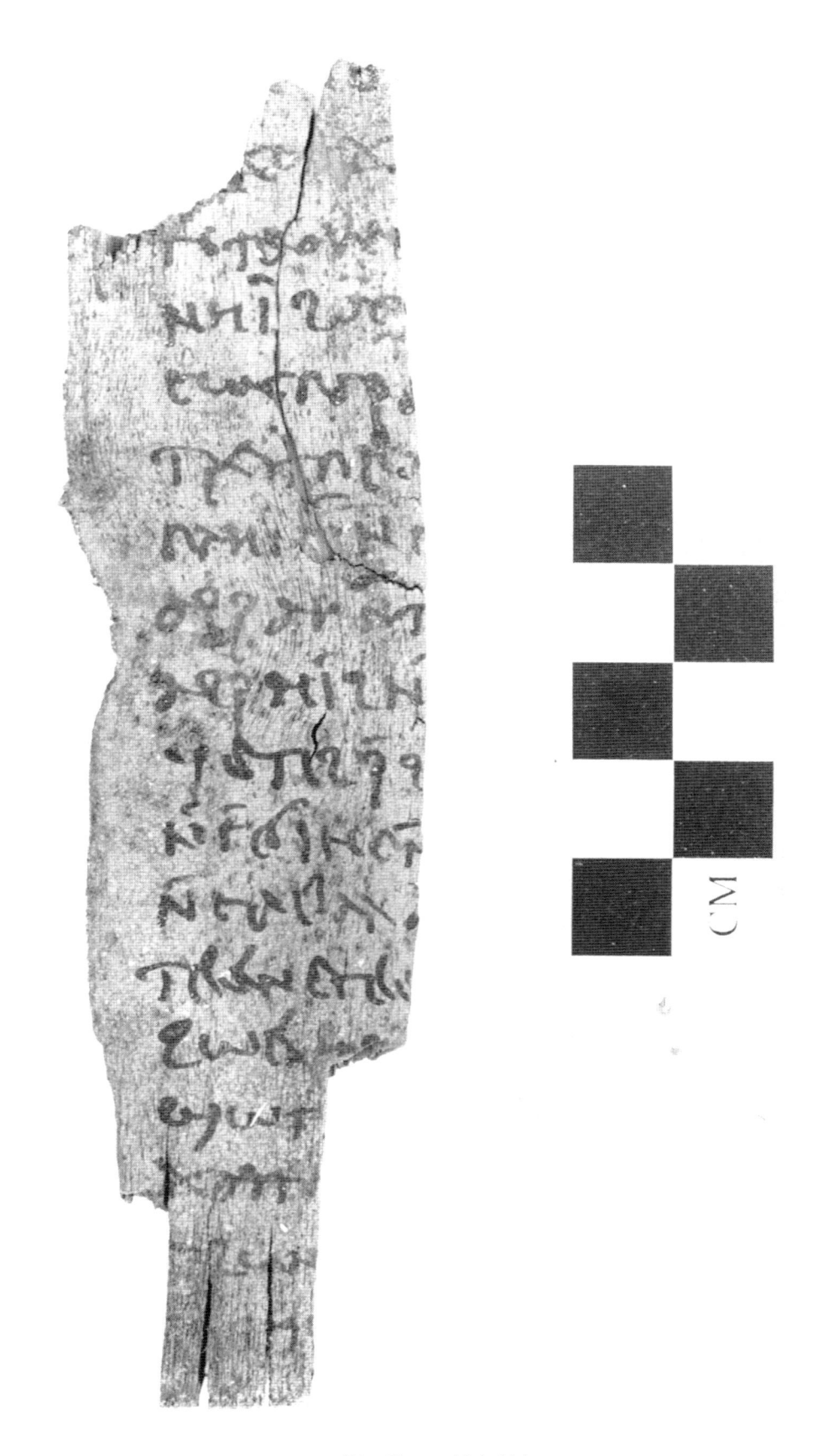

P. Kellis Copt. 131 (A)

P. Kellis Copt. 131 (B)